KT-210-071

The **Rough Guide** to

Sicily

written and researched by

Robert Andrews and Jules Brown

ROUGH
GUIDES

www.roughguides.com

Contents

Food and wine in Sicily
colour section
following p.248

Outdoor adventures
colour section
following p.344

◄◄ Villa Palagonia, Bagheria ◄ Scala dei Turchi, near Agrigento

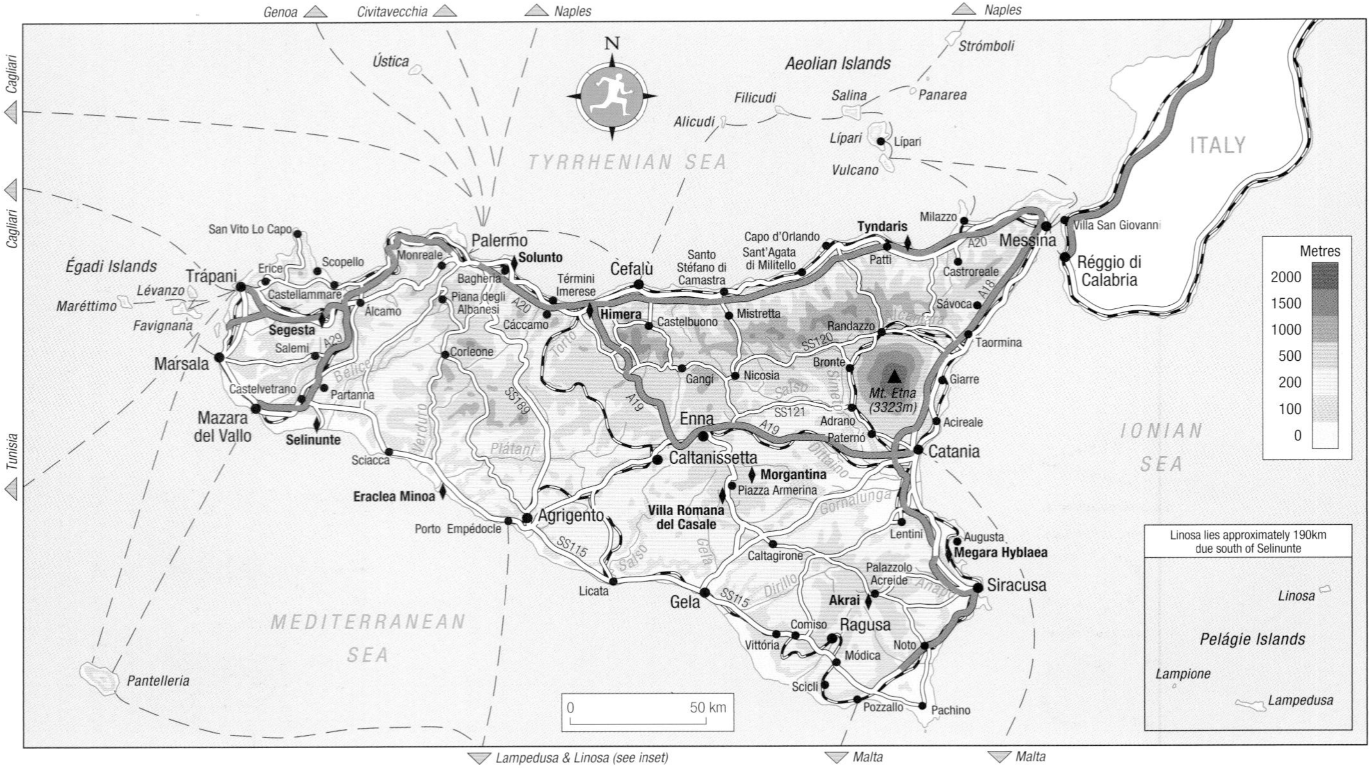

Genoa
Civitavecchia
Naples
Naples
Cagliari
Cagliari
Tunisia
Lampedusa & Linosa (see inset)
Malta
Malta
N
Ústica
Aeolian Islands
Strómboli
Filicudi
Salina
Panarea
Alicudi
Lípari
Lipari
Vulcano
TYRRHENIAN SEA
ITALY
Villa San Giovanni
Réggio di Calabria
Messina
Milazzo
A20
Tyndaris
Capo d'Orlando
Sant'Agata di Militello
Santo Stéfano di Camastra
Patti
Castroreale
Sávoca
A18
Taormina
Giarre
Acireale
Catania
Mt. Etna (3323m)
Randazzo
Bronte
Adrano
Paternò
SS120
SS121
A19
Mistretta
Nicosia
Gangi
Castelbuono
Cefalù
Términi Imerese
Himera
Palermo
Solunto
Bagheria
Piana degli Albanesi
Cáccamo
Monreale
Corleone
SS189
Égadi Islands
Trápani
Erice
San Vito Lo Capo
Scopello
Castellammare
Lévanzo
Maréttimo
Favignana
Segesta
Salemi
A29
Álcamo
Mársala
Castelvetrano
Partanna
Mazara del Vallo
Selinunte
Sciacca
Eraclea Minoa
Porto Empédocle
Agrigento
SS115
Licata
Gela
Enna
Caltanissetta
Morgantina
Piazza Armerina
Villa Romana del Casale
Caltagirone
Lentini
Augusta
Megara Hyblaea
Siracusa
Palazzolo Acreide
Akrai
Ragusa
Comiso
Vittória
Módica
Scicli
Noto
Pozzallo
Pachino
Belice
Verduro
Plátani
Torto
Salso
Simeto
Dittaino
Gornalunga
Dirillo
Anapo
Alcantara
MEDITERRANEAN SEA
IONIAN SEA
Pantelleria
0
50 km
Metres
2000
1500
1000
500
200
100
0
Linosa lies approximately 190km due south of Selinunte
Linosa
Pelágie Islands
Lampione
Lampedusa

Introduction to
Sicily

To say that Sicily isn't Italy is trite but true – only 3km of water separate the island from the Italian mainland, but the historical and cultural gulf is much wider than that. The locals see themselves as Sicilians first and Italians a very firm second, a difference that is celebrated at every turn and that's obvious even to first-time visitors. On this strategically located island at the heart of the Mediterranean some of the western world's richest civilizations have left their indelible mark, from ancient temples to stunning mosaic-decorated churches. A distinct Sicilian language survives, and indeed thrives, while many place names are derived from the Arabic that was once in wide use across the island. Couscous is as much a part of the Sicilian menu as pasta, while markets brim with produce that speaks firmly of the south – oranges, lemons, olives, rice, almonds and peppers.

Moreover, the historic combination of island mentality and wild, lawless, mountainous interior has fostered an us-and-them attitude that still defines the relationship between modern-day Sicily and Italy. The island was probably the most reluctantly unified Italian region in the nineteenth century, with Sicilians almost instinctively suspicious of the intentions of the latest in a long line of rulers, whether Phoenicians, Greeks, Romans, Arabs, Normans or the Spanish. For many Sicilians, their place in the modern Italian state is illustrated every time they look at a map to see the island being kicked – the perpetual football.

Fact file

- Sicily is the largest and one of the most densely populated islands in the Mediterranean, with extensive areas of mountains in the north and east, the highest being Mount Etna (3323m) – Europe's largest active volcano. Apart from Etna's sporadic eruptions, Sicily is also prone to seismic upheavals – massive earthquakes destroyed Messina in 1908, and rocked the western part of the island in 1966.

- Sicily has a semi-autonomous status within the Italian republic, with its own parliament and president, and limited legislative powers in such areas as tourism, transport, industry and the environment. There is no separatist movement to speak of, though suspicion of central government runs deep.

- Compared to north Italy, the economy has remained relatively underdeveloped. Though there are pockets of oil-refining and chemical-industrial activity, Sicily is mainly agricultural, devoted to the cultivation of wheat, barley, corn (maize), olives, citrus fruit, almonds, wine grapes and some cotton. Tuna and sardine fishing are also important, while the last thirty years or so have seen tourism playing an increasingly crucial role.

- The population – mainly concentrated in the two main cities of Palermo and Catania, on the northern and eastern coasts – is something over five million.

▼ Festa di San Paolo, Palazzolo Acréide

And Sicilians do have a point. Pockets of the island have been disfigured by bleak construction projects and unsightly industry, and despite Sicily's limited political autonomy, little has really been done to tackle the more deep-rooted problems: emigration is still high, poverty seemingly endemic, and there's an almost feudal attitude to business and commerce. Aid and investment pour in, but much has been siphoned off by organized crime, which is still widespread. Visitors, of course, see little of this. Mafia activity, for example – almost a byword for Sicilian life when viewed from abroad – is usually an in-house affair, with little or no consequence for travellers.

What Sicily does offer, however, is a remarkably fresh Mediterranean experience. Its main resorts and famous archeological sites have attracted visitors for many years, but budget airline routes have opened up lesser-known parts of this fascinating island, while boutique accommodation and sustainable tourism projects have mushroomed in recent years. The rewards are immediate, notably the dramatic landscapes that range from pin-prick outlying islands to the volcanic heights of Mount Etna. Much of the island is underpopulated and outside the few tourist zones crowds are rare, which means plenty of opportunity to make your own personal discoveries – dazzling white- and black-sand beaches, sparkling coves, rolling wheat plains, upland wildflower meadows and precarious mountain passes. The island was an important power-base during Greek and Roman times, and its excavated ancient cities and temples especially are superb, standing comparison with any ruins in Greece itself. There are stunning Arab and Norman palaces, churches and castles across the island, while the devastation wrought by the great earthquake of 1693 provided a blank slate for some of the most harmonious Baroque architecture to be seen in Europe.

Perhaps above all, there's a distinct way of day-to-day living that separates Sicily from the rest of Italy – an almost operatic exuberance that manifests itself in some extraordinarily vibrant festivals and celebrations. You're unlikely to forget the intensity of the Sicilian experience, whether you're shopping for swordfish in a raucous souk-like market, catching a concert in a dramatic open-air Greek theatre, bathing in a hidden hot spring or island-hopping by hydrofoil across azure seas.

▲ Ceramics shop, Santo Stéfano di Camastra

7

Catacombs, caves and holes in the ground

Sicily is home to some of the world's creepiest tourist destinations, in the form of its catacombs and caves, used as burial places for thousands of years and accessible to anyone with a flashlight and a strong nerve. The oldest, the rock-cut tombs of the great necropolis at Pantálica, were first used in the thirteenth century BC. Another huge swathe of tombs is on view below the Greek temples at Agrigento, while catacombs riddle the ground in the city of Siracusa. But for sheer hands-in-the-air horror, there's no beating the infamous preserved bodies that line the catacombs of Palermo's Convento dei Cappuccini, or the smaller-scale show in the little village of Sávoca, near Taormina. Bodies were placed here as late as the nineteenth century, and the locals used to pay daily visits, often standing in the adjacent niches to accustom themselves to the idea of the great ever-after.

Where to go

Set in a wide bay at the foot of a fertile valley, the capital, **Palermo**, is an essential part of any Sicilian visit, with a vibrant, almost Middle Eastern, flavour and featuring some of the island's finest churches, historic treasures, markets and restaurants. It gets hot and stuffy here in summer, though, which makes escapes out of the city all the more tempting, either to the local beach at Mondello or the hilltop sanctuary on Monte Pellegrino, or further afield to the offshore island of **Ústica**, the Baroque villas of **Bagheria** or the extraordinary church mosaics at **Monreale**. An hour east of Palermo, meanwhile, lies one of Sicily's premier resorts, **Cefalù** (also with its own fabulous church mosaics), with several other smaller-scale beach towns strung out further east along the Tyrrhenian coast. Cefalù is also the jumping-off point for the **Madonie** natural park, whose mountains are the highest on the island after Etna.

Ferries and hydrofoils depart from various points on the Tyrrhenian coast to the **Aeolian Islands**, a stunning chain of seven volcanic islands – including the famed Strómboli – that attracts sun-worshippers, celebrities and adventurous hikers alike. They are the easiest of Sicily's offshore islands to visit, and, many would argue, the best. Otherwise, the northeastern tip of the island is marked by the bustling city of **Messina** – crossing-point to mainland Italy – with the fashionable resort of **Taormina** to the south, the latter perhaps the single most popular holiday destination in Sicily. Further south, halfway down the Ionian coast, dark, Baroque **Catania** is the island's second city, dominated entirely by the graceful cone of **Mount Etna**, Europe's largest and most active volcano.

The finest concentration of historical and architectural sites is arguably in **Siracusa**, where classical ruins and stunning Baroque buildings decorate Sicily's most attractive city. In the southeast region beyond, beautiful towns like **Noto**, **Ragusa** and **Módica** were rebuilt along planned Baroque lines after a devastating earthquake in the seventeenth century, though the unique Neolithic cemeteries of **Pantálica** survived to provide one of Sicily's most atmospheric backwaters.

After the richness of the southeast towns, many find the isolated grandeur of the interior a welcome change. This is the most sparsely populated region, of rolling hills and craggy mountains, yet it hides gems like the historic stronghold of **Enna**, the well-preserved Roman mosaics at **Piazza Armerina**, the majestic Greek excavations of **Morgantina** and the Baroque ceramics town of **Caltagirone**. Away from these few interior towns, remote roads wind back and forth, towards Palermo or Catania, through little-visited destinations like Corleone, whose names chime with the popular image of Sicily as a nest of Mafia intrigue.

Along the south coast, only the spectacular ancient temples of **Agrigento** and the Greek city and beach at **Eraclea Minoa** attract visitors in any numbers. Further around the coast, the up-and-coming city of **Trápani** anchors the west of the island, a great base for anyone interested in delving into the very different character of this side of Sicily. The Arabic influence is stronger here than elsewhere, especially in **Marsala** and **Mazara del Vallo**, while **Selinunte** and **Segesta** hold the most romantic sets of ancient ruins on the island. It's from ports on the south and west coasts, too, that Sicily's most absorbing outlying islands are reached. On **Lampedusa**, on the **Égadi Islands** and, above all, on distant **Pantelleria**, the sea is as clean as you'll find anywhere in the Mediterranean, and you truly feel you're on the edge of Europe.

▲ San Vito lo Capo

Piazza IX Aprile, Taormina

When to go

Sicily can be an extremely uncomfortable place to visit at the height of summer, when the dusty *sirocco* winds blow in from North Africa. In **July** and **August**, you'll roast – and you'll be in the company of tens of thousands of other tourists all jostling for space on the beaches, in the restaurants and at the archeological sites. Hotel availability is much reduced and prices will often be higher. If you want the heat but not the crowds, go in May, June or September, while swimming is possible right into November.

Spring is really the optimum time to come to Sicily, and it arrives early: the almond blossom flowers in February, and there are fresh strawberries in April. **Easter** is a major celebration, a good time to see traditional festivals like the events at Trápani, Érice and Piana degli Albanesi, though again they'll all be oversubscribed with visitors.

Winter is mild by northern European standards and is a nice time to be here, at least on the coast, where the skies stay clear and life continues to be lived very much outdoors. On the other hand, the interior – especially around Enna – is very liable to get snowed under, providing skiing opportunities in the Monti Madonie or on Mount Etna, while anywhere else in the interior can be subject to blasts of wind and torrential downpours of rain.

Average daytime temperatures

	Jan	Feb	Mar	Apr	May	Jun	Jul	Aug	Sep	Oct	Nov	Dec
Palermo												
°C	10.3	10.4	13	16.2	18.7	23	25.3	25.1	23.2	19.9	16.8	12.6
Taormina												
°C	11	10.6	13.1	16.2	20.1	24.1	27.1	27.1	23.7	20	16	12.6

things not to miss

It's not possible to see everything Sicily has to offer in one trip – and we don't suggest you try. What follows is a selective taste of the island's highlights – architecture, dramatic landscapes, and exciting experiences. They're arranged in five colour-coded categories, so you can browse through to find the very best things to see and do. All highlights have a page reference to take you straight into the Guide, where you can find out more.

01 **Lampedusa** Page **303** • Explore superb beaches and crystal-clear waters on a remote island that's halfway to Africa.

02 **Siracusa** Page **217** • Sicily's finest ancient city, Siracusa, has an enjoyable Baroque old town with plenty of places to sit and relax.

04 **Ragusa Ibla** Page **251** • The restorers have been to work in Ragusa Ibla, now one of the best-looking Baroque old towns on the island.

03 **Riserva Naturale dello Zíngaro** Page **320** • Sicily's first and most beautiful nature reserve offers great walks and spectacular marine scenery.

06 Duomo, Cefalù Page **99** • The glittering mosaics in Cefalù's cathedral are the most impressive on the island.

07 Aeolian Islands Page **115** • Island-hopping, Sicilian-style – jump on a ferry or hydrofoil to see the seven Aeolians, each with a distinct flavour of its own.

05 Monreale Page **79** • The delicately sculpted columns are immaculate examples of medieval craftsmanship.

08 Monti Madonie Page **107** • The Madonie mountains, inland from the coast at Cefalù, offer magnificent walks, drives and views.

09 **Valle dei Templi, Agrigento** Page **290** • Agrigento's "Valley of the Temples" is a stunning series of ancient Greek temples lining the ridge below town.

10 **Égadi Islands** Page **338** • Although they are easy to reach from Trápani, the three west-coast Égadi Islands retain a real air of adventure, offering boat tours, fishing trips and excursions.

11 **Villa Romana del Casale, Piazza Armerina** Page **271** • Uncovered at a Roman hunting lodge near Piazza Armerina, these brightly coloured mosaics are unrivalled in the Roman world in their quality and extent.

12 **Segesta** Page **322** • Transport yourself back in time with a visit to the dramatic Greek temple at Segesta.

13 Pescheria, Catania Page **195** • The city's vibrant fish market lives up to its top reputation.

14 Pantálica Page **235** • This high ravine would be spectacular even without the thousands of prehistoric tombs that honeycomb its sheer walls.

15 San Vito Lo Capo Page **334** • Some of the best sands in Sicily are found at the lively resort of San Vito Lo Capo.

16 Teatro Greco, Taormina Page **175** • This magnificently located ancient theatre offers wonderful views towards Etna and down to the sea, and is still used to stage concerts and dramas.

17 **Noto** Page **238** • The whole town is a marvel of Baroque building, filled with glorious honey-coloured palaces and churches.

18 **Museo delle Marionette, Palermo** Page **65** • Explore the history of Sicilian puppet theatre, or even catch a show, at Palermo's specialist puppet museum.

19 **Mount Etna** Page **203** • Europe's greatest volcano – still very active – is the ultimate Sicilian adventure trip.

Basics

Basics

Getting there

Budget airlines fly direct to Sicily from all over Europe and, outside peak holiday periods, the taxes often exceed the price of the ticket. The island has two main airports, at Palermo in the west and Catania in the east, though Ryanair and others use Trápani airport in the far west, and there are also airports on the main outlying islands of Pantelleria and Lampedusa. No direct flights go to Sicily from the US, Canada, Australia or New Zealand: the main points of entry to Italy are Rome and Milan, from where it's easy to pick up a connection to any of the Sicilian airports. If you want to see some of France or Italy en route, or are taking a vehicle, various overland combinations of ferry, rail and road are possible, though these will nearly always work out pricier than flying direct. European rail passes will save you some money, but most need to be purchased before you leave. Finally, package holidays and tours can be good value – from beach holidays to escorted historical tours – while airlines, travel agents and specialist operators can all also provide car rental, hotel bookings and other useful services. Car rental, in particular, is usually best arranged before you leave.

Air fares are seasonal, at their highest at Easter (a big celebration in Sicily), Christmas and New Year (as Sicilian émigrés come home), and between June and August (when the weather is hottest and the island the busiest). The **cheapest flights** from the UK and Europe are usually with no-frills budget and charter airlines, especially if you're prepared to book several weeks in advance or chance a last-minute deal. Budget airline tickets are sold on a one-way basis, so you may find the outward or return leg of your journey significantly more expensive depending on demand. Cheap flights also tend to have fixed dates and are non-changeable and non-refundable. Major **scheduled airlines** are usually (though not always) more expensive, but tickets remain valid for three months and usually have a degree of flexibility should you need to change dates after booking.

Flights from the UK and Ireland

There are daily **direct flights to Sicily** (around 3hr) with easyJet (London Gatwick to Palermo, ⓦwww.easyjet.com), Ryanair (Stansted, Luton and Liverpool to Trápani, ⓦwww.ryanair.com) and British Airways (Gatwick to Catania, ⓦwww.britishairways .com), while Thomsonfly (ⓦwww.thomsonfly .com) has a weekly seasonal service (May to Oct) from either Gatwick or Manchester to Catania. Prices on all routes can range from as little as £7.99 plus taxes each way to over £300 return. **From Ireland**, Ryanair offers a direct flight from Dublin to Trápani.

The alternative from the UK or Ireland is to fly to one of the many airports on the **Italian mainland**, and travel onwards from there. Ryanair alone flies to around twelve Italian airports, and uses Trápani as its Sicilian hub, easyJet flies from Milan to Catania, while Alitalia and British Airways have decent connections from Rome, Milan and others to Palermo, Catania, Trápani, Lampedusa and Pantelleria. Meridiana (ⓦwww.meridiana .it) has daily services from London Gatwick to Florence with onward connections to Catania, as well as connections between half a dozen other Italian cities and Palermo, Lampedusa and Pantelleria. There are also flights to Sicily with the budget and holiday airlines of other countries (like Germany) with an established tourist connection. In the end, you'll have to weigh up the extra travelling time flying via mainland Italy, or elsewhere, with the savings you might make.

Six steps to a better kind of travel

At Rough Guides we are passionately committed to travel. We feel strongly that only through travelling do we truly come to understand the world we live in and the people we share it with – plus tourism has brought a great deal of **benefit** to developing economies around the world over the last few decades. But the extraordinary growth in tourism has also damaged some places irreparably, and of course **climate change** is exacerbated by most forms of transport, especially flying. This means that now more than ever it's important to **travel thoughtfully** and **responsibly**, with respect for the cultures you're visiting – not only to derive the most benefit from your trip but also to preserve the best bits of the planet for everyone to enjoy. At Rough Guides we feel there are six main areas in which you can make a difference:

• Consider what you're contributing to the **local economy**, and how much the services you use do the same, whether it's through employing local workers and guides or sourcing locally grown produce and local services.

• Consider the **environment** on holiday as well as at home. Water is scarce in many developing destinations, and the biodiversity of local flora and fauna can be adversely affected by tourism. Try to patronize businesses that take account of this.

• Travel with a purpose, not just to tick off experiences. Consider **spending longer** in a place, and getting to know it and its people.

• Give thought to how often you **fly**. Try to avoid short hops by air and more harmful night flights.

• Consider **alternatives to flying**, travelling instead by bus, train, boat and even by bike or on foot where possible.

• Make your trips **"climate neutral"** via a reputable carbon offset scheme. All Rough Guide flights are offset, and every year we donate money to a variety of charities devoted to combating the effects of climate change.

Flights from the US and Canada

There are **no direct flights** from the US and Canada to Sicily, so you'll have to fly first to Rome or Milan (9 hours from east coast US/Canada, 12 hours from Chicago, 15 hours from west coast US/Canada). For the connection to Sicily add on another hour and a half or so, plus any time spent waiting for the connection itself.

Alitalia (W www.alitalia.com) flies direct every day between the US or Canada and Italy, and their great advantage is the ease of making the connecting flight to Sicily with the same airline. But several other airlines – including Delta (W www.delta.com), Continental (W www.continental.com) and Air Canada (W www.aircanada.com) – fly to Rome or Milan, and can arrange an onward connection for you. Or you can fly to Italy with airlines like British Airways, Air France, Lufthansa and Iberia, which travel via their respective European hubs.

Generally, the cheapest round-trip fare from the US to Palermo or Catania, via Rome or Milan, starts at around US$600, rising to US$1000 during the summer. From Canada, low-season fares start at around Can$800, increasing to around Can$1400 in high season. The alternative option is to pick up a discounted flight to the UK, and then fly on to Sicily with one of the European budget airlines (see section above). It depends on how soon in advance you book, and the season, as to whether this will be a realistic way to save money.

Flights from Australia and New Zealand

Although there are **no direct flights** from Australia or New Zealand to Sicily, many airlines offer through tickets with their partners via European or Asian hubs. Round-trip fares from the main cities in Australia start from around Aus$1600 in low season, going up to around Aus$2000 in high season; from

New Zealand, fares cost from NZ$3000. Fares don't vary as much between airlines as you might think, and in the end you'll be basing your choice on things like flight timings, routes and possible stop-offs on the way. If you're seeing Sicily as part of a wider European trip, you might want to aim first for the UK in any case, since there's a wider choice of cheap options to Sicily once there – or consider a **Round-the-World** (RTW) fare, though note that these tend to include only Rome or Milan as standard stopovers.

Package holidays and tours

Most **package holidays** are to Taormina, Sicily's most chic resort, and its less glamorous beachside neighbour Giardini-Naxos (on the east coast), and to the historic beach town of Cefalù (north coast, near Palermo), though you'll also see holidays in the Aeolian Islands, and special tours of the major historical sights which take in overnight stops in several towns. It's obviously cheapest to go out of season, something to be recommended anyway as the resorts and sights are much less crowded, and the weather warm without being oppressive.

From the UK, a flight and a week's self-catering apartment accommodation starts at around £350 per person. Staying in a three-star hotel on a B&B basis starts from around £450, and for four- and five-star properties you're looking at more like £800–1000. Obviously, special deals and last-minute offers can undercut these prices; for the best current deals consult any high-street or online travel agent. Some tour operators organize **specialist holidays** to Sicily, particularly walking tours, culinary trips, and art and archeology holidays, but they are usually more expensive as accommodation, food, local transport and the services of a guide are nearly always included. Walking tours tend to be cheapest, based on simple rural two- and three-star hotels, but a week's fully inclusive cultural holiday can easily cost £2000, and a ten-day cruise from around £3000.

From the US, dozens of companies operate group travel and tours in Italy, ranging from all-inclusive escorted bus tours to smaller specialized groups out biking and hiking.

Although specifically Sicilian options are less common, most general operators usually offer tours at least partly based on the island. You can also, of course, simply book a hotel-plus-flight deal, or rent a villa or a farmhouse for a week or two. Prices vary wildly, so check what you are getting for your money (most don't include the cost of the airfare, though that can always be arranged for you). Reckon on paying at least US$2000 for a standard ten-day touring vacation without flight, and up to US$6000 for a fourteen-day escorted specialist package.

Trains

It's a long journey **from the UK to Sicily** by train (2672km from London to Messina). The fastest route (via Paris, Rome and Naples) is scheduled to take around 30 hours, but delays on the Italian stretch are not uncommon. Tickets include seat reservations, though for any degree of comfort it's also worth reserving a couchette or sleeping car for the overnight part of the journey. The easiest way is to take the **Eurostar** service (ⓦwww.eurostar.com) from London to Paris (from £69 return), then the **overnight train from Paris to Rome** (from £66 return), followed by the direct Intercity express **from Rome to Sicily** (calling at Messina, Taormina, Catania and Siracusa, or to Palermo, from around £70 return). There's also an overnight Rome-to-Sicily service. You can book tickets online with Rail Europe (ⓦwww.raileurope .co.uk, www.raileurope.com), and with Italian Railways (ⓦwww.trenitalia.com, English-language version available) – the Italian Railways sites also post fares and full Italian train timetables.

The invaluable train travel website ⓦ**www .seat61.com** tells you exactly how to book the entire journey, down to precise details about the various sleeper-train options. It also has a "Railpasses" section which will help you decide whether or not buying a rail pass is a good idea. InterRail and Eurail are the best known of these, giving unlimited rail travel throughout Europe, as well as providing discounts on Eurostar and cross-Channel ferry crossings. For details of rail passes, including those for use solely within Italy, see "Getting around", p.24.

Buses

It's difficult to make any case for travelling to Sicily by bus, especially as there's no direct service from the UK. **Eurolines** (🌐www .nationalexpress.com) has a service from London Victoria to Naples, but that takes at least 35 hours depending on connections in Paris and Milan, and then you'll have to take a second overnight bus with Italian bus company SAIS (🌐www.saistrasporti.it) on to Sicily (another 6 hours to Messina, 10 to Palermo). Even with book-in-advance promotional fares (up to thirty days in advance) you're looking at from £77 each way for the London–Naples section, and another €35 each way for Naples–Sicily. It hardly compares with most budget airline fares, and you'll be half-dead when you arrive.

By car and ferry

Driving to Sicily from the UK, using the standard **cross-Channel services or Eurotunnel** (🌐www.eurotunnel.com) through the Channel Tunnel, takes at least two full days. From the France/Italy border, it's possible, with a bit of luck, to reach the Straits of Messina in a long day if you keep on the motorways. While not a cheap option (factoring in the cross-Channel trip, tolls, overnight stops and meals), it is a good way of seeing something of France and Italy on the way.

The shortest crossing from the Italian mainland, over the Straits of Messina, is from **Villa San Giovanni by ferry**; or, fifteen minutes further south – at the end of the motorway – by hydrofoil or fast ferry from **Réggio di Calabria**. All the details are given in the box on p.152.

To cut the driving time in Italy, you could use one of the earlier ferry or hydrofoil crossings from the Italian mainland to Sicily, **from Genova** (to Palermo, 20hr), **Salerno** (to Palermo, 12hr, or Messina, 8hr), **Civita-vecchia** (ie, Rome, to Palermo, 12hr, or Catania, 18hr) or **Naples** (to Palermo 11hr, or Aeolian Islands 4–6hr). Non-drivers could even combine a cheap flight (say Ryanair to Genoa) with one of these ferry crossings. You can also approach Sicily by travelling **via Corsica or Sardinia**, though obviously this is a somewhat complicated route involving two

lengthy crossings – it's not recommended for a short trip to Sicily. The Genova, Salerno and Naples crossing schedules are seasonal, and with several different operators, but there are daily sailings in summer and at least two or three per week throughout the year. The best places to check schedules and fares, and book tickets, are the exhaustive websites 🌐**www.directferries.co.uk** and **www.viamare.com**, which contain details about every Italian ferry service.

Booking flights and services online

🌐**www.cheapflights.co.uk, www.cheap flights.com** Price comparison on flights, short breaks, packages and other deals.

🌐 **www.ebookers.com, www.ebookers.ie** Flights, hotels, cars and holiday packages.

🌐 **www.expedia.co.uk, www.expedia.com, www.expedia.ca, www.expedia.co.nz, www.expedia.com.au** Discount airfares, all-airline search engine, and daily deals on hotels, cars and packages.

🌐**www.lastminute.com, www.travelocity .com** Destination guides, hot fares and good deals on car rental, rail passes and accommodation, with dedicated sites for UK, US, Canada, Ireland, Australia and New Zealand.

Discount flight agents

North South Travel UK ☎01245/608 291, 🌐www.northsouthtravel.co.uk. Friendly, competitive travel agency, offering discounted fares worldwide. Profits are used to support projects in the developing world, especially the promotion of sustainable tourism.

STA Travel UK ☎0871/2300 040, US ☎1-800/781-4040, Australia ☎134 782, New Zealand ☎0800/474 400, South Africa ☎0861/781 781, 🌐www.statravel.com. Worldwide specialists in independent travel; also student IDs, travel insurance, car rental, rail passes, and more. Good discounts for students and under-26s.

Trailfinders UK ☎0845/058 5858, Republic of Ireland ☎01/677 7888, Australia ☎1300/780 212, 🌐www.trailfinders.com. One of the best-informed and most efficient agents for independent travellers.

Tour operators

Art and culture

Martin Randall Travel UK ☎0208/742 3355, 🌐www.martinrandall.com. Small-group cultural tours, led by experts on art, history, archeology and music, to the classic sites of Sicily. Tours depart two or three times a year, costing from £3550 for thirteen days, including flights, meals and transport. Also shorter tours of Palermo (7 days, £1940) or gastronomic Sicily (8 days, £2370).

Tabona and Walford UK ☎0208/767 6789, ⓦwww.tabonaandwalford.com. Tailor-made cultural walking holidays in Érice and the west or the Madonie and Lípari, with bike and market excursions, vineyard visits and other activities. From around £800.

Botanical

Naturetrek UK ☎01962/733 051, ⓦwww.naturetrek.co.uk. Offers an all-inclusive eight-day "Wild Flowers of Sicily" tour (£1195) around Etna and the Madonie mountains, with an annual spring departure.

Food and drink

Arblaster & Clarke UK ☎01730/263 111, ⓦwww.arblasterandclarke.com. Deluxe seven-night wine tours, including flights, meals and tastings, plus an expert guide, from £1999. There's also a wine cruise of Italian islands, including Sicily and its offshore islands.

The International Kitchen US ☎1-800/945-8606, ⓦwww.theinternationalkitchen.com. Six-night all-inclusive Sicilian culinary tours and cooking school holidays, from US$2750, with winery and market visits included.

Italian Connection Canada ☎1-800/462-7911, ⓦwww.italian-connection.com. The "Savoring Sicily" walking and culinary tour (seven days, from US$3960) ranges across the island from east to west. But there are also more specialist cooking and cultural tours, all accompanied by local experts.

General

Citalia UK ☎0800/232 1802, ⓦwww.citalia.com. Italian holiday specialist, offering short breaks, resort holidays, tailor-made island tours, villas and car rental.

CIT Holidays Australia ☎1300/361 500, ⓦwww.cit.com.au. Italian travel specialists, offering Sicily tours, hotel reservations, car rental and rail passes.

Italiatours US ☎1-800/283-7262, ⓦwww.italiatours.com. Low-cost Italy tour specialist with a range of escorted bus-tour programmes, from three days to a week exploring the island highlights (from around US$1200). Also hotel bookings, flights and transfers.

Sunvil Holidays UK ☎0208/758 4722, ⓦwww.sunvil.co.uk. Holidays in the best of Sicily's resorts and historic cities, as well as island-based stays on Lípari. Prices vary according to standard of accommodation offered; tailor-made routes and fly-drive holidays also available.

Sailing

Nautilus Yachting UK ☎01732/867 445, ⓦwww.nautilus-yachting.co.uk. Yacht holidays, operating out of Sant'Agata di Militello (for the Aeolians) and Marsala (the Égadis). Prices start from £1060 for the boat for a week, though if you have no experience you can add the services of a skipper from around another £150 a day.

Walking

Adventure Center US ☎1-800/228-8747, ⓦwww.adventurecenter.com. The worldwide adventure and hiking specialist has an eight-day "Sicilian Volcano Hike" walking tour that ranges from Etna to the Aeolian islands, from US$1630.

Alternative Travel Group UK ☎01865/315 678, ⓦwww.atg-oxford.co.uk. Inclusive eight-day walking holidays (April–June & Sept/Oct) in the Monti Madonie, from Enna to Cefalù. Accommodation is mostly two- and three-star standard, and prices start at £895 for the self-guided option or £2125 for a fully inclusive escorted walking holiday. Seven-night best of western/eastern Sicily walking trips in four/five-star hotels start at £2575.

Ramblers Worldwide Holidays UK ☎01707/331 133, ⓦwww.ramblersholidays.co.uk. Eight-day walking holidays based in Francavilla (near Taormina) for seeing eastern Sicily (from around £619), or a twelve-day touring holiday of the island (from around £1119). Weekly departures Feb, March–May, Sept, Oct & Dec.

Getting around

You don't have to rent a car to see Sicily's major towns and sights, but getting around by public transport is not always as easy as it should be. The rail system is slow, few buses run on Sundays and route information can be frustratingly difficult to extract, even from the bus and train stations themselves. Sicily's geography makes it a push to get right across the island – say from Siracusa to Trápani – in a single day, though you'll be able to travel most of one of the coastlines easily enough. On the positive side, public transport prices are among the cheapest in Europe.

The "Travel details" section at the end of each chapter in this book gives the full picture on transport schedules and frequencies. Note that unless specified, these refer to regular working-day schedules, ie Monday to Saturday; services are much reduced, or even nonexistent, on Sundays. Note also that comments such as "every 30min" are approximations – on the railways in particular, there are occasional gaps in the schedule, typically occurring just after the morning rush hour, when the gap between trains may be twice as long as normal.

One thing to bear in mind is that travelling by train is not the best way to see all of the island. Some stations are located a fair distance from their towns – Enna and Taormina are two notable examples (though there are bus connections) – while much of the west and centre of Sicily is only accessible by bus or car.

By train

Italian State Railways, **Ferrovie dello Stato** (FS), operates the trains in Sicily (for details of Sicily's only private railway, the Ferrovia Circumetnea route around the base of Mount Etna, see p.208). The FS website Ⓦ www.trenitalia.com has a useful English-language version, where you can view timetables and book tickets. Trains connect all the major Sicilian towns, but are more prevalent in the east of the island than the west. On the whole they *do* leave on time, with the notable exception of those on the Messina–Palermo and Messina–Catania/Siracusa routes that have come from the mainland. These latter can be delayed by up

to three hours, though around an hour late is more normal.

Of the various types of train, the most expensive are the **Intercity** (IC) trains that link the main cities. **Diretto** and **Interregionale** trains are long-distance expresses, calling only at larger stations, while the **Regionale** services (also called Locale), which stop at every place with a population higher than zero, are usually ones to avoid. A **seat reservation** (*prenotazione*) is obligatory on Intercity services and advisable on other trains where possible, especially in summer when trains can get crowded. You can buy tickets and make reservations at any major train station, or buy online on the FS website (both regional and Intercity services) and print your own tickets. **Fares** are very reasonable – a typical journey, say Palermo to Catania, costs around €16. Children aged 4–12 pay half price, while the under-4s travel free provided they do not occupy a seat. If you jump on the train without a ticket you'll pay the full fare plus a fine to the conductor.

Information boards and **timetables** are displayed at stations. "Departures" are *Partenze*, "Arrivals" *Arrivi*, "Delayed" *In Ritardo*, while some services are seasonal (*periódico*) or only operate between certain dates (*Si effetua dal... al...*). *Feriale* is the word for the Monday-to-Saturday service, symbolized by two crossed hammers; *festivo* means that a train runs only on Sundays and holidays, with a cross as its symbol.

Unless you're visiting Sicily as part of a wider Italian or European tour, the major pan-European **rail passes** (InterRail and Eurail) are not worth considering. Both

Stamp it

All rail stations and platforms have validation machines in which passengers must stamp their ticket before embarking on their journey. Failure to **validate your ticket** may land you with an on-the-spot fine, so if the machine at your departure station doesn't work, tell the train ticket-inspector as soon as possible (*"le macchine di validazione non funzionano"*).

schemes do also have single-country Italy rail passes, but given the relative cheapness of local train tickets, and the restricted service in some parts of Sicily, buying one of these probably won't save you any money either. The **InterRail Italy** pass (@ www .raileurope.co.uk/inter-rail) is only available to European residents, and allows three, four, six or eight days' train travel in one month (from £105 for three days, under-26s from £69). For anyone else, Eurail (@ www.rail europe.com) has various Italy passes available, typically offering three days' travel in two months (from US$195, under-26s from $159). All passes have to be bought before you leave home, and you'll still be liable for supplements and seat reservations on Intercity trains.

By bus

Almost anywhere you want to go will have some kind of **regional bus** (*autobus* or *pullman*) service, usually quicker than the train (especially between the major towns and cities), but generally more expensive.

Between them, four main **companies** – SAIS Trasporti (@ www.saistrasporti.it), SAIS Autolinee (@ www.saisautolinee.it), AST (@ www.aziendasicilianatrasporti.it) and Interbus (@ www.interbus.it) – cover most of the island. Other companies stick to local routes. Many routes are linked to school/ market requirements, which can mean a frighteningly early start, last departures in the afternoon, and occasionally no services during school holidays, while nearly every-where services are drastically reduced, or nonexistent, on Sundays.

The local **bus station** (*autostazione*) is often in a central piazza, or outside the train station, though in some towns different bus companies have different bus terminals. Timetables are available on the companies' websites, and also from company offices and bus stations. You usually buy tickets on the bus, though on longer routes (and to be sure of a place) you can buy them in advance from the companies' offices. On most routes, it's possible to flag a bus down if you want a ride. If you want to get off, ask *"posso scéndere?"*; "the next stop" is *"la próssima fermata"*.

City buses usually charge a flat fare of around €1, and the tickets are often valid for ninety minutes, allowing you to change services for free within that time. Invariably, you need a ticket *before* you get on. Buy them in *tabacchi*, or from the kiosks and vendors at bus stops, and then validate them in the machine in the bus. Checks are frequently made by inspectors who block both exits as they get on, though if you don't have a ticket you'll usually get off with an earful of Sicilian and be made to buy one; some inspectors might hold out for the spot fine.

real sicily **Sunvil** discovery

find the real Sicily with Sunvil- tailor-made trips & fly-drives.

call **020 8758 4722**
or visit **Sunvil.co.uk/sicily**

find the real country

ATOL 808, ABTA V6218, AITO PROTECTED

By car

Driving in Sicily is almost a competitive sport, and although the Sicilians aren't the world's worst drivers they don't win any safety prizes either. However, with a car you'll be able to see a lot of the island quickly, and reach the more isolated coastal and inland areas.

Most **main roads** are prefixed SS (Strada Statale) or SP (Strada Provinciale), and signposting is pretty good. On the whole they are two-lane roads with passing places on hills, though some stretches near towns and cities are dual carriageway. **Road maintenance**, however, is very patchy and even major routes can be badly potholed. In the interior, on long routes like the SS120, SS121 or SS189, you should expect road washouts, resurfacing work and other interruptions on any journey.

Some roads provide spectacular cross-country driving routes (see the "best drives" box), as do the impressive Sicilian **motorways** (autostradas), which are carried on great piers spanning the island. These link Messina–Catania–Siracusa (A18), Catania–Palermo (A19), Palermo–Trápani/Mazara del Vallo (A29) and Messina–Palermo (A20), while work continues on extending the motorway network towards Agrigento and

Gela. The Messina–Catania–Siracusa and Messina–Palermo autostradas are **toll-roads** (*pedaggio*, toll; *autostrada a pedaggio*, toll-motorway). Take a ticket as you come on, and pay on exit; the amount due is flashed up on a screen.

Rules of the road are straightforward: drive on the right; at junctions, where there's any ambiguity, give precedence to vehicles coming from the right; observe the speed limits (50km/h in built-up areas, 110km/h on country roads, 130km/h on autostradas); and *don't* drink and drive. Speed cameras and traffic-calming humps are becoming more evident, but this doesn't seem to deter Sicilians from travelling at any speed they choose.

Italian **fuel prices** are roughly in line with those in the UK, with unleaded petrol (*senza piombo*) slightly cheaper than leaded (*super*). Blue lines in towns signify authorized **parking zones**, where you'll pay around €1 an hour, either in a meter or to an attendant hovering nearby. You can also often buy a *biglietto parcheggio*, a scratch card, from *tabacchi* or local bars, where you scratch off the date and time and leave it in the windscreen. However, if you've parked in a street that turns into a market by day, you'll be stuck until close of business, while if you park in a *zona di rimozione* (tow-away zone), your car will most likely not be there when you get back. Most cities also have official **car parks** and garages, charging between €8 and €12 a day. **Never leave anything visible in the car** when you leave it (hide away or remove MP3 players and satnavs), and always depress your aerial and tuck in the wing mirrors.

To drive in Sicily, you need a valid **driving licence** and, if you are a non-EU licence holder, an international driving permit. It's *compulsory* to carry your car documents and passport while you're driving, and you'll be required to present them if you're stopped by the police – not an uncommon occurrence. You are also required to carry a triangular danger sign, which will be provided with rental cars. Many car insurance policies cover taking your own car to Italy; check with your insurer when planning your trip (you'll need an international green card of insurance). You'd also be advised to take

Sicily's six best drives

1. **SS120, Nicosia to Polizzi Generosa** – bare landscape punctuated by isolated hilltop villages, with Etna dominating the eastern horizon.

2. **SS185, Tyrrhenian coast to Giardini-Naxos** – across the Peloritani mountains to Etna and the sea.

3. **Ávola to Cava Grande** – winding up the mountainside to where eagles dare.

4. **SP624 and SP5, Palermo to Piana degli Albanesi** – past jagged fangs and towers of rock, with glimpses of lakes and lingering views over fertile valleys.

5. **Trápani to Erice** – for the startling interplay of coast and mountain.

6. **SS118, Agrigento to Corleone** – remote western valleys and crags, rock tombs and Mafia towns.

The Sicilian driving experience

If all you had to do was drive on Sicilian **motorways** – light traffic, fast travel, dramatic scenery – things would be fine. Unfortunately, you have to come off them sooner or later and drive into a town, and then all bets are off. The good news is that the swirling town **traffic** isn't as horrific as it first looks – the secret is to make it *very* clear what you're going to do, using your horn as much as your indicators and brakes. There are established **rules** of the road in force, though Sicilians, needless to say, ignore most, if not all, of them as a matter of principle. A character in Andrea Camilleri's Inspector Montalbano novels drives "like a dog on drugs", which is a pretty fair assessment of local driving skills, and if you go your entire holiday without being cut up on the inside, jumped at a junction or overtaken on a blind bend, you'll have done well. You'll switch your satnav off the first time you encounter a Sicilian **one-way system** – installed by traffic engineers with a sense of humour – which lead you into old-town areas where the streets grow ever narrower until the point that you can't back out or turn round. It usually works out fine if you rigidly follow the one-way signs, though matters aren't helped by it being accepted local **parking** practice simply to drive your car up on the pavement, or stop where it's most convenient for the driver – this can include the middle of the street, or pausing for a chat with a mate at a major road junction. Out in the **countryside** it's generally less of a hassle, though you do have to allow for shepherds and their sheep (and there aren't many places in Europe you can still say that about), idling around the next bend. Pedestrians, meanwhile, deal with the general mayhem by taking a deep breath, staring straight at the drivers and strolling boldly across the road. If in doubt, follow someone old and infirm, or put out your hand policeman-like, but *never* assume that you're safe on a pedestrian crossing – they're regarded by most drivers as an invitation to play human skittles.

out extra cover for motoring assistance in case you break down, and **motoring organizations** like the RAC (ⓦwww.rac.co.uk) or the AA (ⓦwww.theaa.co.uk) can help. Alternatively, by dialling ☎116 you can get 24-hour assistance from the Automobile Club d'Italia (ⓦwww.aci.it).

Car rental

Car rental in Sicily costs from around €250 per week for a three-door, a/c Fiat Punto, with unlimited mileage. It's usually cheaper arranged in advance through one of the large international chains (Avis, Budget, Europcar, Hertz, Holiday Autos, Thrifty, for example) – check websites for competitive Internet deals and special offers – or with your travel agent or tour operator. Otherwise, rental agencies – including local companies, like Maggiore (ⓦwww.maggiore.it) – are found in the major cities and at Palermo, Catania and Trápani airports.

It's essential to check that you have adequate **insurance cover** for a rental car. Going by the dents and scratches on almost

every car on the road, you want to make sure that your liability is limited as far as possible. Ensure that all visible damage on a car is duly marked on the rental sheet. It's worth paying the extra charge to reduce the "excess" payment levied for any damage, and most rental companies these days offer a zero-excess option for an extra charge. You can also avoid excess charges by taking out an annual insurance policy (from £49) with ⓦwww.insurance4carhire.com, which also covers windscreen and tyre damage.

Scooters, quads and mokes

Virtually everyone in Sicily – kids to grandmas – rides a **moped or scooter**, although the smaller models are not suitable for any kind of long-distance travel. They're ideal for shooting around towns, and you can rent them in Taormina, Cefalù and other holiday centres – check the Guide for details. Crash helmets are compulsory, though you'll see many Sicilian youths just riding with one slung over one arm. Lampedusa and other offshore islands also have **quad-bikes** and **mini-mokes** available for rent, which are great for bashing around local roads to beaches and beauty spots – just be aware that there's a high accident rate with machines like these.

Ferries and hydrofoils

There are **ferries** (*traghetti*) and **hydrofoils** (*aliscafi*) to the Aeolians, the Égadi and Pelágie islands, and Pantelleria and Ústica, and there's also a summer hydrofoil service that runs along the northern Tyrrhenian coast, from Palermo to the Aeolians, stopping at a couple of towns on the way. The main **operators** are Siremar (www.siremar.it), SNAV (www.snav.it), NGI (www.ngi-spa.it) and Ústica Lines (www.usticalines.it), and you'll find full details about services, schedules and fares in the relevant sections of the Guide. Timetables are also available online, pinned up at the dockside or are available from the ferry offices and tourist offices.

You can **island-hop** year-round in the Aeolians and Égadis. Services are heavily used in summer, making early booking advisable, though you should always be able to get on a ferry if you just turn up. Both passenger and **car-ferry** services operate, though it's debatable how much you'll need a car on any of the islands – only Lípari, Pantelleria and Lampedusa are of any size, and in any case you can rent a vehicle there if you need to.

Internal flights

If you're short on time, consider flying to **Lampedusa** or **Pantelleria** from Trápani, Palermo or Catania – otherwise, the alternative is an overnight ferry ride. Flights are with Meridiana (www.meridiana.it), and prices start at around €60 one-way – check the website for timetables and the latest offers. Meridiana also connects Sicily to destinations on the Italian mainland, including Rome, Milan and Venice, while Alitalia (www.alitalia.it), together with its low-cost partner Air One (www.flyairone.it), has services to a dozen or more Italian airports.

Accommodation

On the whole, accommodation in Sicily is slightly cheaper than in the rest of Italy, starting at around €60 a night for a basic double or twin room (though prices can double in summer in the most popular resorts). The only accommodation cheaper than this comes in the form of the very few youth hostels and the many campsites across the island. Hotels run across the entire range, from crumbling townhouses to five-star palaces, from restored country villas to resort hotels. There's also a large number of "bed and breakfast" places and "*agriturismo*" rural properties, where the attraction is mixing with your hosts and experiencing something of Sicilian life.

All hotel accommodation is officially graded and the tariffs fixed by law. In tourist areas, there's often a low-season and high-season **price**, but whatever it costs, the rate should be posted on the door of the room. In summer (usually in August) some places – especially in major resorts or on outlying islands – insist on half-board accommodation (*mezza pensione*, full-board *pensione* *completa*), when the price will also include lunch or dinner, and there may even be a three-night or longer minimum stay. Few single rooms are available anywhere and, in high season especially, lone travellers will often pay most of the price of a double. B&Bs are also regulated by law, but such is their proliferation that many – while offering a perfectly fine experience – operate outside the tax regime and may not be interested in seeing your passport or providing you with a receipt. **Breakfast** is usually included in the price in hotels (save perhaps in the very cheapest places), but not when you stay in *afittacamere* ("rooms") places or apartments – while, sometimes, in "bed and breakfast" places, you'll be given a voucher instead for breakfast at a nearby bar.

Hotels

Sicilian hotels are known by various titles (**pensione**, **albergo** – plural *alberghi* – or even simply "hotel") and are graded with one to five stars. Some cheaper hotels, especially in town centres, are located in old mansion buildings or palaces, which can be characterful places to stay. However, not all have been modernized, so plumbing, heating and decor might occasionally be on the primitive side, and they probably won't take credit cards either.

A room in a one-star hotel starts at around €60 and there's usually a choice of rooms, with or without en-suite bath- or shower-room. Facilities in a one-star hotel tend to be minimal (there are exceptions), but once you're up to three-star level (€90–120) you can expect an en-suite room with satellite TV, air conditioning and, increasingly, internet and wi-fi. Four-star hotels, plus hotels in resorts and on islands, can charge pretty much what they like, especially in August when room prices can top €300, while the dozen or so five-star hotels on the island (notably in Palermo, Taormina, Catania and Siracusa) charge international rates. There are some bargains around out of the summer season, when even the classier hotels drop their room rates by as much as forty percent, and in cheaper places you

might be able to negotiate a lower rate for a longer stay (ask "*C'è uno sconto per due/ tre/quattro notti?*").

In the cheaper places especially, you can always **ask to see the room** before you take it ("*Posso vedere?*") – and check if it's en suite ("*La cámera ha un bagno privato?*") or air conditioned ("*C'è aria condizionata?*"). It's worth noting that smaller, cheaper places don't have much in the way of heating in the winter – you can freeze in some of the older *palazzi*.

Private rooms and B&Bs

Private rooms (*cámere*, *affitacamere*) for rent are common in beach resorts and on the Aeolian and Égadi Islands. Facilities vary, but the best are clean and modern, with private bathroom and often with a kitchenette. Prices start at about €50, with variations depending on the season and location – in August in Taormina and on the Aeolians you might pay as much as €100 a night for a room. Breakfast isn't usually included, but is sometimes available for an extra charge.

Recent years have seen a huge growth in the number of "**bed and breakfasts**" (as they term themselves). Pretty much every Sicilian town now has some B&B choices, all liberally signposted as you tour around, and in many places they've taken over from the old-fashioned family-run pensions. Many are actually little different from private rooms, with the owners either not living on the premises or not always available throughout the day – often, you have to call a mobile phone number to summon attendance. Prices start at around €30 per person per night, usually for an en-suite room in a nicely maintained building where you'll get a flavour

---

Accommodation price codes

All establishments listed in this guide have been coded according to price. The codes represent the cheapest available double/twin room in high season (Easter & June–Aug), though rates may be lower at other times. August itself is often an exception in resorts, when prices can be double the normal rate. For youth hostels we give a per-person euro price for a dorm bed instead. The categories are:

❶ €60 and under   **❹** €121–150   **❼** €251–300

❷ €61–90   **❺** €151–200   **❽** €301 and over

❸ €91–120   **❻** €201–250

A dozen unusual places to stay

Alla Giudecca, Siracusa. Ancient Jewish houses, renovated as boutique hotel. See p.220.

L'Atelier sul Mare, Castel di Tusa. Extraordinary "art hotel" on the northern coast. See p.104.

Dammuso houses, Pantelleria. Native domed cube-houses, available for rent. See p.366.

Eremo della Giubiliana, Ragusa. Medieval feudal estate and hermitage, now five-star country retreat. See p.250.

Grand Hotel Villa Igiea, Acquasanta, near Palermo. Luxury Art Nouveau seaside villa. See p.57.

Azienda Agricola Silvia Sillitti, Caltanissetta. Stay on a working, organic olive, almond and wheat farm. See p.268.

Ostello del Borgo, Piazza Armerina. Ancient Benedictine convent, now backpackers' hostel and budget hotel. See p.269.

Palazzo Il Cavaliere, Módica. Stylishly restored Baroque B&B. See p.246.

La Salina Borgo di Mare, Salina. Aeolian Island chic in an old saltworks. See p.133.

Stenopus Greco, Porticello. Boutique rooms in a working fishing port near Palermo. See p.85.

Suite d'Autore, Piazza Armerina. Every artwork and piece of furniture is for sale in Piazza Amerina's outrageously quirky designer hotel. See p.269.

Tonnara di Bonagia, Bonagia, near Trápani. Stylish lodgings in a converted tuna-fishing village. See p.334.

---

of Sicilian home life. Some B&Bs are truly magnificent, based in remarkable Baroque *palazzi* or elegant country houses, and you can pay as much as €90 per person. The southeast particularly has lots of B&Bs, and tourist-friendly towns like Siracusa, Ragusa, Módica and Noto are awash with stylishly converted old homes. Touring Club Italiano publishes an annual "Bed and Breakfast" guide to Italy, available in local bookshops, or check the very useful websites **Bed and Breakfast Italia** (Wwww.bbitalia.it) and **Caffèlletto** (Wwww.caffelletto.it), where you can view scores of properties.

Self-catering villas and apartments

Private holiday apartments are available in places like Taormina, Cefalù, Siracusa and the Aeolians, and are generally rented for anything from a couple of nights to a month. Although these can be very expensive in the peak summer season – when Italian families come on holiday – real bargains can be found in May or late September, and during the winter. Ask in the tourist offices or a local

estate agency (*agenzia immobiliare*) and keep an eye out for local advertisements.

Tour operators and villa companies also have self-catering **villas, farmhouses and apartments** located right across the island, usually in beautiful locations, often with swimming pools. Rates vary wildly, from €600 a week (sleeps four) to thousands for a place suitable for a house party. For an idea of what's available, contact companies like Think Sicily (Wwww.thinksicily.com), Bridgewater (Wwww.bridgewater-travel.co .uk), Travel Sicilia (Wwww.travelsicilia.com), Italian Breaks (Wwww.italianbreaks.com), Solo Sicily (Wwww.solosicily.com) or Dolce Vita Villas (Wwww.dolcevitavillas.com).

Rural accommodation

Rural tourism has expanded significantly in Sicily in recent years, and every region now holds a choice of interesting places to stay, from working farms and wine estates to restored palaces and architect-designed homes. Accommodation is in private rooms or apartments, and many establishments also offer activities such as cooking courses, horseriding, mountain-biking, walks and excursions. Hosts often speak English or French, and sometimes offer meals, or there might be a restaurant attached serving home-produced food, as is the case in many farmhouse-style places. We've recommended some of our favourites in the Guide, but many others fall within various umbrella schemes like Agriturist (@www.agriturist.it) and Agriturismo (@www.agriturismo.com), whose websites have sections on Sicily, with links to the properties. Rooms usually cost €80–120, depending on the establishment, and note that some places will require a minimum stay of three nights.

Hostels, campsites and mountain huts

There are only seven or eight **hostels** on the whole island, though they do crop up in useful tourist destinations like Palermo, Catania, Taormina, Noto, Siracusa, Lípari and Piazza Armerina. Dorm beds cost €15–20 a night, depending on season, and all have some kind of self-catering facility available. Some are official IYHF hostels, others are independent backpackers' (ie no membership required), but the official ones at least are detailed on the Hostelling International website (@www .hihostels.com), and if you aren't already a member of your home hostelling organization you can join upon arrival at any hostel.

There are approximately ninety officially graded **campsites** dotted around the island's coasts, on the outlying islands, and around Mount Etna. Few are open all year round; indeed, campsites generally open or close whenever they want, depending on business, but there are more details on the comprehensive website @www.camping.it. Many of the sites are large, family-oriented affairs, often complete with pools, bars, shops and sports facilities. Charges are usually between €5 and €7 per person per day, usually the same again for a tent and vehicle. Many campsites also have bungalows, caravans or apartments for rent (often with self-catering facilities) – demand and prices are high in summer (when a week's minimum stay might be required), but out of season you can expect to pay €35–50 a night.

Staffed **mountain huts** (*rifugio*, plural *rifugi*) are available in certain magnificent locations, particularly in the Madonie and Nébrodi ranges and on Mount Etna. They're used mainly by hikers and outdoor enthusiasts, and operated by the Club Alpino Italiano (@www.cai.it) – non-members can use them for around €20 a night, but advance reservations are essential.

Food and drink

There's much to be said for coming to Sicily just for the eating and drinking. Often, even the most out-of-the-way village will boast somewhere you can get a good lunch, while places like Catania, Palermo, Ragusa, Trápani and Siracusa can keep a serious eater happy for days. And it's not ruinously expensive either, certainly compared to prices in the rest of mainland Italy: a full meal with local wine generally costs around €30 a head, a pizza, drink and ice cream around half that.

Contemporary Sicilian cooking leans heavily on locally produced foodstuffs and whatever can be fished out of the sea, mixed with the Italian staples of pasta, tomato sauce and fresh vegetables. Red chillies, tuna, swordfish, sardines, olives, pine nuts and capers all figure heavily, while the mild winter climate and long summers mean that fruit and vegetables are less seasonal (and much more impressive) than in northern Europe: strawberries appear in April, for example, while oranges are available right through the winter. The **menu reader** in the "Language" section (p.409) covers all the basics, as well

Ice cream

A cone (*un cono*) of famous Sicilian **ice cream** (*gelato*) – or perhaps a dollop in a brioche – is the indispensable accessory to the evening *passeggiata*. The best choice is at a **gelateria**, where the range is a tribute to the Italian imagination and flair for display. If they make their own on the premises, there'll be a sign saying "*produzione propria*"; sadly, however, this increasingly means they make the stuff from pre-packed commercial pastes and syrups. Anyhow, there's no trouble in locating the finest *gelateria* in town: it's the one that draws the crowds. And as it's hard to find decent ice cream in restaurants these days (it's mostly *confezionato*, ie mass-produced), many locals also head to the *gelateria* for dessert.

as including a full rundown of Sicilian specialities, some of which crop up in nearly every restaurant.

Breakfast, snacks and markets

For most Sicilians, **breakfast** (*prima colazione*) is an espresso or cappuccino, and the ubiquitous *cornetto* – a jam-, custard- or chocolate-filled croissant. Many bars and patisseries (a *pasticceria*) also offer things like an *iris* (a pastry ball stuffed with sweet ricotta cheese), an *arancino* (a deep-fried ball of rice, either *rosso*, filled with meat, or *bianco*, with butter and cheese) and *cannoli* (pastry tubes with sweet ricotta cheese and candied fruit). On the other hand, breakfast in a hotel or B&B will usually be a limp affair of bread rolls and bad coffee, though the better places make far more of an effort with cheese, eggs, salami, fruit and fresh pastries.

There are **sandwich** (*panini*) bars in the bigger towns, though alternatively, in most places, you can simply go into an *alimentari* (grocer's shop) and ask them to make you a sandwich from whatever they've got. Bakeries sometimes sell *panini* or *pane cunzati*, crusty bread rolls filled with pungent combinations such as tuna, tomato, anchovy and capers. *Tramezzini* are ready-made sliced white-bread sandwiches with mixed fillings, while toasted sandwiches (*toste*) tend to be a variation on cheese with ham or tomato.

You'll get most of the things already mentioned, plus small pizzas, ready prepared pasta, and full hot meals in a **tàvola calda** (literally, "hot table"), a sort of stand-up snack bar. In the larger cities, you'll occasionally come across an old-fashioned **focacceria** – takeaway establishments selling *focaccia* (an oven-baked flat bread, with a topping or filling) and other bread-based snacks. Or there's the ubiquitous **rosticceria** in every Sicilian town, a takeaway grill-house where the speciality is spit-roast chicken (*pollo allo spiedo*).

Grocers' shops and **markets** are the best places for fruit, veg and picnic food, and you'll usually be able to jazz up your picnic lunch with sweet peppers, olives, seafood salad, and pickled vegetables. Some markets also sell **traditional takeaway food**, loved by Sicilians, though perhaps a challenge for some visitors – usually things like boiled artichokes, cooked octopus, raw sea urchins and mussels, and fried offal sandwiches.

Pizza

Outside its home of Naples, Sicily is the best place to eat pizza in Italy. It comes flat, not deep-pan, and there are some fairly distinctively Sicilian combinations – using pecorino cheese instead of mozzarella, oregano instead of basil, and lots of anchovies, capers and hot peppers. It's also easy to find pizzas cooked in the traditional way, in **wood-fired ovens** (*forno a legna*), so that they arrive blasted and bubbling on the surface, with a distinctive charcoal taste. Unfortunately, because of the time it takes to set up and light the ovens, *forno a legna* pizzas are usually only served at

---

Sicilians are not hung up on restaurant formality. Asking for just pasta and a salad, or the main course on its own, won't outrage the waiter. Equally, asking for a dish listed as a first course as a second course, or having pasta followed by pizza (or vice versa), won't be frowned upon either.

night, except on Sundays and in some resorts in summer.

Restaurant meals

For a full meal, rather than just a pizza, you'll have to go either to a **trattoria** or a **ristorante**. A *trattoria* is usually the cheaper, more basic choice, offering good home cooking (*cucina casalinga*), while a *ristorante* is often more upmarket (tablecloths, printed menu and uniformed waiters). In small towns and villages, the local trattoria is often only open at lunchtime, there may not be a menu and the waiter will simply reel off a list of what's available. In tourist resorts and larger towns you'll come across hybrid establishments (a *trattoria-ristorante*, say, or *ristorante-pizzeria*) that cater to all tastes, while there are also more youthful pasta-oriented restaurant-bars called *spaghetterias*. Signs or blackboards announcing "*pranzo turístico*" or "*pranzo completo*" are advertising a limited-choice **set menu** which can be pretty good value at €15–30.

Traditionally, lunch (*pranzo*) or dinner (*cena*) starts with an **antipasto** (literally "before the meal"), at its best when you circle around a table and help yourself to a cold buffet selection. If you're moving on to pasta and the main course you'll need quite an appetite to tackle the *antipasti* as well. Otherwise, the menu starts with soup or pasta, **il primo**, and moves on to **il secondo**, the meat or fish dish. Note that fish will either be served whole (like bream or trout) or by weight (usually per 100g, *all'etto*, like swordfish and tuna) so ask to see what you're going to eat and check

the price first. The second course is generally served unadorned, except for a wedge of lemon or tomato – **contorni** (vegetables and salads) are ordered and served separately, and often there won't be much choice beyond chips and salad. If there's no menu, the verbal list of what's available can sometimes be a bit bewildering, but if you don't hear anything you recognize just ask for what you want: everywhere should have pasta with tomato or meat sauce. Dessert (**dolci**) is almost always fresh fruit, fruit salad or ice cream, though restaurants may also have a choice of cakes, tarts and puddings – unfortunately, though, many of these are mass-produced (by such brands as Ranieri), and a restaurant *tiramisù* or *cassata*, say, can be a poor substitute for the real thing.

Although Sicily has hardly any specifically **vegetarian** restaurants, most pasta sauces are based on tomatoes or dairy products, and it's easy to pick a pizza that is meat- (and fish-) free. Pizzas are also available without cheese, though soups are usually made with a fish or meat broth.

In many places, the **bill** (*il conto*) doesn't amount to much more than an illegible scrap of paper so, if you want to be sure you're not being ripped off, ask for a receipt (*una ricevuta*). Nearly everywhere, you'll pay a small **cover charge** per person for the bread (*pane e coperto*); **service** (*servizio*) will be added as well in many restaurants, usually ten percent, though fifteen or even twenty percent isn't unheard of. If service isn't charged, leaving ten percent would do, though most pizzerias and trattorias won't expect it.

The original fusion food

Historically, **Sicilian cuisine** has been held in high regard: one of the earliest of cookbooks, the *Art of Cooking* by Mithaecus, derived from fifth-century BC Siracusa, while in medieval times Sicilian chefs were much sought after in foreign courts. As the centuries passed, the intermittent waves of immigration left their mark, from the use of prickly pears (originally imported from Mexico by the Spanish) to the North African influence evident in the western Sicilian version of couscous or in orange salads. The **Arab influence** is also apparent in the profusion of sweets – marzipan is used extensively, while *cassata*, the most Sicilian of desserts, derives from the Arabic word *quas-at*, referring to the round bowl in which it was traditionally prepared. Indeed, virtually every dish – though apparently common-or-garden Italian/Sicilian – calls upon 2500 years of cross-cultural influences, from the Greeks and Romans to the Arabs, Normans and Spanish.

Coffee, tea and soft drinks

One of the most distinctive smells in a Sicilian street is that of fresh **coffee**. The basic choice is either an espresso (or just *caffè*) or a cappuccino. The latter is primarily a breakfast drink – no Italian would order a cappuccino after a meal. A watered-down espresso is a *caffè lungo*, with a drop of milk it's *caffè macchiato* ("stained"), while coffee with a shot of alcohol is *caffè corretto*. In summer you might want your coffee cold (*caffè freddo*), or try a *granita di caffè* – cold coffee with crushed ice that's usually topped with whipped cream (*senza panna*, without cream). **Tea**, too, can be drunk iced (*tè freddo*), usually mixed with lemon. Hot tea (*tè caldo*) comes with lemon (*con limone*) unless you ask for milk (*con latte*).

For a fresh fruit juice (usually orange, lemon or grapefruit), squeezed at the bar, ask for a **spremuta**. Fruit juice mixed with crushed ice is that Sicilian speciality, **granita**; a **frullato** is a fresh fruit shake, while a **succo di frutta** is a bottled fruit juice. As an alternative to Coke try the homegrown Italian alternative, Chinotto (Coke-like, but not so sweet, with a tamarind flavour). Tap water (*acqua normale*) is drinkable almost everywhere and you won't pay for it in a bar. But **mineral water** (*acqua minerale*) is the usual choice, either still (*senza gas* or *naturale*) or fizzy (*con gas*, *gassata* or *frizzante*).

Beer, wines and spirits

Beer (*birra*) – generally lager in Sicily – usually comes in 33cl (*piccolo*) or 66cl (*grande*) bottles. The Sicilian brand Messina, and the Italian Peroni and Dreher, are widely available – ask for *birra nazionale*, otherwise you'll be given a more expensive imported beer, and note that draught beer (*birra alla spina*) is usually more expensive than the bottled variety. So-called "dark beers" (*birra nera*, *birra rossa* or *birra scura*) are also available, which have a slightly maltier taste, and in appearance resemble stout or bitter.

Local **wine** (*vino locale*) is often served straight from the barrel in jugs or old bottles, and costs as little as €5 a litre. You may be flummoxed by the *vino locale* not being the colour you've ordered, but you'll get whatever they make – in the west, for example, it's often a tart but refreshing rosé, in Marsala it's amber. Bottled wine is more expensive, though still good value, from around €8–10 in a restaurant (though often much higher in tourist resorts).

The most famous Sicilian **dessert wine** is *marsala*, made in the western town of the same name – see the box on p.350 for more. If you're heading to the offshore islands, watch out for *malvasia* (from the Aeolians) and *moscato* (from Pantelleria), while around Taormina the local speciality is *vino alla mándorla*, almond wine, served ice cold. **Spirits** are known mostly by their generic names, except brandy which you should call *cognac* or ask for by name – again, for cheaper Italian brands, ask for *nazionale*. At some stage you should also try an **amaro** (literally "bitter"), a remarkably medicinal after-dinner drink supposed to aid digestion. The favourite brand is Averna (from Caltanissetta) but there are dozens of

Sicilian wine

Although they don't necessarily qualify for the strict Italian DOC and DOCG denomination systems, Sicilian wines have an increasing reputation (and the island often produces more wine in a year than any other Italian region, and as much as Australia). Typical of the wines making waves are those made from the local **Nero d'Ávola** grape variety (a hearty red, similar to a Syrah/Shiraz) – it's well suited to the dry climate, and Planeta's Santa Cecilia (from Noto) is as good an example as you'll find. Other Sicilian regions produce very distinct tastes, too, like the dry reds and whites made from grapes grown on the volcanic slopes of **Etna**, the white **Bianco d'Alcamo** from Trápani province and **Cerasuolo di Vittoria** (red and white) from vines in the area around Ragusa. Boutique wineries are springing up all over Sicily, perhaps just making a particular wine, though the major brands you'll see everywhere include Corvo, Donnafugata and Regaleali.

different kinds. Look out, too, for a feisty red liqueur called Fuoco dell'Etna, mostly sold on the east coast.

Where to drink

In most town and village **bars**, it's cheapest to drink standing up at the counter (there's often nowhere to sit anyway), in which case you pay first at the cash desk (*la cassa*), present your receipt (*scontrino*) to the bar person and give your order. There's always a list of prices (the *listino prezzi*) on display, and when you present your receipt it's customary to leave a small tip on the counter – though no one will object if you don't. It's more expensive to sit down inside than stand up (the difference in price is shown on the price list as *távola*) and it costs up to twice the basic price if you sit at tables outside (*terrazza*).

Although bars have no set **licensing hours**, outside the cities it's often difficult to find a bar open much after 9pm. Children are allowed in and bars, like restaurants, are smoke-free (strictly enforced), though if you're drinking or eating outside it's fine to smoke. Tourist bars and cafés are open later, but they're more expensive than the typical chrome-counter-and-Gaggia-machine local bar – any stylish bar that fancies itself tends to be called an "American Bar", a designation that you'll see all over Sicily.

Most Sicilians tend to drink when they eat, and young people especially don't make a night out of getting wasted. When they do go out on the town, it's to a **birreria** (literally "beer shop") or something calling itself a "pub" or even a "Drinkeria". Needless to say, they're not much like English pubs, though in the various "Irish" **pubs** that are springing up in the cities and resorts, you'll be able to get a pint of Guinness and watch the big game.

Festivals and events

There's nothing to beat arriving in a Sicilian town or village to discover that it's festival time. Many annual feast days have remained unchanged for decades, if not centuries, celebrating the life of a patron saint or some notable event lost in the mists of time. But whatever the reason for the party, you are guaranteed the time-honoured ingredients for a Sicilian knees-up – old songs and dances, a costumed procession, perhaps a traditional puppet show, special food and sweets, and noisy fireworks to finish. The most famous annual celebrations are covered below, but there's also a box listing the best regional festivals at the beginning of each chapter.

Carnevale

Carnevale (Carnival, or Mardi Gras) is celebrated in the five days immediately before the start of Lent (in practice, some time between the end of February and the end of March). Traditionally, its significance is as the last bout of indulgence before the abstinence of Lent, which lasts for forty days and ends with Easter. True, Sicily isn't Rio de Janeiro, but most towns manage to put on a little bit of a show and a costumed parade.

The best carnival festivities on the island are generally judged to be at **Acireale** on the Catania coast, where flower-filled floats, parades and concerts keep the townspeople occupied for days.

Easter

All over the island, **Easter** week is celebrated with slow-moving processions and ostentatious displays of penitence and mourning. Particularly dramatic events take place at

The weird and wonderful

Sicily can boast some of the Mediterranean's most idiosyncratic festivals. The conquest by the Normans is echoed in August's **Palio dei Normanni** in Piazza Armerina, a medieval-costumed procession with jousting knights, while the similar **La Castellana** throngs the streets of Cáccamo in September. The island's fishermen have their own rituals, such as the festive boat parade and fish-fry of **Sagra del Mare** at Sciacca. During May's **Pesce a Mare** festa at Aci Trezza, on the Catania coast, as the local tourist brochure puts it, "a fisherman pretends to be a fish and excitedly the local fishermen catch him". Unmissable, for different reasons, is the **pilgrimage** every May in the Etna foothills, when the pious run, barefoot and shirtless, up to the sanctuary at Trecastagni.

Érice, Marsala and Taormina, while at **Enna** in the interior, thousands march in silent procession behind holy statues and processional carts. It's in **Trápani**, however, that the procession of statues is raised to an art form. Just as they have been every year since the seventeenth century, the city's "Misteri" figures, portraying life-sized scenes from the Passion, are paraded through the streets on Good Friday (see box, p.327). Meanwhile, at the Albanian village of **Piana degli Albanesi**, near Palermo, the villagers retain their ancient Orthodox traditions and costumes. Other, less conventional parades take place at Prizzi in the western interior, and at San Fratello above the Tyrrhenian coast, where masked and hooded devils taunt the processions.

Ferragosto

The biggest island-wide celebration, bar none, is high summer's **ferragosto**, the Feast of the Assumption of the Virgin Mary. The day is actually August 15, but anywhere with a celebration of any size makes a meal of it, perhaps starting with services and parties a few days earlier before culminating, like all *ferragosto* celebrations, with spectacular fireworks on the night of the 15th. This is a particularly good time to be in **Messina**, where the procession of the city's enormous patron giants is followed by a mad scramble when the elaborate carriage known as the Vara is pulled through the streets. As the night wears on, flowers are thrown to the crowds before fireworks light up the Straits of Messina late at night (see box, p.158).

Traditional entertainment

Puppet theatre (*teatro dei pupi*) has been popular in Sicily since the fourteenth century. The shows are always the same, and all Sicilians know the stories, which centre on the clash between **Christianity** and **Islam**. As each strutting, stiff-legged knight, such as Orlando (Roland) and Rinaldo, is introduced, the puppeteer lists his exploits. There may be a love interest, perhaps a jousting tournament to win the hand of Charlemagne's daughter, before the main business of staged battles between the Christians and the Saracen invaders. Between bouts, Orlando may fight a crocodile, or confront monsters and magicians. Things climax with some great historical battle, like Roncesvalles, culminating in betrayal and treachery as the boys face an untimely and drawn-out death. The whole story plays out regularly in theatre shows in Acireale, and also tourist centres like Siracusa and Taormina, though it's Palermo where you can best explore the tradition (see p.65).

Sports and outdoor activities

As a Mediterranean island, Sicily is well set up for water sports of all kinds, from scuba-diving to windsurfing, while many come in the cooler months either side of summer (April, May, September and October) for the hiking. The volcanoes of Etna and Strómboli offer more adventurous excursions – probably the most emblematic Sicilian outdoor activity is the climb up Strómboli to see the nightly volcanic light show.

Watersports

The best places for **snorkelling** and **scuba-diving** are the limpid waters of the offshore islands, principally Ústica, the Aeolians, Lampedusa and Pantelleria. Diving schools on each of these offer day-trips and courses for beginners and experienced divers alike. Other areas are protected as marine and natural reserves, so even at far more touristed resorts like Mazzarò (Taormina) the water is often remarkably clear. **Windsurfing** gear is available for rent at most of the major resort beaches and lidos, and **kitesurfing** is increasingly popular at places like Mózia on the west coast.

Hiking

Hiking is growing in popularity, though it's nowhere near as established as in alpine Italy. If you're keen to do a lot of walking in a short time, your best bet is to join a **walking holiday** – several tour operators now offer

this as an option (see list on p.23) and the routes used have all been thoroughly tried and tested. The best walking areas are in the interior, around **Etna** in the east, and in the mountain regions of the **Monti Madonie** and **Monti Nébrodi** (between Etna and the Tyrrhenian coast), where a few marked trails have been laid out, making use of existing paths.

On the whole, though, given the paucity of information and services, unsupported hiking in interior Sicily is more for the experienced and well-equipped walker. You'd do well to get hold of *Walking in Sicily* by Gillian Price (Cicerone, ⓦ www.cicerone.co.uk), which details 42 walks across the whole island. However, if all you're looking for is a half-day stroll or short hike you're better off sticking to the coast or outlying islands. The Aeolians and Égadis in particular offer some lovely walking, while the protected coast between Scopello and San Vito Lo Capo (north of Trápani) has an excellent network of well-maintained paths.

National game, national shame

Football (*calcio*) is the national sport (Italy won the World Cup for the fourth time in 2006) and both the two big Sicilian teams – **Palermo** (ⓦ www.ilpalermocalcio.it) and **Catania** (ⓦ www.calciocatania.it) – are currently in Serie A, the top domestic division. However, football in Italy is in crisis. The national team made a dismal showing at the 2010 World Cup (failing to win a single game and drawing with mighty New Zealand), while the domestic game continues to suffer the fallout of a major match-fixing and corruption scandal. There's also a long history of violence at games, notably at a derby match between the Sicilian teams in 2007 that saw a policeman killed and hundreds of spectators injured during rioting. Matches were suspended at the time and many stadiums closed until they met more rigorous safety conditions. Is it safe to go to a match in Sicily? Yes, probably, as there's little or no trouble at most matches, though you would want to avoid going to European cup games involving travelling British teams as such matches have witnessed violence in the past.

Outdoor pursuits

The dramatic volcanic terrain around **Mount Etna** supports a whole **outdoor activities** industry, from guided summit hikes to four-wheel-drive safaris. Local tourist offices and travel agents as far away as Siracusa and Taormina are geared up to book visitors onto trips. The small mountain towns of Nicolosi and Linguaglossa are the centres for Etna's surviving **skiing** (ski lifts keep being destroyed by eruptions), and winter sports are also available in the Monti Madonie

around Piano Battáglia, where you can rent ski gear. Really, though, no one comes to Sicily just to ski. Volcanoes are a different matter, though, as few in the world are as active as Etna and **Strómboli** – the latter (the furthest flung of the Aeolian Islands) is another great base for guided crater treks (day and night), volcano-watching cruises and the like.

Finally, **horseriding and pony-trekking** are available in some areas – sometimes offered by *agriturismo* (rural tourism) properties.

Travelling with children

Children are revered in Sicily and will be made a fuss of in the street, and welcomed and catered for in bars and restaurants. It's perfectly normal for Sicilian children to stay up until they drop, and in summer it's not unusual to see young-sters out at midnight, and not looking much the worse for it.

Pharmacies and supermarkets carry most **baby requirements**, from nappies to formula food. However, you may not see the brands you are used to at home, and don't expect there to be a full range of (or indeed any) organic food products, especially in smaller towns. Otherwise, **food** is unlikely to be a problem as most children eat pasta and pizza, and while specific children's menus are not common, many restaurants are happy to provide a smaller version of an adult meal.

Hotels normally charge around thirty percent extra to put an additional bed or cot in the room. However, self-catering apartments, or rooms or B&Bs with the use of a kitchen, are quite common and most Sicilian resorts offer such options. Generous **discounts** apply for children at most sights and attractions, and also when travelling on trains.

In high summer, the **heat and sun** can be exhausting for children. Make sure they are well covered with sun block, which can be bought in any pharmacy and many super-markets. Also, do as the Sicilians do and dress your children in bonnets or straw hats, available from most markets, and take advantage of siesta time to recover flagging energy. If you're using public transport, try and travel during the less busy periods – mornings and evenings – and make sure your children drink plenty of water.

Southern Mediterranean stereotypes certa-inly still apply in Sicily, with children firmly ensconced in their **gender roles** at an early age: the girls' clothes on sale are all frills and flounces, while the toy, candy and nut trolleys that you find in every piazza have one side devoted to guns and hammers, the other to dolls, tiaras and manicure kits.

Travel essentials

Beaches

You'll have to pay for access to many of the island's better beaches (known as *lido*), with lounger, parasol and use of the showers often included in the price (usually €5–10 a day). Many lidos also have other facilities like pedalo- and windsurf-hire, bars and restaurants, and thus make a good bet for families. Elsewhere, beaches are free though not always clean – during the winter most look like dumps, as it's not worth anyone's while to clean them until the season starts at Easter.

Costs

Sicily isn't particularly cheap compared to other Mediterranean holiday spots, though it is usually better value than the popular tourist parts of mainland Italy. The single biggest cost is generally **accommodation**, with simple one-star hotels, private rooms and bed and breakfasts all starting at around €60 a night. A decent three-star hotel, on the other hand, will set you back up to €120. Of course, you'll pay a lot more in summer in the big tourist spots – Érice, Cefalù, Siracusa and Taormina – and more all year round on most of the offshore islands, particularly the Aeolians and Pantelleria.

Most other items are fairly inexpensive. The Sicilian staple, a pizza and a beer, costs around €10 just about everywhere, while a full **restaurant meal** can cost as little as €20 a head. Of course, there are some excellent Sicilian restaurants where the bill comes in much higher, up to say €50 or €60 a head, but even these are remarkably good value for the quality on offer. A carafe of local house wine rarely comes to more than €5, a bottle €10, and the same wine in a supermarket might cost a third of that. Other snacks and drinks soon add up, especially in fancy resorts, and you should note that if you sit down in a café (rather than stand at the counter) it'll cost twice as much. **Public transport**, on the other hand, is very cheap, while even the island's showpiece museums,

archeological ruins and attractions rarely cost more than €6 – and under-18s and over-65s usually get in for free.

Overall, apart from accommodation, you could reasonably expect to spend €50 a day – taking the train, eating picnics, cheap meals and pizzas, seeing the sights and so on. For a more comfortable daily experience (meals in better restaurants, plus taxis, evening drinks, concerts and the like) you're looking at €80 and upwards.

Crime and personal safety

Although Sicily is synonymous with the Mafia, you'll forget the association as soon as you set foot on the island. Cosa Nostra is as invisible to the average tourist as it is ingrained for the islanders, and the violence that sporadically erupts is almost always an "in-house" affair. Of more immediate concern is **petty crime**, mainly in crowded streets or markets, where gangs of *scippatori*, or bag-snatchers, strike on foot or on scooters, disappearing before you've had time to react. As well as handbags, they whip wallets, tear off visible jewellery and, if they're really adroit, unstrap watches. Carry shoulder bags, as you'll see many Sicilian women do, slung across your body. It's a good idea, too, to entrust most of your money and valuables to hotel safes or management. The vast majority of cases occur in Catania and Palermo, and at or on the way to and from the airports. On the whole it's common sense to avoid badly lit areas at night, or run-down inner-city areas at all times.

Emergency phone numbers

Police (Carabinieri) ☎112
Emergency services (Soccorso Pubblico di Emergenze) ☎113
Fire brigade (Vigili del Fuoco) ☎115
Road assistance (Soccorso Stradale) ☎116

Women's safety

Although Italy has a reputation for **sexual harassment of women** that is well known and well founded, there's no reason to presume unwarranted intrusion at every turn. A woman travelling alone, or with another woman, can expect a certain amount of attention, including tooting and whistling, though bear in mind that local custom dictates that every friend and acquaintance is greeted with a toot. If you follow common-sense rules, the most that should worry you is the occasional try-on. Off the beaten track, you're more likely to be subjected to stares (from both sexes). For greater anonymity, dress smartly and, as a deterrent, flaunt a wedding ring.

If the worst happens, you'll be forced to have some dealings with the police. Most conspicuous are the **Carabinieri** – the ones with the blue uniforms – who are a branch of the armed forces and organized along military lines, dealing with general crime and public disorder. They are also the butt of most of the jokes about the police, usually on the "How many Carabinieri does it take to…?" level. They share a fierce turf rivalry with the **Polizia Statale**, or state police, to whom you're supposed to report any theft at their local HQ, the Questura. The **Polizia Urbana**, or town police, are mainly concerned with directing the traffic and punishing parking offenders. The **Guardia di Finanza**, often heavily armed and screaming ostentatiously through the cities, are responsible for investigating smuggling, tax evasion and other similar crimes, and the **Polizia Stradale** patrol the autostrada.

Electricity

The supply is 220V, though anything requiring 240V will work. Plugs have two or three round pins (and some sockets have larger holes than others); a travel adaptor plug is very useful.

Entry requirements

British, Irish and other EU citizens can enter Sicily and stay as long as they like on production of a valid **passport**. Citizens of the United States, Canada, Australia and New Zealand don't need a visa, but are limited to stays of three months. Most other nationals will have to apply for a visa from an Italian embassy or consulate.

Legally, you're required to register with the police within three days of entering Italy,

though if you're staying at a hotel this will be done for you. Although the police in some towns have become more punctilious about this, most would still be amazed at any attempt to register yourself down at the local police station while on holiday.

Italian embassies abroad

Australia ☎ 02/6273 3333, ⓦ www.ambcanberra .esteri.it.

Canada ☎ 613/232-2401, ⓦ www.ambottawa .esteri.it.

Republic of Ireland ☎ 01/660 1744, ⓦ www .ambdublino.esteri.it.

New Zealand ☎ 04/473 5339, ⓦ www.amb wellington.esteri.it.

UK ☎ 020/7312 2200, ⓦ www.amblondra.esteri.it.

USA ☎ 202/612-4400, ⓦ www.ambwashingtondc .esteri.it.

Gay and lesbian Sicily

Homosexuality is not illegal in Italy, and the age of consent is 16. That said, attitudes towards homosexuality are much less tolerant in Sicily than in Rome or the industrial north. Taormina is the only place in Sicily where there is any kind of gay scene, and even this is very low-key. Even so, physical contact between men is fairly common in Sicily, on the level of linking arms and kissing cheeks at greetings and farewells – though an overt display of anything remotely ambiguous is likely to be met with hostility. The main national gay organization, **ArciGay** (ⓦ www.arcigay.it) has branches all over the country, including Sicily, and its English-language website is a good place to look for information. The ⓦ www.gay.it website also has a wealth of information for gays and lesbians in Italy.

Health

Sicily poses few health problems for visitors; the worst that's likely to happen to you is suffering from the extreme heat in summer or from an upset stomach. Vaccinations are not required, but you should take insect repellent and strong sun protection. The water is perfectly safe to drink (though bottled water tastes better). You'll find public drinking fountains in squares and city streets everywhere, though look out for "*acqua non potabile*" signs, indicating the water is *not* safe to drink.

An Italian **pharmacist** (*farmacia*) is well qualified to give you advice on minor ailments, and to dispense prescriptions. There's generally one pharmacy open all night in the bigger towns and cities. A rota system is used, and you should find the address of the one currently open late/all night on any *farmacia* door or listed in the local paper.

As an EU country, Italy has reciprocal health agreements with other member states, and EU citizens can simply show their **European Health Insurance Card** (ⓦwww .ehic.org.uk) and passport at a health centre or hospital. This basically entitles you to the same treatment as an insured person in Italy, but you're still advised to have a travel insurance policy as well.

Every town and village has a **doctor** (*médico*). To find one, ask at a pharmacy, or consult the local yellow pages (*Págine Gialle*) under "Azienda Unità Sanitaria Locale" or "Unità Sanitaria Locale Pronto Soccorso". If you're eligible, take your EHIC with you to the doctor's, which will enable you to get free treatment and prescriptions for medicines at the (much cheaper) local rate. For repeat medication, take any empty bottles or capsules with you to the doctor's – the brand names often differ. Out of hours (ie weekends, holidays and night-time), the local **Guardia Médica** first-aid clinic is available in most towns and, though sometimes minimally equipped, will be able to treat stings, bites, fevers and minor accidents.

In an **emergency**, dial ☎113 and ask for "*ospedale*" or "*ambulanza*". The nearest hospital will have a **Pronto Soccorso** (casualty) section, while on smaller islands, or places with no hospital, there is usually a Guardia Medica clinic.

Insurance

It's essential to take out a travel insurance policy to cover against theft, loss, illness or injury during your travels. A typical policy will provide cover for the loss of baggage, tickets and – up to a certain limit – cash, as well as cancellation or curtailment of your journey. Most policies exclude so-called dangerous sports, unless an extra premium is paid: in Sicily this can mean things like scuba-diving, windsurfing and volcano trekking. If you need to make a claim, you should keep receipts for medicines and medical treatment, and in the event you have anything stolen, you must obtain an **official statement from the police**. This is sometimes easier said than done in Sicily, but persevere; without it, you'll not be able to claim your money back.

Internet

There are internet places all over Sicily, with access costing up to €5 an hour. Note that you will be asked to show some form of

---

Rough Guides travel insurance

Rough Guides has teamed up with WorldNomads.com to offer great **travel insurance** deals. Policies are available to residents of over 150 countries, with cover for a wide range of **adventure sports**, 24-hour emergency assistance, high levels of medical and evacuation cover and a stream of **travel safety information**. Roughguides.com users can take advantage of their policies online 24/7, from anywhere in the world – even if you're already travelling. And since plans often change when you're on the road, you can extend your policy and even claim online. Roughguides.com users who buy travel insurance with WorldNomads.com can also leave a positive footprint and donate to a community development project. For more information go to ⓦ**www .roughguides.com/shop**.

ID to use a public internet point. However, free **wi-fi** access is increasingly available in B&Bs, hotels and bars, and there are wireless "hot spots" in many public spaces (though you might need to sign up and pay for an hour's or day's use for these). If you take your own laptop, make sure you've got insurance cover and all the relevant adapters and chargers.

Laundry services

Coin-operated laundries are very rare. More common is a *lavanderia*, a service-wash laundry, where you'll be able to get your laundry done for €10 or so. Many B&Bs offer a laundry service as well. Although you can usually get away with it, washing clothes in your room can be problematic – simply because the ancient plumbing often can't cope with all the water. It's better to ask if there's somewhere you can wash your clothes.

Mail

Post office opening hours are usually Monday to Saturday 8.30am to 6.30pm; offices in smaller towns close on a Saturday, and everywhere else post offices close at noon on the last Saturday of the month. You can also buy stamps (*francobolli*) in some gift shops in tourist resorts, and in shops called *tabacchi*, recognizable by a sign displaying a white "T" on a black or blue background (these also sell cigarettes, sweets and stationery). The Italian postal service is among the slowest in Europe – if your letter is urgent, consider paying extra for the express service, or *posta prioritaria*.

Maps

The best large-scale **road map** of Sicily is published by the Touring Club Italiano (*Sicilia*, 1:200,000), available from map and travel bookshops or from online retailers like Stanford's (🌐www.stanfords.co.uk) or Rand McNally (🌐www.randmcnally.com). Rough Guides also has a Sicily map (1:200,000), printed on waterproof, untearable paper. Otherwise, the Automobile Club d'Italia issues a good, free 1:275,000 road map, available from the State Tourist Offices, while local tourist offices in Sicily often have free

road maps of varying quality. Local tourist offices also hand out reasonable town plans and regional maps.

Hiking maps (scale 1:25,000 and 1:50,000) for the Monti Madonie and other areas can be ordered from the Istituto Geográfico Militare (🌐www.igmi.org), or check what's available at the Palermo stationer's shop Cartoleria de Magistris, Via A. Gagini 23 (☎091.589.233). Note, however, that most of these maps were drawn up in the 1970s, and, particularly at altitudes above 1500m, many of the paths shown on them no longer exist. The Club Alpino Siciliano, Via A. Paternostro 43, Palermo (🌐www.clubalpinosiciliano.it) or – sometimes – tourist and regional park offices in Palermo or Cefalù can supply you with 1:50,000 maps of the Monti Madonie, but again, these should be treated with caution. However, all national parks and nature reserves (Madonie, Nebrodi, Pellegrino, etc, see 🌐www.parks.it) have walking itineraries on their websites, while the various park offices listed in the Guide can supply rudimentary hiking maps and, occasionally, English-language route guides.

Media

The centre-left *La Repubblica* and authoritative and rather right-wing *Il Corriere della Sera* are the two most widely read national **newspapers**, based in Milan but published with local supplements. But Sicily also has its own **regional papers**, useful for transport schedules, reviews, film listings and suchlike. In Palermo, the best is *Il Giornale di Sicilia*; in Catania, *La Sicilia*; in Messina, *La Gazzetta del Sud*. The most widely read paper, though, is the pink *Gazzetta dello Sport*; essential stuff for the serious sports fan. **English-language newspapers** can be found in Palermo, Catania, Messina, Taormina and Cefalù, usually a day late.

Italian **television** is deregulated, with the three state-run channels, RAI 1, 2 and 3, suffering in the face of a massive downmarket independent onslaught. The output is pretty mainstream, with a heavy helping of Brazilian soaps, American sitcoms and films, and ghastly Italian cabaret shows, though the RAI channels have less advertising and mix some good reporting in among the dross. **Satellite and cable TV** is widely available, and at most bigger hotels and upmarket B&Bs you'll often get a couple of foreign-language channels (BBC World, CNN, Eurosport, MTV) plus perhaps pay-for-movie channels.

The situation in **radio** is even more anarchic, with the FM waves crowded to the extent that you can pick up a new station just by walking down the corridor. Again, the RAI stations are generally more professional, though daytime listening is virtually undiluted, nonstop dance music.

Money

Italy's currency is the **euro** (€), and notes are issued in denominations of 5, 10, 20, 50, 100, 200 and 500 euros, and coins in denominations of 1, 2, 5, 10, 20 and 50 cents and 1 and 2 euros. Up-to-the-minute currency **exchange rates** are displayed at ⓦ www.xe.com.

By far the easiest way to get money is to use your bank debit card to withdraw cash from an **ATM** (known as *bancomat* in Italy). These are found even in the smallest towns and on some of the more remote islands, as well as on arrival at the three main airports. Instructions are available in English, and the daily withdrawal limit depends on your bank or credit card company, usually €250 a day. Make sure that you have a PIN number that's designed to work overseas, and check with your bank whether you can use your debit card directly in shops and petrol stations etc, as not all systems are available in Sicily.

Credit cards can also be used for cash advances over the counter in banks and for payment in most hotels, restaurants, petrol stations and some shops. MasterCard and Visa are the most widely accepted cards. Cash advances on credit cards are treated as loans, with interest accruing daily from the date of withdrawal; there may also be a transaction fee on top of this.

The main **banks** you'll see in Sicily are the Banco di Sicilia, the Banca Popolare Sant'Angelo, the Cassa di Risparmio, the Banca Nuova and the Banca Nazionale del Lavoro. **Banking hours** vary slightly from town to town, but generally banks are open Monday to Friday 8.30am to 1.20pm and

again around 3pm to 4pm. Outside these times you can change foreign currency at large hotels, the airports at Palermo and Catania, and some main train stations.

Opening hours and public holidays

Basic opening hours for most **shops and businesses** are Monday to Saturday from 8am or 9am to around 1pm, and from around 4pm to 7pm or 8pm, though some offices work to a more standard European 9am to 5pm day. Everything, except bars and restaurants, closes on Sunday, though you might find cake shops, and fish shops in some coastal towns, open until lunchtime. Local religious holidays and festivals don't generally close down shops and businesses, but everything except bars and restaurants will be closed on the public holidays listed in the box.

Most **churches** open in the early morning (around 7am or 8am) for Mass and close around noon, opening up again at 4pm or 5pm, and closing at 7pm. More obscure ones will only open for early morning and evening services; some only open on Sunday and on religious holidays. One problem you'll face all

Public holidays

January 1 *Primo dell'anno*, New Year's Day

January 6 *Epifania*, Epiphany

Good Friday *Venerdì Santo*

Easter Monday *Pasquetta*

April 25 *Giorno della Liberazione*, Liberation Day

May 1 *Festa dei Lavoratori*, Labour Day

June 2 *Festa della Repubblica*, Republic Day

August 15 *Ferragosto*, Assumption of the Blessed Virgin Mary

November 1 *Ognissanti*, All Saints Day

December 8 *Immaccolata*, Immaculate Conception of the Blessed Virgin Mary

December 25 *Natale*, Christmas Day

December 26 *Santo Stefano*, St Stephen's Day

over Sicily is that lots of churches, monasteries, convents and oratories are **closed for restoration** (*chiuso per restauro*). We've indicated the more long-term closures in the text, but even if there's scaffolding up you might be able to persuade a workman or priest/curator to show you around.

Museums are generally open daily from 9am to 1pm, and again for a couple of hours in the afternoon on certain days; likely closing day is Monday, while they close slightly earlier on Sunday, around 12.30pm. **Archeological sites** are usually open from 9am until an hour before sunset (in practice until around 4pm from November to March, 7pm from April to October, though never bet against a custodian bunking off early on a slow day). Sites are also sometimes closed on Mondays.

Shopping

Sicilian street **markets** provide some of the best experiences on the island – the Vucciria in Palermo and Catania's fish market, for example, are sights in themselves, while any market can provide inexpensive souvenirs and gifts like stove-top coffee pots or espresso cups. You'll be taken for an imbecile if you don't haggle for everything except food – ask for "*uno sconto*" (a discount). Other day-to-day items, toiletries and basic supplies can be bought in local supermarkets. **Food and drink** souvenirs are almost endless – a bag of dried wild oregano or salted capers from the Aeolians, pistachios from Bronte, almonds from the Agrigento area, *frutta di martorana* from Palermo, marsala wine from Marsala. Taormina is probably the best single place on the island for clothes **boutiques**, while all the main Italian labels and brands have outlets in the three main cities of Palermo, Catania and Messina. Sicily has a reputation for its **ceramics**, widely available in tourist shops

in the major resorts but best sourced at the production centres, like Santo Stéfano di Camastra (Tyrrhenian coast), Sciacca (south coast) and especially Caltagirone (southern interior). You'll see **lace and embroidery** in gift shops in places like Palermo, Taormina and Cefalù, and the quality isn't too bad. The same tourist outlets usually sell gift versions of traditional Sicilian **theatre puppets** and **hand-painted carts**. Anywhere near Etna, you're also guaranteed to find things in shops fashioned from **lava** – paperweights to sculptures.

Telephones

Public **telephones** operated by Telecom Italia come in various forms, usually with clear instructions in English. Coin-operated phones are increasingly hard to find, so you will probably have to buy a phonecard (*scheda telefónica*), available in various denominations from €5 from *tabacchi* or newsstands. Bars will often have a phone you can use: look for the yellow phone symbol. Alternatively, telephone offices in major towns have a *cabina a scatti*, a sound-proofed and metered kiosk: ask to make the call and pay at the end. Phone tariffs are among the most expensive in Europe, especially if you're calling long-distance or internationally – it's always cheapest to buy a phonecard. Specifically, don't make any calls from hotel phones, which always have very high rates.

Dialling ℡170 or 176 will get you through to an English-speaking operator. You can **find numbers online** with the Italian Yellow Pages (ⓦwww.paginegialle.it) or White Pages (ⓦwww.paginebianche.it). To **call Sicily from abroad**, dial your international access number + 39 (Italy country code) + number.

Most **cellphones** bought in the UK and Ireland, Australia and New Zealand, will work in Sicily, though a mobile phone bought for

---

Visiting churches, museums and ruins

To visit churches and religious buildings you should **dress modestly** (which means no shorts, not even Bermuda-length ones, and covered shoulders for women), and avoid wandering around during a service. At otherwise free **chapels, museums and archeological sites**, if you're shown around by a custodian or caretaker it's customary to give a small tip – say €1 each.

use in the US might not work here unless it is triband or supporting GSM. Prices are coming down, but it's expensive to use your cellphone exclusively to make national and internationals calls in Sicily. You might simply be able to buy a replacement SIM card for your own phone, though this depends on the model, contract and service provider. Or, if you're coming for more than a couple of weeks, you could even buy a mobile in Sicily – basic models cost as little as €39. A mobile phone is *un cellulare* or *telefonino*, a recharger is *un ricaricatore*, and a text message is *un messaggio SMS*.

Time

Sicily (and Italy) is always one hour ahead of the UK, except for one week at the end of October when the time is the same. Italy is seven hours ahead of Eastern Standard Time and ten hours ahead of Pacific Time.

Tourist information

The **Italian Government Tourist Board** (Ⓦwww.enit.it) has a useful website for general information, or you can contact the state tourist office organization in your own country. In Sicily, most towns, main train stations and the two principal airports have a **tourist office** (*ufficio di turismo*) or a **Pro Loco** office, usually funded by the *Comune*, overseeing cultural events and providing tourist information. Other than in the main tourist areas staff aren't likely to speak English, but you should at least be able to get a free town plan and a local listings booklet in Italian, and some offices will reserve you a room and sell places on guided tours.

Likely summer (April–Oct) **opening hours** are Monday to Friday 9am to 1pm and 4pm to 7pm, Saturday 9am to 1pm, though some offices in tourist areas open for longer. From November to March hours may be reduced. If the tourist office isn't open and all else fails, the local Sicilian telephone office and most bars with phones carry a copy of the local *Tuttocittà* (Ⓦwww.tutto citta.it), a listings and information magazine which details addresses and numbers of most of the organizations you're likely to want to know about. It also has indexed street maps for local towns and adverts for

restaurants and shops. The Palermo version (with an interactive map) is available online.

Plenty of other material about Sicily is available online. The following **websites** are a good place to start: Ⓦwww.bestofsicily .com (an informative site detailing history, the arts, books, food and wine, sights and travel); Ⓦwww.siciliaonline.it (some information in English, with details on everything from folklore and the weather to transport and festivals); and Ⓦwww.press.sicilia.it (mostly Italian, extracts from all sorts of articles about Sicily, plus news and reviews). All the major regions, towns, cities and islands have their own websites too, detailed where appropriate in the Guide.

Italian state tourist offices

Australia & New Zealand ☏02/9262 1666, Ⓦwww.italiantourism.com.au.
Canada ☏416/925 -4882, Ⓦwww.italiantourism .com.
UK ☏020/7408 1254, Ⓦwww.italiantouristboard .co.uk.
USA ☏212/245-5095, Ⓦwww.italiantourism.com.

Travellers with disabilities

Although most Sicilians are helpful enough if presented with a specific problem, the island is hardly geared towards accommodating travellers with disabilities. In the medieval city centres and old villages, few budget hotels have elevators, let alone ones capable of taking a wheelchair, and rooms have rarely been adapted for use by disabled visitors. Narrow, cobbled streets, steep inclines, chaotic driving and parking are hardly conducive to a stress-free holiday either. Crossing the street in Palermo is a major undertaking even if you're fully mobile, while Taormina, the most popular resort, poses great accessibility challenges for anyone in a wheelchair.

If the thought of negotiating your own way around the island proves too daunting, an **organized tour** may be the way to go. While that will cost more than planning your own trip, you can request accommodation in higher-category hotels that should at least have some facilities for disabled travellers, and you'll also have someone on hand who speaks Italian to help smooth the way. Accessible Italy (Ⓦwww.accessibleitaly.com)

is an Italian organization offering tours and advice to foreigners, and though it's mainly useful for mainland Italy, you can ask for advice on travelling in Sicily. You can also contact one of the organizations in your own country dedicated to people with disabilities. Tourism For All (Ⓦwww.tourismforall.org.uk), for example, publishes an information pack about holidaying in Italy for disabled travellers.

Guide

Guide

Palermo and around

CHAPTER 1 # Highlights

* **Cappella Palatina in the Palazzo dei Normanni** There's a breathtaking beauty in the chapel's glorious Byzantine mosaics. See p.63

* **Museo delle Marionette** Catch a performance and admire the swashbuckling wooden Sicilian puppets in all their finery. See p.65

* **Galleria Regionale della Sicilia** If you only visit one Palermo museum, make it the island's finest collection of medieval art. See p.67

* **La Vucciria** Dive into the capital's most frenetic market and don't come out without a souvenir or two. See p.68

* **The Duomo at Monreale** Don't miss the mosaics and cloisters at the medieval cathedral in the hills above the city. See p.79

* **Bagheria and Porticello** Over-the-top Baroque villas, boutique lodgings and harbourside fish restaurants make for a great side trip from the city. See p.83

* **A trip to Ústica** Take the ferry or hydrofoil out to the relaxed island of Ústica for a spot of hiking, diving and snorkelling. See p.88

▲ Byzantine mosaics, Cappella Palatina

Palermo and around

U nmistakably the capital of Sicily, **Palermo** is fast, brash, loud and exciting. Hub of the island since the ninth century AD, it borrows heavily from the past for its present-day look, showing a typically Sicilian fusion of foreign art, architecture, culture and lifestyle. In the narrow streets of Palermo's old town, elegant Baroque and Norman monuments exist cheek by jowl with Arabic cupolas, while Byzantine street markets swamp the medieval warrens, and the latest Milanese fashions sit in shops squeezed between Renaissance churches and Spanish *palazzi*. And, ricocheting off every wall, the endless roar of traffic and wail of police sirens adds to the confusion. Palermo is probably the noisiest city in Italy, which – coupled with the oppressive summer climate and frenetic street scenes – conjures up visions of North Africa or the Near East. Indeed, there's little that's strictly European about

Festivals

January
6 Orthodox Epiphany procession at **Piana degli Albanesi**; traditional costumes and the distribution of oranges.

Easter
Holy Week Traditional Orthodox processions and celebrations at **Piana degli Albanesi**, best on Good Friday and Easter Sunday.

April
23 Costumed processions at **Piana degli Albanesi** to celebrate St George's Day.
Last week Annual World Windsurfing Festival at **Mondello**; races, food, drink and entertainment.

July
11–15 The festival of St Rosalia – who saved the city from plague – in **Palermo**. A procession of the saint's relics, fireworks and general mayhem.

September
4 Pilgrimage to Monte Pellegrino in **Palermo** in honour of St Rosalia, patron saint of the city.

October/November
Last week in October and first week in November A week of ecclesiastical music concerts at **Monreale** cathedral.

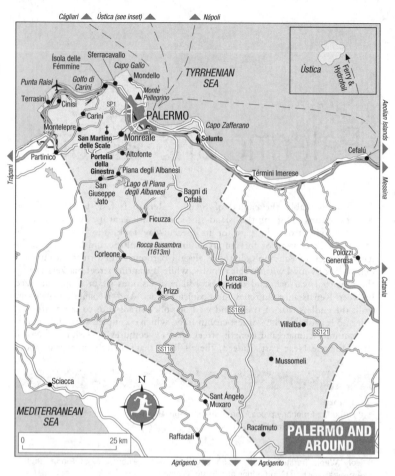

Palermo, and its geographical isolation has forced this vibrant city of 700,000 to forge its own distinct identity. You'll need at least three or four days to fully explore the historic sights, fascinating medieval quarters and chaotic markets, and a week wouldn't be too long if you plan to use the city as a base for day-trips. The most essential of these is to the medieval cathedral of **Monreale** and its celebrated mosaics, which is a hugely popular (ie, tourist-thronged) destination – spending the night allows you to see Monreale at a more leisurely pace. Fewer visitors head east along the coast, where you can spend an unhurried day at **Bagheria** and its Baroque *palazzi*, before taking in the fishing port of **Porticello** and nearby Roman site at **Solunto**. West of the city, a series of small family resorts lines the **Golfo di Carini**, while south of Palermo an enticing route heads to **Piana degli Albanesi**, a surviving Albanian Orthodox enclave in a stridently Catholic island, and then further into the mountains to the royal hunting lodge at **Ficuzza** and the notorious Mafia town of **Corleone**. For a real change of air, though, jump on a ferry or hydrofoil to the island of **Ústica**, as little as an hour and a quarter from the city. With its good, clean swimming and lazy feel, you may end up staying longer there than planned.

Palermo

In its own wide bay underneath the limestone bulk of Monte Pellegrino, and fronting the broad and fertile Conca d'Oro (Golden Shell) valley, **PALERMO** is stupendously sited. Originally a Phoenician colony, it was taken by the Carthaginians in the fifth century BC and became an important Punic bulwark against the Greek influence elsewhere on the island. It was named Panormus (All Harbour) after its obvious mercantile attractions, and it remained in Carthaginian hands until 254 BC, when the city fell to the Romans. Yet Palermo's most glorious days were still to come. In 831 AD the city was captured by the Arabs, under whose rule it thrived as an Islamic cultural and intellectual centre – the River Papineto that now flows beneath the city was said to speak with the Nile and abide by its tides. Two centuries later under the Normans, the settlement continued to flower as Europe's greatest metropolis – famed for the wealth of its court, and unrivalled as a nexus of learning.

Palermo's later fortunes fluctuated with a succession of other foreign rulers, but the city always retained its pre-eminence on the island. However, Allied bombs during World War II destroyed much of the port area and turned large parts of the medieval town into a ramshackle demolition site – a state of affairs that is only now gradually being resolved. Regeneration has been aided by funds from the European Union (when not siphoned off by illicit means; see box below) and, nowadays, although decay and deprivation are still apparent in Palermo, a more positive spirit animates the city, typified by a burgeoning number of boutique B&Bs sited in the old-town areas. Although there are notable relics from the ninth to the twelfth centuries – Palermo in its prime – it's the rebuilding of the sixteenth and seventeenth centuries that shaped the city as it appears today: essentially a straightforward street-grid confused by the memory of an Eastern past and gouged by war damage. Traditionally, Palermo has been a city of rich churches, endowed by the island's ruling families and wealthy monastic orders, from the mighty Cattedrale to the nearby mosaic-decorated Cappella Palatina, tucked inside the Palazzo dei Normanni. Each old quarter features countless other fascinating

The Mafia in Palermo

The most glaring symptom of decay in Palermo, the **Mafia problem**, is intimately connected with the welfare of the city. For years it has been openly acknowledged that a large part of the funds pouring in from Rome and the EU, ostensibly to redevelop the city centre, are unaccounted for – channelled to dubious businessmen, or simply raked off by Mafia leaders. The subtle control exerted by the Mafia is traditionally referred to only obliquely, though it periodically erupts into the news.

The problem is deeply rooted and unlikely to disappear completely any time soon, despite the courageous efforts of various individuals. Prominent among these is **Leoluca Orlando**, mayor of Palermo from 1985 to 1990 and 1993 to 2000, who attempted to combat corruption at municipal level by removing companies suspected of links with organized crime from the tenders list for new contracts. Resistance to Mafia corruption has also emerged at a more local level, notably with many owners of shops and business in Palermo banding together and refusing to pay *pizzo*, the protection money traditionally demanded by local crime gangs. A thriving organization, **Addiopizzo** (@ www.addiopizzo.org), coordinates the local resistance – their *consumo critico* (critical shopping) list publicizes the hundreds of enterprises now offering a *pizzo*-free Palermo experience (look for the stickers), including restaurants, bars and B&Bs.

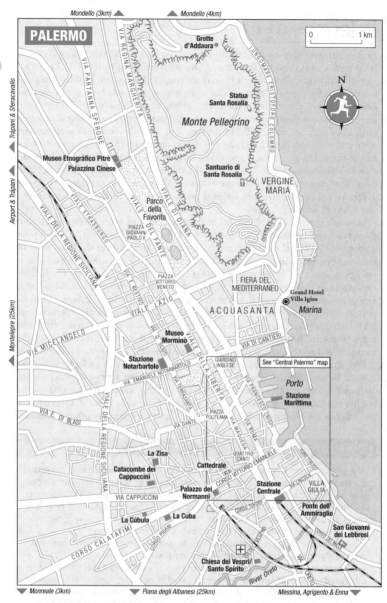

PALERMO

Mondello (3km)

Mondello (4km)

0   1 km

N

Trápani & Sferracavallo

Airport & Trápani

Grotte
d'Addaura

Statua
Santa Rosalía

Monte Pellegrino

LUNGOMARE CRISTOFORO COLOMBO

VIA REGINA MARGHERITA

VIA PARTANNA SPERONE

Museo Etnográfico Pitrè
Palazzina Cinese

Santuario di
Santa Rosalía

VERGINE
MARIA

VIALE DI DIANA

Parco
della
Favorita

PIAZZA
GIOVANNI
PAOLO II

VIALE DEL FANTE

VIALE STRASBURGO

Montelepre (25km)

VIALE DELLA REGIONE SICILIANA

VIA E. RESTIVO

PIAZZA
VITTORIO
VENETO

FIERA DEL
MEDITERRANEO

VIALE LAZIO

ACQUASANTA

Grand Hotel
Villa Igiea

Marina

VIA MICELANGELO

Museo
Mormino

Stazione
Notarbartolo

VIA EMANUELE NOTARBARTOLO

VIA TERRASANTA

VIALE DELLA LIBERTÀ

GIARDINO
INGLESE

VIA DI CANTIERI

See "Central Palermo" map

Porto

Stazione
Maríttima

VIA FRANCESCO CRISPI

VIA E. DI BLASI

VIA DANTE

PIAZZA
POLITEAMA

VIA ROMA

VIA MAQUEDA

VIA CRISPI

La Zisa

Catacombe dei
Cappuccini

Cattedrale

QUATTRO
CANTI

CORSO VITTORIO EMANUELE

TORI TRINI

VIALE DELLA REGIONE SICILIANA

VIA CAPPUCCINI

Palazzo dei
Normanni

Stazione
Centrale

VIA LINCOLN

VILLA
GIULIA

La Cúbula

La Cuba

CORSO CALATAFIMI

CORSO PISANI

CORSO TÚKORY

CORSO TÚKORY

VIA DEI BENEDETTINI

Ponte dell'
Ammiraglio

San Giovanni
dei Lebbrosi

CORSO DEI MILLE

VIA ORETO

Chiesa dei Vespri/
Santo Spírito

River Oreto

Monreale (3km)

Piana degli Albanesi (25km)

Messina, Agrigento & Enna

churches and chapels, while enthusiasts can trace the city's Norman and Baroque heritage in a series of landmark buildings and sights. But just to see Palermo in terms of an architectural tour would be to ignore much of what makes it unique, from its rollicking markets and traditional street food to the back-street puppet theatres and creepy catacombs. There's certainly never a dull moment in Sicily's feistiest city.

Arrival

Palermo's Falcone Borsellino **airport** is at Punta Raisi, 31km west of the city. It's not the island's main airport (that's Catania), but it has all the facilities you may need on arrival, including ATMs, post office and English-speaking tourist office (Mon–Fri 8.30am–7.30pm, Sat 8.30am–2pm; ☎091.591.698). Prestia & Comandè buses (ⓦ www.prestiaecomande.it) run into the city every thirty minutes (daily 5am–midnight; €5.80; 45min journey) and stop outside the Politeama theatre, at Stazione Maríttima and at <u>Stazione</u> Centrale. Urban (*metropolitana*) trains (daily 6am–10pm, €5.50) run from the airport to Stazione Centrale roughly twice an hour (works on this line may close it during 2011 and beyond), or a taxi costs around €50. All the **car rental offices** are in a separate building about 400m from the Arrivals hall – follow the footpath signs or wait for the free shuttle bus (*navetta*) that leaves every eight minutes or so.

Palermo's main train station is **Stazione Centrale** in Piazza Giulio Césare, at the southern end of Via Roma. Some trains (from Trápani/Álcamo) stop first in the northwest of the city at Stazione Notarbártolo; sit tight and you'll end up at Stazione Centrale.

Buses operate from a variety of terminals across the city, though nearly all though the main bus arrivals and ticket offices are in the streets around the train station – notably Via Paolo Balsamo and Via Rosario Gregorio. Other termini are Piazza Marina (down by the old port) and Piazzale John Lennon (near the intersection of Via Leonardo da Vinci with Viale Regione Siciliana, bus #102 from Stazione Centrale) – the latter mostly used by AST services to and from places west of Palermo.

All ferry and hydrofoil services – from Ústica, the Aeolians, Civitavecchia, Genoa, Naples and Cágliari (in Sardinia) – dock at the **Stazione Maríttima**, from where it's a ten-minute walk to Piazza Politeama and the modern city centre.

Driving and parking

Driving into Palermo can be a bit traumatic, as directional signs are confusing and the traffic unforgiving of first-time visitors. Following signs for "Stazione Centrale" – or anything that reads "Centro" – should at least get you into the city, while Piazza Politeama is a convenient first place to get your bearings and leave your vehicle. **Leaving the city** by car, you need Via Oreto (behind Stazione Centrale) for the Palermo–Messina (A19) and Palermo–Catania (A20) autostradas; Corso Vittorio Emanuele (westbound) for Monreale; and Viale della Libertà (northbound) for the airport and Trápani.

Finding a **parking space** can be a real problem, though you'll find somewhere eventually if you drive around for long enough. Metered parking costs €1 an hour (maximum 3hr) – either feed the ticket machine or buy a parking scratch card (*biglietto parcheggio*) from a nearby shop. In some areas, you will be ushered into a parking space by an unofficial attendant, who will expect a tip of 50 cents to €1. It's much less hassle to use a **garage**, especially if you have to leave your car in Palermo's old quarter overnight: useful ones include L'Oasi Verde (Corso Tukory 207, southwest of Stazione Centrale), Central Garage (Piazza Giulio Césare 43, in front of Stazione Centrale), Via Guardione 81 (near Stazione Maríttima, behind Via Francesco Crispi) and Via Sammartino 24 (town centre, off Via Dante). It costs €10–20 per day to garage-park, usually less when arranged through a hotel.

If it's not already abundantly clear from the above, it's far better not to have to drive in Palermo – you won't need a car to get around, and can pick up a rental car on the day you leave.

Information

Palermo's helpful city-centre **tourist office** is at Piazza Castelnuovo 34 (Mon–Fri 8.30am–2pm & 2.30–6pm; ☎091.605.8531, Ⓦ www.palermotourism.com), hidden behind the trees across from the bandstand. There are free maps and plenty of information about the city, and details of accommodation throughout the province. Other **information kiosks** (all open Sat–Wed 9am–1pm & 3–7pm, Thurs & Fri 9am–1pm & 3–6pm) are scattered through the city centre, in places like Piazza Politeama, Piazza Bellini and at the Stazione Centrale. For a rundown of what's on, the free **Agenda Turismo** lists useful contact details, museum times, transport links and cultural events in and around the city. For a more detailed look at arts and entertainment, there's **Lapis** (Ⓦ www.palermoweb.com/lapis), published fortnightly and widely available from cultural venues, bars and cafés. The local edition of the daily newspaper *Il Giornale di Sicilia* also details forthcoming events.

City transport

The **city buses** run by AMAT (☎848.800.817, Ⓦ www.amat.pa.it) cover every corner of Palermo, and run out as far as Monreale and Mondello. Most services run from around 4am until 11pm or midnight (sometimes earlier on Sundays). Flat-fare **tickets** (valid for 90min) cost €1.30, or you can buy an all-day ticket for €3.50, while tickets for the circular minibus services (*Linea Gialla*, *Linea Rossa* and *Linea Verde*) which weave in and out of the *centro storico*, cost just €0.52 for a day's use. All tickets are available from AMAT's glass kiosks (outside Stazione Centrale, and in Piazza Politeama and Piazza Verdi), in *tabacchi*, or wherever else you see the sign "*Véndita Biglietti AMAT*" – validate one in the machine on the bus at the start of your journey (or on just the first ride with an all-day ticket). You can also buy tickets on board from the driver for a small supplement (€0.40). **Fare dodging** – seemingly commonplace – is punishable by large spot fines from roving gangs of inspectors who board buses at random. Don't think that tourists are exempt, though unless you happen across a particularly venomous inspector you'll just be made to buy a ticket.

Bus routes are covered in the text where useful, but Stazione Centrale is a handy starting-point for many, including the #101 and #102 to Piazza Politeama, the #109 to Piazza dell'Indipendenza (for Palazzo dei Normanni and buses to Monreale), and the #139 to Piazza Marina/Corso Vittorio Emanuele and Stazione Maríttima. Stazione Centrale is also the hub for the minibuses of the **Linea Gialla** (to Orto Botanico, La Kalsa, Via Alloro, Quattro Canti, Ballarò and Corso Tukory) and **Linea Rossa** (Via Roma, Vucciria, Piazza Politeama, Giardino Inglese, Viale della Libertà, Teatro Mássimo and Via Maqueda).

There are **taxi** ranks all over the centre (see "Listings" for locations), though don't count on flagging one down on a busy street. Few trips within the city will cost more than €15, but drivers are notoriously reluctant to switch on the meter, which means it's best to agree a price before leaving.

To get an overview of the city, you could do worse than take a **sightseeing tour**. City Sightseeing (☎091.589.429, Ⓦ www.palermo.city-sightseeing.it) operates a hop-on-hop-off open-top bus service around the sights with a multilingual commentary. Departures are daily, every 30 to 60 minutes from Piazza Politeama; buy tickets on board (€20).

Accommodation

Most of Palermo's traditional budget **hotels** lie on and around the southern ends of Via Maqueda and Via Roma, close to Stazione Centrale. However, you will get far more for your money by staying in one of the city's **B&Bs**, many of which are charming and extremely well run. Prices tend to stay the same year-round (except out on the nearby coast, where usual summer rates apply), but advance reservations are recommended if you want to be sure of a room in a particular place (and also around the time of Palermo's annual festival, July 11–15). For an **apartment** stay, try the Palazzo Conte Federico (℡091.6511881, ⓦwww.contefederico .com), a magnificent (if chilly) palace built over the city walls, close to the Ballarò market, which has several apartments for rent for €150 per night.

The two nearest **campsites**, as well as Palermo's **youth hostel**, are actually all at the beachside town of Sferracavallo (see p.82), 16km northwest of the city, or a good half an hour on the bus – convenient for beach or airport but not really for city sightseeing or nights on the town.

Old town

Alla Kala Corso Vittorio Emanuele 71 ℡091.743.4763, ⓦwww.allakala.it. Five stylish rooms with magnificent views of the sailing marina, and a keen following among those in the know. ❸

BB22 Palazzo Pantelleria, Largo Cavalieri di Malta 22 ℡091.611.1610 or 335.790.8733, ⓦwww.bb22.it. Faultless Milanese designer-chic (resinated cement floors, perspex chairs, matte-coloured walls) fused with a home-from-home feel (free wi-fi, coffee and water) in a historic *palazzo* a few steps from the Vuccaria market. Breakfast is served on a small roof terrace. ❹

La Casa dei Limoni Piazza Giulio Césare 9 ℡334.834.3888 or 338.967.8907, ⓦwww .lacasadeilimoni.it. A friendly B&B right opposite the train station that's great value for money, and the perfect place to stay if you arrive late or have to leave early. ❶

La Dimora del Genio Via Garibaldi 58 ℡347.658.7664, ⓦwww.ladimoradelgenio .it. Four cosy rooms (not all en suite) in a centrally heated seventeenth-century *palazzetto*, furnished with a tasteful blend of antiques, modern furniture and original paintings by Palermo artist Maurizio Muscolino. The cheery owner is a talented cook and offers cooking courses for guests, as well as a splendid Sunday dinner for €30 a head. ❷

La Dimora del Guiscardo Via della Vetriera 83–85 ℡328.662.6074, ⓦwww.ladimoradelguiscardo.it. Funky little B&B in the heart of La Kalsa, close to the area's bars and restaurants, with simple rooms sharing a single bathroom. ❶

Giardino dell'Alloro Vicolo San Carlo 8 ℡091.617.6904 or 338.224.3541, ⓦwww.giardinodellalloro.it. Lovely B&B in La Kalsa with books for guests to borrow, a courtyard where breakfast is served, a small spa in the garden and a living room used as exhibition space by contemporary Sicilian artists. The five rooms also feature original works of art, and there's a small kitchen for guests. ❷

Letizia Via dei Bottai 30 ℡091.589.110, ⓦwww .hotelletizia.com. Each room in this delightful hotel,

just off Piazza Marina, has its own individual colour scheme and furnishings. There's an enclosed courtyard for breakfast. ❷

Orientale Via Maqueda 26 ℡091.616.5727, ⓦwww.albergoorientale.191.it. One of the most atmospheric of old-town hotels, an eighteenth-century *palazzo* with a columned courtyard and marble staircase, a frescoed salon, and two cavernous, vaulted double rooms (nos. 6 and 7, where Mussolini once stayed) complete with a long balcony overlooking Via Maqueda. Other doubles – some en suite – are plainer and quieter, looking down onto the courtyard and the Albergheria market. ❷

Paradiso Via Schiavuzzo 65 ℡091.617.2825. The windows of this basic, old-fashioned first-floor *pensione* overlook the Piazza della Rivoluzione. The ten rooms (all share a bathroom) are among the cheapest in town, and the couple who run it are a delight. No credit cards. ❶

Quattro Quarti Palazzo Arone di Valentino, Corso Vittorio Emanuele 376 ℡091.583.687, or 347.854.7209, ⓦwww.quattroquarti.it. A superior B&B with four elegant rooms and a plush suite furnished with antiques, occupying part of a huge *palazzo* owned by the Arone di Valentino family. Guests are very well looked after, making this a good place to consider if you are a little nervous about finding your feet in Palermo. ❸

Modern city

Grand Hotel et des Palmes Via Roma 398 ℡091.602.811, ⓦwww.grandhoteletdespalmes .com. The four-star *Grand Hotel* is very definitely of the old school, and though it no longer has the social cachet of its nineteenth-century heyday, it remains a comfortable and convenient base on the main Via Roma. Some of the rooms are huge, and there are often substantial discounts for online bookings. ❺

Grand Hotel Villa Igiea Via Belmonte 43, 3km north of the centre ℡091.631.2111, ⓦwww .villaigiea.hilton.com. This classic Art Nouveau building of 1900, originally a villa of the Florio family (the people who pioneered tuna canning), stands outside the city centre above the marina of Acquasanta. The swimming pool overlooking the port is a plus, but otherwise it's a bit too self-important (with its endless photos of famous guests) and often filled with tour groups. The best rates are on the website. ❽

🏃 **Palazzo Pantaleo** Via Ruggero Séttimo 74 ☎091.325.471 or 335.700.6091, 🌐www .palazzopantaleo.it. An outstanding B&B with seven huge, light, airy rooms in an eighteenth-century *palazzo* on a quiet piazzetta, a short walk from Piazza Politeama. There's internet access in all rooms, and a small kitchen where you can make drinks or snacks. ❸

Ucciard Home Via Enrico Albanese 34–36 ☎091.348.426, 🌐www.hotelucciardhome.com. Designer hotel opposite the prison, with sixteen comfortable, stylish rooms and lovely, luxurious bathrooms. Check the website for the best rates. ❻

Vecchio Borgo Via Quintino Sella 1–7 ☎091.611.8330, 🌐www.hotelvecchioborgo.eu. An appealing hotel sited between Piazza Politeama and one of Palermo's best weekend markets. Comfortable rooms feature bold printed fabrics, while an excellent breakfast includes home-made cakes. There's also garage parking (€10 a night) and limited spaces in a free outdoor car park. ❸

The City

Historical Palermo sits compactly around a central crossroads, the **Quattro Canti**, which is the intersection of Corso Vittorio Emanuele and Via Maqueda, two streets that date from the city's reconstruction in the sixteenth century. Parallel to Via Maqueda, and running north from Stazione Centrale, **Via Roma** was a much later addition, linking the old centre with the **modern city**. At the heart of this nineteenth-century grid of shops, apartments and office blocks are the double squares of Piazza Castelnuovo and Piazza Ruggero Séttimo – together known to Palermitans as **Piazza Politeama** – a lengthy 25- to 30-minute walk from the train station (or a quicker bus ride).

Four distinct medieval quarters lie around Quattro Canti: the **Albergheria** and **Capo** districts lie roughly west of Via Maqueda, **Vucciria** and **La Kalsa** to the east, closest to the water. In the past, the inhabitants of these quarters had their own dialects, trades, palaces and markets – even intermarriage was frowned upon. Today, the areas hold most of Palermo's most interesting sights and buildings, concealed within a tight, undisciplined web of alleys and piazzas. Often, you'll come across tranquil gardens or chapels containing outstanding works of art, or even stabling for a goat – a world away from the din of the urban assault course outside. Beyond the old centre, on the outskirts of the modern city, are other attractions, from Palermo's best park, the **Parco della Favorita**, to the ghoulish **Cappuccini monastery**, while the other quick retreat is to **Monte Pellegrino**, the mountain that looms beyond the city to the north.

Given that cars, let alone buses, can't get down many of the narrow streets in the old city centre, you'll have to walk around most of what is detailed below – although for certain specific sights, don't hesitate to jump on a bus, as it's no fun at all slogging up and down the long thoroughfares of the modern city.

Around the Quattro Canti

The **Quattro Canti** or "Four Corners" is the centre (if anywhere is) of the medieval town area. Erected in 1611, this is not so much a piazza as a set of Baroque crossroads that divides central Palermo into quadrants. In each concave "corner" are tiers of statues – respectively a season, a king of Sicily and a patron of the city – where, in previous centuries, the heads of convicted rebels were hung from poles. Only a few steps from here lie some of Palermo's most opulent piazzas and buildings, including several of the city's most extraordinary churches.

On the southwest corner (entrance on Corso Vittorio Emanuele), the early seventeenth-century **San Giuseppe dei Teatini** (summer Mon–Sat 7.30–11am & 6–8pm, Sun 8.30am–12.30pm & 6–8pm, winter Mon–Sat 7.30am–noon & 5.30–8pm) is the most harmonious of the city's Baroque churches. The misleadingly simple facade conceals a wealth of detail inside, from tumbling angels holding the holy water on either side of the door to the lavish side chapels and ceiling encrusted with writhing putti. Outside, adjacent to the church, is the main building of the **Università**, a dull nineteenth-century restoration job replacing what was originally a convent adjoining San Giuseppe. There are generally plenty of students around here, and a couple of good bars in the little piazza across from the entrance. Nearby, just down the Corso, the impressive **Palazzo Riso**, Corso Vittorio Emanuele 365, has been restored as the **Museo d'Arte Contemporanea della Sicilia** (exhibitions vary, current programme on Ⓦwww.palazzoriso.it), another good place to escape from the hubbub in its cool bar, courtyard and arty book and gift shop.

Cross Via Maqueda instead, to **Piazza Pretoria**, and you're confronted by the gleaming-white nude figures of its racy sixteenth-century Florentine fountain, protected by railings to ward off excitable vandals. The piazza also holds the plaque-studded and pristine **Municipio** and, towering above both square and fountain, the massive late sixteenth-century flank of the church of **Santa Caterina** (summer Mon–Sat 9.30am–1.30pm & 3–7pm, Sun 9.30am–1.30pm; winter Mon–Sat 9.30am–1pm & 3–5.30pm, Sun 9.30am–1pm; enter from Piazza Bellini), the antithesis of San Giuseppe over the road. This is Sicilian Baroque at its most exuberant, with every inch of the enormous interior covered in wildly decorative, pustular relief work, deep reds and yellows filling in between sculpted cherubs, Madonnas, lions and eagles. One marble panel (in the first chapel on the right) depicts Jonah about to be devoured by a rubbery-lipped whale, with a Spanish galleon above constructed from wire with string rigging.

Piazza Bellini, San Cataldo and La Martorana

Just around the corner from the Pretoria fountain, **Piazza Bellini** is largely a car park by day, with vehicles jammed together next to part of the city's old Roman wall, and beneath two more wildly contrasting churches. The little Saracenic red golf-ball domes belong to **San Cataldo** (summer Mon–Sat 9am–2pm & 3.30–7pm, Sun 9am–2pm; winter daily 9am–2pm; €1), a squat twelfth-century chapel on a palm-planted bank above the piazza. Other than the crenellations around the roof it was never decorated, and in the eighteenth century the chapel was even used as a post office. It still retains a good mosaic pavement in an otherwise bare and peaceful interior.

The understatement of this little chapel is more than offset by the splendid interior of **La Martorana** opposite (Mon–Sat 9.30am–1pm & 3.30–5.30pm, summer until 6.30pm, Sun all year 8.30–9.45am & noon–1pm), one of the finest surviving buildings of the medieval city. It was paid for in 1143 by George of Antioch, King Roger's admiral, from whom it received its original name, Santa Maria dell'Ammiraglio. After the Sicilian Vespers, the island's nobility met here to offer the Crown to Peter of Aragon, and under the Spanish the church was passed

---

Frutta di Martorana

When Palermo's religious houses were at their late medieval height, many supported themselves by turning out remarkable sculpted confectionery – fruit and vegetables made out of coloured almond paste. La Martorana was once famous for the quality of its almond "fruits", which were sold at the church doors, and today most Sicilian *pasticcerie* continue the tradition. In Palermo these creations are known as *frutta di Martorana*, and cake-shop windows usually display not only fruit but also fish and shellfish made out of the same sickly almond mixture. The best time to see the displays is in October, before the festival of Ognissanti (All Saints).

Ferries to Cagliari, Genoa, Livorno, Ústica & Naples; hydrofoils to Ústica, ▲ Cefalù & Aeolian Islands

CENTRAL PALERMO

ACCOMMODATION

Alla Kala	G
BB22	F
La Casa dei Limoni	N
La Dimora del Genio	M
La Dimora del Guiscardo	I
Giardino dell'Alloro	K
Grand Hotel et des Palmes	E
Grand Hotel Villa Igeia	A
Letizia	H
Orientale	O
Palazzo Pantaleo	D
Paradiso	L
Quattro Quarti	J
Ucciard Home	B
Vecchio Borgo	C

RESTAURANTS

Bellini	28
Casa del Brodo	14
Dietro la Cattedrale	20
Il Garage	31
Lilia e Toduccio	19
Mi Manda Picone	1
Michele alla Brace	4
Il Mirto e la Rosa	3
Osteria lo Bianco	29
Osteria dei Vespri	10
Pizzeria Italia	13
Santandrea	2
Trattoria Piccolo Napoli	27
Trattoria Primavera	17
Trattoria Torremuzza	11
Le Tre Sorelle	C

BARS, CAFÉS, STREET FOOD & ICE CREAM

American Bar	21
Antica Focacceria San Francesco	18
Bar Malox	26
Caffè Letterario Malavoglia	30
Cama Enoteca	23
Casa Obatola	22
Champagneria del Massimo	8
I Cuochini	5
Franco 'U Vastiddaru	15
Kursaal Kalhesa	25
Ilardo	16
Mazzara	6
Obika	12
Oriol	7
Palazzo Riso	24
Rosciglione	32
La Taverna	31

Stazione Marittima

Bus to Airport ★

Ucciardone Prison

Giardino Inglese

Acquasanta & ▲   La Favorita & Mondello ▲

Museo Mormino ▼

Sferracavallo Campsites ▼

VIA DI GIARDINO · VIALE DELLA LIBERTA · VIALE DELLA LIBERTA · VIA P. CALVI · VIA CARINI · VIA LA LUMIA · VIA G. DAITA · VIA MAZZINI · VIA E. ALBANESE · VIA ARCHIMEDE · CORSO DOMENICO SCINA · VIA FRANCESCO CRISPI · VIA EMERICO AMARI · VIA PRINCIPE BELMONTE · VIA BENEDETTO GRAVINA · VIA MARIANO STABILE · VIA PRINCIPE GRANITELI · VIA CERDA · VIA MICHELE AMARI · VIA ROMA · VIA CAVOUR · VIA GUARDIONE · VIA XIII VITTIME · VIA WALTER · VIALE DELLA LIBERTA · VIA SIRACUSA · VIA XX SETTEMBRE · VIA DANTE · VIA PRINCIPE DI VILLAFRANCA · VIA SAMMARTINO · VIA MESSINA · VIA CATANIA · VIA PARISI · VIA GENNARO · VIA CAROLGA · VIA RUGGERO SETTIMO · VIA VILLAREALE · VIA SAMMARTINO

PIAZZA CRISPI · PIAZZA MORDINI · PIAZZA CASTELNUOVO · PIAZZA RUGGERO SETTIMO · PIAZZA POLITEAMA · PIAZZA UCCIARDONE · PIAZZA STURZO · PIAZZA FLORIO · PIAZZA XIII VITTIME

Teatro Politeama Garibaldi

Bus to Airport ★

N

③ Hotel Garibaldi, Via Emerico Amari, 146

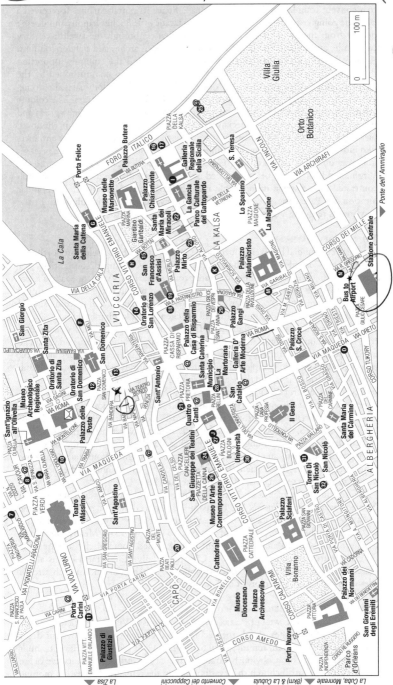

1

100 m

0

Villa Giulia

Orto Botánico

Ponte dell' Amminaglio

PIAZZA DELLA KALSA

Porta Felice

FORO ITALICO

VIA LINCOLN

VIA ARCHIRAFI

Palazzo Butera

S. Teresa

VIA DELLA VITTORIA

Museo delle Marionette

Palazzo Chiaramonte

Galleria Regionale della Sicilia

La Cala

Porta Felice

Santa Maria della Catena

Palazzo Garibaldi

Santa Maria di Miracoli

La Gancia

Parco Culturale del Gattopardo

Lo Spasimo

PIAZZA MAGIONE

La Magione

CORSO DEI MILLE

Stazione Centrale

Giardino Garibaldi

San Francesco d'Assisi

Palazzo Mirto

LA KALSA

Palazzo Aiutamicristo

VIA DELLA VITTORIA

Bus to Airport

San Giorgio

Santa Zita

VIA DELLA CALA

Oratorio di San Lorenzo

Palazzo della Casa di Risparmio

Palazzo Gangi

Palazzo S. Croce

VIA MAQUEDA

VIA ORETO

Museo Archeologico Regionale

Oratorio di Santa Zita

San Domenico

Sant'Antonio

Santa Caterina

La Martorana

Galleria D'Arte Moderna

San Cataldo

Il Gesù

Santa Maria del Carmine

Sant'Ignazio all'Olivella

Oratorio di San Domenico

Palazzo delle Poste

Municipio

Quattro Canti

Teatro Massimo

Sant'Agostino

San Giuseppe dei Teatini

Museo D'Arte Contemporanea

Università

Torre Di San Nicolò

San Nicolò

Palazzo Sclafani

ALBERGHERIA

Porta Carini

Palazzo di Giustizia

Cattedrale

Villa Bonanno

Museo Diocesano

Palazzo Archescovile

CAPO

Porta Nuova

Parco d'Orleans

CORSO AMEDO

San Giovanni degli Eremiti

Palazzo dei Normanni

61

to a convent founded by Eloisa Martorana – hence its popular name. It received a Baroque going-over and its curving northern facade in 1588, but happily this doesn't detract from the great power of the interior; enter through the twelfth-century campanile, an original structure that retains its ribbed arches and slender columns. A series of spectacular **mosaics** are laid on and around the columns supporting the main cupola – animated twelfth-century Greek works, commissioned by the admiral himself, who was of Greek descent. A gentle Christ dominates the dome, surrounded by angels, with the Apostles and the Madonna to the sides. The colours are still strong, a golden background enlivened by azure, grape-red, light-green and white, and, in the morning especially, light streams in through the high windows, picking out the admirable craftsmanship. On both sides of the steps by the entrance, two more original mosaic panels (from the destroyed Norman portico) have been set in frames on the walls: a kneeling George of Antioch dedicating the church to the Virgin, and King Roger being crowned by Christ – the diamond-studded monarch contrasted with a larger, more simple and dignified Christ. The church is a popular location for Palermitan weddings, spectacular events that often culminate in the newlyweds releasing a dozen white doves from the steps of the church.

The Albergheria

The district bounded by Via Maqueda and Corso Vittorio Emanuele, just northwest of Stazione Centrale – the **Albergheria** – can't have changed substantially for several hundred years. Although there are proud *palazzi* on Via Maqueda itself, the real heart of the quarter is in the sprawling warren of tiny streets away from the main roads. The central core taken up by a lively street market, and there are several fine churches interspersed among the tall, blackened and leaning buildings.

The most spectacular of the churches is **Il Gesù**, or **Casa Professa** (daily 7am–noon & 4–6.30pm), on Via Ponticello, topped by a green-and-white-patterned dome. The first Jesuit foundation in Sicily, it was begun in the mid-sixteenth century and took over a hundred years to complete. It was later almost entirely rebuilt following bomb damage in World War II, and there are still signs of the devastation in the surrounding streets. The reconstruction has been impressively thorough, and the church's awesome interior, a glorious Baroque swirl of inlaid marble, majolica, intricate relief work and gaudily painted ceiling, takes some time to absorb. Continuing down the road leads to **Piazza Ballarò**, the focus of a raucous daily fruit and vegetable market that starts early in the morning. Gleaming fish curl their heads and tails in the air, squashes come as long as baseball bats, and vine leaves trail decoratively down from stalls. There are some very cheap snack bars here, too, where you can sidle in among the locals and sample sliced-open sea urchins, fried artichokes and beer.

At one end of the piazza on Via Nasi, climb the 84 steps of the **Torre di San Nicolò** (usually open Tues & Sat 10.30am–12.30pm; donation expected) for one of the best city views. It started life as a watchtower in the thirteenth century and was joined to the adjacent church of San Nicolò in about 1518. Meanwhile, at the southern end of Via Ballarò, the bright majolica-tiled dome of the seventeenth-century church of **Santa Maria del Cármine** (daily 9.30–11am) looms above Piazza del Cármine, a singular landmark amid the market stalls and rubbish-strewn alleys, with an adjoining cloister and convent.

San Giovanni degli Eremiti

Any of the long streets west of Piazza del Cármine leads to Via dei Benedettini, across which, behind iron gates, stands the deconsecrated church of **San Giovanni degli Eremiti** (daily 9am–5pm, summer until 6.30pm; €6) – St John of the Hermits. Built in 1132, this is the most obviously Arabic of the city's Norman relics, its five ochre domes topping a small church that was built upon the remains of an earlier mosque (part of which, an adjacent empty hall, is still visible). It was especially favoured by its founder, Roger II, who granted the monks of San Giovanni 21 barrels of tuna a year, a prized commodity controlled by the Crown. A path leads up through citrus trees to the church, behind which lie some celebrated late thirteenth-century cloisters – perfect twin columns with slightly pointed arches surrounding a wilted garden.

Immediately behind the church, on Corso Re Ruggero, the **Palazzo d'Orleans** is also set in its own garden. Home to the exiled Louis-Philippe, duke of Orleans (later the last king of France), between 1810 and 1814, it's now the official residence of Sicily's president.

Palazzo dei Normanni

A royal palace has always occupied the high ground above medieval Palermo, and the vast length of the **Palazzo dei Normanni**, or Palazzo Reale, still dominates the western edge of the old town. Originally built by the Saracens in the ninth century, the palace was enlarged considerably by the Normans, under whom it housed the most magnificent of medieval European courts. The long front was added by the Spanish in the seventeenth century, and most of the interior is now taken up by the Sicilian regional parliament (hence the security guards and limited access).

Visitors can tour the **Royal Apartments** (Mon–Sat 8.15am–5.45pm, last entry at 5pm, Sun & hols 8.15am–1pm, last entry at 12.15pm; €8.50, includes Cappella Palatina; ⓦwww.federicosecondo.org), whose showpiece is the **Sala di Ruggero**, one of the earliest parts of the palace and richly covered with twelfth-century mosaics of hunting scenes. Other rooms, such as the **Sala del Duca di Montalto**, are used for occasional exhibitions. The highlight of the entire palace, however – and the undisputed artistic gem of central Palermo – is the beautiful **Cappella Palatina** (closed for services on Sun between 9.45am and 11.15am), the private royal chapel of Roger II, built between 1132 and 1143. Its intimate interior is immediately overwhelming, with cupola, three apses and nave entirely covered in **mosaics** of outstanding quality. The oldest are those in the cupola and apses, probably completed in 1150 by Byzantine artists; those in the nave are from the hands of local craftsmen, finished twenty-odd years later and depicting Old and New Testament scenes. The colours are vivid and, as at Monreale and Cefalù, it's the powerful representation of Christ as Pantocrator that dominates the senses, bolstered here by other secondary images – Christ blessing, open book in hand, and Christ enthroned, between Peter (to whom the chapel is dedicated) and Paul. The chapel also has a delightful Arabic ceiling with richly carved wooden stalactites, a patterned marble floor and an impressive marble Norman candlestick (by the pulpit), 4m high and contorted by manic carvings.

You should note that the Royal Apartments can close without warning for parliament sessions, weddings and other events (weekends are usually most reliable for access).

The Cattedrale and around

Walking down Corso Vittorio Emanuele from the Quattro Canti, there's no preparation for the sudden, huge bulk of the **Cattedrale** (Mon–Sat 7am–7pm, Sun 7am–1.30pm & 4.30–7pm; closed during services; ⓦwww.cattedrale.palermo .it), an even more substantial Norman relic than the royal palace. Founded in 1185 by Palermo's English archbishop Gualtiero Offamiglio (Walter of the Mill), the cathedral was intended to be his power base in the city. Yet it wasn't finished for centuries, and in any case was quickly superseded by the glories of William II's foundation at Monreale. Less-than-subtle late-eighteenth-century alterations added a dome – completely out of character – and spoiled the fine lines of the tawny stone. Still, the triple-apsed eastern end (seen from a side road off the Corso) and the lovely matching towers are all twelfth-century originals and, despite the fussy Catalan-Gothic facade, there's enough Norman carving and detail to give the exterior more than mere curiosity value. The same is not true, however, of the overblown interior, which was modernized by Fuga, the Neapolitan architect responsible for the dome. Instead, the main interest inside resides in the **Area Monumentale** (Mon–Sat: March–Oct 9.30am–5.30pm; Nov–Feb 9.30am–1.30pm; €2.50, or €5 including Museo Diocesano, see below), where you can view the **royal tombs**, Palermo's pantheon of kings and emperors. Gathered together in two crowded chapels are the mortal remains of some of Sicily's most famous monarchs, notably Frederick II (left front) and his wife Constance (far right), Henry VI (right front) and Roger II (rear left). In a reliquary chapel to the right of the choir the remains of city patron, Santa Rosalia, are housed in a silver casket, while in the **treasury**, or *tesoro*, is a rare twelfth-century jewel- and pearl-encrusted skullcap and three simple, precious rings removed from the tomb of Constance of Aragon in the eighteenth century. Finally, the **crypt** is home to 23 impressive marble tombs, many of which are actually ancient sarcophagi with interesting decoration – no. 12 is a Greek sarcophagus boasting an imposing effigy by Antonello Gagini, one of a prolific dynasty of talented medieval sculptors who covered Sicily with their creations.

At the western end of the cathedral, over the road, stands the **Palazzo Arcivescovile**, the one-time archbishop's palace, entered through a fifteenth-century gateway. One wing of it holds the **Museo Diocesano** (Tues–Fri 8.30am–1.30pm, Sat 10am–6pm, Sun 9.30am–1.30pm; €4), which brings together religious art from the cathedral and from city churches destroyed during World War II. There's some marvellous work here from the medieval and Renaissance periods, including a twelfth-century mosaic of the Madonna, a startling flagellation of Christ by Antonio Veneziano (1388), and a couple of lovely fifteenth-century triptychs, both showing the *Coronation of the Virgin* (one with angels blasting on trumpets).

A little way up Via Bonello (left out of the archbishop's palace) there's usually some activity in the open-air **Mercato delle Pulci**, an antique-cum-junk market in Piazza Peranni displaying chandeliers galore. Back on the Corso, the road runs up to the royal palace, on the northern side of which lies the commanding **Porta Nuova**. Erected in 1535, it commemorates Charles V's Tunisian exploits, with suitably grim, turbaned and moustachioed figures adorning the western side.

Il Capo

Around the back of the Cattedrale lies the **Capo** quarter, one of the oldest areas of Palermo and another labyrinthine web of run-down streets. The only touch of grace is in the tree-planted **Piazza del Monte**, while former grandeur is indicated by a few surviving sculpted portals in the decaying palaces. One alley, Via Porta Carini, climbs past shambolic buildings and locked, battered churches to reach the decrepit **Porta Carini** itself, one of the city's medieval gates. There are market stalls packed into Via Porta Carini, and the entire area is reminiscent at times of an Arab souk, though with a decidedly Sicilian choice of wares.

The market extends on either side of Via Porta Carini, west to the edge of the Capo district and east, along **Via Sant'Agostino** – the closer you get to Via Maqueda, the more it's devoted to clothes and shoes rather than food. Keep an eye out for the church of **Sant'Agostino** (Mon–Sat 7am–noon & 4–6pm, Sun 7am–noon), built by the Chiaramonte and Sclàfani families in the thirteenth century. Above the main door (on Via Raimondo) there's a gorgeous latticework rose window and, inside through the adjacent side-door, some fine seventeenth-century stuccoes by Giácomo Serpotta. Another door leads to a quadrangle of calm sixteenth-century cloisters. Otherwise, turn the corner, and along Via Sant'Agostino, behind the market stalls, the church sports a badly chipped, sculpted fifteenth-century doorway attributed to Domenico Gagini.

Along Via Roma

Starting out from Stazione Centrale, there doesn't seem too much along modern **Via Roma** to get excited about, but many of the side streets are traditionally devoted to particular trades and commerce. Ironmongery, wedding dresses, baby clothes and ceramics all have their separate enclaves, while the pavements of narrow Via Divisi are chock-full of stacked bikes from a series of cycle shops. Via Divisi itself runs to **Piazza della Rivoluzione**, from where the 1848 uprising began, marked by an oddly elaborate fountain. From here, **Via Garibaldi** marks the route that Garibaldi took in May 1860 when he entered the city; at Via Garibaldi 23, the immense, battered fifteenth-century **Palazzo Aiutamicristo** keeps bits of its original Catalan-Gothic structure.

North of Piazza della Rivoluzione, Via Aragona leads to Piazza Aragona, the first of a confusing jumble of squares. On the adjacent **Piazza Croce dei Vespri**, marked by a cross for the French who died in the 1282 Sicilian Vespers rebellion, stands the huge entrance to the **Palazzo Valguarnera Gangi**, where Visconti filmed the ballroom scene in *The Leopard*; you may be able to get a glimpse of the inside by smooth-talking the porter. West of Piazza Croce dei Vespri, back towards Via Roma, the **Galleria d'Arte Moderna** (Tues–Sun 9.30am–6.30pm; €7) occupies an elegantly restored ex-convent in Piazza Sant'Anna. The artworks here are all Sicilian, from the nineteenth century onwards, best of which is the sculpture, including a small bronze study of an exhausted horse by Enrico Quattrociocchi. International touring exhibitions often visit too.

Along Corso Vittorio Emanuele to the waterfront

From the Quattro Canti, **Corso Vittorio Emanuele** stretches east towards the water. Via A. Paternostro cuts away to the right to the thirteenth-century church of **San Francesco d'Assisi** (daily 8am–noon & 4–6pm), whose well-preserved portal, picked out with a zigzag decoration, is topped by a wonderful rose window – a harmonious design that is, for once, continued inside. All the Baroque trappings have been stripped away to reveal a pleasing stone interior, the later side chapels showing

---

Sicilian puppet theatre

Sicily's most vibrant traditional entertainment is its puppet theatre, and in the engaging **Museo delle Marionette** (Mon–Sat 9am–1pm & 2.30–6.30pm, Sun 10am–1pm; Ⓦ www.museomarionettepalermo.it; €5) you'll find the country's definitive collection of puppets and painted scenery; the museum is just down Via Butera at Piazzetta Antonio Pasqualino. It's fairly wide-ranging, so the museum also encompasses puppet figures from Rajasthan, glittering dragons from Rangoon and the British Punch and Judy in their traditional booth, but it's the Sicilian puppets that steal the show. Best of all is to see a theatrical performance – enjoyably rowdy affairs of battles, chivalry, betrayal and shouted dialect, based around French and Sicilian history and specifically the exploits of the hero Orlando (Roland). The museum puts on its own **puppet shows** (*Spettácolo dei Pupi*), most regularly every Tuesday and Friday between October and June, but also at other times (details on the website, tickets €8). There are also shows staged at other backstreet **puppet theatres**, run by the same families for generations, including Figli d'Arte Cuticchio (Via Bara all'Olivella 95, near Teatro Mássimo, Ⓦ www.figlidartecuticchio.com), Teatro Argento (Via Pietro Novelli 1, off Corso Vittorio Emanuele, opposite the Cattedrale) and Teatro Ippogrifo (Vicolo Ragusi 6, near Quattro Canti, off Corso Vittorio Emanuele).

beautifully crafted arches – the fourth on the left is one of the earliest Renaissance works on the island, sculpted by Francesco Laurana in 1468. To the side of the church, at Via Immacolatella 5, the renowned **Oratorio di San Lorenzo** (Mon–Sat 9am–5pm; €2) contains another of Giácomo Serpotta's stuccoed masterpieces, namely intricately fashioned scenes from the lives of St Lawrence and St Francis.

Otherwise it's a straight run along the Corso down to the water, with the old city harbour of **La Cala** to the left. This thumb-shaped inlet was once the main port of Palermo, stretching as far inland as Via Roma, but the harbour was in decline from the sixteenth century, when silting caused the water to recede to its current position. With all the heavy work transferred to new docks to the northwest, La Cala's surviving small fishing fleet now plays second fiddle to the yachts of Palermo's well-heeled. The little harbour is overlooked on one side by the church of **Santa Maria della Catena**, named after the chain that used to close the harbour in the late fifteenth century. The Corso, meanwhile, ends at the Baroque **Porta Felice** gate, begun in 1582 as a counterbalance to the Porta Nuova, visible way to the southwest. From here, you can judge the extent of the late medieval city, which lay between the two gates.

The whole area beyond the Porta Felice was flattened in 1943, and has since been rebuilt as the **Foro Italico** promenade (also known as Foro Umberto I), complete with small amusement park, from where you can look back over the harbour to Monte Pellegrino. This is one of the liveliest places in the city on summer evenings, when the locals take to the street armed to the teeth with cellphones and ice creams. A street back, on Via Butera, the seventeenth-century facade of the **Palazzo Butera** faces out over the Foro Italico. Once the home of the Branciforte family, at one time the wealthiest family in Sicily, it was gradually partitioned and sold off, and is now only open for conferences or groups of visitors, but numerous films have been shot here, including *The Talented Mr Ripley* and *The Godfather Part III*.

Piazza Marina and around

The large square of **Piazza Marina** encloses the tropical **Giardino Garibaldi**, famed for its enormous banyan trees. It's a popular venue for the city's elderly card-players, who gather around green baize tables at lunchtime for a game. The square itself was reclaimed from the sea in the tenth century, subsequently used for jousting tournaments and executions, and is now surrounded by pavement restaurants and *palazzi*, including the second-largest of Palermo's palaces, the **Palazzo Chiaramonte**, flanking the east side of the square. Dating from the fourteenth century, the palace was the home of the Inquisition from 1685 to 1782, before becoming the city's law courts (until 1972). Today, it is the administrative centre of the university and is only open to the public for occasional art exhibitions.

The other side of Piazza Marina is marked by the lovely Renaissance church of **Santa Maria dei Mirácoli**, while just up from here, off the piazza, head down the narrow Vícolo della Neve all'Alloro for the **Parco Culturale del Gattopardo** (Mon & Wed–Sun 11am–9pm; ⓦ www.parcotomasi.it), a cultural centre with café-bar dedicated to Giuseppe Tomasi di Lampedusa and his iconic book *The Leopard*. The centre hosts concerts, film shows and readings, and runs guided walking tours in Italian and English focusing on places associated with the author, the book and the film (minimum numbers may be required, contact the centre). The bar is a nice place in any case to relax over a *granita* or a glass of wine in its cobbled garden.

From Santa Maria dei Mirácoli, turn right off Via Lungarini to reach the **Palazzo Mirto**, Via Merlo 2 (daily 9am–7pm; €4), a late eighteenth-century building that's one of the few in the city to retain its original furnishings, thus giving a rare insight into *palazzo* life. The exquisite ceilings, intimate Chinese Room, imposing *baldacchino*, vibrantly coloured tapestries and overblown Baroque fountain are perhaps all to be expected, but the family's more modest living quarters have also been preserved, while visits also take in the servants' kitchen and the carriages in the stables.

Galleria Regionale della Sicilia

Sicily's finest medieval art collection is displayed in the **Galleria Regionale della Sicilia** (Tues–Sun 8.30am–6.30pm, last entry 5.30pm; €8), which occupies the princely Palazzo Abatellis, Via Alloro 4, a fifteenth-century building that still retains elements of its Catalan-Gothic and Renaissance origins. There are some wonderful works here, by all the major names encountered on any tour of the island, starting with the fifteenth-century sculptor **Francesco Laurana**, whose white marble bust of *Eleonora d'Aragona* is a calm, perfectly studied portrait. Another room is devoted to the work of the **Gagini** clan, mostly statues of the Madonna, though Antonello Gagini is responsible for a rather strident *Archangel Michael*, with a distinct military manner. Highlight of the ground floor, though, is a magnificent fifteenth-century **fresco**, the *Triumph of Death*, by an unknown (possibly Flemish) painter. It's a chilling study, with Death cast as a skeletal archer astride a galloping, spindly horse, trampling bodies slain by his arrows. He rides towards a group of smug and wealthy citizens, apparently unconcerned at his approach; meanwhile, to the left, the sick and the old plead hopelessly for oblivion.

There are three further frescoes (thirteenth- and fourteenth-century Sicilian, and rather crude) above the steps up to the first floor, which is devoted to painting. The earliest works (thirteenth- to fourteenth-century) are fascinating, displaying marked Byzantine characteristics, like the fourteenth-century mosaic of the *Madonna and Child*, eyes and hands remarkably self-assured. For sheer accomplishment, though, look no further than the collection of works by the fifteenth-century Sicilian artist **Antonello da Messina**: three small, clever portraits of saints Gregory, Jerome and Augustine (with a rakish red hat), followed by an indisputably powerful *Annunciation*, a placid depiction of Mary, head and shoulders covered, right hand slightly raised in acknowledgement of the (off-picture) Archangel Gabriel.

La Kalsa

The Galleria Regionale stands at the edge of the neighbourhood of **La Kalsa** (from the Arabic *khalisa*, meaning "pure"), one of the oldest quarters in Palermo, originally laid out by the Saracens and heavily bombed during World War II. It's still a little on the rough side, with some unkempt squares and alleys, although the area is showing some signs of gradual gentrification, with the opening of new bars, restaurants and some chic B&Bs.

There's more work by the Gagini family (sculpted fragments and reliefs) in the fifteenth-century church of **La Gancia** – or Santa Maria degli Angeli – next door to the gallery on Via Alloro (Mon–Sat 9.30am–noon & 3–6pm, Sun 10am–12.30pm). From here, turn down Via della Vetriera (where the assassinated anti-Mafia judge Paolo Borsellino was born and bred), past a rather bleak park area, to find the former church and convent of **Santa Maria dello Spasimo** on Via dello Spasimo. None other than Raphael painted *Lo Spasimo di Sicilia* for the church, installed here in 1520 (though now in the Prado in Madrid). Since then, the church has been variously used as a theatre, barracks, plague hospital and rubbish tip, but is now undergoing restoration; it remains a popular concert venue, known as Lo Spasimo, and concerts continue to be held in the courtyard outside. To the side of the church is a small building (ask an attendant for the key if it's locked) which houses a large model of Palermo in wooden bricks.

La Kalsa's main highlight is the lovely church of **La Magione** (Mon–Sat 9.30am–noon & 3–6.15pm; donation requested), standing in isolation on Piazza Magione and approached through a pretty palm-lined drive and garden. A fine example of

Arab-Norman architecture, it was originally built in 1151 for the Cistercians, but given to the Teutonic knights as their headquarters by Henry VI in 1197. The cloister resembles that at Monreale, and houses a rare Judaic tombstone re-carved into a basin for holy water. In the room between the cloister and the chapel, there's a fresco of the crucifixion and – far more interesting and rare – a plaster preparation of the fresco, opposite. It's the only example of a fresco model in Sicily, and its near-mathematical sketch lines show the care and detailed planning that went into the creation of such works.

To escape La Kalsa and the city noise, walk a few minutes along Via Lincoln to the eighteenth-century gardens of **Villa Giulia**. There's a children's train ride, plus bandstand, deer and ducks, while the **Orto Botánico** (daily 9am–dusk; €5), next to the park, dates from 1795 and features tropical plants from all over the world.

La Vucciria and around

North of Corso Vittorio Emanuele and east of Via Roma, one of Palermo's oldest and busiest markets, **La Vucciria**, is said to be named after the French *boucherie*, for butcher's shop. Winding streets radiate from a small enclosed piazza, wet from the ice and waste of the groaning fish stalls – you'll see swordfish heads stuck to marble slabs and huge sides of tuna from which fishmongers carve bloody steaks. There are a couple of excellent little trattorias tucked away in the alleys (best at lunchtime), and some very basic bars where the wine comes straight from the barrel. The market is also *the* place to buy porcelain pasta bowls, espresso cups and coffee-makers.

The northern limit of the market is marked by the church of **San Domenico** (Tues–Sun 8.15am–noon, Sat & Sun also 5–7pm), whose fine eighteenth-century facade, with its double pillars and slim towers, is lit at night to great effect. Inside, a series of tombs contains a horde of famous Sicilians – parliamentarians, poets and painters – of little interest to foreigners except to shed some light on Palermitan street-naming.

Behind San Domenico, along Via dei Bambinai, is a greater treat, the sixteenth-century **Oratorio del Rosario di San Domenico** (Mon–Sat 9am–1pm; donation

---

Shopping in Palermo

The old city sometimes seems like one big market. Apart from the stalls of Il Capo, Vucciria and Ballarò, where a range of household items are on offer alongside the fruit and veg, the old city has several **flea markets** (*mercati delle pulci*) – with the occasional antique lurking amid the knick-knacks and curios – notably on Piazza Peranni near the cathedral and the Albergheria's Piazza San Francesco Saverio off Corso Tukory (this last on Sunday). You're more likely to find jewellery, watches – often convincing copies of branded products – and "designer" clothing on Via Sant'Agostino and the back streets of the Capo quarter. More upmarket **boutiques** are scattered along Via Roma and Via Ruggero Séttimo, and on and around Viale della Libertà.

Sicilian **puppets and ceramics** of varying quality are sold along Corso Vittorio Emanuele, Via Divisi and around Piazza Marina, or in the new city around Piazza Castelnuovo and along Viale della Libertà. You'll also find model **Sicilian carts** in abundance in all these areas – a typical, if rather corny, souvenir. For **frutta di Martorana** look in any decent *pasticceria* – these are sold by weight, and do not need to be kept chilled.

One of the best **supermarket** chains is Oviesse, which has branches on Viale della Libertà (on the corner with Via Siracusa) and at Via Marco Polo 12 (northwest of the Palazzo di Giustizia), both open until 8pm. The ubiquitous SISA, CRAI and GS supermarkets are also perfectly adequate, though prices are much higher than at the street markets.

requested), built and still maintained by the Knights of Malta, and adorned by the acknowledged master of the art of stucco sculpture, **Giácomo Serpotta**. Born in Palermo in 1656, Serpotta devoted his entire life to decorating oratories like this – here, the figures of *Justice, Strength* and suchlike (resembling fashionable society ladies, who often served as models) are crowned by an accomplished Van Dyck altarpiece.

There's more stucco splendour further up Via Bambinai, behind the late sixteenth-century church of Santa Zita (or Santa Cita) on quiet Via Squarcialupo. The marvellous **Oratorio del Rosario di Santa Zita** (entrance on Via Valverde; Mon–Fri 9am–1pm, ring the bell if closed, or ask in the church; €2) contains some of the wildest flights of Serpotta's rococo imagination – a dazzling confusion of allegorical figures, bare-breasted women, scenes from the New Testament, putti galore, and, at the centre of it all, a rendering of the Battle of Lepanto. It's a tumultuous work, depicted with loving care – notice the old men and women, or the melancholy boys perched on the ledge, and look for Serpotta's symbol on the left wall, the golden snake.

Via Squarcialupo continues down to **Piazza XIII Víttime**, where five tall V-shaped steel plates splinter out of the ground, commemorating the officials who have lost their lives in Palermo's enduring struggle with the Mafia. It replaces a monument commemorating thirteen citizens shot by the Bourbons in the 1860 revolt, which now stands along Via Cavour. West instead, along Via Valverde from Santa Zita, you'll end up back on Via Roma, opposite Palermo's main post office, the gargantuan **Palazzo delle Poste**, built by the Fascists in 1933. Its empty pretensions are put to shame by what hides behind it, around the corner in Piazza Olivella. Here, the church of **Sant'Ignazio all'Olivella** (Thurs–Sat 9–10am & 5–6pm, Sun 9–10am) displays an opulent Baroque touch in its great chandeliers, rich side chapels and paintings by Pietro Novelli. Next door, meanwhile, the cloisters and surviving buildings of a sixteenth-century convent – once the property of the church – now house the city's archeological museum.

Museo Archeologico Regionale

Palermo's **Museo Archeologico Regionale**, Via Bara all'Olivella 24, gathers together artefacts found at all western Sicily's major Neolithic, Carthaginian, Greek and Roman settlements. It's a magnificent collection, unmissable if you have any interest in the island's archeological history, though unfortunately the museum has been closed since 2009 for long overdue renovations. These should improve the frankly old-fashioned displays, but you may have to take the projected re-opening date of 2012 with a pinch of salt. It's also impossible to know what the new layout will be, but a rundown of the highlights is still useful, to give an idea of what will be on display.

In particular, the museum is the repository of the extraordinary finds from the Greek site of **Selinunte** on the southwest coast, gathering together the rich stone carvings that adorned the various temples (known only as Temples A–G). The oldest are single panels from the early sixth century BC, representing the gods of Delphi, the Sphinx, the rape of Europa, and Hercules and the Bull. Other reconstructed friezes are more vivid works from the fifth century BC, like Perseus beheading Medusa, while the most technically advanced tableaux are those from Temple E, portraying a lithe Hercules fighting an Amazon, the marriage of Zeus and Hera, Actaeon savaged by three ferocious dogs, and Athena and the Titan. Other Greek relics include the famous stone lion's-head water-spouts from the fifth-century-BC Victory Temple at **Himera** – the fierce animal faces tempered by braided fur and a grooved tongue that channelled the water. Finds from the sites at Términi Imerese and Solunto are also here, as well as rich bronze sculptures like the naturalistic figure of an alert and genial ram (third century BC) from **Siracusa**,

The Ucciardone – no need to escape

A couple of blocks east of the Giardino Inglese is Palermo's notorious **Ucciardone prison**, connected by an underground passageway to the maximum-security bunker where the much-publicized *maxi processi* (maxi-trials) of Mafia suspects were held in the 1980s. At the time, the gloomy Bourbon prison was dubbed "the best-informed centre in Italy for gossip and intelligence about the operations of organized crime throughout the world", not least because it was home to a good percentage of the biggest names in the Italian underworld. Mafia affairs were conducted here almost undisturbed, by bosses whose food was brought in from Palermo's best restaurants and who collaborated with the warders to ensure that escapes didn't happen – something that might increase security arrangements and hamper their activities. However, following the murders of Mafia investigators Falcone and Borsellino in 1992, many of the highest-risk inmates were transferred to more isolated prisons in different parts of the country.

once one of a pair (the other was destroyed in the 1848 revolution). There's **Etruscan** funerary art, a wide range of **Neolithic** finds (including casts of the incised drawings from Addaura, on Monte Pellegrino, and Lévanzo), and a series of beautifully preserved **Roman mosaics** – the largest of which measures nearly 10m in length – excavated from Piazza della Vittoria in Palermo.

The modern city

Via Maqueda assumes an increasingly modern aspect as it progresses north from Quattro Canti. Barring the bustle of activity around **Via Candelai** – a busy shopping street by day, a hubbub of cafés at night – the interesting medieval alleys are gradually replaced by the wider and more nondescript streets around Piazza Verdi, site of the late nineteenth-century **Teatro Mássimo**. Claimed as the largest theatre in Italy, a monument to rival Europe's great opera houses, it was constructed by Giovanni Battista Basile, whose Neoclassical design was possibly influenced by Charles Garnier's contemporary plans for the Paris Opéra. **Tours** with an English-speaking guide take place throughout the year (Tues–Sun, every 30min, 10am–2.30pm, except during rehearsals; E5), showing you the rich, gilded, marble Sala Pompeiana, where the nobility once gathered, and the domed ceiling in the six-tiered auditorium, constructed in the shape of a flower head, its centre and petals adorned with an allegorical portrayal of the triumph of music. Francis Ford Coppola shot the long climactic opera scene of *The Godfather Part III* here, using the theatre's sweep of steps to great effect.

Beyond the theatre Via Maqueda becomes Via Ruggero Séttimo, which cuts through gridded shopping streets on its way to the huge double square that characterizes modern Palermo. Known as **Piazza Politeama**, it's made up of Piazza Castelnuovo to the west and Piazza Ruggero Séttimo to the east. Dominating the whole lot is Palermo's other massive theatre, the late nineteenth-century **Politeama Garibaldi**, built in overblown Pompeiian style and topped by a bronze chariot pulled by four horses.

A few hundred metres further up Viale della Libertà are the **Giardino Inglese** gardens. Nearby, at Viale della Libertà 52, the **Museo Mormino** (Mon–Fri 9am–1pm & 3–5pm, Sat 9am–1pm; €4) houses a beautifully presented collection of artefacts and paintings in the sumptuous Banco di Sicilia building. There's a wide selection of Italian majolica from the fifteenth to the eighteenth centuries, and an extensive collection of Greek vases, Etruscan finds, old maps and ancient coins, while nineteenth-century paintings on show include the seascapes and tuna-fishing scenes of Antonino Leto.

Parco della Favorita and Museo Etnográfico Pitrè

North of the centre, around 3km from Piazza Politeama, lies the **Parco della Favorita** (bus #101 from Stazione Centrale to Piazza Giovanni Paolo II, ex-Piazza A. de Gasperi, then change to the #645), a long, wooded expanse at the foot of Monte Pellegrino, with sports grounds and stadiums at one end, and formal gardens laid out a couple of kilometres beyond. The grounds were originally acquired in 1799 by the Bourbon king Ferdinand during his exile from Naples, and for three years he lived here in the **Palazzina Cinese** (closed to the public), a small Chinese-style pavilion. Next door is the **Museo Etnográfico Pitrè** (currently closed for restoration, though open for occasional exhibitions, ☏091.740.4879), which contains a wide-ranging exhibition on Sicilian folklore and popular culture, including its two best-known emblems, traditional puppets (*pupi*) and brightly painted carts (*carretti*). The carts, in particular, are fascinating and in the past provided a clue as to a person's status, judged by the skill and extent of the decorations on their cart (which could be any two-wheeled vehicle, from barrows to horse-drawn wagons). Less well-known Sicilian handicrafts are also on display, from sculpted and painted terracotta figures to wooden *ex voto* (votive) tablets depicting the often gruesome death of the dedicatee. There are also dolls, games, tapestries, tools, masks and costumes, not to mention a fine display of *presepe* (nativity scenes) complete with perky camels and a dramatic killing of the innocents.

Other remnants of Norman Palermo

Palermo's best Norman buildings are, with a couple of exceptions, in and around the old-town area of the city. But to be thorough in tracking down the rest of the Norman relics you'll have to poke around the southern and western outskirts in built-up areas that were once rolling parkland owned by successive kings.

The palatial king's retreat of **La Zisa** (daily 9am–6.30pm; €4.50; bus #124 from Piazza Sturzo and Piazza Politeama) – from the Arabic *al-aziz* or "magnificent" – was begun by William I in 1160, and later finished by his son William II. At one time its beautiful grounds were stocked with rare and exotic beasts, though a raid on the palace by disaffected locals in 1161 released some of the wild animals, which probably came as a bit of a shock to William's neighbours. It's now besieged by modern apartment blocks, but has been thoughtfully restored to something approaching its former glory. The centrepiece is the Sala della Fontana, comprising an elaborate fountain in a marble-sided chamber with glittering mosaic decoration. These are appropriate surroundings for a modest collection of Islamic art and artefacts, mostly inscribed copper bowls from periods much later than when La Zisa was constructed, and from different parts of the Mediterranean. The latticed windows afford impressive views over the surrounding greenery.

To the south, about 1km beyond the Porta Nuova, at Corso Calatafimi 100 (opposite Via Quarto dei Mille), **La Cuba** (Mon–Sat 9am–6.30pm, Sun 9am–1pm; €2) is the remains of a slightly later Norman pavilion that was sited in part of La Zisa's royal park (and now lies within a military barracks). Frankly, there's not a great deal to see save an Arabic inscription and the traces of a water gate, evidence that the pavilion once stood in the middle of an artificial lake. A room to one side holds a model showing how the palace once appeared, as well as the inscription that supplied the date of the building's foundation (1180), and there's also an exhibition explaining its history and construction. Buses #105, #309, #339 or #389 all run along Corso Calatafimi from Porta Nuova, past La Cuba and up to its sister pavilion, **La Cúbula** (on the right, at the end of Via Aurelio Zancla, between nos. 443 and 459 on the main road). This domed kiosk, once a summerhouse in the extensive grounds of La Zisa, now looks rather uncomfortable in the midst of the modern buildings on all sides.

Around 1.5km southeast of Stazione Centrale is the restored domed church of **San Giovanni dei Lebbrosi** (Mon & Wed–Sat 9–11am & 4–6pm, Tues 9–11am; buses #226, #227 or #231 from the northern end of Corso dei Mille), one of the oldest Norman churches in Sicily, reputedly founded in 1070 by Roger I. The church's name (St John of the Lepers) derives from a building nearby, which was once a leprosy hospital. Corso dei Mille itself is named for the route Garibaldi and his "Thousand" took into the city in May 1860, crossing the Norman **Ponte dell'Ammiraglio**, the site of a brief last stand by Bourbon troops. Built in 1113 by George of Antioch, founder of La Martorana, this slender bridge once straddled the River Oreto, though the water has since been diverted and it's now surrounded by a little garden.

Last of the Norman attractions is the cemetery-surrounded church of **Chiesa dei Vespri** (daily 8am–noon; bus #246 from Stazione Centrale to Cimitero Sant'Orsola), also known as Santo Spírito. Founded in 1173, and now restored to its original, rather severe state, this was where the **massacre of the Sicilian Vespers** began in 1282, ostensibly sparked by a French officer insulting a bride on her way to church. The ringing of the vesper (evensong) bell was the signal to drive the French out of Sicily; most were eventually slaughtered by the oppressed islanders.

Catacombe dei Cappuccini

Of all the attractions on the edge of Palermo, it's the **Catacombe dei Cappuccini** (daily: summer 8.30am–noon & 2.30–6pm, winter 9am–12.30pm & 3–5.30pm; €3) that generates the most interest among visitors; get there by taking bus #327 from Piazza dell'Indipendenza to Via Pindemonte, and then follow the signposts for a couple of hundred metres. For several hundred years the Cappuccini placed its dead brothers in catacombs under the church and later, up until 1881, rich laymen and others were interred here too. Some 8000 bodies in all were preserved by various chemical and drying processes – including dehydration, the use of vinegar and arsenic baths, and treatment with quicklime – and then placed in niches along rough-cut subterranean corridors, dressed in a suit of clothes that they had previously provided for the purpose. In different caverns reserved for men, women, the clergy, doctors, lawyers and surgeons, the bodies are pinned with an identifying tag, some decomposed beyond recognition, others complete with skin, hair and eyes, fixing you with a steely stare. Those that aren't arranged along the walls lie in stacked glass coffins, and, to say the least, it's an unnerving experience to walk among them. Times change, though, as Patrick Brydone noted in his late eighteenth-century *A Tour Through Sicily and Malta*:

Here the people of Palermo pay daily visits to their deceased friends ... here they familiarize themselves with their future state, and chuse the company they would wish to keep in the other world. It is a common thing to make choice of their nich, and to try if their body fits it ... and sometimes, by way of a voluntary penance, they accustom themselves to stand for hours in these niches ...

Of all the skeletal bodies, saddest are the many remains of babies and young children, nothing more than spindly puppets. Follow the signs for the sealed-off cave that contains the coffin of two-year-old Rosalia Lombardo, who died in 1920. A new process, a series of injections, preserved her to the extent that she looks as though she's asleep. Perhaps fortunately, the doctor who invented the technique died before he could tell anyone how it was done.

Monte Pellegrino

North of the city, and clearly visible from the port area, the massive bulk of **Monte Pellegrino** separates Palermo from the bay at Mondello. The mountain is a nature reserve (ⓦ www.riservamontepellegrino.palermo.it), and there are marked paths across it, though for most locals Monte Pellegrino is primarily a venue for

La Festa di Santa Rosalia

Next to nothing is known for sure about Rosalia, who was probably a member of the Norman court in the twelfth century, except that at some point she rejected her wealthy background and lived as a hermit on Monte Pellegrino, outside the city. Nothing more was heard of her until the early seventeenth century, when a vision led to the discovery of her bones in a mountain cave. Pronounced sacred relics, these were carried around the city in procession in both 1624 and 1625, thus staying the ravages of a terrible plague. It's a ceremony that is now re-enacted every July 15 (and also Sept 4), with a torchlight procession to the saint's sanctuary that forms part of Palermo's annual jamboree, **La Festa di Santa Rosalia** – "U Fistinu" in dialect. An ebullient blend of devotion and revelry, U Fistinu is the central event of the year for locals, while for tourists it's an uproarious party, perhaps the most exhilarating you'll see anywhere in Italy. The annual ritual includes both solemn processions and gaudy entertainment, with the passionate and vociferous participation of hundreds of thousands of Palermitani. The central event is a long parade through the centre of town, from the Palazzo dei Normanni along Corso Vittorio Emanuele to the seafront, headed by a candle-lit statue of the saint borne aloft on the "Carro Trionfale". There are puppet re-enactments of the saint's miracles, concerts, exhibitions, and a gastronomic feast on Foro Italico, where heaps of food are consumed – most famously, snails, nuts, watermelons and *dolci*. The celebrations culminate in a spectacular display of fireworks over the harbour.

Sunday picnics and strolls. It's also a significant place of pilgrimage, the site of the shrine of the city's patron saint, St Rosalia.

The half-hour ride up the mountain (bus #812 from Piazza Sturzo or Teatro Politeama every one or two hours) provides wide views over Palermo and its plain. At the very end of the road stands the **Santuario di Santa Rosalia** (daily 7am–12.15pm & 2–6pm), part of a ramshackle collection of huts and stalls, entered through a small chapel erected over a deep cave in the hillside where the saint's bones were discovered in 1624. Inside, a bier contains a reclining golden statue of the saint, thought by Goethe to be "so natural and pleasing, that one can hardly help expecting to see the saint breathe and move". The water trickling down the walls is supposedly miraculous.

A small road to the left of the chapel leads to the cliff-top promontory – a half-hour's walk – where a more restrained statue of Santa Rosalia stares over the sprawling city. Another path, leading up from the sanctuary to the right, takes you to the top of the mountain – 600m high, and around a forty-minute walk. Elsewhere, the trails that cover Monte Pellegrino are dotted with families picnicking, while kids play on rope swings tied to the trees.

Eating

You can eat well and cheaply in Palermo, either snacking in bars and at market stalls or sitting down in one of dozens of good-value restaurants throughout the old town serving *cucina casalinga*. Pizzas and pastries, in particular, are among the best in Sicily, while fish is another local highlight – a typical Palermo speciality is **pasta con le sarde**, macaroni with fresh sardines, fennel, raisins and pine kernels. Traditional **street food** is enjoying something of a renaissance, and in hole-in-the-wall outlets and fancy bars alike you can try the sort of earthy snacks and fritters the locals have eaten for decades. The other prime glory is **ice cream** – Palermo's best *gelaterie* (ice-cream parlours) are famed all over Italy.

Restaurants tend to close early, especially in the central old town, where if you turn up at 10pm the waiters are likely to be packing up around you. For the most popular places, go before 8pm or be prepared to wait in line.

Cafés, street food and ice cream

Antica Focacceria San Francesco Via A. Paternostro 58. This old-fashioned place has been in the same family for five generations. Downstairs they serve authentic Sicilian street food (fritters, *focaccia*, croquettes and pizza), there are full meals upstairs (and several fixed-price menus from €7) and an associated *gelateria* across the piazza, the *San Francesco*, that stays open very late in summer. *Antica Focacceria* closed Tues, *San Francesco* closed Oct–March.

Casa Obatola Via Alloro 16. Relaxed little bar with outdoor seats, good for a break after seeing the Galleria Regionale. Serves delicious sandwiches and salads, and good pastries. Closed Sun.

I Cuochini Via Ruggero Séttimo 68. The pristine *friggittoria* – all gleaming white tiles and zinc – was founded in 1826, and is concealed behind an arched gateway (the only sign is a small ceramic plaque). For under €1 a portion you can sample some amazing traditional snacks, like *panzerotti* (deep-fried savoury-stuffed pastries), *pasticcino* (an ancient Sicilian speciality with Arabic roots, being a sweet pastry with minced meat), *timballini di pasta* (deep-fried pasta) and *besciamelle fritte* (bechamel fritters). Closes 2.30pm, and all Sun.

Franco 'U Vastiddaru Piazza Marina. A good place for no-nonsense *palermitani* fast food such as *pane e panelle, arancini, crocche* and *pani cu' la meuza*, which you can munch at plastic tables on the busy corner of Piazza Marina and Via Vittorio Emanuele.

Ilardo Foro Italico 12 (at the end of Via Alloro towards the water). The *Ilardo* has been in business for decades and is well known for its very good (and luridly coloured) ice cream. Opens 4pm till late. Closed Oct–May.

Mazzara Via Magliocco 15, off Via Ruggero Séttimo. Long-established bar-*pasticceria* where Giuseppe Tomasi di Lampedusa is reputed to have penned some of *The Leopard*. These days it serves light meals and lunches alongside a dangerous selection of pastries and ice creams. Closed Mon.

Obika Rinascente, 4th floor, Via Roma at Piazza San Domenico. On the top floor of the Rinascente department store, this exclusive bar specializes in *mozzarella di bufala*, which appears in exquisitely presented salads and other light dishes. It's a great lunchtime escape from the city heat, or a good place for an aperitif (daily 6.30–9pm) as the drinks are accompanied by a selection of mouthwatering mozzarella tasters. There's also a sushi bar on the same floor.

Oriol Piazza Ungheria 68. Fabulous fresh fruit ice creams from a parlour just off Via Ruggero Séttimo.

Palazzo Riso Corso Vittorio Emanuele 365. Cool white minimalist bar with shady courtyard belonging to Palermo's contemporary art museum. It's great for things like hazelnut and chocolate-flavoured coffees, herbal teas, *cornetti* with forest fruits and light lunches.

Rosciglione Via Gian Luca Barbieri 5. Watch *cannoli* being made as you eat them at this traditional bakery (which exports worldwide) on the edge of the Ballarò market. Closed Sun.

Palermo's street food

Street food in Palermo is pretty distinctive – away from pizza slices and pastries there are plenty of things you may not have come across before (and a few you may not wish to encounter again). Many of the more **traditional snacks** are straight out of the market, and while chopped boiled octopus (*purpu* in Sicilian), cooked artichokes and charcoal-roast peppers and onions are at least familiar, you might be less inclined to hover at the stalls selling *pani cu' la meuza* – bread rolls filled with sautéed beef spleen or tripe, which either come unadorned (*schiettu*, meaning "nubile") or topped with fresh ricotta and caciocavallo cheese (*maritatu*, "married"). Meanwhile, any old-fashioned **friggittoria** (deep-fry takeaway) – and there are still plenty in Palermo – serves up *arancini* (savoury rice balls), *pane e pannelle* (chickpea-flour fritter served in a bread roll) and *crocchè* (potato croquettes with anchovy and caciocavallo cheese). **Markets** are a great place to sample all these kinds of street food, especially the Vucciria, (off Via Roma between Corso Vittorio Emanuele and the San Domenico church), the Ballarò market (in Piazza del Cármine), at Vecchio Borgo and along Via Sant'Agostino. The Ballarò market, in particular, has a few very basic *hosterie* – wooden tables scattered around the market stalls – where you can accompany your snack with a beer or two.

Restaurants and pizzerias

Bellini Piazza Bellini ☎091.616.5691. At the back of the Teatro Bellini, with outdoor tables underneath La Martorana church, this is one of the city's more romantic locations – inevitably touristy (queues form after 8pm) but a reliable place for pizzas, pastas and fish (pizzas from €5, other dishes €8–15). You'll need to book for the best tables outside or upstairs by the window. Closed Mon.

Casa del Brodo Corso Vittorio Emanuele 175 ☎091.321.655. Exuberant family-run place on the edge of the Vucciria market, which has been serving up its speciality *bollito di manzo con patate e zafferano* (meat cooked in broth with potatoes and saffron) for over a century. There are other dishes too, including fresh fish, and prices are reasonable, with *primi* at €6–8, *secondi* from €10, and set menus from €16. Closed Sun in summer, Tues in winter.

Dietro La Cattedrale Piazza Santíssimi 40 Mártiri ☎091.611.5364. Excellent choice for sightseers looking for a budget-priced lunch, with a €12 menu that includes dishes like spaghetti with mussels followed by grilled meat. It hits no gastronomic heights, but it is a friendly place with outdoor tables in a quiet piazza, not far from the cathedral. Closed Tues.

Il Garage Via San Nicolo all'Albergheria 34 ☎333.490.6356. A great little hole-in-the-wall trattoria in the Ballarò market, whose affable Tunisian owner cooks very good fish, lamb and couscous dishes (you'll eat for around €25). It's quite hard to find, but ask anyone in the vicinity for "Mario" and they'll direct you. Dinner only.

Lila e Toduccio Via Bara all'Olivella 91 ☎320.292.6255. The top end of Via Bara all'Olivella is lined with rough-and-ready places to eat – think street food with tables – with displays of *antipasti* laid out on stalls and hearty helpings of *pasta al forno* and the like (dishes start at €5). This one also has fresh fish and meat ready to be grilled on an outdoor brazier.

Mi Manda Picone Via A. Paternostro 59 ☎091.616.0660. This old-town *enoteca* has a fine choice of mostly Sicilian wines and a simple if inspired menu that changes with the seasons. Spring dishes might include a *frittata* of fava beans, artichokes and peas served with fresh ricotta, while in summer expect spaghetti with mint, courgettes and capers followed by swordfish with a pistachio crust. Meals from €30 a head and up. Dinner only, closed Sun.

Michele alla Brace Piazza Borgo Vecchio, no phone. At the square's tiny market, you can't miss this huge grill with a couple of plastic tables and a steaming cauldron of vegetables. Buy your fish from one of the nearby stalls and bring it to Michele, who will grill it and provide you with veg, drinks and cutlery – around €15, all in. Closed Wed.

Il Mirto e la Rosa Via Príncipe di Granitelli 30 ☎091.324.353. This began life as a vegetarian restaurant and although carefully sourced local fish and meat have now joined the menu, the emphasis on veggies is still strong. Signature dishes include *caponata* with pistachio-spiked couscous, and home-made *tagliolini* with tomato sauce, grilled aubergine and cheese from the Nébrodi mountains. Desserts are fantastic, and you should finish up with a home-made cinnamon liqueur. Eating à la carte costs from around €25, but there are menu deals at €10 and €15. Closed Sun.

Osteria lo Bianco Via E. Amari 104 ☎091.251.4900. Decorated with Juventus souvenirs and religious bric-a-brac, this is one of the cheapest places to eat in town. It's a traditional menu through and through, from *pasta con le sarde* to a stew of beef, peas and carrots. Two courses with wine and fruit costs under €15. Closed Sun.

Osteria dei Vespri Piazza Croce dei Vespri ☎091.617.1631, ⓦwww.osteriadeivespri .it. Palermo's best restaurant started life as a hobby and it continues to be run with passion by brothers Andrea and Alberto Rizzo. Complex, artfully presented dishes rely on quality Sicilian ingredients – say, rabbit terrine with pistachios from Bronte, black *tagliolini* served with red mullet, ginger, red onion and fava beans, or quail stuffed with prunes served on a purée of cannellini beans and celeriac. It's a real special-occasion place (*primi* around €20, *secondi* €20–30, *degustazione* menus from €70), but as good as contemporary Sicilian cooking gets. Closed Sun.

Pizzeria Italia Via Orologio 54 ☎091.589.885. Come here for the best pizzas in Palermo – the queue tells you you're in the right place. The crisp, oven-blistered pizzas (€4–10) are sensational, including the "Palermitana" with tomato, anchovies, onion, artichokes, caciocavallo cheese and breadcrumbs. Dinner only; closed Mon.

Santandrea Piazza Sant'Andrea ☎091.334.999 or 328.131.4595. Chic but relaxed family-run place a stone's throw from Piazza San Domenico and the Vucciria. Everything is spanking fresh, straight from sea or market, and inventive dishes (€10–15) include things like mixed raw fish served with a fruit salsa, pasta with anchovies or *tagliata di tonno*, slices of seared tuna fillet. Book in advance to eat *al fresco*. Closed Sun.

Trattoria Piccolo Napoli Piazzetta Mulino a Vento 4 ☎091.320.431. Lively trattoria off the Vecchio Borgo market run for over fifty years by three generations of the same family. They have two boats at nearby Terrasini, from which fish is brought in daily, and anything not eaten is sold on to the local market traders. Try their wonderful *caponata* to start, followed by a seafood pasta or the freshest of prawns, and grilled fish. Dishes start at €5–10, with fish and shellfish sold by weight. Lunch only, plus Fri & Sat dinner; closed Sun.

Trattoria Primavera Piazza Bologni 4 ☎091.329.408. Excellent neighbourhood trattoria with a little terrace in the square, serving genuine home-style dishes like *pasta con le sarde, bucatini con broccoli* or a serving of tuna with a sweet-sour onion dressing (dishes €8–10). Closed Mon.

Trattoria Torremuzza Via Torremuzza 17 ☎091.252.5532. Your fish is grilled on an outdoor brazier at this great no-frills trattoria, where you can eat *al fresco* in summer, inside in winter. It's bargain-priced, with most *antipasti, primi* and simple meat grills at €5, fish (fried or grilled, prawns, bream or seabass) from €7–10, and wine a dangerous €3 a litre, so lunch here could well write off your afternoon. Closed Sun evening.

Le Tre Sorelle Via Volturno 110 ☎091.585.960. The "Three Sisters" is a traditional trattoria – check tablecloths, posters and pictures – with some good pasta dishes, including tasty *bucatini con le sarde* (with sardines) or *casarecce alla lido* (fresh pasta with swordfish and aubergine). *Primi* run around €7–10, meat and fish mains €8–12, and you can sit outside on a nice day. Closed Sun.

Bars and clubs

After dark and over much of the city, Palermo's frenetic lifestyle stops, pedestrians flit quickly through the shadows, and the main roads are given over to speeding traffic and screaming police sirens. The only place for a civilized, fume-free *aperitivo al fresco* is the pedestrianized **Via Príncipe di Belmonte**, off the upper part of Via Roma, which has a glitzy selection of bars and *pasticcerie*. For a livelier scene, head to the clutch of bars in the streets **behind the Museo Archeologico** – Via Spinuzza, Via Bara all'Olivella and Piazza Olivella – while things are grungier in the student-filled bars along and around **Via Candelai**, not far from the Quattro Canti, off Via Maqueda. There's also a burgeoning bar scene down in La Kalsa, on and off Via Alloro. Palermo's clubs are almost exclusively found in the northern part of the city, especially on and around **Viale della Regione Siciliana**, a bus- or taxi-ride away. They're mostly expensive dance clubs, rarely worth the long journey (and note that you may have to pay to "join" the club before they'll let you in). In summer, the scene switches to the coastal resorts of Mondello and Isola delle Fémmine, while the beach at Capo Gallo, between Mondello and Sferracavallo (about 30min north of the city), is popular with students for ad hoc weekend parties until dawn.

Bars

American Bar Grande Albergo Sole, 5th floor, Corso Vittorio Emanuele 291 (near the Quattro Canti). Stunning hotel roof-terrace bar, from where you can gaze across the rooftops of the city's church domes and the mountains behind. It's an excellent place for a sunset drink and well worth the slightly inflated prices.

Bar Malox Piazzetta della Canna. Hidden away off an old-town alley near the Quattro Canto, this convivial student bar has plenty of tables outside where the drinking continues till late. Closed Mon & alternate Sun.

Caffè Letterario Malavoglia Piazzetta Pietro Speciale. You could easily miss this small, backstreet "literary café" near Corso Vittorio Emanuele, but it's a good find, with sofas, books, occasional exhibitions and live music, cheap drinks from 6–9pm, and late hours.

Cama Enoteca Via Alloro 105. Cosy, candlelit wine bar with welcoming, knowledgeable staff and an almost overwhelming wine list. It's closed in the summer months, when the owners shift operations to a bar on the Égadi island of Maréttimo. Closed Mon.

Champagneria del Mássimo Via Salvatore Spinuzza 59. Charming wine bar with outdoor seating near the Teatro Mássimo; along with the neighbouring bars, it's a lively spot on summer nights, and stays open till the early hours. Closed Sun.

Kursaal Kalhesa Foro Italico 21 @www .kursaalkalhesa.it. Set deep in the echoing stone vaults of the *foro*, this impressive café and wine bar (closed Mon) is furnished with traditional Sicilian furniture and has a huge fire in winter. In summer, the Palermo address closes and the bar shifts to an atmospheric ex-tuna-fishing station at the foot of Monte Pellegrino in the seaside town of

Vergine Maria (bus #731) – at *Il Kursaal Tonnara* (🌐www.kursaaltonnara.it) there are indoor and outdoor bars, a jasmine-scented courtyard, a fancy sea-facing restaurant, and frequent concerts.

La Taverna Piazza Ballarò. This tiny place for beers and wines gets incredibly busy, with a mostly student crowd spilling out across the road. It's open late and has low prices.

Clubs

Biergarten Viale Regione Siciliana 6469. Long-established venue for rock, punk and metal acts.

Caffè 442 Piazza Don Bosco 1 🌐www .caf€442.it. Lounge bar near Viale Lazio and La Favorita, with nightly DJ sets and dancing to house music.

I Candelai Via Candelai 65 🌐www.candelai.it. Live rock and DJ sets on Fri & Sat in the heart of an area popular with a student crowd.

Zsa Zsa Mon Amour Via Angelitti 32 🌐www .zsazsamonamour.com. Live rock, metal and funk bands. It's west of Stazione Notarbártolo, off Piazza Campolo. Closed July–Sept.

Music, culture and the arts

There's always something going on in Palermo, and you can check the current cultural calendar at the tourist office, in the arts publication *Lapis* or the daily newspaper *Il Giornale di Sicilia*. Teatro Mássimo is the first choice for **classical music**, but lots of other smaller theatres and concert halls have good music programmes too. Independent **arts centres** put on a really mixed bag of concerts and events, and although there's no major venue for **live bands** (top British and American artists rarely make it further south than Naples) the *Comune* regularly stages open-air gigs in the summer, usually in the Giardino Inglese and other city parks. Mainstream Italian-language **theatre** is less accessible to foreign visitors, but a couple of more offbeat venues are worth checking out, while for **puppet theatre** (easily the best night out at the theatre in Palermo) see box on p.65. **Cinemas** show the latest films dubbed into Italian – it's rare to find films in their original language with subtitles – and the main central screens, *ABC* and *Imperia*, are right next to each other at Via Emerico Amari 160–166.

The biggest traditional **festival** of the year is La Festa di Santa Rosalia, in honour of the city's patron saint (see box, p.73). Palermo's most interesting arts festival over the last few years has been **Kals'Art**, a cultural extravaganza of live music, theatre and cinema that takes place at a number of venues in the old-town La Kalsa neighbourhood (usually between mid-July and mid-September). However, at the time of writing, its existence was threatened by a lack of funding.

Agricantus Via XX Settembre 82A ☎091.309.636, 🌐www.agricantus.org. Arts centre near the Giardino Inglese, owned by and named after Italy's most outstanding World Music band (check out the album *Tuareg* or the soundtrack to the film *Bagno Turco*). Regular live music and dance sessions, as well as theatre, readings, festivals and events, and a bar that's open until 1.30am. Closed Mon.

Nuovo Montevergini Via Montevergini 8 ☎091.612.4314, 🌐www.nuovomontevergini .com. Alternative culture, Palermo-style, in a monumental deconsecrated convent that supports its own theatre, arts festivals and events programme, from dance and live music to poetry and film. The bar is open daily until late.

Lo Spasimo Via dello Spasimo, La Kalsa ☎091.616.1486. The former church hosts an excellent series of concerts, classical and jazz, many of them free.

Teatrino Ditirammu del Canto Popolare Via Torremuzza 6, La Kalsa ☎091.617.7865, 🌐www .teatrinoditirammu.it. An intimate venue for Sicilian folk music and traditional dance performances.

Teatro Franco Zappalà Via Autonomia Siciliana 123A ☎091.543.380. Traditional theatrical productions, but in Sicilian dialect.

Teatro Libero Salita Partanna 4, Piazza Marina ☎091.617.4040, 🌐www.teatroliberopalermo.it. Palermo's long-standing avant-garde theatre, with an annual festival that incorporates theatre, dance, music and performance art.

Teatro Mássimo Piazza Verdi ☎091.605.3580, 🌐www.teatromassimo.it. The concert and dance programme (classical music, opera and ballet) at Palermo's most prestigious venue runs from October to June, while in summer shows shift to the Teatro del Parco di Villa Castelnuovo for concerts and outdoor performances of ballet and operetta.

Listings

Airport Falcone Borsellino airport (☎ 800.541.880, ⓦ www.gesap.it) is at Punta Raisi, 31km west of the city. Prestia & Comandè buses run from Stazione Centrale (at 4am, then every 30min, 5am–11pm; €5.80, 45min), or there are trains, also from Stazione Centrale (every 30 minutes 7am–8pm).

Bike and scooter rental City Bike (Via Maqueda 139 ☎ 331.750.7886) charges around €10 per day for bikes. For scooters, there's Rent a Scooter (Via E. Amari 63 ☎ 091.336.804, ⓦ www.renta scooters.com) and Motorent (Via E. Amari 91 ☎ 091.602.3455), from €21 per day.

Bookshops There's a large selection of English books at Mondadori Multicenter, Via Ruggero Séttimo 18; Feltrinelli, Via Cavour 139; and Libreria Flaccovio, Via Ruggero Séttimo 37.

Buses Most bus companies have their terminals near Stazione Centrale, especially on Via Paolo Balsamo: these include AST (☎ 091.680.0038, ⓦ www.aziendasicilianatrasporti.it; for Bagheria, Castelbuono, Corleone, Montelepre); Cuffaro (☎ 091.616.1510, ⓦ www.cuffaro.info; Agrigento); Interbus (☎ 091.616.7919, ⓦ www.interbus.it; Catania and Siracusa); Randazzo (☎ 091.814.8235, ⓦ www.autobusrandazzo.altervista.org; Cáccamo and Términi Imerese); SAIS (☎ 091.616.6028, ⓦ www.saisautolinee.it; Caltagirone, Catania, Cefalù, Enna, Gela, Messina and Piazza Armerina); and Segesta (☎ 091.616.919, ⓦ www.segesta.it; Álcamo, Messina, Partinico, Trápani). On nearby Via Rosario Gregorio there's Salemi (☎ 0923.981120, ⓦ www .autoservizisalemi.it; Castelvetrano, Marsala and Mazara del Vallo), while Prestia & Comandè run from Stazione Centrale (☎ 091.586.351, ⓦ www.prestiae comande.it; airport and Piana degli Albanesi). Russo is at Piazza Marina (☎ 0924.31.364, ⓦ www .russoautoservizi.it; Castellammare del Golfo and San Vito Lo Capo), and AST also has a terminus at Piazzale John Lennon, near Viale Regione Siciliana (☎ 091.685.8015; Capaci, Carini and Partinico).

Car rental Most agencies have outlets at the airport and in the city: Avis (☎ 091.586.940, ⓦ www.avis.co.uk); Hertz (☎ 091.323.439, ⓦ www.hertz.it); Maggiore (☎ 091.681.0801, ⓦ www.maggiore.it); Sicily By Car (☎ 091.581.045, ⓦ www.sbc.it).

Consulates UK, Via Cavour 117 ☎ 091.326.412; USA, Via Vaccarini 1 ☎ 091.305.857; South Africa, Largo degli Abeti 16 ☎ 348.340.0219. Other major consulates are in Milan or Rome.

Ferry and hydrofoils Grandi Navi Veloci (Grimaldi) to Livorno, Rome and Tunis (☎ 091.587.404, ⓦ www.gnv.it); NGI to Ústica (☎ 091.743.7393, ⓦ www.ngi-spa.it); Siremar to Ústica (☎ 091.749.3111, ⓦ www.siremar.it); Ústica Lines to the Aeolian Islands, Cefalù and Naples (☎ 091.333.333, ⓦ www.usticalines.it); Tirrenia to Naples and Cágliari (☎ 892.123 ⓦ www.tirrenia.it).

Hospitals Ospedale Cívico, Via Carmelo Lazzaro ☎ 091.666.1111; Policlinica, Via Carmelo Lazzaro ☎ 091.655.1111. For an ambulance call ☎ 118.

Internet There are places along Via Maqueda near the train station, or Aboriginal Café, Via Salvatore Spinuzza 51, near Teatro Mássimo (Mon–Sat 9am–3am, ⓦ www.aboriginalcafe.com).

Left luggage Stazione Centrale by track 8 (daily 7am–11pm; €3.80 for the first 5hr, then cheaper); Stazione Maríttima (daily 7am–7.30pm; €2 for 12hr).

Newspapers Foreign newspapers and magazines are sold at kiosks at Stazione Centrale, Piazza Verdi and Piazza Castelnuovo, and at *Kursaal Kalhesa*, Foro Italico 21.

Pharmacies All-night service at Lo Cascio, Via Roma 1; Di Naro, Via Roma 207; and Farmacia Inglese, Via Marina Stabile 177. Other chemists operate a rota system, with the address of the nearest open chemist posted on the door.

Post offices Palazzo delle Poste, Via Roma 320 (Mon–Sat 8am–6.30pm).

Taxis There are taxi tanks at Stazione Centrale (Piazza Giulio Césare), Piazza Castelnuovo, Piazza Giuseppe Verdi, Piazza Indipendenza, Piazza San Domenico, Piazza Matteotti, and along Via Malta and Via Roma. To call a taxi (24hr service), try ☎ 091.513.311 or 091.225.455.

Trains For information and timetables call ☎ 892.021 or consult ⓦ www.trenitalia.com.

Mondello

On a hot summer's day, when the city heat is oppressive, the most obvious escape from central Palermo is the 11km run to **MONDELLO**, a small seaside resort tucked under the northern bluff of Monte Pellegrino. A 2km-long sandy beach fronts the town, and there's also a tiny working harbour, a jetty from which you can try your luck fishing, and the remnants of a medieval tower. In July and

August, like most Sicilian resorts, it's a bit of a zoo, featuring tacky souvenir stalls, hot-dog and burger vans, pumped-up pizza places and packed lidos. At night, there's a crush in the bars in the main square while the roads around are filled with cruising cars and preening youth. In winter it's more laid-back and rarely busy, but many of the restaurants and snack stalls stay open and it's usually warm enough to swim until well past the end of the official season.

There's a line of **trattorias** – some with outdoor terraces – though the quality is patchy (have a good look at the fish on display in the fridges before you decide where to eat). The best traditional choice is *Da Calógero*, on the seafront at Via Torre 22 (☎091.684.1333), where you stand up at the window and eat freshly caught and cooked octopus (they do have chairs and tables these days, but standing at the window is *de rigueur*). To get to Mondello, take **bus** #806 or #833 from Piazza Politeama or Viale della Libertà – a thirty-minute ride. The last bus back to town leaves around midnight, or a taxi costs about €35. Driving to Mondello, exit at the Tommaso Natale junction from the main road.

Monreale and around

The major excursion from the city – rated almost unmissable – is to **MONREALE**, a small hill-town 8km southwest of Palermo. It commands unsurpassed views down the Conca d'Oro valley, with the capital shimmering in the distant bay, and while the panorama from the "Royal Mountain" alone is worth making the trip for, the real draw is the mighty Norman cathedral and its celebrated mosaics. These form one of the most extraordinary and extensive areas of Christian medieval mosaic-work in the world, and are the apex of Sicilian-Norman art. Monreale is an easy day-trip from Palermo, but once the tourists leave in the late afternoon the prospect of a quiet night in town might appeal, and there are plenty of characterful B&Bs in the medieval alleys near the cathedral.

The cathedral owes its existence to young King William II's rivalry with his powerful Palermitan archbishop, the Englishman Walter of the Mill. Work had started on Walter's fine cathedral in the centre of the city in 1172. Determined to quickly break the influence of his former teacher, William endowed a new monastery in his royal grounds outside the city in 1174, and its abbey church – the Duomo at Monreale – was thrown up in a matter of years. Monreale was made an archbishopric in 1183, two years before Walter's cathedral was finished, and this unseemly haste had two consequences. As a highly personal project, Monreale's power lasted only as long as William did: although he wanted to create a royal pantheon, he was the last king to be buried here. But the speed with which the Duomo was built ensured the splendid uniformity of its interior art – a galaxy of mosaic pictures bathed in a golden background.

The Town

Monreale's **Duomo** (Mon–Sat 8.30am–12.45pm & 2.30–6pm, Sun 8am–10am & 2.30–5.30pm; ⓦwww.cattedraledimonreale.it) presides magisterially over the town centre, facing two open squares and flanked by alleys teeming with souvenir stalls and gift shops. Bear in mind that, despite the continual influx of tourists, you may not be allowed in if dressed inappropriately.

The gleaming **mosaics**, almost certainly executed by Greek and Byzantine craftsmen, are a magnificent achievement, thought to have been completed in just ten years. They were designed for worshippers to be able to read the Testaments straight from the walls, and eyes are drawn immediately to the all-embracing half-figure of

Christ in benediction in the central apse. The head and shoulders alone stand almost 20m high, face full of compassion, curving arms with outstretched hands seemingly encompassing the whole beauty of the church. Underneath are an enthroned Virgin and Child, attendant angels and, below, the ranks of saints – each subtly coloured and identified by name. The two side-apses are dedicated to saints Peter (right) and Paul (left), the arches before each apse graphically displaying the martyrdom of each – respectively, an inverse crucifixion and a beheading. The nave mosaics then start with the Creation (above the pillars to the right of the altar) and run around the whole church, while the aisle mosaics depict the teachings of Jesus. Most scenes are instantly recognizable: Adam and Eve; Abraham on the point of sacrificing his son; positively jaunty Noah's-ark scenes showing the ship being built, recalcitrant animals being loaded aboard, Noah's family peering out of the hatches; the Feeding of the Five Thousand; and the Creation itself, a set of glorious, simplistic panels portraying God filling His world with animals, water, light ... and Man.

Above the two **thrones** (royal and episcopal) are more mosaics: William receiving the crown from Christ; and the king offering the cathedral to the Virgin. Both William I and William II are buried here in side chapels, the latter resting in the white marble sarcophagus to the right of the apse. A ticket desk provides access to the **tower and terrace** (€1.50) for some sweeping views, and there's a combined ticket (€2) to see the collection of reliquaries in the **treasury**. You also shouldn't miss the **Chiostro dei Benedettini**, or cloisters (daily 9am–7pm, last entry 6.30pm; €6; enter from Piazza Gugliemo, in the corner by the right-hand tower of the cathedral), an elegant arcaded quadrangle with 216 twin columns supporting slightly pointed arches – a legacy of the Arab influence in Sicilian art. No two of the carved capitals are the same: on one, armed hunters do battle with winged beasts; another has two men lifting high a casket of wine; while flowers, birds, snakes and geometric shapes dip and dance from column to column. One final point of interest in the Duomo is its enormous triple **apse**, a polychromatic jumble of limestone and lava, supported by slender columns and patterned by a fine series of interlacing arches. To see it, go through the arched alley (Arco degli Angeli) to the left of the Duomo entrance.

It's hard to look beyond the Duomo, but Monreale itself is a handsome small town with a dense latticework of streets and (mostly locked) Baroque churches. For the famous view down the valley, stroll into the courtyard of the new convent (built in 1747) behind the cathedral cloisters to the **belvedere** (the entrance is from the other corner of Piazza Gugliemo). Come *passeggiata* time the main **Via Roma** pulses with life, and you don't have to walk very far along here to swap touristy mosaic galleries and gift shops for butchers, grocers and hardware stores.

Practicalities

Bus #389 runs frequently from Palermo's Piazza dell'Indipendenza (outside the Porta Nuova, reached by bus #109 from Stazione Centrale) through the western suburbs and up the valley, and takes around twenty minutes. A taxi from Palermo costs around €30 each way. Parking is restricted in Monreale's old town and visitors are advised to use one of the signposted **car parks** – there's one on Via Cappuccini, below the Duomo and belvedere (from where a pedestrian way leads up past souvenir stalls into the town) and another (Parcheggio Duomo) down Via D'Acquisto to the side of the Palazzo Communale. Parking costs €1 an hour, and it's free overnight after 8pm.

There's only a limited number of **hotels** actually in town, most reasonable of which is the somewhat old-fashioned three-star *Carrubella Park*, Via Umberto I 233 (℡091.640.2187, ⓦwww.carrubellaparkhotel.com; ❸), a short walk from the centre with great views over the valley from one side. However, there are charming **B&Bs**

and "rooms" places much nearer the Duomo, especially in the tangle of alleys by the Duomo's apse. *La Ciambra*, Via Sanchez 23 (T 091.640.9565 or 335.842.5865, W www.laciambra.com; no credit cards; ❷), is a quaint, family-run place wedged into a plant-filled alley, and there are several others signposted nearby, or you can ask about rooms in the gift shops hereabouts – pretty much everyone either has rooms or knows someone who does.

There are plenty of **restaurants**, though prices are generally on the high side. *Peppino*, Via B. Civiletti 12 (T 091.640.7770; closed Tues), is a popular local pizzeria tucked away down on a side street off Via Roma (past San Giuseppe church). It has a shady summer terrace, some *antipasti* to start and crisp pizzas (€5–10). Otherwise, *Bricco & Bacco*, Via B. D'Acquisto 13 (T 091 641 7773; closed Sun June–Aug), is a brasserie that's serious about its meat – steaks, chops and lamb grills for €10–15, with the Angus beef also available with a classy balsamic vinegar and honey salsa. It's a definite cut above the family tourist restaurants in town, and there's a cool little corner **bar**, *Al Solito Posto*, just next door, ideal for a street-side *aperitif*.

Around Monreale: San Martino delle Scale and Báida

Seven kilometres west of Monreale, the impressive white monastery of **San Martino delle Scale** is an ancient religious settlement that has been taken over in recent years as a summer hill resort – holiday homes and Sunday-trippers are much in evidence. The Benedictine monks are still here, however, and you can visit their **Abbazia di San Martino** (Mon–Sat 9am–noon & 4.30–6.30pm, Sun 9–11am & 5–6.30pm) – supposedly founded by Gregory the Great in the sixth century – to see its frescoes, grand fountain and eighteenth-century marble staircase. There are local buses here from Monreale, or there's a direct Virga service four times a day from Palermo's Piazza Verdi (by the Teatro Mássimo). This approaches San Martino through the wooded "Paradise Valley", at the eastern end of which a road leads from the village of **Boccadifalco** (about 5km out of the capital) 2km north to **BÁIDA**, a tenth-century Saracen village (*baidha* is Arabic for "white") with another medieval convent. Báida, too, is a pretty village, ringed by hills, and again there are direct buses from Palermo, most convenient of which is the #462 from Piazza Príncipe di Camporeale (itself reached by #122 from Stazione Centrale, or #110 from Piazza dell'Indipendenza).

Golfo di Carini

If you're looking for a beach to while away a few hours, then the small fishing ports and holiday resorts along the **Golfo di Carini**, northwest of the capital, are perfectly adequate, and certainly less intense than Mondello. However, few tourists venture inland from the coast into the dry, bare hills behind, although the SP1 road from Palermo to Montelepre and Partinico would make an interesting alternative to the much busier coastal route for those heading west. The castle at **Carini** is an obvious stop, while romanticized tales of banditry still hold sway in places like **Montelepre**, where for centuries, poverty, desperation and outlawry have been ingrained in the local culture.

Along the coast

The adjacent towns of Sferracavallo and Isola delle Fémmine, 16km northwest of the city, are the best bet for an easy beach getaway – the *isola* in question at the latter is a tiny offshore islet. **SFERRACAVALLO** has the closest official campsites to Palermo – the *Ulivi* (ⓦ www.campingdegliulivi.com) and the pricier *Trinacria* (ⓦ www.campingtrinacria.it) – as well as the regional youth hostel, the *Baia del Corallo* (ⓣ 091.769.7807, ⓦ www.ostellopalermo.it; dorms from €18). To get out to Sferracavallo, take bus #101 from Stazione Centrale to Piazza Giovanni Paolo II (ex-Piazza A. de Gasperi) and then bus #628.

The same bus also runs to **ISOLA DELLE FÉMMINE**, though there's a more convenient direct train from Stazione Centrale. A kilometre west of town, *La Playa* campsite (ⓦ www.campinglaplaya.net; closed mid-Oct to Feb) lies close to a sandy beach, while for a decent restaurant you need only head to the main beach road where you'll have your pick from nearly a dozen fish and seafood places. *La Scogliera Azzurra* (ⓣ 091.867.7874, ⓦ www.scoglieraazzurra.it; ❷) is good, with a set-price menu for €25; it's also a small hotel popular with families, with access to a pool and private beach.

The train from Palermo runs further out along the Golfo di Carini, with **TERRASINI**, forty minutes out of the city, typical of the small ports along the gulf. There's a sandy beach, a clutch of small hotels and several trattorias, like the excellent *Turiddu* (ⓣ 091.881.0588), on the seafront, good for fresh fish and pizzas.

Carini

Five kilometres from the coast, **CARINI** is distinguished by a pair of sixteenth-century churches set around a typically chaotic market square-cum-car park, and a first-rate castle (Tues–Sun 9am–1pm & 3–7pm; €4), whose walls overlook the spreading coastal plain below. The battlemented fortress dates from Norman times

Sicily's bandit king: Salvatore Giuliano

Salvatore Giuliano (1922–50) was Sicily's most dashing anti-establishment hero – and villain. Known to his comrades as Turiddu, he embodied the hopes and frustrations of the Sicilian people more than any other individual in recent history. Part of his charm lay in his long defiance of the government. Starting out as a petty criminal and black-marketeer, he was a hunted man after his murder of a Carabiniere who had challenged him as he transported stolen grain in 1943. Gathering a band of followers in the mountains around his home in Montelepre, he was pursued by platoons of hand-picked soldiers who combed the maquis for him. As his legend grew, so did his charisma, enhanced by such madcap gestures as writing to President Truman and offering the annexation of Sicily to the United States, in a last-ditch attempt to sever the island from the Italian State.

Giuliano's separatist ambitions led him into some disreputable alliances, and his fall from grace occurred when he was shown to be behind the massacre of villagers at Portella della Ginestra in 1947 (see p.85). Just three years later, he was betrayed and killed, his body found in a courtyard in Castelvetrano, in the south. No one knows exactly what happened or who was responsible for his death, though his deputy, Gaspare Pisciotta, chose to confess to the crime. Many doubt that he was the one who pulled the trigger, and Pisciotta himself was on the verge of making revelations at his trial that would have implicated high-ranking Italian politicians, when he too was assassinated in his cell at Ucciardone prison. Whatever the truth, there's a pungently Sicilian flavour to the affair, full of corruption, betrayal and counter-betrayal, and Giuliano's legend has since grown to Robin Hood dimensions, nowhere more so than in his home territory around Montelepre. As his biographer Gavin Maxwell was told: "They should change the name of that village, really – anything else but Montelepre would do. No one can look at it straight or think straight about it now – it just means Giuliano."

and was subsequently held by some of Sicily's leading feudal dynasties: in 1508 an infamous murder occurred here when the local count killed his errant daughter and her lover, immortalized in an anonymous contemporary poem considered to be the highest example of Sicilian popular versifying, *La Baronessa di Carini*. Inside you can see grand courtyards and a series of restored chambers, some holding period furniture, with wooden ceilings, frescoes and coats of arms. You can get to Carini by bus (the train station is a long way from town), but it's an unlikely destination unless you're driving and fancy a coffee break.

Montelepre

A minor road climbs 11km south of Carini through the hills to the small town of **MONTELEPRE** (there's a direct AST bus from Palermo), occupying a view-laden notch in the mountains but notable only for its notorious history. To Sicilians, Montelepre is instantly familiar as the birthplace and home of the bandit **Salvatore Giuliano**, who hid out in the hills and caves around here, slipping into town at night to see family and friends. If you are genuinely interested, you may be able to persuade his nephew to show you around the house in which Giuliano lived, to see personal effects including the various musical instruments that he played, the bike he rode, and the bed he was born and slept in. The nephew runs the *Castello di Giuliano*, Via Pietro Merra 1, at the top of town on the road in from Carini (☏091.894.1006, ⓦwww.castellodigiuliano.it; ❷), an eccentric hotel and restaurant built to look like a castle, with more Giuliano memorabilia on display and faux-rustic rooms; the baronial restaurant (most dishes €6–11) serves pasta, meat and fish grills and pizzas in the evening.

Bagheria and around

The Palermitan nobility of the seventeenth and eighteenth centuries chose to sit out the enervating summer heat in their Baroque country villas scattered around the small town of **BAGHERIA**, 14km east of the city. Here – as described by Dacia Maraini in her memoir *Bagheria* – they enjoyed "the atmosphere of a summer garden enriched by lemon groves and olive trees, poised between the hills, cooled by the salt winds". Some of the villas are open for visits, and Bagheria still has the air of a summer retreat. Give yourself a full day and you can also see the ancient ruins at **Solunto** and the working fishing port of **Porticello**, the latter boasting a boutique hotel and a ring of harbourside fish restaurants that might just persuade you to make a night of it.

Bagheria

Best-known – or perhaps that should be most notorious – of Bagheria's Baroque villas is the **Villa Palagonia** (daily: April–Oct 9am–1pm & 4–7pm, Nov–March 9am–1pm & 3.30–5.30pm; €5; ⓦwww.villapalagonia.it), at the end of Via Palagonia, whose grounds boast an eccentric menagerie of grotesque gnomes, giants, gargoyles and assorted mutants. The villa was the work of Ferdinand, Prince of Palagonia, a hunchback who – in league with the architect Tommaso Napoli – took revenge on his wife's lovers by cruelly caricaturing them. Although only 64 of the original 200 statues remain, they certainly add entertainment to a wander around the garden, before you climb the stairs into the crumbling sandstone villa to view a selection of frescoed halls and the dramatic Salone degli Specchi, covered in mirrors and marbling.

The nearby **Villa Valguarnera** (also by Napoli) displays Bagheria's most sumptuous facade, pink and festooned with a royal coat of arms and Attic statues. **Villa Butera**, meanwhile, has within its grounds a collection of wax figures in Carthusian apparel. Legend has it that their creator, Ercole Branciforti, had promised the erection of a Carthusian abbey in return for the granting of a prayer, and took the crafty way out when the prayer was answered. The Valguanera and Butera villas, and many others, are still privately owned, and only open to the public on occasion. However, a further villa is always open, the **Villa Cattólica**, 500m from the train station on Via Rammacca (the main SS113), which has been restored to hold the **Museo Guttuso** (Tues–Sun: April–Oct 9.30am–2pm & 3.30–7.30pm, Nov–March 9am–1pm & 2.30–7pm; €5; Ⓦwww.museoguttuso.it), dedicated to Bagheria's most famous son, Renato Guttuso (1912–87), whose brilliant use of colour and striking imagery made him one of Italy's most important modern artists; his tomb, designed by his friend, the sculptor Giacomo Manzù, is in the garden.

Practicalities

There are frequent local trains from Palermo to Bagheria, and it's a good ten minutes' walk from the **train station** to Villa Palagonia (turn left out of the station onto Corso Butera, then left onto Via Palagonia). AST **buses** from Stazione Centrale drop you much closer, on Corso Umberto I, from where it's a straight walk to the villa. There's free **parking** nearby, though you might find yourself sucked into the narrow streets of the old town trying to find it. Eventually, though, you should be directed into a space by a parking guy, to whom you tip a euro. A town map outside the gates of Villa Palagonia shows you the local layout, but basically anything else you need – like drinks and ice cream – is easily found down the pleasant, long, traffic-free Corso Umberto I that runs from the villa. Best place for a **meal** is the atmospheric *Antica Osteria Zzá Maria*, Via Paternò 11 (Ⓣ091.931.388; closed Mon) – all wine barrels and old photos – where there's no actual menu (and you might have to hammer at the door for entrance), but you'll get a good plate of home-made *pasta con le sarde* or similar for €7. Find it by walking down Corso Umberto I to the free-standing columns at Piazza IV Novembre and you'll see a restaurant sign on your right, down Via Pasquale.

Solunto

It's a 5km, ten-minute drive from Bagheria to the dramatically sited remains of the important Greco-Roman settlement at **Solunto**, just to the east. You can also get there on the train, getting off one stop beyond Bagheria (at Santa Flavia-Solunto-Porticello station), crossing over the tracks and walking down the main road towards the sea; after 300m there's a signposted left turn up the hillside, altogether a twenty-five-minute walk. Beautifully sited on the slopes of Monte Catalfano, ancient Solus, a Phoenician settlement, was originally founded in the eighth century BC, resettled in the fourth century BC, and later Hellenized, finally surrendering to Rome after the First Punic War, when its name was changed to Solentum. Ruins at the **site** (Mon–Sat 9am–7pm, Sun 9am–2pm, last entry 1hr before closing; €2) date mostly from the Roman period, notably the impressive remains of wealthy houses – one, with a standing column, was built on two floors, the stairs still visible, and retains a complete geometric mosaic floor. The main street leads past houses and shops to the agora itself, a piazza with nine clay-red-coloured recessed rooms at the back. Above it sit the fragmentary ruins of a theatre and a smaller odeon, deliberately sited so as to give marvellous views away to the coast. Beyond the agora are the remains of a water cistern and storage tanks – necessary, as Solentum had no natural springs. Two "pavilions" interpret the site and display many of the finds, one at the entrance (before you see the ruins) and one at the exit, though there's nothing in English.

Porticello

Six kilometres east of Bagheria, **PORTICELLO** makes a great bolt-hole from the city, with views across the bay towards Cefalù and up to the line of rounded peaks on the horizon. Fishermen have been working out of the port for centuries, and an old *tonnara* (tuna fishery) is still preserved near the medieval Castello di Sólanto, which guards one side of the bay. It's a real, working harbour, and Porticello's fish market is one of the most important in Sicily, with boats unloading here in the early hours before the catch is shipped across Italy and beyond. Ice-house chutes channel ice into containers for the fish, and boats and nets are still hauled under great stone arches back from the harbour to be repaired.

Palermitani come here at weekends and in summer to eat fish and seafood at the harbourside **trattorias**. For a superb meal seek out *Arrhais*, in Largo Marino, just above the fish market (☎091.947.127; closed Wed in winter) – it's not on the harbourside itself, but has a covered outdoor terrace where you'll eat off-the-boat specials like *fritto misto*, pasta with cuttlefish ink, oven-roast seabass and huge grilled shrimp (dishes from €10, but the sky's the limit). To wake up to harbour views, stay at ꞁ*Stenopus Greco* (☎091.958.851 or 320.799.2011, ⓦwww.stenopus greco.com; ❷, July & Aug ❸), a boutique dockside **hotel**, which charming owner Stéfano has imbued with real artistic flair. There are eight lovely rooms in bold colours with terracotta floors and beamed ceilings, original art above the handmade beds, painted ceramics and carved Indonesian chests. Three rooms have harbour-view balconies, others either partial harbour or town views. It's a surprising find in such a working town, but perhaps a sign of things to come if plans for a new harbour and marina development for Porticello come to fruition.

Piana degli Albanesi and around

Less than an hour's bus ride south of the capital, **PIANA DEGLI ALBANESI** sits placidly in an upland plain above a pleasant lake. The town was founded by fifteenth-century Albanians uprooted from their homes in flight from the Turkish invasions, and the six thousand inhabitants here still follow the Orthodox rite and proudly retain many of their old traditions – signs here are in Albanian as well as Italian, and on Sunday mornings there are traditional Orthodox services in the three churches lining the steeply sloping main street, Via Giorgio Kastriota. At Easter, out

---

The massacre at Portella della Ginestra

The mountain pass 4km southwest of Piana degli Albanesi, **Portella della Ginestra**, was the scene of one of the most shocking episodes in recent Sicilian history. On May 1, 1947, when the Albanians and villagers from neighbouring San Giuseppe Jato had assembled for their customary May Day celebrations, gunfire erupted from the crags and boulders surrounding the plain, killing eleven and wounding 55, many of them children. This massacre was the work of the bandit Salvatore Giuliano, whose virulent anti-Communist feelings were exploited by more sinister figures high up in the political and criminal hierarchy: only two weeks previously, the people of the town, together with most other Sicilians, had voted for a Popular Front (left-wing) majority in the regional parliament. The cold-blooded killings erased at one stroke the bandit's carefully nurtured reputation as defender of the poor and friend to the oppressed. There's a car park at the pass and the site is marked by a memorial of sculpted rocks inscribed in blood-red lettering – slightly unkempt, and a haunting place still.

come the handsome traditional costumes – black with gold brocade on Good Friday, brightly coloured on Easter Sunday – and you can see examples of these in the **Museo Cívico** (Tues, Thurs & Sat 9.30am–1pm & 4–7pm, Wed & Fri 9.30am–1pm, Sun 10am–1pm; free), just a few steps from Piazza Vittorio Emanuele, the small square at the top of the main street. Rural life and local history is well covered in this fascinating little museum, with reconstructions of room interiors containing anything from dental tools to cheese-making equipment as well as grainy photographs and other memorials to the infamous massacre at Portella della Ginestra.

Prestia & Commandé **buses** run to Piana from Palermo's Stazione Centrale; the last one back leaves at around 4pm. Buses stop at the top of town, 500m from Piazza Vittorio Emanuele, at the Villa Comunale gardens (there's free parking here too). Cross the road viaduct to reach Via Kastriota and the centre of town. For **food**, the best choice is *Trattoria San Giovanni*, Via G. Matteotti 34 (℡091.857.1070; closed Tues), right by the bus stop and Villa Comunale, where pastas and mains go for €7–8.

Ficuzza

South of Piana degli Albanesi, a highly scenic driving route skirts the lake and then winds through rolling hills to reach the junction for **FICUZZA** after 20km. Another 1km from here, up the lane, you emerge in a dead-end hamlet that is completely dominated by the honey-coloured stone **Palazzo Reale di Ficuzza** (daily 9.30am–1.30pm & 3–6pm, last tour 30min before closing; free), set against a dramatic mountain backdrop. This stately royal palace, fronted by a grassy piazza, was actually once the hunting lodge of Ferdinand III, and guided group visits (in Italian) set off every thirty minutes to show you the parts that survived destruction and burning by Mussolini's troops, notably the hunting scenes in the Sala da Pranzo. An information board in the piazza also shows the local waymarked **walks** (between 45min and 3hr) on mountain paths that crisscross the wooded heights of Rocca Busambra (1613m), or you can simply grab a drink or a simple meal in one of the two or three bars and trattorias in the piazza.

Corleone

From Ficuzza, another 20km on a quick country highway sees you in **CORLEONE**, a fairly large inland town squeezed between a couple of fortified rocks and girded by crags. It attracts a trickle of tourists, mostly on the scent of the Mafia since the town lent Mario Puzo's fictional Godfather, Don Corleone, his adopted family name. However, it is also the real-life name of Sicily's most notorious Mafia clan, and post-war Corleone was certainly a desperate place of murder and inter-family bloodletting. You wouldn't, of course, know it from the quiet streets today and if it wasn't for the notoriety there would be no compelling reason to stop in Corleone, pleasant though the town centre is. A flurry of signs do their best to interest you in the various churches and small local museums, but more to the point is the Anti-Mafia Museum known (and signposted) as **CIDMA** (ie, the International Centre for the Documentation of the Mafia and the Anti-Mafia Movement), at Via Orfanotrofio 7, off the central Piazza Garibaldi, close to the *Comune* (open daily, with guided tours available, though best to email or call first ⓔinfo@cidma.it; ℡091.845.242.95). Here you can trace the violent history of both Corleone and the Mafia, not only through brutal photographs (taken and donated by photographer Letizia Battaglia) of the so-called "Mafia Wars" but also by examining displays of original documents used in the maxi-trials of the 1980s. It's a sobering experience, though current street names in town at least demonstrate a contemporary *corleonese* desire to make amends

Corleone and the Mafia

Whether by luck or with foresight, when Mario Puzo chose the name **Corleone** for his central character in *The Godfather* (published 1969), he picked a little-known place that later came to have a huge significance in Mafia circles, as the native town of many of the so-called *capo di tutti capi* (literally "boss of all the bosses"). Even before Puzo's novel, the name Corleone had a certain resonance, due to the activities of **Luciano Leggio** (also known as Liggio), who had a reputation as a dashing figure and was hailed for his long-running evasion of the forces ranged against him. He was, however, responsible for one of the most notorious political killings of the twentieth century, that of the trade union leader **Plácido Rizzotto**, who had been trying to organize peasants into staging occupations of uncultivated Mafia-owned lands. Two years after Rizzotto's disappearance in 1948, the fire brigade hauled out his dismembered corpse from a 30m crevice near Corleone (along with sackfuls of other bodies of Mafia victims). His killers were eventually acquitted for lack of evidence, the most common end to murder charges brought against *mafiosi*. Leggio was finally imprisoned in 1974 and died in jail in 1993.

At the time of his arrest in 1993, Leggio's trusted deputy from Corleone, **Salvatore Riina**, was the most wanted man in Italy, allegedly responsible for ordering at least 150 murders, 40 of which he's said to have committed himself. His capture came as a complete surprise and triggered a wave of accusations, since it became clear that for over twenty years Riina had been living in Palermo while making clandestine visits to his family in Corleone. This, it's said with some justification, could only have been the case if he had enjoyed a degree of high-level protection.

The most notable among several further members of the Corleonese clan who have been put away since Riina's arrest is **Bernardo Provenzano**, known as "the Tractor" on account of his brutal methods and also as "the Accountant" for the way in which he increasingly blurred Mafia operations with legitimate business interests. He was finally captured in 2006, having been convicted in absentia of a string of murders, including the 1992 killings of the two anti-Mafia investigators Giovanni Falcone and Paolo Borsellino. For more on all these characters, and the ongoing saga of the Sicilian Mafia, see Contexts, p.387.

(Piazza Víttime della Mafia, Piazza Falcone e Borsellino, etc). And at dusk in the town gardens, when couples, teenagers and families stroll under the soaring palms and flowering oleanders, the dark dealings of earlier times seem an age away. This more enlightened view of town is the one promoted by two local women under the name "Corleone, Come and See" (call ☎340.402.5601), who, with a couple of days' notice, can arrange a tailor-made tour with an English-speaking guide and including a typically rustic *corleonese* lunch.

Practicalities

Corleone is 60km from Palermo and while it's an unlikely day-trip, it is a reasonable stop en route to the south coast or to interior destinations. There are plenty of bars and cafés in the centre, while for a decent **trattoria** follow the signs to *Al Capriccio*, Via Sant'Agostino 39 (☎091.846.7938; closed Tues; dishes €5–10, or a bargain €10 tourist menu). Two **hotels** do the honours, one at each end of town, the better being the three-star, villa-style *Leon d'Oro* (☎091.846.4287, ⓦwww.leondorocorleone.it; ❸), just off the roundabout on the northern (Palermo) approach road. The rooms are spacious and smart, and you can enjoy excellent crisp pizzas (€4–6), pasta and regional cuisine (dishes €6–13.50) in the shady garden courtyard. Otherwise, the *Belvedere* (☎091.846.4000, ⓦwww.hotelbelvedere corleone.it; ❷) on the southern side, has a pool, views over Corleone from some rooms, and its own restaurant further up the hill, *A'Giarra*.

Off the beaten track in Palermo province

Corleone might only be 60km from Palermo, and still in the same province, but the dry hills, rolling farmland and isolated rural outposts are far removed from the bustling capital. If you're in no hurry, there's a circular driving route back to Palermo that shows you a wilder side of the island, with a few Mafia connections to boot to add a certain *frisson*. It's a quick 25km southeast over the hills on the SS118 to **Prizzi** – the name borrowed for that of a New York mob family in John Huston's 1985 black comedy *Prizzi's Honor*. On Easter Sunday here, giant statues of Christ and the Virgin Mary are taunted by masked figures representing Death and the Devil, to whom onlookers are forced to give money. Another 20km east along the SS189, the main claim of **Lercara Friddi** is as the birthplace in 1897 of the Sicilian-American gangster Lucky Luciano, whose family emigrated in 1907. While in prison in the US, Luciano was enlisted by the Americans to aid their Sicilian campaign (which was fully backed by the Mafia in its desire to end the Fascist rule) and his reward when the war was over was to be freed, on the condition that he returned to Sicily. The town's main piazza was packed to welcome him home in 1946, and he repaid the adulation by opening Lercara Friddi's first cinema – apparently with a screening of the gangster movie, *Little Caesar*. A few kilometres north of Lercara, you pick up the SS121, which winds across the entire length of Sicily from Catania to finish its run in Palermo. One final (signposted) stop is at **Bagni di Cefalà**, eleventh-century Arab baths, still flowing with thermal waters which the locals use for washing clothes, though you can swim here too. Few other examples of Arab architecture in Sicily are in such good condition.

Ústica

A turtle-shaped volcanic island, 60km northwest of Palermo, **ÚSTICA** is ideal for a few days' rest and recreation. The island's fertile nine square kilometres are just right for a ramble and what it lacks in sandy beaches it more than makes up for in the limpid waters of a marine reserve that many consider to provide the best snorkelling and dive-sites in the Mediterranean. If tourism has rescued isolated Ústica, it has also been at the risk of spoiling its charms – the population of 1300 quadruples in the summer months, and you'll see the island at its best if you can avoid coming in August.

Colonized originally by the Phoenicians, the island was known to the Greeks as Osteodes, or "ossuary", a reference to the remains of six thousand Carthaginians they found here, abandoned to die on the island after a rebellion. Its present name is derived from the Latin *ustum* – "burnt" – on account of its blackened, lava-like appearance. Ústica had a rough time throughout the Middle Ages, its sparse population constantly harried by pirates who used the island as a base. In the Bourbon period the island was commandeered as a prison for political enemies, a use to which the island continued to be put well into the twentieth century – Antonio Gramsci, the great theorist of the Italian Communist Party, was interned here in 1926, while Mussolini similarly exiled many other political prisoners. Only in recent decades has Ústica shaken off its chains and become a holiday destination.

Arrival and information

Siremar (Ⓦ www.siremar.it) **ferries** (€16.35; 2hr 30min) and **hydrofoils** €20; 1hr 15min) operate daily from Palermo (from the Stazione Maríttima); summer

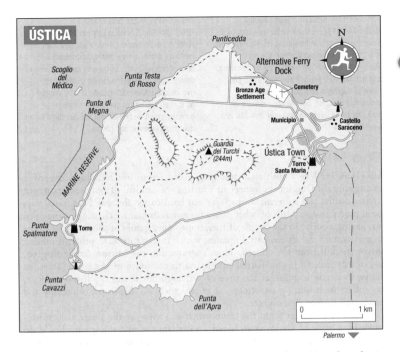

departure times from Palermo are 7am, 8.15am, 1pm and 5.15pm, though are liable to change. Note that there's also a summer Ústica Lines (Ⓦwww.ustica lines.it) hydrofoil service connecting Ústica with the Égadi Islands, Trápani and Naples.

You arrive at **Ústica Town**, the island's only port, with the town centre up the flight of steps leading from the harbour. You'll emerge in the main square, which is really three interlocking squares – piazzas Umberto I, della Vittoria and Vito Longo. From Piazza della Vittoria, an efficient **minibus** service (pay on board) plies Ústica's one circular road every hour or so until around 7pm. There is no tourist office here, but you can glean some information from the **websites** Ⓦwww.ustica .net and www.ustica.org.

Accommodation

In summer hotels fill up quickly, and in winter only a few remain open. However, there are plenty of opportunities to rent rooms (*cámere*) – ask around in the shops or at the *Bar Centrale*, in Piazza Umberto I.

Ariston Via della Vittoria 5 ☏091.844.9042, Ⓦwww.usticahostels.it. A smart, central hotel with eleven rooms and impressive sea views. Diving trips and scooter rental can be arranged. Sizeable reductions in winter. No credit cards. ❸

Caminita Vittorio Via Tufo 1 ☏091.844.9212. The friendly couple at this address rents out two attractive self-contained mini-apartments, each with kitchenette, bathroom, terrace and separate entrance. One has a sweeping view down over the town to the sea. It's just a few minutes from the main square – at the church, turn right along Via Calvario and Via Tufo is the sixth on the left. No credit cards. ❷

Giulia Via San Francesco 16 ☏091.844.9007, Ⓦwww.giuliahotel.net. Open year-round, with ten perfectly acceptable two-star rooms right off the main piazza (single rooms also available), above a lovely restaurant. No credit cards. ❷

Stella Marina Residence Stella Marina
☎091.844.8121, ⊛www.stellamarinaustica.it.
Seventeen smart, self-catering mini-apartments
in a small complex right above the port.
There's also a nice big terrace for sun-soaking,
and a small spa. Rentals are from €660 per
week in Aug for a two-person apartment,
including breakfast, but they're available on
a nightly basis between May and July and in
Sept & Oct. ❷

Da Umberto Piazza della Vittoria 7
☎091.844.9542, ⊛www.usticatour.it. As well as
running the *Da Umberto* restaurant, Gigi Tranchina
rents out rooms in over twenty apartments and
houses around Ústica, some with great sea views,
others more rustic in the middle of the island
overlooking a few grazing cattle. Prices depend
on size and quality of the accommodation. In
summer, count on prices from €55 per night for an
apartment sleeping two people.

The island

ÚSTICA TOWN is built on a steep slope, many of its low buildings covered in
fading murals. Despite the veneer of tourism – a handful of hotels, restaurants,
diving outfits and souvenir shops – it's not hard to see that life here has always
been pretty tough. Most of what passes for entertainment – chatting in the open
air, having a coffee in the couple of bars, impromptu games of soccer – takes place
in and around the three central squares, which merge into each other, tumbling
down the hill from the church. There's a museum, the **Museo Archeologico**,
previously housed in the Torre Santa Maria to the south of the town (about to
move to a new location at the time of writing), but it too is a low-key affair,
its collection a motley assortment of crusty anchors, shipwreck oddments and
excavated Bronze Age objects.

What you don't get from the town centre is a view of the water and, consequently, a sense of Ústica as an island, so perhaps the first thing you should do
is climb up to the remains of the **Castello Saraceno**, which gives you a good
initial view of the island's layout: from the top of the square to the right of the
church, the path runs left of the fancy cross at the end of Via Calvario, an easy
twenty-minute walk to an old fort pitted with numerous cisterns to catch the
precious water.

From here you can see Ústica's highest point, the **Guardia dei Turchi** (244m),
at the summit of a ridge that cuts the island in two, and topped by what looks
like a giant golf ball – in fact a meteorological radar system. You can also climb
up to the summit from the town, in about an hour or so: take Via B. Randaccio
to the right of the church, turn left at the top and then right, and you'll come to
the Municipio, where you turn left along Via Tre Mulini for the summit – keep
straight ahead on the cobbled path, cutting off to the left when you reach the
stepped path.

To explore the rest of Ústica you could use the minibus service, rent a scooter,
or even walk – it doesn't take much more than two or three hours to walk round
the entire island. There's a path running right round the rocky coastline, with just
a brief stretch where you have to follow the road, and there are ample opportunities to stop for a swim or sunbathe along the northern coast. Keep straight on past
the Municipio and then bear off the road to the right, down past the cemetery.
The path starts at the remains of a **Bronze Age settlement** – the foundations of
the closely packed huts are still clearly visible. From here the path hugs the cliffs
along the island's north side as far as the **Punta di Megna** (where path and road
converge). There's excellent snorkelling at Punta di Megna and at the offshore
rock of **Scoglio del Médico**, where the clear water is bursting with fish, sponges,
weed and coral. The road then keeps to the west coast as far as the old *torre* (tower)
at **Punta Spalmatore**, where you'll find some of the island's best bathing spots;
try below the tower, or – below the nearby lighthouse – at **Punta Cavazzi**,
where there's a *piscina naturale*, a perfect, sheltered pool of seawater that can get

uncomfortably crowded in high season. Above here, the *Rosa d'Eventi* restaurant-bar offers the only refreshments and shade along the route.

Eating and drinking

There are several places to eat on and around the central squares, and most of the hotels have **restaurants**, often with roof terraces and sea views. Most restaurants not attached to hotels close during the winter. Of the **bars**, *Kiki's Bar*, overlooking the harbour on Via Colombo, is a cool place to hang out, while *Il Faraglione*, close by, is another good nightspot above the harbour, with food, an outdoor lounge and dance area, and occasional live music. Finally, don't neglect to visit Maria Cristina, just above the piazzas at Via Petriera 5, who sells Ústica lentils, home-made preserves, pestos and sauces, and other island treats to savour, from a tiny room in her home.

Giulia Via San Francesco 13 ☏091.844.9007. The simple trattoria attached to this hotel is the best bet on the island for genuine home-cooking. Try *pennette al uticese* (with herbs, chilli, garlic, pine-nuts, raisins, anchovies, capers and olives), fish-balls (*polpettine*) with local capers and olives, or *totano* (a big squid) stuffed with shrimp, tomatoes, cheese and breadcrumbs. Fish couscous is available for a minimum of two people. Expect to spend around €30–40 per person. No credit cards.

Da Umberto Piazza della Vittoria ☏091.844.9542. Tables on the terrace and a menu chiefly consisting of pasta dishes (from €7–8) and seafood main courses that depend on the day's catch (€10–16).

Listings

Bank Monte dei Paschi di Siena, Via Cap. V. di Bártolo, on the left-hand side of the church, has an ATM.

Bike, boats and tours Associazione La Ciprea (☏340.336.8475) for bikes and donkey rides, and boat tours. Usticamare Noleggio (☏091.844.9548 or 339.218.5630) also has bikes, boats and cars to rent, while the restaurant *Da Umberto* (☏www.usticatour.it) rents out scooters and boats and arranges tours. Boat excursions from the quay cost around €15 per person for three hours – it's best agree a price beforehand.

Ferries and hydrofoils The R&S Militello ticket agency, just off the piazza at Via Cap. di Bártolo 15 (☏091.844.9002), dispenses all tickets; there's also a ticket kiosk at the harbour, open just before sailings.

Pharmacy Piazza Umberto I 30 ☏091.844.9382 (Mon–Sat 8.30–1pm & 5–8.30pm). Closed Wed afternoon Nov–April.

Post office Largo Ameria off the main piazza (Mon–Fri 8am–1pm, Sat 8am–12.30pm).

Diving on Ústica

The island is well set up for divers, and facilities include a decompression chamber, though medical facilities are limited to the pharmacy and the *guardia médica*. The waters are protected by a natural marine reserve, divided into several zones with restrictions on where you can swim, dive and fish. **Profondo Blu** (☏091.844.9609 or 349.672.6529, ☏www.ustica-diving.it), run by an Italo-Belgian couple, is the island's most experienced and experienced dive-operator, arranging diving courses, holidays and accommodation in their own self-contained resort with apartments outside town. It is open from May till the end of October, with prices from €400–620 per week for an apartment sleeping two, depending on the season. Meals are available (breakfast €5; dinner €35). There are various diving packages – a single dive costs €40; a ten-dive package €330 and a six-day open water diver PADI course €360.

Travel details

Trains

Palermo to: Agrigento (12 daily Mon–Sat, 7 daily Sun; 2hr 15min); Bagheria (2–3 hourly; 10min); Caltanissetta (6 daily Mon–Sat, 2 daily Sun; 2hr); Capaci (hourly; 40min); Carini (hourly; 45min); Castellammare del Golfo (hourly; 1hr 30min); Castelvetrano via Álcamo (5–6 daily; 2hr 25min); Catania (3 daily Mon–Sat, 1 daily Sun; 3hr 45min); Cefalú (hourly; 45min–1hr); Enna via Caltanissetta (3 daily; 2hr 10min–3hr 15min); Isola delle Fémmine (hourly; 30–45min); Marsala via Trápani (5–6 daily; 3hr–3hr 45min); Mazara del Vallo via Álcamo (6 daily; 3hr); Milazzo (13 daily; 2hr 30min–3hr); Messina (13 daily; 3–4hr); Soluto (1–2 hourly; 15min); Términi Imerese (2–3 hourly; 25–40min); Trápani (5 daily; 2hr 15min–3hr 45min).

Buses

Palermo to: Agrigento (5 daily; 2hr 30min); Bagheria (1–2 hourly Mon–Sat; 1hr 15min); Cáccamo (4 daily Mon–Sat; 1hr); Caltagirone (1 daily except Sat; 3hr); Caltanissetta (7–10 daily Mon–Sat, 5 daily Sun; 1hr 40min); Capaci (Mon–Sat 1–2 hourly; 1hr); Carini (Mon–Sat 1–2 hourly; 1hr–1hr 30min); Castelbuono (5 daily Mon–Sat, 1 daily Sun; 1hr 40min–2hr 30min); Castellammare del Golfo (6 daily Mon–Sat, 1–3 daily Sun; 50min); Catania (hourly; 2hr 40min); Cefalù (3 daily Mon–Sat, 1 daily Sun; 1hr); Corleone (hourly Mon–Sat; 1hr 30min); Enna (5–7 daily; 1hr 35min–1hr 50min); Gela (3–4 daily; 2hr 45min–3hr); Marsala (hourly; 2hr 30min); Messina (6 daily Mon–Sat; 2hr 45min); Piana degli Albanesi (6 daily Mon–Sat; 1hr); Piazza Armerina (3–6 daily Mon–Sat, 4 daily Sun; 2hr–2hr 20min); San Martino delle Scale (2 daily Mon–Sat; 30min); San Vito Lo Capo (2–4 daily Mon–Sat, 1–3 daily Sun; 2–3hr); Siracusa (3 daily Mon–Sat, 2 daily Sun; 3hr 15min); Términi Imerese (6 daily Mon–Sat; 40min); Trápani (1–2 hourly Mon–Sat, 11 daily Sun; 2hr).

Ferries

Palermo to: Cágliari (1 weekly; 14hr 30min); Civitavecchia (13 weekly; 12–13hr); Genoa (5–7 weekly; 20hr); Livorno (3 weekly; 17hr); Naples (2–3 daily; 10hr 30min); Salerno (1–2 weekly; 9hr); Tunis (1–2 weekly; 10–11hr); Ústica (1 daily; 2hr 30min).

Hydrofoils

Palermo to: Aeolian Islands (June to mid-Sept 2 daily; 2hr–5hr 45min); Cefalù (June to mid-Sept 1 daily; 1hr 10min); Ústica (June–Sept 2–3 daily; Oct–May 1–2 daily; 1hr 15min).
Ústica to: Favignana (June–Sept 3–4 weekly; 2hr); Lévanzo (June–Sept 3–4 weekly; 2hr 25min); Naples (June–Sept 3 weekly; 4hr); Palermo (June–Sept 2–3 daily; Oct–May 1–2 daily; 1hr 15min); Trápani (June–Sept 3–4 weekly; 2hr 50min).

Cefalù and the Monti Madonie

CHAPTER 2 # Highlights

✳ **Duomo mosaics, Cefalù** The Byzantine mosaics in Cefalù's cathedral are one of the glories of Sicily. See p.99

✳ **Castello at Cáccamo** Perched high on a spit of land, this impressive Norman castle can be seen for miles. See p.103

✳ **Santo Stéfano di Camastra** A ceramics town with a beach, Santo Stéfano is a resort with a difference. See p.105

✳ **Fiumara d'Arte** Follow the dramatic sculpture trail from Castel di Tusa through the nearby hills and valleys. See p.105

✳ **Castelbuono** The charming old centre of Castelbuono is the northern gateway to the peaks and valleys of the Monti Madonie. See p.108

✳ **Petralia Sottana** Pretty mountain town at the heart of the Parco Regionale delle Madonie. See p.111

▲ The Norman castle at Cáccamo

2

Cefalù and the Monti Madonie

Visitors to Palermo don't have to travel very far for good beaches and mountain scenery, and at the major holiday resort of **Cefalù** – an hour east of the capital – there's easy access to both. It's a well-known package holiday destination, but the town has more about it than sea and sand, principally a stupendous medieval cathedral that contains some of the best mosaic-work on the whole island. A short way inland, the attractive small town of **Castelbuono** is backed by the **Monti Madonie**, a high mountain range (now a regional park) that's easy to explore by car – even in just a day-trip from the coast you'll be able to circle the high mountain passes between Castelbuono and the twin towns of **Petralia Soprana** and **Petralia Sottana**. Back on the coast, Cefalù can also serve as the base for day-trips, by road or rail. West, en route to Palermo, lies the archeological site

Festivals

February/March
Carnevale celebrated in **Cefalù** with three days of events, including a costumed children's procession on the last day.

Easter
Holy Week On the Thursday and Friday, bizarre happenings at **San Fratello**, the Festa dei Giudei, with processions and devils' costumes.

September
A medieval procession, La Castellana, in **Cáccamo**, composed of five hundred characters representing all the notables in the town's history from the eleventh to the nineteenth centuries.
7–8 Procession with Madonna delle Luci and her guardians at **Mistretta**.
8 Pilgrimage at **Gibilmanna**, south of Cefalù.

October
Horse fair in **San Fratello**.

November
Historical fair held in **Sant'Agata di Militello**.

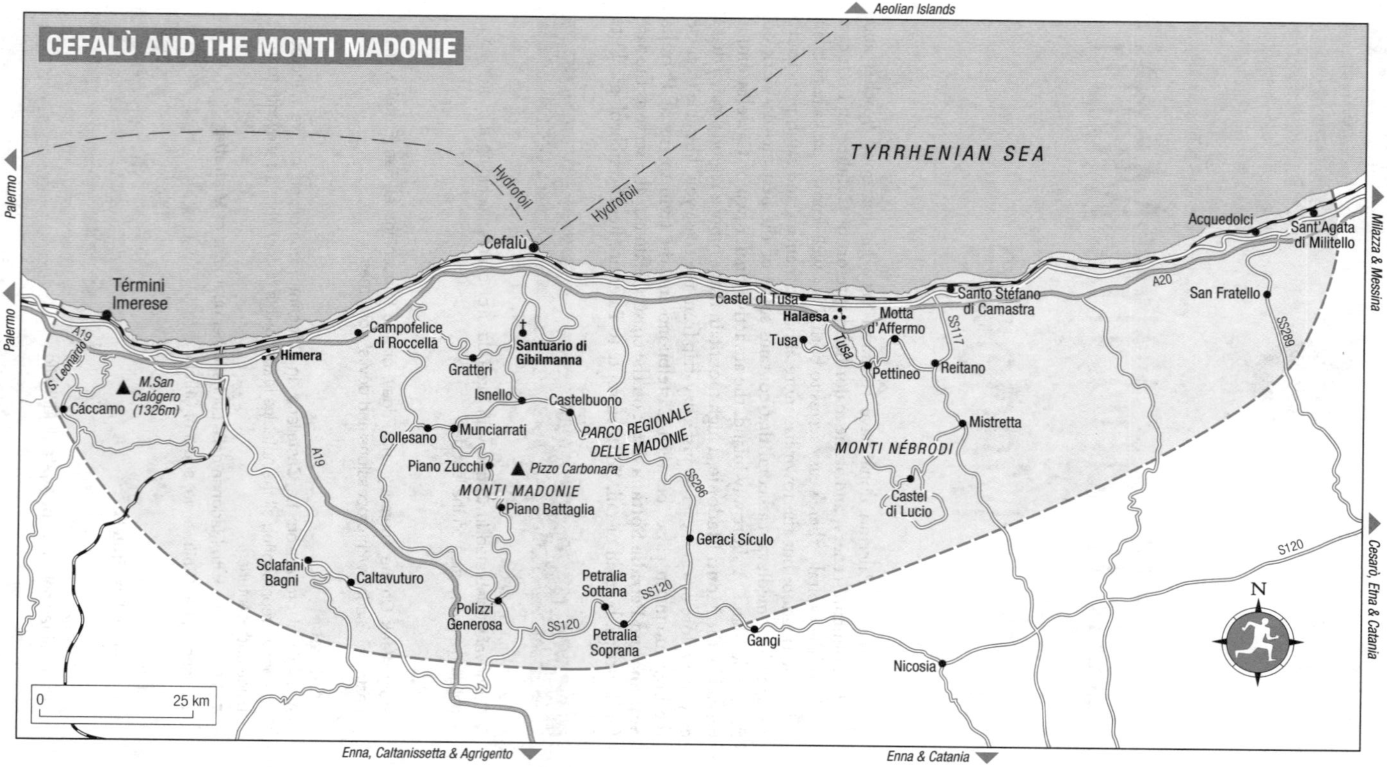

CEFALÙ AND THE MONTI MADONIE

Milazza & Messina

Cesarò, Etna & Catania

Aeolian Islands

TYRRHENIAN SEA

Sant'Agata di Militello

Acquedolci

San Fratello

SS289

A20

SS117

Santo Stefano di Camastra

Motta d'Affermo

Pettineo

Reitano

Mistretta

Castel di Lucio

MONTI NÉBRODI

Tusa

Halaesa

Castel di Tusa

Nicosia

Enna & Catania

Hydrofoil

Hydrofoil

Cefalù

Santuario di Gibilmanna

Castelbuono

PARCO REGIONALE DELLE MADONIE

Pizzo Carbonara

Geraci Siculo

Gangi

SS286

Isnello

Munciarrati

Piano Zucchi

MONTI MADONIE

Piano Battaglia

Petralia Sottana

Petralia Soprana

SS120

SS120

Gratteri

Collesano

Polizzi Generosa

Campofelice di Roccella

Caltavuturo

Himera

A19

Sclafani Bagni

Enna, Caltanissetta & Agrigento

Términi Imerese

M. San Calógero (1326m)

Cáccamo

SS120

Palermo

Palermo

0   25 km

of Greek **Himera**, the old spa town of **Términi Imerese** and the blustery hill-top stronghold of **Cáccamo**, which features the best-preserved of Sicily's Norman castles. To the east (towards Messina), it's the Tyrrhenian coast that holds sway, at its best an eye-catching succession of cliff and cove, sandy strips and citrus groves, though all too often eclipsed by monotonous tourist developments. Still, in the cheery ceramics town of **Santo Stéfano di Camastra** there's one of the coast's nicest small resorts, while from **Castel di Tusa** you can trace the mammoth sculptures of the fascinating **Fiumara d'Arte** trail.

A good train service makes it easy to see any of the coastal destinations from Cefalù, and buses link to some inland destinations, though a car is definitely required if you're intent on seeing much of the mountains. Driving can be slow on the SS113 coastal road, along which traffic sometimes files at a snail's pace – it's much faster on the A20 autostrada (a toll-road), which features some outstanding feats of road-engineering in the form of long tunnels and soaring viaducts. It's also worth knowing that Ústica Lines operates a useful summer hydrofoil service between Palermo, Cefalù and the Aeolian Islands.

Cefalù

The finest resort on the long Tyrrhenian coast between Palermo and Messina is **CEFALÙ**, 70km from the capital, with a long sandy beach and a dramatic setting under the fearsome crag known as La Rocca. Roger II founded a mighty cathedral here in 1131 and his mosaic-filled church still dominates the skyline: the great twin towers rear up above the flat roofs of the medieval quarter, with the whole structure framed by the looming cliff behind. The shady tangle of old streets and gift shops, and nearby beach and promenade, are certainly touristy but also retain a real charm. Cefalù, in fact, is nowhere near as developed as Sicily's other main package resort, Taormina. It's busy in July and August, but never overwhelmingly so, and there's a lot to be said for making the town your base. Palermo is less than an hour away by train, and there are smaller beaches and resorts on the rail line to the east, while it's an easy drive into the Monti Madonie to the south.

Arrival and information

The **train station** is south of the centre, ten minutes' walk from the main old-town street, Corso Ruggiero; **buses** pull into the square outside the station. It's residents-only parking in the old town and the best advice is to park on the seafront, either in the metered places along the promenade (€1 per hour, free between midnight and 8am) or in the patrolled **car park** (€6 for 12hr), just after the *Riva del Sole* hotel beyond Via Archimede. The summer Ústica Line **hydrofoil** service to and from Palermo and the Aeolian Islands operates from the port east of town, a twenty-minute walk away around the headland; the boat currently leaves Cefalù for the Aeolians at 8.15am, or for Palermo at 8.10pm.

There's a **tourist office** at Corso Ruggiero 77 (daily 8am–8pm, winter until 7pm; ☎0921.421.050), where you can pick up a free town map and an accommodation list, as well as information about summer concerts, theatre performances and other events. The **websites** ⓦwww.cefaluonline.com and www.cefalu.it are also useful for accommodation, restaurants and local services. The park office for the Monti Madonie, the **Ente Parco delle Madonie**, Corso Ruggiero 116 (Mon–Sat 8am–8pm, reduced hours in winter; ☎0921.923.270, ⓦwww.parco dellemadonie.it), has some information about the mountains in English, and a map of walking routes.

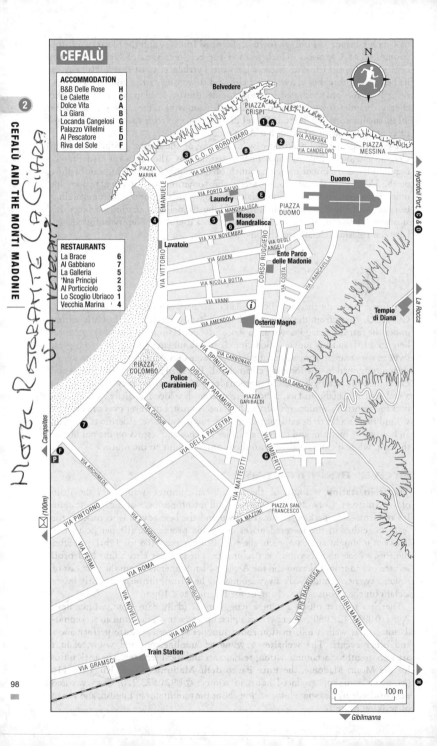

CEFALÙ

ACCOMMODATION
B&B Delle Rose	H
Le Calette	C
Dolce Vita	A
La Giara	B
Locanda Cangelosi	G
Palazzo Villelmi	E
Al Pescatore	D
Riva del Sole	F

RESTAURANTS
La Brace	6
Al Gabbiano	7
La Galleria	5
'Nna Principi	2
Al Porticciolo	3
Lo Scoglio Ubriaco	1
Vecchia Marina	4

Belvedere

PIAZZA CRISPI

VIA PORPORA
VIA CANDELORO
PIAZZA MESSINA

VIA C.O. DI BORDONARO
VIA VETERANI

PIAZZA MARINA

Duomo
PIAZZA DUOMO

VIA PORTO SALVO
Laundry
VIA MANDRALISCA
Museo Mandralisca

VIA DEGLI ANGELI
VIA COSTA
VIA TRANCAVILLA

Hydrofoil Port. C & D

La Rocca

VIA XXV NOVEMBRE
Lavatoio

Ente Parco delle Madonie

CORSO RUGGIERO

VIA VITTORIO EMANUELE

VIA GIOENI

VIA NICOLA BOTTA

VIA VANNI

Tempio di Diana

VIA AMENDOLA

Osterio Magno

VICOLO SARACENI

VIA CARBONARI

PIAZZA COLOMBO

VIA SPINUZZA

DISCESA PARAMURO

Police (Carabinieri)

PIAZZA GARIBALDI

VIA CAVOUR

VIA DELLA PALESTRA

VIA UMBERTO I

Campsites

VIA ARCHIMEDE

VIA MATTEOTTI

PIAZZA SAN FRANCESCO

VIA MAZZINI

(100m)

VIA PINTORNO

VIA S. PASQUALE

VIA FERMI

VIA ROMA

VIA NOVELLI

VIA GIGLIO

VIA MORO

VIA PIETRAGROSSA

VIA GIBILMANNA

Train Station

VIA GRAMSCI

0   100 m

Gibilmanna

CEFALÙ AND THE MONTI MADONIE

Accommodation

Most of the resort **hotels** are out of the centre, by the beaches and bays to either side of town. There are, however, lots of central **B&Bs** and rooms places, though vacancies can be hard to find in August (when prices everywhere double) and some are on pretty noisy streets with restaurants and bars below. Self-catering **apartments** are widely available too, though again summer is very busy and there's usually a minimum stay of three or even seven nights. Try the website Ⓦ www .casevacanzecefalu.it or ask at the tourist office. The local **campsites** are 4km west of town at Contrada Ogliastrello, the large, resort-style *Costa Ponente* (Ⓦ www .campeggio-sicilia.it) and smaller, nicer *Camping San Filippo* (Ⓦ www.campingsan filippo.com).

B&B Delle Rose Via Gibilmanna ☎0921.421.885, Ⓦ www.dellerosebb.it. Charming B&B that has its own parking, and some rooms with views and spacious terraces (worth the supplement). Breakfast includes cheese and salami as well as rolls and jam. The main drawback is its distance from the centre, a 15–20min walk along the continuation of Via Umberto I (up the Gibilmanna road, heading out of town). ❷

Le Calette Via Vincenzo Cavallaro 12, Contrada Caldura ☎0921.424.144, Ⓦ www.lecalette.it. On the eastern side of the headland, overlooking the hydrofoil port, this four-star villa-style hotel is beautifully sited above a little cove, and has its own pool, restaurant and gardens. All rooms face the sea and those on the second floor have large balconies. Half board is from €130 per person in August, but B&B at other times is more reasonable and online rates are best. ❸

Dolce Vita Via C.O. Bordonaro 8 ☎0921.923.151, Ⓦ www.dolcevitabb.it. The top choice for B&B – right in the heart of the old town but with the sea on one side, so rooms with a view are nice and peaceful. Two face the street, three the sea, and all are en suite and spacious (sleeping up to four), with high ceilings and restored tile floors. Best of all is the glorious terrace, a perfect haven with uninterrupted sea views, while the cheery owner can arrange boat trips, airport transfers, etc. Breakfast is taken in a bar in the cathedral piazza. Usually closed two months between Nov and Feb. ❷, Aug ❸

La Giara Via Veterani 40 ☎0921.421.562, Ⓦ www.hotel-lagiara.it. The three-star *La Giara* is very central, on an old-town street close to the Duomo, and has decent rooms and a top-floor terrace with town and ocean views. Expect some noise from street-facing rooms. ❷

Locanda Cangelosi Via Umberto I 26 ☎0921.421.591, Ⓦ www.locandacangelosi.it. The cheapest place in town is this pension with pretty basic facilities. There are four rooms – two with balconies overlooking the busy street – with a shared bathroom, but the better option is one of the four small self-catering apartments available in a quieter position. No credit cards. ❶

Palazzo Villelmi Corso Ruggiero 149 ☎0921.923.057 or 339.852.0161, Ⓔ info@villelmi.com. Stylish, elegant B&B in a beautifully restored old *palazzo* on the main street, very near the Duomo. High painted ceilings give a hint of the its former grandeur, and a rooftop breakfast terrace looks right on to the cathedral. ❷, Aug ❸

Al Pescatore Località Caldura ☎0921.421.572, Ⓦ www.hotelalpescatore.it. Around the headland, near the port, this family-run hotel is pretty good value for most of the year, with simply furnished rooms with tile floors offering sea or mountain views. There's no restaurant, though, and it's a fair walk into town. ❸

Riva del Sole Lungomare G. Giardina ☎0921.421.230, Ⓦ www.rivadelsole.com. The most central seaside hotel has rooms overlooking the promenade and beach, and it's very close to the parking area. As long as you don't mind the summer noise from the bars and restaurants, it's a great location – it's just steps from the sand and has its own chic terrace-café. Half board in August is around €100 per person. ❹

The Town

The sandy **beach** is one of Sicily's best, jam-packed in summer, with sheltered swimming in clear waters and marvellous views from the lungomare (promenade) over the red roofs of the town. This is understandably the focus of summer visits, but central to the town's historic existence is the majestic **Duomo** (daily: summer 8am–7pm; closes 5.30pm in winter), set back in a pretty square under the cliffs.

Apocryphally, it was built in gratitude by Roger II, who found refuge at Cefalù's safe beach in a violent storm, though it's more likely that the cathedral owed its foundation to his power struggle with Pope Innocent II. Shortly after his coronation in 1130, Roger had allied instead with Anacletus, the anti-pope, whose support enhanced the new king's prestige. Roger's cathedral benefited from Anacletus's readily granted exemptions and privileges, and it is at once rich and showy, from the massive, fortress-like exterior to the earliest and best preserved of all Sicilian church **mosaics**. With all the former Baroque decoration finally stripped away after years of "restoration", the impact of the mosaics is profound. Dating from 1148 (forty years older than those at Monreale), they are thoroughly Byzantine in concept and follow a familiar pattern: Christ Pantocrator, right hand outstretched in benediction, open Bible in the left, dominates the central apse; underneath is the Madonna flanked by archangels; then the twelve Apostles, in two rows of six.

The cathedral is very much the cultural highlight in town, though just down the road, at Via Mandralisca 13, the **Museo Mandralisca** (daily 9am–1pm & 3–7pm, July & Aug daily 9am–7pm; €5) houses a small collection of quality objects. On the first floor you'll find its most famous exhibit, the wry and inscrutable *Portrait of an Unknown Man* by the fifteenth-century Sicilian master **Antonello da Messina**. Look out, too, for the quirky Greek *krater* (fourth century BC) showing a robed tuna-fish salesman, knife in hand, disputing the price of his fish.

Otherwise, the old-town streets themselves are the best thing about Cefalù – a cobbled, tangibly Arabic jumble of alleys with rows of washing stretched between houses, hidden arches and flower-filled courtyards. The main Corso Ruggiero is lined with attractive buildings in various stages of well-tended decay. The **Osterio Magno**, on the corner of Via Amendola and the Corso, is the surviving part of a medieval palace, now regularly used for art exhibitions, while the **lavatoio** is a relic of the Saracen occupation – a wash-house at the bottom of a curving staircase, with cold water pouring forth into the basins. At the head of the Corso, a **belvedere** gives onto the old Greek walls of Cefalù, largely incorporated into the later sixteenth-century defensive bastion. A modern path has been cut into the rocks below, running in the direction of the hydrofoil port, and you can clamber down here to explore the rock pools and sunbathe on the slabs. Further around the headland, at the **port**, is a bay full of fishing and leisure boats, and more strange rock stacks to investigate.

Towering above cathedral and town is the mountain of **La Rocca**; access is from the steps at the side of the Banco di Sicilia in Piazza Garibaldi. A steep twenty-minute climb takes you to the so-called **Tempio di Diana**, a megalithic structure adapted in the fifth century BC by the addition of classical doorways, their lintels still in place. A path continues upwards, right around the crag, through pinewoods and wild fennel, dipping in and out of a surviving stretch of medieval wall to the sketchy fortifications at the very top. You can then cut down to the temple and rejoin the path back into town, the whole walk taking a little over an hour – take water with you, as it's a strenuous climb.

Eating and drinking

There are dozens of **restaurants** in town, though many trade on their sea view and are overpriced. Menus are broadly similar – fish and seafood, of course, is the local highlight – and the best deals are often in the form of set menus for €20–30 a head. The **cafés** in Piazza del Duomo are a nice place to start the day, with breakfast in front of the cathedral. For sunset drinks and views, there's a line of restaurants, **bars** and *gelaterie* along the prom by the beach, including a little garden bar in Piazza Colombo, while the local *passeggiata* runs all the way up the main Corso to Piazza Garibaldi and its streetside bars and ice cream shops.

La Brace Via XXV Novembre 10 ☎0921.423.570. An attractive place to dine, to classical music in a room formed by three stone arches. Most of the pasta dishes (€6.50) are veggie-friendly, while mains (€11–14) like *involtini di melanzane* (stuffed aubergine rolls) and *spiedini di pesce spada* (swordfish kebabs) are recommended. Closed Mon, & mid-Dec to mid-Jan.

Al Gabbiano Lungomare G. Giardina ☎0921.421.495. Best of the seafront promenade restaurants, this place has a good *antipasto al buffet*, spicy *zuppa di cozze* and pizzas at lunch and dinner (pizzas €6–10, otherwise mains mostly €10–12). Closed Wed in winter.

🏃 La Galleria Via Mandralisca 23, also entrance on Via XXV Novembre ☎0921.420.211, ⓦwww.lagalleriacefalu.it. Billed as a "literary café", and incorporating courtyard bar, exhibition space and cultural centre, *La Galleria* is also a great place for classy, contemporary Sicilian cooking – think chic, white dining room and a menu featuring pasta with swordfish, lemon zest and wild fennel, and tuna sashimi on *caponata* (dishes €8–18). Closed Thurs.

🏃 'Nna Principi Corso Ruggiero 192 ☎0921.421.578. The best set menu deal in town gets you three courses for €15 in a rustic

family restaurant on the main street. Otherwise, dishes run €7–16, pizzas from €6, on a menu that's strong on fish (smoked swordfish to grilled bream) but also has steaks, rabbit, chicken and chops.

Al Porticciolo Via C.O. Bordonaro 66 ☎0921.921.981. Walk through the low-vaulted restaurant to their wonderful terrace at the back, built over the coastal rocks. There are no menu surprises, but the food's good (pizzas €7–11, otherwise dishes €10–20 or so), and a fixed-price menu offers seafood spaghetti and grilled swordfish for €25. There's another *Porticciolo* up the street at no. 90, though this branch doesn't serve pizzas. Closed Wed.

Lo Scoglio Ubriaco Via C.O. Bordonaro 2–4 ☎0921.423.370. The "Drunken Rock" is a slick, reliable restaurant with a sea-facing terrace. It's good for fish (mains up to €13.50), and also serves pizzas (€6–10) in the evening. Closed Tues Sept–June.

Vecchia Marina Via Vittorio Emanuele 73 ☎0921.420.388. If you're going to go for a seafood blowout this is where Italian families come, inspecting their meal first on the fish slab and in the tank. It's not cheap (pasta and starters €10–15, fish dishes €15–25, catch of the day by the kilo), though the €29 set menu isn't a bad deal. Closed Tues & Jan.

Listings

Bike and scooter rental Scooter for Rent, Via G. Matteotti 13 ☎0921.420.496 or 338.230.9008, ⓦwww.scooterforrent.it. Mountain bikes from €10 per day, scooters €25–35 per half-day, €35–50 per day.

Car rental Meditravel, Piazza Garibaldi 12 ☎0921.420.441, ⓦwww.meditravel.it; Siciltravel, Piazza Garibaldi 8 ☎0921.420.090, ⓦwww .siciltravel.it.

Hospital Contrada Pietrapollastra ☎0921.920.111.

Hydrofoils There's a ticket kiosk at the port, or you can buy tickets in town in advance from Agenzia Pietro Barbaro, Corso Ruggiero 82 ☎0921.421.595.

Laundry Lavanderia e Tintoria, Via Porto Salvo 21. Self-service wash from €5, or service wash and dry from €12.

Pharmacies Battáglia, Via Roma 13, ☎0921.421.789; Cirincione, Corso Ruggiero 144,

Shopping in Cefalù

If you're looking for more than *Godfather* T-shirts, Sicilian puppets or mass-produced cookbooks in Japanese and German, you need to dig a bit deeper in Cefalù's old town. For contemporary **ceramics** look in A Lumera (Corso Ruggiero 176), or browse the hand-painted **silk and cotton** in Celanie (Cortile Vazzana, bottom of Via Vittorio Emanuele). For **bric-a-brac**, antiques and junk there's the treasure trove that is Robinson (Via degli Angeli), while any number of flashy stores along Corso Ruggiero specialize in classy **jewellery** at very high prices. There's also a lot of serious **wine shops and enotecas**, like Cantina di Cicerone (Via Vittorio Emanuele 13), where tastings are often offered, while at the back of Vinum et Ambrosia (Corso Ruggiero 151) you can buy huge chunks of Madonie mountain **cheese**. Finally, it's worth buying sun cream or aspirin just to have a look at the beautifully carved cabinets inside the traditional Farmacia Cirincione (Corso Ruggiero 144).

0921.421.209 (both Mon–Fri 9am–1pm & 4.30–8.30pm). There's a rota system for evening and late-opening pharmacies posted in the window.
Police Carabinieri, Discesa Paramuro 0921.421.412.
Post office Via Vazzana 2 (between Via Roma and the seafront), Mon–Fri 8am–6.30pm, Sat 8am–12.30pm.

Taxis Taxi rank outside the train station at Piazza Stazione 0921.422.554.
Tours Agencies throughout town offer daily trips in season to all sorts of destinations, from Palermo to Etna. For boat excursions, call into SMIV, Corso Ruggiero 83 800.077.822, which offers daily trips along the coast (€30) or to the Aeolian Islands (€60–80).

Himera

Around 20km west of Cefalù, on the coast, stands the site of the ancient Greek city of **Himera** (Mon–Sat 9am–6.30pm, Sun 9am–1pm; €2), though the visible remains are few and it's probably one for dedicated stone-hunters only. It's around halfway on the drive between Cefalù and Términi Imerese – take the Buonfornello exit from the autostrada and keep a keen eye out for signs once you're on the SS113 coastal road.

Himera was the first Greek settlement on Sicily's northern coast, founded in 648 BC as an advance post against the Carthaginians, who controlled the west of the island. The town inevitably became a flashpoint, and in 480 BC the Carthaginian leader Hamilcar landed a huge force nearby. Pitted against the combined armies of Akragas (Agrigento), Gela and Syracuse, the invading force was demolished and Hamilcar himself perished – either assassinated by Greek spies before the battle, or killed when he threw himself onto the pyre afterwards, depending on whose version you read. The outcome of the battle marked a significant upheaval of the classical world – and, in the case of Sicily, a new balance of power, with the Greeks in the ascendant. But their glory was short-lived: in 409 BC Hamilcar's nephew, Hannibal, wreaked his revenge and razed the city to the ground, forcing the surviving citizens west to what is now Términi Imerese.

All that's left of the important Chalcidinian settlement that once stood here is the massive **Tempio della Vittoria**, erected to commemorate the defeat of the Carthaginians – indeed, the labour was carried out by the captured Carthaginians themselves. It's a conventional Doric construction, with six columns at the front and back, and fourteen at the sides. Despite the paucity of the remains, and the proximity of the road and rail line, the solitary ruin does have a powerful appeal. It's said to stand on the very site of the 480 BC battle, and after the victory some of the rich Carthaginian spoils were pinned up inside. The acropolis lay just inland, and, though excavations have uncovered a necropolis and some smaller temples, much work remains to be done at the site. There is a good **museum** (same hours and ticket), housing some of the items dug up at the site (others are in museums in Términi and Palermo), including a few of the striking lion's-head water-spouts that drained the temple's roof. One strangely moving display is of the grave of a married couple, the wife curled up next to her husband, her leg resting on his.

Términi Imerese

Around 35km west of Cefalù, **TÉRMINI IMERESE** is the last major town before the capital, Palermo. The coast on either side is largely industrial, but Términi has the magnificent backdrop of Monte Calógero (1326m) as some compensation and – once you've negotiated the congested streets – an airy upper town with a stunning belvedere that's worth the trip. Términi was originally settled by Greeks from Zancle (Messina) in the seventh century BC, and grew in importance as it absorbed the influx of survivors from the destroyed city of Himera, 13km to the east. Later, as Therma Himeraia, it flourished under the spa-loving Romans, and today the town is still famous in Italy for its waters, reputed to be good for arthritis and pasta-making.

Términi is split between its lower town, where the **train station** is located, and the far more scenic upper town. Turn right outside the station, walk past Piazza Crispi and down Corso Umberto e Margherita to Via Roma, the stepped street that climbs to the upper town (a good 15min walk). **Buses** arrive at and depart from immediately outside the station, though some also make a stop in the upper town. Drivers would do best to follow signs for "Museo" and "punto panoramico", as there's plenty of **parking** up by the belvedere.

At the centre of the upper town is a spacious piazza dominated by the monumental, pink-fronted, seventeenth-century **Duomo**. Inside are renowned sculptures by Marabitti, notably his *Madonna del Ponte* in the fourth chapel on the right. Opposite, down a lane to the side of the Palazzo Margherita, the excellent **Museo Cívico** (Tues–Sat 9am–1pm & 4–6.30pm, Sun 9am–1pm; free) has more art treasures, including work by Antonello Gagini, a fine sixteenth-century Flemish *Annunciation* and some grisly scenes of martyrdom. There are also coins, ceramics and other finds from Greek Himera, as well as the marble bust of an elegant second-century Roman matron.

Really, though, the views are the thing in Términi, so stroll beyond the Duomo along the palm-fringed **belvedere**, which offers an extensive panorama over town, mountain, port and sea. The promenade continues around the headland to the shady **Villa Palmieri** gardens, which shelter the remnants of a public building from the Roman era as well as the remains of an **Anfiteatro Romano** – this lies just up from the Porta Palermo, the former entrance to the city. Outdoor cafés and kiosks between cathedral, belvedere and gardens offer drinks, ice creams and a shady place to sit.

There's absolutely no need to stay the night in Términi, and no great choice of accommodation anyway, though in the lower town the landmark, four-star *Grand Hotel delle Terme* in Piazza delle Terme (℡091.811.3557, Ⓦwww.grandhoteldelleterme.it; ❹) might tempt some. It's a *fin de siècle* hotel, full of gilt and swagger, that houses Términi's **thermal spa**, where the waters issue forth at a constant 42°C – some of the original Roman structure is still visible in the stone and mosaic baths, and modern spa facilities are available for guests and day visitors.

Cáccamo

Randazzo buses from Términi's train station run regularly to the small town of **CÁCCAMO**, 10km to the south and set amid green hills. It's worth visiting chiefly for its remarkable **castello** (daily 9.30am–1pm & 3–8pm; €2), a chalk-white array of towers and battlements dominating the town and commanding the heights above the deep San Leonardo river valley. Built originally in the twelfth century, the castle has over 130 rooms, though only a fraction are open to the public – there's usually a multilingual guide on hand, able to churn out colourful background stories for a few euros. The highlight is the grand Sala della Congiura, where the barons' plot against William I ("the Bad") was hatched in 1160; it has a fine painted wooden ceiling and walls festooned with arms. Other rooms hold more weapons, costumes, coats of arms and reproductions of period furniture, and a terrace allows you to savour the glorious views.

Cáccamo itself is not much more than an overgrown village, disturbed only by the weight of traffic along the one main street, Corso Umberto I. In Piazza del Duomo, behind the castle crag, sits the **Chiesa Madre**, with reliefs around the sacristy door attributed to Francesco Laurana, the Renaissance sculptor who left his mark all over the region, particularly in Palermo. Look out, too, for the seventeenth-century tablet depicting St George and the Dragon over the main portal. To the right of the Chiesa Madre as you enter the piazza, the **Chiesa dell'Anime del Purgatorio** (erratic hours) is more compelling, specifically its catacombs, reached down crumbling steps – fully clothed and collapsing bodies lie in niches in the walls, topped by a row of white skulls, the remains of the town's nobility and clergy who made their last journey here between the seventeenth and mid-nineteenth centuries. If the church is closed, ask around for the custodian, who expects a tip for letting you in (though you can get a glimpse of the niches and skulls by peering through the grate beneath the front entrance).

For a **meal** right by the castle, there's the medieval-looking *A Castellana* (T091.814.8667; dishes from €6–8; closed Mon), a pizzeria-*ristorante* housed in its old grain store, with a long list of grilled meats and pizzas.

Castel di Tusa and around

Some 25km east of Cefalù, the coastal village of **CASTEL DI TUSA** features the remnants of a defensive castle and some good rocky beaches. In recent years, however, the place has become rather better known for its modern art, thanks to the efforts of **Antonio Presti** (born in Messina in 1957), who in the late 1980s and early 1990s invited artists from around the world to create a group of large-scale sculptures along the river bed (*fiumara*) and valley of the Tusa river, which flows down from the Nébrodi mountains just east of the village. After a protracted legal battle with the authorities, the sculptures were formally inaugurated as the **Fiumara d'Arte** sculpture park in 2006. You can pick up a brochure and map from Presti's other venture, the equally arresting "**art hotel**" in Castel di Tusa, which itself has become something of a tourist attraction. At the 🕮 *L'Atelier Sul Mare*, just metres from the sea on Via Cesare Battisti (T0921.334.295, Wwww .ateliersulmare.com; ❹, art rooms ❺), many of the rooms have been given the designer-art treatment by individual artists: one is adorned with Arabic and Italian poetry and sports a mammoth window looking onto the sea, with a shower that works like a car wash, while another is bathed in a red glow at night. Other rooms are more conventionally styled, though still with original artworks and furnishings. Non-residents, meanwhile, can be shown around the art rooms on guided tours (daily at noon, €5, call to check).

Halaesa

Just 3km up the road from Castel di Tusa, on the way to the village of Tusa, are the sparse ruins of **Halaesa** (daily 9am–1hr before sunset; €2), a fifth-century BC Sikel settlement that enjoyed some success under Rome. The name derives from the Greek *alaomal*, meaning to wander aimlessly, and refers to the original settlers here, the peripatetic Alesini, who had tried settling just about everywhere else. You can make out the chequered layout of the streets, remains of the agora, and – at the highest point – foundations of two third-century BC temples, with lofty views down over the Tusa valley.

A tour of the Fiumara d'Arte

All the structures and sculptures along the **Fiumara d'Arte** lie south of Castel di Tusa, and seeing the lot entails a 50km round trip by car through some magnificent countryside. Follow the signposts and you can't go far wrong, starting at the turn off the SS113 for Pettineo, a couple of kilometres east of Castel di Tusa (Santo Stéfano/Messina direction). One of the earliest commissions – *La Materia Poteva Non Esserci*, resembling two giant hands joined in prayer – comes almost immediately into view, standing right under the motorway viaduct. It's 6km further up the valley to **Pettineo** itself, a gorgeous little village with the shards of a ruined castle at its highest point and a couple of bars in the old centre for drinks. More signs then direct you another 6km up the nearby mountain to the precariously located village of **Motta d'Affermo** for *Energia Mediterranea* – a graceful concrete curving wave in mottled blue astride a dusty hilltop. Beyond lies the dramatic cliff-top pyramid that is *38° Parallelo* (also known as *La Piramide*), after which you backtrack to Pettineo. There's a further cluster of works a twisting 10km south of Pettineo, in the environs of the striking hilltop hamlet of **Castel di Lucio**, from where you can either return the way you came, back to the coast, or continue on to Mistretta, which offers an alternative way back down to Santo Stéfano di Camastra (or on over the mountains to Nicosia).

Santo Stéfano di Camastra

Cefalù aside, quite the nicest stop along the Tyrrhenian coast is **SANTO STÉFANO DI CAMASTRA**, reached on frequent trains or a quick drive along the SS113. It's actually much the better for being split in two – beach and harbour below (where the train station is) and town high above, the latter forming a handsome old grid on a panoramic shelf of land. A steep cobbled path connects the two. Santo Stéfano is renowned for its colourful ceramic work and the road through town is lined with shops selling platters, plates, cups, jugs, statues, household goods and decorative pottery. Off the main road, the old town is kept largely free of traffic and there's a small public garden, a belvedere with sea views and a pedestrianized main street, Via Vittorio Emanuele, of shops, cafés, boutiques and grocery stores. It's touristy certainly, but all very charming, while in the signposted **Museo della Ceramica** (Tues–Sun 9am–1pm & 4–8pm; free), in the handsome Palazzo Trabia, you can admire the best historic examples of the local pottery.

    Accommodation is relatively easy to find, except perhaps in August. The best central option is the signposted ☘ *Girasole*, a B&B at Via Antonio Garofalo 19 (☎0921.339.586 or 347.131.8900, ⓦwww.girasole.me.it; ❷), with big, airy, majolica-tiled en-suite rooms; turn up Via Dante opposite the main T-junction in town (where all the signposts are) and it's two blocks up, on the right (you can park outside). The **cafés** in town opposite the gardens liven up on summer nights, while you'll easily find *Fantasy*, on Via Vittorio Emanuele 32 (☎0921.339.672), on the main pedestrianized street – in summer, at least, it's a typically raucous terrace **pizzeria-restaurant** for the holiday crowd, but the food is excellent, pasta to pizzas, and nothing costs more than €9. Across the street from here, and a few metres down Via Garibaldi (signposted), *Trattoria da Giannino* (☎0921.331.748) is also recommended; there are only a few outdoor tables, but it's a good-value (*primi* from €7, *secondi* from €10) family restaurant that's a nice place for fish.

The Monti Nébrodi

The **Monti Nébrodi** – a sparsely populated expanse of high forest and rocky peaks – covers a huge wedge of land between Santo Stéfano di Camastra and Mistretta in the west and Randazzo and the Etna foothills in the east. Much of the mountain range is protected as the **Parco Naturale dei Nébrodi** (the largest such area in Sicily), though it's difficult to get a good impression of the whole by car since few roads connect the scattered villages within the park and even the towns on the periphery are minor attractions for the most part. However, adventurous hikers can follow any number of trails through the hills and valleys – there are some detailed on the useful park website, ⓦwww.parcodeinebrodi.it – while there is a road up to the highest peak, **Monte Soro** (1847m), between San Fratello and Cesarò (SS289), from which extensive views reach to the Aeolian Islands to the north and Etna to the southeast. There's plenty more park information on the website (including in English), and there are also **visitor centres** in Sant'Agata di Militello (☏0941.702.524), Santo Stéfano di Camastra (☏0921.331.199), Cesarò (☏095.773.2061), Randazzo (☏095.799.1611) and several of the mountain villages. Most visitor centres are open weekday mornings only, and are only intermittently useful – you should be able to pick up maps, accommodation details and walking itineraries, but English-speaking assistance is rare and there's not much more help for hikers than what can be gleaned from the printed information. The best single visit is probably to the **Palazzo Zito**, the official headquarters in Sant'Agata di Militello (Mon–Sat 9am–1pm & 3.30–7.30pm, Sun 9am–1pm & 4–7.30pm), which contains a museum covering the park's social and natural history and heritage.

Mistretta

From Santo Stéfano, a high viaduct flies off 16km inland to one of the biggest of the nearby hill villages, **MISTRETTA** – there are several daily buses up here as well. The handsome old centre of eighteenth- and nineteenth-century buildings and cobbled alleys is largely unspoiled by modern construction: wrought-iron balconies and flower-boxes overlook the long main street, the seventeenth-century cathedral has the hoary look of a medieval monument, while the population is largely composed of brown-suited pensioners milling around their veterans' associations. There's not much else to it, save some old-fashioned barbers' shops, the public gardens, and castle ruins atop a small hill, but it makes a good side trip from the coast. The *Gran Bar*, halfway up the main Corso at Via Libertà 164, has a mighty doorway flanked by giant sculpted figures – an old-fashioned place perfectly in keeping with Mistretta's prevailing sepia tone. Spending the night here would be equally eccentric, but you might be tempted by the *Agriturismo Santa Sofia*, Via Nazionale 1 (☏0921.383.032 or 338.125.8747, ⓦwww.agriturismo santasofia.it; ❷) – just 200m from the centre down the Nicosia road – which offers robust country furnishings, extensive grounds and stupendous views. In any case, its restaurant is a find, offering a good range of *antipasti*, hearty pastas and traditional mountain dishes (a set lunch or dinner costs €22).

Sant'Agata di Militello

The next reasonable stop on the coast is **SANT'AGATA DI MILITELLO**, 28km east of Santo Stéfano, a small Tyrrhenian resort that's moribund for most of the year. In truth, it can hardly be called attractive, though the very long pebbled beach and calm sea is popular with holidaying Italian families who pack the town's apartments for a few weeks each summer. There's a fishing harbour at one end, a palm-studded promenade, and a gridded town centre set back up the hillside, while a restored castle speaks of more important times. Best bet for drivers is to follow the "porto" signs and drive in along the seafront, where there's plenty of free parking. The only **restaurant** with an actual ocean view is *Asteria* (ⓣ327.044.9308) – try their *pennette ai gamberi e pistacchio*, a deliciously creamy shrimp and nut pasta (€7), or grilled fish for €10–15, plus pizzas lunch and dinner, under a shady canopy with sea and port views.

There are hourly buses along the coast from Santo Stéfano to Sant'Agata, and it's also a frequent stop on the coast train line. Beyond Sant'Agata, road and rail are bound for Capo d'Orlando, Milazzo and Messina, all covered in Chapter 4.

Parco Regionale delle Madonie

The Madonie mountain range and valleys south of Cefalù fall within the limits of one of Sicily's most accessible regional parks, the **Parco Regionale delle Madonie** (official site ⓦwww.parcodellemadonie.it, also ⓦwww.madonie.it). It's an area of beech and pinewoods, flower-filled upland plains, craggy rocks, high passes and soaring peaks (including the highest mountains in Sicily after Etna). Villages and towns are few and far between, but a couple of places in particular make good bases for tours and walks, while several remote resort hotels and *rifugi* offer a real mountain escape. There's a minor ski scene in winter, though not one for which you'd travel to Sicily.

Northern gateway to the Madonie park (pronounced Mad-on-*ee*-eh) is the attractive town of **Castelbuono**, 20km southeast of Cefalù, while right across the mountains on the south side is the smaller settlement of **Petralia Soprana**. There is a bus from Cefalù to Castelbuono, which would show you something of the region, but realistically you'll need a car to get around, particularly as accommodation outside the towns is extremely limited and fairly remote. A good **driving route** runs from Castelbuono to Geraci Siculo and on to Petralia Soprana, before twisting back across the mountains to the ski and hiking area of Piano Battàglia and round again to Castelbuono. You could do this in a day (about a 90km, 3hr, drive), but spending at least one night in the mountains would give you time for a walk, a country picnic or two and endless stunning views.

Devils in the hills

Fifteen kilometres up in the hills from Sant'Agata, the large village of **San Fratello** was once populated by a Lombard colony, introduced to Sicily by Roger II's queen, Adelaide di Monferrato. On the Thursday and Friday of Holy Week, before Easter, the town puts on the **Festa dei Giudei** (Feast of the Jews) – a unique carnival-type celebration when locals dress up in red devils' costumes, complete with black tongues and horses' tails (a reminder of their traditional trade of horse-raising), to the cacophonic accompaniment of trumpets, bells and drums. Needless to say, the ecclesiastical authorities take a dim view of these proceedings, but have to make do with having the Easter Sunday church congregations in suitably contrite and sober mood. For a panoramic picnic spot, head for the Norman church of **Santi Alfio, Filadelfio e Cirino**, isolated on top of a hill outside the village (follow the rough track from the cemetery). The church is dedicated to three brothers horribly martyred by the Romans: the first had his tongue torn out, the second was burnt alive, and the third hurled into a pot of boiling tar. Enjoy your picnic.

There's useful **information** on the official park website (though largely in Italian), plus park information offices in Cefalù, Castelbuono and Petralia Soprana, and a network of waymarked **hiking paths**. However, it's not as straightforward as it might be to go walking in the mountains – you'll be lucky to get any first-hand advice (or English-speaking assistance) in the information offices, while the only available walking **map** (*Carta dei Sentieri e del paesaggio*; 1:50,000), although almost insanely informative, is not of a good enough scale to route-find. There are also some other "geological pathway" route guides, translated loosely into English, for out-of-the-way places like Caltavuturo and Sclafani Bagni – they aren't as useful as they seem and require a high degree of tolerance for getting lost. Some local **tour operators** organize hikes, pony treks and other mountain activities, which might be your best bet for getting to grips with the Madonie – check posters and brochures in local information offices.

Castelbuono

CASTELBUONO – self-styled "capital" of the Monti Madonie – doesn't actually feel much like a mountain town at all, but it is a pretty place that makes a good day-trip from Cefalù, even if you plan to go no further and higher into the Madonie park. It owes its origins to the Ventimiglia family, who made the town something of a thriving cultural centre in the fifteenth century, and their seat was the squat **Castello Ventimiglia** that's visible from miles around. Once restoration works are complete, it should be open again for visits (highlights include a small stuccoed chapel from the Serpotta workshop), but it's a useful landmark in any case. From the restored gateway and enclosed castle piazza, a charming tree-lined street runs down to central Piazza Margherita, where terrace cafés overlook the fourteenth-century **Matrice Vecchia** (daily 11am–1pm & 5–7pm), fronted by a pretty loggia. Inside, you pay fifty cents to descend well-worn steps into the crypt to view a series of remarkably well-preserved sixteenth-century frescoes of the *Passion of Christ*.

Beyond Piazza Margherita runs the main street, Via Umberto I, which is closed to traffic for much of the day. Like the rest of town, it makes for an enjoyable stroll, with a maze of cobbled streets on either side opening on to occasional churches and shady piazzas. For three days every June, the streets are laid with amazing floral designs and pictures during the **Infiorata Castelbuonese**. The lovely freestanding "Venus and Cupid" **fountain** on Via Umberto I is a good thirst-quencher on a hot day, while if you stroll around for any length of time you'll also probably come across Castelbuono's **eco-donkeys** – the town has replaced its garbage trucks with a unique door-to-door donkey collection service for household waste and recycling.

A pilgrimage to the holy hill

Coming from Cefalù, your first stop in the mountains might be the **Santuario di Gibilmanna**, a twisting 14km up from the coast and en route to Castelbuono; there are daily buses from Cefalù's train station. The sanctuary lies in a spot made sacred by the Arabs, who recorded miraculous deeds by the Madonna on the hillside. There's a church at the highest point (daily, summer 7.30am–1pm & 3.15–7.30pm, winter 8am–1pm & 3.15–5.30pm; free) that's the goal of pilgrimages which culminate on September 8 each year. Otherwise you can stop to admire the superb view back down to the coast from the belvedere, or strike off on the woodland trails through the cypress trees. A museum beside the church (Mon–Sat 11am–1pm & 3.30–5.30pm, Sun 10.30am–1pm & 3.30–6pm; €2) contains artefacts from other churches, convents and monasteries in the area, and there's a restaurant and bar just below the car park.

Arrival and information

There are regular **buses** to Castelbuono from outside Cefalù's train station, a forty-minute ride. If you're staying in Cefalù, you might as well leave the car and take the bus; otherwise, **park** where you can and walk into the old town area ("*centro storico*"). Traffic loops through town on a convoluted one-way system, and it has to be said that initial impressions of Castelbuono by car are not good; it's much nicer once you're on foot. There is a **tourist and park office** at Via Umberto I 75 (May–Sept Mon–Sat 9am–1pm & 4–7pm, Sun 9am–1pm; Oct–April Mon–Sat 9am–1pm & 3–6pm; ☎0921.671.124, ⓦwww.comune.castelbuono.pa.it), but other than dispensing leaflets it's pretty hopeless.

Accommodation

There's plenty of fine accommodation for all budgets, though not too much in the centre itself. The tourist office has a stack full of cards and brochures for local B&Bs and hotels.

Azienda Agrituristica Bergi Contrada Bergi, SS286, Geraci Siculo road, 3km southeast of town ☎0921.672.045, ⓦwww .agriturismobergi.com. A laidback organic estate in a gorgeous valley just outside town, with spacious, country-style one- and two-room units set around landscaped gardens and a pool. It's a working farm of orchards and olives – home-made preserves and fruit from the trees are served at breakfast, while a good four-course dinner (€25, or included in the €70 half-board rate) uses more of their produce. ❸

4 Cannola Via Dafni 7 ☎0921.671.587 or 333.242.1018, ⓔ4cannola@virgilio.it. The town's most central B&B is in a restored house just behind the Venus fountain on the main street. ❶

Relais Santa Anastasia Contrada Santa Anastasia ☎0921.672.233, ⓦwww.santa-anastasia-relais.it. For a sumptuous stay, there's this rather grand restored twelfth-century abbey 8km outside town,

with honeyed stone walls, elegant rooms in deep colours, and a glorious outdoor pool. Rates can run up to €360 per night, depending on the room or suite, but contact them for special deals. Dinner in the lovely restaurant is €40 per person. ❺

Rifugio Francesco Crispi Piano Semprià ☎0921.672.279. The nearest mountain refuge to Castelbuono is at 1300m above sea level, and a good two hours' strenuous walk away in the Milocca forest. It's open all year, providing simple, hostel-style accommodation (dinner, bed and breakfast costs around €40 per person) – and another 3hr walk the next day gets you to Piano Battáglia, where there's another *rifugio*. ❶

Villa Calagioli Contrada da Calagioli ☎0921.676.153 or 333.588.4421, ⓔvillacalagioli abbate@libero.it. For a rural B&B, though only a few hundred metres from the centre, follow the signs from the through road in town to this pretty olive-oil-producing country house. ❷

Eating and drinking

A line of appealing cafés and restaurants with outdoor terraces lies between the castle and Piazza Margherita, while yet more places are hidden away in the surrounding alleys. Pork, beef and especially wild mushrooms are typical menu items in this mountain region.

Antico Baglio Piazza Ten. Schicchi 3 ☎0921.679.512. It's a couple of hundred metres off the beaten track, but this restored old *baglio* (warehouse) has both a cool interior and shady outdoor deck, where you can sample things like home-made pasta with a sausage-meat and mushroom *ragù* (dishes €8–10). At night there are pizzas too. Follow the signs from Piazza Matteotti at the end of Via Umberto I.

Fiasconaro Piazza Garibaldi 10 ☎0921.671.231. A seat here in the charming old-town square, a home-made ice cream or a dish of strawberry *granita* takes some beating on a hot day.

Nangalarruni Via delle Confraternite 5 ☎0921.672.045. The town's best-known address for serious mountain cuisine is an upmarket rustic tavern that does amazing things with wild mushrooms. They appear in soups, sauces and pasta dishes, with pork and beef to follow, while finishing with a shot of the sweet, local *digestivo*, Elisir di Fontana, is always a good idea. Dishes are €9 to €18, or a couple of tasting menus at €22 and €30 offer a good deal. It's just down Via Umberto I from Piazza Margherita, second alley on the right. Closed Wed in winter.

Geraci Sículo

For an initial taste of the mountains, make the half-hour drive from Castelbuono up the winding SS286 to **GERACI SÍCULO**, 20km away. If ever a town was buttoned up tight against the threat of winter, it's this one, with its packed houses lining streets so narrow that laundry is strung across from balcony to balcony. At the highest point, up back-breaking cobbled alleys, the scant, restored ruins of a castle and an ancient chapel stand amid wild flowers and scented pines. Amazing 360-degree panoramas unfold, while back down the valley Castelbuono and its own mighty castle are easily seen. The road south of town climbs even higher before dropping down to the SS120 Gangi–Petralia road, where you can pick up the route into the central park region. There is a bus to Geraci a couple of times a day from Cefalù/Castelbuono, which runs on to Gangi, but realistically Geraci is only a coffee stop for drivers.

Piano Zucchi and Piano Battáglia

The heart of the Madonie lies southwest of Castelbuono, in the upland slopes and valleys below the two peaks of Pizzo Antenna Grande (or Pizzo della Principessa, 1977m) and Pizzo Carbonara (1979m). These are the highest of Sicily's mountains after Etna, with a winter ski business based at the two resort areas of Piano Zucchi and Piano Battáglia – though "resort" is pushing it, since there are no villages here and only very limited facilities. Outside winter time, it's an enjoyable drive up into the high mountains, with plenty of places to park up, take a walk through the alpine meadows and have a picnic.

From Castelbuono, drive 9km west to Munciarrati (also known as Mongerati), between Collesano and Isnello, where there's a turn-off up into the mountains. With the *Rifugio Orestano* still closed, there's nothing much at all at **Piano Zucchi** (1100m), 17km from the junction, save a little mountain chapel, a children's playground and views of peaks to all sides. It's another 7km up to **Piano Battáglia**, sited at 1600m (ⓦwww.pianobattaglia.it), a rather nicer area for walks in the high plains and picnics under the beech trees. On the way up from Piano Zucchi you'll have passed two resort-style hotels, the *Piano Torre Park Hotel* (ⓣ0921.662.671, ⓦwww.pianotorreparkhotel.it; ❸, half board €75 per person) and the *Hotel Baita del Faggio* (ⓣ0921.662.194, ⓦwww.baitadelfaggio.it; ❸, half board €60 per person), both with panoramic views and restaurants. Rather more in keeping with the rugged surroundings is the Sicilian Alpine Club's *Rifugio Piero Merlino* (ⓣ0921.649.995 or 347.851.1511, ⓦwww.rifugiopieromerlino.it; ❶), right at Piano Battáglia, which has small, plain, multi-bedded pine-clad rooms, and a bar-restaurant with outdoor terrace; it's open all year round, and dinner, bed and breakfast runs to around €40 per person. If you're interested in the hike up to the summit of Pizzo Carbonara (5hr round trip), the refuge is the place to ask for advice and route directions.

From Piano Battáglia, it's another 20km, or half-hour drive, over the tops and down to the Petralia towns.

Petralia Soprana and Sottana

The southern edge of the Madonie range is marked by the twin towns of Petralia, which lie on opposite sides of a hill. There are some wonderful views, as you might imagine, from the upper town of **PETRALIA SOPRANA**, which sits at an altitude of nearly 1150m. This was the birthplace of the craftsman Fra Ùmile da Petralia (1580–1639), whose wooden crosses are found in churches all over southern Italy. From the edge of the village you get a long view over the Madonie and Nébrodi mountains, as well as an occasional sight of Etna.

However, it's the lower town, 3km away, **PETRALIA SOTTANA**, that acts as the mountain base for the region. Clinging to the hillside, it's an evocative place with one long main street, Corso Paolo Agliata, lined with weathered medieval churches, small piazzas and shuttered houses, culminating in the usual castle ruins. The **tourist office** at Corso Paolo Agliata 100 (daily 8.30am–2pm & 3–8pm; T0921.641.811, Wwww.petraliasottana.net) is one place you can find out more about the Madonie park; it shares its premises with the **Museo Civico Antonio Collisani** (same hours; €2), which showcases both the geological and archeological heritage of the region. The other is the **Ente Parco delle Madonie** office at Corso Paolo Agliata 16 (daily 8am–2pm; T0921.684.011, Wwww.parcodellemadonie .it), which should be able to tell you something about hiking, skiing and escorted excursions. For a day out in the trees above town you can drive 4km beyond Petralia Sottana, on the Piano Battáglia road, to the **Parco Avventura** (April–June, Sept & Oct weekends 10am–6pm, July & Aug daily 10am–8pm; park entrance €2; Wwww.parcoavventuramadonie.it), where as well as picnic areas and marked trails there's a thrilling high-ropes adventure course (€24) through the pines – booking is a good idea.

Petralia Soprana has the only concentration of **accommodation** on this side of the range, much of it along and around the main street. Decent **B&Bs** include *Al Casale*, Via Rocca 25 (T0921.641.973 or 348.749.6860; no credit cards; ❷), which has four boldly painted rooms with en-suite bathrooms and views of the village from the windows. Or for a more old-world-style hotel, there's *Il Castello*, Via Generale di Maria 27 (T0921.680.105, Wwww.il-castello.net; ❷), which along with its stone walls, tiled floors and beams has a cosy, rustic restaurant.

The best **trattoria** is *Petra Leium*, Corso Paolo Agliata 107 (T0921.641.947; closed Fri evening except in Aug), which features local mountain dishes – notably grilled meats and wild mushrooms – and has generous tourist menus for €15 and €18. There's more of a bar scene at the *Saxum* pub and pizzeria, Via Gangi 3 (T0921.680.444; open evenings only until late; closed Wed), just up from the war memorial.

Polizzi Generosa

A twenty-minute drive west of the Petralias, the small town of **POLIZZI GENEROSA** is another possible Madonie base. Mountain views aside, the grand old Chiesa Matrice contains the area's greatest work of art, a triptych of the *Madonna and Child* flanked by saints. Attributed to a mysterious fifteenth-century Fleming known only as the "Maître au Feuillage brodé", it's reckoned to be his finest achievement. Just up from here, *U Bagghiu* (T0921.551.111; closed Tues; dishes from €6) serves a great pasta speciality, *penne al Bagghiu* (cheesy penne with tomato and garlic), and pizzas in the evening, while *L'Orto dei Cappuccini* (T0921.688.535; closed Mon), Via Cappuccini 3, on a side street off the road up to town, has a nice cloistered garden and a creative menu (meals €15–20). There are a couple of B&Bs in town, though at Contrada Santa Venera, 7km to the north (towards the Scillato autostrada junction), the same family that runs *U Bagghiu* also operates a comfortable farmhouse **agriturismo**. *Santa Venera* (T0921.649.421, Wwww.santavenera.com; ❷) is surrounded by vineyards and orchards, with seven en-suite rooms, a swimming pool and good views in all directions. You can eat in the restaurant here for €15–25, or there's a half-board deal for €55 per person.

Travel details

Trains

Cefalù to: Messina (12 daily; 2hr 15min–3hr); Milazzo (12 daily; 1hr 40min–2hr); Palermo (1–2 hourly; 1hr); Sant'Agata di Militello (hourly; 1hr); Santo Stéfano di Camastra (hourly; 30min); Términi Imerese (1–2 hourly; 25min).

Buses

Cáccamo to: Cefalù (2 daily; 45min); Palermo (4 daily Mon–Sat; 1hr 15min); Términi Imerese (8 daily Mon–Sat; 15min).
Castelbuono to: Cefalù (7 daily Mon–Sat, 1–2 daily Sun; 40min); Collesano (6 daily Mon–Sat; 45min); Gangi (1 daily; 1hr–1hr 20min); Geraci (2 daily Mon–Sat, 1 daily Sun; 45min); Isnello (1 daily Mon–Sat; 25min); Palermo (3 daily Mon–Sat; 1hr 45min); Términi Imerese (2 daily Mon–Sat; 1hr 30min).
Cefalù to: Cáccamo (2 daily; 45min); Castelbuono (7 daily Mon–Sat, 2 daily Sun; 40min); Gangi (1 daily; 1hr 45min–2hr); Geraci (2 daily Mon–Sat, 1 daily Sun; 1hr 25min); Gibilmanna (3 daily; 30min); Palermo (3 daily Mon–Sat, 1 daily Sun; 1hr); Petralia (1 daily Mon–Sat; 2hr).
Polizzi Generosa to: Caltavuturo (1–3 daily Mon–Sat, also 1 daily Sun in July & Aug; 35min); Palermo (2 daily; 1hr 20min); Términi Imerese (1–2 daily Mon–Sat; 1hr 45min).
Sant'Agata di Militello to: Cesarò (1 daily Mon–Sat; 1hr 30min); San Fratello (6 daily; 20min); San Marco d'Alunzio (4 daily; 20min).
Santo Stéfano di Camastra to: Mistretta (6 daily Mon–Sat, 3 daily Sun; 35min); Nicosia (1 daily Mon–Sat; 1hr 30min).
Términi Imerese to: Cáccamo (9–10 daily Mon–Sat; 15min); Castelbuono (2 daily Mon–Sat; 1hr 30min); Collesano (2 daily Mon–Sat; 45min).

Hydrofoils

Cefalù June to mid-Sept to: Alicudi (1 daily; 1hr 15min); Filicudi (1 daily; 1hr 50min); Lípari (1 daily; 3hr 15min); Palermo (1 daily; 55min); Panarea (1 daily; 3hr 45min); Rinella (1 daily; 2hr 30min); Santa Marina (1 daily; 2hr 45min); Strómboli (1 daily; 4hr 25min); Vulcano (1 daily; 3hr 35min).

The Aeolian Islands

CHAPTER 3

Highlights

* **Upper town, Lípari** The ancient citadel, high above two harbours, shelters the island's magnificent archeological museum. See p.123

* **Hotel Signum, Salina** This stylish, yet personable hotel, with fabulous restaurant and views out to Strómboli, is many people's Aeolian favourite. See p.134

* **Boat trip, Panarea** Swim in the sparkling waters above bubbling fumaroles and Roman remains, and explore the craggy outcrops off the celebrity-filled island of Panarea. See p.136

* **The ascent of Strómboli** Don't miss the guided climb up one of the world's most active volcanoes. See p.141

* **Zucco Grande, Filicudi** This remote village, abandoned to emigration, makes a great target for a hike along the mule tracks of Filicudi. See p.143

* **La Sirena, Filicudi** It's not quite the hotel at the end of the world, but this charming oasis is hard to beat. See p.144

* **A sojourn in Alicudi** Few places in Europe are more remote than Alicudi. Join its population of 80 in low season for a true isolation experience. See p.145

▲ Boats on the beach, Lípari

The Aeolian Islands

The **Aeolian Islands**, or Isole Eolie, are a mysterious apparition when glimpsed from Sicily's northern coast. Sometimes it's clear enough to pick out the individual white houses on their rocky shores; at other times they're murky, misty and only half-visible. D.H. Lawrence, on his way to Palermo by train in bad weather, thought they resembled "… heaps of shadow deposited like rubbish heaps in the universal greyness". The sleepy calm that seems to envelop this archipelago masks a more dramatic existence: two of the islands are still volcanically active, and all are buffeted alternately by ferocious storms in winter and a deluge of tourists in summer. But their unique charm has survived more or less intact, fuelled by the myths associated with their elemental and unpredictable power.

Closest island to the mainland is the day-tripper magnet of **Vulcano**, with its mud baths, hot springs, black sand beaches and smoking main crater. Across the channel lies the main island, **Lípari**, which is the hub of the ferry and hydrofoil system and so makes the best base for island-hopping. It also has the widest choice of accommodation and restaurants, and is the only island with any kind of life outside the main summer season. Of the central group of islands, **Panarea** is the smallest and most elite, and in August the conspicuously rich float in to commune with nature from their multi-million-euro yachts and villas and €500-a-night hotel rooms, overlaying the gentle lapping of the waves with a cacophony of extremely loud music. Though the regular fireworks of its volcano bring droves of trekkers to **Strómboli**, this island too attracts its share of fashionistas – Dolce and Gabbana have a house here – while the chic whitewashed Piscità quarter is full of stylish villas. Twin-peaked **Salina** springs perhaps the best surprise – second in size only to Lípari, it attracts a less flamboyant crowd, and being unusually fertile, remains green year-round, making walking in its mountains pleasant at all times. **Filicudi**, long favoured by the trendy left, has something of a radical-chic feel, though it is all very understated and relaxed; wandering its mule tracks, it's not hard to get taste of what life in the archipelago was like twenty – or a hundred – years ago. If this is what you are looking for, make the effort to get out to distant **Alicudi**, an uncompromising kind of place, and some would say, the hardest to like.

Individual identity aside, each Aeolian island is embraced by water of a limpid quality rarely found along the coast of Sicily. Sandy beaches are sparse, and tend to be ash-black, but **boat tours** (available at every Aeolian harbour) provide access to any number of secluded coves, hidden caves and quiet snorkelling and scuba-diving waters. Lípari and Salina are the only two islands you might consider taking a car across to, but that's hardly necessary (best leave it in a garage on the mainland). Both islands have a good bus network, while you can rent bicycles, mopeds and scooters on all the main islands, or simply walk around the smaller

Festivals

March

19 Festival of San Giuseppe at Malfa, **Salina**, with locals dressed up as the Holy Family, and feasting for all on pasta and *ceci* (chickpeas) cooked in huge cauldrons, along with *antipasti* and puddings made by local people. Repeated in April at Lingua, and on May 1 in Leni.

Easter

Holy Week Procession in **Lípari**, reenactment of the Passion of Christ, Good Friday, Salina.

June

29 Festival of San Pietro on **Panarea**.

July

17 Festival of Santa Marina in **Santa Marina di Salina**, Salina.

23 Festival of St Mary of Terzito at the **sanctuary of Madonna del Terzito** on Salina.

August

10 Festival of San Lorenzo in **Malfa**, Salina.

24 Procession of San Bartolomeo's statue and relics in **Lípari town**, accompanied by fireworks. Celebrations, too, on **Alicudi**.

ones. **Aeolian food** is among the most distinctive in Italy, fish of course providing the mainstay but with the traditional crops of capers, olives and mountain herbs flavouring most dishes, while the malvasia grapes provide one of Sicily's more ancient wines. Other foods (as well as much of the water on some islands) have to be imported, so restaurants tend towards the expensive, as does **accommodation**. Places offering simple rooms vie with boutique and resort hotels throughout the islands, but high prices and limited availability in high season (Easter, July & Aug) are common to them all, when many also insist on half board (*mezza-pensione*, ie dinner, bed and breakfast) and multi-night stays.

Ferries and hydrofoils ply between the islands year-round – their arrival is often the high point of the day in a place like Alicudi, with a permanent population of around a hundred. Services are reduced **out of season** (basically Oct to May), but you should still be able to reach most islands daily. Indeed, visiting outside peak season is highly recommended, since there's a refreshing absence of other tourists, and accommodation rates plummet accordingly. However, be warned that many hotels and restaurants close their doors for the entire winter, while if the weather turns, you're in danger of being stuck for days – the archipelago is frequently lashed by storms between October and March. Even in summer high winds and storms can strike, and heavy seas can mean the cancellation of ferry and hydrofoil services to both the mainland and the other islands. If this happens, there's no alternative to sitting and waiting the storm out.

Legends and history

Volcanoes have always been identified with the mouths of hell, and it was in the Aeolians that Jupiter's son, **Vulcan**, had his workshop. Vulcano is named after this god of fire and metalworking, while another island takes its name from Liparus, whose daughter Ciane married **Aeolus**, ruler of the winds and master of navigation; Aeolus, in turn, lent his name to the whole archipelago. These winds were

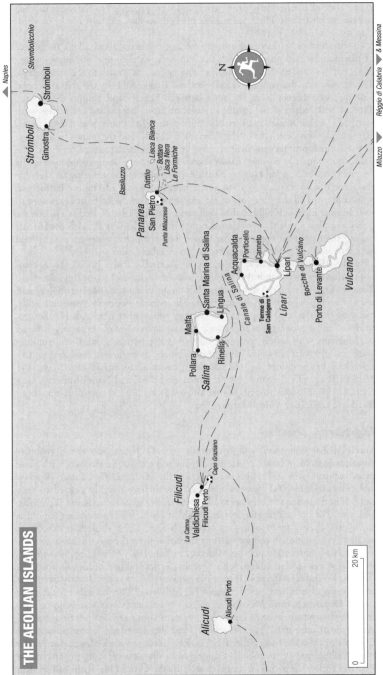

THE AEOLIAN ISLANDS

0   20 km

kept in one of the Aeolians' many caves, and were presented to Odysseus in a bag to take on his travels. His curious crew opened the bag and, as a result, blew his ship straight back to port.

The first historic settlers exploited the volcanic resources, above all the abundance of **obsidian**, a hard glass-like rock that can be worked to produce a fine cutting edge, and was traded far and wide, accruing enormous wealth to the archipelago. The islands were drawn more closely into the Greek ambit by the arrival, around 580 BC, of refugees from the wars between Segesta and Selinus (Selinunte). Those Greeks based at the fortified citadel of Lípari later allied themselves with Carthage, which made Lípari its base during the First Punic War. For its pains, Greek Lípari was destroyed by the Romans in 251 BC and the islands became part of the Roman province of Sicily, paying hefty taxes on exports of obsidian. The islands subsequently changed hands several times before being abandoned to the frequent attacks of wide-ranging North African **pirates**, culminating in a terrible slaughter that took place in 1544 at the hands of Khair ed-Din, or Barbarossa, who consigned all the survivors of the massacre to slavery – a figure estimated to have been as high as 10,000. Italian unification saw the islands used as a prison for political exiles, a role that continued right up to World War II, with the Fascists exiling their political opponents to Lípari. The last political detainee to be held here was, ironically, Mussolini's own daughter, Edda Ciano, in 1946.

By the 1950s **emigration**, especially to Australia, had reduced the Aeolian population to a mere handful of families, when the release of Rossellini's *Stromboli: Terra di Dio* (1949) and the story of his affair on the island with star Ingrid Bergman put the archipelago under the spotlight. The curious began to visit the islands, many of them buying properties for a song, while other film-makers followed, many of them pioneers in underwater photography. Today's economy is based on **tourism**, with hotels sprouting on previously barren ground, and running water and electricity installed (almost) everywhere. Nonetheless, enough primitive splendour has remained for the islands to continue to attract film crews, and Michael Radford's *Il Postino* (1994), filmed on Salina, and Nanni Moretti's *Caro Diario* (1994) still draw tourists in their droves. Since 2000, the Aeolians have been listed as a UNESCO World Heritage Site.

Getting there

Ferries (*navi* or *traghetti*) and **hydrofoils** (*aliscafi*) depart year-round (weather permitting) from Milazzo, Messina, Palermo and Cefalù. Services are with three main companies, namely **Siremar** (Ⓦ www.siremar.it), **Ústica Lines** (Ⓦ www .usticalines.it) and **NGI** (Ⓦ www.ngi-spa.it), with fares roughly pegged to each other. The most frequent services to all islands are in high season, June to September inclusive. The car-carrying ferries take roughly twice as long to most destinations as the hydrofoils, but are around sixty percent cheaper. The hydrofoils are also more prone to cancellation in bad weather, particularly out to the more distant islands.

The main embarkation point is **Milazzo**, an hour from Messina by bus or train, with daily, year-round sailings with Siremar (ferries and hydrofoils), Ústica Lines (hydrofoils) and NGI (ferries). In summer, services depart almost hourly from here to the main islands, and most services from Milazzo call first at either Vulcano or Lípari. Departures from **Messina** are more convenient if you're coming directly from Catania airport. Ústica Lines runs hydrofoils out to the islands from here all year (at least once daily, even in winter), and also operates summer connections from mainland Italy, from either Réggio di Calabria (some via Messina) or Naples (these calling first at Stromboli). Coming from the west of Sicily (or arriving at Palermo airport), it makes far more sense to use the Ústica Lines hydrofoil services from either **Palermo** or **Cefalù**, which run daily in summer. However, note that these services are routed first via Alicudi and Filicudi, which makes for a long and expensive trip if you're heading directly for Strómboli, for example.

Tickets are sold at the companies' harbourside offices before departure, and timetables are posted at every office – or up-to-date schedules are available online on the company websites. Only in August might you need to buy tickets in advance (for which there is a surcharge); otherwise, services are rarely full. Sample one-way high-season **fares** from Milazzo are around €16 by hydrofoil, €10 by ferry, to Lípari; €21/14 to Strómboli; and €28/16 to Alicudi. Hydrofoils from Messina to Lípari cost around €23, while from Palermo you'll pay around €26 to Alicudi, €38 to Lípari and €54 to Strómboli. Transporting a car on the car-ferry starts at around €30 one-way (Milazzo to Lípari), while on all services children under 4 go free and under-12s go half-price. All fares cost a couple of euros less between October and May.

Lípari

LÍPARI is the busiest, biggest and most diverse island in the Aeolian archipelago, with a long history of settlement and trade. The main town – also called Lípari – is a thriving little port, dominated by impressive castle walls that surround an upper citadel housing the bulk of the archeological remains and a terrific museum. The road that circles the island from town takes in several much smaller villages, some good beaches and excellent views out to the neighbouring islands, though development has not been carefully controlled. While parts of the island are beautiful and unspoilt, getting there inevitably means passing through villages cluttered with brassy holiday houses, or with rusting machinery and ghostly abandoned factories – relics of the island's now defunct pumice mining industry.

Historically, it has always been Lípari that has guided the development of the Aeolians. In classical times, after obsidian had been superseded by metals, the island's prosperity was based on its sulphur baths and thermal waters, while its alum, too, was much prized, and was found more abundantly here than anywhere else in Italy. More recently, its main industry was mining pumice – the reason why huge chunks of the mountains on the east coast are missing – but under the auspices of UNESCO this has now been banned, and today the economy is firmly based on tourism.

Arrival, information and transport

Hydrofoils and ferries dock at Lípari town's **Marina Lunga** (sometimes called Porto Sottomonastero). The quickest services from Milazzo take between forty-five minutes and an hour, or it's roughly ninety minutes from Messina. Dockside offices sell tickets and post timetables; Siremar and Ústica Lines are in the same building, just up from the gangways. A fifteen-minute walk south of Marina Lunga, down the main Corso Vittorio Emanuele, is **Marina Corta**, a smaller harbour used by excursion boats. Virtually everything of note lies between these two marinas.

The **tourist office**, Corso Vittorio Emanuele 202 (Mon–Fri 8.30am–1.30pm & 4–7.30pm; July & Aug also Sat 8.30am–1.30pm; ☎090.988.0095, ⓦwww .aasteolie.191.it) is the most reliable place for information on all the islands, and can advise on accommodation, boat excursions and current events; there's also lots of material in English on the website.

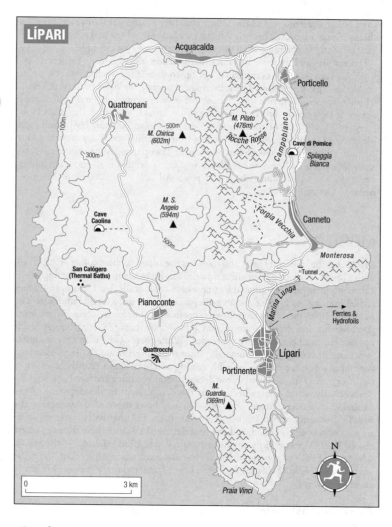

Buses leave Lípari town approximately every hour for the rest of the island (every 15–30min in summer for Canneto, less often on all routes on Sun and outside July and Aug). They depart from an obvious stop at Marina Lunga, opposite the petrol station, close to the quayside ticket agency, and current timetables are posted at the kiosk window; buy tickets on board. Nowhere is more than thirty minutes' ride away.

Accommodation

Although there's more accommodation in Lípari town than anywhere else, you can still find yourself stuck for a room in July and August, so if you don't have a reservation it makes sense to listen to the offers of **rooms** as you step off the boat. Many of the owners of places reviewed below meet arrivals at the quayside. Prices vary so much (often doubling in Aug) that the codes below show the possible range over much of the year; for the cheapest rooms, as a rule, expect to pay €50 per person in August, around €25–30 (even €20 if you're very lucky) at other times. In high summer there's often a minimum stay (usually three or four nights), while hotels will probably require you to take half-board terms. The island's only **campsite** and the archipelago's only **youth hostel** are both out at the beach strip of Canneto, 3km north of town, which is easily reached by bus, though Canneto is not a patch on Lípari town as a base.

Hotels and B&Bs

Carasco Porto delle Genti ☏090.981.1605, ⓦwww.carasco.it. Superbly located three-star hotel, with its own terraces, rocky cove, good pool and sparkling views. There's a wide range of rooms (up to suites with lounge and jacuzzi), though not all standard rooms have sea views. It's out of the centre, but not too far from Portinente beach and the Marina Corta. Closed Nov–March. ❹–❻

Casajanca Marina Garibaldi 109, Canneto ☏090.988.0222, ⓦwww.casajanca.it. If you don't mind being out at Canneto, you might prefer the boutique style of Casajanca to the resort hotels of town. It's a charming townhouse hotel, three-star standard, 20m back from the beachfront promenade, with ten stylish rooms and personal service. You can also ask about their simpler B&B in Canneto. ❸–❺

Diana Brown Vico Himera 3 ☏090.981.2584 or 338.640.7572, ⓦwww .dianabrown.it. Run by a jovial South African and her Sicilian husband, this is a really friendly and well-organized B&B, located in a tiny lane parallel to Corso Vittorio Emanuele. Seven smart rooms have a/c, heating, fridges and kettles, while another five also have small kitchenettes, and there's a great roof terrace where you eat breakfast. There's a book exchange and laundry service available, while Diana and her family know lots about the island, and can advise about walks and boat tours. Breakfast is €5, though not available in Aug. ❸

Enza Marturano Via Maurolico 35 ☏368.322.4997, ⓦwww.enzamarturano.it. Four bright, modern rooms with a/c, cooking facilities and views, ranged around a communal lounge, with a terrace overlooking the Corso. No credit cards. ❸

Enzo Il Negro Via Garibaldi 29 ☏090.981.3163, ⓦwww.enzoilnegro.altervista.com. "Enzo the black" takes its name from the bronzed owner's local nickname. Just up from Marina Corta, its eight rooms, all with a/c and fridge, share one of the best private roof terraces in town. ❹

Tritone Via Mendolita ☏090.981.1595, ⓦwww .bernardigroup.it. This superior four-star on the southern edge of the town centre is the best of the resort-style hotels, set away from the town bustle amid quiet gardens, and is extremely competitively priced. There's a good pool, a lovely spa, and rooms all have balcony or terrace. At the associated *Residence Mendolita*, a collection of self-contained villas and apartments set in mature gardens just down the road, accommodation is slightly cheaper throughout the year. ❹

Villa Meligunis Via Marte 7 ☏090.981.2426, ⓦwww.villameligunis.it. A converted *palazzo*, this elegant central four-star has excellent views of the citadel and sea from its rooftop restaurant, which sports a pool alongside. Rooms are tastefully turned out, many with sea views and balconies; there is also a beautifully restored eighteenth-century annexe with apartments. ❼

Hostel and campsite

Baia Unci Canneto ☏090.981.1540, ⓦwww.lipari casevacanze.it. The hostel (closed Nov–March), occupying a townhouse above the beach at the southern end of the seafront, is more like mini-apartments, with two five-bedded dorm rooms sharing a kitchen and terrace area. Advance reservations are essential; their bus picks up guests from Lípari harbour. Dorm beds cost €20, less out of season. The hostel is virtually next door to the island's only campsite, also called the *Baia Unci* (☏090.981.1909, ⓦwww.baiaunci.com; closed Oct–March), with cabins available and its own bar and restaurant. No credit cards. The *Ristorante del Pescatore* is between the two, and the bus from Lípari stops outside.

Lípari Town

LÍPARI TOWN is split into upper and lower sections. Virtually everything of historic interest lies in the upper town, or citadel, protected by the sturdy walls of the castle, while all the shops and services are in the lower town, mostly along and off the main Corso Vittorio Emanuele, with the town's two harbours at either end. The most impressive approach from lower to upper town is from Via Garibaldi, from which long steps cut straight up through the thick defensive walls, emerging right outside the Duomo.

The lower town

The main **Corso Vittorio Emanuele** runs the length of the lower town – it's closed to traffic in summer during the evening *passeggiata*, when its cafés come into their own. Most of the gift shops are found along here, but tourism has never

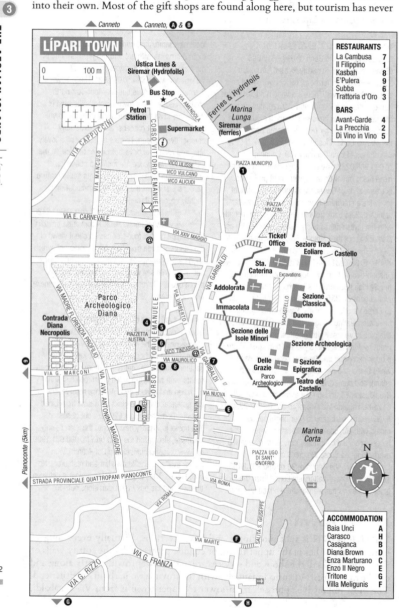

LÍPARI TOWN

0   100 m

▲ Canneto   ▲ Canneto, Ⓐ & Ⓑ

Ústica Lines &
Siremar (Hydrofoils)

Bus Stop ★

Petrol
Station

VIA AMENDOLA

Ferries & Hydrofoils ➤

Marina
Lunga

Siremar
(ferries)

Supermarket

ⓘ

VICO ULISSE
VICO VULCANO
VICO ALICUDI

PIAZZA MUNICIPIO

Ⓞ

VIA CAPPUCCINI

VIA MANCUSO

CORSO VITTORIO EMANUELE

PIAZZA
MAZZINI

VIA E. CARNEVALE

✉
❷
@

✝

VIA XXIV MAGGIO

Ticket
Office

Sezione Trad.
Eoliare

Castello

Sta.
Caterina

Excavations

Ⓒ

Addolorata

Immacolata

Sezione
Classica

Sezione
Archeologica

VIA MADRE FLORENZA PROFILO

Parco
Archeologico
Diana

Contrada
Diana
Necropolis

CORSO VITTORIO EMANUELE

VIA UMBERTO

VIA GARIBALDI

VICASTELLO

Duomo

Ⓓ

PIAZZETTA
AUSTRIA

Ⓕ

Ⓖ

VICO TINDARIS

Sezione delle
Isole Minori

Ⓒ Ⓗ

VIA MAUROLICO

Ⓖ

VIA G. MARCONI

Ⓓ

VIA AVV. ANTONINO MAGGIORE

VICO S. SELINUNTE

VIA NUOVA

Ⓔ

Delle
Grazie

Sezione
Epigrafica

Parco
Archeologico

Teatro del
Castello

VIA GARIBALDI

Marina
Corta

STRADA PROVINCIALE QUATTROPANI PIANOCONTE

Pianoconte (5km) ◀

◀ Ⓖ

PIAZZA UGO
DI SANT'
ONOFRIO

VIA ROMA

VIA ROMA

SALITA S. GIUSEPPE

Ⓕ

VIA MARTE

N

VIA G. RIZZO

VIA G. FRANZA

▼ Ⓖ   ▼ Ⓗ

RESTAURANTS
La Cambusa   7
Il Filippino   1
Kasbah   8
E'Pulera   9
Subba   6
Trattoria d'Oro   3

BARS
Avant-Garde   4
La Precchia   2
Di Vino in Vino   5

ACCOMMODATION
Baia Unci   A
Carasco   H
Casajanca   B
Diana Brown   D
Enza Marturano   C
Enzo Il Negro   E
Tritone   G
Villa Meligunis   F

completely dominated life in Lípari, so among the carved obsidian trinkets, coral jewellery and Etna postcards there are still shops selling screwdrivers, fishing tackle and goldfish, along with a very useful supermarket and some great bakeries. Just off the Corso, the **Parco Archeologico Diana** (daily 9am–noon & 2.30–6.30pm, though sometimes locked because of staff shortages; free), also known as Parco Diana, preserves more remains of ancient buildings and houses, as well as a children's playground, though the more interesting sight is the nearby **Contrada Diana necropolis**, closed for access but visible off Via G. Marconi, where Graeco-Roman tombs stud a sunken field.

Other than this, the best place to explore is down around the **Marina Corta**, overlooked by parasol-shaded cafés. It's where most of the boat excursions depart from, while behind the chapel and up the steps you can get lost in the narrow alleys of the old fishing quarter.

The upper town

Most of what remains of Lípari's formidable citadel is sixteenth-century Spanish in style, though it incorporates fragments of earlier medieval and even Greek buildings. Until the eighteenth century, this upper zone was the site of Lípari town itself, which explains the presence of the island's most important church, the **Duomo**, along with the dilapidated ruins of several other Baroque churches. Scattered in between are the excavations of superimposed layers of occupation, from the Neolithic to the Roman age, a continuous record covering almost two thousand years and a unique sequence that has allowed archeologists to date other Mediterranean cultures. The wide excavated trenches don't tell you much, though spare a glance at least at the **Parco Archeologico** at the southern end of the citadel walls (Mon–Sat 9am–dusk; free), which has some Greek and Roman tombs on display, a modern amphitheatre and nice views over the rooftops and Marina Corta.

All the archeological finds are displayed in Lípari's superb **Museo Eoliano** (daily 9am–1.30pm & 3–7pm; €6), which is housed in various buildings sited on either side of the Duomo. Despite the official opening hours most of the sections are usually only accessible in the mornings – only the **Sezione Classica** tends to keep the full opening times. This holds classical and Hellenic material retrieved from various necropoli, and includes re-creations of both a Bronze Age burial ground and of the Lípari necropolis (eleventh century BC), where bodies were either buried in a crouching position in large, plump jars or cremated and placed in bucket-shaped jars (*situlae*). Most eye-catching of all are the towering banks of amphorae, each 1m or so high, dredged from shipwrecks under Capo Graziano (Filicudi), many still encrusted with barnacles. There are also shelves of vases decorated in polychrome pastel hues – showing sacrifices, bathing scenes, mythical encounters and ceremonies – with many identified as those of an individual known as the Lípari Painter (300–270 BC) and his pupils and rough contemporaries. Other poignant funerary goods include toy vases and statuettes from the grave of a young girl, and delicate clay figurines of working women using mortar and pestle or washing children in a little bath.

The museum, though, is best known for what comes last in the Sezione Classica, namely the oldest and most complete range of Greek **theatrical masks** in existence. Many are models, found in fourth-century BC graves, and covering the gamut of Greek theatrical life from the tragedies of Sophocles and Euripides to satyr plays and comedies. One room has a collection of small terracottas grouped in theatrical scenes, while there are also statuettes representing actual dancers and actors – nothing less than early Greek pin-ups of the period's top stars.

The seventeenth-century bishop's palace contains the **Sezione Archeologica**, where you can trace the early exploitation of obsidian, made into blades and exported all over the western Mediterranean – glass cases contain mounds of shards, worked flints, adzes and knives. Meanwhile, the pottery finds from ancient burial sites allowed archeologists to follow the development of the various Aeolian cultures, as burial techniques became gradually more sophisticated and grave goods more elaborate – as in the lid of a mid-sixth-century BC *bothros*, or sacred repository of votive articles, embellished with a reclining lion.

Other museum sections cover subjects as diverse as the prehistory of the minor islands or Aeolian traditions and customs, while the **Sezione Epigrafica** contains a little garden of tombs and engraved stones, and a room packed with more inscribed Greek and Roman tombstones and stelae. Unless you're really keen, though, there are diminishing returns to be had from soldiering on to the bitter end.

Around the island

Buses run in two directions around the island, clockwise to Quattropani, and anticlockwise to Canneto, Porticello and Acquacalda. There are enough departures (up to ten daily in summer) to be able to get around the whole island easily in a day, although if you're really pushed for time the bus company operates a ninety-minute **tour of the island** (*giro dell'isola*), usually twice a day from July to the end of September (€5) – though if they don't have a minimum of 12 passengers, trips are cancelled. Or you could drive or scooter around Lípari's winding roads in a couple of hours flat, stopping at places like Monte Guardia, Quattrocchi, Quattropani and Monterosa for some amazing views out across the archipelago.

Canneto and Campobianco

It's around 3km north from Lípari town to the nearest village, **Canneto**, an extended resort set on a wide bay on the other side of the headland. A long stony beach fronts the village, which has a rather abandoned feel outside summer when most businesses are closed, which may however be preferable to the gaudiness and noise when they are open. For more secluded swimming, stay on the bus until it reaches a stop at the far northern end of the lungomare, at a steep rise. From here, a stepped path runs up, around and down to the **Spiaggia Bianca**, an expansive sand-and-pebble beach that is worth the effort to reach. Refreshments and parasols are available here in summer.

Boat excursions

Tour operators all over town offer year-round **boat excursions**, both around Lípari and to all the other islands, which is an easy way to do some sightseeing without bothering about bus timetables and hydrofoil schedules. The boats mostly run from Marina Corta, but agencies are prominent at the main port too. Universally recommended is Da Massimo, Via Maurolico 2 (℡090.981.3086, 🖢www.damassimo.it), where there will be someone who can speak English, and where boats are clean, well-maintained, and have freshwater showers and canopies. Prices are pitched roughly the same everywhere, from €15 for a Lípari and Vulcano tour, €25 Lípari and Salina, and from €30 to Panarea and Strómboli. Da Massimo work with the excellent Magmatrek (see p.142) for boat trips to Strómboli, including a night ascent of the volcano (from €70). If you want to rent a **gommone** (rubber boat) and putter around yourself, expect to pay around €100 per day for a 5m-long boat with shower and canopy and space for six people. Most operators also run **beach shuttles** in summer to good beaches on Lípari that are otherwise tricky to reach, like Praia Vinci.

Buses continue north of Canneto, through the Cave di Pomice at **Campobianco**, where pumice workings have left huge white scars on the hillside. For 2 or 3km all around, the ground looks as if it's had a dusting of talcum powder, while years of accumulation of pumice sediment on the sea bed have turned the water a piercing aquamarine colour.

Above Campobianco, a path leads up the slopes of **Monte Pilato** (476m), thrown up in the eruption from which all the pumice originally came. The last explosion occurred in around 700 AD, leading to the virtual abandonment of Lípari town and creating the obsidian flows of Rocche Rosse and Forgia Vecchia, both of which can be climbed. Although it's overgrown with vegetation, you can still make out the outline of the crater at the top, and you may come across the blue-black veins of obsidian.

Porticello and Acquacalda

From the bus stop above the stony beach at **Porticello**, a road (and a quicker, more direct path) winds down to a small bay, which sunbathers share with the forlorn Heath Robinson-style pumice-work machinery that connects the white hillside with the pier. After storms, this is ripe hunting ground for hunks of obsidian, washed up on the strand. There's no shade here, and the pebble beach soon reaches scalding temperatures. A couple of summer vans sell cool drinks and snacks.

Buses all terminate a couple of kilometres further on at **Acquacalda**; you could walk between the two villages in about half an hour, if you wanted some aerial views of the azure waters and pumice quarries, and pick up the return Lípari bus in either place. Acquacalda itself is just a one-street village – not a very attractive one – with more abandoned pumice machinery, a long, usually deserted stone beach, an industrial pier and a couple of waterfront bars.

Quattrocchi to Quattropani

Heading west from Lípari town, a 3km climb through lush and fertile country leads to **Quattrocchi**, a noted viewpoint over Vulcano and the spiky *faraglioni* rocks, which puncture the sea between the two islands. The curious name (meaning "Four Eyes") is said to derive from the fact that newly wedded couples traditionally come here to be photographed, so gracing every shot with two pairs of eyes.

Just before the fragmented village of Pianoconte, a side road slinks off down to the old Roman thermal baths at **San Calógero**. It's a particularly pleasant route to follow on foot, across a valley and skirting some impressive cliffs, with the baths hidden behind a long-disused spa hotel: there's usually an unofficial guide to show you around and allow you a dip, if you dare, in the scummy 57°C Roman pool. For a really great coastal hike, stay on the bus from Lípari, asking the driver to drop you at the **Cave Caolina**, a quarry of multi-coloured clays used as pigments by the ancient Greek artist responsible for the polychrome painted vases in Lípari's museum, known simply as "the Lípari painter". From here an easy-to-follow path leads down through the quarry, and back to San Calógero, passing sulphurous fumaroles, a hot spring, and a couple of places where you can scramble down the cliffs for a swim. If you feel happier with a map (though it really isn't necessary), there are large-scale Isole Eolie maps on sale in many shops along the main Corso.

The bus from Lípari ends its run at **Quattropani**, a dispersed settlement with more fine views. If it isn't too hot you could always walk the 5km or so, further along the winding road, to complete the island circle at Acquacalda, and catch the bus back from there.

Eating, drinking and entertainment

There's a fair choice of **restaurants** in Lípari town, though note that many close between October and March. Prices are on the high side, but a couple of the restaurants rank among the best in the archipelago. For self-catering, there's a **supermarket** on the main Corso, near the tourist office, and several other *alimentari* and bakeries.

Bars along the Corso fill up from early evening onwards, as the *passeggiata* swings into action. Alternatively, for a drink with a sea view, head down to the Marina Corta where a line of tables belonging to late-opening bars spills out across the harbourfront.

Every summer (June–Sept), Lípari town puts on **dramas and concerts**, including some spectacularly sited events at the Teatro del Castello, the modern Greek-style theatre up at the citadel's Parco Archeologico. There are annual **processions** in town at Carnevale (Feb/March) and at Easter, but Lípari's main **festival**, dedicated to the island's patron, St Bartholomew, takes place over three days around August 24.

Restaurants

La Cambusa Via Garibaldi 72. About the cheapest trattoria in town (*primi* €7, *secondi* €10), and a reliable place for a straightforward meal of Sicilian dishes, from stuffed sardines to swordfish. Closed Nov–Easter.

Il Filippino Piazza Municipio ☎090.981.1002, ⊛www.filippino.it. This stupendous fish restaurant – Lípari's best, in business since 1910 – really knows its stuff. It's in the upper town and has a shaded outdoor terrace where you can eat classy Aeolian specialities like borlotti bean, sardine and fennel soup, *risotto nero* (coloured with squid ink), grouper-stuffed *ravioloni* and local fish in a *ghiotta* sauce (tomatoes, onions, celery, capers and olives). Choose carefully and you might get away with €35 a head, though you could easily spend €60 – and more if you give any serious thought to the massive wine list. Closed Mon in Oct to Nov & Jan to March, & closed mid-Nov to Dec.

Kasbah Via Maurolico 25 ☎090.981.1075. Chic but unpretentious restaurant, with a beautiful long garden, where the Anglo-Aeolian owner will advise on the best ways to sample the spanking fresh fish. *Antipasti* (€8–9) and *primi* (€10–12) make creative use of local ingredients – try *treccine* with local shrimps, aubergine and cherry tomatoes, or *tagliolini* with clams, zucchini flowers, basil and black pepper. They also make their own bread – and the island's best pizza (€6–8.50), using stone ground flour. Closed Mon & Oct–March.

E'Pulera Via Diana ☎090.981.1158. A romantic courtyard-garden restaurant specializing in classic Aeolian food: swordfish *involtini*, caper salads, home-made pasta with wild fennel and prawns, almond biscuits and malvasia wine. The super cuisine is well worth the highish prices, and it stays open till late (kitchen closes at midnight). Expect to pay €35 plus a head excluding wine. Dinner only; closed Oct–Mar.

Subba Corso Vittorio Emanuele 92 ☎090.981.1352. The island's best and most traditional café, since 1930, has a nice shaded terrace at the rear in the square. Try *Lulus*, clouds of *crema*-filled choux pastry, or the pistachio- and almond-studded *eoliana* ice cream.

Trattoria d'Oro Via Umberto I 32 ☎090.981.1304. A cut above the town's cheaper trattorias, this shady, rustic place is a cool haven on a hot day, and it's very welcoming to families. *Pasta con le sarde* (with sardines and wild fennel) and stuffed squid are typical dishes, with pasta from €7 and fish mains from €8. Open all year.

Bars & cafés

Avant-Garde Corso Vittorio Emanuele 135. You get a huge plate of nibbles with your drink here, where there are tables outside (along with a rowdy TV) and the occasional DJ in the evening.

La Precchia Corso Vittorio Emanuele 191. A cosy spot in winter for a glass of wine or any of a vast range of hot chocolates – white chocolate, dark chocolate with chilli, chocolate and hazelnut, chocolate and orange, for example – a treat if you've done the night trip to Strómboli. Not a bad place for breakfast, too.

Di Vino in Vino Corso Vittorio Emanuele 102. This classy enoteca has a well-researched range of wines, along with hams and cheeses from the Nébrodi mountains (tasters of which you'll be given with your glass of wine at aperitif hour). They also serve a choice of salads, *bruschette* and toasted sandwiches.

Listings

Banks and exchange There are plenty of ATMs down the main Corso, and you can exchange cash at the post office and some travel agencies. All the other islands, except Alicudi, have ATMs, but it's best to make sure you have enough cash before you set off island-hopping, as other island ATMs do occasionally run out of money at inconvenient times.

Bike, scooter and car rental Rental agencies line the dockside at Marina Lunga (the ferry and hydrofoil port); you'll have to leave your passport, credit card or a hefty deposit as security. Bikes from €10/day, scooters from €15–20, small cars from €40 for most of the year, skyrocketing in August.

Books and newspapers La Stampa, Corso Vittorio Emanuele 170, sells English-language newspapers, books, local maps and guides.

Buses The bus company, Urso Guglielmo, has its office at Via Cappuccini 29, by the Marina Lunga ☎090.981.1262.

Diving Many of the larger hotels can put you in touch with a diving school, or contact Diving Centre La Gorgonia, Salita S. Giuseppe, Marina Corta ☎090.981.2616 or 335.571.7567, ⓦwww .lagorgoniadiving.it. Single dive from €30 (€50 including equipment); three dives from €85 (€125 including equipment), PADI courses from €350.

Hospital Ospedale Civile, Via Sant'Anna ☎090.98.851. The hospital also has a walk-in 24hr first aid service on ☎090.988.5267. Or for emergencies or an ambulance, call ☎118.

Ferry and hydrofoil companies Ticket offices are all at Marina Lunga – with the hydrofoil offices by the hydrofoil dock, the ferry offices on the other side by the ferry dock. NGI ☎090.981.1955; Siremar, hydrofoils ☎090.981.2200, ferries ☎090.981.1312; Ústica Lines ☎090.981.2448.

Left luggage The Siremar/Ústica Lines office at Marina Lunga has a small left-luggage facility (daily from 8.30am; €4 for 12hr).

Internet Internet Point, Corso Vittorio Emanuele 185 (daily 9am–1pm & 5.30pm–midnight, reduced winter hours); Net Café, Via Garibaldi 61 (daily 9am–1pm & 4–10pm).

Pharmacies Cincotta, Via Garibaldi 60 ☎090.981.1472; Internazionale, Corso Vittorio Emanuele 28 ☎090.981.1583; Sparacino, Corso Vittorio Emanuele 95 ☎090.981.1392. Pharmacies open late according to a rota system, detailed on the doors of the shops.

Police Carabinieri, Via Madre Florenzia Profilio, near Via G. Marconi ☎090.981.1333.

Post office Corso Vittorio Emanuele 207 (Mon–Fri 8.30am–6.30pm, Sat 8.30am–1pm).

Vulcano

Closest of the Aeolians to the Sicilian mainland, and just across the narrow channel from Lípari, **VULCANO** is the usual first port of call for ferry and hydrofoil services from Milazzo, and as such suffers the bulk of the archipelago's day-trippers. As on more distant Strómboli, volcanic action defines the island, with the main crater hanging menacingly over its northern tip and constant vapour trails issuing from its flanks. It's a very old volcano, in the last, smoking, phase of its life, and although it's highly unlikely to erupt again you often don't even have to disembark to experience its other apparent trait – the disconcerting sulphurous, rotten-egg smell that pervades the island's entire inhabited area when the wind is in the right direction. The volcano was threatening enough to dissuade anyone from living here before the eighteenth century, since when there have been some hasty evacuations – subterranean activity is still monitored round the clock, just in case. In the nineteenth century a Scot called Stevenson bought the island to exploit the sulphur and alum reserves, but all his work was engulfed by the next major eruption. Although the volcano's last gasp of activity occurred between 1886 and 1890, its presence gives Vulcano an almost primeval essence. Everything here is an assault on the senses, the outlandish saffron of the earth searing the eyes, as violent as the intense red and orange of the iron and aluminium sulphates that leak out of the ground in the summer, to be washed away with the first autumn rains.

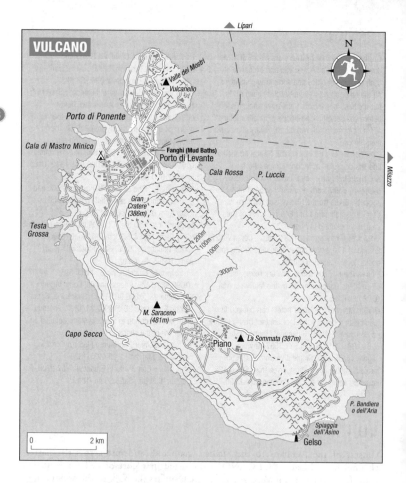

However, none of the summer trippers and B-list celebs bronzing themselves on Vulcano's black sand beaches are discouraged, while many others come to dip themselves in the sulphurous mud baths. That said, it's difficult to recommend a night's stay, even if the lingering smell doesn't put you off. Accommodation is mostly overpriced, while restaurants tend to command exorbitant prices for barely edible food. In fact, you can climb the crater, and cycle or bus across the island and back, all on a day-trip from the far pleasanter Lípari, just a ten-minute hydrofoil ride away. If you need provisions, there's a small supermarket tucked into an alley at the end of the main street.

Around the island

Ferries and hydrofoils dock at **Porto di Levante**, the main harbour, backed by just a couple of streets of restaurants, villas and shops. Walk to the right, towards the multi-coloured rock pinnacles, to find the famed **fanghi**, or mud baths (Easter–Oct daily 7am–9pm, though at other times of the year you can just walk in and wallow; €3), more exactly one pool containing a thick yellow soup of foul-smelling sulphurous mud, in which people flop belly-up, caking every inch of their bodies with the stuff.

The smell is indescribable, and the degree of radioactivity makes it inadvisable to immerse yourself for any length of time, and unsuitable for young children or pregnant women. Avoid contact with the eyes (it stings mightily) and remove contact lenses as well as any silver or leather jewellery, which will be ruined just by coming into contact with the sand hereabouts. When you've had enough, hobble over to rinse yourself off in the nearby sea, where natural hot water springs bubble up.

A narrow neck of land separates Porto di Levante from **Porto di Ponente**, a fifteen-minute walk past the *fanghi*. Here, a perfect arc of fine black sand lines a bay looking onto the towering pillars of rock that rise out of the channel between Vulcano and Lípari. There are a couple of seafront cafés here, and some large hotels set back from the sands. From the beach, the only road heads north through the trees to **Vulcanello**, thrown up out of the sea in a famous eruption in 183 BC, and joined to the main island by another flurry of activity a few centuries later. The walk takes less than an hour. On the north side of Vulcanello, the **Valle dei Mostri** – literally the "Valley of the Monsters" – is an area of lava rock formations, blackened and sculpted by the elements.

In the other direction from Porto di Levante, a road (and bus service) runs south across the island, past **Monte Saraceno** (481m) and the settlement of **Piano**, as far as the coastal hamlet of **Gelso** – *gelso* is Italian for "mulberry" and they're cultivated here, along with capers. There's a tiny patch of black sand here (and a seasonal trattoria, *Da Pina*), and a better beach at **Spiaggia dell'Asino**, a larger cove accessible from a steep path which you'll have passed on your way into Gelso (there's a bus stop). This is a great spot for a swim, with a summer café and umbrellas and deck chairs available.

Practicalities

From the **ferry and hydrofoil** dock, walk to the right for the *fanghi* and Porto di Ponente; Porto di Levante and the village are straight ahead, up past the traffic circle and the *Cantine Stevenson* bar. The ticket offices are in various buildings near the dock, while there's a **bank** with an ATM, 100m or so up the crater road. Da Paolo (℡090.985.2112) and Sprint (℡090.985.2208), also on this road, opposite each other, rent out **mountain bikes/scooters** (€5–15 a day).

Buses run from the dockside, year-round to Piano (Mon–Sat 7–8 daily; 10min), and summer only to Gelso (mid-June to mid-Sept, Mon–Sat 3 daily; 20min). Otherwise, it's a 15km drive out to Gelso, though most **boat tours** (around €15 per person) offered at the port in summer come out this way to visit the caves and bays on the island's west side.

> ## Climbing Vulcano's volcano
>
> Vulcano's main crater, the **Gran Cratere**, is just to the south of Porto di Levante – follow the road immediately to the left of the dock and walk up it for 500m or so until you're directed off the road to the left and up the slope (€3 fee charged to climb in season). It takes an hour to reach the crater, and it's a toughish climb, totally exposed to the sun, so do it early or late in the day in the summer months, and do it in strong shoes. The only vegetation consists of a few hardy gorse bushes on the lower slopes, nibbled at by goats whose bells echo across the scree. The first part of the path ascends a virtually black sand dune before reaching the harder volcanic crust, where it runs above the rivulets caused by previous eruptions. Reaching a ledge with views over all the other Aeolian islands, you look down into the vast crater itself, where vapour emissions – acrid and yellow – billow from the surrounding surfaces. Nerves are not exactly steadied by the admonitory notices at the start of the climb reading "Do not sit down, Do not lie down".

Accommodation

Eden Park Porto di Ponente ☎090.985.2120, ⓦwww.isolavulcano.it. This agreeable holiday site, set in its own peaceful grounds on the south side of the bay and slightly inland, is by far the island's best budget option. Campers can pitch tents on real grass, or even bivouac on the lawn, while there are also single-room apartments (with terrace, shower and kitchen; ❹) and "economic" double rooms (two bunk beds, shared bathroom; ❷) available. Breakfast available for a charge, and campers pay extra for showers. No credit cards. Closed Dec–Feb.

Orsa Maggiore Porto di Ponente ☎090.985.2018, ⓦwww.orsamaggiorehotel.com. It's a few hundred metres from the black sand beach, but this small hotel does have a rather nice pool, terrace and gardens. Closed Nov to March. ❸–❹

Les Sables Noirs Porto di Ponente ☎090.9850 or 06.8339.6880, ⓦwww.framonhotels.com. The finest resort hotel on the island (four-star) fronts the black sand beach, with stylish rooms almost all opening to big private terraces with views. Gardens and terrace-restaurant also make the most of the panoramic bay, and you get your own private bit of beach as well as a small, shaded outdoor pool. Check for good online deals. Closed Nov–March. ❺–❻

Salina

The ancient name of **SALINA** was Didyme, or "twin", referring to the two volcanic cones that give the island its distinctive shape. Both volcanoes are long extinct, but their past eruptions, combined with plenty of ground water – unique in the Aeolians – have endowed Salina with the most fertile soil of all the islands. The slopes are verdant, the island's tree cover contrasts strongly with the denuded crags of its neighbours, and both capers and malvasia grapevines – classic Aeolian staples – are vigorously cultivated. The island's central position in the archipelago makes it a good alternative base to Lípari for exploring the others, while Salina

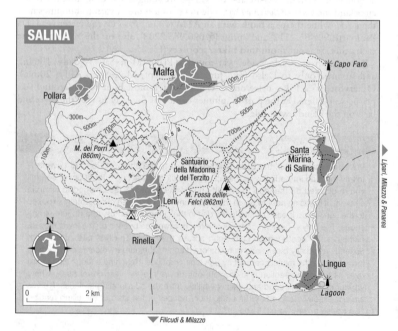

Walking on Salina

There are well-maintained, waymarked hiking trails right across Salina, in particular to the heights of Monte Fossa delle Felci and the sanctuary of Madonna del Terzito. It's great walking country, since most of the island has been zealously protected: wild flowers are much in evidence, and hunting and shooting are banned, which helps keep the bird numbers high.

For a good day out on the tops, first take the bus to the sanctuary – all buses except those between Malfa and Pollara pass right by. **Madonna del Terzito** is set in the saddle between the two peaks of Salina, with fine views over the sea. A signposted track leads up to the summit of **Monte Fossa delle Felci** (962m), the archipelago's highest peak. It's a steady climb through forest and mountain parkland, which takes the best part of two hours – only in the latter stages does it become tougher, with a final 100m clamber over rocks to reach the stone cairn and simple wooden cross at the top, from where the views are magnificent.

You can come back the same way to the sanctuary and catch the return bus, but signposts point out alternative approaches and **descents** to Malfa, Lingua or Santa Marina. However, not all the tracks are clear, and they can be very steep, and soil erosion and the crumbling volcanic underlay can make getting a grip a tricky business, so if you are not an experienced walker, best to stick to the main track. Count on another two hours back down, whichever descent you follow.

itself holds a network of hiking trails, some good beaches and several distinct villages. Tourism here is fairly sophisticated, with some charming boutique-style accommodation and excellent restaurants, especially in the main port, **Santa Marina di Salina**, and in the main town of **Malfa**, but the island certainly isn't a summer fleshpot like Vulcano or Panarea. It's quieter, more relaxed, still very much part of the ebb and flow of traditional Aeolian life, which makes it many people's favourite island.

There are two ports on Salina, Santa Marina di Salina in the east and smaller *Rinella* on the south coast. Not all services call at both ports, so it's essential to check timetables carefully if time is tight and connections crucial. There is, however, a regular bus service between both ports, vaguely timed to connect with arrivals, though if your boat is late, don't expect the bus to have waited.

Santa Marina di Salina and around

The main island port, **Santa Marina di Salina**, on the east coast, is where most of the services are located. A village of whitewashed Aeolian houses and elegant townhouses built in the nineteenth century by those who made their fortunes with Malvasia wine, it's a relaxed place, with a couple of pebble beaches. A long lungomare reaches north from the harbour, running from the town beach to the more secluded beach of Punta Barone, backed by the relics of an ancient Roman fish farm. Along the narrow pedestrianized main street, Via Risorgimento, which runs parallel to the water, one block back, chic boutiques mingle with grocery shops, fruit shops and butcher and baker. A couple of the gift shops sell a decent map of the islands.

Three kilometres south, **Lingua** is a prettier base, its entire waterfront traffic-free, so ideal for anyone on holiday with kids. It's connected to Santa Marina by bus, though the undulating road makes a fine forty-minute stroll, weaving around the coves in between the two settlements. Lingua itself is not much more than a seafront promenade and a narrow beach, backed by a tiny cluster of hotels and trattorias facing the shore of Lípari. At the end of the road is the salt lagoon from which Salina takes its name, and a car park where locals used to gather after bumper anchovy-catches to salt fish en masse. Overlooking the lake, two typical Aeolian houses have been converted into museums: a small **ethnographic museum** (May–Oct Tue–Sun 9am–1pm & 3–6pm; free) holds examples of rustic art and island culture – mainly kitchen utensils and mill equipment, much of it fashioned from lava rock, while the **archeological museum** (May–Oct Tue–Sun 9am–6pm; free) has finds from Bronze Age and Roman Salina.

Practicalities

Santa Marina is around 25 minutes by hydrofoil from Lípari. The Siremar (☏090.984.3004) and Ústica Lines/NGI (☏090.984.3003) **ticket offices** stand close to the dock on the waterfront piazza, on either side of the church, and usually open thirty minutes before sailings. There is a seasonal **tourist information point** with flexible opening hours just up the hill from the piazza, below *Bar Matarazzo*, with bus timetables, maps, contacts for hotels and restaurants and information on the island's various cultural happenings.

The bus stop for Lingua is right by the port, opposite the bar *La Cambusa*; buses to Malfa, Rinella and Pollara stop on the other side of the piazza, by the Siremar office (7–8 daily throughout the year, roughly every 90min, hourly in summer; pay on board). In winter you may have a lengthy wait in Malfa, the island hub, for an onward connection. If that is the case, better to get off the bus at Malfa's bank, and chance hitching – if you don't get a ride, all buses stop there anyway. All the usual boat tour options are available in summer, mostly from booths in the piazza by the harbour, while bike, moped and car hire is available from Nino Bongiorno at the beginning of the road to Lingua. **Services** along Via Risorgimento include a clinic with emergency doctors and ambulance, a pharmacy, the post office, an internet point and a bank with ATM (with another ATM on the seafront just beyond the Ústica Lines office).

Salina holds little in the way of out-and-out budget **accommodation**, though on this side of the island you might have some luck with private rooms and B&Bs, either touted at the harbour in summer or advertised in shops and bars. Hotels tend to demand half-board stays in August, while properties down at Lingua send shuttle-buses to pick up guests, and will give you a ride back to Santa Marina if you have eaten in their restaurants.

Restaurants are largely seasonal, and if you are coming in low season, it may be wise to get an apartment and self-cater. For aperitifs or after-dinner drinks in Santa Marina, try *Layla*, underneath the Portobello restaurant, with a relaxed ethnic-chic terrace above the water and cool music, or *Bagghiu Lisciu*, on the traffic-free back road up the steps from Bongiorno's car rental, more minimalist in style, and with free snacks including home-made hummus, salads and dips to accompany your drinks.

Accommodation

A Cannata Lingua ☏090.984.3161 or 339.575.4240, ⓦwww.acannata.it. Set a few metres back from the sea near the church, there are simple rooms above a decent restaurant, and several apartments of various sizes and styles to rent around the village, starting from around €500 a week in mid-season (€350 in low). ❹–❺

I Cinque Balconi Via Risorgimento 38, Santa Marina Salina ☏090.0943517, ⓦwww.icinquebalconi.it. Simple rooms in an eighteenth-century townhouse on Santa Marina's pedestrianized main street, whose most striking feature are the floors of subtle, carefully preserved original tiles. Behind the hotel, you can while away afternoons in an enchanting secluded garden, shaded by citrus and fig trees. There are eight rooms, several with sea views, and a romantic suite overlooking the garden with its own terrace and access. ❹–❺

Il Delfino Lingua ☏090.9843.024, ⓦwww .ildelfinosalina.it. Smart new rooms with marvellous terraces and views, set back from Lingua's lungomare, and older rooms opening directly onto

it, that are a good bet if you have children. The restaurant is lovely, with tables on the lungomare. Half-board obligatory in Aug at €120 per person. ❷
Il Gámbero Lingua ☏090.984.3049, ⓦwww .ilgamberosalina.it. Above *Il Gámbero* restaurant (see below) are three rooms and a fabulous shared terrace with 360-degree views of Lípari, Panarea, Strómboli and Monte Fossa. The family live half the year in Australia, so speak perfect English. ❸

🏃 Mamma Santina Via Sanità, Santa Marina Salina ☏090.984.3054, ⓦwww.mamma santina.it. The affable Mario presides over a highly personal, boutique-style restaurant-with-rooms, set on wide terraces above the town. The sixteen rooms are in bright seaside colours, with gorgeous Mediterranean tile floors and big bathrooms with walk-in showers, while guests can lounge in hammocks or around the pool. Call to be picked up from the port, or find the hotel signposted to the left off Via Risorgimento (after no. 66). Guests pay an extra €30 per person per night for half board. Closed mid-Dec to mid-March. ❺–❻

Mercanti di Mare Piazza Santa Marina 7, Santa Marina Salina ☏090.984.3536, ⓦwww .hotelmercantidimare.it. Harbourfront three-star hotel with nine white, airy rooms and an attractive terrace overlooking the water. ❺
Da Sabina Via Risorgimento 5c, Santa Marina Salina ☏090.984.3134 or 332.272.6025, ⓦwww.bbsalina.it. Classy B&B at the far end of the village from the port (10min walk). Three smart en-suite rooms open onto a big sea-view terrace, where breakfast is served. No credit cards. ❸
La Salina Borgo di Mare Lingua ☏090.984.3441, ⓦwww.lasalinahotel.com. This impressive four-star hotel is set in the restored buildings of the old salt-works, by Lingua's lagoon. The lovely rooms are individually furnished, and most have sea views and private terraces, while public areas are enhanced by traditional tile- and stonework. There's no restaurant, but you can eat at nearby *Il Gámbero* on a half-board basis. ❺

Eating and drinking

🏃 Da Alfredo Lingua. Right on the seafront piazza, this little café is famous throughout Italy for its fresh fruit *granita* – the summer yachties and boat-trippers queue up for a taste. The other speciality is *pane cunzato*, a huge round of grilled bread piled with various combinations of home-cured tuna, capers, tomatoes, baked ricotta and olives.
Il Gámbero Lingua ☏090.984.3049. This restaurant serves excellent fish – try the mixed fish *antipasto* (€10) and *involtini di pesce spada* (€15) – as well as pizza and *pane cunzato*. In low season there's a fixed menu at €20.

🏃 Mamma Santina Via Sanità, Santa Marina Salina ☏090.984.3054. The restaurant at the lovely Mamma Santina is marvellous and open to non-guests, with outdoor service for most of the year. The emphasis is on island specialities, like a grilled *antipasto* platter of vegetables and seafood, spaghetti with a pesto of fourteen herbs, or grilled seabass (pasta from €10, fish from €13). Closed mid-Dec to mid-March.
Bar Matarazzo Via Risorgimento, Santa Marina Salina. The best *cornetti* – home-made in the kitchen every day – filled with *crema*, ricotta, jam or chocolate, that you are ever likely to taste, along with

traditional biscuits, featuring lots of almonds, pista-chios and a jam made of citron. *Cannoli* are filled to order. Good *granita* in summer, as well as savoury snacks such as *arancini* and mozzarella in *carrozza*, all best enjoyed on the terrace overlooking the sea.
Nni Lausta Via Risorgimento 188, Santa Marina Salina ☏090.984.3486. Cool bar-restaurant whose New York-trained owner-chef gives an adventurous twist to local dishes – like raw tuna dressed with wild fennel and capers, or crispy fish cakes made from the day's catch. A full meal will cost at least €40 without wine, though you can just have a drink at the bar (until 2am) – €5 will buy you a glass of decent Salina wine, with crostini and home-made dips, pestos and salsas. Closed Nov–March.
Porto Bello Above the harbour, Santa Marina Salina ☏090.984.3125. Reliable and longstanding restaurant owned by a local writer that serves excellent local *antipasti*, pasta with capers and tomatoes, slabs of swordfish and good wine. A full meal will cost from around €40 without wine, and from the outdoor terrace you can gaze on the sparkling necklace of lights across the water on Lípari. A good choice for a splash-out. Closed Nov & Wed in winter.

Malfa and Pollara

Salina's only road climbs from the harbour at Santa Marina and traces the coast north, turning west at Capo Faro, before winding in through the outlying districts of **MALFA**, easily the island's biggest town and with its grandest accommodation.

The town spills down from the wide terrace outside its peach-coloured church to a tiny pier at the bottom. The bus stops up by the church, and again a few hundred metres below, above the tiny fishing harbour. A devilishly twisting road runs down to the port, across which cuts a more direct series of paths and steps. A little further along, by the *Punta Scario* hotel, steps lead down to Malfa's beach, stony but picturesquely backed by vertiginous cliffs. It was closed in summer 2010 because of the danger of falling rocks. If this is still the case when you visit, do as the locals do and swim instead from the harbour.

Just out of Malfa, a minor road (served by several buses a day) snakes off west to secluded **POLLARA**, raised on a cliff above the sea and occupying a crescent-shaped crater from which Salina's last eruption took place some 13,000 years ago. Scenes from Michael Radford's 1994 film, *Il Postino*, were shot in a house here that is available for rent, though it is pretty basic and quite expensive (call Pippo Cafarella on ☏339.425.3684). More scenes were shot down on the narrow beach at the base of cliffs below the village, but the popularity of the beach with boat tours and film pilgrims has caused severe erosion over the years. Boats are no longer permitted to anchor close to the shore, and the beach has recently been closed to land visitors due to falling rocks. You can swim instead from ramps in front of the so-called *balate*, caves in which fishermen traditionally kept their boats and equipment, or clamber and splash along the rocky coast to more private swimming spots.

Accommodation and eating

Capo Faro 3km east of Malfa ☏090.984.4330, ⓦwww.capofaro.it. At the five-star Tasca d'Almerita malvasia wine estate, a series of stunning, contemporary rooms occupy seven Aeolian-style houses that look down across the vineyards. Facilities are top-notch, from magnificent pool to classy bar and restaurant, and you can tour the vineyards on request. Prices start at €200, though for the suites or an Aug stay, you're looking at double that. No children under 12. ❻–❽

Al Cappero Pollara ☏090.9843.968. Simple, family-run place, with something of a Greek taverna feel, where you should be sure to arrive in time to watch the sun sink over the isles of Filicudi and Alicudi. *Frittelle di zucchine* (deep-fried courgette fritters) come free, after which there will be two or three pasta dishes of the day (€7–10), inevitably including one dressed with a pesto of their own capers. Fish (€8–12) comes grilled or fried, but the signature dish is a tasty *coniglio in agrodolce*, rabbit stewed in a typical Sicilian sweet-sour sauce. Wines from €12.

La Locanda del Postino Pollara ☏090.984.3958, ⓦwww.lalocandadelpostino.it. Ten rooms with terraces in tranquil Pollara – a great choice if you want to turn your back on the world and collect sunsets. The best room is no. 10, with a large, private terrace (the rest of the terraces are divided by potted plants, so are pleasant but lack privacy). The restaurant is known for its seafood. ❸–❺

🏃 **Signum** Via Scalo 15, Malfa ☏090.984.4222, ⓦwww.hotelsignum.it. Island hotels don't come much better than this, deftly balancing style and luxury with friendly and relaxed service. Thirty comfortable rooms (some classed as superior and deluxe) display a seamless blend of antique furniture and contemporary style and have either terraces or balconies, sea or garden views. Swimming in the splendid infinity pool here at night and catching sight of Strómboli's eruptions across the water takes some beating, and the exquisite spa, tapping into a hot volcanic spring and offering treatments such as an anti-cellulite caper-rub, is also not to be missed. The restaurant, probably the island's best, serves Aeolian specialities (reservations recommended for non-guests). ❹–❼

Rinella

The smaller port of **RINELLA**, on the island's south coast, is 15km from Santa Marina, at the very bottom of a steep and winding road. It has clear water, a popular beach and the island's only campsite, so it gets a fair number of visitors in summer, though it's otherwise rather remote in feel. Buses meet the boat arrivals on the quayside (and call here several times a day otherwise), and you might be offered a room for rent. There's also a very nice little **hotel** and **restaurant**, *L'Ariana* (℡090.980.9075, Ⓦwww.hotelariana.it; ❺–❼), above the port to the left, occupying an old villa with a frill of terracotta busts around its roof. The *Campeggio Eolie* **campsite** (℡090.980.9052, Ⓦwww.campeggioeolie.it; closed Oct–April; bungalows ❹) is 200m up the road from the port, with its pitches for tents and caravans, a bar-restaurant, small shop and seven tiny bungalows ranged across pine-shaded terraces. It also has an internet point and can arrange boat trips. Great home-cooked food is served at the amiable 🍴 *Bar Papero*, tucked behind the main road with tables and canopies prettily arranged on Piazzetta Anna Magnani, and there's an excellent pizzeria, *Da Marco* (℡090.980.9120; open weekends only in winter), just up the road from *L'Ariana*.

Panarea

Halfway point between the central island group and Strómboli is **PANAREA**, at just 3km by 1.5km the smallest island in the archipelago, and indisputably the prettiest. It's almost Greek in aspect, with freshly painted white houses, their terraces decked with bougainvillea and oleander, and swept narrow lanes shaded by fruit trees. Panarea also holds one of the region's most important archeological sites, located on the dramatic Punta Milazzese, while the entire island is surrounded by clusters of islets set in dazzlingly clear water. It's hardly surprising then that Panarea's cosy intimacy has put it on the radar of the rich, famous and aspirational, and August in particular sees the island resemble the set of "I'm a Celebrity…" as Hollywood stars, fashionistas and wealthy Italians descend for a month of diving off blinding white yachts and wading knee-deep in the crystalline water. When the big names do arrive, Panarea kowtows, so if you turn up at some sleek hotel or bar for a sundowner and find it closed, don't be surprised – it simply means that Armani is in town and throwing a private party.

Around the island

Panarea's population divides itself between three hamlets on the eastern side of the island – Ditella, San Pietro and Drauto – though, as they meld into one another, it's a distinction that hardly matters. No cars can squeeze onto the island's narrow lanes to disturb the tranquillity, though heavily laden three-wheelers are common, zipping down to the port and back.

Boats arrive at **San Pietro**, tucked onto gentle terraces and backed by gnarled outcrops of rock. It's here that you'll find most of the accommodation, restaurants and facilities, while just to the north, passing through **Ditella**, you'll see evidence of volcanic activity in the steaming gas emissions (*fumarole*) on the stone beach below here, the **Spiaggia Fumarole**.

Ferries & Hydrofoils to Lipari & Salina ▼

Out to the islands: boat tours, snorkelling and diving

The islets and rocks off Panarea make for a great day out. You can either go on a tour (from around €15 per person) – there'll be plenty of time for swimming – or rent your own boat (from around €100 for a half-day excluding fuel). Check out the seafront kiosks at San Pietro or look for the signs advertising "*Noleggio barche*" (boat rental) in nearly every bar, shop and restaurant. Or, for snorkelling and scuba-diving (including introductory and PADI courses), contact the island's dive centre, Amphibia, in San Pietro (☏335.613.8529, ⓦwww.amphibia.it), which also offers day tours and children's activities.

The nearest of the islets to Panarea, **Dáttilo**, points a jagged, pyramidal finger skyward and has a minuscule beach. There's better swimming at **Lisca Bianca**, the stark setting of Antonioni's 1960 film *L'Avventura*, where the tranquil water is sheltered by **Bottaro** opposite. Just offshore, submarine fumaroles, created during the last major eruption of Strómboli in 2002, send columns of bubbles rising to the surface – a great snorkelling experience – though check before leaving if access is permitted, as gas emissions can occasionally be dangerous. Nearby Lisca Nera and Le Formiche (The Ants) are mere wrinkles on the sea surface, albeit a constant hazard to shipping. The largest islet is **Basiluzzo**, which retains the remains of a Roman fort and port (the latter now submerged) but is currently only used for caper cultivation.

South of San Pietro through the tangle of lanes, a gentle thirty-minute stroll above the coast leads to the mainly stone beach below **Drauto**. Just beyond here, the path descends to **Zimmari**, a popular, dark-gold sandy beach – the only one on the island – overlooked by a seasonal and expensive bar-trattoria. Steps at the far end of the beach climb up and across to the headland of **Punta Milazzese**, passing the trailhead of a waymarked path (look for the signposts) that wends into Panarea's interior, passing below the island's highest peak, the craggy **Punta del Corvo** (421m), before descending back to San Pietro – a hike of two to three hours on a path that is easy to follow.

Before taking the path, however, take time to see the archipelago's best-preserved Bronze Age village and to swim in one of its most magnificent bays. Atop Punta Milazzese a Bronze Age village of 23 huts was discovered in 1948; the oval outlines of the foundation walls are easily visible. This beautiful site, occupying a hammerhead of land overlooking two rocky inlets, is thought to have been inhabited since the fourteenth century BC, and pottery found here (displayed in Lípari's museum) shows a distinct Minoan influence – fascinating evidence of a historical link between the Aeolians and Crete that goes some way towards corroborating the legends of contact between the two in ancient times. Steps descend from Punta Milazzese to **Cala Junco**, a delightful stony cove whose aquamarine water, scattered stone outcrops and surrounding coves and caves make it a popular spot for snorkelling.

Practicalities

The quickest services take around an hour from Lípari, 25 minutes from Salina. **Ferries and hydrofoils** all dock at San Pietro's harbourside, where the Siremar (☏090.983.007) and Ústica Lines (☏090.983.344) ticket offices are almost next door to each other. Don't expect to see any celebs here buying tickets, though – they are more likely to use Air Panarea's **helicopter** service (☏090.983.4428 or 340.366.7214, ⓦwww.airpanarea.com), which runs a summer scheduled service from Réggio di Calabria airport (from €200 one-way) plus panoramic fly-overs of Strómboli and the other islands.

Although there's no tourist office, you can get **information** at ⓦwww.panarea .com (in Italian), which has links to a few hotels and rooms places. San Pietro has a pharmacy, an ATM and a summer-only police post and *guardia medica*, while in the warren of alleys behind the harbour is a little supermarket, two or three *alimentari* and a bakery. The little electric buggies down at the harbour act as taxis. However, all the hotels provide a free pick-up service.

Accommodation is insanely expensive in July and August (over €300 a night in many places) and, although there are cheaper rented rooms (still well over €100 double), the supply simply can't meet the demand in high summer. Prices do drop considerably come September, while many places close between October and Easter (you will always find somewhere to stay, however). **Nightlife** in summer revolves around the bars in the coolest hotels, though the *Bar del Porto* is always good for a harbourside drink and snack. Otherwise, the terrace of the *Raya* is all the rage, where sophisticated dance parties can carry on until late on summer nights, though it occasionally closes for private events.

Accommodation

Girasole Drauto ☎090.983018 or 328.861.8595, ⓦwww.hotelgirasole-panarea.it. Family-run hotel at Drauto, out on the way to the sandy beach at Zimmari. It's a great place to stay in low season, but even this part of the island is busy in August. ④–⑥

Lisca Bianca Via Lani, San Pietro ☎090.983.004, ⓦwww.liscabianca.it. This typical Aeolian building – covered wide terraces, blue shutters, white walls – has gorgeous views, with stylish rooms overlooking either the sea or the bougainvillea-clad gardens and port. You can see Stromboli from the breakfast terrace, and the bar is one of the best on the island. The *Casa Nonna* annexe on Via Ditella (in the village) has a few cheaper rooms, and prices outside August are quite reasonable at either place (look for special deals on the website). Closed Nov–March. ④–⑥

Peppe and Maria Soldini Ditella ☎090.983.061 or 334.703.5010. One of the least expensive places to stay on Panarea, these rooms lie up the hill behind the port in Ditella (beyond the Carabinieri barracks). Spotlessly clean, they are set in a garden and have their own terraces. Out of season (when rates are considerably lower) Pippo and Maria will provide meals. ③

A Quartara Via San Pietro, San Pietro ☎090.983.027, ⓦwww.quartarahotel.com. Very classy four-star boutique hotel run by a cheerful family, where the thirteen fashionable rooms have elegant wood furniture and stone floors. A terrace jacuzzi overlooks the port at the back, and there's a well-regarded restaurant. Closed Nov–March. ⑤–⑦

Raya Via San Pietro ☎090.983.013, ⓦwww .hotelraya.it. Opened in the 1960s, this is the hotel that put Panarea on the party map. It remains one of the hippest and priciest hotels in the Aeolians – however, ordinary folk paying €500 for a room might find it a little overrated. Bar, club and restaurant are located above the harbour, rooms (whitewashed walls, teak furniture, hand-batiked textiles, citronella candles) are a fair distance away, built into the hillside at the back of the village, but with wonderful views to the sea over groves of olives, hibiscus and bougainvillea. ⑤–⑧

Rodà Via San Pietro ☎090.983.006. One of the cheaper places on the island, a straightforward pensione with a garden-restaurant serving pizzas in the evening. Obligatory half board in Aug costs €120 per person. Closed Nov–March. ③

Eating

Da Adelina ☎090 983246. Relaxing and unpretentious candlelit restaurant overlooking Panarea's port, with a simple menu of seasonal dishes, such as *moscardini* (tiny octopus, cooked with tomato, capers, wild fennel and chilli) appearing alongside year-round dishes like *pennette adelina*, dressed with anchovies, aubergine, capers, olives, mint and basil. For the main course opt for the mixed fish of the day, either fried or grilled, along with a selection of grilled vegetables. Closed Nov–Feb.

Da Francesco ☎090.983.023. With views over the harbour, this offers pretty good value for meals of pasta (around €9) – including the signature dish,

"*disgraziata*", with peppers, chilli, capers, olives, aubergine, tomatoes and baked ricotta – and fish (from €13). It also has rooms to rent in summer. Closed Dec–Feb.

Da Paolino ☎090.983.008. Walking north towards Ditella, after ten minutes or so you'll reach this family-run restaurant whose terrace has fine views of Strómboli. You'll spend quite a bit if you order a full meal, but you can pick up a very decent plate of pasta with a salad and a glass of wine for around €20. Try the rich *mille baci* pasta with greens – and the fish is whatever the family has caught that day. Closed Nov–March.

Strómboli

The most spectacular of all the Aeolians, **STROMBÓLI** is little more than a volcanic cone thrust out of the sea. It's very much alive and kicking, throwing up showers of sparks and flaring rock from the craters at regular intervals, while a handful of more serious eruptions over the last century have caused major lava flows. That of 1930 led to serious damage to many homes and sparked a spate of emigration from the island, while threatening eruptions in 2002 and 2003 spewed volcanic rock into the sea, spawning tsunami and ejecting rocks onto rooftops. In 2007, two new craters opened on the summit, creating new lava streams into the sea, and in July 2010 fiery boulders set the mountain alight, though the fire was swiftly extinguished.

Amazingly, perhaps, people have chosen to live here for centuries, reassured that, historically, the main lava flows have been confined to the channel of the Sciara del Fuoco, down the western side of the island. This leaves the eastern parishes of San Vincenzo, San Bártolo and Piscità (often grouped together simply as Strómboli), and the solitary southern community of Ginostra, to lead something of a charmed life, their white terraced houses adorned with bougainvillea, plumbago and wisteria, remote from the fury of the craters above. The island's permanent population numbers perhaps five hundred, plumbing is often rudimentary, and access sometimes restricted because of winter storms, but despite this, Strómboli has become a chic resort, attracting a eclectic moneyed crowd that range from gay fashionistas to hip intellectuals, a mix leavened with a generous dose of holidaying families and hardy mountain types. Its black-sand beaches are overlooked by attractive terraced hotels, while thrill-seekers come from all over the world to climb one of the planet's most accessible volcanoes.

Around the island

The main settlement of **Strómboli** spreads for a distance of around 2km between the lower slopes of the volcano and the island's beaches. It's an utterly straightforward layout of two largely parallel roads and steep, interconnecting alleys, though the profusion of local place names keeps visitors on their toes. From the scruffy quayside area known as **Scari**, the lower coastal road (Via Marina and Via Regina Elena) runs around to the main beach of **Ficogrande**, a long black stretch overlooked by several hotels. Further on is **Piscità**, around 25 minutes' walk from the port, with the island's most beautiful and secluded ashy beach at its far end. There's also a sand-and-stone stretch south of Scari, past the fishing boats, and if

---

Strómboli boat tours

The main daytime boat tour offered is the **round-island excursion** (2hr 30min; around €20) calling at Ginostra and Strómboli's extraordinary basalt offspring, Strombolicchio. You usually get half an hour to scramble around Ginostra, which is plenty of time to see it, while at Strombolicchio there's swimming and a 200-step climb up the battlemented rock to the lighthouse on its top.

At night, the stock-in-trade is the cruise to see the **Sciara del Fuoco** (1hr 30min; around €15), the lava channel rising sheer out of incredible deep-blue sea water. Boats aren't allowed to dock on the shoreline, since it's too unpredictably dangerous, but through the gloom you'll see orange and red flashes from the crater above.

You can book tours at any of the stands (prices are broadly similar), where you can also charter a boat for longer tours or rent your own, or from Paola and Giovanni (☎338.431.2803) who work from opposite the *Sirenetta* hotel in Ficogrande.

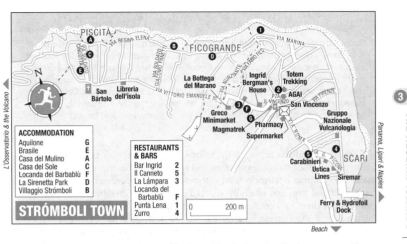

you clamber over the rocks at the end of this beach, there's a further sweep of lava-stone beach that attracts a fair bit of nude sunbathing.

The other road from the quayside cuts up into what could loosely be described as "the village", where, as Via Roma, it runs as far as the church of **San Vincenzo**, whose square offers glorious views of the Strombolicchio basalt stack. Beyond the square, it's another fifteen minutes' or so walk to the second church of **San Bártolo**, above Piscità, just beyond which starts the path to the crater. Once you've got this far, you've seen all that Strómboli village has to offer. The only "sight", apart from the churches, is the house in which **Ingrid Bergman** lived with Roberto Rossellini in the spring of 1949, while making the film *Strómboli: Terra di Dio*. A plaque records these bare facts on the pink building, just after San Vincenzo church, on the right.

Without seeing its name on timetables, you might not even be aware of the existence of **Ginostra**, the hamlet on the southwest side of the island. From the minuscule harbour, zigzag steps climb into a cluster of typical white Aeolian houses on terraces. It's a refreshingly simple place: donkeys are tethered to posts outside homes; ancient exterior stone ovens lie idle; and cultivated hedges and volcanic stone walls snake up the hillside. Weather permitting, a couple of hydrofoils run to and from Strómboli town per day in summer (once daily in winter), though a boat tour is a more realistic way to see Ginostra (unless you fancy actually staying here at the one small hotel). A century ago, there was also a maintained path that skirted the shore back to Strómboli, but assault by the elements has done for most it. However, you don't need to go very far, following the coast anticlockwise, to find spots where you can swim off the rocks.

Practicalities

Several **ferry and hydrofoil** services from Lípari call first at Ginostra, though the main port is Strómboli. It's a good hour and three-quarters by hydrofoil, and can take up to four hours by ferry. There are also direct summer hydrofoils to Strómboli from Naples (4hr) and Réggio di Calabria (up to 3hr 30min). The Siremar (℡090.986.016) and Ústica Lines (℡090.986.003) **ticket offices** are both by Strómboli harbour, which is a hive of activity in summer, especially with tour agencies and accommodation touts. If you've come without a reservation, accepting a **room** (from €50, cheaper out of season) from one of the touts is as good an idea as any – there's no obligation to stay, if you don't like what you see.

Getting around Strómboli

Strómboli has no network of **public transport** – indeed the only transport on the island is by three-wheeler pick-up (known locally as *lapa*), motorbike or one of the licensed taxis that resemble electric golf cars. If your hotel is any distance from the port you might appreciate the use of a taxi – though as these require ten hours' charging for every two hours' driving, they're not always available. Of the official taxis, Sabbia Nera, based near the port (☏090.986.399), are reliable and friendly. Alternatively, ask your hotel at the time of booking if they have, or can organize, transport for you.

Most other **facilities** are up in the village, including several small supermarkets, a pharmacy, police station, post office and an ATM. La Bottega del Marano on the main Via Vittorio Emanuele is an outstanding deli-supermarket, with fabulous fresh fruit and veg, and carefully sourced cheeses, hams, salamis and wines (you can also get there by climbing the steps directly above the beach at Ficogrande). Further along Via Vittorio Emanuele is the chic little bookshop, Libreria dell'Isola (open Easter–Sept), with frequent **film screenings** in its garden along with exhibitions by jewellers and other artisans; it also has **internet** access. This and several other shops sell a good map of Strómboli showing local hiking trails. The **bars** down at the harbour see a lot of action during the day, while at night there's no better spot than *Bar Ingrid* (☏090.986.385; open until midnight, up to 3am in high summer) in the square by San Vincenzo church.

Accommodation

Aquilone Via Vittorio Emanuele 29 ☏090.986.080. Up an alley opposite the Greco minimarket, this friendly place is ranged around a rose garden and lemon grove, though rooms are plain, almost monastic. There's also a cosy mini-apartment round the back with cooking facilities. Closed Nov–March. ❸

Brasile Via Soldato Cincotta, Piscità ☏090.986.008, ⓦwww.strombolialbergobrasile.it. Tranquil spot at the far end of town, with friendly management and simple rooms with plain tiled floors. Two nicer suites have their own private terraces, or there's a large roof terrace that everyone can use. Half board at their restaurant is obligatory from mid-June to Aug (€70–85 per person per night). Closed Nov–March. ❷

Casa del Mulino Piscità ☏090.986.701 or 338.540.8931, ⓔmichele.wegner@gmail.com. Friendly, laid-back, scruffy-bohemian sort of place, in an old windmill perched right on the lava-cliff edge above a cove. There are four simple rooms, including two adjacent triples with their own terrace and kitchen. ❶–❷

Casa del Sole Via Soldato Cincotta, Piscità ☏090.986.300, ⓦwww.casadelsolestromboli.it. A cheapie in an old building within metres of the sea, offering ten simple rooms, including five-bedded rooms with shared bathrooms, and en-suite doubles. Kitchen facilities are available, and there's a sun terrace. No credit cards. Closed Dec–Feb. ❷–❸

Locanda del Barbablù Via Vittorio Emanuele 17 ☏090.986.118, ⓦwww .barbablu.it. An old Aeolian house, with antique rooms, four-poster beds and original tile floors, provides the most relaxed accommodation on Strómboli. It's combined with a restaurant where you can dine under the stars. Closed Nov–Feb. ❺–❻

Petrusa Ginostra ☏090.981.2305. Ginostra's only official accommodation (you may find other places by asking around) has three large rooms with their own terraces, sharing a bathroom. Half board is obligatory in July and Aug. Their bar-restaurant, *L'Incontro*, has fairly high prices but is pretty good. No credit cards. Closed Oct–April. ❷–❸

La Sirenetta Park Via Marina 33, Ficogrande ☏090.986.025, ⓦwww.lasirenettahotel.it. Four-star hotel set opposite the black sands of Ficogrande. It's got a decent-sized outdoor pool, a summer nightclub and access to watersports facilities. The room rates drop considerably outside summer and at the beginning or end of the season you can stay for around €120. Closed Nov–March. ❹–❻

Villaggio Strómboli Via Regina Elena ☏090.986.018, ⓦwww.villaggiostromboli.it. With simple rooms jutting up against the breaking waves, this pleasant, quiet place is one of the nicest seaside stays; it also has a good terrace restaurant where you can gaze out over the water. ❸–❺

Eating

Il Canneto Via Roma ☎ 090.986.014. A rustic trattoria where the waiters reel off a list of daily specials, such as spaghetti *alla strombolana* (with chilli, anchovies and capers) with clams, or coloured with squid ink, followed by fresh fish. Outside August there is a fixed price menu at €23 for a *primo, secondo* and salad or grilled vegetables; drinks and dessert extra. Closed Nov–March.

La Lámpara Via Vittorio Emanuele ☎ 090.986.009. Dine on pizza, pasta and grilled meat and fish on the large raised terrace under a pergola of climbing vines among huge pots of basil and rosemary. Closed Nov–March.

Locanda del Barbablù Via Vittorio Emanuele 17 ☎ 090.986.118. Stylish restaurant, specializing in fresh fish and vegetables. There are just two menus that change daily: the full *degustazione* (tasting) menu costs €50, and the "piccolo" *degustazione* menu €38, with wine extra. Worth the splurge, though it's not particularly child-friendly.

Punta Lena Via Marina, Ficogrande ☎ 090.986.204. Smart place with a marvellous position at the water's edge, and great for fish (*secondi* from €15) – the choice basically depends on the day's catch. Their version of spaghetti *alla strombolana* is good, with wild fennel, anchovies, chilli, cherry tomatoes and garlic. Closed Nov–March.

Zurro Via Marina ☎ 090 986 283. Named for its bearded, piratical-looking chef, a one-time fisherman, this place a short walk from the port isn't exactly romantic, with its startlingly bright lights and aluminium-framed windows, but you're guaranteed a good meal. Dishes might include razor-thin slices of raw aubergine flecked with chilli flakes and served with balsamic-dressed rocket and parmesan, spaghetti *alla strombolana*, with cherry tomatoes, anchovies, mint, chilli and garlic, or *pietre di mare*, black ravioli stuffed with *ricciola* (amberjack) and dressed with capers, cherry tomatoes and basil. The chocolate cake is a must.

Climbing the volcano

Climbing the volcano is big business, and for safety reasons it's no longer the free-for-all it used to be. Public access was only reopened in 2005 (after the eruptions of preceding years), and while you can freely walk along the trails below 400m, to go any higher you have to be accompanied by a licensed guide. Numbers at the crater are also limited, so it's essential to reserve a place on an **organized excursion** (from €28; see below for contact details and other information) as soon as you can – on the day is usually fine for most of the year, but advanced booking is advised in high summer – and be prepared for the trip to be postponed because of poor weather or other climatic or geological reasons. You need to be in decent health, have proper hiking boots and clothes (you can rent these in the village), and carry plenty of water and sun protection. Guides usually supply helmets.

Most excursions leave in the late afternoon, taking around five or six hours – this lets you catch the amazing sunsets and gives you around an hour or so at the top, watching the fireworks. The explosions occur roughly every twenty minutes and vary in intensity, but it's always nothing less than impressive, the noise alone something like an express train thundering directly below you. Ignore the warning signs at your peril.

The **route** starts a few minutes' walk beyond San Bártolo church, climbing to the first orientation point, *L'Osservatorio*, a bar-pizzeria (closed in winter) which has a wide terrace and a view of the volcano. You can come this far without a guide. Beyond, you'll see the frighteningly sheer volcanic trail that channels all the lava outflows, known as the **Sciara del Fuoco**, plunging directly into the sea. This is a huge blistered sheet down which thousands of years' worth of volcanic detritus has poured, scarring and pock-marking the hillside. Menacing little puffs of steam dance up from folds in the bare slope, where absolutely nothing grows. If ever a place warranted a "Here Be Dragons" sign, this is it.

Guides, equipment and information

AGAI (Associazione Guide Alpine Italiane) Piazza San Vincenzo ☎ 090.986.211 or 090.986.263. One of the main guided operations.

Gruppo Nazionale Vulcanologia Near the harbour ☎ 090.986.708, ⓦ gnv.invg.it. The national vulcanology organization has an office with useful background information on the volcano. It's open most days and shows a video about Strómboli, while the national website has photos, technical information and some scary seismograph readings from previous eruptions.

 Magmatrek Via Vittorio Emanuele, just off the piazza ☎090.986.5768,

ⓦwww.magmatrek.it. Local climbing guru, Zazà, and his colleagues have daily volcano treks throughout the year. Guides are knowledgeable and experienced and in constant contact with the vulcanological centre.

Totem Trekking Piazza San Vincenzo 4 ☎090.986.5752. Useful little shop that sells and rents out hiking equipment and accessories.

Filicudi

FILICUDI is the larger of the two minor, westerly islands, and closest to the main pack. The small harbour consists of a few colour-trimmed cubes of buildings, and promises little at first sight, but Filicudi turns on its charm the longer you stay. Climb away from the port, and the rest of the pretty island is easily accessible on well-kept paths that crisscross the slopes, lined with volcanic boulders interspersed with great flowering cacti whose pustular blooms erupt upon elephant-ear leaves. You can clamber down to pebble beaches and swim in deserted coves, or make your way around the terraced headlands to deserted villages and phenomenal viewpoints. Filicudi's sheer slopes are all painstakingly lined with stone terracing, a reminder that before mass emigration in the 1950s and 1960s there was a great deal of agricultural activity here. Many terraces were subsequently abandoned, and cultivation is now down to a few vines and olives, but they do serve to reduce soil erosion. Today, there are only 250 or so permanent island residents, and while this number swells perhaps tenfold in August with visitors, a coterie of left-wing villa owners (including former Rome mayor Francesco Rutelli), and returned *emigranti*, Filicudi is still a long way from being overdeveloped.

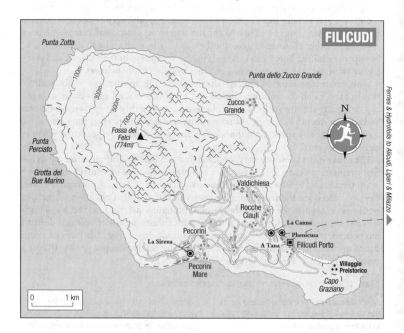

The walk to Zucco Grande

Many footpaths on Filicudi have been restored in recent years, notably the excellent route to the derelict village of **Zucco Grande** on the island's eastern flank. The path starts from just below Valdichiesa church, at a bend in the road (a 20min walk from Rocche Ciauli), where a signpost says "*Sentiero, Zucco Grande, m1900*" – there are subsequent fingerposts all the way, so you can't go wrong. It's a good path, beautifully cut, that follows the contours around the cliffs through gorse and prickly pear, until finally reaching the village after another thirty minutes. Abandoned forty years ago – the inhabitants mostly left for Australia – the houses are in a parlous state, clinging to the cliffside, with sweeping views out to sea. The current population is three. One of them, Giovanni, who has a couple of rooms and can provide a basic dinner (☎347.813.2579 or 368.407.544), has lived here for years, while the others are solace-seeking souls who have bought houses to renovate. Here, amid the ruins, is a great place to sit and dwell on the isolation and hardship that forced the original inhabitants to flee to the other side of the world. Either return the way you came, or continue on the path through the village, which eventually climbs up and over the top, back towards Valdichiesa.

Around the island

The only real settlement is **Filicudi Porto**, where almost all accommodation and services are found. There's only one road, too, which runs southeast, up away from the harbour and stone beach – where it makes a sharp turn to the right you'll find the start of a steep stone path up to the renowned archeological site, the **Villaggio Preistorico** at Capo Graziano. This occupies a grassy plateau, high above the harbour, a twenty-minute walk all told from the dockside. Here, the remains of a dozen or so oval huts mark the place that gave its name to the local Bronze Age Capo Graziano culture that immediately preceded Panarea's Punta Milazzese, from the eighteenth to thirteenth centuries BC. The site is always open and though there's not much to see, it's a fine place from which to watch the comings and goings at the harbour below.

The island road winds around and up to the **Rocche Ciauli** district, where the road forks (at the *Villa La Rosa* hotel and restaurant). You can get to this point more directly on a heart-bursting stepped path from the harbour, a fifteen-minute climb. Turn left at the junction and the road swings around to **Pecorini**, no more than a few houses grouped around a church, below which, down the switchbacks, is the little harbour of **Pecorini Mare**. This is 7km by road from Filicudi Porto, though a short cut, by vertiginous donkey track, starts to the side of the church in Pecorini and takes just fifteen minutes down to the harbour (or an hour's total walk from Filicudi Porto). Pecorini Mare is a mere scrap of a fishing hamlet with a small dockside, a Carabinieri post, a "Saloon", which sells drinks and *gelati*, and a couple of trattorias. It's a gorgeous, end-of-the-line place, with a long pebble beach backed by fishermen's houses and holiday homes, and perfectly clear water that's surprisingly warm for swimming.

Turning right instead at the Rocche Ciauli junction, a twenty-minute walk up the switchback road brings you to the dispersed central village of **Valdichiesa**, where the church (*chiesa*) itself is set back on a terrace with splendid views. This is the way to come for the fantastic walk to Zucco Grande (see box above), while above church and village lie the heights of **Fossa dei Felci** (774m), reached by vague paths that climb through the terraces.

To explore the island's uninhabited northern and western coasts you'll need to **rent a boat** (about €15–20 a head, depending on numbers). In summer, there's usually someone at Filicudi Porto or Pecorini Mare touting for custom, and any

3

Cars on Filicudi

In the summer of 2010, in a measure designed to cut down on the density of tourist traffic, cars were permitted to enter Filicudi only for drivers staying on the island for at least a week, whether in a hotel or in private accommodation. Proof of booking was required by the ferry companies before issuing tickets. Whether the initiative continues remains to be seen, so check with your hotel, or the ferry companies.

hotel, shop or restaurant can point you in the right direction too. The main sights include the fine natural arch of **Punta Perciato** and the nearby **Grotta del Bue Marino** ("Seal Grotto" – there aren't any), a wide rocky cavity 37m long by 30m wide, its walls of reddish lava barely visible in the pitch black of the interior. Near the island's northwest coast, the startling **Canna**, a rugged obelisk 85m tall, is the most impressive of all the *faraglioni* of the Aeolian Islands.

Practicalities

Filicudi Porto is an hour by hydrofoil from Lípari, and three hours from Palermo. The Siremar (☎090.988.9960) and Ústica Lines (☎090.988.9949) **ticket offices** are on the dockside, both open before departures. The one-street port has a pharmacy (limited opening), general store, ATM and two or three bar-restaurants, with terraces overlooking the water and Salina in the distance. One of them, *Da Nino sul Mare* (☎090.988.9984), also sells ice cream, postcards and island maps showing some of the footpaths.

There's usually a red **minibus taxi** waiting at the harbour (*bus navetta*), which will take you where you want to go on the island. It costs €12 to Pecorini Mare, less per head if there's a group of you. If it's not there, call D&G Servizio Navetta (☎347.757.5916 or 347.517.1825). There's also summer **scooter rental** at the port, and a seasonal **scuba-diving** outfit, Apogon (☎090.988.9955, ⓦwww.apogon.it) – alternatively many of the hotels can arrange scooter rental and diving sessions.

Outside the summer months, it's usually no problem just turning up and finding **accommodation**, though as options are limited a call is still recommended to be on the safe side. Reservations are essential in summer, though you can always try asking around for private rooms – a few are available, or contact the house agent Vincenzo Anastasi (☎336.926.560, ⓦwww.eolie-filicudi.com), who rents out two- to six-bed houses across the island (from around €500 per week, double that in summer). In July and August, you'll be obliged to have dinner at your hotel, though this is rarely a hardship as the quality is uniformly excellent. Otherwise, a full meal in any of the hotel **restaurants** (all open to non-guests) costs about €30 a head plus wine.

Accomodation and eating

🏃 **La Canna** Via Rosa 43, Rocche Ciauli ☎090.988.9956, ⓦwww.lacannahotel.it. The best choice near the port, though it's a stiff climb up the steps to Rocche Ciauli; call ahead and they'll pick you up from the dock. Ten lovely bright rooms with tiled bathrooms open onto a spacious terrace with a magnificent view over the bay below, and there's a small pool (summer only). The food in the restaurant (open to all) is excellent – home-made pasta, fresh fish, local caper salads and plenty of home-produced wine and fruit. Half board in Aug is up to €100 a head, though more reasonable at other times. ❸–❺

Phenicusa Filicudi Porto ☎090.988.9946, ⓦwww.hotelphenicusa.com. The only hotel right by the harbour opens for just four months a year – it's a traditional three-star, with reasonable rooms, though not all have sea views (and you pay a supplement for those that do). Breakfast is served on the sun-soaked terrace, and the decent restaurant has the same sea and harbour views. Half board is required in Aug at €110 per person. Closed Oct–May. ❸–❺

🏃 **La Sirena** Pecorini Mare ☎090.988.9997, ⓦwww.pensionelasirena.it. An oasis you won't want to leave, this cosy inn sits right on the Pecorini Mare seafront, with the fishing boats drawn up alongside. A varied selection of rooms is available, some with antique furniture and little waterfront balconies, others in self-contained houses not far away. Out on the shaded terrace is the island's most relaxed restaurant (open to all, lunch and dinner). It gets very busy in Aug, but at most times of the year all you can hear is the sound of lapping water as you tuck into such dishes as spaghetti with almond sauce and spanking fresh grilled tuna. Half board is obligatory in July and Aug (€110–120 per person). Closed Oct–May. ❹

A Tana Filicudi Porto ☎090.988.9089. At this little restaurant just a minute or two's walk along the seafront from the port, you can dine on simple dishes such as *pasta con cozze e vóngole* and other seafood specials on a lovely terrace overlooking the stone beach. Closed Oct–May.

Alicudi

Ends of the line in Europe don't come much more remote than **ALICUDI**. Two and a half hours from Milazzo by hydrofoil, or five by ferry, the island forms a perfect cone, a mere Mediterranean pimple, and its precipitous shores are pierced by numerous caves. Up the sheer slope behind the only settlement, terraced smallholdings and white houses cling on for dear life, decorated with tumbling banks of flowers. Indeed, Alicudi's ancient name of Ericusa was the word for the heather that still stains its slopes purple in spring. Its rocky isolation was formerly exploited by the Italian government, who used the island as a prison for convicted Mafiosi, but now it's virtually abandoned by all but a few farmers and fishermen.

It's this quietude, of course, that attracts tourists; not many, it's true, but enough for there to be some semblance of facilities in the village to cater for visitors. Electricity arrived at the start of the 1990s, so now there's TV, too. There are two general stores, plenty of fancy boat hardware, even a car or two parked at the dock (though, since there are no navigable roads, it's not clear whether this is bravado or forward planning on behalf of the owners). You have to walk to reach anywhere and the network of volcanic stone-built paths behind the village is extremely steep and tough – all the heavy fetching and carrying is still done by donkey or mule, whose indignant brays echo across the port all day.

The island

Once you disembark at **ALICUDI PORTO**, things to do are simply enumerated. The most exhausting option is the hike up past the castle ruins to the island peak of **Filo dell'Arpa** (675m). The path runs up through the village houses from the port and there's a proper stone-built track most of the way. Unfortunately, the track looks as though it was created by a malevolent giant emptying a bag of boulders from the top and letting them fall where they will. There's absolutely no shade, and it will take at least two hours to get up, though the magnificent views make it worthwhile.

Otherwise, you'll probably get all the exercise you need clambering over the rocky **shore** to the south of the port. The path soon peters out beyond the island's only hotel and the power station, but the rocks offer a sure foothold as they get

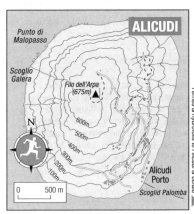

larger the further you venture. The water is crystal clear and, once you've found a flat rock big enough to lie on, you're set for more peace and quiet than you'd bargained for. The only sounds are the echoed mutter of offshore fishermen, the scrabbling of little black crabs in the rock pools and the lap of the waves.

Practicalities

From the dock, walk to the left past the beached fishing-boats and in the almost cave-like dwellings in front of you are the Siremar **agency** (open before departures; (℡090.988.9795), Ústica Lines (℡340.301.5047) and – in the arched terrace above – one of the island's **general stores** (the other one is along the path to the hotel).

The modern, twelve-roomed *Ericusa* **hotel** is a five-minute walk south along the shore (℡090.988.9902, ⓦwww.alicudihotel.it; closed Oct–May, half board only €75–95 per person), with sea views, terrace and restaurant. **Apartment or room rental** is usually quite straightforward too, and available all year round: ask around at the port, or contact *Da Rosina Alla Mimosa*, up in the village, with a handful of simple rooms to rent (℡090.988.9937 or 368.361.6511, ⓦwww.rosina-barbuto .it; ❷), or *Casa Mulino* (℡090.988.9681, ⓦwww.alicudicasamulino.it; ❸), which has small apartment rooms with terraces sleeping two, four or six people.

If you don't want to **eat** at the *Ericusa*, try *Da Rosina Alla Mimosa* (see above), where virtually everything is produced or – in the case of rabbit and fish – caught by the family. In autumn there are wild mushrooms, and from autumn to spring wild pickings such as fennel and borage. Alternatively, call in on Signore Silvio during the day, who lives up the hill behind the Siremar office (anyone can point you in the right direction). He cooks dinner on request – spaghetti, fresh fish, salad, fruit and wine – for around €25 a head, served on his bougainvillea-covered terrace in the company of whoever else happens to turn up. If you want to fend for yourself, pick up provisions from either of the village stores, including bread, cheese, cured meats, olives, beer, ice cream, and whatever fruit and vegetables arrived on the boats.

Travel details

Ferries and hydrofoils year round connect the Aeolians with Milazzo, Messina, Palermo and Cefalù; additional summer (June to Sept) services operate from Naples and Réggio di Calabria on the Italian mainland. Main services are with Siremar (ⓦwww.siremar.it), Ústica Lines (ⓦwww.usticalines.it) and NGI (ⓦwww.ngi-spa.it), whose websites are the best places to consult up-to-date timetables and ticket prices.

Ferries	Hydrofoils
Lípari to: Alicudi (at least 3 weekly, 1 daily in summer; 3hr 45min); Filicudi (at least 3 weekly, 1 daily in summer; 2hr–2hr 40min); Ginostra (at least 4 weekly, 1 daily in summer; 3–4hr); Milazzo (4–5 daily; 2hr); Panarea (at least 4 weekly, 1–2 daily in summer; 2hr); Salina (2 daily; 50min); Strómboli (at least 4 weekly, 1 daily in summer; 3–4hr); Vulcano (2–3 daily; 25min).	**Lípari** to: Alicudi (1–4 daily; 2hr); Cefalù (1 daily in summer; 3hr 30min); Filicudi (1–4 daily; 1hr 15min); Ginostra (1 daily; 1hr 30min); Messina (1–5 daily; 1hr 30min–2hr 10min); Milazzo (approximately hourly; 45min–1hr); Palermo (2 daily in summer; 3–4hr); Panarea (3–5 daily; 1hr); Salina (approximately hourly; 25min); Strómboli (3–5 daily; 1hr 45min); Vulcano (approximately hourly; 10min).

Messina, Taormina and the northeast

CHAPTER 4 # Highlights

* **Ferragosto in Messina**
  Giant puppets and dazzling
  fireworks over the Straits
  are the highlights of this
  mid-August party, which takes
  over the entire city. See p.158

* **Fish supper in Ganzirri** A few
  kilometres north of Messina,
  dine on seafood alongside
  the lakes or facing the Straits.
  See p.159

* **Tíndari** Spend time with the
  lizards exploring the Roman
  remains of Tyndaris, loftily
  located by the sea. See p.165

* **Sávoca** This hill-village offers
  a gruesome set of mummified
  bodies and a location seen
  in *The Godfather* movie.
  See p.168

* **Teatro Greco, Taormina** The
  island's most dramatically
  sited classical theatre makes
  a superb summer venue for
  concerts, films and dramas.
  See p.175

* **The Gole dell'Alcántara**
  Wade through the water in the
  deep gorge of the Alcántara
  River. See p.181

▲ The basilica at Tíndari

Messina, Taormina and the northeast

With its dramatic backdrop of mountains, Sicily's **northeastern corner** includes the island's most visually exotic coastline, crammed with brilliant displays of colourful vegetation. Perhaps not surprisingly, the coast is also dominated by an almost unbroken ribbon of development, for this is one of Sicily's most popular resort areas, with both Italian and foreign tourists lured by the stunning views down to a turquoise sea. Still at heart the hill-village it once was, **Taormina** is the most illustrious resort – on the entire island, never mind this coast – and its famous ancient theatre, grand hotels and engaging small-town charm captivate most visitors. The local beaches are all a short ride below town, including the extensive sands that line the curving bay at **Giardini-Naxos**.

It's **Messina**, just across the busy Straits from mainland Italy, that's the major city in this region, though an unfortunate history has left only scant attractions. If it's **beaches** you're after, then some of the best lie west of Messina, beyond the fortified town of **Milazzo** or just below Tíndari at **Marinello**; other more crowded swathes lie around small resorts like **Capo d'Orlando**, which also makes a lively stopover.

Inland, you soon leave the crowds behind in the venerable old hill-village of **Castroreale**, west of Messina, while south of the city **Mili San Pietro** and **Itala** are distinguished by impressive Norman churches built by Count Roger in the eleventh century, and mummified bodies are on display in the Cappuccini monastery at **Sávoca**. Further south, beyond Taormina, the only road that penetrates any distance inland takes in the **Alcántara valley** and its spectacular gorge, before heading up to the gnarled old towns of **Francavilla** and **Castiglione di Sicilia**.

By road, the toll autostradas (the A18 south and A20 west) are the fastest way to get around, plunging through some fairly dramatic scenery as they cruise above the sea. Palermo-bound trains running west from Messina stop at Milazzo and Capo d'Orlando, though fast buses are the most convenient link between Messina and Milazzo. Travelling south down the coast, local buses get snarled up in the succession of towns and villages along the coast – an excruciatingly slow ride – while, again, fast buses via the autostrada are best for going direct to Taormina. The train line traces the shoreline pretty much all the way, allowing sparkling views across to Calabria on a clear day.

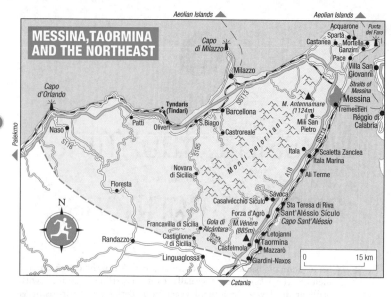

Messina and around

MESSINA may well be your first sight of Sicily, and from the ferry it's a fine one, stretching out along the seaboard, north of the distinctive hooked harbour from which the city took its Greek name – Zancle (Sickle). The natural beauty of its location, looking out over the Straits to the forested hills of Calabria, is Messina's best point; Shakespeare (who almost certainly never laid eyes on the city) used it as the setting for his *Much Ado About Nothing*. Yet the city itself holds only a few buildings of any historical or architectural interest, dotted along streets that are either traffic-choked or used as racetracks by drivers who rank among the most reckless in Sicily. The unedifying appearance is not entirely Messina's own fault: the congestion is largely the result of the surrounding mountains, which squeeze the traffic along the one or two roads that link the elongated centre with the northern suburbs. Messina's modern aspect is more a tribute to its powers of survival in the face of a record of devastation that's high even by Sicily's disaster-prone standards.

The greatest damage has been caused by the unstable geological belt on which Messina stands, responsible for a series of catastrophic **earthquakes**. The most notable of these occurred in 1783 and 1908; on the latter occasion the shore sank by half a metre overnight and around 80,000 Sicilians lost their lives (plus around 15,000 across the Straits in Calabria). The few surviving buildings, along with everything that had been painstakingly reconstructed in the wake of the earthquake, were subsequently the target of Allied bombardments, when Messina achieved the dubious distinction of being the most intensely bombed Italian city during World War II. Consequently, the attractions of Messina itself are limited, and can be seen quickly. However, if you're here in summer, you'll notice the passage of the tall-masted *felucche*, or **swordfish boats**, patrolling the narrow channel, attracted to these rich waters from miles up and down the Italian coast. You can enjoy their catch the same day in a good choice of restaurants, especially a little way north at **Ganzirri**, where lakeside fish restaurants provide some welcome relief from the city. Beyond, and around the corner of **Punta del Faro**, lidos line the coast at **Mortelle**, whose beaches, bars and pizzerias are where the city comes to relax.

Arrival, information and city transport

Driving into Messina, leave the autostrada at the Boccetta exit for the centre and ferries. Arriving **by train,** disembark at **Stazione Centrale**, at Piazza della Repubblica, unless you're coming from the mainland, in which case you might as well disembark at Messina's **Stazione Maríttima** – even if you're changing trains, as it takes a good hour to reassemble trains from the ferry – and walk 100m on to the Stazione Centrale. Piazza della Repubblica is also where most of the local and long-distance **buses** arrive and depart, including buses to Milazzo for the Aeolian Islands.

Ferries from Villa San Giovanni or Réggio di Calabria also dock at the Stazione Maríttima, apart from Caronte ferries which pull in further up, adjacent to Via della Libertà (ten minutes' walk north along the harbour). At either place,

---

Festivals

January
1–6 New Year celebrations in **Taormina**. Puppet shows, folk-singing and concerts, ending on Twelfth Night.

February/March
Carnevale Carnival celebrations in **Taormina** and **Giardini-Naxos**: processional floats, fireworks and music for three days.

May
Festival in **Milazzo** dedicated to San Francesco di Paola.

4th week Classical dramas at **Tyndaris** staged in the ancient theatre through to mid-June.

June
2nd/3rd week International Film Festival in **Taormina**, with screenings in the Teatro Greco.

2nd/3rd week Start of the theatrical performances and concerts at the castle in **Milazzo**; runs through to August.

July
3rd week onwards, until late August Dance, drama and music in **Taormina**; many of the performances are held in the Teatro Greco.

4th week, until late August More theatre and concerts in the ancient theatre at **Tyndaris**.

Late July and early August In the mountain village of **Castroreale**, Castroreale Jazz attracts international musicians in a series of open-air concerts.

August
12–14 Procession of the *giganti* in **Messina**.

15 Ferragosto procession and fireworks in **Messina**, and procession of boats along the coast in honour of Madonna di Porto Salvo at **Capo d'Orlando**.

September
8 Informal pilgrimage to the sanctuary of the Black Madonna at **Tyndaris**.

December
20 onwards Christmas and New Year celebrations in **Taormina**. Puppet shows, folk-singing, parades and concerts.

MESSINA, TAORMINA AND THE NORTHEAST | Messina and around

Crossing the Straits of Messina is arguably the most evocative entry into Sicily. The main embarkation point is **Villa San Giovanni**, 12km north of Réggio di Calabria, from where two ferry services, the state-railway-run Bluvia (℡090.678.6478) and the private firm Caronte (℡800.627.414, ⓦwww.carontetourist.it), and one hydrofoil (*aliscafo*) service, Metromare (℡0923.873.813, ⓦwww.metromaredellostretto.it), operate.

Drivers should follow signs from the Villa San Giovanni autostrada exit, a straight-forward run with ferry ticket offices clearly marked. The most frequent service is operated by Caronte, which has two ticket kiosks en route to the port; the second one, past the railway, can be a bit of a scramble, with nowhere to park. The FS/Bluvia ticket office lies across the square from here, with plenty of parking space. Tickets are €28–30 for a car one way; returns valid for sixty days cost €55–60, three-day returns €30–35. The queue for boarding involves an average wait of around 15 minutes – even in the peak times of August and rush hour, it's rarely more than 25.

Note that Caronte also operates a ferry service direct to Messina **from Salerno**, leaving once or twice daily all year and taking 8 hours; fares are €19–24 depending on season, more for an armchair or berth, and €60–90 for a car.

Travelling **by train**, you might want to stay on it if you're crossing at night (though you'll probably be woken by the clanking din as the train is loaded onto the Bluvia ferry), but by day it's quicker to leave the train at Villa San Giovanni station and skip the shuttling operation, boarding an earlier ferry by foot. In this case, following the signs from the platform, descend to sea level, where there are ticket offices for Bluvia ferries (one-way tickets €1.50) and Metromare hydrofoils (€2.50). Overhead signs tell you which bay leads to the first departure, or follow everyone else. There are enough Bluvia ferries (1–2 an hour) to make it unnecessary to walk the 500m to the Caronte ferries; hydrofoil departures are roughly hourly (Sat & Sun 4–5 daily).

Journey time for crossings is 20–30 minutes on Bluvia and Caronte ferries, hydrofoils take 20 minutes. On ferries, a bar on board serves snacks (including some good *arancini*), coffee and refreshments. Drivers might as well leave their vehicles, though look sharp as the ferry approaches Messina, as disembarkation is a rushed affair (and a suitable introduction to driving in Messina).

From Réggio di Calabria to Messina, there are hydrofoil services from the port, a couple of hundred metres back from Réggio Lido station, operated two or three times daily by Ústica Lines (℡346.011.6552, ⓦwww.usticalines.it) and roughly hourly (Sat & Sun 5 daily) by Metromare, taking about 15 and 30 minutes respectively. Tickets cost €4.30 on Ústica Lines, €3.50 on Metromare. Meridiano Lines (℡0965.810.414, ⓦwww.meridianolines.it) runs a **car ferry service** from Réggio di Calabria to Messina and to Tremestieri, south of Messina (useful for the autostrada to Taormina and Catania). On weekdays, these run twice daily to Messina and every couple of hours to Tremestieri, but on Saturday there are only departures every two hours to Messina, and on Sunday there are no departures at all. The crossing takes 40 minutes and tickets, costing just €12 per car including passengers, can be bought before departure from the kiosk at the port.

For information on hydrofoil and ferry tickets for the **return journey**, see "Listings", p.158.

---

drivers not stopping at Messina should follow the green signs for the Palermo (A20) and Catania (A18) autostradas. **Hydrofoils** (from the Aeolian Islands, Villa San Giovanni and Réggio di Calabria) dock at the terminal in the port area signposted "aliscafi".

Both of Messina's tourist offices should be able to provide a town map, accommodation listings and information about getting to the Aeolians. The handiest one lies outside the train station on Piazza della Repubblica (Mon–Fri 9am–1.30pm, also June–Sept Mon & Wed 3.30–6.30pm, Tues & Thurs 3–5pm; ☎090.672.944). Most of Messina's hotels are scattered around this area, and it's just a short walk to Piazza Cairoli, which holds banks, shops and a **local tourist office** upstairs at no. 45 (Mon–Wed 8am–2pm & 3–6.30pm, Thurs & Fri 9am–2pm; ☎090.293.5292). The independent **website** Ⓦ www.messinacitymap.com has a detailed street map and some useful contact numbers but is quite out of date.

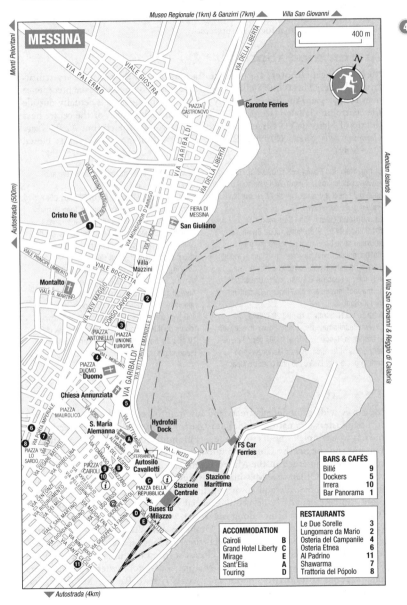

BARS & CAFÉS

Billé	9
Dockers	5
Irrera	10
Bar Panorama	1

RESTAURANTS

Le Due Sorelle	3
Lungomare da Mario	2
Osteria del Campanile	4
Osteria Etnea	6
Al Padrino	11
Shawarma	7
Trattoria del Pópolo	8

ACCOMMODATION

Cairoli	B
Grand Hotel Liberty	C
Mirage	E
Sant'Elia	A
Touring	D

153

You can walk easily from the station or harbour to the centre of town, but to venture anywhere further, take the city's single **tram line** (#28), running between Annunziata in the north (for the Museo Regionale) to Gazzi in the south, with departures from Piazza della Repubblica, Piazza Cairoli and Piazza Municipio every ten minutes (30min on Sun), or **buses**, including #79 to Ganzirri, and #80 and #81/ (*barrato*) to Ganzirri and Mortelle. All city lines are run by ATM (℡090.228.5263, Ⓦwww.atmmessina.it), with tickets (€1.25 valid 90min; €1.70 valid 2 journeys per day, or €2.60 all day) available at *tabacchi* and from Autosilo Cavallotti, the terminal for most services.

Accommodation

Messina's cheaper **hotels** are near the station, though they're not very scintillating choices. This is one Sicilian city where business travellers take precedence over tourists, and the best reasonably priced accommodation is actually outside the centre, in Ganzirri (see p.159). There's a **campsite** north of the centre near the tip of Sicily at Via Circuito, Torre Faro, beyond Ganzirri (bus #79): *Nuovo Camping dello Stretto* (℡090.322.3051, Ⓦwww.campingdellostretto.it; closed Oct–May).

Cairoli Viale San Martino 63 ℡090.673.755, Ⓦwww.hotelcairoli.it. Large, old-fashioned, central hotel right next to Piazza Cairoli. All rooms have a/c and en-suite bathrooms. ❷

Grand Hotel Liberty Via I Settembre 15 ℡090.640.9436, Ⓦnh-hotels.com. Swish, Art Nouveau-style hotel right opposite the train station, popular with business travellers – though there's no garage and no restaurant, and the only internet access is in the lobby. Breakfasts on the roof terrace are nice though. Closed July to mid-Sept. ❹

Mirage Via N. Scotto 3 ℡090.293.8844, Ⓦwww.hotelmiragemessina.it. Down an alley off Piazza della Repubblica, this 1960s period piece sports lots of formica, plaster Madonnas and curling posters of Padre Pio and obscure local beauty spots. All rooms have phones, a/c and en-suite bathrooms. ❶

Sant'Elia Via I Settembre 67 ℡090.601.0082, Ⓦwww.hotelsantelia.com. Central, friendly and reliable three-star hotel, primarily for business travellers but good value. Most rooms have tall ceilings, spacious bathrooms and balconies. Internet access is free but slow. ❸

Touring Via N. Scotto 17 ℡090.293.8851, Ⓦwww.hoteltouring-me.it. Just up from the *Mirage* and a cut above it, this hotel has bare but spacious rooms, each with bathroom, telephone and a/c (and some have a safe). Try and avoid rooms on the ground floor, where the desk clerk's TV and the hot-drinks machine can be noisy. No credit cards. ❷

The City

Messina's wide remodelled streets and low reinforced buildings guard against future disasters of a natural kind, but make for a pretty uninspiring spectacle. It only takes a couple of hours to see the few monuments that remain – chiefly, the Duomo and the nearby Chiesa Annunziata dei Catalani – though the treasure-trove of art contained in the Museo Regionale makes up for what the rest of the city lacks. Otherwise, Messina's pleasures are to be found in kicking around its portside promenade and absorbing the views across the Straits. Messina by night can be particularly beautiful, especially from the high **Via Panoramica** (which changes its name along its route west of the centre from Viale Gaetano Martino to Viale Príncipe Umberto and Viale Regina Margherita) – from here, with the city at your feet, there's a long, sparkling view across to mainland Italy. From the centre, the closest sections of this route are the Viale Príncipe Umberto and Viale Regina Margherita stretch, where there are bars and pizzerias around two floodlit sanctuaries (Cristo Re and Montalto) and plenty of scope for pleasant evening strolling.

The Duomo and around

Messina's most important monument, the **Duomo** (Mon–Fri 9am–7pm, Sat & Sun 9am–noon & 3.30–7.30pm), epitomizes the city's phoenix-like ability to re-create itself from the ashes of its last disaster. It's the reconstruction of a twelfth-century cathedral erected by Roger II, one of a series of great Norman churches that included the sumptuous cathedrals of Palermo and Cefalù. Formerly, the building dominated medieval Messina, and was the venue for Archbishop Palmer's marriage of Richard the Lionheart's sister Joan to the Norman-Sicilian king, William II. Devastated by the earthquake in 1908, it was rebuilt in the years following World War I, only to fall victim to a firebomb in 1943 that reduced it once more to rubble. What you see today is mostly a faithful copy, which took years to complete, with few elements remaining of the original fabric.

The Romanesque facade is its best aspect, the lower part mostly authentic and dominated by a richly decorated, late-Gothic **central portal**, extravagantly pointed, with good detail, and flanked by two smaller contemporary doors. Almost everything in the undeniably grand **interior** is a reproduction, from the marble floor to the elaborately painted wooden ceiling. Two rows of sturdy columns line the nave, topped by cement capitals faithfully copied from originals, some of which survive in the Museo Regionale. The **mosaicwork** in the three grand apses holds most interest, though it pales into insignificance beside the island's other examples of the genre, and only the mosaic on the left – of the Virgin Mary with St Lucy – is original. All the same, try to find someone to switch on the lights, as the mosaics then take on a majesty that's entirely lost in the gloom that normally shrouds the cathedral's interior. Little else here predates the twentieth century, apart from some salvaged tombs, most handsome of which is that of Archbishop de Tabiatis from 1333, on the right of the altar and heavily graffitied. The **tesoro** (Aug daily 9.30am–1pm & 4–7.30pm, other times vary according to whether cruise ships are in port, but usually Mon–Sat 9.30am–1pm; €3, or €5 including campanile) holds precious reliquaries, the bejewelled *Manta d'Oro* – a holy adornment for sacred images, of a kind more commonly used in Orthodox rites – and a collection of skilfully crafted silverware.

In front of the cathedral and its belltower, the graceful **Fontana di Orione** was daintily carved in the mid-sixteenth century by Montorsoli, a Florentine pupil of Michelangelo. The fountain depicts Orion, the city's mythical founder, surmounting a collection of cherubs, nymphs and giants, and surrounded by four figures (representing the rivers Nile, Ebro, Camaro and Tiber) reclining along the balustrade. The upper part was carefully restored after earthquake damage in 1908.

Messina's roaring clocktower

The Duomo's detached **campanile**, or belltower, claims to be the largest astronomical clock in the world, and puts on its best show at noon every day, when a bronze lion (Messina's ancient emblem) unleashes a mighty roar over the city – quite alarming if you're not expecting it. On the side facing the cathedral two dials show the phases of the planets and the seasons, while above them a globe shows the phases of the moon. The elaborate panoply of moving gilt figures facing the piazza, activated on the hour, half-hour and quarter-hour, ranges from representations of the days of the week and the four Ages of Man to Dina and Clarenza, two semi-legendary women who saved the city from a night attack by the Angevins during the Wars of the Vespers.

You can climb to the top of the tower to enjoy a great view of the piazza and city (mid-April to mid-Sept Mon–Sat 9am–1pm & 4.30–6.30pm, Sun 10am–1pm & 4.30–6.30pm; mid-Sept to Oct Mon–Sat 9am–1pm, Sun 10am–1pm; Nov to mid-April Sun 10am–1pm; €3.50, or €5 including *tesoro*).

Just back from the Duomo, the truncated section of the twelfth-century **Chiesa Annunziata dei Catalani** (usually Mon–Sat 9.30–11.30am, but often closed; call ☎090.675.175 to check) squats below pavement level, Messina's only surviving example of Arab/Norman church-building. The blind arcading around the apses and the Byzantine-style cupola are the perfect antidote to the ugly cement facade surrounding its three portals, and the interior is suitably simple, with the transept and apse true to their original construction. In front, a martial statue by the sculptor Andrea Calamecca (Calamech) stands half-hidden under the trees, depicting a proud Don Giovanni of Austria, victor of the Battle of Lépanto (the victorious Christian fleet sailed from Messina in 1535).

From here, it's a short stroll to the **harbourside**, with its combination of constant activity and compelling vistas over the Straits. Sicily's deepest natural harbour is a port of call for freighters and cruisers of all descriptions, as well as for frequent NATO warships. But the greatest traffic consists of ferries, endlessly plying back and forth, which are Sicily's chief link with the mainland.

The Museo Regionale

Messina's **Museo Regionale**, at Via della Libertà 465 (Mon & Fri 9am–2pm, Tues, Thurs & Sat 9am–2pm & 4–7pm or 3–6pm in winter, Sun 9am–1pm; last entry 30min before closing; €3), is a repository for some of the city's greatest works of art, many of them carefully rescued from earthquake rubble, and includes what is perhaps Sicily's finest collection of fifteenth- to seventeenth-century art. A much larger museum building is being built next door, where the collection is due to be transferred (for an update call ☎090.361.292): until then, the layout of the museum is as described below.

The collection starts with some lovely Byzantine work, larded with a good helping of Gothic, well evident in a fourteenth-century triptych of the *Madonna with Child between Sts Agatha and Bartholomew*, and a remarkably modern-looking wooden crucifix from the fifteenth century, with a sinuous, tragic Christ. The highlight is **room 4**, which holds marvellous examples of fifteenth-century art, notably the museum's most famous exhibit, the *St Gregory* polyptych, by Sicily's greatest native artist, **Antonello da Messina** – a masterful synthesis of Flemish and Italian Renaissance styles that's a good example of the various influences that reached the port of Messina in the fifteenth century. The statue of *Scilla*, the classical Scylla who terrorized sailors from the Calabrian coast (as described in Homer's *Odyssey*), is on display in **room 6** – an alarming spectacle, with contorted face and eyes awash with expression. Sculpted by Montorsoli in 1557, it was once adjoined to an imperious figure of Neptune in the act of calming the seas, a copy of which stands on the seafront just up from the hydrofoil terminal. Also here are a couple of large shadowy canvases by **Caravaggio**, commissioned by the city in 1609, the better of which is the atmospheric *Raising of Lazarus*. The last room on the ground floor has a monstrous ceremonial carriage from 1742, hauled out for viceregal and other high-ranking visits. Though faded and tarnished, its gilt bodywork is still awesomely grandiose, showing an impressive array of detail.

Many more items will be displayed in the new museum, including an ethereal statue of the *Madonna and Child*, attributed to Francesco Laurana, and a collection of mainly ecclesiastical silverware, an art at which Messina once excelled.

To reach the museum, take tram #28 to the last stop, Annunziata; the museum lies on the left, immediately after the Regina Margherita hospital.

Eating and drinking

Messina has a good range of inexpensive **restaurants**, though you should head away from the port and Piazza Cairoli for a more relaxed atmosphere. If you're here in early summer, make a point of sampling the local **swordfish**; May and June are the best months for this, before the water gets too warm. The streets around Piazza Lo Sardo (also known as Piazza del Pópolo) hold a good mix of rough-and-ready trattorias and more serious eating places, while the area around Piazza Cairoli is best for **bar life**, though some of the bars close in August when everyone's at Ganzirri or Mortelle. For a picnic lunch, tasty panini and other cold **snacks** are on offer at *Salumeria Nucita*, an *alimentari* at Via Garibaldi 125.

Cafés, bars and birrerias

Billé Piazza Cairoli 7. Superb and rather refined *pasticceria* where the piazza joins Via T. Cannizzaro, with ice cream, *granite*, pastries and chocolates, as well as salads and *arancini*. There are tables inside and out.

Dockers Via Vittorio Emanuele 31. Cheerful portside pub, with Guinness on tap and a range of snacks, including *piadine* (filled flatbread), salads and fish & chips. Closed daytime Sat & Sun.

Irrera Piazza Cairoli 12. In business since 1910, serving cakes, *frutta di martorana* (marzipan fruits), ices and pastries of renowned quality.

🦅 Bar Panorama Viale Príncipe Umberto (next to the Santuario Cristo Re). Known as the *Bar del Pappagallo* – a fixture here for 38 years – this serves the best ice cream and *granite* in town, along with traditional snacks like *arancini*. A great view to boot.

Restaurants

🦅 Le Due Sorelle Piazza Unione Europea 4 ☎090.44.720. With only nine tables, this is a small and select trattoria, but also innovative and memorable. Specialities such as *padella* – a local version of paella – and *couscous con pesce* cost about €16, with main courses up to €18. Booking advised. Closed Sat lunch, Sun lunch & Aug.

Lungomare da Mario Via Vittorio Emanuele 108, with an entrance also on Via Garibaldi ☎090.42.477. A fine choice for a fish lunch opposite the port, though it can be noisy if you sit outside. Pastas and (in the evening) pizzas are around €8, fish courses cost €10–12, and there are three-course fixed-price menus for €16. Closed Wed Sept–July.

Osteria del Campanile Via Loggia dei Mercanti 7 ☎090.711.418. Reliable little trattoria with outdoor tables to the rear of the Duomo. Try the filling, fresh *maccheroni alla Norma* (€7) or the *linguine inferno di mare* with spicy seafood sauce (€11), and in the evening you can eat pizza too. Set menus range between €10 and €17. Closed Sun except July & Aug.

Osteria Etnea Via Martino 38. Abundant portions and low prices (all dishes €6–9) make this tidy little place near Piazza Lo Sardo popular with locals. The menu is long and service brisk. Closed Sun.

🦅 Al Padrino Via S. Cecilia 54–6. This bare, frills-free neighbourhood trattoria specializes in traditional Sicilian fare, such as *maccu* (mashed fava or broad beans), and the house specialities, *melanzane al Padrino* (aubergines stuffed with fresh pasta and ricotta) and *pasta con legumi riposata* (with beans), both €6–8. A three-course meal will cost under €20. Closed Sat eve & Sun.

🦅 Shawarma Via M. Giurba 8 ☎090.712.213. Tagines, couscous and a range of potato dishes share menu space with pizzas (€6–10) at this popular trattoria off Piazza Lo Sardo, with some outdoor seating. Hubble-bubbles and occasional belly-dancing (usually Fri & Sun) add to the atmosphere. Closed lunchtime & all Mon.

Trattoria del Pópolo Piazza Lo Sardo ☎090.671.148. You can eat outside at this friendly trattoria, making the most of the rare calm of this corner of the city. Dishes include *sarde allinguate* (fried sardines dressed with vinegar) and *franceschini* (baby squid fried in breadcrumbs); pasta dishes cost €5–6, mains €6–9. Closed Sun & mid-Aug.

Nightlife and entertainment

Exhibitions and classical concerts take place near the port at the church of Santa Maria Alemanna (Via I Settembre), while free **concerts** of light music are staged in Piazza del Duomo in July and August. During the same period, some years, **free films** are shown, (usually at 8.30pm), generally in the Villa Mazzini public gardens near the hydrofoil dock or nearby next to the church of San Giuliano off Via della Libertà, around the Fiera di Messina – though the venue may change. If films are showing, arrive early, as these events tend to get crowded. Ask at the tourist office for details of all of these.

Ferragosto

If you're in Messina in midsummer, you might catch the festivals around the Feast of the Assumption, or **ferragosto**. Although all the villages on both sides of the Straits hold festivals around this time, with some pretty spectacular fireworks lighting up the sky on any one night, Messina's festivities are grander, beginning around August 12, when two plaster giants (*giganti*) are wheeled around town, and finally stationed near the port opposite the Municipio. These are said to be Messina's two founders, Mata and Grifone, one a white female, the other a burly Moor, and both mounted on huge steeds. On *ferragosto* itself, August 15, another towering carriage, the Vara, is hauled through the city centre. It's an elaborate column supporting dozens of papier-mâché cherubs and angels, culminating in the figure of Christ stretching out his right arm to launch Mary on her way to Heaven. This unwieldy construction is towed on long ropes, pulled by hundreds of penitents – semi-naked if they're men, all in white if they're women – and cheered on by thousands of people along the way. The whole thing is a sweaty and frenetic performance, finishing up at Piazza del Duomo, where flowers are thrown out to the crowds, many of whom risk being crushed in the mad scramble to gather these luck-bearing charms. Late at night, one of Sicily's best **firework displays** is held on the seafront near Via della Libertà.

Listings

Airport Nearest is Aeroporto dello Stretto, outside Réggio di Calabria, for internal services and summer charters only (℡0965.640.517, ⓦwww .sogas.it). There's a summer weekday hydrofoil service connecting the airport directly with Messina in 35min (℡0923.873.813, ⓦwww.metromare dellostretto.it), and a year-round bus service linking the airport with Reggio's port.

Bus companies AST, from Piazza della Repubblica or Autosilo Cavallotti, near the train station ℡090.662.244 or 840.000.323, ⓦwww.aziendasicilianatrasporti.it (for Barcellona and Patti); Giuntabus, from Piazza della Repubblica 52 ℡090.675.749, ⓦwww .giuntabustrasporti.com (for Milazzo and the Aeolian Islands); Interbus, from Piazza della Repubblica 6 ℡090.661.754, ⓦwww.interbus .it (for the coast south to Letojanni, Taormina and Catania, also thrice-weekly connections to Umbria and Tuscany); Jónica, from Autosilo Cavallotti ℡090.771.400, ⓦwww.insicilia.com (for Forza d'Agrò, Itala, Santa Teresa di Riva and Sávoca); SAIS Autolinee, from Piazza della Repubblica 6 ℡090.771.914, ⓦwww.sais autolinee.it (for Palermo, Catania and Catania airport, also regular connections to Umbria, Tuscany, Bologna and Milan); SAIS Trasporti, from Piazza della Repubblica ℡091.617.1141, ⓦwww.saistrasporti.it (for Catania, Naples and Rome); TAI/Magistro, from Via Santa Maria Alemanna, near the train station ℡090.675.184, ⓦwww.autolineetai.it (for Capo d'Orlando, Patti and Tíndari).

Car rental Avis, Via Garibaldi 109 ℡090.679.150; Maggiore, Via Vittorio Emanuele II 75 ℡090.675.476; Sicilcar, Via Garibaldi 187 ℡090.46.942.

Ferry tickets All tickets across the Straits are on sale at the respective terminals; for Villa San Giovanni, contact ℡090.678.6478 (Bluvia) or ℡800.627.414, ⓦwww.carontetourist.it (Caronte); for Réggio di Calabria, contact ℡090.641.3234 or 335.825.5909, ⓦwww.meridianolines.it (Meridiano).

Hospital Ospedale Piemonte, Viale Europa ℡090.2221. For emergencies call ℡113.

Hydrofoil tickets To Réggio di Calabria, Villa San Giovanni and the Aeolians, on sale at the hydrofoil terminal; call Metromare ℡0923.873.813, ⓦwww.metromaredellostretto.it or Ústica Lines on ℡090.364.044, ⓦwww.usticalines.it.

Internet Imbogames, Via N. Fabrizi 20c, off Piazza Cairoli (Mon–Sat 9am–1pm & 2–8pm).

Left luggage Office on Platform 1 at the train station (Mon–Fri 6am–4pm, Sat & Sun 6am–2pm); €3 per bag for 12hr, then €2 for every subsequent 12hr.

Pharmacy There's an all-night service on a rotating basis: consult any pharmacy window to find out current *farmacie notturne*.

Police Carabinieri, Via Nino Bixio ℡112 or 090.771.330; Questura, for the police, Via Plácida 2, near Villa Mazzini ℡113 or 090.3661.

Post office Main office at Corso Cavour 138, behind Piazza Duomo (Mon–Fri 8am–6.30pm, Sat 8am–12.30pm, but Aug Mon–Fri 8am–1.30pm, Sat 8am–12.30pm).

Shopping Messina is renowned for its pastries and biscuits. There's a cluster of classy *pasticcerie* around Piazza Cairoli – look out for the typical local *pignolata*, a sugary confection covered with brown or white icing with a doughy filling. Oviesse is a convenient supermarket for food, clothes and other items on Piazza Cairoli (daily 9am–1pm & 4–8pm), while the lanes running off the square hold smart boutiques and leather shops.

Taxis Ranks at Piazza Cairoli (℡090.293.4880), Piazza della Repubblica, outside Stazione Centrale (℡090.673.703), and at the Caronte terminal; 24hr radio taxi (℡090.6505).

Travel agents Albertours, Piazza della Repubblica 25 ℡090.712.035; Lisciotto Viaggi, Via Garibaldi 106a ℡090.719.001. For all air, rail and sea tickets.

Around Messina

Several mountain or coastal destinations, all well worth a visit, are less than thirty minutes from the centre of Messina by bus or car. If you're driving, you might wish to follow the high-level Via Panoramica north rather than the congested coastal road, which is the route the bus takes; but make a point of taking this lower road – an extension of Via della Libertà – at least once, passing fishermen's houses that back onto short sandy strips in areas that must once have justified their idyllic names of Paradiso, Contemplazione and Pace. In Pace, look out for the British cannons lining the esplanade, pulled out of the Straits where they were sunk during the Napoleonic Wars.

Ganzirri and Punta del Faro

Buses #79, #80 and #81 make a stop in **GANZIRRI**, 10km north of the centre of Messina. There's mussel-farming on Ganzirri's lake, which in summer especially is the hub of milling crowds. You can eat plenty of fresh shellfish, swordfish or whatever else has been hauled in that day by the many boats operating around here. Most of the **trattorias** are squeezed into the wedge of land between lake and sea, and you can eat outside at nearly all of them. Prices tend to be high and the quality variable, but for very reasonably priced, exquisitely cooked seafood dishes, seek out ⚐ *Lilla Currò*, signposted on the right side of the lake at Via Lido di Ganzirri 10 (℡090.395.064; no credit cards; closed Mon), where you can enjoy a feast for €20–25 – booking is essential for evening meals, and service can be slow. Fifty metres further up at Via Lago Grande 96, *La Sirena di Mancuso* (℡090.391.268; closed Wed) also puts on a very good spread, again at low prices, with lake views from its covered veranda.

Ganzirri would make a good place to stay, too: the pleasant, family-run **hotel** *Donato* at Via Caratozzolo 8 (℡090.393.150, Ⓦwww.hoteldonato.com; ❷) has airy, smartly restored rooms – all with bath – undisturbed by the scream of Vespas, and situated just 50m from the sea shore. It's signposted off the lake, just beyond *Lilla Currò*.

Punta del Faro (also called Capo Peloro) is the very tip of Sicily, the nearest point to mainland Italy, and on summer evenings it's the venue for open-air **free films**.

A bridge too far

Plans to build the **world's longest suspension bridge**, over the Messina Straits, have been in the air for years. Spearheaded by Berlusconi but fiercely opposed by the environmental lobby and seismologists, the bridge would have to span the 3km Straits suspended from pylons as high as the Eiffel Tower, in order to support a twelve-lane motorway and a two-track railway. Seismologists fear that any bridge would be unable to resist a severe earthquake, while environmentalists claim that its pylons would affect the delicate water table that feeds the lakes of Faro and Ganzirri. In the current economic climate it's unlikely to get the go-ahead any time soon, but if construction contracts are ever tendered, both the Calabrian and the Sicilian Mafia are potentially set to make a killing.

The lighthouse here (the *faro*) is dwarfed by the towering pylon supporting the massive cables that tether the island to the mainland. Here, too, was where the legendary **Charybdis** once posed a threat to sailors – along with Scylla on the opposite shore – still remembered in the locality's name of Cariddi.

Mortelle and Acquarone

A couple of kilometres further up the road, on the Tyrrhenian coast, **MORTELLE** is the focus in summer for Messina's bronzed youth, who throng the orderly lidos and sleek bars and pizzerias, filling the air with the screech of motorbikes. The fine sandy **beaches** extend west from here, most easily accessed from such villages as **ACQUARONE** (also called Acqualadrone), 7km from Mortelle, reachable on bus #80 (not Sun) from there or Messina's Autosilo Cavallotti.

Inland to the Monti Peloritani

Inland from Messina, the ridge-top of the **Monti Peloritani** offers the best vantage-point of the Tyrrhenian and Ionian coasts and also has some excellent walking in the pinewoods, which get denser the further up you go. You can reach some good spots along the SS113 (Via Palermo) from Via Garibaldi in the city (bus #70 or #71 from Autosilo Cavallotti). Turning left at the crossroads at **Colle San Rizzo** (where bus #71 stops), it's another 10km south to reach the panoramic **Monte Antennamare** sanctuary, a shabby building in a sublime spot (1124m high). Back at Colle San Rizzo, you could make a round trip by descending north to Castanea, another wooded area favoured by hunters, and down to the Tyrrhenian coast at Spartà, on the Messina road.

Milazzo

If it weren't for the industry besieging **MILAZZO** – the first major town as you head west along the Tyrrhenian coast – it wouldn't be a bad-looking place. A long plane- and palm-tree-lined promenade looks across the sparkling sea, while behind the town a rambling old castle caps Milazzo's ancient acropolis. Most people, though, are put off by the unsightly oil refinery that occasionally produces a yellow smog overhead, and only stop long enough to get out again, taking the first ferry or hydrofoil to the Aeolian Islands (see Chapter Three), for which Milazzo is the major embarkation point. But Italian tourists know the town well, and regularly crowd the beaches and campsites strung along **Capo Milazzo**, the finger of land behind the town.

Sailings to the Aeolians from Milazzo operate daily and are frequent enough to make it unnecessary to book (unless you're taking a car), although bear in mind that there is a reduced service between October and May. For schedules and prices from Milazzo, see pp.118–119.

The **shipping agencies** listed below are all by Milazzo's port and open usual working hours as well as before all departures – Siremar for ferries and hydrofoils, Ústica Lines for hydrofoils only, and NGI for ferries only. You can pick up useful ferry/hydrofoil **timetables** from any of them. There are also daily **excursions** in summer on cruises, usually sailing from Milazzo at 8.15am or 9am, stopping at two or three of the islands, and returning at around 6pm (tickets €40–60).

If you need to leave a car in Milazzo, you can do so at one of several **garages**, the most convenient of which are also listed below; expect to pay around €15 per day (worth negotiating for longer periods). Some offer a shuttle service to the port.

Shipping agencies
Navigazione Generale Italiana (NGI) Via dei Mille 26 ℡090.928.3415 or 800.250.000, ℗www.ngi-spa.it.
Siremar Via dei Mille 19 ℡090.928.3242 or 892.123, ℗www.siremar.it.
Ústica Lines Catalano, Via dei Mille 33 ℡090.928.7821 or 0923.873.813, ℗www.usticalines.it.

Cruise lines
Navisal Via dei Mille 27 ℡090.922.4926, ℗www.navisal.com.
Tar.Nav Via dei Mille 17 and 43 ℡090.922.3617 or 340.070.7285.

Garages
Central Garage Via Cumbo Borgia 60 ℡090.928.2472. By the Duomo Nuovo, 5min from the port.
Mil Nautica Via Acquaviole 49 ℡090.928.1912. South of the port, on the road to the train station.
Ullo Via Nino 40 ℡090.928.3309. Signposted up Via Minniti from the port.

Arrival and information

Buses (including the Giuntabus service from Messina) stop right on the quayside. The **train station** is a good 3km south of the centre, but local buses run into town every 15–30 minutes during the day, dropping you on the quayside or further up in Piazza della Repubblica. Buy tickets (€0.85) aboard, or take a taxi (around €10). Milazzo's **tourist office** is at Piazza Duilio 20 (Mon–Fri 8.30am–1.30pm & 3.30–6pm, Sat 8.30am–1.30pm; ℡090.922.2865), just back from the harbour. There's **internet** access at Bet 1128 at Via Manzoni 14 (daily 9am–8pm) and Redac at Via Cosenz 29c (Mon–Sat 8.30am–1pm & 4–8pm).

For **ferries** and **hydrofoils** to and from the Aeolian Islands, see p.118; shipping agencies in Milazzo are listed in the box above. Note that Ústica Lines also operate a summer hydrofoil service to Cefalù and Palermo – see "Travel details", p.183, for schedules.

Accommodation

There are plenty of reasonable **hotels** handy for the port; if you have a car and the inclination to get out of town, you can stay by the sea. The two nearest **campsites** lie on the cape, around 5km north of town, and are accessible in summer by bus #6 from Piazza della Repubblica: *Cirucco* (℡ 090.928.4746, ⓦ www.cirucco.it; April–Oct) and the smaller *Riva Smeralda* (℡ 090.928.2980, ⓦ www.rivasmeralda.it). Both also have bungalows for rent (❷–❹), available by the week only in high summer and considerably cheaper in low season; the *Cirucco* also has B&B rooms (❹).

Cassisi Via Cassisi 5 ℡ 090.922.9099, ⓦ www .cassisihotel.com. Upmarket hotel with a sober, minimalist style. Its up-to-date facilities include wi-fi, but there's no restaurant. ❸

Cosenz Via E. Cosenz 5 ℡ 090.928.2996. Good budget choice, with clean, quiet rooms, each equipped with a fridge, a/c and fan, and private bathroom. ❶

Petit Via dei Mille 37 ℡ 090.928.6784, ⓦ www.petithotel.it. Right opposite the port, this "ecological" hotel has ceramic tiles on the walls and floors, a great roof terrace and nourishing breakfasts. Garage parking is available for extra charge, but the left-luggage service is free. Rates drop outside the peak season. ❹

Piazza Roma Via Pistorio 1 ℡ 320.726.0946, ⓦ www.bbpiazzaroma.it. Smart, modern B&B with spacious, well-equipped rooms (including top-notch

mattresses), though there is some traffic noise. Two of the six rooms share a bathroom, and breakfast is taken in a nearby bar. No credit cards. ❷

Solaris Via Col. Berte 70, ℡ 090.928.4739 or 333.605.0091, ⓦ www.bbsolaris.eu. Cheerful B&B a block from the port, with five colour-themed rooms with a/c, fridges and balconies, and one has a small covered terrace. No credit cards. ❷

Il Vicolo Via Salemi 14 ℡ 349.504.6851, ⓦ www .ilvicolobeb.it. Located in a quiet side street on the Ponente (eastern) side of town, 30m from the beach and just five minutes' walk from the port, this B&B has three spick-and-span rooms with en-suite bathrooms and a fourth with a bathroom outside. All have use of a fully-equipped kitchen, and there's a courtyard for outside dining. Facilities include a washing machine, and the use of bikes. Upstairs are three larger apartments rented out by the week. ❷

The Town

If you're in a hurry, Milazzo is easy enough to handle. You could be on an outward-bound ferry or hydrofoil within an hour of arriving. But there's enough in and around town to make it an enjoyable overnight stop, before or after your Aeolian trip, with one major sight – the castle – that stands comparison with any in Sicily.

Historically, the site's strategic importance made it one of the most fought-over towns in Sicily. The Greeks arrived in 716 BC, after which the town was contested by successive armies, from the Carthaginians to the Aragonese. It even became a base for the British during the Napoleonic Wars, while fifty years later Garibaldi won a victory here that set the seal on his conquest of Sicily. None of this is evident from the fairly nondescript modern streets behind the port, but a fifteen-minute walk north along Lungomare Garibaldi and up through the **Borgo**, the old hilltop citadel, offers a pleasing change in aspect. Here, the views open out over bay and plain, while the higher you climb, the older and more decrepit the buildings become – some churches and *palazzi* on the approach to the castle are little more than precariously balanced shells.

To appreciate the citadel's size, walk round to the north side, where the formidable defences erected by the Spanish still stand almost in their entirety. The massive walls are magnificent, pierced by a suitably imposing tunnelled gateway. The **castello** itself (guided tours Tues–Sun 9.30–11.30am & 3–5pm, check winter times at tourist office; free) is steeped in military history: built by Frederick II in the thirteenth century on the site of the Greek acropolis and on top of Arab foundations, it was enlarged by Charles V, and restored by the Spanish in the seventeenth century. Inside the castle walls is the **Duomo Antico**, a central Norman keep, the old Sala del Parlamento and the remains of the Palazzo dei Giurati, later used as a prison.

Milazzo has a couple of other churches worth looking at. Directly opposite the castle's entrance, the Dominican **Chiesa del Rosario**, together with its convent, was formerly a seat of the Inquisition, while below, in the new town, the silver-domed

Duomo Nuovo has some excellent Renaissance paintings in the apse: four panels of Sts Peter, Paul, Rocco and Thomas Aquinas; between the last of these, an *Adoration of the Child* by Antonello de Saliba, and an *Annunciation* by Andrea Giuffrè above that. Large, graceful chandeliers adorn the nave.

Capo Milazzo

The thin promontory north of town is the focus of most of the summertime activity. A few fine hotels, a couple of well-equipped campsites and a decent restaurant or two are grouped around the headland of **Capo Milazzo**, 6km out of town; it's a fifteen-minute bus ride away on #6 from the port (June–Sept). There are plenty of good **beaches** all around here, but the sandiest is close to the centre of town, on Milazzo's western, less-developed side (at the end of Via Colombo).

Eating and drinking

There's a small but worthy range of **restaurants and trattorias** in Milazzo's centre; those furthest from the port tend to do the best food. The town's *passeggiata* is one of the liveliest in Sicily, with baby buggies, scooters and cars clogging up Lungomare Garibaldi, and a swarm of couples and families dropping in for ice cream at the **bars** along the way, most of which stay open late in summer. There are plenty of pubs dotted around the Borgo too, open every evening in summer, at weekends in winter.

Restaurants

Bagatto Via M. Regis 11 ☎090.922.4212. You can sample local salami and cheeses as well as more substantial dishes (€10–14) at this chic wine bar. There's a great selection of wines and a cool, laid-back ambience, with some tables outside. Closed daytime.

La Casalinga Via R. D'Amico 13 ☎090.922.2697. Local favourite for fish, where the speciality is spaghetti *polpa di granchi* (with crab sauce). First courses are around €8, mains €7–15. Worth booking. Closed Sun Oct–April.

Il Covo del Pirata Lungomare Garibaldi 47–48 ☎090.928.4437. With wooden ceilings, stone walls and piratical decor, this has more atmosphere than most local eateries, and the food is occasionally superb. Downstairs is a pizzeria, but you should go upstairs for the sea view. First courses include *linguine tuttomare*, a seafood extravaganza (€14) – other pasta dishes are around €10. Closed Wed.

Bars

Bar Dama Piazza Battisti. Excellent little café for a daytime snack, with a few outdoor tables. The fruit *granite* are terrific. Closed Mon Oct–June.

Caffè Antico Via Duomo Antico. Pleasant spot for a drink, just downhill from the castle, with an outdoor terrace for distant views of the coast.

Castroreale

Heading west along the coast, you can make a rewarding detour at the uninspiring town of Barcellona to the Peloritan hill-village of **CASTROREALE**, 8km south. Favoured by Frederick II of Aragon, who came here for the hunting, the town enjoys magnificent views over the hills and out to sea. At its highest point a single tower is the only remaining fragment of Frederick II's fort, built in 1324 and subsequently ruined by earthquakes.

The rest of Castroreale is creakingly medieval, and it's enough just to stroll along the quiet, sloping streets, dropping in at the couple of basic bars for a drink. The village hosts the annual festival **Castroreale Jazz** over ten days in late July and early August (ⓦwww.castrorealejazz.it), featuring evening performances by international jazz musicians in Piazza Peculio. Tickets for each are around €17.

There's an excellent **agriturismo** just outside town on Via Porticato – 🍴 *Green Manors* (☎090.974.6515 or 338.434.0917, 🌐www.greenmanors.it; ④), run by a Belgian-Italian family and dishing up some of the best meals around. Guests can make use of a swimming pool, "tropical garden", library and wi-fi. Cheaper accommodation includes an attractive and friendly, if rather rudimentary, **hostel**, located in the highest part of the village next to the old Aragonese tower: *Ostello delle Aquile* (☎333.900.3308 or 333.373.6535, 🌐www.ostellodelleaquile.com). Both male and female dormitories hold ten beds (€12–13.50 each); the minimal facilities include a kitchen (there's no restaurant), washing-room and luggage deposit, and there are organized excursions into the Peloritani mountains.

To get to Castroreale by **public transport**, take a bus from the bus station at Ponte Longano, in the centre of Barcellona (last departure at 5pm, 4pm in winter, or 2.30pm on Sat). If you're arriving by train, buses connect Barcellona's train station, some way north of the centre, with the bus station (7 daily Mon–Sat; last departure at 2.20pm; tickets from the bar in the station). Alternatively, it would not be inconceivable to walk up, by following the valley of the Longano river inland for about three hours – the steep bit's at the end.

Roman remains at San Biagio, Tíndari and Patti

West of Milazzo lie a trio of **Roman remains**, most impressive of which is the Greco-Roman site at **Tíndari**, sharing a high promontory with a popular pilgrimage spot. Lacking the physical splendour of Tíndari's site, the villas at **San Biagio** and **Patti** are less enticing, though neither requires a great effort to visit if you're travelling under your own steam. There's a marvellous beach at **Marinello**, below Tíndari, while an incursion inland will bring you to the mountain village of **Novara di Sicilia**, a great spot to unwind away from the crowded coast.

San Biagio and Novara di Sicilia

Around 8km west of Milazzo, you can quickly take in the modest Roman remains at the unremarkable coastal town of **SAN BIAGIO**, just off the SS113. The excavations of the first-century AD **Roman villa** here (daily 9am until 1hr before sunset; €2) have revealed interesting evidence on the construction of baths, but above all it's the vivid mosaics that make this worth stopping for – one in particular depicting a fishing scene at sea.

From San Biagio, the SS185 branches inland into the mountains, the only road connecting the Tyrrhenian and Ionian coasts, ending at Giardini-Naxos. This is one of the finest routes on the island, climbing gently into the hills through some handsome countryside to **NOVARA DI SICILIA**, whose main street is dotted with bars and shops that sell the strong local sheep's cheese, *maiorchina*. For somewhere to **stay**, try *Sganga Kondé King* on the main Via Nazionale (☎0941.650.526; no credit cards; ①), a pleasant B&B in a huge *palazzo* that once accommodated Mussolini. On the same road is a traditional **trattoria**, *La Pineta* (☎0941.650.522; closed Mon), where you can sample the local ricotta, deep-fried *crespelle* (little pancakes) stuffed with fresh vegetables, and home-made pasta.

The dense woods above, with expansive views over the sea, are a favourite spot for the locals, who come out here on a Sunday armed with picnic hampers and portable stoves, though there are enough shady nooks and glades to find your own space. Soon after Novara, the road climbs to 1270m before descending, in sight of Etna's dramatic slopes, to Francavilla and Castiglione.

Tíndari

With your own transport, you could drive a further twenty minutes (11km) from San Biagio along the coastal road to the area's most complete collection of classical remains at **TÍNDARI**. Originally founded in 396 BC, **Tyndaris**, as it was known, was one of the last Greek settlements in Sicily, built and fortified by settlers from Syracuse (Siracusa) as a defence against Carthaginian attacks along this coast. Almost impregnable on its commanding height, the town prospered even under Rome, when it was given special privileges in return for its loyalty.

Climbing the hill to the site, however, the first thing you see, glistening from its cliff-top position, is the **Santuario di Tíndari** (Mon–Sat 6.45am–12.30pm & 2.30–7pm, Sun 6.45am–12.45pm & 2.30–8pm; closes 1hr earlier in winter; ⓦ www.santuariotindari.it), a lavishly kitsch temple erected in the 1960s to house the much-revered *Madonna Nera*, or Black Madonna. A plaque underneath this Byzantine icon proclaims *Nigra sum, sed hermosa* ("I am black, but beautiful"), a reference to the esteem in which she has been held for a thousand years since the icon appeared from the east to perform a series of miracles, such as producing a soft mattress in the nick of time to save a child who was hurtling to the rocks below. Pilgrims throng to the sanctuary to pay their respects, especially around the Black Madonna's feast day on September 8. There's a great view from the top, overlooking a long tongue of white sand and the Marinello lagoons below (see p.166). Buses stop in the car park over 1km from the sanctuary, from where minibuses shuttle every ten minutes or so up to the litter of cabins and stalls at the foot of the church (return tickets €0.60). The car park charges €1 per hour.

The archeological site

The **archeological site of Tyndaris** (daily 9am–2hr before sunset; €4) lies at the end of a path that starts in front of the sanctuary. Most of the visible remains are Roman, including some houses and shops along the main street, the decumanus – one of them (probably a caldarium, or bathhouse) with traces of plumbing still surviving – and an impressive **basilica** at the eastern end. The basilica would have been the entrance to the agora lying beyond (now covered by tourist shops). It was restored in the 1950s, using modern materials, though it still retains a certain grandeur. You can just about make out the manner of its construction, bridging Greek and Roman building techniques, and designed in such a way that the central gallery could be shut off at either end and used for public meetings, with the market traffic diverted along the side passages.

The decumanus has streets running off it, and at the bottom of one is the **Casa Romana**, a Roman house in good condition, with mosaic floors. At the other end of the main street, the **teatro**, cut into the hill, boasts a superb view over the sea, as far as the distant Milazzo promontory. A part of the stage remains from the original third-century BC Greek edifice, but most of the rest is Roman, dating from the Imperial Age when the theatre was converted for use as a gladiatorial arena. Later, it was partly dismantled to furnish stone for the **city walls** that once surrounded the settlement, of which a good portion remain. You'll have seen some of them on the road up, including the ancient city's **main gate**, built to the same "pincer" design as the one at the Euryalus castle outside Siracusa.

The site's **museum** contains some of the best finds from the excavations, including a massive stone head of Augustus. There's also a reconstruction of the theatre's scene-building, and some eighteenth-century watercolours showing how the basilica looked before its overhaul.

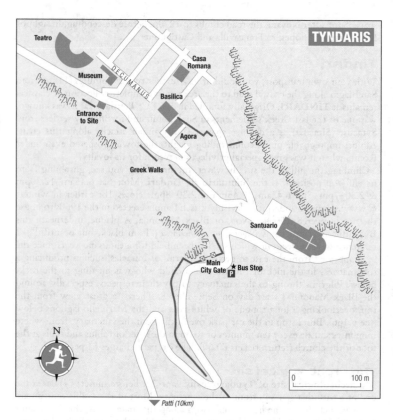

TYNDARIS

Teatro

Casa Romana

DECUMANUS

Museum

Basilica

Entrance to Site

Agora

Greek Walls

Santuario

Main City Gate

Bus Stop

N

0   100 m

▼ Patti (10km)

You can experience the theatre here at its best by attending one of the **classical dramas** staged on alternate evenings from late May to mid-June or the dramas and **concerts** taking place between late July and late August; performances normally start at 9pm, with tickets costing around €20 for the best seats, otherwise about €14. Ask at the ticket office by the entrance to the archeological site or contact the box office directly (☎0941.240.912 or 800.031.922, ⓦwww.teatrodeiduemari .net) for details. You can also pick up a programme from the **tourist office** here, right next to the site on Via Teatro Greco (Mon–Fri 9am–1pm; ☎0941.369.184, ⓦwww.pattietindari.com). Note that there's a **free bus service** from Messina's Piazza Duomo timed to arrive before the start of performances and returning afterwards; call ☎0941.240.912 to book a place.

Directly below Tíndari and west of Oliveri lies one of Sicily's most entrancing **beaches**, forming part of the **Riserva Naturale Laghetti di Marinello**, where saltwater lagoons, sand dunes and dramatic rocky cliffs provide a sanctuary for migratory birds. The lagoons, fine sand and clean water are irresistible, and there are bars and a campsite (see opposite), but precious little shade on the beach.

Patti

Five buses daily (not Sun) connect Tíndari with the main Piazza Marconi at **PATTI**, which has more charm than many of the centres on this coast. At the top of the town, Patti's **Cattedrale** has a powerful *Madonna* by Antonello de Saliba and, in the right transept, the tomb of Adelasia, much-loved first wife of Roger I, with the date of her death inscribed at the bottom, 1118. East of the town, close to the train station and under an autostrada viaduct, lie the remains of a fourth-century AD **Roman villa** (daily 9am–1hr before sunset; €2), where you can view a few poorly maintained mosaics and the ruins of a bathhouse; a small **antiquarium** (same ticket) shows finds from the site.

Practicalities

There are two **train stations** within reach of the main sites: Patti–San Piero Patti station is the stop for Patti; for Tyndaris you can either take a bus from Patti station direct to the site, or stay on the train for a few more kilometres to Oliveri-Tíndari, from where it's about a 3km (uphill) walk. There's one daily bus here from Messina and one from Milazzo (both Mon–Sat).

Perfectly located for the Laghetti di Marinello, there's a well-equipped **campsite** at the bottom of the cliffs holding the Tíndari sanctuary at Località Marinello, the *Marinello* (☎0941.313.000, ⓦwww.villaggiomarinello.it), within steps of the lovely sandy beach and with bungalows (❷) and mini-apartments rentable by the week. There's another, smaller and more basic site at Oliveri: *Baia del Príncipe* (☎0941.313.302, ⓔbaiadelprincipe@hotmail.it; closed mid-Nov to mid-March). There are also some decent beachside **hotels** in and around Patti; *Villa Romana*, a few metres from the sea on Via Playa (☎0941.361.268, ⓦwww.hotelvillaromana patti.com; ❷), offers the best value; at least half board is required in peak season (€60 per person).

Capo d'Orlando and Naso

Occupying a headland that was the site of a historic defeat for the Aragonese king, Frederick II, at the hands of a group of rebellious barons in 1299, **CAPO D'ORLANDO**, 30km west of Patti, is a slick holiday town today, surrounded by good rocky and sandy beaches. If you're sufficiently charmed by the **swimming**, which is best on its eastern side (around the San Gregorio area), you might well want **to stay**. The cheapest accommodation choice is the 1960s-style *Hotel Faro*, Via Libertà 7 (☎0941.902.466, ⓦwww.nuovohotelfaro.com; ❸), with spacious rooms and balconies fronting the beach; half board is usually compulsory in August, at €70 per person. Turn right out of the station and walk along Via Crispi, head for the sea at Piazza Matteotti, and the hotel is a few blocks to the right. The town has plenty of restaurants, bars and birrerias, with a choice of discos in summer.

From Capo d'Orlando there are daily **excursions to the Aeolian Islands** between June and September, with departures at 8am, returning at 7pm: contact any travel agency in town for further information and bookings, for example Agatirso Viaggi, Via Consolare Antica 332 (☎0941.912.756, ⓦwww.agatirso .com) or La Rosa, Via Piave 67 (☎0941.904.045, ⓦwww.larosaviaggi.it). For general tourist **information**, ask at the kiosk on the seafront (summer daily 9am–1pm & 4–8pm, winter usually Mon–Fri 9am–1pm & 3–7pm but hours can be reduced; ☎0941.918.134) or at the regular **tourist office**, Via Améndola 20, on the corner of Via Volta (Mon–Fri 8am–2pm & 4.30–7.30pm; ☎0941.912.784, ⓦwww.aastcapodorlando.it).

Inland from Capo d'Orlando, the oddly named town of **NASO** ("Nose") sits at the end of a 12km bus ride, where you can see (just before entering the town, up a steep lane on the left) the partly ruined **Convento dei Minori Osservanti** – a fifteenth-century affair, with an interesting tomb of the same period decorated with allegories of the six virtues. The SS116 continues up, another 33km, to **FLORESTA**, lying on a grassy plain and, at 1275m, claiming the distinction of being Sicily's highest village, then down to Randazzo and the foothills of Mount Etna. If you need a break, you can **eat** well for €20–25 at Floresta's *Trattoria Il Fienile*, Via Vittorio Emanuele 70 (℡0941.662.313; closed Mon), good for *antipasti* and meat dishes, with views of Etna from the terrace.

South of Messina: Mili San Pietro to Itala

Messina's ungraceful suburbs extend south almost as far as the autostrada turn-off at Tremestieri. Shortly beyond, a minor road leads off inland from Mili Marina to **MILI SAN PIETRO**, a nondescript little place 2km up the road. As the village swings into view, the grey cupolas of the monastery-church of **Santa Maria** are just visible below the road on the right. The Basilian monastery of which this was a part was founded by Count Roger in 1082, but is now abandoned – and irreverently occupied by assorted farmyard animals and permeated by their pungent rural smells. The church survives – just – its exterior displaying some nice interlaced blind arcading on one wall, and a semicircular apse. But the inside is derelict and not particularly interesting, although it's said to contain the burial place of Roger's son, Jordan; ask at the church in the centre of the village for the key. You can get here from Messina on bus #8 from the terminal at Zir (Mon–Sat every 1–2hr), for which there are frequent tram connections from Autosilo Cavallotti; on Sunday bus #10 from Cavallotti goes to the village directly.

Further down the coast by 7 or 8km, **SCALETTA ZANCLEA** is a popular resort with the impressive eleventh-century **Castello Rufo Ruffo** at its highest point (Mon–Sat 9am–noon, also Fri & Sat 4–7pm; €2), containing such heraldic knick-knacks as Bourbon armour and medals. The next village down, Itala Marina, has an inland parent, **ITALA**, 2.5km up the road from the coast, just beyond which – over the bridge on the road to Croce – is the church of **San Pietro**. Built by Count Roger in 1093, in thanksgiving for a victory over the Arabs, the building has features in common with Santa Maria in Mili San Pietro, and provided the model for the church near Casalvécchio Sículo built eighty years later. This domed, red-brick construction has been restored and is still in use; indeed the best time to see it is before or after the 10.30am service on Sunday. Failing that, contact the priest for the key; find him on Itala's main street, Via Umberto 26 (call first at ℡090.952.154).

Sávoca

Around 30km south of Messina, the small resort of Santa Teresa di Riva is the jumping-off point for the foothills of the Monti Peloritani and, in particular, the evocatively sited village of **SÁVOCA**. That sits at the end of a winding 4km run up from the coast, its houses and three churches perched on the cliffsides in clumps, with a tattered castle (originally Saracen) topping the pile. Two pincer-like streets, Via San Michele and Via Chiesa Madre, reach around to their respective churches, the grandest being the square-towered thirteenth-century **Chiesa Madre**. Seated on a tiny ridge between two opposing hills, it's a fine vantage point from which to look down the valley to the sea and across the surrounding hills. Spare a glance, too, at the house next door, lovingly restored and displaying a fifteenth-century stone-arched double window; the house is one of many in the village that have had a face-lift as outsiders move in to snap up run-down cottages as second homes. These days, Sávoca lies within the Taormina commuter belt and most of the people who live here work elsewhere. That's to its advantage: during the day the streets and hillside alleys are refreshingly empty, and the medieval atmosphere still intact.

Signs in the village point you to the **Cappuccini monastery**, whose catacombs (April–Sept Tues–Sat 9am–1pm & 4–7pm, Sun 4–7pm; Oct–March Tues–Sat 9am–1pm & 3–6pm, Sun 3–6pm; donations requested) contain a selection of gruesome mummified bodies. These are the remains of local lawyers, doctors and the clergy: two hundred to three hundred years old, they stand in niches dressed in their eighteenth-century finery, the skulls of less-complete colleagues lining the walls above. An added grotesque touch is the green paint with which the bodies have been daubed, the work of vandals and hard to remove without damaging the cadavers. Ask the custodian and you'll probably be shown the church **treasury** as well, which holds a small collection of liturgical books and seventeenth- and eighteenth-century bibles.

More offbeat delight is at hand in the village's ⚘ *Bar Vitelli*. An appealing wood-panelled, eighteenth-century stone-flagged building, it (and the village) were used as the scene of Michael Corleone's betrothal to Apollonia in Coppola's film *The Godfather*. A few words of Italian might nudge the woman behind the bar into recounting her memories of the shoot – she's something of an expert on all the *Godfather* films. There are numerous mementoes of other episodes in the bar's past inside, and tables under the pergola outside. In summer, the signora at the *Bar Vitelli* will probably persuade you to sample her delicious lemon *granita*, which she makes daily. Sávoca also has a *paninoteca* for snacks below the Capuchin monastery and a popular **trattoria**, *La Pineta* (☎0942.761.094; closed Wed in winter), with a panoramic terrace, near the bar.

You could easily see the village on a day-trip from either Messina or Taormina. Frequent Jónica **buses** connect Messina with Santa Teresa di Riva (not Sun), from where there are six connections daily to Sávoca. From Taormina, take an Interbus service to Santa Teresa and change there for Sávoca and Casalvécchio. For taxi transport locally, call ☎0942.751.566, or 338.433.9568. The **tourist office** on Via Pineta (daily: mid-July to Sept 9am–1pm & 4–8pm; Oct to mid-July 9am–1pm plus some afternoons; ☎0942.761.125) can provide information on the nearest accommodation options.

Casalvécchio Sículo

The only road beyond Sávoca (and served by the same bus from Santa Teresa di Riva) careers another 2km along the ridge to **CASALVÉCCHIO SÍCULO**, which, if anything, has even better views of the valley from its terraces. There's not much to detain you here, except the quiet village atmosphere, but walk through Casalvécchio and, after about 500m, a rough road drops away to the left (signposted), snaking down into a lush, citrus-planted valley. It's about a twenty-minute hike to the Norman monastery of **Santi Pietro e Paolo**, glori-ously situated on a high bank above the river. Built in the twelfth century, its battlemented facade and double domes are visible from a distance through the lemon groves. Though considered Sicily's best example of Basilian architecture, the church betrays a strong Arabic influence, particularly in the polychromatic patterns of the exterior. If it's locked, there should be someone around in one of the adjacent buildings with a key.

Either head back up to the main road and wait for the return bus to pass, or continue downhill for a longer **walk**, beyond the monastery to the River Agrò. It's about another hour's tramp, alongside the wide (and mostly dry) river bed to Rina, back towards the sea. The main (SS114) coastal road is signposted from Rina, and in another twenty minutes, through a small tunnel, you're back in Santa Teresa di Riva, on the Messina–Catania bus route.

Forza d'Agrò

The only other worthy diversion into the hills is just a few kilometres south, where the turn-off at **Capo Sant'Aléssio** gives the first views of Taormina. The cliffs here support a sturdy castle, which has been for sale for years; you can climb up to it, but you can't get in.

Four kilometres inland of here, atop a corkscrew road – and most easily reached by four daily Interbus buses from Taormina and Letojanni – is **FORZA D'AGRÒ**. Like so many Sicilian villages, it's a breezy place defiantly crumbling all around its mostly elderly inhabitants, and with little left of the Norman **castello** that crowns it. A memorable clamber will take you up to the top: the streets become ever more perilous, and the stone cottages increasingly neglected and held together by rotting spars of wood. One push, it seems, would bring the whole lot down. The lower parts of the village are better maintained, but not much – shops are tucked into tiny cottage interiors, and a couple of churches are locked and decrepit.

Still, this is close enough to Taormina to attract the tour buses, which deposit their passengers in the village square, where there are a couple of bars to help idle the time away. And there's a fine, moderately priced **restaurant** too, known to both tourists and locals: *L'Abbazia* (☎0942.721.226; closed Mon Nov–May). Specialities here include a mixed vegetable grill made with local mushrooms, aubergine, peppers and radicchio, which you can eat on a terrace with great views; fixed-price three-course menus cost €25 and €28. There's a decent **hotel** if you are tempted to overnight here, the small and simple *Villa Souvenir* on Viale delle Rimembranze (☎0942.721.078, ⓦwww.villasouvenir.com; ❷), where half board is compulsory in August (€60 per person).

Taormina and around

TAORMINA, dominating two grand, sweeping bays from high on Monte Tauro, is Sicily's best-known and classiest resort. Although it has no beach of its own – they are all sited quite a way below town – the outstanding remains of the classical theatre and the sheer beauty of the town's site, framed by a distant Etna, amply compensate. Beloved of writers, artists and celebrities across the decades, it's an expensive place to stay (perhaps the most expensive in Sicily), but the air of exclusivity at least is only skin-deep – at heart, what was once a small hill-village still can't seem to believe its good luck. Much of its late medieval character is still intact, with the one main traffic-free street presenting an unbroken line of aged *palazzi*, flower-decked alleys and intimate piazzas. The downside is that most of the time, and particularly between June and September and at New Year and Easter, Taormina simply seethes as the narrow alleys are filled shoulder-to-shoulder with tourists. Things get a little quieter in winter, and this is also the time when the views of Etna are incomparably clearer, while the spring brings flamboyant hillside displays of flowering plants and shrubs. Inland, the town is overlooked by the lofty mountain village of **Castelmola**, visited for the superb views in all directions, and an easy trip from Taormina. Down on the coast, the local **beaches** soak up the day trade all summer – the best ones are at **Giardini-Naxos**, a resort that's cheaper and less pretentious than Taormina in every way.

Arrival, information and transport

Taormina-Giardini **train station** is way below town, on the water's edge – it's actually one of Italy's most attractive stations, in Sicilian-Gothic style with Art Nouveau decoration, and there's a small **tourist office** (Mon–Fri 8.30am–1.30pm; ☏0942.52.189). To get up to town, you either need to take a taxi (around €15) or catch one of the Interbus buses leaving once or twice hourly (fewer on Sun) from outside the station; buy your ticket from the driver. All buses stop in Taormina's **bus station** on Via Luigi Pirandello.

The main street, Corso Umberto I, runs right through town, from Porta Messina to Porta Catania. In the crenellated Palazzo Corvaja, off Piazza Vittorio Emanuele, the English-speaking **tourist office** (Mon–Thurs 8.30am–2pm & 4–7pm, Fri 8.30am–2pm; ☏0942.23.243, ⓦwww.gate2taormina.com) is a useful stop for maps, leaflets, tour brochures and local bus and train timetables. The website ⓦwww.taorminaservizipubblici.it gives information on such public services as car parks and local transport.

A free **minibus service** (*bus navetta*) shuttles from Piazza San Pancrazio (just below Porta Messina) to and from the Lumbi car park. Other local bus services depart hourly from Piazza San Pancrazio up to Madonna della Rocca (for the castle) and Castelmola, and down to the beach at Spisone/Letojanni, while most other buses – including those to Giardini-Naxos – leave from the bus terminal. For the beach below town at Mazzarò, there's a **cable-car** (*funivia*) service from Taormina (Mon 9am–8pm, Tues–Sun 8am–8pm, until 1am daily in summer; €2, €3.50 return); the station is on Via Luigi Pirandello, between Porta Messina and the bus terminal.

Accommodation

The mushrooming number of B&Bs and rental rooms provide the cheapest **accommodation** in Taormina, but even in these you can easily pay €90 or €100 for a double in July and August, perhaps €70 for the rest of the year. Hotels all charge more than their equivalents anywhere else in Sicily (up to €200 for a mere three-star), but nowhere else has such a range of charmingly sited establishments (many of them elegant old villas) with such sweeping views. Wherever you choose, it's a good idea to book in advance, and look for special offers online or by telephoning. Drivers should enquire about parking facilities (if any). The tourist office has full accommodation lists, as does their

---

Parking in Taormina

Unless there's parking at your hotel, drivers will have to use one of the long-stay **car parks** signposted on the approaches to Taormina, notably outside Porta Catania at the southwestern end of town or at the Lumbi car park northeast of the centre; Lumbi car park is further from the centre, and is a lengthy walk up steps to Via Cappuccini, though a free minibus service saves you the ten-minute climb. Alternatively, park near the coast at Mazzarò, and take the cable-car up to town. **Tariffs** (€5–7 for 2hr 30min, €12.50–16 for 24hr, €20.50–28 for 48hr) are slightly higher at Porta Catania, and higher at all car parks in August.

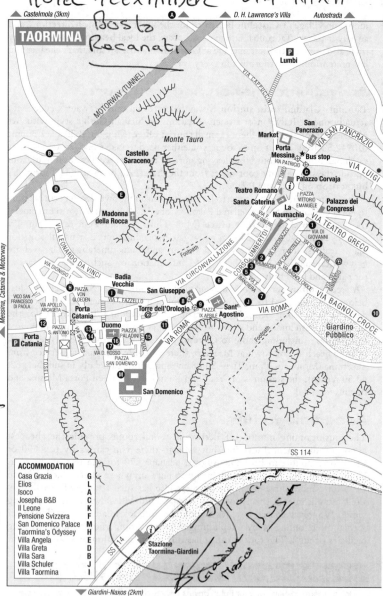

TAORMINA

Handwritten notes at top: HOTEL ALEXANDER VIA NIXA / Basta / Rocanati

Map labels: Castelmola (3km) · D. H. Lawrence's Villa · Autostrada · Lumbi · Monte Tauro · Castello Saraceno · Madonna della Rocca · San Pancrazio · Market · Porta Messina · Bus stop · Palazzo Corvaja · Teatro Romano · Santa Caterina · La Naumachia · Palazzo dei Congressi · Badia Vecchia · San Giuseppe · Torre dell'Orologio · Sant' Agostino · Porta Catania · Duomo · San Domenico · Giardino Pubblico · Stazione Taormina-Giardini · Giardini-Naxos (2km)

ACCOMMODATION

Casa Grazia	G
Elios	L
Isoco	A
Josepha B&B	C
Il Leone	K
Pensione Svizzera	F
San Domenico Palace	M
Taormina's Odyssey	H
Villa Angela	E
Villa Greta	D
Villa Sara	B
Villa Schuler	J
Villa Taormina	I

Side margin: MESSINA, TAORMINA AND THE NORTHEAST | Taormina and around · Messina, Catania & Motorway

website (and see ⓦwww.taohotels.com for places belonging to Taormina's hotel association). The nearest **campsite** is at Letojanni (see p.180).

You can usually save a bit of money (though not necessarily in July and August) by staying down at the **beach** in the less exclusive resort of Giardini-Naxos, though then you'll be travelling up to Taormina fairly frequently. At Mazzarò, the closest and most beautiful stretch of local coastline, beachfront accommodation comes at a real premium, typified by five-star-deluxe properties.

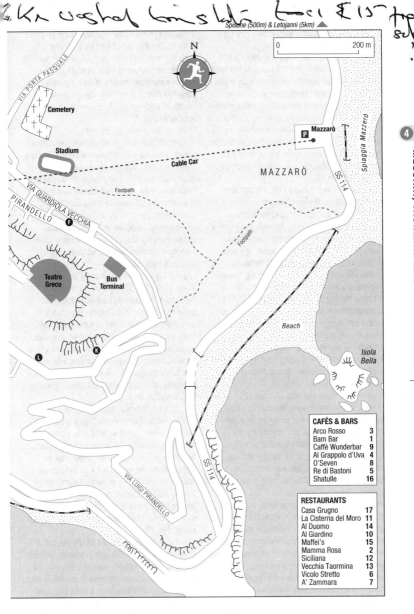

Spisone (500m) & Letojanni (5km) ▲

N

0   200 m

VIA PORTA PASQUALE

Cemetery

Stadium

Cable Car

Mazzarò

P

MAZZARÒ

Spiaggia Mazzarò

SS 114

VIA GUARDIOLA VECCHIA

PIRANDELLO

Footpath

Footpath

Teatro Greco

Bus Terminal

Beach

Isola Bella

VIA LUIGI PIRANDELLO

SS 114

CAFÉS & BARS

Arco Rosso	3
Bam Bar	1
Caffè Wunderbar	9
Al Grappolo d'Uva	4
O'Seven	8
Re di Bastoni	5
Shatulle	16

RESTAURANTS

Casa Grugno	17
La Cisterna del Moro	11
Al Duomo	14
Al Giardino	10
Maffei's	15
Mamma Rosa	2
Siciliana	12
Vecchia Taormina	13
Vicolo Stretto	6
A' Zammara	7

Hotels and B&Bs

Casa Grazia Via Iallia Bassia 20 ☎0942.24.776, Ⓔcasagrazia@libero.it. You won't find anything much cheaper than this in the centre, nor such positively mothering management. Most of the basic but clean rooms have fridges and private bathrooms and balconies – the best ones are at the top, with use of a panoramic terrace. Free wi-fi. No credit cards. ❷

Elios Via Bagnoli Croce 98 ☎0942.23.431, Ⓦwww.elioshotel.com. A smartish two-star hotel a short walk from the town centre, where rooms have en-suite bathrooms, minibars, safes and a/c (these may be charged extra). Most rooms have a sight of the sea or Etna, but the best views are from the broad roof terrace. ❸

🏃 **Isoco** Via Salita Branco 2 ☎0942.23.679, ⓦwww.isoco.it. The five rooms in this small boutique hotel are quirkily themed on such artists as Botticelli and Keith Haring, and each has its own entrance, a/c, safe and minibar, with a private bathroom across the corridor. Amazing breakfasts are served round a large table in the shady garden, where there's also a hot tub, while the roof terrace has sunbeds and views extending north up the coast as far as Calabria. Free wi-fi. No credit cards. Closed Dec–Feb. ❸

Josepha B&B Vico Zecca 31 ☎0942.628.871 or 348.844.2971, ⓦwww.bbtaormina.com. In a little courtyard, through a hacked-out archway, immediately inside the Porta Messina, this has two doubles and two singles, sharing two bathrooms. There's also a kitchen, laundry facility and terrace for guests. It's pretty flexible, since families or groups can rent all or part of the building. Breakfast is taken at a nearby bar. No credit cards. ❷

Il Leone Via Bagnoli Croce 126 ☎0942.23.878, ⓔinfo@camereilleone.it. This no-frills B&B is best for the extraordinary bay views from its balconies. There's a bar at street level where the meagre breakfast is served, and a couple of small, plain apartments with basic cooking facilities are also available. A voucher allows guests discounted parking rates. No credit cards. ❷

Pensione Svizzera Via Luigi Pirandello 26 ☎0942.23.790, ⓦwww.pensionesvizzera.com. Nearly all the rooms in this spotless though rather old-fashioned three-star hotel (family-owned since 1925) have balconies with sea views, and the gardens and terracing are lovely – you can eat breakfast outside in summer. There's also a shuttle service to a private beach, wi-fi access and parking. Closed Nov–Feb. ❸

San Domenico Palace Piazza San Domenico 5 ☎0942.613.111, ⓦwww.amthotels.it. Taormina's grandest hotel, a five-star of immense charm, is stunningly situated in a fifteenth-century convent whose cloisters, rooms and corridors have been retained. Views and facilities are unsurpassed – whether it's the bougainvillea-clad terraces leading down to the heated outdoor pool (summer only), the baronial lounge bar or stylish dining in one of four restaurants. Prices start at around €250, though more like €350 for a sea view and twice that for the luxurious suites. Parking available. ❼

🏃 **Villa Angela** Via Leonardo da Vinci ☎0942.27.038, ⓦwww.hotelvillaangela .com. Ever wondered what rock stars do in their spare time? Jim Kerr of Simple Minds, a devotee of Taormina, plumped for opening a boutique four-star

hotel, high on the Castelmola road above town. It's a swish, contemporary take on a traditional villa, with terrific views from soaring picture windows, an open-air pool and a terrace restaurant. The staff are especially friendly. It's a steep walk from Taormina itself, but the hotel lays on an efficient shuttle to town and beach, and there's a bus stop directly outside. ❺

Villa Greta Via Leonardo da Vinci 46 ☎0942.28.286, ⓦwww.villagreta.it. This bolthole above town on the Castelmola road offers amazing views over town, bay and volcano, with all rooms having either a terrace or balcony. It's a relaxing base, away from the central hubbub, and there's a good restaurant (open to non-guests), with al fresco seating in summer, featuring typical Sicilian dishes alongside speciality vegetarian dishes and couscous. The hotel is a steep 15min walk from Taormina, but the bus passes right outside. Closed Jan. ❸

🏃 **Villa Sara** Via Leonardo da Vinci 55 ☎0942.28.138, ⓦwww.villasara.net. Behind unprepossessing bare walls, this great-value B&B close to *Villa Greta* reveals itself to be a gracious villa with period furnishings. The welcoming host family rents out three good-size rooms, each with a/c, fridge, bathroom and a large terrace commanding spectacular views. As with *Villa Greta*, the downside is the steep hike up from the centre, though it's only a brief bus or taxi ride. Wi-fi available. ❷

Villa Schuler Piazzetta Bastione ☎0942.23.481, ⓦwww.hotelvillaschuler.com. This fine old hotel has been in the same family for over a century, and retains something of an elegant yesteryear feel. There are scintillating bay views from the tranquil, palm-shaded terrace, and an extensive jasmine-draped garden at the back. Staff are friendly and breakfasts superb. Borrow a mountain bike, or use the shuttle service to the beach. Free wi-fi and limited parking available. Closed late Nov to early Feb. ❹

Villa Taormina Via T. Fazzello 39 ☎0942.620.072, ⓦwww.hotelvillataormina.com. A superior four-star townhouse that oozes old-fashioned charm – and with only eight antique-filled rooms, the feel is more private house party than hotel. It's also blessedly quiet, off the main drag, and with a terrace that has a hot tub and excellent views. Check online for the best last-minute deals. Parking and beach shuttle available. Closed Nov–Feb. ❺–❻

Hostel

Taormina's Odyssey Via Paternò di Bíscari 13, near Porta Catania ☎0942.24.533 or 349.810.7733, ⓦwww.taorminaodyssey.com.

Catering to an international crowd, this independent hostel lies in a residential neighbourhood at the western end of town, around a 5min walk from the Corso. There are two dorms, holding four and six beds (€20–22), and a range of private rooms (€40–70) with TVs, ceiling fans and separate or en-suite bathrooms. You can use the cooking facilities on the outdoor terrace, and there's also a laundry service and internet access. Drivers get a 40 percent discount voucher to use at the car park.

The Town

Entering Taormina's old centre from Porta Messina, you'll find yourself immediately on the town's axis, Corso Umberto I, where a useful first stop would be the fourteenth-century **Palazzo Corvaja** – home to Taormina's tourist office, accessed through a courtyard. From here, a staircase rises to the chamber where the Sicilian "parliament" met in 1410 to choose a successor to the Aragonese line, now housing the engaging **Museo Siciliano d'Arte e Tradizioni Popolari** (Tues–Sun 9am–1pm & 4–8pm; €2.60), a collection of quirky folklore items ranging from painted Sicilian carts to cork-and-wax nativity scenes. One of the highlights is the 25 panel paintings of the 1860s showing people being saved by miraculous intervention from such terrible fates as falling onto a stove or being attacked by cats.

Opposite Palazzo Corvaja, the church of **Santa Caterina** was built almost on top of a small, brick-built odeon, known as the **Teatro Romano** (originally used for musical recitations): peer down at it through the railings around the back, and then enter the church to take a closer look at bits of the theatre exposed in the floor of the nave.

The Teatro Greco

The crowds flowing from Piazza Vittorio Emanuele past an unbroken parade of tourist shops will point you towards Taormina's **Teatro Greco** (daily 9am to 1hr before sunset; €8), one of Sicily's unmissable sights – and best visited in the early morning or near closing time to avoid the throngs. Nothing, however, can detract from the site's natural beauty. Carved out of the hillside, the theatre gives a complete panorama of the Sicilian coastline, the mountains of southern Calabria across the water and snow-capped Etna – a glorious natural backdrop for the audiences of classical times. Despite its name, and though founded by Greeks in the third century BC, the existing remains are almost entirely Roman,

---

D.H. Lawrence in Taormina

If you've got twenty minutes to spare you can turn literary sleuth, though there's nothing to see except the back of a house. From Porta Messina, follow Via Cappuccini and then Via Fontana Vecchia, before dropping down to Piazza Franz Pagano. Follow the road around and a steep left fork – Via David Herbert Lawrence – puts you on the right track for the villa in which **D.H. Lawrence** lived for three years in the 1920s. It's up the hill and just around the corner, on the right-hand side of the road, a pink-and-cream-coloured building, now a private house, and marked by a simple plaque reading: "D.H. Lawrence, English author, lived here 1920–1923". He wrote many of his short stories and essays here, and much of Lady Chatterley's Lover, which was supposed to have been inspired by the exploits of an Englishwoman living in Taormina who had fallen for a local farmer. Lawrence wasn't always enamoured of the town; in a letter of December 1921 he described Corso Umberto as "one long parade of junk shops ... things dearer than ever, more faked, food tiresome as it always was. If only Etna would send down 60,000,000 tons of boiling lava over the place and cauterise it away."

dating from the end of the first century AD, a period when Taormina enjoyed great prosperity under Imperial Roman rule. The reconstruction completely changed the character of the theatre, though not always for the better – the arched apertures, niches and columns of the impressive Roman scene-building, for example, must have obscured the views of Etna that were presumably a major reason for the theatre's original siting. As the spectacles of the Imperial Roman era were strictly gladiatorial, the stage and lower seats were cut back to provide more room, and a deep trench was dug in the orchestra to accommodate the animals and combatants.

Along the Corso

Further up the Corso, a side alley to the left (Via Naumachia) brings you to the 122m-long niched wall of **La Naumachia**, a Roman water cistern and gymnasium, while if you continue downhill, along Via Bagnoli Croce, you reach the shady **Giardino Púbblico** (open dawn–dusk; free), from where there are some outstanding views. The gardens were endowed by a Scot, Florence Trevelyan, who settled in Taormina in 1899 having been "invited" to leave England in the wake of a romantic liaison with the Prince of Wales, the future Edward VII. She also contributed the curious *apiari* ("beehives") – pavilions, variously resembling rustic log cabins and stone- or brick-built pagodas, and now holding caged birds, plants and a children's play area.

Tourists and locals all collide bang in the middle of Corso Umberto I, at **Piazza IX Aprile**, Taormina's "balcony". The restored twelfth-century Torre dell'Orologio (clocktower) straddles the Corso here, while sweeping views from the terrace overlook Etna and the bay. It's hard to resist the lure of a café seat here – just be warned that you'll be presented with a big bill, even for an *espresso*. The two small churches in the square, incidentally, give an indication of how small-scale Taormina was until fairly recently. Squat fifteenth-century **Sant'Agostino** is now a library, while **San Giuseppe**'s seventeenth-century facade is adorned with plaques depicting skulls and crossbones.

Through the clocktower, the next small square – fronted by a pretty seventeenth-century fountain – contains the battlemented **Duomo**, originally built in the thirteenth century, though much restored since. Stepped alleys climb up from here towards the Via Circonvallazione, where the **Badia Vecchia** survives as one of the old town's most graceful buildings. It's the sole remnant of a fifteenth-century abbey, with the swallow-tailed battlements and twin Gothic windows characteristic of Taormina. The local **Museo Archeologico** has been installed inside, displaying a few relics of the Roman town, including a marvellous carved sarcophagus, though the building was closed for restoration work at the time of writing. When it's open, it offers excellent views out through the windows over the rooftops to the sea.

Eating and drinking

As with accommodation, so with **restaurants**; Taormina can be the most expensive town in Sicily in which to eat, though there are plenty of places offering competitively priced tourist menus. While there are lots of restaurants, menus are pretty standard across the board, although a few at the top end stand out as pretty special. Because of the demand, pizzas are widely available here at lunchtime too (unlike most other places in Sicily), usually costing €8–10.

Cafés and **bars** are particularly pricey, though, barring a few chic retreats, the nightlife scene isn't especially exclusive, with people milling around the streets all night in summer, hopping from bar to bar until the small hours. Taormina also has

Festivals and parades are staged at Christmas and Carnevale, but summer is the best time for cultural events. Between June and September, **Taormina Arte** (@www .taormina-arte.com) features a varied theatre, music and dance programme, from rock bands and symphony orchestras to classical dramas, held either at the spectacular Teatro Greco or the Palazzo dei Congressi in Piazza Vittorio Emanuele. Tickets cost from around €15. The events kick off with the **Taormina FilmFest** (@www .taorminafilmfest.it), which runs for a week every June, previewing new movies – from around the world in their original versions – on a big screen at the Teatro Greco (tickets €8–12).

Tickets for all events are available on line or at the Palazzo dei Congressi, Piazza Vittorio Emanuele.

a fairly discreet **gay** scene, mostly centred on the style bars around Piazza Paladini. At least the buzzing evening *passeggiata* along the Corso is free, and you could always bus down to the resort-strip of Giardini-Naxos for a waterfront stroll and a cheaper bite to eat – by no means the worst way to spend an evening.

Restaurants

Casa Grugno Via Santa Maria dei Greci ☎0942.21.208, @www.casagrugno.it. One of the top places in town, if not the region. Chef Andreas Zagerl takes traditional Sicilian cuisine as his starting-point but presents a very modern Mediterranean menu that changes with the seasons – thus, ravioli with ricotta and aubergines, or suckling pig roast with wild fennel seeds and beer. Two courses here will cost you around €50, three courses €70, and tasting menus start from around €80. Reservations are essential, especially for the summer courtyard dining. Closed lunchtime; Nov–April closed Sun, also closed Jan & Feb.

La Cisterna del Moro Via Bonifacio 1 ☎0942.23.001. This is basically an all-day pizza joint – they are good and crisp – though with the low lights and bougainvillea-draped terrace it's also a romantic spot for local couples on a night out. Pizzas €8–10. Closed Mon Oct–Easter.

Al Duomo Vico Ebrei 11 ☎0942.625.656, @www.ristorantealduomo.it. Fine restaurant with a serious commitment to local ingredients and local dishes such as *maccu* (broad bean soup), pasta with sardines and wild fennel, and lamb stew. Mains cost €20–22, and the tasting menu rings in at €60. There's a lovely terrace above the Duomo square and a simple, pretty interior. Closed Wed Nov–March.

Al Giardino Via Bagnoli Croce 84 ☎0942.23.453, @www.algiardino.net. With pasta €8–10 and standard meat and fish dishes from €9, this is what passes for inexpensive in Taormina. It's in an out-of-the-way spot opposite the public gardens,

and is usually busy, with amiable and enthusiastic service. Closed Mon.

Maffei's Via San Domenico de Guzman 1 ☎0942.24.055. If you want one really good fish meal, this formal but not overpowering restaurant is the place. The day's specials (from around €20) are written on the board – seabass to lobsters – while oysters, sea urchins, pastas and carpaccios are offered as appetizers. English-speaking staff guide you through the menu, and all you can hear on the bougainvillea-covered terrace is the gentle clatter of cutlery and contented murmurs. It's small, so it's an idea to book ahead if you don't want to miss out.

Mamma Rosa Via Naumachia 10 ☎0942.24.361. This does a roaring trade in *forno a legna* pizzas, served at tables spilling down the stepped alley. There's also a full menu, though you'll easily pay €30 a head for a couple of courses and wine. Closed Tues Nov–Feb.

Siciliana Salita Ospedale 9 ☎0942.24.780. Just outside the Porta Catania, and raised above the square on a cheery terrace, this trattoria is pretty good value (pasta from €8, mains around €14), especially as the menu rings the changes a bit. There's smoked swordfish and tuna as an appetizer, lamb as well as fish, and crispy roast potatoes with parsley and parmesan instead of chips. Closed Wed.

Vecchia Taormina Vico Ebrei 3 ☎0942.625.589. Taormina's best pizzeria has a stack of olive wood outside the door for the fire, and tables outside in a sheltered courtyard. Pizzas are light, crispy, blisteringly hot and also available at lunchtime.

Vicolo Stretto Vicolo Stretto 6 ☏ 0942.625.554. Reached up the slimmest of alleys off the Corso, by Piazza IX Aprile, this is a chic place to try "real Sicilian cuisine" – from pasta with swordfish and mint to beef in a Nero d'Ávola wine sauce (mains range €16–22, though fresh fish is sold by weight). There's a small terrace for eating *al fresco*. Closed lunchtime July & Aug, also Mon Oct–March.

A' Zammara Via Fratelli Bandiera 13 ☏ 0942.24.408. A lovely secluded garden of orange trees entices you in, but this is also one of the best places in town to try authentic Sicilian dishes, such as *tagliolini* with shrimps and Bronte pistachios or *risotto al finocchietto selvático* (with wild fennel). Most dishes are €12–18. Closed Wed Oct–July.

Cafés, bars and clubs

Arco Rosso Via Naumachia 7. Quite a rarity is this proper little old-fashioned bar, tucked down steps just off the Corso, which sells wine by the glass or bottle and doesn't charge the earth for it. Closed Sun lunch, also Wed Oct–Easter.

Bam Bar Via Di Giovanni 45. Taormina's no. 1 spot for ice cream and *granite*, coming in a lip-smacking range of flavours – recommended choices include watermelon, coffee with almond and nutella. The owner will show you photos of all the celebs who have dropped by.

Caffé Wunderbar Piazza IX Aprile. Once the haunt of Garbo and Fassbinder, this remains the most favoured spot in town for the see-and-be-seen brigade, with outdoor seats beneath the clocktower and a determinedly elitist pricing policy. The piano is wheeled out every night for ivory-tinkling beneath the stars.

Al Grappolo d'Uva Via Bagnoli Croce 6–8. A tourist-friendly *osteria* (wine bar) with a dozen Sicilian wines available by the glass (try before you buy) and local cheeses. You get a decent-sized glass and it's not too expensive. Closed Nov–Feb.

O'Seven Largo La Farina 6, off the Corso behind the clocktower. An Irish pub in genteel Taormina? Don't worry, there are pretty candles on the tables and they don't usually show the football.

Re di Bastoni Corso Umberto I 120. The Corso's most popular pub has a bohemian, folksy feel, and there's regular live jazz (usually Wed & Fri). The house special is a strawberry caipirinha. Closed Mon Oct–June, daily Jan to mid-March.

Shatulle Piazza Paladini 4. Currently the main focus of Taormina's gay and lesbian scene, with a chill-out feel, cosy seats and soft lights in the pretty piazza. There are several other cool bars around here too. Closed Mon Sept–June & all Nov–Feb.

Shopping in Taormina

Corso Umberto I can lay fair claim to be the flashiest shopping street in southern Italy, and here you'll have no trouble tracking down a Gucci bag, a €10,000 necklace or a genuine Baroque candelabra. Of course, you can also pick up mass-produced ceramic dishes, Sicilian puppets, model Etnas and AC Milan football shirts. The bulk of the out-and-out tourist gift shops are up Via Teatro Greco on the way to the theatre, but for quirkier boutiques and souvenirs, delve into the side alleys and stepped streets off the Corso.

A few outlets are especially worth seeking out. The **ceramic workshop** at Kerameion (Corso Umberto I 198; ⓦ www.kerameion.com) turns out brilliantly coloured tiles, plates, vases and espresso cups, among other items. Signor Pancrazio's grandmother first opened the Arte Antica Cacopardo **antiques** store (Corso Umberto I 27, corner Via F. Ingegnere; ⓦ www.cacopardoarteantica.com) in 1902 (he's got postcards showing her sitting outside it), and he continues to set out the furniture, porcelain and *objets* on the pavement every day, rain or shine. La Boutique del Tonno Rosso (Via Bagnoli Croce 6; ⓦ www.iltonno.com) is the shop you never knew you needed, devoted entirely to **tuna** fish from the Égadi Islands, including smoked slices, hideously expensive tins of *ventresca* (belly tuna) and not forgetting *lattume di tonno* ("tuna semen") – no, we don't know what you do with it either.

Meanwhile, there's a daily indoor **market** (Mon–Sat) for fruit and veg off Via Cappuccini, and a weekly **Wednesday market** for household items, above town at Parcheggio von Gloeden, off Via Leonardo da Vinci; both are open till around 1.30pm.

Listings

Bus information Interbus ☏ 0942.625.301, ⓦ www.interbus.it, runs regular services to Messina and Catania, and points in between, from the bus terminal. There's a full timetable posted there, plus one outside the train station and more inside the tourist office.

Car and scooter rental Avis, Via S. Pancrazio 7 ☏ 0942.23.041; California, Via Bagnoli Croce 86 ☏ 0942.896.203; City, Piazza Sant'Antonio 5 ☏ 0942.23.161; Italia, Via Luigi Pirandello 29 ☏ 0942.23.973; Sicily By Car, Via Apollo Arcageta 4 ☏ 0942.21.252.

Hospital Ospedale San Vincenzo, in Via Crocefisso, Contrada Sirina, south of Porta Catania (☏ 0942.5791; for emergencies ☏ 0942.579.297). Otherwise there's a first-aid point (Guardia Médica) in Castelmola at Via De Gásperi 49 (☏ 0942.28.256; summer only).

Internet Las Vegas, Salita Alexander Humbolt, opposite Corso Umberto I 186 (daily 10am–10pm, may close later in summer).

Pharmacy British Pharmacy, Corso Umberto I 152 (corner of Piazza IX Aprile) ☏ 0942.625.735; open June–Sept daily 8.30am–9.30pm, Oct–May Mon–Fri 8.30am–1pm & 3.30–8pm; outside these hours pharmacies operate according to a rota system, indicated on pharmacy doors.

Police Carabinieri, Piazza Vittorio Emanuele 4 ☏ 0942.23.232 or 112.

Post office Piazza Sant'Antonio, outside Porta Catania (Mon–Fri 8am–6.30pm, Sat 8.30am–1pm).

Supermarket Upim/Punto SMA supermarket outside Porta Catania (and to the right) on Via Apollo Arcageta.

Taxis There are ranks at the train station (☏ 0942.51.150), at Porta Catania (☏ 0942.628.090), in Piazza San Pancrazio and in Piazza Vittorio Emanuele (☏ 0942.23.000).

Tours Lots of tours are offered to Etna, the Alcántara gorge and Siracusa, or further afield to places like Palermo and Piazza Armerina, from around €35 for a day for the Alcántara gorge and the Etna foothills to €75 for an Etna summit jeep tour. The tourist office has flyers and brochures, or contact an agency directly, like Saistours, Corso Umberto I 222 ☏ 0942.620.671, ⓦ www.saistours .com, and SAT, Corso Umberto I 73 ☏ 0942.24.653, ⓦ www.sat-group.it.

The Castello Saraceno, Madonna della Rocca and Castelmola

Immediately above Taormina, the cliff-top cross and chapel of **Madonna della Rocca** and, just above, the remains of Taormina's tumbledown medieval **Castello Saraceno**, are well worth a visit for the glorious views, down to theatre, town and coastline, and there are a couple of restaurants and cafés here too. Buses taking just a few minutes run up the winding road once or twice hourly from town, but it's more evocative to **walk up** – there's a steep processional path to the chapel (signposted "Castel Taormina/Via Crucis") from Via Circonvallazione, starting just past the Q8 petrol station, and taking around twenty minutes.

From the castle, an obvious signposted concrete path continues all the way up the mountain to **CASTELMOLA**, about 5km by road above Taormina and around an hour in total on foot. The tiny hill-village seems to sprout out of the severe crag beneath it, with just a jumble of precipitous alleys to explore and the remnants of a long-demolished castle. Drivers should park in the car park before entering the village. Hourly buses stop 200m below the main square, disgorging visitors for a quick potter around and a gawp at the stupendous views.

Hardly surprisingly, Castelmola is entirely given over to tourism, with souvenir shops and up to a dozen bars and restaurants flanking the cobbles. *Bar San Giorgio* in the square is the doyen, smartened up over the years, but purveying drinks and views for decades, as the old newspaper cuttings in the corner attest. Try a glass of *vino alla mándorla* (almond wine) here, the sweet local brew. Alternatively, for a diversion in questionable taste, drop into the *Bar Turrisi* in Piazza Duomo – dedicated to the phallus in all its manifestations, and without the slightest hint of irony. The views from the terrace are good too.

Above Castelmola, intrepid hikers can embark on the roughly two-hour climb to the top of **Monte Vénere** (885m), the highest peak hereabouts. The **walk down** from Castelmola is *much* easier than the ascent of course, and the views are better, too; it's an easy fifteen minutes to Madonna della Rocca, thirty minutes to town. Otherwise, hourly **buses** take about fifteen minutes to the centre.

Local beaches

The **coastline below Taormina**, north and south, is immensely appealing – a mixture of grottoes, rocky coves and good sand beaches – although much of it is either sectioned off as private lidos (which you have to pay to use; prices vary from around €5 to €15 a day) or simply gets very packed in summer. Easiest to reach, by bus or cable car, are the small, stony stretches around Mazzarò. For decent expanses of sand you'll have to travel to Giardini-Naxos, around a 5km, fifteen-minute bus ride south of Taormina, and very much a separate town, with its own holiday trade and nightlife.

Mazzarò, Spisone and Letojanni

The closest beaches to town are the scintillating pebbled coves at **MAZZARÒ**, which you can reach by cable car (*funivia*) from Via Luigi Pirandello in Taormina. There's also a steep path, which starts just below the cable-car station. Of the two beaches, the southernmost is usually the most packed, fronting its much-photographed islet, the **Isola Bella**, protected as a marine-life sanctuary. The waters are remarkably clear, and you can rent boats, snorkelling and scuba gear down here.

A little further north are the beach bars and restaurants at **SPISONE**, which you can either walk to from Mazzarò (10min) or directly down from Taormina (path from below the cemetery, off Via Guardiola Vecchia, around 30min), though hourly buses from Taormina's Piazza San Pancrazio also run here, passing Isola Bella and Mazzarò on the way. **LETOJANNI**, 5km north of Taormina, is a little resort in its own right, with a few fishing-boats on a sandy beach and several modest seafront hotels and restaurants. The nearest **campsite** to Taormina lies here: *Euro Camping Marmaruca*, Via Leto (☎0942.36.676; April–Sept). Hourly buses head back to Taormina, passing Spisone and Isola Bella, while local trains link the village with Taormina-Giardini station.

Giardini-Naxos

The best sand beaches close to Taormina are those at **GIARDINI-NAXOS**, south of town, where a long strip of sand curves around the wide bay, backed by a busy promenade of bars, cafés, restaurants and hotels. It's much more of a resort in the Italian style than Taormina – packed and noisy until late September each year, and then largely drawing up the shutters until the following spring. But it's a nice place for a stroll by the sea at any time of year. Half of the beach is free ("*spiaggia libera*"), although the better sands further around the bay towards the cape are partitioned off as private lidos, complete with sun-loungers, shades, watersports gear, bars and restaurants.

Significantly, the bay was the site of the first Greek colony in Sicily. As an obvious stop for ships sailing between Greece and southern Italy, there was a settlement here by 734 BC, named **Naxos** after the Greek island from which the colonists came, though it was never very important. The **excavations** on the site of the ancient settlement (daily 9am until 1hr before sunset; €2) lie right on the cape, Capo Schisò, with the entrance right by *La Sirena* restaurant, overlooking the harbour. The remains are disappointingly sketchy, though they stretch across a large area of the cape and it's pleasant to stroll through the olive and lemon groves around the site. There's scarcely any interpretation of what you're seeing – scant foundations of a large, gridded town and a long stretch of ancient, lava-built city wall – and the small museum on site that houses some of the finds doesn't really help either.

Practicalities

Buses run every thirty minutes to Giardini from Taormina's bus terminal (until around midnight in summer), passing the train station en route. Or you can walk from the train station itself (turn left) in about fifteen minutes. The seafront promenade road is Via Tysandros, with the **tourist office** at no. 54 (Mon–Thurs 9am–1pm & 3.30–6.30pm, Fri 9am–1pm; ☎0942.51.010, ⓦwww.strgiardini .it), next to *La Riva* hotel. The road curves round as far as the fishing harbour and excavations (changing its name from Via Tysandros to Via Schisò), while Via Naxos runs parallel inland. The tourist office is the best first stop for accommodation in summer (it posts a list outside), or just take a walk along the seafront and look for vacancies.

Giardini's **restaurants** are consistently better value than those in Taormina, including the moderately priced *Fratelli Marano*, Via Naxos 187, with fresh pasta and fish and fine pizzas, and ⚔ *La Sirena*, by the harbour and excavations at the end of Via Schisò (☎0942.51.853; closed Mon in winter), where you can eat *forno a legna* pizzas, pasta and seafood on the terrace, with views stretching across the bay to Taormina (there are rooms here too; ❷). Most dishes cost €10–15 in each.

The Alcántara gorge

Etna aside, the main local tour touted in Taormina is to the gorge of the **Alcántara river**, located around 20km west of town. You can also do the trip yourself easily enough, as four buses a day (1 on Sun) run out this way from Taormina's bus terminal, through gentle hills covered with citrus groves, olive trees and wild flowers. The road runs over and alongside the river, and the various bridges are a reminder that the name, Alcántara, is a corruption of the Arabic word for bridge.

The river itself has its source up in the Monte Nébrodi and flows for 50km towards the Ionian sea. Interrupted thousands of years ago by a flow of lava from Etna, the Alcántara eventually wore its way through the rock, forming a spectacular gorge. It's an hour's ride all told to the entrance to the **Gole dell'Alcántara** (open daily; ⓦwww.parcoalcantara.it), where there's a car park, bar and restaurant. Since the gorge has been protected as the Parco Fluviale dell'Alcántara, access is controlled by the park office, where you pay €7 to descend in a lift to the bottom and to follow a geological and botanical itinerary extending for 1.5km above the river. There's also a free public entrance, 200m beyond the main entrance (Francavilla direction), though it's two hundred steps down and back. Within the gorge, you can hire waders and wetsuits in summer in order to slosh along the river (it's always icy) through pools and into the main gorge. Terralcantara (☎0942.985.010, ⓦwww.terralcantara .it) organizes **river-trekking and canyoning expeditions** (€18 and €40 respectively) which you can book at the ticket office. Note that the last bus back to Taormina leaves at 6.15pm.

Francavilla di Sicilia

Walk 4km further up from the Alcántara gorge, or pick up the next bus onwards, to reach **FRANCAVILLA DI SICILIA**, alongside the river and overlooked by the few surviving walls of its hillside castle. This was the site of one of the bloodiest battles fought in Sicily, when the Austrian army (given logistical support by the British) engaged with the Spanish in 1719, to no obvious result apart from the loss of some 8000 lives. There's a path up to the ruins, and although much of the town is newly built there's a fair amount of interest in the couple of old central streets, and there's a well-marked path that winds down to the river through groves of citrus and nut trees, where you'll find a series of waterfalls and natural round ponds where you can swim. Taking the signposted right turn as you approach the village, you might drop in to the **Convento dei Cappuccini** that peers over town and river, where a modest little **museum** (Easter–Oct daily 11am–1pm & 3.30pm–sunset, in winter call ☎0942.981.017 or 338.941.8324; €2.50) shows how the monks – now reduced to two – passed their time in baking, brewing and crafting. You can also inspect the herbarium and buy some of their honey, perfumes or almond- or lemon-flavoured liqueurs.

A good **hotel** in Francavilla offers a quiet alternative to staying in Taormina; in fact, in high summer, it's often easier to get a room here than at the beach. A *Hotel d'Orange d'Alcántara* (☎0942.981.374, ⓦwww.hoteldorange.it; ❸), on the way in from the Gole dell'Alcántara on Via dei Mulini, is a friendly, family-run three-star that has a small pool and restaurant-pizzeria; the hotel can rent you a car, book you onto local tours and dispense advice about hikes in the area.

Castiglione di Sicilia

Five kilometres above Francavilla, and across the border in Catania province, the numerous church spires and the lofty, ruined rock-built castle of **CASTIGLIONE DI SICILIA** make an inviting target as you approach up the switchback road. It's easy to spend a couple of hours just wandering the quiet streets of this old mountain settlement, which meander up as far as a small piazza at the top of town, where there's a flight of steps leading up to the shattered castle, or **Fortezza Greca** (always open), supposedly founded in the fifth century BC by Greek exiles from nearby Naxos and offering grand panoramic views. There are plenty of old churches to poke around, too, including a perfectly restored Byzantine chapel in the valley below, known as "**La Cuba**" for its perfect symmetry. Behind La Cuba, a path leads to the river where there are little waterfalls and pools.

A short walk beyond the piazza, and well signposted all over town, you'll find an excellent **restaurant**, the *Belvedere d'Alcántara*, whose rooftop terrace takes full advantage of the soaring views and which has a €20 tourist menu and pizzas in the evening (☎0942.984.037; closed Mon). The village has some tasty items to take away, too: Alcantara Formaggi, Via Federico II, offers a range of local cheeses, mostly made of sheep's milk, while *Dispensa dell'Etna*, a wine bar and restaurant at Piazza Sant'Antonio 2, has wines, preserves and other local produce.

Castiglione would make a nice **overnight** stop, with the smart little *Hotel Federico II* off the main piazza at Via Maggiore Baracca 2 (☎0942.980.368, ⓦwww.hotelfedericosecondo.com; ❷), and it has a great restaurant. If you don't want to hang around for the return bus to Giardini, you could walk down the hill to Francavilla, an easy hike of about an hour, and pick up one of the more frequent buses from there.

Travel details

Trains

Messina to: Catania (1–2 hourly; 1hr 30min–2hr); Cefalù (12 daily; 2–3hr); Milan (8–10 daily, most with change at Villa S. Giovanni and Rome; 11hr–17hr 45min); Milazzo (10–14 daily; 20–35min); Naples (7–10 daily, most with change at Villa S. Giovanni; 5–7hr); Rome (10 daily, most with change at Villa S. Giovanni; 7–10hr); Palermo (8–11 daily; 2hr 30min–4hr); Taormina (1–2 hourly; 40min–1hr 10min).

Milazzo to: Cefalù (9–12 daily; 1hr 20min–2hr 30min); Messina (12–18 daily; 20–30min); Palermo (9–11 daily; 2hr 10min–3hr 30min).

Taormina to: Catania (1–2 hourly; 45min–1hr); Messina (1–2 hourly; 40min–1hr); Siracusa (4–7 daily; 2hr–2hr 30min).

Buses

Barcellona to: Castroreale (9–10 daily Mon–Sat; 30min).

Messina to: Barcellona (1–2 hourly Mon–Sat; 1hr–1hr 30min); Capo d'Orlando (12 daily Mon–Sat; 1hr 15min–1hr 45min); Catania (11–19 daily Mon–Sat, 8 daily Sun; 1hr 35min); Catania airport (9–15 daily Mon–Sat, 8 daily Sun; 1hr 50min); Forza d'Agrò (1 daily Mon–Sat; 1hr 35min); Giardini-Naxos (8–9 daily Mon–Sat; 45min–2hr); Itala (4 daily Mon–Sat; 50min); Letojanni (6–10 daily Mon–Sat, 2 daily Sun; 1hr 30min); Milazzo (fast service hourly Mon–Sat, 3 daily Sun; 50min); Naples (2 daily; 6hr 30min–7hr); Palermo (4–8 daily Mon–Sat, 4 daily Sun; 2hr 40min); Patti (1–2 hourly Mon–Sat; 1hr–1hr 20min); Rome (3 daily; 9hr–9hr 20min); Santa Teresa di Riva (13 daily Mon–Sat; 1hr); Scaletta Zanclea (1–2 hourly Mon–Sat; 30min–1hr); Taormina (5–8 daily Mon–Sat, 2 daily Sun; 1hr 45min); Tíndari (1 daily Mon–Sat; 1hr).

Milazzo to: Catania airport (July–Sept 3 daily; 1hr 50min); Messina (fast service hourly Mon–Sat, 3 daily Sun; 50min).

Patti to: Tíndari (Mon–Sat 5 daily; 20min).

Taormina to: Castelmola (hourly Mon–Sat, 9 daily Sun; 15min); Castiglione di Sicilia (2 daily Mon–Sat; 1hr 20min); Catania (1–2 hourly Mon–Sat, 12 daily Sun; 1hr 10min–1hr 50min); Catania airport (15 daily Mon–Sat, 11 daily Sun; 1hr 25min); Forza d'Agrò (2 daily; 40min); Francavilla di Sicilia (3 daily Mon–Sat, 1 daily Sun; 1hr); Giardini-Naxos (1–2 hourly Mon–Sat, every 1–2hr Sun; 15min); Gole dell'Alcántara (4 daily Mon–Sat,

1 daily Sun; 1hr); Messina (6–7 daily Mon–Sat, 2 daily Sun; 55min–1hr 45min); Santa Teresa di Riva (8–9 daily Mon–Sat, 3 daily Sun; 35min).

Taormina–Giardini train station to: Castiglione di Sicilia (6 daily Mon–Sat; 45min–1hr 10min); Francavilla di Sicilia (8 daily Mon–Sat, 1 daily Sun; 30–55min); Gole dell'Alcántara (9 daily Mon–Sat, 1 daily Sun; 35–50min); Randazzo (4–5 daily Mon–Sat, 1 daily Sun; 55min–1hr 40min).

Ferries

Messina to: Salerno (1–2 daily; 8hr); Réggio di Calabria (2–7 daily; 40min); Villa San Giovanni (Bluvia 1–2 hourly, Caronte every 20min, every 40–60min at night; 20–30min).

Milazzo June–Sept to: Alicudi (7 weekly; 6hr); Filicudi (7 weekly; 5hr); Ginostra (4 weekly; 5hr 20min); Lípari (5–8 daily; 2hr–2hr 30min); Naples (2 weekly; 17hr); Panarea (4 weekly; 4hr 20min); Rinella (8 weekly; 3hr 30min); Santa Marina (4–5 daily; 3hr–3hr 30min); Strómboli (6 weekly; 5hr 50min–6hr 40min); Vulcano (5–8 daily; 1hr 30min–2hr).

Milazzo Oct–May to: Alicudi (6 weekly; 6hr–6hr 30min); Filicudi (6 weekly; 5hr 10min); Ginostra (3 weekly; 5hr 45min); Lípari (3–5 daily; 2hr–2hr 30min); Naples (2 weekly; 17hr 30min); Panarea (4 weekly; 4hr 10min–5hr); Rinella (6 weekly; 3hr 45min); Santa Marina (2–4 daily; 3hr–3hr 30min); Strómboli (5 weekly; 5hr 45min–7hr); Vulcano (3–5 daily; 1hr 30min–2hr).

Tremestieri to: Réggio di Calabria (2–7 daily; 40min).

Hydrofoils and fast ferries

Messina to: Lípari (5 daily June to mid-Sept, 1 daily mid-Sept to May; 1hr 20min–3hr 25min); Panarea (2 daily June to mid-Sept; 2hr 5min); Réggio di Calabria (1–2 hourly Mon–Fri, 7 daily Sat & Sun; 15–25min); Réggio di Calabria airport (mid-July to mid-Sept 5 daily Mon–Fri; 35min); Santa Marina di Salina (3 daily June to mid-Sept, 1 daily mid-Sept to May; 2hr–2hr 45min); Strómboli (2 daily June to mid-Sept; 1hr 25min); Villa San Giovanni (hourly Mon–Fri, 4–5 daily Sat & Sun; 20min); Vulcano (3 daily June to mid-Sept, 1 daily mid-Sept to May; 1hr 20min–2hr 50min).

Milazzo June to mid-Sept to: Alicudi (3–4 daily; 2hr 35min–3hr 15min); Cefalù (1 daily; 4hr 50min); Filicudi (3–4 daily; 2hr 20min–2hr 35min); Ginostra (4 daily; 1hr 20min–2hr 30min); Lípari (15–18 daily; 1hr); Palermo (2 daily; 5hr 15min–6hr);

Panarea (3–6 daily; 1hr 15min–2hr); Rinella
(7 daily; 1hr 35min–1hr 55min); Santa Marina
(11–13 daily; 1hr 25min–2hr); Strómboli (6 daily;
1hr 5min–2hr 50min); Vulcano (15–18 daily;
40min–1hr 10min).
Milazzo *Oct–May* to: Alicudi (1 daily; 2hr 35min);
Filicudi (1 daily; 2hr); Ginostra (2 daily; 1hr

20min–2hr 30min); Lípari (12 daily; 50min–1hr);
Panarea (1–3 daily; 1hr 40min–2hr 5min);
Rinella (7 daily; 1hr 40min–2hr 20min); Santa
Marina (11 daily; 1hr 20min–2hr); Strómboli
(2–3 daily; 1hr 5min–2hr 45min); Vulcano (12 daily;
45min–1hr 10min).

Catania, Etna and around

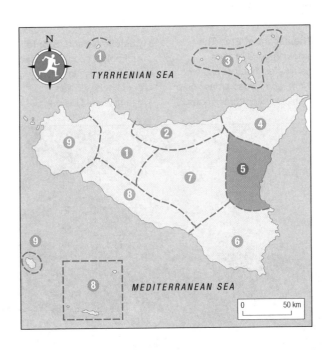

CHAPTER 5   # Highlights

* **Pescheria, Catania** Eat a sea urchin, buy some swordfish, have spaghetti and clams for lunch – Catania's raucous fish market is the best of its kind on the island. See p.195

* **Teatro Mássimo Bellini, Catania** Enjoy a night at the opera with the music of Catania's most famous native son. See p.199

* **The ascent of Etna** The smoking cone of Etna dominates much of eastern Sicily, and invites an ascent of its blackened upper slopes, not least for the awesome views. See p.203

* **Nicolosi** The best base on Etna's south side, ideal for winter skiing or summer walking. See p.205

* **Ferrovia Circumetnea** A day-trip by public transport that takes some beating – riding the volcano-train for over 100km around the base of Mount Etna. See p.208

* **Castello Nelson, Bronte** An English country house with a fascinating history, deep in the Sicilian countryside. See p.209

▲ Hiking on Etna

Catania, Etna and around

atania is Sicily's second largest city, sited on the eastern (Ionian) coast, its airport the point of arrival for many of the island's foreign visitors. Few stay long – it's by no means a prime tourist destination – yet Catania deserves a thorough exploration. An intensely vibrant city, it has a uniformly grand appearance, bestowed upon it following the 1693 earthquake that wrecked the whole region. The jagged volcanic coast to the north sustains a series of small resort-villages around the Baroque town of **Acireale**, while to the south the main driving routes to Siracusa, Ragusa and Enna cross the fertile plain of the **Piana di Catania**. This rich agricultural region was known to the Greeks as the Laestrygonian Fields after the Laestrygonians, a race of cannibals who devoured several of Odysseus's crew. It's a pretty enough ride through the windmill-dotted flat fields, but the only detour of interest is to the archeological museum at **Lentini**, one of the earliest Greek colonies to be founded in Sicily.

There's absolutely no mistaking the single biggest draw in the province, namely **Mount Etna**, Europe's highest volcano, whose foothills start a few kilometres north of Catania. It's still highly active and its massive presence dominates the whole of this part of the coast, with every town and village in the neighbourhood built at least partly from the lava that it periodically ejects. A road and a small single-track railway, the **Ferrovia Circumetnea**, circumnavigate the lower slopes, passing through a series of hardy towns, such as **Randazzo**, almost foolishly situated in the shadow of the volcano and surrounded by swirls of black volcanic rock. Meanwhile, higher villages and ski stations like **Nicolosi** and the **Rifugio Sapienza** are the base for escorted tours and ascents to the **summit craters**. Depending on the weather and volcanic conditions, you should be able to experience the heights of Etna at first hand between April or May and September or October.

Catania

First impressions don't say much at all for **CATANIA** – there's heavy industry here, a large port and some depressing suburbs, while the traffic-choked city centre is largely constructed from suffocating, black-grey volcanic stone. Indeed, the influence of Etna is pervasive, with the city's main thoroughfare named after

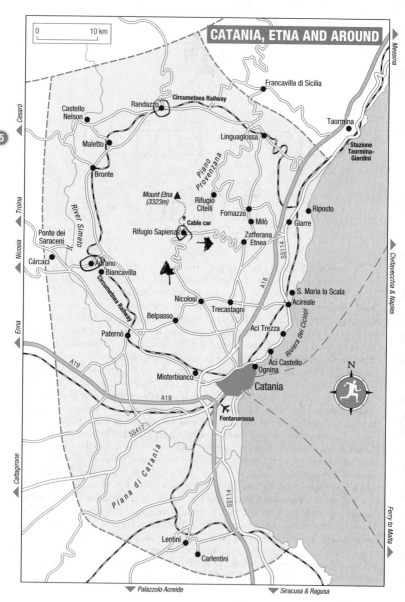

the volcano, which looms threateningly just to the north. Still, Catania is Sicily's only large urban centre outside the capital, and while overshadowed in terms of historical monuments by Palermo, it has a more lively, international, radical outlook, and is well worth a day or two's visit. It is first and foremost a commercial place, boasting arguably the island's best two markets, while if you look beyond the darkened shadows of the buildings you'll detect some of the finest Baroque architecture in Sicily, dating from the eighteenth-century rebuilding. A large student population enlivens the city centre – this is another area where Catania outdoes Palermo, and the thronged piazzas and bars make for one of the island's most exuberant evening promenades. The city is also a major transport terminus, for buses and trains south to Siracusa and west to Enna, Agrigento and Palermo, and if you're Etna-bound by public transport you'll have to leave from Catania itself – drivers usually choose to see the volcano from the prettier towns and villages to the north.

Some of the island's first **Greek colonists**, probably Chalcidinians from Naxos, settled the site as early as 729 BC, becoming so influential that their laws were eventually adopted by all the Ionian colonies of Magna Graecia. Later, the city was among the first to fall to the **Romans**, under whom it prospered greatly. Unusually for Sicily, Catania's surviving ancient relics are all Roman (albeit lava-encrusted, after successive historic eruptions). In the early Christian period

Festivals

January
15 Festa di San Mauro in **Aci Castello**.
17 Festa di Sant'Antonio in **Nicolosi**.

February
3–5 Festa di Sant'Agata in **Catania**: boisterous street events, fireworks and food stalls, and the procession of the saint's relics.

February/March
Carnevale Five days of floats, flowers and traditional music in **Acireale** – one of Sicily's best annual events. Smaller-scale affair at **Paternò**.

March/April
Easter Good Friday procession in **Acireale** in traditional costume. Easter Sunday ceremony in **Adrano**, the Diavolata – a symbolic display showing the Archangel Michael defeating the Devil.

May
9–10 Traditional high jinks at **Trecastagni**: a pilgrimage by athletic souls who, barefoot and shirtless, run the main road linking Catania to the sanctuary at Trecastagni, and also assorted costumes, painted carts, etc.

June
24 Pesce a Mare, a highly symbolic fishing ceremony enacted at sea, at **Aci Trezza**.

July
19–26 Festival commemorating St Vénera in **Acireale**.

August
15 Procession of the *vara* in **Randazzo**: an 18m-high column with decorative figures representing the Assumption.

November
11 San Martino's Day celebrations in **Catania**.

December
Christmas week Display of eighteenth-century cribs in **Acireale**.

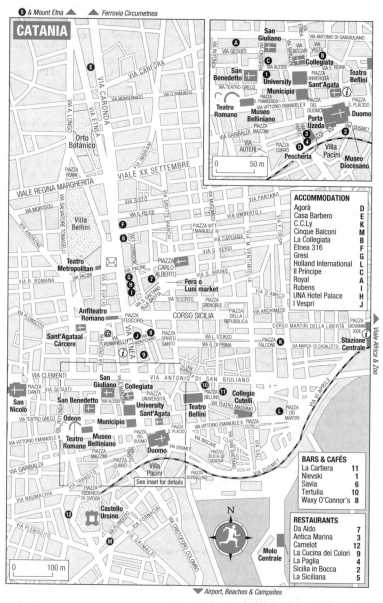

CATANIA

5 & Mount Etna ▲▲   ▲ Ferrovia Circumetnea

▼ Airport, Beaches & Campsites

Catania witnessed the martyrdom of **Agatha**, who, having rejected the improper advances of the praetor, Quintianus, was put to death in 252. She was later canonized (becoming the patron saint of Catania), and it was her miraculous intervention that reputedly saved the city from complete volcanic destruction in the seventeenth century. Even with the saint's protection, Catania has had its fair share of disasters: Etna erupted in 1669, engulfing the city in lava, while the **great earthquake** of 1693 devastated the whole of southeastern Sicily. But making full use of the lava as building material, the eighteenth-century architect **Giovanni Battista Vaccarini** gave central Catania a lofty, noble air that endures today.

Arrival

From Fontanarossa **airport**, 5km south of the city, the cheapest way into the centre is to take the Alibus #457 (every 20min, daily 5.30am–midnight) from right outside, which runs to the central Piazza Stesícoro (on Via Etnea) and to Stazione Centrale in around twenty minutes (longer in heavy traffic); buy tickets (€1) from the machine or the bookshop, both in the Arrivals hall. Most regional express buses (to Siracusa, Taormina, Ragusa, Agrigento, Enna and Palermo) also stop at the airport, and you can get a direct bus from the airport to Messina or Milazzo (for the Aeolian Islands). The **taxi** ride from the airport to the centre costs around €20.

Trains pull in at **Stazione Centrale** in Piazza Giovanni XXIII, just east of the centre. It's easy to jump on a city bus outside to reach Piazza del Duomo or Via Etnea (see "City transport"), or to take a taxi (around €10). Otherwise, the walk to the Duomo takes twenty minutes. **Regional buses** stop at the terminal across from Stazione Centrale. This whole area isn't particularly salubrious, and at night it's a bit off-putting – if you're going to take a taxi, ignore the touts and use the official rank by the train station. The other city station, the **Stazione Catania Borgo** (on Via Caronda, off the northern end of Via Etnea) is for trains on the Ferrovia Circumetnea (the round-Etna line) – a metro connection from here (see p.192) delivers you to Stazione Centrale.

Driving into Catania isn't too difficult (just follow signs for "centro" for Via Etnea), but driving around the city once there is a different matter, because of the chaotic traffic, the fiendish one-way system and the utter impossibility of **parking**. Some hotels have their own parking or arrangements with nearby garages, but as you really don't need a car in Catania, the best advice if you're picking up a rental car is to do so on the day you leave the city.

Information

There are **info points** covering the whole of Catania province at the Stazione Centrale (Mon–Sat 9am–2pm; ☏095.093.7024; ⓦturismo.provincia.ct.it) and at Via Etnea 63 (Mon–Fri 9am–1.30pm plus Tues & Thurs 3.30–5.30pm; ☏095.401.4070), but the **main tourist office** specifically for the city is just up

---

City tours and excursions to Etna

To see a lot of Catania in a short time and without too much walking, join one of the **bus tours** operated by Katane Live (☏095.354.704, ⓦwww.katanelive.it), which offers a hop-on hop-off service (daily 9am–7pm; €5, tickets on board) around the centre, taking in Via Etnea, Piazza del Duomo and Villa Bellini, with stops at those places plus the train station, Piazza Stesícoro and Piazza Verga, among other places. Alternatively there's the **Trenino Turístico** (☏095.820.4281), a mini-train on wheels of special appeal to children, which leaves from Piazza Duomo and performs a wide circuit of the centre including Via Vittorio Emanuele II, Via Etnea and Via Crocíferi lasting one hour (€5).

There are numerous **tours to Etna**, for example Geo Etna Explorer (☏349.610.9957, ⓦwww.geoetnaexplorer.it) and Etna Experience (☏349.305.3021, ⓦwww.etna experience.com), which offer a range of half-day and full-day tours from around €45, with pick-up points in the city centre (some operators will pick you up from your hotel). Ask the tourist office for the full list of Etna excursions.

from the Duomo at Via Vittorio Emanuele II 172 (Mon–Fri 8.15am–1.15pm & 1.45–7.15pm, Sat 8.15am–12.15pm; ℡800.841.042 or 095.742.5573, ⓦwww .comune.catania.it/turismo), where you should find a list of accommodation, a city map, information about the sights and someone who speaks English. There are also info points at the port (open for ship arrivals) and at the airport (daily 8am–8pm; ℡095.093.7023), though as the latter is funded by the tourist administration of Siracusa, it only has information on that city.

City transport

AMT city buses have a terminal immediately **outside Stazione Centrale**, where a staffed booth sells tickets (€1 valid for 90min, or all-day ticket for €2.50; punch it inside the bus on the first ride). You can also buy bus tickets at any *tabacchi*. Information boards at the bus ranks detail the routes but, among others, circular bus #1–4 runs along Via VI Aprile and Via Vittorio Emanuele II to Piazza del Duomo, while #448 runs along Corso Sicilia to Piazza Stesícoro. The other central bus terminal is **Piazza Borsellino** (below Piazza del Duomo by the Villa Pacini gardens), where there's a stop for the airport bus and for buses out to the local beaches and coast.

The city's **Metropolitana** underground system runs on a limited route from Stazione Centrale, south to Catania Porto and north to Catania Borgo (the terminal for the Ferrovia Circumetnea). There are future plans to run the metro out to the airport and to provide new city-centre stations, but for now it's an under-used facility. Services operate Monday to Saturday every fifteen minutes between 7am and 8.45pm, and tickets are valid for ninety minutes.

Accommodation

Catania's **hotels** have raised their game over recent years, and many of the grubby old pensions have disappeared, replaced by renovated three- and four-star hotels and a few stylish boutique places. It's always wise to reserve in advance, especially in July and August, with prices usually determined by availability. There's also a burgeoning number of city-centre **B&Bs** – you'll see several signposted just by walking up Via Etnea – and an excellent central **youth hostel**. Local coastal **campsites** are all a bus ride out of the centre and overpriced; the best is *Europeo*, south of town at Viale Kennedy 91 (℡095.591.026, ⓦwww.villaggioeuropeo.it; late May to Sept), where bungalows are available (❷).

Hotels and B&Bs

Casa Barbero Via Caronda 209 ℡095.820.6301, ⓦwww.casabarbero.it. Contemporary colours and design in a beautifully restored Liberty-era *palazzo* with six quiet rooms set around a courtyard. Breakfast is served either in the courtyard or in the stuccoed and frescoed dining room. There's a/c, free wi-fi and bikes for guests' use (free but deposit required). ❷–❸

Cinque Balconi Via Plebiscito 133 ℡095.723.4534 or 338.727.2701, ⓦwww.5balconi.it. This clean, relaxed B&B has artistically decorated rooms with vintage furnishings and plenty of personality. The young Anglo-Sicilian couple who run it are full of local tips. Bathrooms are shared, and there's a/c, free wi-fi and a choice of breakfasts. It's on a busy road, but noise intrusion is minimal. No credit cards. ❶

La Collegiata Via Vasta 10 ℡095.315.256, ⓦwww.lacollegiata.com. A rather elegant choice in a restored building, just off the main street, with a dozen rooms (half of them with street views) reflecting its nineteenth-century style. ❷

Etnea 316 Via Etnea 316 ℡095.250.3076, ⓦwww.hoteletnea316.it. Real care has gone into the maintenance of this charming old B&B, where ten spruced-up rooms retain their original tile floors and lofty proportions. There's a pretty lounge and breakfast room, and a calm air envelopes all. ❷

Gresi 2nd floor, Via Pacini 28 ℡095.322.709, ⓦwww.gresihotel.com. This old-fashioned three-star in a big old building is redeemed by its rather splendid frescoed ceilings and original proportions. It has a convenient central location, and rooms have minibars and a/c, with some overlooking the main street. ❷

Holland International Via Vittorio Emanuele II 8 ☎095.533.605, ⓦwww.hollandintrooms.it. On the first floor of an ageing *palazzo* that retains most of its old frescoed ceilings, this budget place on the edge of the centre (near the station) is run by a Dutchman who speaks good English. It has few frills and no breakfast is served, but the rooms have a/c, free wi-fi and tea- and coffee-making facilities. There are four en-suite doubles, while one cheaper double and a single share a bathroom, and parking is available in the courtyard. ❶

Il Principe Via Alessi 24 ☎095.250.0345, ⓦwww.ilprincipehotel.com. This boutique four-star in an old *palazzo* at the foot of the Alessi steps holds spotless and spacious rooms with woodblock floors and handsome beds. Bathrooms can be a bit of a squeeze, though superior rooms have spa baths. The general tone is sleekly smart and facilities are up-to-the-minute. Parking is €12 per day. Book online for the best deals. ❸

Royal Via Antonio di San Giuliano 337 ☎095.250.3347, ⓦwww.hotelroyalcatania.it. Four-star hotel occupying a Baroque *palazzo*, presenting twenty rooms in rich colours with traditional period furniture but all mod cons (including free internet access). Some rooms are small and all are a bit gloomy, but it has a comfortable, hideaway feel, despite the central location, and a big outdoor terrace lets you breakfast above the Catania rooftops. Staff are efficient, and there's a restaurant, sauna and Turkish bath, and parking. ❸

Rubens Via Etnea 196 ☎095.317.073, ⓦwww.rubenshotel.it. A good-value choice if you want to stay on the main Via Etnea, with seven spacious, air-conditioned rooms with minibars and free wi-fi, mostly facing the side and back. The friendly owner speaks English, and the decent breakfast in a dining room overlooking Via Etnea includes ham, cheese, boiled eggs and croissants. ❷

UNA Hotel Palace Via Etnea 218 ☎095.250.5111, ⓦwww.unahotels.it. This contemporary four-star applies Catania's dominant colours – lava-black and Etna snow-white

– to its designer rooms, from the marble floors and crisp linen to the signature beds with black headboards and inset medallions. There's plenty of space, a good buffet breakfast and free use of the Turkish bath and fitness centre, but above all there's a fantastic roof-terrace bar and fine-dining restaurant with the best views in town – reserve for dinner (most dishes €10–20). Garage parking costs €20 per day. ❹

I Vespri Via Montesano 5 ☎095.310.036, ⓦwww .ivesprihotel.it. A budget "rooms" place, right in the centre, with helpful owners. Not all rooms are en suite but shared facilities are well kept, and a buffet breakfast is included (to be eaten in your room). There's a laundry service too, free wi-fi and a good-value self-catering option. ❶

Hostels

Agorà Piazza Currò 6 ☎095.723.3010, ⓦwww.agorahostel.com. The location is fantastic, very near the Pescheria fish market (follow the signs), but secluded. Non-guests come here to eat in the excellent bistro-style restaurant, catch a DJ or gig, sit out at the laid-back outdoor terrace or drink in the unique cellar wine bar (housed in a natural lava-cave with one of Catania's underground streams running through it). Consequently it can get noisy. The basic dorms (six to ten beds) have bunks and lockers, with separate bathrooms for men and women, and there are some small private double rooms. Free internet access, use of kitchen, washing facilities and bike rental are also offered, and there's 24hr access. Dorms from €15, Aug €20, rooms ❶

C.C.Ly Piazza Falcone ☎095.746.2399, ⓦwww .ccly-hostel.com. On the top floor of a 19th-century *palazzo*, this hostel – pronounced "Sicily" – is fantastically kitsch, the swirling decor harking back to the 1960s – but it's very friendly and has low prices and a central location close to the bus station. The eight beds in each of the single-sex dorms (€16–18) share a bathroom, and there are also en-suite doubles (❶). Guests have lockers, internet access, use of a kitchen, laundry facilities and parking.

The City

You could see the whole of central Catania in a busy day's strolling, but the city really deserves more time if you can spare it. Most of the sights are confined within a small area, centred on Piazza del Duomo and the cathedral, from where the wide main avenue, Via Etnea, steams off to the north up to the city's Bellini gardens. Fish market and castle lie to the south, and the landmark Teatro Bellini to the east. Much of this entire area, sections of Via Etnea included, is closed to traffic, so walking around is quite enjoyable, especially at night when certain areas become bar and café zones.

Piazza del Duomo and around

Piazza del Duomo is one of Sicily's most elegant Baroque piazzas, rebuilt completely in the first half of the eighteenth century by the Palermitan Giovanni Battista Vaccarini, who was made Catania's municipal architect in 1730. With the majestic cathedral as his starting-point, he produced a dramatic open space – kept traffic-free today – softened by the addition of a central fountain, no less than a **lava elephant** supporting an Egyptian obelisk on its back. The elephant has been the city's symbol since at least the thirteenth century, a talismanic protection against Etna eruptions, and this one also features an inscription, *Agatina MSSHDEPL* – an acronym for "The mind of St Agatha is sane and spontaneous, honouring God and liberating the city".

Agatha herself is both Catania's patron saint and the dedicatee of Vaccarini's grandest project, the **Duomo** (Mon–Sat 7am–noon & 4–7pm, Sun 7.30am–noon & 4.30–7pm), which flanks the eastern side of the piazza. The original cathedral here was founded in the eleventh century, and built on the site of earlier Roman baths, but of this medieval church only the beautifully crafted apses survived the 1693 earthquake; you can see them through the gate at Via Vittorio Emanuele II 159. Vaccarini added an imposing Baroque facade, on which he tagged granite columns filched from Catania's Roman amphitheatre, while the interior is adorned by a rich series of chapels. The Cappella di Sant'Agata is to the right of the choir, and houses the relics that are paraded through the city on the saint's festival days. Next to it, entered through a fine sixteenth-century doorway, the Cappella della Madonna holds a Roman sarcophagus that contains the ashes of the Aragonese kings – Frederick II, Louis and Frederick III. The tomb of the composer **Bellini**, a native of the city, is set in the floor before the second column on the right as you enter, inscribed with a phrase from his opera, *La Sonnámbula* (The Sleepwalker).

To the right of the Duomo, the **Museo Diocesano** (Mon–Fri 9am–5pm, Sat & Sun 9am–1pm; €7) houses the cathedral's collection of religious art and silverware, with items dating back to the fourteenth century, including pieces recovered from the pre-1693 cathedral. Below here, the piazza ends in the late seventeenth-century **Porta Uzeda**, a towering gateway, with the **Villa Pacini** gardens just beyond.

On the other side of the Duomo, across Via Vittorio Emanuele II, the church of **Sant'Agata** is another of Vaccarini's works, though the lighter, pale grey Rococo interior post-dates his death. A little further up the street at Via Vittorio Emanuele II 140, there's the minor curiosity that was the home of Catanese erotic poet and philosopher **Domenico Tempio** (1750–1821). It's now desperately neglected,

---

The Festa di Sant'Agata

Catania's biggest annual festival, the **Festa di Sant'Agata**, takes place each year between February 3 and 5. It's a 500-year-old celebration of the life and death of the virtuous Agatha, born in the city around 230 AD and destined for dreadful tortures once she had spurned the unwelcome advances of the Roman praetor, Quintianus, in 252 AD; prison, whipping, mutilation and burning followed. The three days of the festival see hundreds of thousands processing through the streets following a silver, bejewelled reliquary that holds the relics of the saint. There's also a procession of decorated candlesticks, up to 6m high, carried for hours at a time by groups representing different trades. On the morning of February 5, the saint's relics are carried back into the Duomo, where they remain until the following year. Meanwhile, there are fireworks, food stalls, special services and concerts throughout the *festa*.

though you can still make out the raunchy figures of men and women playing with themselves, which support the balcony above the blackened doorway.

The Pescheria

Catania's best-known food and fish market, the **Pescheria** (Mon–Sat until around 2pm), is reached from the back of Piazza del Duomo by nipping down the steps behind a gushing marble fountain. This takes you right into the main part of the fish market, where vendors shout across slabs and buckets full of twitching fish, eels, crabs and shellfish. Brandishing wicked-looking knives, they slice off swordfish steaks to order, while others shuck oysters, mussels and sea urchins for browsing customers. The side alleys off the fish market are dense with fruit, vegetable and dried goods and herb stalls, as well as cheese counters and bloody butchers' tables. There are also two or three excellent trattorias down here, great for lunch, or follow the "hostel" signs through the market to **Piazza Currò** where the *Agorà* hostel has an open-air terrace-café just a stone's throw from all the action. Just opposite the hostel you can also see the remains of the **Terme dell'Indirizzo**, more old Roman baths.

Castello Ursino

Beyond the market and Piazza Currò, the roads wind through a dilapidated neighbourhood to Piazza Federico di Svevia, dominated by the **Castello Ursino**, once the proud fortress of Frederick II. Originally the castle stood on a rocky cliff above the sea, but the 1669 eruption resulted in this entire area becoming landlocked, and left just the keep standing. The latter still presents a formidable appearance, and it now houses the **Museo Cívico** (Mon–Sat 9am–1pm & 3–7pm, Sun 9am–1pm; free), part of whose ground floor is taken up with temporary exhibitions, while permanent exhibits include retrieved mosaic fragments, stone inscriptions, elegant painted Greek amphoras and terracotta statuettes. Upstairs the Pinacoteca (art gallery) holds mainly religious art from the 17th century.

Along Via Crocíferi

The best place to appreciate the eighteenth-century rebuilding of Catania is along its most handsome street, **Via Crocíferi**, where the wealthy religious authorities and private citizens competed with each other to construct dazzling houses, palaces and churches. They were building on the very bones of the Roman and medieval city: the arcaded **Piazza Mazzini** (straddling Via Garibaldi) was constructed from 32 columns that originally formed part of a Roman basilica, while just to the west, at Via Vittorio Emanuele II 260, is the entrance to the **Teatro Romano** (Tues–Sat 9am–1pm & 2.30–7pm, Sun 9am–1pm; €4) of the second century AD, which preserves much of the Roman seating and underground passageway. A small antiquarium here displays finds from the site. The smaller **Odeon**, adjacent, was used for music and recitations.

At the bottom of Via Crocíferi, opposite San Francesco church, the house where the composer Vincenzo Bellini was born in 1801 is now open as the **Museo Belliniano** (Mon–Sat 9am–1pm; free), displaying photographs, original scores, his death mask and other memorabilia. Born into a musical family, Bellini supposedly composed his first work at the age of 6, and later studied in Naples, where he produced his first opera in 1825. Ten more operas followed during the next decade – his first big success was *Il Pirata* (1827) – with Bellini living largely in Milan until his early death in Paris, aged only 33. His body was transported back to his native Sicily to be buried, and Catania subsequently did her favourite son proud, with the airport, a piazza, the city's main theatre and a park all named after him, as well as the ultimate accolade – a pasta dish, *spaghetti alla Norma*, named after Bellini's famous 1831 opera *Norma* (see p.198 for the recipe).

Staying safe in Catania

Of all Sicilian cities, Catania has the worst reputation for **petty crime**. Hoteliers and locals often warn tourists to be on their guard against pickpockets and, without being too alarmist, it doesn't do any harm to follow their advice. If you're happy with security at your hotel, leave your passport and valuables there before going out. Be careful on your own at night, and don't flash your cash, phones or cameras in run-down areas or in the middle of the teeming markets.

North of Piazza San Francesco, narrow Via Crocíferi runs under an imposing Baroque arch, announcing the start of a series of arresting religious and secular buildings, little changed since the eighteenth century. Amble up and you can peer into the courtyards of the *palazzi* (one holds a plantation of banana trees) and poke around the churches. About halfway up on the right, the finest of these, **San Giuliano** (usually only open for services), has a facade by Vaccarini and an echoing elliptical interior.

San Nicolò

To see Sicily's biggest church, strike west off Via Crocíferi up to the crescent of Piazza Dante, opposite which looms the unfinished facade of **San Nicolò** (Mon–Sat 9am–1pm), studded by six enormous, lopped columns. It was conceived on a ridiculously grand scale, and the work was ultimately curtailed by earthquake damage and soaring costs. What's left is a stark 105m-long interior, virtually undecorated save for the sculpted choir stalls and a meridian line etched in marble across the floor of the transept, embellished with zodiacal signs. The famous organ, admired by earlier visitors, was destroyed in the nineteenth century.

The church is part of an adjoining Benedictine convent, with equally impressive dimensions   it's the second largest convent in Europe after Mafra in Portugal. Through a gate to the left of the church lie the remains of some Roman walls, and, behind, the massive conventual buildings. These are now used by the university's language and literature faculties, but you should be able to stroll in for a look around the once grand cloistered courtyards.

Along Via Etnea

The main city thoroughfare, **Via Etnea**, runs north from Piazza del Duomo and out of the city. Following its full length would eventually lead you right to the foothills of Mount Etna – and from the street's northern end there are photogenic views of the peak in the distance.

The first square off the street, Piazza dell'Università, holds some outdoor cafés and the main building of the **University**, founded by the Aragonese kings in the fifteenth century. The earthquake postponed its completion until the 1750s. The tangled streets off to the east form the heart of the student nightlife zone, converging eventually on the restored Piazza Bellini, overlooked by the flagship **Teatro Mássimo Bellini** (1890).

Halfway up Via Etnea, **Piazza Stesícoro** marks the modern centre of Catania, with its western side almost entirely occupied by the sunken black remains of the **Anfiteatro Romano** (Tues–Sun 9am–1pm & 3–7pm; free), built from lava blocks in the second or third century AD. Much is still concealed under the surrounding buildings, but a diagram shows the original dimensions of the theatre, which could hold sixteen thousand spectators – it's quite evident that the section you can walk through represents only one tiny excavated corner.

At the back of the amphitheatre, you can wind around to find the twelfth-century church of **Sant'Agata al Cárcere**, built on the site of the prison where St Agatha was confined before her martyrdom at the hands of the Romans. When it's open (hours are sporadic), a custodian will let you into the third-century crypt and show you the chapel's medieval stone doorway, topped by evil, grinning, sculpted heads and ape-like creatures.

Off the east side of Via Etnea, back at Piazza Stesícoro, the stalls are out from early in the morning ranged up Via San Gaetano alla Grotta, heralding the city's rumbustious **Fera o Luni market**, centred on the broad Piazza Carlo Alberto. It's not just for food but has all kinds of clothes, shoes, accessories and household goods. It's all here, from tat piled high on a wooden cart to cut-price designer labels, or copies thereof, all accompanied by the constant patter ("*buongiorno bella!*") of cheery traders. The market is a great spot for souvenir-hunting, even more so on Sundays when an antiques fair takes over the space.

For tourists Via Etnea finishes at the **Villa Bellini**, just beyond the post office, a large, ornamental public garden that provides a welcome touch of greenery. The stand-up drinks bar here is where the local police hang out, whiling away time between meal breaks; rather touching photos of the regulars are pinned up, posing stiffly in uniform on horseback or motorbikes.

Zo centre for contemporary culture

Across in the east of the city, up Viale Africa near Stazione Centrale, Catania's former sulphur works, Le Ciminiere, has been transformed into a cultural centre known as **Zo** (Ⓦ www.zoculture.it). The original red-brick chimneys and lava-block walls have been wrapped in a contemporary glass-and-steel frame, while inside are theatre and performance spaces and a café-restaurant. It's an interesting place to visit even if you don't come for an exhibition or event, and it holds two museums as well, both self-explanatory: the **Museo del Cinema** (Tues–Sun 9am–12.30pm, also Tues & Thurs 3–4.30pm; €4), and the **Museo Stórico dello Sbarco in Sicilia 1943** (Tues–Sat 9am–12.30pm, plus Tues & Thurs 3–5pm; €4), or the Museum of the Allied Invasion of Sicily.

Eating, drinking and nightlife

Unusually for Sicily, Catania's streets teem until late, especially in summer, as seemingly half the population heads out for a stroll, a drink and a meal. **Restaurants** are pretty good value, thanks to the presence of so many students, who also go a long way to ensuring the island's best city nightlife. The whole ambience is helped by the fact that the *Comune* closes old-town streets and

Street food

The Catanese do a lot of eating on the hoof, from grazing in the Pescheria on raw mussels and sea urchins to munching ice cream as they parade up Via Etnea in the evening. February's Festa di Sant'Agata sees food stalls selling traditional nougat and sweets, while during summer kiosks offer that thirst-quenching Catania speciality, soda water and crushed lemon, served with or without salt (*seltz e limone con/senza sale*). In autumn the roast-chestnut vendors are out in force, and around San Martino's Day (November 11) it's the time for *crispelle* – fritters of flour, water, yeast and ricotta or anchovies. A great place to try these and other traditional fried snacks is *Friggitoria Stella* (Via Monsignor Ventimiglia 66; closed Sun), a backstreet establishment off Via Giovanni di Prima that's been going for years.

squares to traffic (the so-called *café concerto*) and bars spill tables outside until the small hours. For outdoor **cafés**, those in Piazza del Duomo and Piazza dell'Università have the best views in the most touristy locale, while the cooler **bars** are found around Piazza Bellini (particularly down Via Teatro Mássimo, in Via Rapisardi and in adjacent piazzas Ogninella and Scammacca). The sole exception is the funky, most un-Sicilian café, bar and restaurant at the *Agorà* youth hostel, near the Pescheria market (see p.193).

While the Bellini theatre is the traditional centre of opera, music and ballet, Catania's new focus for **culture and the arts** is the Zo centre (see p.197). You can check what's on in town in the comprehensive, free fortnightly arts and entertainment leaflet, *Lapis* (Ⓦwww.lapisnet.it), available at the tourist offices and elsewhere, or get hold of a copy of Catania's daily newspaper, *La Sicilia* (Ⓦwww .lasicilia.it), which has city **entertainment listings**. Summer is the best time for **concerts and events**, from open-air jazz in the Villa Bellini gardens to classical concerts in churches and theatres across the city. In summer, there are open-air venues for dancing until the early hours along the coast on the outskirts of town – ask around and look for posters and flyers for the latest spots.

Restaurants

Da Aldo Piazza G. Sciuti 2 ☎095.311.158. The best choice near the Fera o Luni market is this amiable first-floor lunchtime grill-house, where bustling waiters reel off the daily specials (*pasta alla Norma*, stuffed squid or a simple grilled seabass or steak). It's great value, less than €20 for a full meal. From Piazza Carlo Alberto, take the first left off Via Pacini, down Via al Carmine. No credit cards. Lunch only; closed Sun.

Antica Marina Via Pardo 29 ☎095.348.197. The fancier of the two Pescheria market trattorias serves excellent seafood pastas and fresh fish, with most dishes around €10–15. Closed Wed.

Camelot Piazza Federico di Svevia 75 ☎095.723.2103. Rough-and-ready but lively spot in front of the Castello Ursino where you can feast for a song on Sicilian *antipasti* and barbecued meat, and drink local wine from plastic cups. Most dishes are under €5, though pizzas and salads cost

Spaghetti alla Norma

Catania's tribute to the composer Vincenzo Bellini, *spaghetti alla Norma* – cooked with tomato and aubergine (*melanzane* in Italian) – is served in most local restaurants. Here's how to prepare it:

Ingredients (serves 4)
Two aubergines, cut into 1/2 inch (1cm) slices (or cubed if you prefer)
Two tablespoons (30ml) olive oil
Two cloves of garlic, peeled and crushed
One tablespoon tomato purée
1lb (454g) fresh plum tomatoes, chopped roughly (use tinned if unavailable)
10oz (300g) spaghetti
Grated hard ricotta salata cheese (or use parmesan or an aged pecorino)
Two tablespoons chopped basil leaves
Salt, black pepper

Fry the aubergine until golden brown (use a low heat). Put to one side. Gently fry the garlic in two tablespoons of olive oil for two minutes, then add chopped (or tinned) tomatoes, one tablespoon tomato purée, and a pinch of salt and pepper, and sauté for thirty minutes, or until the sauce reduces slightly. Add half the chopped basil leaves to the sauce and stir.

  Cook the spaghetti in boiling water until *al dente*. Spoon the tomato sauce on top of the spaghetti, add slices of fried aubergine and top with cheese and the remainder of the basil leaves. Eat with a robust red wine, and sing lustily.

around €8. Some tables outside. Open eves only, closed Mon.

La Cucina dei Colori Via San Michele 9 ☏ 095.715.9893. Organic, vegan and wholefoods predominate in this modern, fresh-looking eatery, where you can order such dishes as *sformato di miglio* (a peppery millet flan with courgettes), couscous salad, non-dairy lasagne and *panelle* (chickpea fritters) with spinach. Beers are locally produced and there are some lip-smacking desserts, for example almond cream and fig tart. Dishes are €6–9 at lunch, €10–15 in the evening. Closed Sun.

La Paglia Via Pardo 23 ☏ 095.346.838. Simple trattoria (wipe-clean tablecloths, panel-board walls) that's the best place for a reasonably priced fish-market lunch – when the *signora* runs out of something she just bellows through the kitchen window for more. Starters cost €5–10, for example pasta with spaghetti and clams; mains, such as grilled tuna, are around €10, and the house wine is the kind that you can run your car on. Closed Sun.

Sicilia in Bocca Via Dusmet 35 ☏ 095.250.0208. One of the nicest places to sit outside, this is pizzeria one side, restaurant the other (though in practice you can mix and match menus), sharing a shaded terrace. It's set in the old arched sea wall (through Porta Uzeda from Piazza del Duomo and turn left), and service is friendly and English-speaking. Pizzas are €6–10, pasta dishes €8–12, mains €12–20.

La Siciliana Viale Marco Polo 52a ☏ 095.376.400. Renowned as one of eastern Sicily's best restaurants, with a thoroughly traditional menu, strong on fish and local specialities like rice with squid ink and fresh ricotta, and they also make their own sensational pastries and desserts. In summer there's outdoor garden-terrace seating. It's expensive, however: count on spending €50–70 for a full meal. You'll need to take bus #628 *rosso* from the station or a taxi as it's way up in the north of the city. Closed Sun evening & Mon.

Cafés and bars

La Cartiera Via Casa del Mutilato 8. Young, studenty Catanese pub where there's often live music. Closed Tues.

Nievski Via Alessi 15–17. They love Che in this "*pub-trattoria alternativo*", where you can come for a plate of organic food, a Fair Trade coffee or a beer. There's internet access, all kinds of concerts and events, and more goatees than you can shake a stick at. It's on the Alessi steps up to Via Crocíferi. Closed daytime & all Mon.

Savia Via Etnea 302 ☏ 095.322.335. Opposite the main entrance to the Villa Bellini, this is the city's most notable *pasticceria*, open since 1897 and always busy with folk digging into savoury *arancini*, ricotta-stuffed *cannoli*, real *cassata* and the like. Closed Mon.

Tertulia Via Rapisardo 1, off Piazza Bellini. Catania's most laid-back bookshop has a café-bar that's open until 1.30am (closed daytime at weekends). Belgian beers, organic drinks and snacky food are served at outdoor tables in the pedestrianized street just up from the Teatro Bellini. Sometimes closed in Aug.

Waxy O'Connor's Piazza Spírito Santo. Hugely popular Irish pub that spills onto the square on summer evenings. And if you don't like *Waxy*, there's always *Joyce* opposite.

Culture and the arts

Teatro Mássimo Bellini Via Perrotta 12, facing Piazza Bellini ☏ 095.730.6111 or 095.715.0921, ⊛ www.teatromassimobellini.it. Catania's impressive opera house has a concert season that runs from Oct until May, and it's not just opera that's offered but also classical music and ballet.

Zo Viale Africa ☏ 095.533.871, ⊛ www.zoculture .it. The centre for contemporary arts is the place for cutting-edge theatre, electronic and world music, experimental art shows, off-the-wall installations and offbeat festivals. It's a 2min walk from Stazione Centrale.

Listings

Airport Fontanarossa, flight information on ☏ 095.340.505, ⊛ www.aeroporto.catania.it. Take the Alibus #457 from Stazione Centrale or Via Etnea (every 20min, 5am–midnight).

Beaches The closest sand beaches to Catania are south of the centre on the wide Golfo di Catania (Viale Kennedy), reached by taking bus #427 from Stazione Centrale or summer bus #D from Piazza Borsellino. This is also where all the big campsites are.

Books and newspapers Libreria Cavallotto, Corso Sicilia 91, has a good selection of English-language books. Some foreign newspapers are sold at kiosks around Piazza del Duomo, but the most reliable source is the newsagents inside Stazione Centrale.

Buses The major companies have terminals around Stazione Centrale, including: AST (Via L. Sturzo 230 ☏ 840.000.323 or 095.723.0535,

Via Etnea is the central spine of the city and its major shopping street, with department and chain stores, designer labels, boutiques and brands. Off here, just before the Villa Bellini, **Via Pacini** is devoted to cheap clothes, shoes, underwear and accessories, while at the far end it melds into the unmissable **Fera o Luni market** (Piazza Carlo Alberto). There's fruit, veg and fish in the square outside the church, and the surrounding streets are a hawkers' bazaar, ideal if you're hankering after a picture of the pope or a five-euro handbag. The nearest big **supermarket** is Punto SMA (Corso Sicilia 50). The other daily market, the **Pescheria**, mainly trades in food (not just fish; it's also great for buying things like salted capers, sun-dried tomatoes, hunks of pecorino cheese or bags of wild oregano), though on the fringes you'll find clothes and jewellery too – **Via Vittorio Emanuele II** has a few "ethnic" shops with carvings, beads and fabrics. Across Piazza del Duomo, in the arches under the Porta Uzeda gateway, there are two or three well-stocked Sicilian souvenir stores, for puppets, postcards, ceramics, painted carts and almond wine. And around the back of the Duomo, look for **Nonna Vincenza** in the old Palazzo Biscari (Piazza San Placido 7), the most traditional place in the city to buy artisan sweets in gorgeous packaging.

www.aziendasicilianatrasporti.it), for services within Catania province, including Etna; Interbus/Etna (Via d'Amico 187 ☏095.530.396, www.interbus.it), for Acireale, Caltagirone, Enna, Giardini-Naxos, Messina, Nicosia, Noto, Piazza Armerina, Ragusa, Siracusa and Taormina; SAIS Autolinee (Via d'Amico 181 ☏095.536.168, www.saisautolinee.it) to Palermo, Messina, Enna and Caltanissetta; SAIS Trasporti (Via d'Amico 213 ☏095.536.201, www.saistrasporti.it) to Messina, Agrigento, Caltanissetta and mainland destinations.

Car rental Most agencies have outlets at the airport and in the city: Avis ☏095.340.500, www.avis.com; Europcar ☏095.348.125, www.europcar.it; Hertz ☏095.341.595, www.hertz.it; Maggiore ☏095.340.594, www.maggiore.it; Sixt ☏095.340.389, www.sixt.it.

City buses AMT city buses (☏800.018.696 or 095.751.9111, www.amt.ct.it) have terminals at Stazione Centrale and Piazza Borsellino.

Ferries Catania's main ferry connections are to Civitavécchia, Naples and Malta. Contact Virtu Ferries (☏095.535.711, www.virtuferries.com) for services to Malta, Grimaldi (☏095.281.300, www.grimaldi-ferries.com) for Civitavécchia and Malta, and TTT Lines (☏800.915.365 or 081.580.2744, www.tttlines.it) for Naples; alternatively, most travel agents have timetables and can sell tickets.

Hospital Ospedale Garibaldi, Piazza S. Maria di Gesù 7 ☏095.759.1111, emergencies ☏095.759.4368.

Internet Internetteria, Via Penninello 44 (Mon–Fri 9am–1am, Sat & Sun 5pm–1am; may close earlier in winter). There's a cluster of other points on Via Vittorio Emanuele II and Via Garibaldi – ID must be presented at all.

Left luggage At Stazione Centrale, Piazza Giovanni XXIII (daily 7.30am–1.30pm & 2.30–8.30pm; €3 per bag for 12hr).

Pharmacies Caltabiano, Piazza Stesícoro 36 ☏095.327.647; Croce Rossa, Via Etnea 274 ☏095.327.232; Europa, Corso Italia 111 ☏095.383.536; Cutelli, Via Vittorio Emanuele II 54 ☏095.531.400.

Police In emergencies call ☏112. Otherwise, Carabinieri, Via Teatro Greco 111 ☏095.326.666; Questura (for police), Piazza S. Nicolella, Via Manzoni 8 ☏095.736.7111.

Post office Main post office, Via Etnea 215, close to the Villa Bellini (Mon–Fri 8am–6.30pm, Sat 8am–12.30pm).

Taxis Ranks at Stazione Centrale, Piazza del Duomo and Via Etnea (Piazza Stesícoro); call Radiotaxi ☏095.330.966 for 24hr service.

Trains Mainline services (principally to Messina and Siracusa, but also to Palermo, Enna and Caltanissetta) from Stazione Centrale in Piazza Giovanni XXIII (information and timetables on ☏892.021, www.ferroviedellostato.it). Round-Etna services are on the Ferrovia Circumetnea, Stazione Catania Borgo, Via Caronda ☏095.541.250, www.circumetnea.it; the same company operates the Metropolitana service between Catania Porto and Catania Borgo via Stazione Centrale.

The coastal route north to Acireale

The main sandy beaches lie south of Catania, but it's actually the coast north of the city that's the most popular resort area. The lava streams from Etna have reached the sea many times over the centuries, turning the coastline into an attractive mix of contorted black rocks and sheer coves, excellent for swimming. Consequently, what was once a series of small fishing villages is now a fair-sized strip of hotels, lidos and restaurants, idle in the winter but swarming in summer with day-trippers. You can get here easily on city AMT bus #534 from Catania's Piazza Borsellino to Aci Trezza, or the AST service from Stazione Centrale to Acireale. Incidentally, the prefix "Aci", given to a number of settlements here, derives from the local River Aci, said to have appeared following the death of the herdsman Acis at the hands of the giant, one-eyed Polyphemus (the river is no longer identifiable).

Ognina, Aci Castello and Aci Trezza

OGNINA, the first stop, is a small suburb on the northern outskirts of Catania, built on lava cliffs formed in the fifteenth century. It holds a few restaurants, overlooking the little harbour, as well as a campsite. Buses run on to **ACI CASTELLO**, 9km from the city, whose castle rises above the sea in splinters from a volcanic rock crag. The base of the rebel Roger di Lauria in 1297, it's remarkably well preserved, despite many threatening eruptions and the destruction wrought by Frederick II of Aragon, who took the castle from Roger by erecting a wooden siege-engine adjacent. The ragged coastline to the north is popular for sunbathing and swimming and, in summer, a wooden boardwalk is built over the lava rocks (you pay a small fee to use the changing rooms and showers).

Aci Castello marks the beginning of the so-called Riviera dei Ciclopi, named after the jagged points of the **Scogli dei Ciclopi** that rise from the sea just beyond town. Homer wrote that the blinded Polyphemus slung these rocks (broken from Etna) at Ulysses as he and his men escaped from the Cyclops in their ships. The largest of the three main sharp-edged islets – also known as *faraglioni* – sticks some 60m into the sky. You could always walk the couple of kilometres north along the rough coast from Aci Castello to **ACI TREZZA**, the fishing village at the heart of nineteenth-century Sicilian novelist Giovanni Verga's masterpiece *I Malavoglia*. Bars, *gelaterie* and seafood restaurants are ranged along the lungomare here.

Acireale

ACIREALE, 16km north of Catania, has the best site of all, high above the rocky shore and the surrounding lemon groves. It's a location best appreciated from the public gardens at the northern end of town, from where you can look right back along the Riviera dei Ciclopi. Known since Roman times as a spa centre (the thermal baths are still heavily used), Acireale is also another striking example of Sicilian Baroque town-planning. This is the fourth successive town on the site, rebuilt directly over the old lava streams after the 1693 earthquake and, as in Catania, it relies on grand buildings, a handsome central square and Duomo and some long thoroughfares for its effect.

The town is well known for its celebrations during **Carnevale** (Feb/March), when it hosts one of Sicily's best festivals, with extraordinarily elaborate flower-decked floats and fancy-dress parades clogging the streets for five noisy days.

Acireale also has a long tradition of Sicilian **puppet theatre**, with regular shows performed in summer by its surviving theatre companies, like that of Turi Grasso at Via Nazionale 195 (☏095.764.8035, Ⓦwww.operadeipupi.com), which also has a small **museum** at the theatre (Wed, Sat & Sun 9am–noon & 6–9pm in summer or 3–6pm in winter; free).

It's easiest to get the bus to Acireale, which stops outside the public gardens or near the Duomo; the train station is well to the south of town, near the thermal baths, and a long walk into the centre along Via Vittorio Emanuele II. Best target for lunch is actually out of town, an easy 2km downhill stroll or drive to the tiny hamlet of **Santa Maria La Scala**, huddled around a minuscule harbour full of painted fishing-boats, where three or four trattorias overlook the bay. To get here on foot, go down Via Romeo (to the side of the Municipio), across the busy main road and then down the steep rural path to the water.

Lentini and around

Half an hour or so south of Catania, **LENTINI** has a long pedigree that puts it among the earliest of the Greek settlements in Sicily, and the first of all the inland colonies. Established in 729 BC as a daughter city of Naxos, Lentini (Leontinoi) flourished as a commercial centre for two hundred years, before falling foul of Hippocrates of Gela. Later, the city was absorbed by Syracuse, sharing its disasters but never its prosperity. It was Leontinoi's struggle to assert its independence, by allying itself with Athens, that provided the pretext for the great Athenian expedition against Syracuse in 415 BC. Another attempt – this time an alliance with the Carthaginians during the Second Punic War – resulted in the Romans beheading two thousand of its citizens, a measure that horrified the whole island, as no doubt it was intended to do. By the time Cicero got round to describing the city, Lentini was "wretched and empty", though it continued as a small-scale agricultural centre for some time, until the great earthquake of 1693 completely demolished it.

Noisy, sprawling, modern Lentini has little to recommend it, though the ancient city survives as an extensive archeological site, a few kilometres out of town. Some of the finds are on display in the town's **Museo Archeologico** in Piazza Studi, east of the centre off Via Piave (Tues–Sun 9am–6pm; €4), though the best artefacts have been appropriated by the museums at Catania and Siracusa. The Zona Archeológica is a twenty-minute walk south of the nearby upper town of **Carlentini**, which you can reach directly by bus from Catania with AST. It has a fairly pleasant central square with bars, though most buses also stop in Piazza San Francesco on the outskirts of Carlentini, closer to the zone, as do local buses from Lentini's train station.

The **Zona Archeologica** (closed at the time of writing; ask at the museum or call ☏095.783.2962 for the latest information) is then a five-minute signposted walk away, spread over the two hills of San Mauro and Metapíccola. The first of these is the more interesting, holding the ancient town's acropolis and the substantial remains of a vast necropolis nearby. You'll see the pincer-style south gate immediately, part of a well-conserved system of fortifications that surrounded the town. Together, the hills make a good couple of hours' rambling, while a dirt road to the side of the main entrance climbs around the perimeter fence to allow views over the whole site and down to Lentini in the valley below.

For a **snack** in Lentini, seek out *Navarria*, a fabulous *pasticceria* at Via Conte Alaimo 8 (anyone can point the way), where pastries and *granite* are to die for.

Mount Etna

One of the world's largest volcanoes, **Mount Etna** (3323m) dominates much of Sicily's eastern landscape, its smoking summit an omnipresent feature for travellers in the area. The main crater is gradually becoming more explosive and more dangerous, with spectacular eruptions in 2001 and 2002 far eclipsing those of the preceding decade (see box on Etna's eruptions, p.206). Despite the risk, the volcano remains a remarkable draw, though the unpredictability of eruptions – they may be expected, but cannot be pinpointed to a precise time – means that it's often impossible to get close to the main crater.

Etna was just one of the places that the Greeks thought to be the forge of Vulcan, a fitting description of the blustering and sparking from the main crater. The philosopher Empedocles studied the volcano closely, living in an observatory near the summit. This terrifying existence was dramatized by Matthew Arnold in his *Empedocles on Etna*:

Alone! –
On this charr'd, blacken'd melancholy waste,
Crown'd by the awful peak, Etna's great mouth.

Certainly, it all proved too much for Empedocles, who in 433 BC jumped into the main crater in an attempt to prove that the gases emitted would support his body weight. They didn't.

A ring of villages circles the lower slopes of Etna, including the ski-centres of **Linguaglossa** (on the Circumetnea rail route) and **Nicolosi**, which hold the bulk of the accommodation, restaurants and tour facilities. The two main approaches to the summit are from north and south. Some of the best scenery is on the north side (signposted "Etna Nord"), though the road beyond **Piano Provenzana** is strictly controlled, and even with a four-wheel drive you will be strongly encouraged to leave your vehicle and take an organized jeep trip. From the south side ("Etna Sud"), beyond Nicolosi, the chief departure point is the mountain refuge-hotel of **Rifugio Sapienza**, connected by daily bus from Catania.

What level you actually reach is dictated by current volcanic activity and weather conditions. Access to the **summit** itself is by 10km of rough track, a large part of it covered by lava, or by means of cable car and 4WD minibus. The higher reaches resemble a lunar landscape, the ground underfoot alternately black, grey or red depending on the age of the lava. The most recent stuff lies in great folds; below, the red roofs and green fields of the lower hills stretch away to the sea. You'll not be in any danger, provided you stay within the limit that is currently deemed safe to reach. Note that ascending the volcano is only possible between about May and October; the rest of the time, it's swathed in snow.

Finally, if you're pushed for time or unable to ascend higher due to adverse conditions, you'll have to make do with the glimpses of Etna's peak and hinterland from

Snow, ice and the bishop

Even in winter, the snow on Etna's southern side tends to lie only in patches, partly melted by the heat of the rocks. On the northern side, however, hollows in the ground are filled year-round with snow. From here, the ice used to be cut, covered with ash and then transported to the rest of the island, the mainland and even Malta, for refrigeration purposes – a peculiar export that constituted the main source of revenue for the Bishop of Catania, who owned the land until comparatively recently.

the Circumetnea railway (see p.208), a circular route from Catania to Riposto that provides one of Sicily's most fascinating rides. Drivers can follow exactly the same route around the volcano foothills as the railway – a minor but perfectly adequate road sticks close to the line.

Etna Nord: the ascent from Piano Provenzana

From Linguaglossa, a tortuous 15km road corkscrews up past the skiing pistes of **Piano Provenzana**. If you don't have your own vehicle, you'll need to take a taxi from Linguaglossa to Piano, from where 4WD minibuses operated by STAR (daily May–Oct, weather permitting; ☎095.371.333 or 347.495.7091) shuttle up and down the upper slopes. At present there is just one option, costing €48.50: a two-hour excursion that brings you to Pizzi Deneri (at a height of 2800m), where there is a ten-minute pause, from where you descend to 2400m for another stop, then down again to 2100m for a thirty-minute walk to a minor crater. If the current regulations change (the situation on the slopes is constantly monitored), there may be other options that bring you closer to the main crater (3200m). The early morning and early evening tours are the best – Etna at dawn or sunset is a spectacular sight – but need booking. The minibuses don't run to a fixed timetable; they simply take off when full, and the operation is a lower-key affair than on the southern side. The extent to which you'll be allowed out to explore independently depends on weather conditions – even in August the wind-chill can make winter clothing advisable, and wind speeds can be strong enough to blow children off their feet. You can also join an **organized hike** to the summit from Linguaglossa or Piano Provenzana – contact Guide Etna Nord for details: Via Roma 93, Linguaglossa (☎095.777.4502 or 348.012.5167, ⓦwww.guidetna nord.com). Solo expeditions are not encouraged.

Two mountain **refuges**, *rifugi*, stand 100m apart in the pinewoods, 5km below Piano Provenzana (follow the road): *Casa Brunek* (☎095.643.015; €26 per person for a private room including breakfast, €40 including dinner too) and the more comfortable *Ragabo* (☎095.647.841, ⓦwww.ragabo.it; ❷, or €50 half board; closed Nov), which has a nice **restaurant** open to all.

Zafferana Etnea and around

Most pleasant of the villages on Etna's southeastern side is **ZAFFERANA ETNEA**, an hour from Catania by bus. Surrounded by vineyards and citrus groves,

---

Etna tours and excursions

If you're short on time, the easiest way to see the volcano and climb its slopes is by **organized tour**. Four-wheel-drive minibuses and guided hikes operate out of the ski stations of Piano Provenzana (see p.206) and Rifugio Sapienza (see p.207), though many tourists simply book an all-day tour from agents and tourist offices in places like Taormina, Giardini-Naxos, Catania and Siracusa. Prices vary according to how high you go and whether or not you take the cable car, but you can expect to pay €45–85 for an excursion leaving at 9am and returning at around 3.30pm or 6.30pm. Departures depend on weather conditions and tours don't generally run between September and April.

For **excursion agencies** in Catania, see box, p.191; for those in Taormina, see Listings, p.179. For more info, contact the tourist offices at Zafferana Etnea, Nicolosi or Linguaglossa.

it's renowned for its honey, the smell of which lingers in the air. Parts of the outskirts were damaged by lava in 1992, when the village became the operational hub of the effort to halt the flow from the volcano. The centre, however, was untouched, and it retains an eighteenth-century air in its buildings and churches, making it a pleasant stop, say for a coffee in the bar on the corner of the elegant central piazza. The previous eruption to threaten Zafferana occurred in 1792, halted on that occasion – according to local tradition – by the intervention of Our Lady of Divine Providence, whose name was again invoked by God-fearing locals during the last volcanic ructions.

Zafferana has acquired a reputation as a low-key hill-resort, and the population of around seven thousand practically doubles at weekends and holidays as the trippers arrive. Certainly, there's some good walking to be done in the green hills behind the village, and if you fancy a longer stay there's a choice of **hotels**, all sited north of the centre. Try the large, fully equipped *Primavera dell'Etna*, Via Cassone 86 (T 095.708.2348, W www.hotel-primavera.it; ❷–❸), set in its own grounds and with superb views from its rooms and terraces, or the smaller *Villa Pina*, Via dei Gerani 19 (T 095.708.1024, W www.albergovillapina.eu; no credit cards; ❶). There's a **tourist office** here at Piazza Luigi Sturzo 3 (Mon–Sat 9am–1pm & 4–8pm in summer, 3–7pm in winter; T 095.708.2825, W www .zafferana-etnea.it).

Five kilometres or so north of Zafferana, **Milò** offers impressive views of the Valle del Bove above. Maps show a road from Milò that climbs northwest, up the volcano to the *Rifugio Citelli*, and back towards Linguaglossa, but frequent landslides often make this route impossible. You should be able to get some of the way up though, for more striking views of the summit and the coastline below. Alternatively, from Zafferana Etnea, there's a road that winds directly up the mountain to *Rifugio Sapienza* (see p.207), a drive of around 45 minutes, while a lower road leads 15km north past various old lava flows – of 1852, 1950 and, near Fornazzo, of 1979 – to Linguaglossa.

Nicolosi and around

The tidy little resort of **NICOLOSI** (698m), which had a narrow escape in the 2002 eruption, is a popular winter ski-centre and the most useful base in the foothills on the south side of the volcano. With several hotels and some good places to eat, it is also well served by frequent AST buses from Catania. It gets pretty busy around here, even in summer, with some good walking possibilities in the area. Best of these, certainly if you're going no further, is the hike up to the **Monti Rossi** craters, around an hour each way. Formed in the eruption of 1669, they're the most important of the secondary craters that litter the slopes of the volcano.

Five kilometres or so east of Nicolosi, **Trecastagni** is worth a look for its main church, the Chiesa Madre, a fine Renaissance building probably designed by Antonello Gagini, and the marvellous views over the coast from its elevated position. Frankly, though, you're hardly likely to come here for just these; better, if you're driving, to look upon Trecastagni as a coffee-stop.

Practicalities

Nicolosi is the last main stop before the steeper slopes begin. There's a helpful **tourist office** on Piazza Vittorio Emanuele (Mon–Fri 9am–1pm, plus Mon, Wed & Thurs 4–6pm; T 095.914.488), just off the main road that runs through town.

Accommodation in Nicolosi is fairly expensive, but there are some exceptions. A good, central B&B is *Al Centro Stórico*, Via Garibaldi 26 (T 095.910.735 or 348.266.4310, W www.alcentrostorico.it; ❷), just off Piazza Vittorio Emanuele,

The eruptions of Etna

Of the scores of recorded **eruptions** of Etna since the 475 BC one described by Pindar, some have been disastrously spectacular: in 1169, 1329 and 1381 the lava reached the sea, while in **1669**, the worst year, parts of Catania were wrecked and its castle was surrounded by molten rock.

During the twentieth century, the Circumetnea railway line was repeatedly ruptured by lava flows, the towns of the foothills were threatened, and roads and farms destroyed. The **1971** eruption destroyed the observatory supposed to give warning of such an event, while in **1979** nine tourists were killed by an explosion on the edge of the main crater. During the **1992** eruption, which engulfed the outskirts of Zafferana Etnea, the American navy joined Italian forces in an attempt to stem the lava flow by dropping reinforced concrete blocks (so-called "Beirut-busters", used to defend military camps) from helicopters into the fissures.

In **2001**, the military helicopters were out again in force, this time water-bombing the forest fires and blazing orchards. Regarded as the most complex in the last three hundred years, the 2001 eruption spewed forth from six vents on Etna's northern and southeastern sides and sent vast, fiery fountains of lava to the skies. Drivers found the roads blocked and air passengers were forced to divert to other island airports, while Catania suffered a rain of black ash day and night. Luckily there were no fatalities; the cluster of buildings around *Rifugio Sapienza* narrowly escaped and the lava flow petered out 4km short of Nicolosi, though the upper cable-car station was destroyed and the hut that held the monitoring live-cam was incinerated (somehow the equipment was saved).

Triggered by an earthquake, the eruption of **2002** saw lava streams pouring down both north and south flanks, destroying restaurants, hotels and a cable car in the ski resort of Piano Provenzana, and threatening the villages of Nicolosi and Linguaglossa below. Emergency teams, however, succeeded in diverting the flow, and a major catastrophe was averted. Some local villagers, on the other hand, preferred to place their faith in parading statues of the Virgin Mary before the volcano, although the devout were far outnumbered by the flocks of sightseers who made excursions as close as they dared, until curtailed by the authorities.

More eruptions followed in 2006, 2007 and 2008, the latter accompanied by minor local earthquakes and continuing at a low intensity for some six months, making it the longest of the eruptions since 2000. A significant eruption of ash also occurred in 2010, producing an ash plume that rose to a height of 800m above the crater.

while the *Etna Garden Hotel*, Via della Quercia 7 (☎095.791.4686 or 347.877.9969, Ⓦ www.etnagardenpark.com; ❷), is stuffed with antiques and has a courtyard garden. *Camping Etna* (☎095.914.309), in a shady pinewood with a pool (summer only), is on Via Goethe, signposted from town just past the hotels.

Restaurants and pizzerias are ten-a-penny in the centre of Nicolosi. For something a bit different and more contemporary, try ⚞ *Nero di Cénere*, a **wine bar and restaurant** at Via Garibaldi 64 (closed daytime & Tues); apart from the wines, it serves samplings of cheese and salami, pastas and various vegetarian dishes, which you can enjoy *al fresco* on the terrace.

Etna Sud: the ascent from Rifugio Sapienza

One or two buses a day from Catania go to Rifugio Sapienza, the mountain refuge/hotel that marks the end of the negotiable road up the south side of Etna. The year-round service leaves from Piazza Giovanni XXIII, outside Catania's

Stazione Centrale, daily at 8.15am, with a stop at Nicolosi; an additional summer service (mid-June to mid-Sept) leaves daily at 11.20am, and necessitates a change at Nicolosi. Altogether, it's a two-hour journey; tickets cost around €5. (You can, of course, catch the bus at Nicolosi, from where departures to the refuge are at 9.15am and – in summer – 12.30pm, an hour-long trip.) The return bus from Rifugio Sapienza leaves for Catania at 4.30pm. It's a bizarre ride: the green foothills give way to wooded slopes, then to bare, black-and-grey seas of volcanic debris, spotted with the hardy endemic plants, the yellow-green Spino Santo and Etna violets, that are the only things to grow on the heights of the volcano. The most recent lava streams lie to the right of the road, where you'll also see earlier spent craters, grass-covered on the lower reaches and no more than black pimples further up.

🏛 **Rifugio Sapienza** (☎095.915.321, ⓦ www.rifugiosapienza.com; €75 per person half board), 1400m below the summit, was the scene of frenetic activity in July and August 2001, when large dams and channels were constructed to contain the molten lava and prevent it from engulfing the tourist complex. As a result, only the lower cable-car station and the car park were damaged, when the lava eventually spilled down and crossed the road in a broad 500m band. It had another narrow escape at the end of 2002, when lava covered a nearby building, causing it to explode. Thirty-two people were injured, but the refuge was untouched – graphic photographs inside illustrate its near escapes.

The refuge is the cheapest place to spend the night, so it's always wise to ring ahead and book. Its modern rooms have clean lines and en-suite bathrooms, and there's a restaurant (excursions can also be arranged from here). Alternative **accommodation** is available at the *Hotel Corsaro* (☎095.914.122, ⓦ www.hotel corsaro.it; ❸, half board €70 per person), a ski-lodge-type place popular with tour groups, set a little apart from the rest of the site and advertising itself as Etna's highest lodging.

The ascent

Organized ascents of the volcano from the south side involve a combination of cable car from *Rifugio Sapienza*, a minibus ride and a guided walk. The **Funivia dell'Etna** cable car (daily: summer 9am–5.30pm, winter 9am–3.30pm; €27.50; ⓦ www.funiviaetna.com) reaches an altitude of 2500m at Monte Montagnola, from where SITAS **minibuses** leave for the crater (April–Oct daily 9am–5pm, weather permitting; ☎095.914.141). The total journey (cable car plus minibus) takes around two and a half hours and costs €52. When the wind is up, or conditions are otherwise difficult, the entire journey is undertaken from *Rifugio Sapienza* by minibus. It's also possible (conditions permitting) to **walk to Etna's summit** from a height of around 2900m, for which you need to contact Etna Touring (☎095.791.8000 or 347.783.8799, ⓦ www.etnatouring.com). Expeditions without an authorized guide are extremely unwise. However you go, take warm clothes, a hat, good shoes or boots and – especially if you wear contact lenses – glasses to keep the flying grit out of your eyes. Weather conditions higher up are often different to those at the *rifugio*, so you might want to take advantage of the padded jackets and boots that are available for rent from the minibus guides.

Depending on conditions, you should be able to reach the so-called **Torre del Filósofo**, a tower that's said to have been the home of Empedocles, but is more likely to be a memorial built by the Romans to celebrate the emperor Hadrian's climb to the summit. Beyond, from the turnaround point for the minibus, you look up to the summit, smoke puffing from the **southeast crater** immediately above. It would be foolish to venture any further – gaseous explosions and molten rock are common this far up. Higher still is the **main crater**: you might see smoke from here too, and, if you're lucky, spitting explosions. Disappointingly, there's often haze or cloud, which can mar the unsurpassed panorama to the sea; for the clearest view, come at sunrise. On the way down, the minibus makes short photo-stops, including the **Valle del Bove**, an enormous chasm almost 20km in circumference, its walls 900m high and streaked with recent lava flows. A massive rent in the side of the volcano, its sunken flank comprises a sixth of the entire surface area of Etna.

The Circumetnea railway

Although there's nothing to beat an ascent of Etna, you can experience something of the majesty of the volcano along the route of the **Ferrovia Circumetnea**, or Circumetnea railway. This is a private line, 110km long, starting in Catania and circling the base of Etna as far as Riposto on the Ionian coast, 30km north of Catania. It's a marvellous ride, running through fertile vegetation – citrus plantations, vines and nut trees – and past the strewn lava of recent eruptions, with endless views of the summit en route. You can easily do the whole round-trip in a day from Catania, although the medieval town of Randazzo also makes an interesting overnight stop. The Circumetnea ends its run 20km southeast of Linguaglossa at Riposto, where you switch to the mainline station Giarre-Riposto for frequent trains south to Catania (or north to Giardini-Naxos).

The Ferrovia Circumetnea trains (℡095.541.250, ⓦwww.circumetnea.it) depart from Stazione Catania Borgo (Via Caronda; metro from Stazione Centrale) in Catania. They take two hours to Randazzo, three to Linguaglossa and three and a half to Riposto (no Sunday service; timetables available on the website), and **tickets** cost €6.85 one way, €11 return. Occasionally, sections of the line are under repair, in which case a replacement bus service operates.

Paternò

The first part of the Circumetnea route runs out through Catania's grim suburbs, with Misterbianco the first stop. Soon, though, the first of the citrus and olive groves are visible and, by the time you reach **PATERNÒ**, you're well within sight of Etna's southern slopes. The busy town clusters around its main street, Via Vittorio Emanuele, with the train station at one end and a medieval castle at the other. Founded by Count Roger in 1073, the castle dates largely from the thirteenth century (though it's much restored) and is worth a look for the view from the terrace at the top – the reason the Germans used it as an observation post during World War II. They proved hard to dislodge, and four thousand people died here during the subsequent aerial bombardment.

Adrano and around

Around 45km from Catania, **ADRANO** is the first town on the route worth more than a quick glance. It was built over the site of ancient Adranon, a town founded by Dionysius the Elder, and parts of the Greek lava-built walls are still visible in town, though they're barely distinguishable from later fortifications. Much more impressive is the squat, solid *castello* in Piazza Umberto I, while the adjacent Chiesa Madre retains some sixteenth-century painted panels in the transepts. The town's shady gardens and faded churches invite a stroll (there are bars across from the castle), while for a reasonably priced lunch, walk 250m down Via Roma alongside the gardens to the car park and turn sharply left to find the Piazza Duca degli Abruzzi and the Teatro Bellini, next to which is the rustic *Hostaria Bellini* (☎095.760.1021; closed Mon; meals €15–20). Afterwards, drivers can follow the signs 8km west of Adrano, near Cárcaci, to the **Ponte dei Saraceni**, a fourteenth-century bridge that arches over the River Simeto (it's at the end of the first road on the right after Cárcaci; keep to the right).

Three kilometres southeast of Adrano, **Biancavilla** was founded by Albanian refugees in 1480. The area around is devoted to growing oranges, and small side roads from here run up through the orchards and onto the higher, southwestern slopes of Etna – a nice little diversion if you're coming this way by car.

Keeping with the Circumetnea route, some of the best views of Etna are revealed between Adrano and Bronte, as the railway line and road climb ever closer to the lava flows.

Bronte and around

BRONTE lies about halfway along the Circumetnea route, another small, unassuming town with a noble past. It was founded by Charles V in 1535, and many echoes of its original layout survive, particularly in the numerous battle-mented campanili that top its ageing churches. The town gave its name to the dukedom bestowed upon Nelson, the English admiral, in 1799, and his ducal seat (see below) lies just to the north of town. Otherwise, Bronte's sole claim to fame these days is as the centre of Italy's **pistachio-nut** production: the plantations around town account for 85 percent of the country's output, but are only harvested in the early autumn of odd-numbered years. The nuts are widely used in Sicilian pasta dishes (including a famously tasty shrimp and nut concoction), while not surprisingly the town's cafés do a great line in pistachio *granite*, ice cream and other goodies – *Bar Conti*, Corso Umberto 247 (☎095.691.165) is first among equals in this *città del pistacchio*.

Castello Nelson

Fifteen kilometres north of Bronte lies the estate given to Lord Nelson as part of his dukedom, granted by King Ferdinand in gratitude for British help in repressing the Neapolitan revolution of 1799, which had forced the Bourbon court to flee to Palermo. Although Nelson never got round to visiting his Sicilian property, his family, the Bridports, only relinquished control in 1978. Surrounded by a wooded estate, it's now owned by the *Comune*, but is still known (and signposted) as the **Castello Nelson** (daily 9am–1pm & 2.30–5pm, summer until 7pm; €3, gardens only €1.50). Its original name was Maniace, after the convent founded here in 1174 on the site of a victory over the Arabs by George Maniakes. The 1693 earthquake destroyed much of this building, but as you pass through the walls you'll see the restored thirteenth-century chapel with its chunky lava columns and Byzantinesque icon, the so-called *Madonna* di *Maniace*. As for the house itself, were it not for the beautiful tiled floors, restored to match the original pattern in yellow, rose and blue, it could easily be mistaken for an English country residence. Its style and furnishings – wallpaper, maritime paintings – were defined by Alexander Hood, one of the Bridports, who lived here for sixty years until the 1930s. The same English-ness is evident in the well-tended garden, planted with box hedges, magnolias and palm trees. On the other side of the river lies the only part of the estate still owned by Nelson's descendants, the English cemetery. Its most celebrated occupant is the Scottish author William Sharp (1855–1905), who wrote under the name of Fiona Macleod and was a regular visitor here. The other literary connection is the origin of the surname of the literary sisters, Anne, Charlotte and Emily; their father, the Rev Patrick Prunty, harboured such an obsession for Nelson that he changed his name to Bronte (and added an umlaut).

Randazzo

Great rivers of volcanic rubble clutter the slopes on all sides of **RANDAZZO**, the closest town to the summit of Etna, just 15km away as the crow flies. Occasionally visible through the black debris, walls belonging to former orchards or vineyards eerily poke through. Despite its dangerous proximity, the town has never been engulfed, though an eruption in 1981 came perilously close. Randazzo has not escaped entirely unscathed, however: as one of the main forward positions of the German forces during their defence of Sicily in 1943, the town was heavily bombed, and most of the lava-built churches and palaces you'll see here, originally dating from the wealthy thirteenth- to sixteenth-century era, are the result of meticulous restoration. The result is a handsome old centre, with enough to occupy a half-day's exploration – and Randazzo is easily the best place to break your Circumetnea trip if you fancy a night in the sticks.

In medieval times, three churches took turns to act as Randazzo's cathedral, a sop to the three parishes in town whose inhabitants were of Greek, Latin and Lombard origin. The largest, **Santa Maria**, on the main Via Umberto I, is the modern-day holder of the title, a severe Catalan-Gothic structure with a fine carved portal with vine decoration. Further up the road, facing a small square, the blackened tower that forms part of the old city walls is all that survives of Randazzo's Castello Svevo, which did duty as a prison from around 1500 until 1973. It's now the **Museo Vagliasindi** (Tues–Sun 10am–1pm & 3.30–7.30pm; €2.60), which holds a good collection of objects from a nearby Greek necropolis, including wine jugs in the form of women's heads, and a vessel in the shape of a spunky little rat. Downstairs you'll find ranks of dangling Sicilian puppets, variously sporting armour, a velvet cloak or a deer-stalker cap – typically for eastern Sicily, they are taller than the puppets you may have seen in Palermo. The museum's other rooms, including the bare, minuscule cells where inmates once rotted, display agricultural tools and other rustic items.

Practicalities

Arriving on the **Circumetnea train**, walk straight up Via Vittorio Véneto to reach the central Piazza Loreto, with the medieval town further on, down Via Umberto I. The **bus station** is a couple of blocks back from Piazza Loreto off Via Vittorio Véneto. You'll find a limited amount of information on Etna and the surrounding area at the Parco dei Nébrodi **tourist office**, on the way to the museum at Via Umberto I 197 (daily 9am–1pm & 3–7.30pm; ☎095.799.1611, Ⓦwww.parcodeinebrodi.it).

Accommodation inside town is relatively uninspiring, typified by the three-star *Hotel Scrivano* (☎095.921.126, Ⓦwww.hotelscrivano.com; ❸), by the Agip petrol station, off Piazza Loreto. It's adequate for the night, and there's a decent restaurant, but the better, more intimate choice is ⚞ *Ai Tre Parchi Bed and Bike*, Via Tagliamento 49 (☎095.799.1631 or 329.897.0901, Ⓦwww.aitreparchibb .it; ❷), an excellent place offering B&B and self-catering apartments, plus bike rental and local bike tours. To reach Via Tagliamento, turn left off Via Vittorio Véneto from the station.

In the evening, a lively *passeggiata* parades up and down Via Umberto I, where you'll also find some nice old-fashioned **bars**, such as the intricately decorated *Arturo* at no. 75. There's also the *Casa Lanza* enoteca at Via dei Lanza 24, off Via Umberto I near Santa Maria church, a bar in a restored fourteenth-century house down a pretty street of overhanging balconies and flower-boxes. Best place in town for a reliable **meal** is *Da Antonio*, Via Pietro Nenni 8 (℡095.799.2534; closed Tues), where typical local dishes and pizzas are served (€5–10); the house *antipasto* is really good. The restaurant is a few hundred metres from Piazza Loreto – walk down the Linguaglossa road, past the petrol stations, and it's up a side road on the right.

Linguaglossa

Road and rail stick close together around the northernmost stretch of the Circumetnea route and it's a 20km ride to **LINGUAGLOSSA**, which is the main tourist centre on Etna's north slopes. It had a narrow escape from the lava flow during the 2002 eruption, when hotels, restaurants and a ski lift were destroyed at the ski-resort of Piano Provenzana, 15km above. There's only really much life here during the winter, especially at weekends, when the town fills with winter-sports enthusiasts – the **tourist office** in Piazza Annunziata (Mon–Sat 9am–1pm & 4–8pm in summer, 3–7pm winter, Sun 9am–noon; ℡095.643.094, ⓦwww .prolocolinguaglossa.it) can fill you in on local ski schools, Etna excursions and the like. For the rest of the year, however, Linguaglossa doesn't have a great deal to recommend it, save perhaps for a ramble in the extensive surrounding pine forests. There's plenty of accommodation, including several bed and breakfasts, all signposted on the way in and out of town.

Travel details

Trains

Catania to: Acireale (1–2 hourly; 10min); Caltagirone (6 daily Mon–Sat; 1hr 45min); Caltanissetta (3–4 daily; 2hr); Enna (4 daily Mon–Sat, 3 daily Sun; 1hr 20min); Gela (5 daily Mon–Sat; 2hr 10min–2hr 45min); Giarre-Riposto (1–2 hourly; 30min); Lentini (11 daily Mon–Sat, 5 daily Sun; 30min); Messina (1–2 hourly; 1hr 30min); Palermo via Caltanissetta or Messina (4 daily; 3hr–6hr 40min); Siracusa (11 daily Mon–Sat, 5 daily Sun; 1hr 30min); Taormina (1–2 hourly; 45min).

Circumetnea trains

Catania to: Paternò, Adrano, Bronte, Maletto, Randazzo, Riposto (up to 7 daily Mon–Sat; up to 2hr 20min).

Randazzo to: Catania (up to 7 daily Mon–Sat; 2hr 20min); Linguaglossa (4 daily Mon–Sat; 35min); Riposto (4 daily Mon–Sat; 1hr 10min).

Buses

Catania to: Acireale (1–3 hourly; 35min–1hr 15min); Agrigento (hourly Mon–Sat, 9 daily Sun; 3hr); Caltagirone (1–2 hourly Mon–Sat, 4 daily Sun; 1hr 30min); Enna (8–11 daily Mon–Sat, 3 daily Sun; 1hr 20min–2hr 35min); Gela (8–10 daily Mon–Sat, 6 daily Sun; 1hr 45min); Giardini-Naxos (5 daily Mon–Sat, 2 daily Sun; 1hr 30min); Lentini (1–2 hourly Mon–Sat; 1hr–1hr 15min); Messina (1–2 hourly Mon–Fri, 12 daily Sat, 9 daily Sun; 1hr 35min); Nicolosi (hourly; 40min); Nicosia (4–5 daily Mon–Sat, 2 daily Sun; 2hr–2hr 45min); Noto (9–11 daily Mon–Sat, 6 daily Sun; 1hr 35min–2hr 40min); Palermo (hourly Mon–Sat, 9 daily Sun; 2hr 40min); Piazza Armerina (4–5 daily Mon–Sat, 2 daily Sun; 1hr 40min); Ragusa (6–10 daily Mon–Fri, 6 daily Sat & Sun; 2hr); Randazzo (1–2 hourly Mon–Sat; 1hr 45min); Rifugio Sapienza (1–2 daily; 2hr); Rome (1 daily; 11hr); Siracusa (hourly Mon–Sat, 7 daily Sun; 1hr 25min); Taormina (1–2 hourly; 1hr 10min–2hr);

Trecastagni (1–2 hourly Mon–Sat, 3 daily Sun; 1hr);
Zafferana Etnea (hourly Mon–Sat, 4 daily Sun;
1hr 15min).

Catania airport to: Agrigento (hourly Mon–Sat,
10 daily Sun; 2hr 40min); Enna (9 daily Mon–Fri,
6 daily Sat, 3 daily Sun; 1hr 15min); Messina
(13 daily Mon–Fri, 8 daily Sat & Sun; 1hr 50min);
Milazzo (3 daily July–Sept; 1hr 50min); Palermo
(hourly Mon–Sat, 9 daily Sun; 2hr 30min); Siracusa
(8 daily Mon–Fri, 6 daily Sat & Sun; 1hr 15min);
Taormina (hourly Mon–Sat, 11 daily Sun; 1hr 25min).

Randazzo to: Bronte (2 daily Mon–Sat; 30min);
Catania (1–2 daily Mon–Sat; 1hr 45min); Cesarò
(2 daily Mon–Sat; 45min–1hr 25min); Giardini-
Naxos (2–3 daily Mon–Sat, 1 daily Sun; 55min–1hr
40min); Maletto (1–2 daily Mon–Sat; 20min);
Messina (1–2 daily Mon–Sat; 1hr 45min).

Ferries

Catania to: Civitavécchia (3 weekly; 18hr 30min);
Naples (1 daily; 12hr); Valletta, Malta (1–5 weekly;
3hr).

6

Siracusa and the southeast

CHAPTER 6

Highlights

* **Piazza del Duomo, Siracusa** Sicily's most graceful piazza has been beautifully restored. See p.222

* **Siracusa's Teatro Greco** Classical dramas and modern productions are still staged in the theatre where Aeschylus attended performances of his own plays. See p.228

* **Pantálica** Walk the gorge to explore the thousands of prehistoric tombs that honeycomb this high ravine. See p.235

* **Noto** The apotheosis of Baroque town planning, Noto offers glorious vistas at every turn, from extra- vagantly balconied *palazzi* to soaring church facades. See p.238

* **Cava Grande del Fiume Cassíbile** Eagles soar high above the Cassíbile River canyon, while a track leads down to secluded swimming spots. See p.242

* **Chocolate-tasting, Módica** The little Baroque town with the big crunch – sample the goods at Sicily's oldest chocolate manufacturer. See p.246

* **Ragusa Ibla** Spend the night in a classy B&B in Ragusa's chic Baroque old town. See p.251

▲ The Duomo, Siracusa

6

Siracusa and the southeast

Sicily's southeast has always ranked among the island's most alluring regions, and in **Siracusa** it boasts a city whose long and glorious history outshines all others on the island. Indeed, Siracusa was once the most important city in the western world, though, with most business activity located elsewhere and all political power centred on Palermo, its status today is as a provincial capital. Yet it remains the most interesting destination in this part of the island, charged with historical resonance, and a useful base for visiting many other regional highlights, few more than 45 minutes' drive from the city.

Festivals

April
Last Sunday St George's Day celebrations in **Ragusa Ibla**: statues paraded through the streets and a costumed procession.

May
1 Procession in **Siracusa**, with the statue of St Lucy carried around town.
Third Sunday Infiorata flower festival in **Noto**.

May/June
Classical drama festival at **Siracusa**, events taking place in the Greek theatre.

August
First Sunday Boat race (*palio*) round Ortigia island in **Siracusa**, in which the five traditional quarters of the city compete with raucous enthusiasm.
27–29 Festivities in **Ragusa** to mark the city's patron St John the Baptist; more processions and statues.
29 Start of Madonna delle Lácrime festival (devoted to the "weeping" Madonna) in **Siracusa**; runs until September 3.
Last Sunday Festival of St Corrado in **Noto**.

December
13 Festival of St Lucy in **Siracusa**: a procession to the church of Santa Lucia.

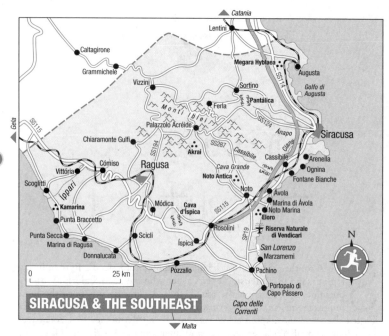

SIRACUSA & THE SOUTHEAST

Inland, the southeast is characterized by the rough and wild **Monti Iblei**, riven by spectacular ravines, or *cave*, which are riddled with rock-cut tombs that prove occupation of the area as far back as the thirteenth century BC. The most famous is **Pantálica**, northwest of Siracusa, Sicily's greatest necropolis, while at the **Cava Grande del Fiume Cassibile**, near Ávola, you can peer into the distant depths of Sicily's own "Grand Canyon". Greek colonists later appropriated many early Neolithic sites, founding towns at **Megara Hyblaea**, on the coast north of Siracusa near **Augusta**, and inland at **Akrai**, just outside the attractive small town of **Palazzolo Acréide**. Several other much smaller archeological sites lie strung along the coast, often set beside otherwise unsung sand beaches.

However dramatic the natural scenery, it's the built environment that most defines the southeast. Damaging earthquakes have repeatedly afflicted the area, none so destructive as that of January 11, 1693, which affected the entire region as far north as Catania. This catastrophe did, however, have one lasting effect: where there were ruins, a confident new generation of architects raised planned towns, displaying a noble but vivacious Baroque style that endures today. The gorgeous small town of **Noto** is the pre-eminent example, though **Ragusa** – capital of its own province – and nearby **Módica**, **Scicli** and **Íspica** all hold Baroque centres of varying refinement, as local authorities have slowly awoken to their tourist potential. There are probably more B&Bs in this area than in any other region of Sicily, many housed in restored Baroque mansions, while tours and activities are increasingly available, from mountain-biking to gorge-walking.

The **coast** is a mixed bag, virtually off-limits north of Siracusa thanks to the petrochemical industry that disfigures the **Golfo di Augusta**, and otherwise largely devoted to small-scale beach dormitory towns aimed squarely at a local clientele. The only real exception is the coastline south of Noto, from **Ávola** to Sicily's southern cape, **Capo delle Correnti**, in between which lie assorted pristine beaches, old tuna-fishing villages and market-garden towns, with the undisputed highlight being the lagoons, paths and bird hides of the **Riserva Naturale di Vendicari**.

Siracusa

More than any other Sicilian city, **SIRACUSA** (ancient Syracuse) has a past that is central not just to the island's history, but to that of the entire Mediterranean. Its greatest splendour belongs to antiquity. Syracuse established its ascendancy over other Sicilian cities for more than five hundred years, and at its height was the supreme power in Europe, home to at least three times its present population. Its central position on the major trade routes ensured that even after its heyday the port continued to wield influence and preserve its prestige. All this is reflected in a staggering diversity of monuments, spanning the Hellenic, early Christian, medieval, Renaissance and Baroque eras – the styles are often shoulder-to-shoulder, sometimes in the same building. It's one of the most enjoyable cities in Sicily, with a fascinating old town and outlying archeological and leisure areas that can easily occupy three or four days, if not a week of your time.

As for two and a half thousand years, the city is still divided between its ancient hub, the island of Ortigia, and the four mainland quarters of Achradina, Tyche, Neapolis and Epipolae. **Ortigia** is the heart and soul of Siracusa, a predominantly medieval and Baroque ensemble of mansions and palaces, containing most of the city's best B&Bs, hotels, cafés and restaurants. Across the bridge on the mainland, the modern city is centred on **Achradina**, now, as in Greek times, the busy commercial centre, traversed by the main street of Corso Gelone. North of Achradina, the old residential quarter of **Tyche** holds Siracusa's celebrated **Museo Archeologico** and the extraordinary Santa Lucia and San Giovanni **catacombs** – after those in Rome, Siracusa's catacombs constitute the largest system of subterranean tombs in Italy, and are the oldest in Sicily. **Neapolis** is the site of the **Parco Archeologico**, containing remains of the Greek city's theatres and some extensive quarries, while spread over the ridge to the west of town, **Epipolae** holds the old defensive walls and the remnants of the **Euryalus fort**. Other obvious trips out of the city are to the local beaches, particularly that at **Fontane Bianche**, or a cruise along the **Fiume Ciane** (Ciane River).

A brief history

The **ancient city** grew around Ortigia, an easily defensible offshore island with two natural harbours on either side, fresh springs, and access to extensive trade routes. Though Corinthian colonists arrived here in 733 BC, apparently at the behest of the Delphic oracle, it wasn't until the start of the fifth century BC that the city's political position was boosted by an alliance with Greeks at Akragas (Agrigento) and Gela. With the transfer of Gela's tyrant, **Gelon**, to Syracuse and the crushing victory of their combined forces over the Carthaginians at Himera in 480 BC, the stage was set for the beginning of the city's long supremacy. The grandest extant monuments are from this period, and more often than not were built by slaves provided from the many battles won by Syracuse's bellicose dictators.

Inevitably, the city's ambitions provoked the intervention of Athens, which dispatched one of the greatest fleets ever seen in the ancient world. This **Great Expedition** was scuppered in 413 BC by a mixture of poor leadership and astute defence: "to the victors the most brilliant of successes, to the vanquished the most calamitous of defeats", commented the historian Thucydides. But Syracuse earned

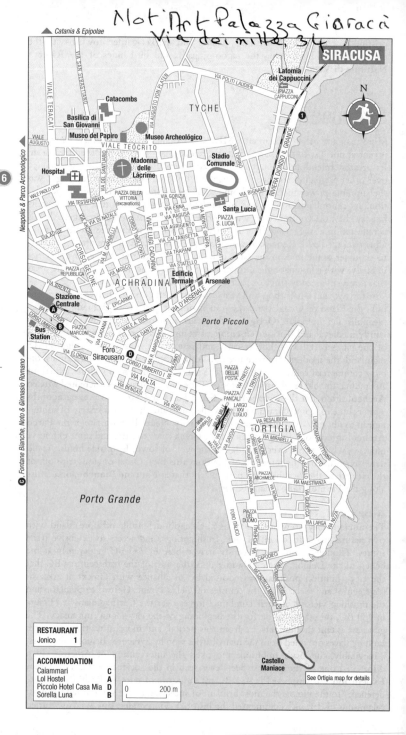

Not Art Palazza Giaracà
via dei mille, 34

SIRACUSA

▲ Catania & Epipolae

VIA POLITI LAUDIEN

Latomia
del Cappuccini

PIAZZA
CAPPUCCINI

N

TYCHE

Catacombs

Basilica di
San Giovanni

Museo del Papiro

Museo Archeológico

Stadio
Comunale

VIALE TEÓCRITO

Madonna
delle
Lácrime

Hospital

PIAZZA DELLA
VITTORIA
(excavations)

VIA GORIZIA

VIA ENNA

Santa Lucia

PIAZZA
S. LUCIA

VIA RAGUSA

VIA AGRIGENTO

VIA CALTANISSETTA

VIA TRAPANI

VIA STATELLO

PIAZZA
REPUBBLICA

ACHRADINA

Edificio
Termale

Arsenale

Stazione
Centrale

Porto Piccolo

Bus
Station

PIAZZA
MARCONI

Foro
Siracusano

PIAZZA
DELLA
POSTA

PIAZZA
PANCALI

LARGO
XXV
LUGLIO

VIA MALTA

ORTIGIA

VIA BENGASI

VIA RODI

Porto Grande

PIAZZA
ANCHIMEDE

PIAZZA
DEL DUOMO

VIA LARGA

VIA CAPODIECI

Castello
Maniace

See Ortigia map for details

RESTAURANT
Jonico   1

ACCOMMODATION
Caiammari   C
Lol Hostel   A
Piccolo Hotel Casa Mia D
Sorella Luna   B

0   200 m

218

SIRACUSA AND THE SOUTHEAST

6

◄ Neapolis & Parco Archeologico

◄ Fontane Bianche, Noto & Gimnasio Romano

the condemnation of the Hellenic world for its seven-year incarceration of the vanquished Athenians – in appalling conditions – in the city's notorious quarries.

Throughout this period Syracuse was in a state of constant tension between a few overweening but extremely capable rulers, and sporadic convulsions of democracy. Occasionally the tyrants displayed a yearning for cultural respectability that sat uncomfortably beside their vaulting ambition. **Hieron I** (478–466 BC), for instance, described by the historian Diodorus as "an utter stranger to sincerity and nobility of character", invited many of the luminaries of the age to his court, including **Pindar**, and **Aeschylus** – who possibly witnessed the production of his last plays, *Prometheus Bound* and *Prometheus Released*, in the city's theatre. **Dionysius the Elder** (405–367 BC) – "cruel, vindictive and a profane plunderer of temples" and responsible for the first of the **Euryalus** forts – comically harboured literary ambitions to the extent of regularly entering his poems in the annual Olympic Games. His works were consistently rejected, until the Athenians judged it politic to give him the prize, whereupon his delirious celebrations were enough to provoke the seizure that killed him. His son **Dionysius II** (367–343 BC) dallied with the "philosopher-king" theories of his tutor **Plato** until megalomania turned his head and Plato fled in dismay. Dionysius himself, recorded Plutarch, spent the end of his life in exile "loitering about the fish market, or sitting in a perfumer's shop drinking the diluted wine of the taverns, or squabbling in the streets with common women".

Rarely, the rulers themselves initiated democratic reforms – men such as **Timoleon** (343–337 BC), who arrived from Corinth to inject new life into all the Sicilian cities, and **Hieron II**, who preserved Syracuse's independence from the assertions of Rome by a novel policy of conciliation, abandoning expansion in favour of preserving the status quo. His long reign (265–215 BC) saw the construction of such monuments as the **Ara di Ierone II**, and the enlargement of the **Teatro Greco** to more or less its existing proportions.

Following the death of Hieron II, Syracuse, along with practically every other Sicilian city, sided with Carthage against Rome in the Second Punic War. For two years the city was besieged by the Romans, who had to contend with all the ingenious contrivances devised for its defence by **Archimedes**, though Syracuse eventually fell in 211 BC, an event that sent shock waves rippling around the classical world. The city was ransacked, and Archimedes himself – the last of the great Hellenic thinkers – was hacked to death, despite the injunctions of the Roman general Marcellus.

Syracuse languished under Roman rule, though its trading role still made it the most prominent Sicilian city, and it became a notable centre of early Christianity, as attested by its extensive **catacombs**. The city briefly became the capital of the Byzantine empire when Constans moved his court here in 663 AD, but otherwise Syracuse was eclipsed by events outside its control and played no active part against all the successive waves of Arab, Norman and other medieval conquerors. The 1693 **earthquake** laid low much of the city, but provided the impetus for some of its Baroque masterpieces, notably the creations of the great Siculo-Spanish architect Giovanni Verméxio, who contributed an imposing facade to the **Duomo**, itself adapted from the bones of an early Greek temple and later Norman cathedral – and thus a building that encapsulates perfectly the polyglot character of modern Siracusa.

Arrival, information and transport

The **train station** is on the mainland at the end of Via Francesco Crispi, while AST and Interbus regional **buses** stop just around the corner on the parallel Corso

Siracusa by bike

Renting a bike is a great way of getting around the city. A council initiative, Go Bike, makes bikes available at a dozen or so key points throughout Ortigia and Siracusa including Stazione Centrale, Piazza Archimede, Fonte Aretusa, Talete car park and Neapolis. Rates are €10 for one day, €20 for three days and €40 for a week. You can sign up at *Bar Oasi*, Corso Umberto I 19 (℡0931.65.598), where you'll be asked to present a passport or other ID. Bikes are kept in locked stands that are released by inserting your *téssera* (plastic card), and need to be returned every night. In 2010, the council was in the process of creating a **cycle route** from Ortigia west along the coast and out of the city.

Umberto I. You can walk from here to Ortigia in around twenty minutes, or there's a taxi rank outside the train station. Most of the orange AST **city buses** also make a stop at the bus terminal off Corso Umberto I, while on Ortigia the main stop is at Riva della Posta (outside the main post office, close to the bridge). The main routes run up Corso Umberto I, stop at the bus terminal and then head up Corso Gelone. Tickets (€1.10 valid for 90 minutes) must be bought in advance; they're available from booths at the bus terminal and in Piazza della Posta, or from any *tabacchi*.

Drivers will find the city a breeze after Palermo and Catania, though driving onto the island of Ortigia is restricted and street parking there is almost impossible for non-residents. However, there is a monumental parking garage called **Talete**, to which all visitors are directed, at the end of Via Trieste (look for the sign) on the lungomare. It's free up until 9pm and you pay just €1 (€2 at weekends) to leave your car there overnight – buy a ticket from the machine. The garage is an easy walk from the centre of Ortigia, though a free **shuttle-bus** (*navetta*) leaves from outside every fifteen minutes, dropping passengers in Piazza Pancali and Piazza Archimede.

The main **tourist office** on Ortigia, at Via Maestranza 33 (summer Mon–Sat 8.30am–1.45pm & 4.30–7pm; winter Mon–Thurs 8.30am–1.45pm & 2.45–5.30pm, Fri 8.30am–1.45pm; ℡0931.464.255, ⓦwww.comune.siracusa.it), can supply current opening hours and bus routes for all city attractions.

Accommodation

Siracusa holds a lot of **accommodation**, much of it in the old town on Ortigia, which is by far the best place to stay. Here you'll find scores of **B&Bs** in the backstreets and a cluster of four-star **hotels** on the waterfront. Unless your chosen establishment has private parking, it's best to leave the car overnight in the Talete garage. The cheapest beds are at the **hostel** by the train station; **camping** is available at a very basic site outside the city or at a much better-equipped site down the coast towards Ávola. For **apartment rentals** contact Lynette Chaplin (℡0931.464.362 or 339.685.8461, ⓦwww.casa-giulietta.it), who has two self-contained studios beneath her home on Ortigia, one double with sitting area (€245–385 per week), and one small single (€175–245).

Hotels and B&Bs

L'Acanto Via Roma 15 ℡0931.449.555 or 331.508.0603, ⓦwww.bebsicilia.it. Central Ortigia B&B with five spacious en-suite rooms in white and yellow tones grouped around two small courtyards. There's a sun terrace, and breakfast

is served at the nearby *Gran Caffè del Duomo*. No credit cards. ❷

Alla Giudecca Via Alagona 52 ℡0931.22.255, ⓦwww.allagiudecca.it. A stunning renovation in the old Jewish quarter has brought an interconnected series of medieval houses back to life as an exquisite little boutique hotel. There's exposed stone, soaring arches, colourful tapestries and dried flowers everywhere, while the 23 rooms feature eye-catching wrought-iron beds, flagged floors and antique furniture. ❸

L'Approdo delle Sirene Riva Garibaldi 15 ⓣ 0931.24.857, Ⓦ www.apprododellesirene .com. B&B in a tastefully renovated Ortigia water-front building. The rooms are mostly nice and bright, though you pay a premium for balconies and views, while great breakfasts are served on a terrace overlooking the bay. There are laptops in the rooms for free internet access, and bikes for free use around town. ❸

Ares Via Mirabella 49 ⓣ 0931.461.145 or 338.788.5867, Ⓦ www.aresbedandbreakfast.it. This Ortigia townhouse has been restored with great flair, the spacious, modern rooms equipped with antique furnishings, wooden beams, pristine stonework and balconies. There's a/c, free wi-fi and a terrific roof garden with colourful floor tiles from Caltagirone; breakfast is by voucher in the *Gran Caffè del Duomo*, a few minutes' walk away. The chatty owner, Enzo, is full of local advice. No credit cards. ❷

Diana Piazza Archimede 2 ⓣ 0931.721.135, Ⓦ www.bbdolcecasa.it. The location of this B&B is unbeatable, in an apartment forming part of the historic Palazzo dell'Orologio on Ortigia's central piazza. The five smallish rooms are fancily old-fashioned, two of them with a balcony overlooking the fountain. Breakfast is served at a café below. Closed Jan & Feb. ❷

Domus Mariae Via Vittorio Veneto 76 ⓣ 0931.24.858, Ⓦ www.sistemia.it/domusmariae. Occupying a former religious school, this three-star is still owned and run by an order of nuns. Half of the rooms have views to the sea, and all are efficiently maintained if a little plain. There's a fitness centre (costing €30), a roof terrace, parking and, of course, a chapel. ❹

Grand Viale Mazzini 12 ⓣ 0931.464.600, Ⓦ www .grandhotelsr.it. This veteran four-star establish-ment enjoys a prime position in Ortigia, overlooking the Porto Grande. The overall style is fin-de-siècle luxury, though rooms are contemporary updates, and for the considerable bill (sea-view rooms around €200) you also get a terrific panoramic restaurant and access to a private beach. ❺

Gutkowski Lungomare E. Vittorini 26 ⓣ 0931.465.861, Ⓦ www.guthotel.it. There's a real seaside feel to this lovely townhouse hotel on Ortigia's east side, whose chic bare-bones rooms have tile floors, stylish furnish-ings and good bathrooms. Seven have face-on sea views, though these are usually only available with an advance reservation. Breakfast includes fresh juice from organic oranges, locally made preserves and, in summer, almond *granita*. There's a roof terrace, internet access, and parking at nearby Talete garage. ❸

Palazzo del Sale Via Santa Teresa 25 ⓣ 0931.65.958, Ⓦ www.palazzodelsale.it. Stylish, relaxed B&B in a nineteenth-century salt-merchant's home and warehouse on a quiet street behind Fonte Aretusa. The six spacious rooms have wooden floors, designer beds and intriguing touches such as driftwood-framed mirrors and lamps with palm-bark shades. Breakfasts are superb, and service is unfussy and friendly. Free wi-fi and a PC for guests' use. ❸

Piccolo Hotel Casa Mia Corso Umberto I 112 ⓣ 0931.463.349, Ⓦ www.bbcasamia.it. Halfway between Ortigia and the train station, this friendly, family-run place B&B has clean and quiet rooms, some in Liberty style with grand old antique beds, and all with wi-fi and a/c. There's a terrace where breakfast is served in fair weather. English spoken. ❷

Roma Via Roma 66 ⓣ 0931.465.626, Ⓦ www.hotelromasiracusa.it. A serene four-star oasis in the old centre, the chic Roma presents spacious, contemporary rooms with wood-block floors and excellent bathrooms. Staff are charming, breakfast is an extensive buffet spread, and there's also a fine-dining restaurant, fitness area and sauna. There's more of a resort feel at the sister hotel, *Caiammari* (Ⓦ www .caiammarisiracusa.it), a restored country villa across the bay, with lovely gardens and two pools – a shuttle service runs to and from Siracusa and nearby Arenella beach. ❺

Sorella Luna Via Francesco Crispi 23 ⓣ 0931.449.679, Ⓦ www.sorellalunasrl.it. A step up in quality from the cheap hotels near the train station, this classy three-star, housed in a renovated conventual building, has tasteful modern rooms in bold colours, and offers breakfast on a sunny terrace under a gazebo. There's free street parking right outside. ❷

Hostel

Lol Hostel Via Francesco Crispi 92 ⓣ 0931.465.088, Ⓦ www.lolhostel.com. This smart, modern youth hostel in a converted old *palazzo* is just a few steps down from the train station, with either dorms holding up to ten beds or private singles and doubles, all air-conditioned and with en-suite bathrooms. Reception is 24hr, no membership is required, and there's internet access and the cheapest bike rental in town, plus use of a kitchen. Dorms €20–26, rooms ❷

Campsite

Paradiso del Mare Contrada Gallina Fondolupo, Avola, 22km south of Siracusa ☏ 0931.561.147, ⓦ www.paradisodelmare.it. The best-equipped local campsite lies some way south of town off the SS115, in a small secluded spot under trees and close to a great beach. To get here by public transport, take any bus for Ávola, get off at Ospedale di Maria and walk a couple of kilometres back up the road – or call for a pick-up. Open April–Oct.

Rinaura Località Rinaura, 4km south of Siracusa ☏ 0931.721.224. Very basic campsite – more a couple of fields, really, with little shade. The washing facilities are fine, though, and there are electric hook-ups as well as self-catering bungalows (❶). Take bus #21, #22 or #23 (also #24 or #25 in summer) from Corso Umberto I; it's less than a 10min walk from the stop on the SS115 (signposted to the right after the *Albatros* hotel).

Ortigia

The ancient nucleus of Siracusa, **Ortigia** best conserves the city's essential spirit. Here the artistic vestiges of over 2500 years of history are concentrated in a space barely 500m across, 1km in length and all within an easy stroll through quiet streets and alleys. Although parts of Ortigia were badly neglected in the past, there's been a lot of sensitive restoration and development in recent years, which has helped to restore the old town's lustre.

The Tempio di Apollo and Piazza Archimede

Siracusa announces its long history immediately across the narrow ribbon of water that severs the island from the mainland. The **Tempio di Apollo**, on Largo XXV Luglio, is thought to have been the first of the great Doric temples built in Sicily (seventh-century or early sixth-century BC) and, though not much survives apart from a couple of columns and part of the south wall of its cella, it's a dignified old ruin. A scale model in Siracusa's archeological museum shows you what it looked like in its heyday – the arched window in the wall dates from a Norman church that incorporated part of the temple into its structure.

Ortigia's **market** (Mon–Sat until around 2pm) spreads along nearby Via Trento, with fish and shellfish sold down the parallel Via de Benedictis. The other way, up the shopping street of Corso Matteotti, leads to **Piazza Archimede**, its centre-piece a twentieth-century fountain depicting the nymph Arethusa (the symbol of Ortigia) at the moment of her transformation into a spring. The square is surrounded by restored medieval *palazzi*, while down the skinny Via Montalto you can admire the facade of the **Palazzo Montalto**, graced by immaculate double- and triple-arched windows, and with an inscription dating the build-ing's construction to 1397. This is one of the few surviving examples of the style favoured by the powerful Chiaramonte dynasty.

Piazza del Duomo

Ortigia's most impressive architecture belongs to its Baroque period, and nowhere does this reach such heights as in the city's (some would say Sicily's) loveliest square, the **Piazza del Duomo**. It's been gloriously restored, and the traffic kept out, so that the encircling seventeenth- and eighteenth-century buildings are now seen at their best from the pavement cafés, notably the **Municipio** (corner of Via Minerva) and the **Palazzo Beneventano** opposite. The southern end of the piazza is marked by the late seventeenth-century church of **Santa Lucia alla Badia** (Tues–Sun 11am–1.30pm & 5–7pm), dedicated to the city's patron saint whose statue is carried through town on her festival day (December 13), when the piazza is thronged. Inside the church, you can marvel at one of the city's greatest treasures, Caravaggio's *Burial of St Lucy*, returned to prominence in the church after a long restoration.

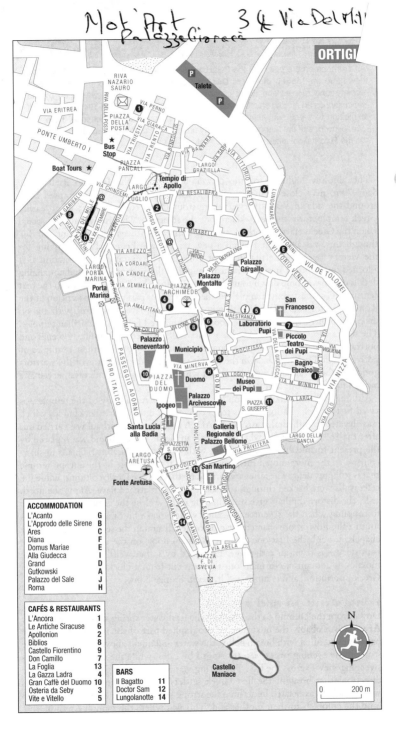

6

Going underground

An entrance on the piazza in the Palazzo Arcivescovile, next to the cathedral, leads down into the **Ipogeo di Piazza Duomo** (Tues–Sat 10am–1pm; €4). This series of underground tunnels and water cisterns, dating back centuries, was used by the *siracusani* as an air-raid shelter during the heavy Allied bombing of 1943, and a small exhibition tells you something of the inhabitants' day-to-day experience. Then you can follow one of the tunnels right the way under the piazza, to emerge by the harbour on the Foro Italico, close to the Fonte Aretusa.

The absolute highlight of the piazza, however, is the **Duomo** itself (daily 8am–7pm, may close earlier in winter), whose great age is first glimpsed from around the side in Via Minerva, where stout Doric columns (part of an earlier Greek temple) form the very skeleton of the structure. The site was already sacred when the Greeks started work on an Ionic temple to Athena here in about 530 BC, though this was abandoned when a new temple was begun in thanksgiving for the victory over the Carthaginians at Himera. The extravagant decoration that adorned this building spread its fame throughout the ancient world, and tantalizing details of it have come down to us through Cicero, who visited Syracuse in the first century BC and listed the temple's former contents as part of his prosecution of the Roman praetor and villain Verres, who appeared to have walked off with a good proportion of them – part of the booty he plundered from many Sicilian temples. The doors were of ivory and gold, and its walls painted with military scenes and portraits of various of Syracuse's tyrants – claimed to be the earliest examples of portraiture in European art. On the temple's roof stood a tall statue of the warrior-goddess Athena carrying a golden shield which, catching the sun's rays, served as a beacon for sailors out at sea.

Although all this rich decoration has vanished, the main body of the temple was saved further despoliation thanks to its conversion into a Christian church, which was elevated to cathedral status in 640 AD. A more drastic overhaul was carried out after the 1693 earthquake, when the Norman facade collapsed and was replaced by the present formidable Baroque front, with statues by Marabitti. This is in sharp contrast to the more muted **interior**, in which it's the frame of the ancient temple that is still prevalent. The aisles are formed by the massive Doric columns, while the cella walls were hacked through to make the present arched nave. Along the north aisle, the distorted pillars give some inkling of how close the entire structure came to toppling when the seventeenth-century earthquake hit Siracusa. The Duomo's south aisle shows more characteristic Baroque effusion in the series of richly ornate chapels, though the first one (nearest the main door, on the right) – actually the baptistery – is from an earlier age. Enlivened by some twelfth-century arabesque mosaics, it contains a Norman font that was cut from a block still marked with a Greek inscription, and is supported by seven bronze lions.

Fonte Aretusa and around

Down from the Duomo to the seafront, the freshwater spring known as the **Fonte Aretusa** is probably the next most photographed part of the island. Planted with papyrus, and filled with bream below the water and ducks above, it's a compulsory stop on the evening *passeggiata*. It's ringed by cafés, while the terrace above offers sweeping views across the bay. The spring was mentioned in the original Delphic directions that brought the first Greek settlers here, and the number of myths with which it's associated underlines the strong sentimental links that continued to bind the colonists to their motherland. This was where the nymph Arethusa rose after swimming across from the Peloponnese, having been metamorphosed into a spring by the goddess Artemis to escape the attentions of the predatory river-god Alpheus; all in vain, though, for the determined Alpheus pursued her here to mingle with her in a watery form. Other legends declared that the spring's water would stain red at the time of the annual sacrifices at the sanctuary of Olympia, and that a cup thrown into the river there would rise here in Ortigia.

The promenade runs both ways from the Fonte Aretusa, south towards the castle and north along the tree-lined Foro Italico (also known as Foro Vittorio Emanuele II) to **Porta Marina**, a fifteenth-century gateway surmounted by a curlicued Spanish heraldic device. The vast, still pool of the **Porto Grande** spreads out beyond, dotted with fishing-boats, liners and tankers, and the odd millionaire's yacht.

Head inland instead, along Via Capodieci, and Siracusa's tradition of architectural hybridism is again apparent in the **Palazzo Bellomo** (Via Capodieci 14), with a courtyard that features thirteenth-century arcading and a Spanish-style stairway leading up to the loggia. The palace is the home of the city's **Galleria Regionale di Palazzo Bellomo** (Tues–Sat 9am–7pm, Sun 9am–1pm; €8), whose treasures include an impressive pair of sixteenth-century sarcophagi – one by Antonello Gagini – and an *Annunciazione* by Antonello da Messina. Just around the corner in Via San Martino, the church of **San Martino** is among Siracusa's oldest. Originally a sixth-century basilica, it was rebuilt in the fourteenth century and smartened up with a good-looking rose window and Gothic doorway. It's usually closed except for ceremonies and concerts, but the dusky interior is a treat – plain stone columns leading to a tiny mosaic half-apse with a fifteenth-century triptych to the right of the choir.

Castello Maniace

The dangling southern limb of Ortigia is entirely taken up by the parade grounds and buildings of the stout **Castello Maniace** (Tues–Sun 10am–1pm; €4), a defensive bulwark erected around 1239 by Frederick II, but named after George Maniakes, the Byzantine admiral who briefly reconquered Syracuse from the Arabs in 1038. Now that the military has moved out, the barracks buildings are used by the university's archeological department, while visitors are allowed to enter through the imposing main gate and wander the echoing halls, chambers and defensive ramparts. Restoration work continues to shore up the neglected castle interior – one of the rooms displays a copy of the famous bronze ram statue, known as *L'Ariete*, a pair of which once guarded the castle gates. The original is now in Palermo's archeological museum.

The Giudecca

Via della Giudecca, off Via Maestranza, recalls Siracusa's old **Jewish quarter**, which existed in the skinny alleys here until the mass expulsion of 1492. The site of the ritual baths has been uncovered on Via G.B. Alagona, underneath the *Alla Giudecca* hotel (no. 52), and there are short guided tours of what's now known as the **Bagno Ebraico** (daily at 11am, noon, 3pm, 4pm, 5pm & 6pm, but visits on Sun afternoons Nov–March must be booked at the hotel; €5). On Via della Giudecca itself, the city's most famous **puppet theatre** company survives – the theatre is at no. 17 (see p.233), but don't miss the tiny **Laboratorio** (Mon–Sat 9.30am–1pm & 4.30–7pm; free), or workshop, down the street at no. 5, where craftsmen create little suits of armour for knights and Saracens, as well as devils and monsters and all the other stage-show paraphernalia. Meanwhile, the **Museo Aretuseo dei Pupi**, on nearby Piazza San Giuseppe (Mon–Sat: June–Aug 10.30am–1pm & 4–6.30pm; Sept, Oct, Dec & March–May 11am–1pm & 4–6pm; €2; Ⓦwww.pupari.com) delves further into the history of puppet theatre in Sicily.

Mainland Siracusa

Modern development in the mainland quarters of Siracusa makes it difficult to picture the ancient city that Plutarch wept over when he heard of its fall to the Romans. Much of the new building dates from after World War II, when Siracusa was bombed twice over – once by the Allies, then, after its capture, by the Luftwaffe in 1943. But even so, some extraordinary relics survive, both in **Achradina**, the nearest mainland quarter to Ortigia, but far more impressively in the northern district of **Neapolis**, where the main archeological park is sited. There's plenty more to see too in **Tyche**, the location of the city's unsurpassed **archeological museum**, while that district in particular is riddled with underground **catacombs**. Regular city buses run to all these places, departing from Riva della Posta on Ortigia or Via Rubino off Corso Umberto I, or you can walk to the museum, catacombs or archeological park in under half an hour from Ortigia.

Achradina

Over the bridges from Ortigia, the main drag of Corso Umberto I runs up to the park area known as the **Foro Siracusano**, once site of the old town's agora. There's not much to see, though the gardens and main street approaches are slowly being restored and improved, so it might become a more pleasant place for a stroll in years to come. On Via Elorina, to the west, the little-visited **Ginnasio Romano** (Mon–Sat 9am–1pm; free) was never actually a gymnasium at all but a small Roman theatre, probably built in the first century AD when the ancient city's much grander Greek theatre was requisitioned for blood sports.

Over on the eastern edge of Achradina, close by the crowded huddle of boats in the Porto Píccolo, you'll find a much less recognizable ruin, the **Arsenale**, by the railway line, which is fenced off to the public. This was a provisions centre, where ships were refurbished, hoisted up from the port by devices that clamped into the ground – and the slots that engaged them are about the only thing to look at here. Adjacent is the **Edificio Termale**, a Byzantine bathhouse claimed to be the very same one in which, in 668 AD, the Emperor Constans was assassinated, knocked on the head by a servant wielding a soap dish. It lies under a modern block of flats, and only a few piles of stones are visible.

Basilica di Santa Lucia

At the northern end of the huge Piazza Santa Lucia (buses #2 and #5 run close by), the church of **Santa Lucia**, built in 1629, supposedly marks the spot where St Lucy, Siracusa's patron saint, was martyred in 304 AD. The church is currently closed for restoration, but when it's open you can view its fine wooden ceiling. You don't need to enter to admire its Norman tower, or, outside in the piazza, Giovanni Verméxio's octagonal chapel of **San Sepolcro**, where the mortal remains of St Lucy were originally preserved before being carried off to Constantinople by the Byzantine admiral Maniakes in 1038, and later shipped to Venice as part of the spoils plundered by the Venetian "crusaders" in 1204.

The main point of a visit, however, is to explore part of the extensive network of **catacombs** lying beneath the site. Tours normally take off at regular intervals during the day, but until church and catacombs are reopened following the restoration work, prebooked visits to the catacombs can be arranged by calling ℡0931.64.694 or asking at the catacombs under the Basilica di San Giovanni (see p.228).

Santuario della Madonna delle Lácrime and Museo del Papiro

The gargantuan **Santuario della Madonna delle Lácrime** (daily 7am–1pm & 3–8pm; bus #1 or #4), fronting Viale Teócrito, dominates the skyline on most approaches to Siracusa. It was completed in 1994 to house a statue of the Madonna that allegedly wept for five days in 1953 (*delle Lácrime* means "of the tears"), and the church was apparently designed to resemble a giant teardrop (it actually resembles one of Tracy Island's missing Thunderbirds). As you can't sink a spade into the ground in Siracusa without turning up a relic or two, it came as no surprise during the building work to discover the extensive remains of **Greek and Roman houses** and streets, which are fenced off but visible just to the south in Piazza della Vittoria.

Across the main Viale Teócrito from the church, next to the archeological museum grounds, the small **Museo del Papiro** (Tues–Sun 9am–1pm; free) is worth a visit to see papyrus art, ancient and modern, including models of boats and even sandals made of the stuff. Ever since papyrus was introduced to Siracusa in the reign of Hieron II, there's been a thriving papyrus industry here, and gift shops on Ortigia are awash with it.

Museo Archeologico

If you have any interest at all in the archeological finds made in this extraordinary city, then all roads lead to Siracusa's **Museo Archeologico**, on Viale Teócrito (Tues–Sat 9am–7pm, Sun 9am–1pm; last entry 1hr before closing; €8; bus #1 or #4). It was purpose-built for Sicily's most wide-ranging collection of antiquities, and it's certainly worth seeing, though there are caveats. It's often extremely confusing to find your way around, with notes in English either nonexistent or mind-numbingly detailed and academic, and to cap it all sections are sometimes closed as continuing renovations attempt to address its organizational shortcomings. The museum is basically split into four sections: prehistoric (section A); items from Syracuse, Megara Hyblaea and the Chalcidinian colonies (B); finds from Gela, Agrigento, Syracuse's subcolonies and the indigenous Sikel centres (C); and Greek and Roman Siracusa (D).

It's section D that's the easiest to understand, where Siracusa in the **Greek and Roman age** is laid bare in an extraordinary series of tomb finds and public statues, none more celebrated than the statue of **Venus Anadiomene**, also known as *Landolina*, after the archeologist who discovered her in 1804. *Anadiomene* means "rising from the sea", which describes her coy pose: with her left hand she holds a robe, while studs show where her broken-off right arm came across to hide her breasts. Probably Roman-made in the first century AD, from a Greek model, the headless statue has always evoked extreme responses, alternately exalting the delicacy and naturalism of the carving, and condemning her knowing sensual attitude that symbolized the decline of the vigorous classical age and the birth of a new decadence. By the statue's feet, the dolphin, Aphrodite's emblem, is the only sign that this was a goddess. Of the tomb finds, pride of place is given to the superb **Sarcófago di Adelfia**, a finely worked fourth-century marble tomb found in the catacombs below San Giovanni. It held the wife of a Roman official, the couple prominently depicted and surrounded by reliefs of scenes from the Old and New Testaments.

Elsewhere, eyes will possibly glaze over at the thousands of pottery shards, burial urns, amphorae, statues, figures and temple fragments. However, **section B** does at least put many of the finds into context, showing where excavations occurred in the city, and even reconstructing useful models of the fallen temples. Among the earlier Hellenic pieces, the museum has some excellent **kouroi** – toned, muscular youths, one of which, from Lentini, is one of the most outstanding fragments still extant from the Archaic age of Greek art – around 500 BC. A striking image from the colony of Megara Hyblaea dates from the same period: a **mother/goddess suckling twins**, its absorbed roundness expressing a tender harmony as close to earth and fertility rites as the *Venus Landolina* is to the cult of sensuality.

The catacombs at Basilica di San Giovanni

Close to the museum lies the most extensive series of catacombs in the city, their presence explained by the Roman prohibition on Christian burial within the city limits (Siracusa having by then shrunk back to its original core of Ortigia). They lie below the ruined **Basilica di San Giovanni** (daily 9.30am–12.30pm & 2.30–5.30pm; €6) off Via San Sebastiano. Fronted by a triple arch, most of the church was toppled in the 1693 earthquake and the nave is now open to the sky, but you can still admire the seventh-century apse and a medieval rose window. This was once the city's cathedral, built over the crypt of St Marcian, first bishop of Siracusa, who was flogged to death in 254.

The tours (departing every 30min) take you down into the crypt to see Marcian's tomb, the remnants of some Byzantine frescoes and an altar that marks the spot where St Paul is supposed to have preached, when he stopped in the city as a prisoner on his way to Rome. Then you're led into the catacombs themselves, labyrinthine warrens hewn out of the rock, though often following the course of underground aqueducts, disused since Greek times. Numerous side-passages lead off from the main gallery (decumanus maximus), often culminating in rotonde, or round caverns used for prayer; other passages are forbiddingly dark and closed off to the public. Entire families were interred in the thousands of niches hollowed out of these walls and floors, anxious for burial close to the tomb of St Marcian. Most of the treasures buried with the bodies have been pillaged, though the robbers overlooked one – an ornate Roman-era sarcophagus unearthed from just below the floor in 1872 and now on show in the archeological museum.

Parco Archeologico della Neapolis

Siracusa's **Parco Archeologico** (daily 9am–2hr before sunset; €10) encompasses the classical city district that was Neapolis. This contained most of the ancient city's social and religious amenities – theatres, altars and sanctuaries – and was thus never inhabited, though these days it's in danger of disappearing under the sheer weight of visitors. The ticket office is hidden beyond a street market of souvenir stalls and ice-cream stands, catering to the busloads of tourists that arrive every few minutes in the summer. Many buses run right past the approach road to the site, including #1, #3, #6, #8, #10, #11 and #12, but basically you can catch anything that goes up Corso Gelone and Viale Teracati/Viale Teócrito.

From the ticket office, you ascend to the **Teatro Greco**, Siracusa's most spectacular monument. One of the largest and best-preserved Greek auditoriums anywhere, its site has been home to a theatre since at least the fifth century BC, though it was frequently added to at different periods. Hieron II expanded it to accommodate 15,000 people, in nine sections of 59 rows (of which 42 remain). The inscriptions around the top of the middle gangway on the west side of the theatre – faint but still visible – date from the third century BC, giving the names of the ruler and his family, with Zeus Olympios in the middle. Most of the

Hear hear

The Orecchio di Dionisio cave owes its name to the painter Caravaggio, who first noted its striking resemblance to a human ear. However, the association with Dionysius derives from a much older story that the tyrant used the cavern's acoustic qualities to overhear the conversations of suspected conspirators – prisoners were routinely kept in the city's high-walled quarries, which made a perfect jail. In fact, Dionysius probably had far more efficient means of extracting information, though the sound-enhancing effect is still there and can be tested by anyone.

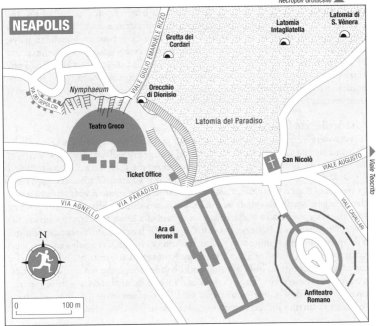

alterations carried out by the Romans were made to adapt the arena for gladiatorial combat, and they also installed some marble-faced seats for privileged spectators, while the seventeenth row was removed, possibly to segregate the classes. The high terrace above the theatre contains the **Nymphaeum**, a large artificial grotto (fed by water from an ancient aqueduct) where a number of statues were found. To the left of here, the overgrown **Via dei Sepolcri** (Street of the Tombs) is deeply rutted by the carts that plied to and fro, and is flanked by more votive niches.

At the ticket office, another path descends to the largest of Siracusa's huge *latomie* (pits or quarries), from which the rock for the city's multifarious monuments was excavated. Now planted with citrus, oleander and bay trees, the so-called **Latomia del Paradiso** is more garden than quarry, and a steady stream of tour parties troops down mainly to see the remarkable ear-shaped cavern known as the **Orecchio di Dionisio** (Ear of Dionysius), which is over 60m long and 20m high. A second cave, the **Grotta dei Cordari**, was used by the ancient city's ropemakers, who found that its damp air prevented rope strands from breaking under stress. However, this and the other two neighbouring quarries remain closed indefinitely to visitors, and most of the garden paths are blocked off, which makes the overrun Latomia del Paradiso a bit of a disappointment – the Cappuccini quarries (see p.230) are far more exciting to visit.

On your way to the ticket office, you'll have passed the ruined base of the **Ara di Ierone II** (no public access), a 200m-long altar erected by Hieron II in the second half of the third century BC. It commemorated the achievements of Timoleon, who liberated the city from tyranny and decline, and was the biggest construction of its kind in all Magna Graecia. It was also the venue for some serious sacrificing: Diodorus records that 450 bulls were led up the ramps at either end of the altar to be slaughtered in the annual feast. Nearby, there's also a separate entrance to the

Anfiteatro Romano (show your park ticket), a large elliptical arena built in the third century AD to satisfy the growing lust for circus games. The rectangular tank in the centre of the arena is too small to have been used for aquatic displays, and is more likely to have been for draining the blood and gore spilled in the course of the combats. But not before the spectators had had their fill: at the end of the contests the infirm, ill and disabled would attempt to suck warm blood from the bodies and take the livers from the animals, in the belief that this would speed their recovery.

Latomie dei Cappuccini

If you were disappointed by the quarries at the archeological park, you'll be charmed by the **Latomie dei Cappuccini** (Mon–Fri 9.30am–1pm, last entry at 12.15pm; €2), gouged out of the hillside below the Cappuccini monastery and *Grand Hotel Villa Politi* in the north of the city. Bus #5 from Via Rubino runs right to the gates (Largo Latomia), and it's a nice idea to combine a visit with lunch at the excellent *Jonico* restaurant (see p.232). Known since at least the sixth century BC, the wide, vertically walled quarries provided a harsh but effective prison for the 7000 Athenian prisoners of war following the fiasco of the Great Expedition. The quarries were acquired by Capuchin monks in the sixteenth century, who turned them into both market garden and contemplative retreat, which is why the cavern floors are so lush. Sinuous paths wind through the overgrown quarries, past natural rock pillars, huge caverns and early Christian tombs – there's even a cavern-theatre down here, sometimes used for performances – and as you delve further and further in, the city noise and traffic slowly dissipates.

Epipolae and the Castello Eurialo

The outlying area of **Epipolae**, 7km west of the city, was the site of ancient Siracusa's military and defensive works. It's a twenty-minute ride on bus #11 or #25 to the village of **Belvedere**, which you can pick up from Corso Gelone and outside the Parco Archeologico.

These heights were first fortified by Dionysius the Elder in about 400 BC, and subsequently modified and extended over a couple of centuries. What remains today consists of a great wall, which marked the city's western limit, and the **Castello Eurialo** (daily: April–Oct 9am–7pm; Nov–March 9am–5pm; €4), just before the village on the right. This is the major extant Greek fortification in the Mediterranean, most of it dating from Hieron II's time, when Archimedes, as his General of Ordnance, must have been actively involved in its renovation. Despite the effort and ingenuity that went into making this site impregnable, the castle has no very glorious history: ignored altogether by the attacking Carthaginians, it surrendered without a fight to the Roman forces of Marcellus in 212 BC.

Assailants had to cope with three defensive trenches, designed to keep the new artillery of the time at bay, as well as siege-engines and battering rams. The first of the trenches (approached from the west, where you come in) lay just within range of catapults mounted on the five towers of the castle's keep, while in the trench below the keep you can see the high piers supporting the drawbridge that once crossed it. Long galleries burrow beneath the walls into the keep, serving as supply and escape routes, and also enabling the defenders to clear out by night the material thrown in by attackers during the day.

Behind the keep is a long, wedge-shaped fortification, to the north of which is the main gateway to the western quarter of the city. This, the **Epipolae gate**, was built indented from the walls, allowing the defenders to shower attackers with missiles, and is reminiscent of the main gate at Tyndaris, a city that shared

A river cruise along the Fiume Ciane

Just southwest of the city, the source of the **Fiume Ciane** (Ciane River) forms a pool said to have been created by the tears of the nymph Cyane when her mistress Persephone was abducted into the underworld by Hades. The pool and the river banks are overgrown by thickets of papyrus, apparently the gift of Ptolemy Philadelphus of Egypt to Hieron II, making this the only place outside North Africa where the plant grows wild. **Boat cruises** operate between early March and November from the bridge over the Ciane, about a 5km signposted drive from Siracusa on the SS115, or take bus #21, #22 or #23 from Via Rubino. There are daily departures between 10am and 6pm, with tickets costing around €10 per person (minimum three people); call ☏346.159.9635 or 368.729.6040 for information. As well as the river, you'll also see the scant but evocative remains of the **Olympieion**, or Tempio di Giove Olimpico, a Doric temple built in the first half of the sixth century BC. The hillock the ruin stands on, a vital strategic point in classical times, was often occupied by Siracusa's enemies when the city was under attack. The pestilential air of the Lysimelia marshes below saved the day on more than one occasion, infecting the hostile armies with malaria.

the same architects. The longest of the underground passages surfaces here stretches 180m from the defensive trenches. From the gate, you can stroll along Dionysius' extensive walls, looking down over the oil refineries and tankers off the coast north of the city, and back over Siracusa itself, with Ortigia clearly visible pointing out into the sea.

Local beaches

You can **swim and sunbathe** from Ortigia off Largo della Gancia, where there are rocks, wooden decks and handy nearby bars, or from the paying beach below the Talete car park, where sunloungers and parasols are available. On the mainland, you'll find more congenial spots if you head north along Riviera Dionisio il Grande, or south at **Isola**, on the far side of Porto Grande – reachable in summer by ferry from the port.

Further north of Siracusa, much of the coast has been contaminated by noxious chemicals, but there are popular swimming spots south at **Arenella** (bus #23 from Via Rubino), mostly consisting of private lidos where you have to pay to use the sandy beach, but there are also rocky stretches to the south where the inlets create clear pools that are good for snorkelling. You can walk to these easily enough from Arenella, or else take bus #21 to **Ognina**, a small fishing port and marina, and walk back a little way. **Fontane Bianche**, 20km south of Siracusa (buses #21 or #22; 30min journey), is another very popular spot with the locals, with a wide arc of sand ringed by hotels, bars and restaurants. There's one free public beach here (signposted *spiaggia libera*, near the car park), but all the others are private lidos.

Eating, drinking and entertainment

Ortigia holds the city's best array of **cafés and restaurants**, most within a short walk of each other. Prices are on the high side for Sicily, though there are few nicer places to sit outside in a medieval street or courtyard and while the evening away. Ortigia also has excellent **bars** – from Italian-style pubs to cocktail joints – and most of the late-night action is concentrated on the streets and alleys near the Fonte Aretusa, particularly around Piazzetta San Rocco and along Lungomare Alfeo. Siracusa is one of the easiest places to catch a traditional Sicilian **puppet theatre** performance, though the best-known cultural entertainments on offer are the open-air classical **Greek dramas**, performed every May and June in the Teatro Greco. Focusing on contemporary music and performance art, the **Ortigia Festival** in September (Ⓦwww.ortigiafestival.it) has lapsed, though may be revived.

Cafés

Le Antiche Siracuse Via della Maestranza 2. Corsino's of Palazzolo Acréide has been making sweets and pastries since 1889, and their outlet in Siracusa – an old-school "*gran caffè*" of mirrors and gleaming counters – stocks a fine range, along with famous ice cream, and has an associated deli-gift shop and a restaurant-pizzeria.

Biblios Via del Consiglio Regionale 11. Locals drop into this relaxing bookshop café more to drink coffee than buy books. Closed Wed morning & Sun morning, all day Sun July–Sept.

Gran Caffè del Duomo Piazza del Duomo 18. The best view in the finest square in Sicily – and, most amazingly of all, prices for drinks and snacks that are entirely reasonable.

Restaurants

L'Ancora di Giancarlo Russo Via Perno 7 Ⓣ0931.462.369. The best of the restaurants near the market has a breezy outdoor terrace, so it's a good place for an *al fresco* lunch. There's a long list of pasta dishes with seafood (mussels, clams, sea urchins, anchovies and breadcrumbs etc), while mains are the day's catch, with most dishes priced at around €10–12. Closed Mon.

🏃 **Apollonion** Via Campisi 18 Ⓣ0931.483.362 or 349.535.4189. You'll feast on some of the best seafood in town at this simple family-run eatery, though there's no menu. Instead, you'll be pampered with a succession of superbly prepared dishes – from such starters as a mix of sardines, swordfish and shrimps in olive oil to mussels in a garlicky broth, baked langoustines and *fritto misto*, served with delicious rustic bread – all for €35 (there's also a €20 option at lunchtime). Booking recommended. Closed Wed.

Castello Fiorentino Via del Crocifisso 6 Ⓣ0931.21.097. The finest pizzas in the city centre – people queue out of the door waiting for tables. It's really good value, and the in-your-face waiters and general mayhem at peak times are all part of the charm. Pizzas are €3–9, other dishes – pastas, seafood and meat – €7–10. Closed Mon.

Don Camillo Via della Maestranza 96 Ⓣ0931.67.133, Ⓦwww.ristorantedoncamillo siracusa.it. If locals want to impress visitors, they bring them to this refined restaurant in the fifteenth-century vaults of a former convent. The fish is fantastically fresh, and the restaurant emphasizes its more unusual Sicilian specialities, like pasta with tuna, mint and tomatoes or a whole fish baked inside a crust of golden bread. It also has Siracusa's finest wine cellar. Prices are high, around €15 for pastas and €20 for mains, and there's a tasting menu for €55. Closed Sun, also part of Feb, July & Aug.

🏃 **La Foglia** Via Capodieci 21 Ⓣ0931.66.233, Ⓦwww.lafoglia.it. The city's most idiosyncratic eatery, from the antique shop-art gallery furnishings to the hippy-chic tableware and place settings. It's actually quite romantic, and a very laid-back place to sample Mediterranean and vegetarian cooking, from rustic soups and home-made ravioli to veggie platters or fish *matalotta* (with tomatoes, onions, capers and olives). You'll pay €12–15 for most dishes, up to around €22 for seafood.

🏃 **La Gazza Ladra** Via Cavour 8 Ⓣ340.060.2428. Most of the restaurants around Via Cavour are very similar, but the "thieving magpie" tries to do things a little differently. The friendly family-run *osteria* has just eight tables and concentrates on authentic Sicilian cuisine with a homestyle touch, using staple ingredients like courgettes, aubergines, tuna, capers, olives, mint and oregano to great effect in their *antipasto* platters and pasta dishes. Mains of fish (mostly fish) are chalked on the board. A full meal will cost you around €25, or you can just drop in for a salad, panino and a drink. Closed Mon and all July & Aug.

🏃 **Jonico** Riviera Dionisio II Grande 194 Ⓣ0931.65.540. A fixture since the 1970s, the rustic Jonico is perched on crags above the sea near the Cappuccini quarries, in the north of the city. Though the menu is written entirely in Sicilian, the owner speaks enough English to guide you through the specialities – say gnocchi with swordfish, wild fennel, pink peppercorns and cherry tomatoes, or spaghetti with dried breadcrumbs, olive oil and parsley, followed by swordfish *involtini* or the grilled fish of the day. It's a bit of a slog from town, but very worthwhile, and a full meal should cost €35–40. Take bus #2 or #3 from Ortigia to Largo Latomia, from where it's a 2min walk, or take a taxi. Closed Tues except June–Sept.

Osteria da Seby Via Mirabella 21 Ⓣ348.926.9114. An exceptional *távola calda* that offers a fabulous selection of grilled vegetables, oven-baked pasta, fish and meat dishes, and home-made cakes at rock-bottom prices. By day it is self-service and takeaway, and you eat on trays with disposable

Shopping in Siracusa

Siracusa's daily **market** (Via Trento, not Sun) offers the usual fruit, veg, meat and fish alongside vendors flogging bead jewellery, sunglasses, big pants and cheap clothes. The biggest concentration of **souvenir stands** in the city is outside the gates of the archeological park, where you can buy typical Sicilian gifts like puppets, ceramics, cowboy hats and Manchester United football shirts. For better, more authentic stuff you can look in the **gift and craft shops** down Via Cavour and around the Fonte Aretusa, where there are some rather good places among the tourist dross. Fish House (Via Cavour 29) is a funky craft gallery offering ceramic fish and driftwood sculpture, while at Sete d'Incanto (Via Roma 27) the owner-artist is inspired by Ortigia's architectural forms and natural elements to produce her hand-painted silk scarves and wall-hangings. At Galleria Bellomo (Via Capodieci 15) you can learn something about the traditional **papyrus** industry in Siracusa – prices here range from a few euros to a few hundred. For designer and high-street **clothes**, most of the best shops and boutiques are down Corso Matteotti.

knives and forks, but in the evening they get out the tablecloths, crockery and cutlery and operate as a trattoria at prices that are still hard to beat – around €25 for a full meal. Closed Mon.

Vite e Vitello Piazza F. Corpaci 1, at Via della Maestranza ☎0931.464.269. A Sicilian steakhouse that's the place for grilled meat (steak, pork, sausages, lamb), plus the best home-made chips in the city. You can expect to pay around €25 for a full meal. There's shaded outdoor seating opposite San Francesco church. Closed Sun and part of Feb & July.

Bars

Il Bagatto Piazza San Giuseppe 1. A cracking little pub, with beat-up wooden tables inside and out, and Belgian and German beers on draught.

Doctor Sam Piazzetta San Rocco 4. The little square is at the hub of Ortigia's night-scene and this funky bar is a popular hangout.

Lungolanotte Lungomare Alfeo. Modish wine bar and restaurant, magnificently sited overlooking the harbour.

Puppet theatre

Piccolo Teatro dei Pupi Via della Giudecca 17 ☎0931.465.540, ⓦwww.pupari.com. Traditional puppet shows by the Vaccaro-Mauceri family, Siracusa's puppeteers, are held at least twice weekly March–October (twice daily in Aug, also daily late Dec to early Jan) in their thriving theatre. You can check up-to-date schedules on the website; behind-the-scenes tours and special shows take place throughout the year. Tickets from €7.50.

Greek dramas

Istituto Nazionale del Dramma Antico (INDA) Palazzo Greco, Corso Matteotti 29 ☎800.542.644 or 0931.487.200, ⓦwww.indafondazione.org. Classical Greek drama is performed each year (May and June, usually Tues–Sun from around 6.30pm) at the Teatro Greco in the Parco Archeologico. It's a real spectacle, though performances are in Italian only. Tickets range from €26 to €62, with cheaper last-minute tickets available for some performances. Get details on the INDA website or from Siracusa's tourist offices; tickets are available at the INDA box office or online.

Listings

Boat trips Ortigia Tours ☎368.317.0711, ⓦwww.ortigiatour.com, offers daily cruises around the city's harbours and local coastline. Boats leave from near the bridge on Ortigia (from 9am in summer, 10am, weather permitting, in winter), and trips last an hour or so; tickets €10 per person. In summer, a kiosk on the quayside provides tickets and information.

Buses All buses depart from Corso Umberto I, near the train station. AST ☎0931.462.711,

ⓦwww.aziendasicilianatrasporti.it (for Augusta, Ávola, Lentini, Catania, Cómiso, Íspica, Módica, Noto, Palazzolo Acréide, Ragusa, Sortino and Vittoria); Interbus ☎0931.66.710, ⓦwww.interbus.it (for Ávola, Catania, Noto, Pachino and Palermo).

Hospital Ospedale Umberto I, Via Testaferrata, near Madonna delle Lacrime church ☎0931.724.111; for the 24hr accident and emergency service call ☎0931.724.285.

Internet Libreria Gabo, Corso Matteotti 38 (daily 9.30am–1pm & 4.30–8pm, opens 10.30am Sun); Chat Internet Point, Via dei Mille 29 (summer daily 9.30am–1pm & 4.30–8pm, winter Mon–Fri 6–8pm, Sat 9.30am–1pm & 4.30–8pm. There's free wi-fi on Piazza del Duomo: apply with a passport at the Municipio (9am–2pm).

Pharmacies Farmacia Centrale, Via Maestranza 42 ☏ 0931.65.320; and Gibiino, Via Roma 81 ☏ 0931.65.760. Outside normal working hours, pharmacies open on a rota system that's posted outside, also available at ⓦ www.comune.siracusa.it.

Police For police, call ☏ 0931.495.111. There's a Carabinieri post in Piazza San Giuseppe, Ortigia ☏ 0931.441.344. Call ☏ 112 in an emergency.

Post office Main post office, Piazza delle Poste 15, Ortigia (Mon–Fri 8am–6.30pm, Sat 8am–12.30pm).

Taxis Ranks in Piazza Pancali ☏ 0931.60.980 and at the train station ☏ 0931.69.722.

Tours Bocca di Fuoco Travel, Via XX Settembre 27 ☏ 0931.483.681, ⓦ www.boccadifuocotravel.com, and Triquetra, Via Roma 10 ☏ 0931.746.855, ⓦ www.triquetraviaggi.net, offer a range of city and regional tours, cultural events and outdoor activities.

Trains The main routes are to Catania and Messina, with a change for Palermo. Other services are to Módica, Noto and Ragusa. Timetables are available on ⓦ www.ferroviedellostato.it.

Augusta and Megara Hyblaea

The coast north of Siracusa, the **Golfo di Augusta**, sports one of the largest concentrations of chemical plants in Europe. This mammoth industrial zone employs one-tenth of the local population, and fills the air with acrid fumes and the sea with chemicals. Hardly surprisingly, it figures on no holiday itineraries, though the industrial port of **AUGUSTA** – half an hour by train or bus from Siracusa – does at least offer the compensation of a handsome, if crumbling, Baroque centre. Despite the town's superficial resemblance to Siracusa – its old centre detached from the mainland on its own islet, surrounded by two harbours – the port has never attained the same importance and didn't even exist until 1232. Frederick II, who founded Augusta, characteristically stamped his own personality on it in the form of a castle (no public access), though everything else of the medieval town was destroyed by the 1693 earthquake. The Villa Comunale below the castle is a shady public garden, on both sides of which are views out to sea, on one side over the port and tankers, on the other to the headland. A few blocks down the main Via Príncipe Umberto, a piazza holds the eighteenth-century Duomo and a solemn Palazzo Comunale, its facade crowned by Frederick II's imperial eagle.

There are a couple of small resorts to the north of Augusta, at **Monte Tauro** and **Brúcoli**, though how tempted you'll be to swim anywhere around here is questionable. Far better for drivers is the short trip out to see the extensive (and well-signposted) remains of **MEGARA HYBLAEA** (daily: June–Sept 9am–7pm; Oct–May 9am–1hr before sunset; last entry 1hr before closing; €4), considered to be the most complete model of an Archaic city still surviving. It prospered as a Greek colony after the Sikel king of Hybla had granted land alongside his own to Greeks from Megara (near Athens). By the middle of the seventh century BC, the population had done so well out of trade and their high-quality pottery that they were able to found some minor colonies of their own, including Selinus in the west, though their city was eventually submerged by Syracusan ambitions and destroyed by Gelon in 482 BC. The town flourished again later in the fourth century BC, but was finally levelled by the Romans in the same avenging campaign that ended Syracuse's independence in 214 BC. Most of the ruins belong to the fourth-century revival, but the fortifications were erected a century later, interrupted by the Romans' arrival. Various buildings lie confusingly scattered over a wide area, though all the finds are in Siracusa's Museo Archeologico.

Pantálica and around

PANTÁLICA, Sicily's greatest **necropolis**, lies in the folds of the Monti Iblei, around 40km northwest of Siracusa. Here, in the deep gorge of the River Ánapo, you can follow tracks past several thousand tombs hollowed out of the valley sides at five separate locations. Several skeletons were found in each tomb, suggesting that a few thousand people once lived in what is now largely a craggy wilderness. This extraordinary location, a UNESCO World Heritage Site, is hard to see by public transport. Drivers, however, will find it an easy and well-signposted diversion en route to either Ragusa or Catania. The approaches are from the small towns of **Sortino** or **Ferla**, at either end of the gorge, with parking at various points near both places. The northern necropolis, approached via Sortino, makes the most dramatic introduction to the area.

The site (always open; free) was first used between the thirteenth and the tenth century BC by Sikel refugees from the coast. After the eighth century BC, it is thought to have been the location of the city of **Hybla**, whose king invited Megarian Greeks to colonize Megara Hyblaea; remains from this era are visible, but all pale into insignificance in contrast with the five thousand or so tombs hewn out of the gorge below. In some were found the traces of several separate skeletons, probably of the same family, while others show evidence of habitation – though much later, when the Syracusans themselves were forced to flee inland from barbarian incursions. The atmosphere is primeval and almost sinister – for Vincent Cronin, even something terrifying: "Here is Sicily of the stone age, intent on nothing higher than the taking of food and the burial of its dead." For Cronin, the free play of nature in this ravine embodied Sicily's own particular contribution to the man-made wonders bestowed later by the island's conquerors, and as such – symbolized by a honeycomb he came across in one of the caves – the object of the quest described in his book, *The Golden Honeycomb* (1954).

The road ends at a parking area at the entrance to the **northern necropolis**, 6km from Sortino (follow the signs). An obvious but rocky path leads around a plateau, then down to the river and up the other side (where there's another parking area, but this time accessed from Ferla – the road was originally planned to span the gorge, but never completed). You'll soon see the **tombs**, first just dotting the walls of the valley in clusters and finally puncturing the whole vertical cliff face – this last view is about 1km, or a thirty-minute walk, from the parking area. There are superb views from the higher reaches, and the path and rock-cut steps remain good all the way.

You can continue down across the river and up the other side of the gorge, where the road begins again and runs west to Ferla, another 9km beyond. This is the upper road to Ferla, with a parking area allowing access to the foundations of the **Anaktoron**, or prince's palace, a building from ancient Hybla, and to the **southern necropolis**, where more rock tombs are visible. A lower road from Ferla has another parking area, from where you can stroll easily along the bottom of the gorge for a while.

Sortino and Ferla

Both Sortino (1hr 15min) and Ferla (1hr 35min) are linked to Siracusa by bus (not Sun), though neither is really close enough to the gorge to make a day-trip feasible. **SORTINO** is a busy, rather sprawling little town, but other than stopping for a quick coffee there's no reason to linger. **FERLA** is much prettier, with a stately church or two and a pleasingly restored square on the long, sloping main street. It has a good pizzeria/trattoria, *Dell'Arco*, off Piazza San Sebastiano at Via Arco

Lantieri 5, and there are also a couple of local B&Bs, one, *La Ginestra*, centrally located at Via Vittorio Emanuele 8 (℡0931.879.442 or 338.312.6885, ⓦwww .bblaginestra.it; no credit cards; ❶), with simple rooms and a roof terrace. You can also stay within the Pantálica natural reserve itself, at *Il Giardino di Pantálica* (℡095.712.2680, ⓦwww.pantalica.it; no credit cards; ❷), an *agriturismo* on an estate with one- and two-bedroomed apartments and a summer swimming pool.

Palazzolo Acréide

Set on a hill some 40km west of Siracusa, **PALAZZOLO ACRÉIDE** is a mainly Baroque town with one of the most interesting of the province's classical sites lying just outside the modern settlement. It's a good excursion, or would make a rather quiet overnight stop, somewhat stranded from the main road and rail links across the province.

AST buses from Siracusa pull up in Palazzolo's main square, **Piazza del Pópolo**. This is the heart of the Baroque town, two sides dominated by the handsome church of San Sebastiano and the gleaming town hall. From here lanes radiate down past opulent facades, hidden courtyards and gargoyled balconies, eventually leading to a trio of fine Baroque churches, the Chiesa Madre, San Paolo and the Annunziata. But the main focus of interest – at least for anyone curious about the roots of Sicilian culture – is the **Casa-Museo di Antonino Uccello** (daily 9am–1pm & 2.30–7pm; free), tucked away in an old house at Via Machiavelli 19. The fruit of one man's thirty-year obsession to preserve the traditions of rural Sicily, it constitutes an important documentation of folk art, showing trousseaux, ceramics, olive presses, puppets, reconstructions of houses and stables, and anything else judged by Uccello to be in danger of extinction.

There's a **tourist office** on Piazza del Pópolo (daily 9am–1pm & 3–7pm, 4–8pm in summer; ℡0931.472.181).

Accommodation

Fattoria Giannavi Contrada Giannavi ☎0931.881.776, ⒲www.fattoriagiannavi.it. A farm with rooms, pool and a restaurant serving home-grown, home-cooked food (meals €12 or €25). It's set high on a bluff with extensive views, 8km from Palazzolo on the Giarratana/Ragusa road (10min drive). Camping also available here. ❷

Santoro Via San Sebastiano 21 ☎0931.883.855, ⒲www.hotelsantoro.com. The town centre's main hotel, just below Piazza del Pópolo, is a simple place, but has a/c, minibars and internet access. No credit cards. ❷

Eating

Il Portico Via Orologio 6 ☎0931.881.532. Dining in this grandly renovated old *palazzo* is something of an occasion, with painted ceilings, period furnishings and such dishes as fresh pasta and grilled meats on the menu. Pizzas are €4–10, all other dishes are €7–15, and tasting menus are €35 and €40. Closed Tues.

Lo Scrigno dei Sapori Via Maddalena 50 ☎0931.882.941. A great spot for a lunch or more substantial dinner, where the inventive menu is strong on meats, for example ravioli with a hare and nut sauce, pork with a pistachio crust, stuffed rabbit, and lamb's ribs, all at reasonable prices. There are pizzas in the evening too. Closed Mon.

Akrai: the ancient city

The **Zona Archeológica** (daily: summer 9am–7pm; winter 9am–5pm; €4) is a twenty-minute walk up from the town centre, or you can park close to the entrance. The first inland colony of Siracusa, **Akrai** thrived during the peace and security that characterized Hieron II's reign during the third century BC. It declined under the Romans, but later re-emerged as an important early Christian centre (as shown by the number of rock-cut tombs in the area), only to be eventually destroyed by the Arabs.

Of the visible remains, the most complete is the small **Teatro Greco**, built towards the end of Hieron's reign. A perfect semicircle, the theatre held six hundred people and retains traces of its scene-building. Behind the theatre to the right is a small **senate-house**, or bouleuterion, a rectangular construction that was originally covered. Beyond lies a 200m stretch of decumanus that once connected the two gates of the city. Crossed at regular intervals by junctions and paved in lava rock, it's in better condition than many of the more recent roads in the area.

Other remains give little impression of their former grandeur. You'll have a job identifying the excavated Roman **Tempio di Persefone**, above the theatre, an unusually round chamber that was formerly covered by a cupola. Equally fragmentary is the much older **Tempio di Afrodite**, sixth- or fifth-century BC, lying at the head of what was the agora. From here you can look straight down into one of the two quarries from which the stone to build the city was taken. Later they were converted into Christian burial chambers, and in the first of them, the **Intagliata**, you can plainly see the recesses in the walls: some of them catacombs, others areas of worship, the rest simply rude dwellings cut in the Byzantine era. The narrower, deeper quarry below it, the **Intagliatella**, holds more votive niches and a relief cut from the rock-face, over 2m long, that combines a typically Greek scene – heroes banqueting – with a Roman one of heroes offering sacrifice. It's thought to date from the first century BC.

There are more niches and chambers in a lower quarry, the **Templi Ferali**, though you'll have to ask the custodian to let you see this, along with the much more interesting **Santoni** further down (a 15min walk from the site). These twelve rock-cut sculptures (carved no later than the third century BC) represent the fertility goddess Cybele, a predominantly eastern deity whose origins are steeped in mystery. There's no other example of so rich a complex relating to her worship, and the local name tagged to these sculptures – *santoni*, or "great saints" – suggests that the awe attached to them survived until relatively recently. To be sure of viewing them, however, you should telephone the day before (𝕋0931.876.602) to make sure staff are available to accompany you, otherwise they are kept locked up.

Noto

The exquisite town of **NOTO** represents the apogee of the wholesale renovation that took place following the cataclysm of 1693, a monument to the achievement of a few architects and planners whose vision coincided with the golden age of Baroque architecture. Although a town called Noto, or Netum, has existed in this area for centuries, what you see today is in effect a "New Town", conceived as a triumphant symbol of renewal. The fragile Iblean limestone used in its construction was grievously damaged by modern pollution, but years of restoration work have gradually shaken off the grime and most of the harmonious buildings have regained their original honey-hued facades. Some characterful B&B accommodation, and traffic-free old-town streets that are at their most charming as the lights come on at dusk, make this one of the island's essential stopovers.

Some history

Noto was flattened on January 11, 1693, and a week later its rebuilding was entrusted to a Sicilian-Spanish aristocrat, **Giuseppe Lanza, Duke of Camastra**, on the strength of his work at the town of Santo Stéfano di Camastra, on the Tyrrhenian coast. Lanza visited the ruins, saw nothing but "*un montón de piedras abandonadas*" (a mountain of forsaken rocks), and quickly decided to start afresh, on a new site 16km to the south. In fact, the ruins weren't abandoned; the city's battered population was already improvising a shantytown, and even held a referendum when Lanza's intentions became known, rejecting the call to relocate their city. But partly motivated by the prestige of the undertaking, partly by the need to refurbish the area's defences, Lanza ignored the local feeling, even pulling down their new constructions and the old town's remaining church.

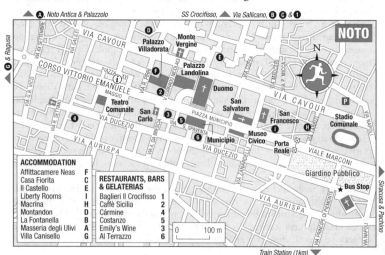

Among the ruins of Noto Antica

Until finally abandoned in 1693, the original town of Noto had several times been a significant historical stronghold: one of the few Sicilian towns to resist the looting of the Roman praetor Verres, it was also the last bastion of Arab Sicily before the Norman conquest of the island. Only sparse remnants of the old town survive, but **Noto Antica** makes a fascinating side-trip nonetheless. It's 16km northwest of Noto, signposted from the western end of the Corso in town (there's no bus) – the turn-off to the site is also that for the convent of Santa Maria delle Scale, with Noto Antica another 5km past the convent. You park outside the surviving gate of the castle (occupied from the eleventh to the seventeenth century), where renovation work has rebuilt some of the circular tower. Early Christian catacombs honeycomb the rock beneath the tumbled walls that line the valley cliff. An unsurfaced country lane pushes on through the castle gate past the now-puzzling, completely overgrown remains of an abandoned city – square-cut stone blocks, shattered arches, bramble-covered courtyards and crumbling walls. If you come out here, you might as well plan the day to take in the Cava Grande canyon too (see p.242), which is only another twenty minutes' drive away – back past the convent to the main road, turn left and look for the signposted right turn.

With the help of the Flemish military engineer Carlos de Grunemburg, Lanza devised a revolutionary new **plan**, based on two gridded sections that were to be almost completely separated from each other – a lower area for the political and religious establishment, the upper town for the people. The best **architects** were to be used: Vincenzo Sinatra, Paolo Labisi and the master craftsman Rosario Gagliardi – not innovators, but men whose enthusiasm and experience enabled them to concoct a graceful synthesis of the latest architectural skills and forms. Their collaboration was so complete that it's still difficult to ascribe some buildings to any one person. Within an astonishingly short time the work was completed: a new city, planned with the accent on symmetry and visual harmony, from its simple street plan to the lissom figures adorning its buildings. It's easily the most successful post-earthquake creation and, for a time, in the mid-nineteenth century, the new Noto replaced Siracusa as the region's provincial capital.

Arrival and information

Noto is 32km southwest of Siracusa. **Buses** stop at the Giardino Púbblico at the eastern end of town, close to the Porta Reale; the **train station** is a good ten to fifteen minutes' walk away down Via Príncipe di Piemonte, and has no facilities – not even a bench – and is often unstaffed. If you have luggage, you may need a **taxi** (☎0931.838.713 or 338.945.8206). Traffic through town is all one-way and while it's easy enough to drive in (follow "centro" signs) or out (destinations are all well signposted), finding a particular spot while driving can be difficult. The best advice is to park first (there's a free waste-ground car park behind the stadium, among others) and get your bearings. Many hotels and B&Bs are signposted through town as well.

There's a well-informed **tourist office** in Piazza XVI Maggio, behind the Hercules fountain (summer Mon–Sat and most Sundays 9am–1pm & 4–8pm, winter Mon–Fri 9am–1pm & 3–7pm; ☎0931.573.779, ⓦwww.comune.noto .sr.it), which has a full list of accommodation. For **tours and excursions**, contact Allakatalla, Corso Vittorio Emanuele 47 (☎0931.574.080, ⓦwww.allakatalla.it) – they also and **rent bikes** and **scooters**.

Accommodation

While **accommodation** is plentiful in Noto, it's worth booking ahead in July and August, when you can expect prices to be at their highest. Even B&Bs charge up to €100 a double in the high summer.

Hotels and B&Bs

Affittacamere Neas Via Rocco Pirri 57,
☎320.238.9548, ⓦwww.affittacamerenoto.it. Five simple, spic-and-span rooms with en-suite bathroom, a/c, fridge and TV in a Baroque *palazzo* just up from the Loggia dei Mercanti, and a hop-and-a-skip from the main Corso. Breakfast is currently at a nearby bar, but more rooms and a breakfast area/internet point are in the pipeline. ❶–❷

Casa Fiorita Via Príncipe Umberto 47,
☎0931/571.576 or 320.113.3813. Run by the easy-going family who own *La Foglia* restaurant in Siracusa, Casa Fiorita has two comfortable mini-apartments (with kitchen), another bedroom (without kitchen) and a two-room apartment with live-in kitchen, all in a pretty eighteenth-century house in the higher town. ❷

La Fontanella Via Rosolino Pilo 3 ☎0931.894.724, ⓦwww.albergolafontanella.it. Thirteen rooms in a sympathetically restored nineteenth-century *palazzo* on a busy road on the northern edge of Noto Alta. It's a three-star place, and the only hotel (rather than B&B) within walking distance of the centre (10min), but there's no restaurant. Parking for once is easy around here. ❷

Liberty Rooms Via Francesco Ferruccio, corner of Corso Vittorio Emanuele ☎338.230.4042, ⓦwww.villacatera.com. This beautiful Art Nouveau "palazzetto" on Noto's central Corso has gracious rooms furnished with antiques. A kitchen and a huge roof terrace on which to eat mean there's no need to dine out. ❷–❸

Macrina Vico Grillo, corner of Via Fabrizi
☎0931.837.202, ⓦwww.b-bmacrina.com. Family-run B&B in a neighbourly street, with three spacious and airy rooms, each with its own terrace. There's also a huge walled garden with a couple of swings plus use of a barbecue, making this a good choice if you have kids. The small breakfast terrace is useful if you want to rustle up a snack or aperitivo. ❷

Masseria degli Ulivi 12km north of Noto, SS287 ☎0931.813.019, ⓦwww.masseriadegliulivi.com. If you prefer country living, this estate deep in the countryside fits the bill. It's been beautifully restored using traditional materials, and there's a good restaurant, plus an outdoor pool under the olive trees. Closed Dec–March. ❸–❹

Montandon Via A. Sofia 50
☎0931.836.389 or 339.524.4607,
ⓦwww.b-bmontandon.com. A real gem, this B&B in a grand *palazzo* in the higher town has three huge rooms, each with its own terrace. Guests have access to an enchanting garden (with swings), which makes a welcome summer retreat from heat and crowds. The owner is a marvellous host, and serves outstanding breakfasts, including eggs, local ricotta, salami, ham, pastries, fruit and home-made jams. ❷

Villa Canisello Via Cesare Pavese 1
☎0931.835.793, ⓦwww.villacanisello.it. An old farmhouse on the western outskirts of town in a quiet residential suburb; rooms open to a patio or terrace, and there's parking. Signs lead you right there from the western end of the Corso – it seems like a bit of a slog, but it's actually only a 10min walk to the centre. Closed Nov–Easter. ❷

Hostel

Il Castello Via Fratelli Bandiera 2,
ⓦwww.notobarocca.com/ostello. Youth hostel housed in a converted *palazzo* in the upper part of town with wonderful views, large dormitories, excellent showers and laundry service. It's accessible from the centre in a few minutes up signposted steps from Via Cavour, behind the Duomo. Beds in dorms €15, in family rooms €18.50.

The Town

From the public gardens on the eastern side of town, the centre of Noto is approached through the monumental **Porta Reale**, built in 1838 and topped by the three symbols of the town's allegiance to the Bourbon monarchy: a dog, a tower and a pelican (respectively, loyalty, strength and sacrifice). The main **Corso Vittorio Emanuele**, running from here through the heart of the lower, patricians' quarter, is lined with some of Sicily's most captivating buildings. Now the traffic's kept out you can stand back and admire them at will, while floodlights, many set into the pavement, show them off to glorious effect at night.

Halfway along, **Piazza del Municipio** forms the dramatic centrepiece of the design, with the imposing twin-towered **Duomo** magnificently restored following the dramatic collapse of its dome in 1996. First completed in 1776, it's said to have been inspired by models of Borromini's churches in Rome – the story of its reconstruction, and some of the Duomo's treasures, are on display around the back of the cathedral (entrance on Via Cavour; usually open 10am–1pm & 5–7pm). The church piazza is bordered by gleaming, restored buildings that look now as they must have done when first built, including the **Palazzo Ducezio** (or Municipio, the Town Hall) opposite, presenting a lovely, convex front of columns and long stone balconies.

The next street west of the Duomo, the steep Via C. Nicolaci, culminates in the elliptical **Monte Vergine** church. It's a perfectly framed view that's enhanced during the annual **Infiorata** flower festival (third weekend of May), when flower petals are laid up the entire street in a swirl of intricate designs. **Palazzo Villadorata**, the palace that flanks the west side of the street, also makes rather an unusual, not to say eccentric, sight. Onto a strictly classical front six extravagant balconies were grafted, supported by the last word in sculpted buttresses – griffins, galloping horses and bald and bearded figures with fat-cheeked cherubs at their bellies. The *palazzo* is currently closed to the public, though it may be open for guided visits – ask at the tourist office. Back on the Corso, at the bottom of Via Nicolaci, there are panoramic views from the top of the belltower of the church of **San Carlo** (daily 9am–1pm & 3.30–7.30pm; €1.50).

The Corso sweeps on to Piazza XVI Maggio, with the tourist office on one side and Noto's **Teatro Comunale** on the other (concert season is Oct–May). A €3 combined ticket lets you into the richly decorated theatre auditorium, as well as the so-called "Hall of Mirrors" in the Municipio with its splendid trompe l'oeil ceiling, and the **Museo Civico**'s collection (closed Mon) of contemporary art on the Corso – the archeological and natural historical collections have been locked away for years in a Siracusan warehouse pending renovation of the rest of the building. Opening hours for all vary, and the theatre and town hall are sometimes closed for rehearsals and events, but the tourist office can tell you the latest.

Finally, it's well worth leaving the Corso to explore the upper part of town, where few tourists tread. It's filled with massive monastic houses and the dwellings of Noto's poorer eighteenth-century citizens, who had their own church, Gagliardi's **Santíssimo Crocifisso**, in Piazza Mazzini. The elegant former monastery of **San Tommaso**, which flanks the square, is now a prison of all things, its cell bars screened by opaque glass windows.

Eating, drinking and entertainment

Although there are surprisingly few **restaurants** in the centre of Noto, you'll be able to ring t e changes over a couple of days, and prices are pretty reasonable. The cafés along the Corso come into their own during the evening *passeggiata*, while the local authorities put on a full range of **concerts and events** throughout the year, from religious processions at Easter to summer music festivals.

Baglieri Il Crocifisso Via Príncipe Umberto 46, ☎0931.571151. Nationally recognised trattoria using seasonal local ingredients in ways that make the taste-buds zing: spaghetti with prawns and wild asparagus, rabbit in *agrodolce* with orange blossom honey, greens, celery, carrots and peppers, and tuna in a pistachio and sesame crust (all €12–14).

Caffè Sicilia Corso Vittorio Emanuele 125. You really shouldn't leave Noto without sampling the ice creams at both of its two rival prize-winning *gelaterie*. The *Sicilia* is the more radical, with flavours such as lemon and saffron, and even basil. Closed Mon.

Cármine Via Ducezio 1 ☎0931.838.705. Locals recommend this trattoria for a good meal at low cost and it's certainly pretty remarkable value, with rustic *antipasto* and pasta dishes running at €5–6, grilled fish from around €9, and a mixed grill at €11. The downside? It's too brightly lit, the house wine is challenging to say the least and the interconnected rooms get very busy, but it defines perfectly the phrase "cheap and cheerful". Closed Mon.

Costanzo Via Silvio Spaventa 7–11. A well-known *pasticceria* and *gelateria*, known for producing what may be the best ice cream in Italy (the other contender is *Sicilia*) in flavours such as mandarin, ricotta, jasmine and rose (depending on the season), as well as sweets and pastries, including dreamy *cassata*. Closed Wed.

Emily's Wine Corso Vittorio Emanuele 70 ☎0931.838.028. A nice place for a glass of good wine and tasty snacks such as *crostini* with ricotta and honey, an unctuous *caponata*, local cheeses and hams. They also have a range of lentil and pulse soups to eat in or take away and heat up at home – useful if you have an apartment.

Al Terrazzo Via A. Baccarini 4–6 ☎0931.839.710. The place for pizza (both at lunch and in the evenings) in the centre, just behind the Municipio, with sheltered outdoor picnic-style tables raked down the sloping street.

Ávola and the Cava Grande

Around 15km northeast of Noto, on the Siracusa road, the agricultural town of **ÁVOLA** also has an old Baroque centre, though in this instance partly reconstructed on a hexagonal design after earthquake damage. An idea of its erstwhile proportions can be gleaned in the huge central Piazza Umberto I, which together with the long main Corso Vittorio Emanuele is lined with gracious *palazzi*. Regular buses and trains come here from Noto (the bus drops you closer to the main piazza), but it hardly warrants a special trip, and you're more likely to call in if you're driving. Glinting in the distance is the seaside settlement of **Ávola Marina**, 2km to the east, where even out of season you'll be able to find somewhere open for lunch. However, the best trip is up into the hills above Ávola to the Cava Grande.

Cava Grande del Fiume Cassíbile

A spectacular winding route northwest of Ávola climbs past the Convento di Ávola Vecchia to the magnificent gorge and nature reserve of the **Cava Grande**. That's about a 15km drive, or you can also approach from Noto up the SS287, past the turn-off for Noto Antica, in which case you can return *down* the switchbacks instead towards Ávola. There's parking by a sensational viewpoint over the Cassíbile River gorge, which really is quite Grand Canyon-esque, with sheer rock walls visible across the divide, birds of prey circling, and the river glistening far below. The very steep path that leads down to the valley bottom is closed at times of high fire risk, and an information booth posts dire warnings of the dangers of the descent. You certainly need to be properly shod, fit enough to climb back out, and to carry plenty of water. The round trip requires a good three hours, plus any time you spend splashing in the natural swimming pools or following the footpath alongside the river, which runs for most of the gorge's 11km length. At the top, at the parking area, you can get a drink or a meal from a rustic tavern, the *Trattoria Cava Grande*.

The coastal route to the cape

South of Noto and Ávola lies the most undeveloped stretch of coast on the east side of the island, sheltering some excellent sand beaches and an extensive nature reserve. Minor roads run all the way south to the **Capo delle Correnti**, the southernmost point of Sicily, while in between a couple of old restored fishing villages serve as small-scale summer resorts. Just inland, the country town of

Pachino stands in the middle of a thriving market-garden region, the fields given over to greenhouses and polytunnels sheltering tomatoes, strawberries and artichokes – the small Pachino cherry tomatoes, particularly, are a staple on local restaurant menus. With a car, you can see the whole of the coast from Noto in a day, as far as the cape and back, though there are also several good rural **accommodation** options. **Buses** operated by Caruso (☏ 0931.836.123) run from Noto to the nearest bit of coast at Noto Marina, and there's also a regular year-round service from Siracusa/Noto to Pachino.

Noto Marina, Eloro and the Riserva Naturale di Vendicari

Noto's local beach, 5km southeast at **NOTO MARINA** (also called Lido di Noto), is fine for a swim and a bite to eat (in summer at least). You can walk from here (though it's easier to drive) just south to the seaside ruins of Helorus, or **Eloro** (Mon–Sat 9am–1.30pm; free), a Syracusan colony founded in the seventh century BC at the mouth of the Tellaro River. It's all a bit ramshackle, and the few remains are quite difficult to make head or tail of, but its position right above the shore is very attractive. The broad expanse of sand below offers good swimming, but direct access is tricky from the site: a road to the south, across the river, leads directly to the beach.

A few kilometres further south down the main Pachino road (SP19), a signposted turn leads to the excellent **Riserva Naturale di Vendicari** (daily: summer 7am–8pm, winter 7am–6.30pm; free entry but parking €2.50; ⓦ www .oasivendicari.net), which protects the local marshes, lagoons, dunes and disused saltpans from future development. There's parking at the entrance, but no other facilities; you can get the Pachino bus to drop you on the main road and walk the short distance to the reserve. Loads of waterbirds can be seen from the hides, including herons, cranes, black storks and even pelicans, though the more than three hundred flamingos can be elusive at times, while sandy tracks and boardwalks fan out north and south through the marshland, leading to some splendid sand crescents. The reserve takes its name from the brick tower, the Torre Vendícari, which looms over a part-restored *tonnara* (tuna-fishing village) by one of the beaches. Its internal courtyards and sandstone pillars gleam brightly against a turquoise sea. Another good beach, signposted **San Lorenzo**, lies just a short drive further south of the reserve, down the main Pachino road, and has very clear water and a small summer lido.

Accommodation and eating

Al Casale dei Mori Fattoria Villa Rosa, Corso da Falconara, Noto Marina ☏ 0931.812.909, ⓦ www.alcasaledeimori.com. Comfortable *agriturismo* with 21 rooms (two with cooking facilities), housed in an enchanting creeper-covered eighteenth-century farmhouse with beautiful grounds. There's a swimming pool suitable for children, a playground and excellent home-cooking in its restaurant (open to all). The farm's rabbits, chickens and goats can all be visited. Half board obligatory July & Aug at €75–100 per person. ❸

Il Roveto Contrada Roveto-Vendicari ☏ 0931.66.024, ⓦ www.roveto.it. This beautifully restored old farmhouse is signposted at the Riserva Naturale turn-off on the SP19 Pachino road. Self-contained apartments with kitchen sleep either two, four or six people, and you're only a few hundred metres from the pristine Torre Vendícari beach. Three-night minimum stay. ❷

Pachino, Marzamemi and the cape

All roads locally zero in on the area's main town, **PACHINO**, which can get pretty lively in summer but slumbers through the winter. A minor road (and local buses) runs 4km out to the coast at **MARZAMEMI**, prettily set around a crescent harbour backed by the port's old *tonnara*. The village is still renowned for its tuna dishes, and is home to a **film festival** in late July (ⓦwww.cinemadifrontiera.it), showing international contemporary and vintage films in open-air venues. Behind the shell of a church and *palazzo*, the restored *tonnara* square shelters bars and restaurants that come into their own in high summer, when tourists descend on the village in droves.

Eight kilometres south of Marzamemi, down the rugged coastal road, **PORTOPALO DI CAPO PÁSSERO** is another low-key summer resort, again with a ruined *tonnara*, and also with several bars along the main street, a **campsite**, *Camping Capo Pássero* (☎0931.842.333), and three or four reasonable hotels, though none that stands out. You might be able to persuade someone to row you over to the little islet that lies just offshore, complete with a seventeenth-century castle. Otherwise, follow the minor cape road out to the southeastern point of **Isola delle Correnti** (the tiny islet just off the cape, linked to it at low tide), where another **campsite** sits in happy isolation behind its own unspoiled sandy bay, *Camping Captain* (☎0931.842.595, ⓦwww.camping captain.it). You're on the southernmost tip of Sicily here, with nothing between you and Africa.

Íspica and the Cava d'Íspica

Inland at **ÍSPICA**, 18km southeast of Módica, human settlement can be traced back 4000 years, to the cave dwellings and tombs carved out of the wide gorge of the **Cava d'Íspica**. These were later used by generations of Sikels, Greeks and early Christians to bury their dead, while during medieval times a strong fortified castle, town and churches were built on the rocky bluff above the southern section of the gorge. Then, in 1693, disaster struck, as the great quake levelled thousands of years of habitation in one swift blow. A new town was rebuilt on the neighbouring hill, which is where modern Íspica thrives today – a rather sprawling place set around a central kernel of restored squares and Baroque churches. The major interest, however, remains in the nearby gorge, signposted "Parco Forza" on the way into town from either Módica or Siracusa. There's parking at the gates to the **Parco Archeologico della Forza** (Mon–Sat 9am–1hr before sunset, Sun 9am–1.15pm; free) – or you can walk there easily enough from the town centre, where a path leads up to a viewing point over the gorge. More paths wind steeply down, past the broken remains of palaces and churches and into the southern section of the gorge itself, where caves were used as houses, storerooms, stables, workshops and cemeteries, right up until 1693. A separate path from the parking area leads to the church of Santa Maria La Cava, cut into the rock and dating back to the very earliest days of Christianity in Sicily – some medieval frescoes can be seen inside.

While there's no great reason to dally in Íspica itself – nearby Módica or Noto make much more pleasant overnight stops – you can get lunch in the central Piazza Regina Margherita (where it's usually easy to park). The *Barone Francesco* (T0932.951.054; closed Mon) serves an inexpensive menu of *antipasto* platters, pasta and grills, plus pizza in the evenings.

Cava d'Íspica Nord

The Íspica gorge actually runs for 13km northwest (towards Módica), with rock-cut dwellings and tombs lining the entire route. It's possible to walk through the gorge, starting either at Íspica or at the northern section, the **Cava d'Íspica Nord** (April–Oct daily 9am–1hr before sunset; Nov–March Mon–Sat 9am–1.30pm; €4), which is around 7km east of Módica (no public transport). There's a direct road route from Módica, while a sign on the main SS115, roughly halfway between Módica and Íspica, points you 6km up a minor road to the site. From the entrance (where there's a café), a landscaped path descends into the gorge, where towering fronds of bamboo and wild fennel grow amid the fig, pomegranate and walnut trees. There are catacombs immediately below the site entrance, while the path meanders back through the site past tombs and dwellings cut into the cliff face. The walking path through the gorge starts on the other side of the road from the entrance, running under the road bridge.

Módica

The small but busy town of **MÓDICA**, 17km northwest of Íspica and 18km south of Ragusa, is another in the region that is enjoying a new lease of life as a select tourist destination, based again on its remarkable late-Baroque heritage. A powerful medieval base of the Chiaramonte family, and later the Cabreras, it was once far more important than Ragusa itself, though ironically, following the reconstruction after 1693 (which has earned it UNESCO World Heritage status) it never regained its erstwhile prestige.

Arrival and information

Regional **buses** drop you right in Módica's centre on Corso Umberto I; the **train station** is a good ten-minute walk away at the other end of town – head to the ornamental fountain at Piazza Rizone and bear left for the Corso. Drivers can **park** on the street, but in most central areas you need to buy a parking voucher (from *tabacchi* to put in your window (charges apply Mon–Sat 9am–1pm & 4.30–8pm; €0.60 per hour). Note also that if you're going to the Cava d'Íspica, you can drive directly to the northern section closest to Módica (there's a brown sign at the ornamental fountain) – you don't need to take the main road to Íspica itself.

The **tourist office** is at Corso Umberto I 149 (currently undergoing reorganization, so contact the *Comune* for latest information at T0932.759.634, Wwww .comune.modica.gov.it).

Accommodation

Módica holds a good selection of quality **hotels** and **B&Bs**, many located in fine *palazzi* and old buildings in the upper town.

Casa Talía Via Exaudinos 1 ☎0932.752.075,
Ⓦwww.casatalia.it. Occupying a cluster of restored
houses in what was once Módica's Jewish ghetto,
Casa Talía is far removed from the bustle of the city
centre, yet just five minutes' walk down a series
of steps and alleyways from the main Corso. A
garden planted with fruit trees adds to the feeling
of seclusion. Rooms, designed by the architect
owners who live on-site, are stylish and practical,
and breakfasts are excellent (freshly squeezed
juices, home-made cakes, jams and breads),
served in a nook-and-crannied whitewashed room
occupying what were once caves used as a cistern
and stables. ④

L'Orangerie Vico de Naro 5 ☎0932.754.703
or 347.067.4698, Ⓦwww.lorangerie.it. Tranquil,
refined B&B with three huge suites (with kitchens)
and four spacious rooms, in a *palazzo* with frescoed
ceilings and private flower-filled terraces. ④

Palazzo Il Cavaliere Corso Umberto I 259
☎0932.947.219, Ⓦwww.palazzoilcavaliere.it.
A down-to-earth aristocratic family run their
eighteenth-century palace as a B&B. The setting is
splendid and authentic – original Caltagirone tiled
floors, frescoed ceilings and antique furniture, and
three of the eight rooms open on to a courtyard. ②

Palazzo Failla Via Blandini 5 ☎0932.941.059,
Ⓦwww.palazzofailla.it. This handsome upper-town
palace by the Santa Teresa church, reborn as a
comfortable four-star hotel, has just seven rooms,
and retains its intimate, aristocratic feel. Rooms
are elegant and traditional, with tiled floors, high,
frescoed ceilings and antique beds. There are also
three contemporary minimalist rooms in an annexe
across the road by the trattoria *La Locanda del
Colonello*, also owned by the hotel. This and the
smarter *La Gazza Ladra* restaurant, on the ground
floor of the main *palazzo*, are reviewed opposite.
Check the website for good last-minute deals. ③

I Tetti di Siciliando Via Cannata 24
☎0932.942.843, Ⓦwww.siciliando.it. Simple,
friendly and unpretentious hotel popular with
budget travellers in the tangle of historic streets
above Corso Umberto I. Rooms are pretty basic,
but it's very reasonably priced and sociable. The
owners are very helpful, and have rental bikes
(€15 per day) and can help organize bike tours of
the surrounding area. Look for the sign opposite
the Agip petrol station towards the top of the Corso
(where you'll have to park), and follow the steps up
around the passageway for the signposted "bed,
bike and breakfast". ①

The upper and lower towns

Módica's upper and lower towns are divided by the long main drag of **Corso
Umberto I** – which originally was a river until a flood of 1902 prompted the
authorities to cover it over. The Corso is flanked by a run of handsome *palazzi*,
whose balconies are buttressed by gargoyles, twisted heads and beasts, while its
churches make grandiose Baroque statements of intent. That of **San Pietro**, for
example, has a wide flight of steps framing the life-sized statues of the Twelve
Apostles. However, it's the warren-like upper town of **Módica Alta** where true
genius lies, in the shape of the magnificent eighteenth-century facade of **San
Giorgio**, a worthy rival to the church of the same name in Ragusa Ibla. It's thought

Sicily's chocolate city

Mention Módica to most Italians and they'll think chocolate. The great Sicilian writer
Leonardo Sciascia declared that "Modican chocolate is unparalleled … tasting it is
like reaching the archetype, the absolute … chocolate produced elsewhere, even the
most celebrated, is an adulteration, a corruption of the original." In fact, the chocolate
sold here is unlike most other chocolate you'll have encountered, from its **grainy,
crunchy texture** to the undertones of cinnamon, orange, vanilla, honey, almonds
and even salt and pepper. You can sample it in a myriad of ways, from ice cream
to Módica's famous **hot chocolate**, but it's most readily available in the traditional
chocolate bar format available from numerous shops in the town. Above all, seek out
Sicily's oldest chocolate manufacturer, the **Antica Dolceria Bonajuto**, up an alley
at Corso Umberto I 159 (Ⓦwww.bonajuto.it), which has been making the stuff since
1880. The shop's a beauty, filled with old display cabinets, and you can sample from
dainty little tasting dishes on the counter before you buy.

that architect Rosario Gagliardi was responsible for this, too: the elliptical facade is topped by his trademark, a belfry, while the approach is characteristically daring – twin flights of stairs zigzag up across the upper town's hairpins, ending in a terrace before the church. From here, and from the tight streets above San Giorgio, you can look back over the grey-tiled roofs and balconies of the town, built up two sides of a narrow valley. There are more views from the remains of the **castle** and its clocktower, which perches on a rocky spur above the main part of town. The local civic collections, from archeology to art, are in the **Museo Civico** on the Corso by the tourist office (Tues–Sun 10am–1pm & 4–7pm; €3).

There's really not much more to Módica – a night would do it full justice – but it is an enjoyable place to visit. There's interest enough in simply strolling the Corso and window-shopping in the boutiques, fancy shoe shops, enotecas and gourmet delis.

Eating and drinking

You'll be spoiled for choice with Módica's fine crop of **restaurants**, and it also has more classy cafés and *pasticcerie* than is seemly for a place of its size.

Borgo Antico Via Pozzo Barone 30 ☎0932.942.423. Family-run place with seats inside and out, and a daily changing menu of home-made pasta and fresh seafood. Dishes may include spaghetti with sea-urchin, and marinated raw fish, but it all depends on the catch of the day. There are tasting menus at €30 and €35, but you can get away with €20 if you limit yourself to two courses. To get here, turn right at the end of Corso Umberto I and follow signs up steps to the left. Closed Mon.

Fattoria delle Torri Vico Napolitano 14 ☎0932.751.286. This is the one everyone talks about in town – a highly regarded restaurant for choice local dishes and an extensive Sicilian wine list. While not exactly economical, it's a memorable gastronomic experience for which booking is advised. It's off the Corso, across from Piazza Matteotti. Closed Sun eve & Mon.

Gargantua Corso Umberto I 261 ☎0932.752.927. The dishes on offer here are more bistro-style than at most other places in town, and are available in a choice of fixed-priced menus (€16–22). You might start with a soufflé of ricotta and *funghi porcini*, perhaps followed by lamb chops or sausage, but the menu changes constantly as the fare is strictly seasonal. Closed Sun eve & Mon.

La Gazza Ladra Via Blandini 5 ☎0932.755.655. Top-class restaurant at the same address as the *Palazzo Failla* hotel, offering creative and exquisitely presented Sicilian cuisine such as spaghetti with anchovies, candied orange, wild fennel flowers and chilli, and fillet of Nébrodi mountain pork with a cream of pine nuts and asparagus. Mains are €22 and tasting menus are €65 and €78 a head excluding drinks. Closed Sun eve & Mon.

La Locanda del Colonnello Vico Biscari 6 ☎0932.752.423. The traditional style of this restaurant, with chequered tiled walls, cantilevered white vaults and evocative photos of old Módica, is counterbalanced by heavy linen napery and efficient service. The mixed *antipasto* (€9) is highly recommended, which includes sardine *polpettine* with wild fennel, a crisp *scacce* (savoury pastry) with a reduced tomato filling, and pepper- and fennel-seed-studded salami. *Primi* are all €8, and make great use of legumes in dishes such as *maccu* (a traditional fava bean purée/soup) and pasta with chickpeas. *Secondi* (€8–9) include sausages and *pancetta* in a stickily reduced tomato sauce.

Osteria dei Sapori Perduti Corso Umberto I 228–30 ☎0932.944.247. Marvellous value, right on the Corso, where you can dine (inside or out) on traditional rustic dishes with a strong emphasis on beans and pulses. The mixed *antipasto* is a good way to start, followed by *lolli con le fave* (hand-made pasta with fava bean purée) or pasta with broth and meatballs. *Secondi* include tripe, grilled meat and pork in tomato sauce. The menu is in Sicilian, but translations are available, and prices are heart-warmingly low.

Taverna Nicastro Via Sant'Antonino 30 ☎0932.945.884. For traditional meat (and especially pork) dishes, try this delightfully old-fashioned and very reasonably priced trattoria with tables outside on a flight of steps in the upper part of the old town. Specialities include sausages and salamis made on the premises, ricotta-filled ravioli in a meaty tomato sauce, rabbit, and stewed lamb. You could eat a four-course meal (including a *cannolo* or a lemon, cinnamon or almond jelly) for under €20, while a carafe of house wine is just €4. The restaurant is signposted from outside San Giorgio, but it's quite a walk, and you may need to seek further directions. Evenings only, closed Sun & Mon.

Scicli

Ten kilometres south of Módica, **SCICLI** is dramatically pitched against the bottom of a knobbly limestone bluff. Like southeast Sicily's other Baroque towns, it has seen quite a restoration in recent years, most strikingly on the main **Piazza Italia** and the pedestrianized **Via Mormina Penna** – a scenographer's dream of a street, lined with exuberant and painstakingly-restored Baroque churches and *palazzi*, including the Municipio fronted by a marvellous sculptural staircase and a small bandstand.

Just off Piazza Italia is one of Scicli's Baroque showpieces, the **Palazzo Beneventano**, complete with spectacularly grotesque grinning faces with lolling tongues and bald heads tucked under the balconies and clinging to the walls. Beyond the *palazzo*, the voluptuously curvy Baroque church of **San Bartolomeo** stands embraced by the towering limestone gorge. Walking on, you'll find yourself in the honeycomb of the old town, clamped to the sides of the gorge, with dwellings at times almost indistinguishable from the natural caves. Although it has a fair number of abandoned houses, the area is by no means deserted, and several of the buildings are now undergoing restoration.

Continuing up the stepped path above Palazzo Beneventano, you can enjoy grand views over Scicli from the terrace of the abandoned church of **San Matteo**. Just below the church, a further stepped path (signposted "Chiesa S. Lucia") leads to the remains of another church; at the top of the ridge here, you're standing right above a series of abandoned **cave-dwellings** that litter the hills around, used from Neolithic times until fairly recently. From the vantage point you can make out bricked-up entrances, caves and doorways in the tree-dotted cliffs below.

Scicli is spiritual home to the **Gruppo di Scicli** group of contemporary artists (Ⓦwww.ilgruppodiscicli.it) – rated by Renato Guttuso no less – whose works can be seen on the walls of the *Hotel Novecento* (see opposite) and at the *Tecnica Mista* gallery on Corso Mazzini, the main drag. Focus of the town's cultural life is *Chiaroscuro*, Via Aleardi 20 (opposite *Hotel Novecento*), a space for exhibitions and arts workshops, with some great music events in the evenings.

Practicalities

Scicli is an easy stop by car en route to or from Módica or Ragusa, and there are buses and trains from either place. The **tourist office** is in Palazzo Spadaro, Via Mormina Penna (Mon–Fri 8am–2pm, also Tues & Thurs 3–6pm; ℡0932.839.608, Ⓦwww.comune.scicli.rg.it). Cafés ring the main piazza, a few restaurants are signposted here and there, and there's even an elegant boutique hotel.

Accommodation

Conte Ruggero Piazza Italia 24 ℡0932.931.840, Ⓦwww.conteruggero.it. Smart old B&B in a restored palace on the main square, fine for a night or two. The spacious rooms have a/c, and some have minibars and balconies. ❷

Puzzling plaques

Intrigued by the plaques that appear in various spots throughout the Siracusa and Ragusa area, featuring a portrait of a bald man, architectural notes, strange quotations and photographs of crime scenes? The explanation is that Italy's most popular TV crime series *Montalbano*, based on books penned by Antonio Camilleri (see Books, p.400), is filmed in the area, especially Scicli itself, which stands for the town of Vigata in the books and TV series.

Food and wine in Sicily

Sicilian cuisine has been described as "the field on which all other cuisines give battle to each other", and dining on the island is like a journey back through history, from the wine and olives that came with the Greek, to the rice, saffron and cinnamon of the Arabs and the meat dishes inherited from Norman and Hohenstaufen invaders. Far from conflicting, these elements coalesce and harmonize, to the point where a good dinner becomes a multicultural experience.

▶▶ There is a full menu reader on pp.409–416.

Fish at Catania's Pescheria ▲

Fishmonger, Siracusa market ▼

Sicilian cuisine

While Italian food and wine are prized the world over, visitors soon learn that there's no such thing as Italian cuisine. Each region has its own specialities, and while Sicilian cooking may lack some of the sophistication of northern Italy, it's often simpler, healthier and cheaper. Even within Sicily, dishes have their own specific provenance. "Locally-sourced ingredients" – an increasingly common boast in countries where food is an industry rather than a life-affirming experience – are taken for granted, and the island's diverse culinary traditions and ingredients are always best sampled on their home turf. So look out for dishes that make the most of pistachios when travelling in the foothills of Etna, walnuts when you're around Agrigento, capers when you're in the offshore islands, and seafood everywhere there's a fishing harbour.

Markets of plenty

"In Baghdad, Valencia or Palermo, a market is more than a market ... it's a vision, a dream, a mirage."

Leonardo Sciascia

All year round, something is always being harvested, fermented, cured or sun-dried somewhere on the fertile island of Sicily. The best place to find what's in season is the local **food market**. Every town, village and neighbourhood has one, either as a constant fixture or a once-a-week affair. In the most famous, the teeming souqs of Palermo and Catania, tables groan under precarious mountains of olives, wedges of glistening fish, slabs of raw meat, lavish boxes of fruit and vegetables of every shape and hue. But the Sicilian market is about much more than food: it's a stage of operatic ardour, sometimes raucous, congested and exhausting, but forever riveting as spectacle and performance.

Fruit market in Siracusa ▼

On the menu

Starters

Any restaurant worth its salt will offer an abundant table of beautifully presented *antipasti*. Typical elements include cold meats and salamis, marinaded anchovies, octopus in various forms, garlic mushrooms, grilled artichokes, aubergines and peppers, and olives flavoured with herbs.

More than any other dish, though, it's pasta – eaten instead of or in addition to *antipasti* – that's the emblem of local pride. Typical in and around Palermo is pasta *con le sarde*, with a rich sauce of sardines, wild fennel, raisins and pine nuts. Spaghetti *alla Norma*, with aubergines, is a speciality of Catania, and in Trápani pasta comes with a pesto-type mix of tomatoes, garlic, basil and almonds.

Main courses

In a land where vegetarianism is still a distant rumour, meat and fish are the solid heart of any Sicilian meal. In inland areas, such hearty dishes as rabbit and sausage spiced with fennel seeds are common, though seafood is always the main event on the coast. *Pesce spada* (swordfish) is ubiquitous between May and September, best sampled around Messina, where the long-masted *felucche* still ply the Straits, while *tonno* (tuna) is the staple in Trápani province.

Desserts and festival food

From the Byzantine Greeks and the Arabs, Sicily has absorbed a taste for sugar-rich cakes and pastries. Once again, the visual impact is as important as the flavour. *Frutti di Martorana*, sugary almond paste delicately fashioned in the shapes of fruits, are an artistic triumph in the Palermo region. Ice cream, too, is a Sicilian celebration of taste and texture, with myriad concoctions available, even in the most humble *gelateria*.

▲ Pasta alla Norma

▼ Selection of *gelati*

Grape harvest, Salina ▲

Marsala wine ▼

The wines of Sicily

Home to more vineyards than any other region in Italy, Sicily is these days respected for the quality as well as the quantity of its wines. Scientific growing techniques and quality control have enabled local producers to make the most of the hot sun, relatively high altitudes and low rainfall. While native grape varieties such as the red Frappato and the white Grillo, Inzolia and Cataratto are still used for blending with other wines to provide body and strength, others, such as Nero d'Ávola, are increasingly appreciated in their own right. In addition, with the introduction of international varieties such as Cabernet Sauvignon and Chardonnay, more Sicilian wines are being shipped all over the world.

Favourite Sicilian wines

▶▶ **Álcamo** This highly rated, robust, dry white from Trápani province is best served with *antipasti* and seafood.

▶▶ **Cerasuolo di Vittoria** A ruby red and cherry-flavoured wine from southeastern Sicily, often with a high alcoholic content.

▶▶ **Etna** Nourished on volcanic soil, and either *rosso* or *bianco*, this can be drunk as an aperitif or used to accompany seafood.

▶▶ **Grecánico** A crisp white from the centre and west of the island that's often blended with Chardonnay.

▶▶ **Malvasia** The variety responsible for these smooth aperitifs or dessert wines is grown all over Italy, and in Sicily in the Aeolian Islands.

▶▶ **Marsala** Sicily's best known export, this fortified wine from the west coast can be either sweet or dry. The quality varies – the best are left to mature in the cask for up to ten years.

▶▶ **Moscato** A sweet, full-bodied, amber-coloured wine from Pantelleria.

Novecento Via Duprè 11 ☎0932.843.817, ⓦwww.hotel900.it. Occupying a Baroque *palazzo* in the heart of town, this stylish hotel has fully equipped rooms with architect-designed beds and arty but sumptuous bathrooms with Bisazza mosaic tiles. The tone is contemporary and arty, and staff are friendly and helpful. ❸

Eating and drinking

Baqqala Piazzetta Ficili ☎0932.931.028. On the steps above Palazzo Beneventano, this shabby-chic osteria has lunchtime snacks and fuller meals in the evening (most dishes €8–9). But it's most fun at night, when you can lounge on the divans outside, soaking up the mellow soundtrack. Closed Mon.

Al Barocco Via Catena 3–5 ☎0932.841.741. Tucked away off the top of Via Penna, this little trattoria has tables outside and within, and it's worth booking ahead to sit outside for a nice atmosphere – the interior is a bit bright. Prices are keen: you can eat well for around €15. Closed Mon except June–Sept.

Ragusa and around

The 1693 earthquake destroyed many towns and cities that were then rebuilt in a different form, but the unique effect on Ragusa was to split the city in two. The old town of **Ragusa Ibla**, on a jut of land above its valley, was comprehensively flattened, and within a few years a new planned town emerged on the higher ridge to the west, known simply as **RAGUSA** (or Ragusa Superiore). However, Ibla was stubbornly rebuilt by its inhabitants and rivalry between the two was commonplace until 1926, when both towns were nominally reunited. For decades Ibla suffered, as all the business and industry relocated to the prosperous upper town – even oil was discovered here, and derricks are scattered around modern Ragusa's higher reaches. But there's been a complete transformation over the last ten years as Ibla has benefited from European funding to tidy up its once dilapidated streets, giving its central core a gleaming veneer. Boutique tourism has taken off here in a big way, with old houses and *palazzi* now given over to classy B&Bs, designer cafés and trendy trattorias. Even so, it's not recklessly touristy – more gourmet deli than gift shop – and Ragusa Ibla makes for a very agreeable night or two's stay.

To the south and west of Ragusa, the largely unsung Baroque towns of **Cómiso** and **Vittoria**, the views from **Chiaramonte Gulfi** or the low-key resorts and beaches along the local **coast** can fill another day's touring, but these are all mere sideshows compared with Ragusa itself.

Arrival and information

If you're coming to Ragusa from Módica, make the journey by road if you can – the train route isn't half as spectacular. Drivers can follow the signs to Ragusa Ibla, where there's a capacious car park below Piazza della Repubblica. **Buses** and **trains**, however, all arrive in the upper town, the adjacent stations near Piazza del Pópolo being a five-minute walk from the Ponte Nuovo and Via Roma.

The most useful **city buses** are #11 and #33 (both every 30–60min; buy tickets in advance from any *tabacchi*), which ply between the upper and lower towns along Via Roma and Corso Italia, stopping outside both Santa Maria and Purgatorio churches, and ending their run in Ibla outside the Giardino Ibleo. For the bus and train stations, #33 is best. In Ibla, you can either board them at the Giardino Ibleo or in Largo Camerina. If you're based in the upper town, the best advice is to walk down to the lower town – less fatiguing and allowing you to enjoy the magnificent view – and catch the bus back. The walk down to Ibla takes about half an hour, heading down Corso Italia and the narrow Via XXIV Maggio.

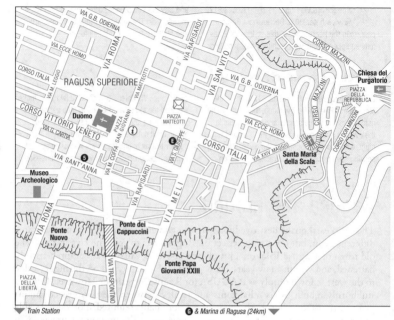

There's a small **tourist office**, marked "Punto Incontro", outside the Chiesa del Purgatorio (Tues–Sun 10am–1pm & 4–7pm, 3–6pm in winter), and another, better informed one in the upper town in front of the Duomo on Piazza San Giovanni (Mon–Fri 8.30am–7.30pm, Sat 8.30am–2pm; ☎0932.684.780, ⊛www.comune .ragusa.gov.it); you can pick up a map and an accommodation booklet from either. There's an **internet point** in Ibla on Piazza Marini.

Accommodation

It's infinitely preferable to stay the night in Ragusa Ibla, where you can stroll the traffic-free streets in the evening and hop from bar to trattoria. It holds more than two dozen **B&Bs** alone, as well as a handful of small, stylish **hotels** – all signposted – and most can find you a parking space outside or nearby. There's a similar number of B&Bs in the upper town, as well as a few largely colourless business-type hotels.

Il Barocco Via Santa Maria la Nuova 1, Ragusa Ibla ☎0932.663.105, ⊛www.ilbarocco.it. A very charming old-town hotel set around a bright courtyard – the rooms are in traditional style, with tile floors and oak furniture, but it's a modern place, all very tasteful and understated. Their excellent restaurant is just a short walk up the street. ❸

Eremo della Giubiliana Contrada Giubiliana, 7.5km south of Ragusa on the Marina di Ragusa road ☎0932.669.119, ⊛www.eremodella giubiliana.it. This five-star country property is housed in the restored buildings of a feudal estate and hermitage dating back to the twelfth century. Rooms (converted from monks' cells), suites and self-contained estate cottages all feature traditional

Sicilian furnishings, the grounds are ravishing, and you can dine on their own organically grown food. It's no surprise to find it also has its own airstrip and private beach, plus pool, nature trails and all sorts of tours and activities available. ❺

Ai Giardini Iblei Via Normanni 4, Ragusa Ibla ☎0932.246.844 or 338.640.1238, ⊛www .aigiardini.it. Right next to the town gardens are three sunny rooms with private bathrooms, simply but tastefully furnished. Free internet. ❷

Locanda Don Serafino Via XI Febbraio 15, Ragusa Ibla ☎0932.220.065, ⊛www .locandadonserafino.it. Beautifully set within the hefty stone walls of a nineteenth-century mansion, this four-star boutique hotel has only ten rooms,

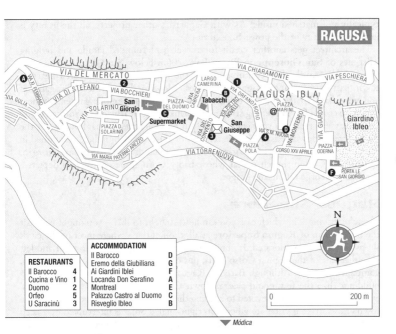

ACCOMMODATION

Il Barocco	D
Eremo della Giubiliana	G
Ai Giardini Iblei	F
Locanda Don Serafino	A
Montreal	E
Palazzo Castro al Duomo	C
Risveglio Ibleo	B

RESTAURANTS

Il Barocco	4
Cucina e Vino	1
Duomo	2
Orfeo	5
U Saracinù	3

0 — 200 m

▼ *Módica*

all gorgeously appointed. The stylish and costly cave-like restaurant (closed Tues), located a 15min walk away, is among the best places to eat in town, offering a modern take on traditional dishes – things like grilled vegetable pie, beef fillet flavoured with tobacco, or rabbit with bacon and pistachios. They also have a lido and restaurant down on the coast at Marina di Ragusa, open April to mid-Oct. ❸

Montreal Via San Giuseppe 8, Ragusa ℡0932.621.133, Ⓦ www.montrealhotel.it. A three-star hotel in the upper town that offers decent prices for reasonable rooms and has garage parking.

🏃 **Palazzo Castro al Duomo** Piazza del Duomo 2, Ragusa Ibla ℡0932.621.887 or 349.266.0528, Ⓦ www.palazzocastro.it. Right on Ibla's majestic cathedral square, rooms in this

B&B run by an elderly and charismatic artist have frescoed ceilings and a blend of antique furnishings and designer touches. There's a courtyard garden as well as a series of rooftop terraces with great views. No credit cards. ❸

🏃 **Risveglio Ibleo** Largo Camerina 3, Ragusa Ibla ℡0932.247.811 or 335.804.6494, Ⓦ www.risveglioibleo.com. A very friendly welcome awaits at this elegant townhouse, where accommodation is in four studio apartments (for couples or families), either in the main house (for more character) or just around the back. The rooms are stylishly decorated, with small kitchenettes, and you come up to the owners' second-floor rooms for a breakfast of fresh bread, home-made preserves and honey, served on the terrace in summer. No credit cards. ❷

Ragusa Ibla

The original lower town of **Ragusa Ibla** is totally charming, its largely traffic-free streets, stepped alleys and dead-end courtyards a delight to wander around. The central focus is the sloping Piazza del Duomo, split by six palms, which ends in impressive wrought-iron fencing, beyond which broad steps lead to the church of **San Giorgio** (Mon & Wed–Sun 10am–12.30pm & 4–6.30pm, Tues 4–6.30pm; enter up the steps to the left-hand side). A masterpiece of Sicilian Baroque, it's the work of Rosario Gagliardi – one of Noto's chief architects – and took nearly forty years to complete. Its three-tiered facade, sets of triple columns climbing up the wedding-cake exterior to a balconied belfry, is an imaginative work, though typically not matched inside. As with Gagliardi's other projects, all the beauty is in the immediacy of the powerful exterior.

The architect gets another credit for the elegant rounded facade and bulging balconies of **San Giuseppe** in Piazza Pola, 200m below San Giorgio. The main Corso XXV Aprile then continues down the hill through the restored heart of town, past stores selling designer sunglasses, "slow food" gourmet delis, galleries and wine bars. At the foot of town, the **Giardino Ibleo** public garden is where everyone comes for an evening stroll and a drink in the nearby cafés. You can enjoy dramatic views from the very edge of the spur on which the town is built, while the violet-strewn flowerbeds set off the remains of three small churches, abandoned in the grounds. To the right of the garden's entrance stands the **Portale San Giorgio**, a surviving Gothic church portal whose badly worn stone centrepiece depicts a skeletal St George killing the dragon.

Ragusa Superiore

If you're driving – in which case you can head straight to Ibla – you might not visit the upper town of **Ragusa Superiore** at all, though that's where most of the city's shops and services are located. It's built on a grid plan, slipping off to right and left on either side of the sloping Corso Italia, just off which stands the sombre Duomo, completed in 1774. Although Baroque Ragusa received its share of good-looking buildings (like the few grand *palazzi* down Corso Italia), most of the architects' efforts seem to have been devoted to keeping the streets as straight as possible, and the town's most striking vistas are where this right-angled order is interrupted by a deep gorge, exposing the bare rock on which the city was built. Three bridges span the gorge: at the Ponte Nuovo, just below Via Roma, the city's **Museo Archeologico** (daily 9am–1.30pm & 4–7.30pm; €4) deals mainly with finds from the Greek site of Kamarina (sixth-century BC), on the coast to the southwest (p.254).

If you're walking back down to Ibla, you could make a stop on the terrace by the restored fifteenth-century church of **Santa Maria della Scala** (which features the remains of an unusual exterior pulpit). A mighty view lies beyond, of the weather-beaten roofs of Ragusa Ibla straddling the outcrop of rock, rising to the prominent dome of San Giorgio. From the church terrace, steps descend beneath the winding road to another church, the **Chiesa del Purgatorio**, from where winding alleys climb back into the heart of Ragusa Ibla.

Eating, drinking and entertainment

Good **restaurants** are easy to find in Ibla, while a few cafés put out tables in the Piazza del Duomo – as night falls, and the lights come on, it's not too much of an exaggeration to suggest that this is the prettiest square in Sicily. The annual entertainment highlight is **L'Estate Iblea**, a series of concerts, recitals and events held throughout the town between late June and September, culminating in a spectacular fireworks display down at the nearby resort of Marina di Ragusa.

Il Barocco Via Orfanotrofio 27–29, Ragusa Ibla ℗0932.652.397. Reliable spot for a good-value meal – there's a rustic interior or streetside tables, but you should get there in good time for the latter. Most mains cost €6–10, though you'll pay a little more for a mountainous platter of grilled meat that you'll struggle to finish. Closed Wed.

Cucina e Vino Via Orfanotrofio 91, Ragusa Ibla ℗0932.686.447. Typical of the more modish operations in Ibla, this old *palazzo* with a

street terrace has separate menus of regional meat (€8–10) and fish (€13–14) dishes, things like lamb with artichokes, ravioli stuffed with ricotta with a pork sauce or fillet of seabass with prawns. Closed Wed except June–Sept.

Duomo Via Capitano Bocchieri 31, Ragusa Ibla ℗0932.651.265, ⓦwww.ristoranteduomo.it. Chef Ciccio Sultano deconstructs his Ragusa roots to produce the glorious concoctions – they're scarcely mere dishes – that have gained his restaurant a name across Sicily. It's highly refined, highly individual and, of course, highly expensive, with main courses around €40–50 and the *menu degustazione* a cool €135. Still, you're unlikely to eat as well or as interestingly anywhere else. Closed Sun & lunchtime Mon.

Orfeo Via Sant'Anna 117, Ragusa ☎0932.621.035. If you're in the upper town it's worth seeking out this place for traditional dishes like broad bean soup, stuffed sardines or

the local pasta, *cavati ragusana* (fresh pasta with a pork *ragù*). Count on spending €20–30 for a full meal excluding drinks. Closed Sun.

U Saracinu Via del Convento 9, Ragusa Ibla ☎0932.246.976. It's been here donkey's years, even before the fancy old-town restoration, and sticks with a traditional Sicilian menu of pasta and meat grills (most dishes €5–10), though pricier couscous and fish specials are also on offer. Closed Sun.

Around Ragusa

Módica apart, there's not much else that need delay you in **Ragusa province**, though if you're driving north into the interior or west to Agrigento you can plot an enjoyable half-day's route. By public transport, to be frank, it's barely worth the trouble to visit any of the places covered below.

Chiaramonte Gulfi

Twenty kilometres north of Ragusa, **CHIARAMONTE GULFI** merits a visit largely for its far-reaching views. This is one of several places dubbed the "balcony of Sicily" and, though hazy in summer, the panorama (west towards Gela and north to Etna) embraces dun-coloured farmland interspersed with solitary villages – a still, silent scene, but for the occasional dog's bark or the whine of a Vespa. An excellent **restaurant** here, *Majore*, Via Mártiri Ungheresi 12, off Piazza Duomo (☎0932.928.019; closed Mon & July), specializes in pig meats – the area is famous for its salamis and cured hams, which you can buy to take away at the restaurant shop.

Cómiso and Vittoria

Heading west, both Cómiso (17km) and neighbouring Vittoria (24km) are on the main train line from Ragusa to Gela, though the road provides the best approach, crossing a barren 600m-high plateau that looks away to the distant sea. A Baroque spirit infuses **CÓMISO**, most prominent in its two major churches, the Chiesa Matrice and the nearby Santíssima Annunziata, which overwhelm everything within reach of their ponderous shadows. Not much of medieval Cómiso survived the 1693 earthquake, save the thirteenth-century church of San Francesco, to which a rich Renaissance chapel was added in 1517 to house the tombs of the powerful Naselli family. **VITTORIA**, meanwhile, holds more Baroque buildings and a rather splendid main square, Piazza del Pópolo, though the town is better known as the source of the well-regarded Cerasuolo di Vittoria wines.

Cómiso's famous sons

Cómiso was the birthplace of both the painter and sculptor **Salvatore Fiume** (1915–97) and his friend, the writer **Gesualdo Bufalino** (1920–96). While the main body of Fiume's paintings, chiefly figurative in style, can be seen in the Vatican museums, he also designed sets for opera houses and worked on architectural projects. Bufalino's career was rather more curious. He began his first book (*The Plague Sower*) in 1950, having spent three years in a Palermitan sanatorium, but declined to let it be published until 1981, when he was finally satisfied with it. After that he picked up steam and wrote several novels and short stories, including the respected *Night's Lies*, which won Italy's most prestigious literary award, the Strega Prize, in 1988.

Marina di Ragusa and Kamarina

Southwest of Ragusa, it's a straight 24km run down to **the coast**, and the start of the so-called "riviera", which extends as far as Gela. Easily reached by Tumino buses from Ragusa (ⓣ0932.623.184, ⓦwww.tuminobus.it), the small resort of **MARINA DI RAGUSA** is a typical Sicilian mix of private lidos and apartments, and bars and restaurants that really only do business for four or five months of the year. A coastal road westwards (served by Tumino buses) offers access to more beaches near Punta Secca and Punta Braccetto, almost as far as the desolate remains of ancient **Kamarina** (also spelt Camerina), a Syracusan colony founded in 599 BC. It lies on a headland overlooking beaches on either side, where a **Museo Archeologico** (daily 9am–1pm & 3–5.30pm; €4) contains everything that wasn't appropriated by Ragusa's museum. Behind the antiquarium is all that's left of a fifth-century BC Tempio di Atena, surrounded by the rubble of city walls and the various ruins of the Hellenistic-Roman city. Note that buses stop a kilometre before the site.

Travel details

Trains

Noto to: Ragusa (1 daily Mon–Sat; 1hr 40min); Siracusa (8 daily Mon–Sat, 1 daily Sun; 35min).
Ragusa to: Cómiso (5 daily Mon–Sat; 30min); Gela (5 daily Mon–Sat; 1hr 20min); Íspica (2 daily Mon–Sat; 1hr); Módica (4 daily Mon–Sat; 20min); Noto (2 daily Mon–Sat; 1hr 30min); Scicli (3 daily; 35min); Siracusa (2 daily Mon–Sat; 2hr); Vittoria (4 daily Mon–Sat; 45min).
Siracusa to: Augusta (7–12 daily; 30min); Catania (7–11 daily; 1hr 15min); Lentini (7–11 daily; 45min); Messina (7–9 daily; 3hr); Módica (5 daily Mon–Sat; 1hr 45min); Noto (7 daily Mon–Sat, 1 daily Sun; 30min); Ragusa (1 daily Mon–Sat; 2hr 10min); Taormina (7–9 daily; 2hr).

Buses

Módica to: Catania (9 daily Mon–Sat, 4 daily Sun; 2hr 10min); Catania airport (9 daily Mon–Sat, 4 daily Sun; 1hr 55min); Íspica (9 daily Mon–Sat, 1 daily Sun; 30min–1hr 10min); Noto (hourly Mon–Sat, 6 daily Sun; 1hr 25min–1hr 45min); Pachino (2 daily Mon–Sat; 1hr 20min–2hr 10min); Ragusa (1–2 hourly Mon–Sat, 4 daily Sun; 25min–1hr); Scicli (1–2 hourly Mon–Sat, 4 daily Sun; 30–40min); Siracusa (10 daily Mon–Sat, 4 daily Sun; 2hr–2hr 40min).
Noto to: Ávola (1–2 hourly; 15min); Eloro (2–4 daily Mon–Sat; 20min); Íspica (11 daily Mon–Sat, 8 daily Sun; 45min); Siracusa (11 daily Mon–Sat, 4 daily Sun; 55min).

Pachino to: Marzamemi (8 daily Mon–Sat; 45min); Portopalo di Capo Pássero (10–11 daily Mon–Sat, 1 daily Sun; 10–30min); Siracusa (5–7 daily Mon–Sat, 2 daily Sun; 1hr 20min).
Ragusa to: Catania airport/Catania (10 daily Mon–Fri, 6–7 daily Sat & Sun; 1hr 45min–2hr); Chiaramonte Gulfi (Mon–Sat 7 daily; 50min); Gela (3 daily Mon–Sat, 1 daily Sun; 1hr 30min); Íspica (6 daily Mon–Sat, 1 daily Sun; 55min–1hr 40min); Kamarina (6 daily; 1hr); Marina di Ragusa (hourly; 1hr); Módica (Mon–Sat 1–2 hourly, Sun 3 daily; 30min–1hr 10min); Noto (6 daily Mon–Sat, 4 daily Sun; 1hr 45min–2hr 15min); Palermo (Mon–Sat 4–5 daily, Sun 2 daily; 4hr); Scicli (9 daily Mon–Sat; 1hr–1hr 50min); Siracusa (6 daily Mon–Sat, 2 daily Sun; 2hr 45min).
Siracusa to: Augusta (11 daily Mon–Sat; 45min–1hr 15min); Ávola (8–12 daily Mon–Sat, 2–3 daily Sun; 40min); Catania (1–2 hourly; 1hr 25min); Catania airport (6–7 daily; 1hr 15min); Ferla (1 daily Mon–Sat; 1hr 35min); Gela (2 daily Mon–Sat, 1 daily Sun; 3hr 45min); Lentini (9–11 daily Mon–Sat; 1hr–1hr 30min); Módica (8 daily Mon–Sat, 3 daily Sun; 1hr 45min–3hr); Noto (12 daily Mon–Sat, 4 daily Sun; 55min); Pachino (6 daily Mon–Sat, 2 daily Sun; 1hr 20min); Palazzolo Acréide (1–2 hourly Mon–Sat, 2 daily Sun; 1hr 10min–2hr 15min); Palermo (2–3 daily; 3hr 20min); Piazza Armerina (1 daily Mon–Sat; 4hr); Ragusa (4 daily Mon–Sat, 2 daily Sun; 2hr 15min–3hr); Sortino (Mon–Sat 10 daily; 1hr 15min).

Enna and the interior

TYRRHENIAN SEA

MEDITERRANEAN SEA

0   50 km

CHAPTER 7

Highlights

✳ **Enna** Spend the night high up in the hill-town of Enna and watch the sun set from its spectacular terraces. See p.258

✳ **Organic agriturismo** The Sillitti family farm near Caltanissetta makes a wonderful base for seeing the unsung interior. See p.268

✳ **Piazza Armerina** Quite apart from the nearby mosaics, the old Baroque town of Piazza Armerina is an undiscovered gem. See p.268

✳ **Villa Romana del Casale** One of the foremost sights on the whole island, the extraordinary Roman mosaics should not be missed. See p.271

✳ **Morgantina** An little-known Greek archeological site in gorgeous rural surroundings. See p.273

✳ **La Scala, Caltagirone** In a town famed for its ceramics, these 142 steps are adorned with beautiful patterned tiles. See p.276

▲ Mosaics in Villa Romana del Casale, near Piazza Armerina

Enna and the interior

... for the last five hours all they had set eyes on were bare hillsides flaming yellow under the sun ... They had passed through crazed-looking villages washed in palest blue; crossed dry beds of torrents over fantastic bridges; skirted sheer precipices which no sage and broom could temper. Never a tree, never a drop of water; just sun and dust.

Giuseppe di Lampedusa, *The Leopard*

O nly in Sicily's vast and mountainous interior – thoroughly depleted by mass emigration – can you truly begin to get off the tourist trail. Outside just three or four decent-sized towns, bunched together almost in the centre of the island, much of the land is burnt dry during the long summer months. The extensive cornfields have been a feature of the Sicilian landscape since Greek times, but the rolling hills are mostly silent and empty, punctuated only by occasional moribund towns and villages wrapped around easily defensible heights. However, travelling through this land has its compensations, not least the fascinating glimpses of a rural life that has all but disappeared in the rest of Sicily.

Symbol of the entire interior is the blustery mountain settlement of **Enna**, which is easy to reach from Catania or Palermo. It's a historic place, with a mighty castle and some even mightier views, and deserves a night's stay. Routes north (towards the Tyrrhenian coast and Palermo) or east (Etna and Catania) head through minor mountain towns and villages on the fringes of the Nébrodi and Madonie mountains, and make good driving circuits provided you don't mind potholed roads and a middle-of-nowhere feel. The largest town in the region is actually **Caltanissetta**, just to the southwest of Enna, though it's also the most disappointing and devoid of much charm. However, it's the gateway to the south coast and the deep west, so you might at least find yourself passing through.

The treasures of the interior, though, are all in the southeast, especially the single biggest draw – the lavish Roman mosaics at the **Villa Romana del Casale**. This lies just outside the enjoyable Baroque town of **Piazza Armerina**, which could also be your base for seeing the extensive and unsung Greek ruins of **Morgantina**. Further south, ceramic-studded **Caltagirone** makes a handy departure point for the Baroque towns of the southeast.

With a car you could pick any of the towns and use it as a base for seeing the rest of the region, since the main roads at least are pretty good and distances not too large. On public transport, with limited time, it's hard to look beyond Enna and Pizza Armerina as the two most important destinations. It's more difficult to travel north and west into the mountains by bus, though there are services out of Enna along the two major routes, the SS120 and SS121.

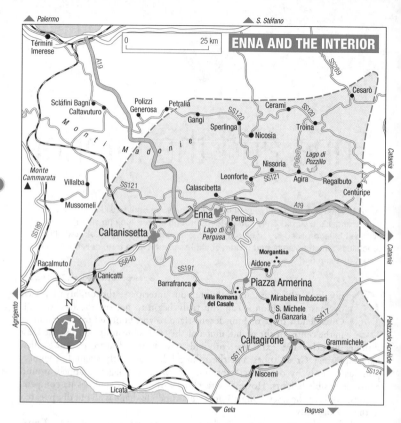

Enna

From a bulging V-shaped ridge almost 1000m up, **ENNA** lords it over the surrounding hills of central Sicily. One of the most ancient towns on the island, Enna has only ever had one function: Livy described it as "inexpugnabilis", and, for obvious strategic reasons, the town was a magnet for successive hostile armies, who in turn besieged and fortified it. The Arabs, for example, spent twenty years trying to gain entrance to Enna before eventually, in 859, resorting to crawling in through the sewers. The approach to this doughty mountain stronghold is still formidable, the road climbing slowly out of the valley and looping across the solid crag to the summit and the town.

Enna remains a medieval hill town at heart, with a tightly packed centre of narrow streets, small squares and hemmed-in churches, where occasional gaps through the buildings reveal swirling drops down into the valleys below. When all is said and done, apart from the castle and the all-encompassing views, there's little enough here to keep you more than a night. However, that night is very definitely worth it, with summer evenings in particular counting among the most enjoyable in Sicily, watching the sun set from some stupendous vantage points. Come in winter and you should expect snow, the wind blowing hard through the streets, and the white slopes beyond blending with the anaemic stone buildings.

Arrival and information

The **bus terminal** is on Viale Diaz, just out of the old centre – to reach central Piazza Vittorio Emanuele from the terminal, turn right, right again down Corso Sicilia, and it's around a ten-minute walk. The **train station**, however, is 5km north of town: a local bus runs roughly hourly to the town centre (less frequently on Sun), or a taxi costs around €12. Having whizzed up the road from below town with comparative ease, the traffic in town is among the most congested in all Sicily and you really don't want to drive around more than you have to. There's a **car park** just off Viale Diaz, by the Cappuccini cemetery and near the bus terminal (look for the blue "P" sign), or lots more free parking up by the castle (follow "castello" signs), and from either place it's under a ten-minute walk into the old town.

Everywhere in Enna itself can be reached very easily on foot, though **local buses** run out to places like Pergusa, Calascibetta and the train station – you'll need to buy a ticket in advance from *tabacchi*, and they are valid for an hour. **Taxi** ranks can be found along Viale Diaz, near the bus terminal, and at Piazza Vittorio Emanuele; alternatively, call ⊕0935.500.905.

There's **information** on Enna on the web portals ⓦwww.ennaturismo.info, www.ennacultura.info and www.turismoenna.it, but only in Italian, while two

---

Festivals

March/April
Easter Holy Week celebrations in **Enna**; including processions, special Masses and the parade of saintly relics. Though it runs all week from Palm Sunday to Easter Sunday, the best day is Good Friday, when thousands march in silent procession dressed in the white-hooded costumes of the medieval fraternities. Other costumed processions can be seen at **Caltagirone**, **Troina** and at **Caltanissetta** (best days Maundy Thursday and Good Friday), featuring processional carts (the *misteri*) and monks. The **motor-racing** season starts at the Autodromo di Pergusa, around the **Lago di Pergusa**, running until Sept.

May
Sagra del Lago Throughout the month at **Lago di Pergusa**, with folk events and fireworks, singing competitions and games.
Penultimate Sunday Festa dei Rami at **Troina**, in which laurel branches are carried to the tomb of St Silvester.

July
Estate Ennese Start of a series of concerts and opera in the open-air theatre at the castle in **Enna**. Runs until end of Aug.
24–25 Festival of San Giácomo in **Caltagirone**, during which the La Scala steps are illuminated.

August
12–14 Il Palio dei Normanni in **Piazza Armerina**, a medieval pageant commemorating Count Roger's taking of the town in the eleventh century. Processional entry into town on the twelfth, ceremonial joust on the fourteenth, along with costumed parades and other festive events. Similar events take place around the same time in a number of surrounding towns, but Piazza's is by far the largest.

December
Annual exhibition of terracotta sculpted cribs in **Caltagirone**.

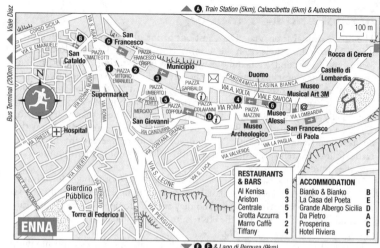

tourist offices in town might be able to help out more (but don't count on it). You can at least pick up a good town map and accommodation details, either at Via Roma 413 (Mon, Tues & Thurs–Sat 8.30am–1.30pm, Wed 8.30am–7pm; ☎0935.528.288), or Piazza Colaianni (Mon–Fri 8am–2pm, plus Wed 2.45–6.15pm; ☎0935.500.875), off Via Roma next to the *Grande Albergo Sicilia*.

Accommodation

There's not a lot of accommodation in Enna itself, just two actual hotels and half a dozen B&Bs, but you should find a room easily enough. The neighbouring village of Calascibetta has a few more B&Bs, and there are plenty more places down by the lake at Pergusa if you're stuck, though that's not as alluring as it sounds (see p.263) and it's a fair drive from Enna itself.

Bianko & Bianko Via Longo 15 ☎331.329.4288 or 327.159.8426, Ⓔgiala81@yahoo.it. An effortlessly cool and uncluttered B&B, with four spacious, light-filled rooms in stylish white. It's handy for the old town, just to the right of the steps of San Cataldo church (bottom of Via Vittorio Emanuele). There's no one on the premises (you have to call first), and breakfast is taken at the bar around the corner. ❷

La Casa del Poeta Contrada da Parasporino, Pergusa, 10km south ☎329.627.4918 or 328.657.2731, Ⓦwww.lacasadelpoeta.it. The most original accommodation hereabouts is this artistically inclined nineteenth-century villa, 1km from Lago di Pergusa, where you're invited to immerse yourself in literature from their library or even write and draw in their "writing room". It's basically a backdrop for fancy B&B, though you may in the end do no more than lounge by the pool. ❷, April–Sept ❸

Grande Albergo Sicilia Piazza Colaianni ☎0935.500.850, Ⓦwww.hotelsiciliaenna.it. Best of the town's two central hotels is the easy-to-find pile in the centre, close to the Duomo. It's a traditional place, with an Art Deco lobby and nicely refurbished rooms, some with hand-painted Sicilian country furniture and others with rooftop views. You can also park right outside, which is a definite bonus. Online bookings and last-minute deals can bring the price down to around €75. ❸

Da Pietro Contrada Longobardi, Calascibetta, 6km north ☎0935.33.647 or 340.276.5763, Ⓔb&bpietrovaccaro@alice.it. Surrounded by a garden, this pleasant B&B, well signposted on the approach to the village of Calascibetta, near Enna, has a wide terrace where breakfast is served. No credit cards. ❶

Prosperina Piazza Scelfo 108, corner with Via Sant'Agata ☎333.299.1957, Ⓦwww.bbenna.it. A tall townhouse B&B right in the historic centre, with seven polished rooms perched on top of one another and reached by lift. They sleep from one to four (including a good family room, with separate bunk-beds), and there's a dining room and little covered terrace area for breakfast. ❷

Hotel Riviera Lago di Pergusa, 9km south ☎0935.541.267, ⊛www.hotelrivieraenna.it. The pick of the hotels down near the race track and lake has reasonable rooms with wooden floors, and an outdoor pool around which pizzas are served at night. You should get better rates online or in advance. ❹

The Town

Despite numerous wars and attacks over the years, most of Enna's medieval remains are in good condition. Prize exhibit is the thirteenth-century **Castello di Lombardia** (daily: summer 8am–8pm, winter 9am–5pm; free), built by Frederick II, which dominates the easternmost spur of town. There's a huge area inside enclosed by the walls, split into various courtyards, while six surviving towers (out of an original twenty) provide lookouts. Climb the tallest, Torre Pisana, for some great views of Enna, the rugged countryside in all directions, and across to Mount Etna.

A road to the side of the castle climbs a little way further to the **Rocca di Cerere**, an exposed outcrop where some scattered foundations are presumed to be the remnants of a temple erected by Gelon in 480 BC. Enna was the centre of the Greek cult of Demeter, the fertility goddess (her Roman counterpart was Ceres, hence the rock's name), and the most famous of the myths associated with the goddess – the carrying off of her daughter, Persephone, to the underworld – is supposed to have taken place just a few kilometres away, at Lago di Pergusa.

Virtually everything else there is to see lies along and around the narrow **Via Roma**, a continuation of Via Lombardia that descends from the castle. Main church is the **Duomo** (daily 9am–noon & 4–7pm), in front of a shady little square, which has been rebuilt several times since its foundation in 1307. It's not much to look at from the outside, but the sixteenth-century interior is a different story, with every surface covered in ornamentation. Look closely at the bottom of the huge supporting dark-grey columns, the bases of which are carved with snarling heads with human hands and snake bodies.

The town's two principal museums are both near the Duomo – and both are closed indefinitely for "works". In the adjacent Museo Alessi are the impressive contents of the cathedral's own treasury, while opposite the cathedral across Piazza Mazzini is the Museo Archeologico, repository of everything dug up in the locality. For now, that just leaves the **Museo Musical Art 3M**, back up the road at Via Roma 533 (Tues–Sun 9am–1pm & 3–7pm; €2), which features projections of the work of artists who have a (sometimes remote) connection with Sicily – for example Caravaggio – all to a rather hammy orchestral accompaniment. A few photographs and costumes are also on show, as well as a reconstruction of a sulphur mine, a reminder of an industry that once dominated this part of Sicily. If you're in a tolerant mood, it'll do to pass twenty minutes or so.

Most of Enna's churches – even the ones in use – have cracked facades and weeds growing out of improbable places, but there are some that catch the eye, like fourteenth-century **San Giovanni** (behind the much larger San Giuseppe, on Piazza Coppola) which has a Catalan-Gothic facade and a tower crowned by a little cupola. Between here and the little Addolorata chapel, there's a small street market, the **Mercato Sant'Antonio**, where you can buy some fruit and watch the fishmonger expertly carve off swordfish steaks.

The western extremity of Via Roma is marked by the sloping, rectangular **Piazza Vittorio Emanuele**, focal point of the evening *passeggiata*. Off here, a long cliff-edge promenade looks out to the little rust-coloured town of Calascibetta over the valley. The plain, high wall of the church of **San Francesco**, which flanks the piazza, has a massive sixteenth-century tower, previously part of the old town's system of watchtowers that linked the castle with all Enna's churches.

One watchtower still stands in isolation in the **Giardino Púbblico**, in the largely modern south of the town. An octagonal tower, 24m high, the **Torre di Federico II** (Mon–Sat 8am–6pm, Sun 8am–1pm; free) is a survivor of the alterations to the city made by Frederick of Aragon, who added a (now hidden) underground passage connecting the tower to the castle. You can climb to the top for more great views.

Eating and drinking

There's only a limited choice of restaurants in the old part of Enna, but enough for a night or two. The cafés and bars around Piazza Vittorio Emanuele fill up during the evening, while during the *passeggiata* dawdling locals hold up the traffic all along Via Roma.

Restaurants

Ariston Via Roma 353 ☏0935.26.038. Long a reliable place for fresh pasta and good, authentic Sicilian dishes, though it's fairly formal and inside an old-fashioned shopping arcade which does its gloomy terrace tables no favours. Expect to pay €30 a head for a meal, though there are pizzas too at night. Closed Sun.

Centrale Piazza VI Dicembre 9 ☏0935.500.963. Attracts a largely local crowd, and has a shady terrace off the main street. The *antipasti* table is impressive, and dishes on a wide-ranging menu cost from €6 to €18, or there are three fixed-price menus. Closed Sat in winter.

Grotta Azzurra Via Colaianni 1 ☏0935.24.328. Run for decades by the charming Giuseppe and Maria, this tiny, no-frills, basement trattoria serves the cheapest meals in town: from €3 for *primi* and €5 or €6 for *secondi*. It's nothing fancy (baked pasta, simple grills and roasts, omelettes, and fruit for dessert), and the house wine could fuel a mission to Mars, but it's a real taste of the past. It's at the very bottom of

Via Roma, past Piazza Vittorio Emanuele and down an alley on the left (there's a sign). Closed Sat in winter. No credit cards.

Tiffany Via Roma 467 ☏0935.501.368. Near the cathedral, and with an outdoor terrace with a glimpse of the distant hills. There are pizzas (€4–8) and regular Italian dishes costing €7–10. Closed Thurs.

Cafés and bars

Al Kenisa Via Roma 481 ⊛www.teatridelcielo.it. The old church next to the Museo Alessi has been stripped bare and revamped as a cultural centre and café. There are warm stone walls, art exhibitions and books inside, and Arab-style lounging outside on the cobbles at low tables and cushions. Closed Mon.

Marro Caffè Piazza Vittorio Emanuele 21. Best perch on the main square is from *Marro Caffè*'s outdoor deck. When you get tired of people-watching, someone has thoughtfully Googled song lyrics for you to read on the back of every chair. Closed Mon.

Listings

Bus companies All are at the bus terminal: SAIS ☏0935.500.902, ⊛www.saisautolinee.it (for Calascibetta, Caltanissetta, Catania, Catania airport, Messina, Palermo and Piazza Armerina); Interbus ☏0935.22.460, ⊛www.interbus.it (for Agira, Catania, Leonforte and Nicosia); ISEA ☏095.464.101, ⊛www.iseaviaggi.it (for Cesarò, Nicosia and Troina).

Cinema Cinema Arena Pergusa (☏0935.542.319 or 335.772.9664), on the road just out of Pergusa

towards Enna, puts on outdoor screenings between July and mid-Sept: pick up a programme from the tourist office.

Emergencies Ambulance ☏118; police ☏113.

Hospital Ospedale Umberto I, Contrada Ferrante in Enna Bassa, on the road to Pergusa ☏0935.45.111.

Pharmacies Librizzi, Piazza Vittorio Emanuele 20 ☏0935.500.908; Farmacia del Centro, Via Roma 315 ☏0935.500.650.

Police Questura at Via San Giuseppe 4
ⓣ 0935.522.111.
Post office Via A. Volta off Piazza Garibaldi
(Mon–Fri 8am–6.30pm, Sat 8am–12.30pm).

Trains Check train timetables at ⓦ www
.trenitalia.com – and remember that Enna train
station is 5km from the town, so allow time to
get there.

Around Enna

The small town you can see from Enna's terraces, hugging a lower hill to the north across the valley, is **CALASCIBETTA**, and it hints at what Enna would be like without the tower blocks. Once a Saracen town, it was fortified by Count Roger in his successful attempt to take Enna in 1087, and the tangled streets seem straight from that age. The tightly packed red-stone buildings perch above a sheer drop on the eastern side, rising to the restored Chiesa Madre at the very top. It's a 6km drive from Enna, or there are frequent buses to Calascibetta from Enna's bus terminal (or every couple of hours from Enna's train station), but only two on Sunday.

It's much harder to recommend a trip to Enna's other local attraction, despite its legendary fame. Nine kilometres south of town (buses every hour from outside Enna's San Francesco church), the **Lago di Pergusa** was the site of Hades' abduction of Persephone to the underworld. The story has it that Persephone, surrounded by nymphs, was gathering flowers on the lush banks of the lake when Hades emerged from a chasm beneath the water and spirited her away. Demeter searched in vain for her daughter, and her grief at the loss of Persephone prevented the corn from growing. To settle the matter, Zeus ruled that Persephone should spend half the year as queen of the Underworld, and live for the other six months in Sicily with her mother as one of the island's goddesses. In her gratitude, Demeter, as goddess of grain and agriculture, made the corn grow again – a powerful symbol in a traditionally fertile land. These days, sadly, the Pergusa road is choc-a-bloc with apartments, hotels and holiday developments, while the lake is encircled by a motor-racing track. It's hard now, despite the pleasant wooded banks beyond the water, to imagine a less romantic spot. Mary Taylor Simeti's journal, *On Persephone's Island*, labels the Lago di Pergusa "a brilliant example of the Sicilians' best efforts to ruin their landscape". There's really no point coming to the lake for any glimpse of the truth behind the legend, though it does make a possible base near Enna.

East towards Etna: along the SS121

There's a great driving route east of Enna, along the minor **SS121** which runs all the way to Adrano and the Etna foothills. It's rolling countryside for the most part, punctuated by a succession of sleepy little towns, villages and viewpoints, and with an occasional coffee and a stretch of the legs the route can occupy half a day. The road is in a bit of a state, with the surface breaking up here and there, though it's perfectly drivable with care. Buses come this way too, though you might find yourself spending longer than you'd want in many of the towns en route – if you're going to get off just once, make it Agira.

LEONFORTE, 20km from Enna, is typical of the small towns hereabouts, with its roots firmly in the seventeenth century and an attractive central square that sprouts bars in profusion. Other than the impressive Duomo and the domineering Palazzo Baronale, Leonforte's most noteworthy sight is **La Granfonte**, overlooking the hills on the edge of town. Built in 1651, it's not so much a fountain as a row of 24 waterspouts set in a sculpted facade of carvings and inscriptions. Once you've filled your water bottle, it's time to move on.

It's another 16km to **AGIRA**, wrapped around a perfect cone of a mountain, with a proud church and the ruins of a medieval castle prominent atop the peak. If you're driving, following "castello" signs should put you at the very top of town, outside the surviving alleys and walls of a once-fortified village. The views are magnificent, while following yet more signs (on foot) through the houses brings you to the *Ristorante Belvedere* (☏0935.696.091), which has a terrace with superb panoramas of the distant Lago di Pozzillo. *Casa Albergo*, a B&B on the road up to the castle at Via Palazzo 16 (☏0935.691.457 or 333.972.7511, Ⓦwww.bebcasalbergo.it; no credit cards; ❷), offers en-suite rooms, a garden and lofty views from its panoramic terrace.

During the short Sicilian campaign of World War II, the hills between Agira and the western slopes of Etna saw most of the heaviest fighting. Just out of Agira, close to the **Lago di Pozzillo**, there's a poignant **war cemetery** sited on a gentle hillside, the resting place of 490 Canadian soldiers killed in July 1943. Eight kilometres beyond, the SS121 continues right through tiny **Regalbuto**, where old men in bars shoot the breeze across the moving traffic.

The final diversion before the Etna towns comes some 15km on from Regalbuto, where a minor road leads south for 8km through orange and olive groves to **CENTÚRIPE**, which faces Etna across the Simeto River valley. Several medieval campaigns destroyed the town, while the last great battle in August 1943 dislodged German forces. Modern Centúripe is an uneasy mix of new building and an untouched central piazza, near which a terrace provides the outstanding views that earned Centúripe the tag "balcony of Sicily". After gazing at the views, you'll exhaust the town's possibilities in around two minutes flat – perhaps ten if you stop for a drink at one of the bars in the central square.

The towns beyond Centúripe are covered in the section on the Circumetnea railway; see p.208.

Nicosia and the SS120

Forty kilometres north of Enna, the small hill town of **Nicosia** is the main stop on the trans-mountain SS120, which cuts across some of the remoter stretches of the Sicilian interior. It's hardly a major destination its own right, though onward routes from Nicosia are all dramatic, especially north over the mountains to Mistretta and the Tyrrhenian coast (see Chapter 2) and **east along the SS120** through a bare landscape dominated ever more dramatically by the giant silhouette of Etna. Again, the road isn't in great condition, with slips and wash-outs common, but it's no problem if you heed the signs and drive carefully.

Nicosia

Sitting under looming crags, **NICOSIA** is a medieval mass of cracked *palazzi* topped by the remains of a Norman castle. Traffic all funnels up to the chatter-filled Piazza Garibaldi, the site of Nicosia's lovely old cathedral, **San Nicola**, a stately construction with a fourteenth-century facade and belltower, and a handsome sculpted Gothic portal. To the side of the cathedral (left side, as you face the church), Via Francesco Salomone rises steeply to the former Saracen district of the town, a jumble of streets occupying one of the four hills on which Nicosia is built. At the top, **Santa Maria Maggiore**, founded in 1267 but rebuilt after an eighteenth-century landslide, has the bells from its campanile piled up outside – they fell down after another earthquake and the sound of them is now electrically reproduced. Inside, amid "No Spitting" notices, you'll find an impressive marble polyptych by Antonello Gagini and a throne used by Charles V when he passed through here in 1535, on the way back from his Tunisian crusade. The views from outside encompass the town's other three promontories, on the highest of which sits the ruined castle.

Practicalities

Buses drop you a few minutes' walk below Piazza Garibaldi. You might be able to park near the square for a short while, but it's better to use one of the signposted **parking areas** as you drive into the centre. To get your bearings, consult the town map outside the *Bar Diana*, Piazza Garibaldi 5 (right-hand side of the cathedral) – while not forgetting to have a scoop of the *Diana's* creamy home-made *gelato*. There's a **B&B** in town, *Umberto I*, Corso Umberto I 34 (℡0935.640.771 or 347.153.5382; no credit cards; ❶), but a better one on the outskirts in Contrada Torretta (around 3km east, SP43 road), *La Torretta* (℡0935.647.325 or 339.896.5507; ❷), with rooms with balconies that look back over the town. There's also *Baglio San Pietro* (℡0935.640.529 or 335.876.7396, Ⓦwww.bagliosanpietro.com; ❸), 1km west of town in Contrada San Pietro (signposted off the Sperlinga road), a restored farm estate originally dating from the seventeenth century. The comfortable rooms here would make a good base for the surroundings, as the farm has its own restaurant, pool and gardens.

Sperlinga

A quick 10km drive or bus ride west of Nicosia, **SPERLINGA** owes its name to the numerous cave-dwellings (from the Latin *spelunca*, cave), some hundreds of years old, that pit the sandstone slopes below the town. Sprouting above is a formidable battlemented **castello** (daily 9.30am–1.30pm & 4–6.30pm; €2), its storerooms, cellars, stables and steps hewn out of the rock. Sperlinga was the only town in Sicily to open its doors to the Angevins, bloodily expelled from other Sicilian towns during the thirteenth-century Wars of the Vespers: barricading themselves inside the castle, the French held out for a year before surrendering. Just below the castle, a small archeological and ethnographical museum (same ticket and times as castle) contains the usual motley collection of historical items and old agricultural and domestic artefacts.

West of Sperlinga, it's a long drive along the SS120 into the heart of the Madonie mountains. The road is in pretty bad shape in parts, particularly around the hilltop town of **Gangi**, where there's a long diversion currently in place, but eventually you reach the Petralia towns, covered in the Parco Regionale delle Madonie section in Chapter 2.

Troina

It's another twisting 30km ride east of Nicosia to what, from a distance, appears like a thimble perched on a hill, 1120m high. This is **TROINA**, which was the focus of heavy fighting in the summer of 1943 during the Allied invasion of Sicily. The town has long played a strategic role, initially coming to prominence during the reconquest of Sicily from the Arabs, when it became one of the first cities to be taken by the Normans. Count Roger withstood a siege here for four months in 1064 that nearly put paid to his Sicilian adventures, a victory he commemorated by founding the monastery of San Basilio, now in ruins. The top of town features an eleventh-century cathedral with an adjacent fifteenth-century church dedicated to San Giorgio (notice the relief of George and the Dragon above the door under the cupola). The wide piazza-terrace in front has a simply magnificent Etna view, while beyond stretches the main street (like the piazza, named for Count Roger). It's laid out along a high ridge, and it makes for an atmospheric stroll down a narrow thoroughfare between noble mansions with a steep drop to either side. A couple of **B&Bs** are signposted off the main street, including *Idria 14*, Via Idria 14 (℡0935.654.589 or 338.744.4897, Ⓦwww .idria14.it; ❷).

Cesarò

Twenty kilometres further east, **CESARÒ** stands under fearsome crags at the crossroads with the SS289, the road that runs north across the Nébrodi mountains to the coast at Sant'Ágata di Militello. On a clear day there are remarkable views over to Etna as you approach town, though the hemmed-in streets of Cesarò itself give no hint of the grandeur of its setting – for a panorama, you must climb or drive up to the mammoth bronze statue of Jesus, the **Cristo Signore della Montagna**, in the cemetery above town.

There's an underwhelming **hotel** and B&B in the town centre, but Cesarò hardly warrants a night (you can be on the coast or in the Etna foothills in an hour). In any case, the best place is actually 2km below town (at the Troina/Randazzo road junction), where the modern *Hotel Fratelli Mazzurco* (℡095.773.2100; ❷) not only has decent rooms but also the town's finest restaurant (closed Thurs except Aug), specializing in local produce (namely mushrooms, pork and pistachios). There's a garden-courtyard for *al fresco* meals and some scintillating views from the front of the hotel.

Caltanissetta

With twice as many inhabitants as Enna, the provincial capital of **CALTANIS-SETTA** (35km to the southwest) is easily the largest town in the interior, though little else about it is remarkable. Moreover, its sprawling modern suburbs give way suddenly to rolling empty fields beyond – the town is very much the last gasp before the almost ghostly rural expanses of Sicily's western interior.

The largely traffic-choked centre breathes a sigh of relief around the prettily restored **Piazza Garibaldi** and its splashing fountain. The handsome Duomo, the wedding-cake confection that is the church of San Sebastiano and the sandstone and salmon-pink Sant'Agata might all be locked but they form a pleasing ensemble, and you can also take a spin around the imposing walls of the seventeenth-century **Palazzo Moncada**, an aristocratic mansion belonging to one of Sicily's great feudal dynasties. Down behind the Duomo (follow Via Pugliese Giannone and Via San Domenico) it's under a ten-minute walk to one of the island's stranger castle ruins, the **Castello di Pietrarossa**, improbably balanced on an outcrop of rock. It's off-limits and looks like it should have fallen down years ago, though it's finally getting some belated attention as restoration work continues on the adjacent church and monastery.

The only other real sights are inconveniently located 3km out of the centre, and you'll need a car to visit both the archeological museum and adjacent Norman church (follow the brown "Museo Archeologico" signs from town and rub the satnav three times for luck). The **Museo Archeologico** (daily 9am–1pm & 3.30–7pm; closed last Sun of month; €4) is a vast circular bunker straight out of the Thunderbirds school of architecture, and contains some of Sicily's earliest

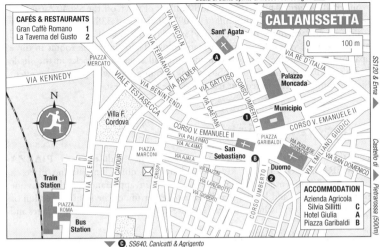

CAFÉS & RESTAURANTS
Gran Caffè Romano   1
La Taverna del Gusto   2

CALTANISSETTA

0   100 m

ACCOMMODATION
Azienda Agricola
Silvia Sillitti   C
Hotel Giulia   A
Piazza Garibaldi   B

finds (from the Bronze Age to the fourth century BC), including treasures like an unusual votive clay model of a temple. It's all beautifully presented, with clear English notes throughout, and there's unlikely to be another soul around save the slumbering attendants. Nearby stands the restored twelfth-century abbey church of **Santo Spírito**, founded by Count Roger and – a rare thing in Sicily – purely Norman in form. The plain structure is only enlivened by three tiny apses at the back, though the interior has a fifteenth-century fresco over the central apse and a twelfth-century font. If the church is locked, you can try ringing at the door on the right (home of the parish priest).

Practicalities

Caltanissetta's **bus and train stations** are at Piazza Roma, about a ten-minute walk from Piazza Garibaldi. (Train travellers **heading to Enna** are advised to take a bus instead from Caltanissetta, as Enna's train station is a long way out of town. Going the other way, the railway line meanders northwest, ultimately to Palermo, through empty upland plains, one of the most desert-like of Sicilian journeys.) There's cheap on-street **parking** all over town: if you follow "centro" signs and dump the car anywhere that looks suitable you shouldn't be too far from things.

Best **café** is the traditional *Gran Caffé Romano*, Corso Umberto I 147, which has an 8m-long counter full of almond (*mándorle*) biscuits (the local speciality), *cannoli* and other treats, and chunky leather sofas outside on the pavement. For lunch or dinner look no further than *La Taverna del Gusto*, Corso Umberto I 146 (☎0934.585.629), just up from the Duomo, which has an excellent-value fixed-price menu (€13, otherwise dishes €6–8) of rustic *antipasti*, home-made *cavati* pasta and grilled meat, and there's pizza too.

There's some uninspiring **accommodation** in a couple of central hotels, like the three-star *Hotel Giulia*, Corso Umberto I 85 (☎0934.542.927, ⓦwww.hotel giulia.it; ❷), but if you're going to stay the night you might as well aim a little higher. *Piazza Garibaldi*, Piazza Garibaldi 11 (☎0934.680.510 or 340.379.5803, ⓦwww.piazzagaribaldi11.it; ❷), is a first-class B&B in a restored palace opposite the Duomo, with colourful bedrooms sporting idiosyncratic murals. Or there's a wonderful *agriturismo* property around 12km out of town off the SS640 Agrigento road: ⚘ *Azienda Agricola Silvia Sillitti* (☎0934.930.733 or 338.763.4601, ⓦwww .sillitti.it; ❷, two-night minimum stay) is a working organic farm of olive and almond groves, wheat fields and vegetable plots. There are rustic rooms in three apartments, expansive terraces with views on all sides, hammocks in the shade and a sparkling swimming pool. Silvia is a charming host who prepares excellent Sicilian dinners (€25) on request using produce from her estate.

Piazza Armerina

Less than an hour's drive southeast of Enna, the small town of **PIAZZA ARMERINA** lies amid thickly forested hills. A quiet, unassuming place, it is mainly seventeenth- and eighteenth-century in appearance, with a skyline pierced by towers and houses that huddle together under the joint protection of decrepit castle and pristine cathedral. Despite the dense traffic that fills its lanes and

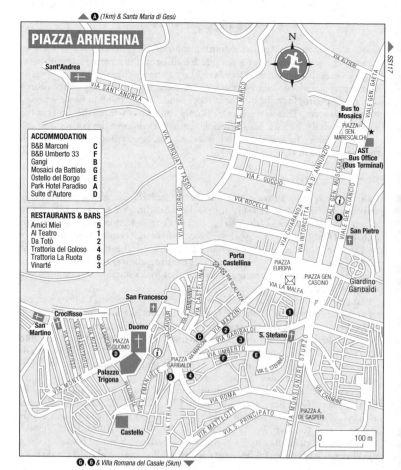

▲ Ⓐ (1km) & Santa Maria di Gesù

PIAZZA ARMERINA

ACCOMMODATION
B&B Marconi	C
B&B Umberto 33	F
Gangi	B
Mosaici da Battiato	G
Ostello del Borgo	E
Park Hotel Paradiso	A
Suite d'Autore	D

RESTAURANTS & BARS
Amici Miei	5
Al Teatro	1
Da Totò	2
Trattoria del Goloso	4
Trattoria La Ruota	6
Vinarté	3

Ⓖ, ❻ & *Villa Romana del Casale* (5km) ▼

thoroughfares, it's a charming place that deserves a detour and even an overnight stop, though many visitors bypass it altogether, given the enticement of the mosaics at the nearby Villa Romana del Casale (see p.271).

Arrival and information

Buses drop you off at Piazza Senatore Marescalchi, a large square on the main road in the lower, modern town, fifteen minutes' walk from the old centre. For bus information and tickets to Aidone, Caltagirone, Catania and elsewhere, ask in the *Bar della Stazione* in Piazza Senatore Marescalchi, or the AST office next door. On the way up to the Duomo in the old town you'll pass the **tourist office**, just up Via Cavour from Piazza Garibaldi, on the raised terrace on the left (Mon–Fri 9am–1pm & 3.30–7.30pm; ☎0935.683.049, ⓦwww.piazza -armerina.it).

There's metered on-street **parking** in the lower town, but you can get closer to the sights by following the signs for "centro" and then "Duomo". The streets narrow and all seems impossible, but actually a fairly sensible one-way system runs along Via Mazzini to Piazza Garibaldi and then dog-legs up Via Cavour to the Duomo – there's a fair amount of metered parking on the way and free parking in Piazza Duomo itself.

Accommodation

Most of Piazza Armerina's few hotels lack character, being mainly geared towards business travellers. However, there's one stand-out boutique choice right in the centre as well as lots of small old-town B&Bs and a decent hostel. If you don't have a reservation, start in Piazza Garibaldi and look for B&B signs in any of the neighbouring streets and lanes.

B&B Marconi Via Marconi 26 ☎0935.682.989 or 329.090.8075, ⓦwww.bedmarconi.com. Above the central *Bar Marconi*, this B&B has four en-suite rooms in warm colours grouped around a quiet courtyard. No credit cards. ❶
B&B Umberto 33 Via Umberto 33 ☎0935.683.344 or 340.558.6002, ⓦwww.umberto33.com. A centrally located B&B with three handsome en-suite rooms. ❷
Gangi Via Generale Ciancio 68–70 ☎0935.682.737, ⓦwww.hotelgangi.it. A three-star hotel housed in a sympathetically restored old *palazzo* in the lower town, featuring exposed stone walls, a cobbled courtyard, and straightforward rooms. You can park nearby as well. ❸
Mosaici da Battiato Contrada Paratore, 3km southwest ☎0935.685.453, ⓦwww.hotelmosaici .com. Out of town, at the turn-off to the Villa Romana, this country inn has reasonable rooms at low prices, and a terrace-restaurant that's subject to an influx of tour groups at lunch. Closed Nov & Dec. ❶
Ostello del Borgo Largo San Giovanni 6 ☎0935.687.019, ⓦwww.ostellodelborgo.it. The refurbished fourteenth-century Benedictine convent has both hostel beds (€17 per person, hostel card required) and 16 other private rooms (singles, doubles and family rooms, with and without

en-suite bathrooms), all converted from former nuns' cells and thus fairly spartan but quiet and clean. ❶, en-suite ❷
Park Hotel Paradiso Contrada Ramaldo ☎0935.680.841, ⓦwww.parkhotelparadiso.it. It's out of the historic centre, 1km beyond the church of Sant'Andrea (signposted from town), but if you want a more resort-style stay this is the place. It's a modern four-star with echoing public spaces aimed at the convention-and-wedding market, but the rooms are pretty spacious and well equipped, and there's a pool, sauna, gym and formal restaurant. ❸
🏃 **Suite d'Autore** Via Monte 1 ☎0935.688.553, ⓦwww.suitedautore.it. Offbeat is hardly the word – fabulously quirky accommodation in a redesigned old *palazzo* across from the Duomo, where the themes come thick and fast ("Strangeness", "Magic and Irony", "Fluidity", etc) in fun-filled rooms that mix contemporary design, stylish artefacts, retro objects, original art and photography. If you're especially taken by your Star Wars bedside table or Philippe Starck chair, everything is also for sale. The top-floor bar, for breakfast and evening drinks, has fabulous town and country views, and there's free parking right outside in the square. ❸, Duomo views ❹

The Town

The central core of town is small enough to cover in a morning's stroll, but its dilapidated yet graceful churches and *palazzi*, narrow streets and skinny alleys soon grow on you. The best views are from the very top of town, from the terrace of Piazza del Duomo, which is backed by the elegant seventeenth-century **Duomo** itself (daily 8am–noon & 4–7pm); you can get in to see the cool blue-and-white interior through the small green door on the Via Cavour side of the building. Across from the cathedral campanile, and its blind Catalan-Gothic windows, stands the spruce facade of the eighteenth-century **Palazzo Trigona**, its simple brick exterior crowned by a spread-eagle plaque. A few outdoor tables at *Bar Duomo* provide the best vantage point for a drink.

Restoration in town has pretty much started and stopped in Piazza del Duomo, and the rest of Piazza Armerina is an endearing jumble of cobbled steps and faded grandeur. There are noble mansions in varying stages of decay along **Via Monte**, formerly the medieval town's main street, while down Via Floresta (to the side of Palazzo Trigona) you soon reach the closed and tumbledown **castello**, built at the end of the fourteenth century and surrounded by once-rich *palazzi* with broken windows and tattered wooden shutters. The other area to explore is the **Castellina** quarter, off Via Mazzini, where steep residential alleys drop to the Porta Castellina, which is a surviving part of the medieval town wall – now with a rough arch hacked through it for traffic access. From pretty **Piazza Garibaldi**, vias Mazzini, Garibaldi and Umberto I are the main old-town shopping streets, all leading eventually to the large twin squares that separate old town from new, with the **Giardino Garibaldi** (gardens) beyond. For a bit more of a leg-stretch, it's only a kilometre's walk to the twelfth-century Norman church of **Sant'Andrea**, north of town and still impressive despite its simple proportions. Another kilometre or so down the same road, through orchards and gardens, stands the sixteenth-century church and convent of **Santa Maria di Gesù**, a low building set amid gentle green hills.

Eating and drinking

The old-town **restaurants** have the most atmosphere and are handy for the B&Bs. The liveliest cafés and bars though are those around **Piazza Generale Cascino**, in front of the Garibaldi gardens. This is where to come at *passeggiata* time for a stroll, an ice cream or a beer.

Amici Miei Largo Capodarso 5 ☎0935.683.541. "My friends" has charming terrace seating outside and a rustic brick-walled dining room, plus a menu that's especially good for seafood, from baked bream to sautéed clams and mussels. Pastas and mains are €6–14, or there are also really good pizzas (€4–8) at night.

Al Teatro Via del Teatro 6 ☎0935.85.662. It takes a bit of finding (easiest from the end of Via Garibaldi), but it's worth it for the terrace tables with nice views over the old theatre and town rooftops. Try the home-made *pappardelle*, or one of the thirty-odd different types of pizza (most dishes €6–10). Closed Wed in winter.

Da Totò Via Mazzini 29 ☎0935.680.153. House speciality in this local institution is the *bocca di lupo*, a steak with prosciutto, aubergine and mozzarella (€11). Otherwise, pastas and main

dishes cost between €8 and €15, or go for pizza at night. Closed Mon.

Trattoria del Goloso Via Garao 4 ☎0935.685.693. Good-value trattoria (most dishes €6–10) just off Piazza Garibaldi, with a little outdoor terrace. Closed Wed in winter.

Trattoria La Ruota Contrada Paratore, 5km southwest ☎0935.680.542. In an attractive rustic setting a little way up the road from the Villa Romana, this handsome former watermill offers shaded outdoor seating and excellent regional food, from home-made pasta to local sausage and rabbit (dishes €6–9). It's only open for lunch, and is the best place to eat near the mosaics (they also have one B&B room).

Vinarté Via Garibaldi 89. A nice little *enoteca* for tasting Sicilian wines, with a couple of stools on the street and a stand-up bar inside.

Villa Romana del Casale

Built on terraces in a sparsely inhabited neighbourhood 5km southwest of Piazza Armerina, the **Villa Romana del Casale** (Ⓦ www.villaromanadelcasale .it) dates from the early fourth century AD and remained in use right up until it was covered by a mudslide in the twelfth century. It was then hidden from view for seven hundred years until excavations began in 1950, revealing multi-coloured mosaic floors that are unique in the entire Roman world for their quality and extent. A roof and walls were added to indicate the original size and shape of the villa, and the mosaics are now protected from the elements, with walkways leading through the various rooms and chambers. It's an essential visit on any trip to Sicily, but the continuous stream of coach parties and tour groups hardly makes for a relaxing trip. If you can, it's best to come early or late in the day in order to avoid the heat and the crowds – the whole visit takes around an hour. In addition, there are ongoing restoration works and it pays to check the website, or ask at Piazza Armerina tourist office, before setting out to see the mosaics. Over the last few years, **opening hours** and **admission charges** have varied, depending on what parts of the villa can be visited, but

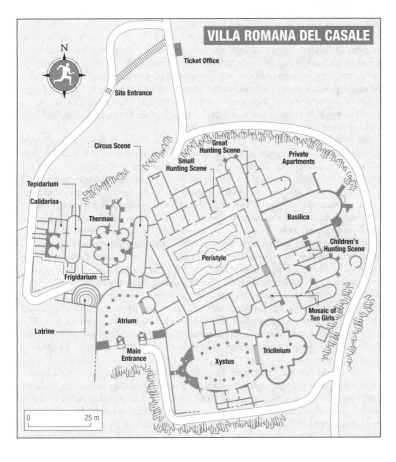

there's usually access to the site on a daily basis (though hours may be limited) and a charge of around €6.

From Piazza Armerina, a **bus** (May–Sept) leaves Piazza Senatore Marescalchi for the Villa Romana on the hour between 9am and noon, and between 3pm and 6pm, with a stop at Piazza Generale Cascino; it's a half-hour ride, and the return service is on the half-hour, starting at 9.30am. A **taxi** from Piazza Generale Cascino in Piazza Armerina costs around €10 each way. There's a **bar-restaurant** at the site, but the best place for lunch is the nearby *Trattoria La Ruota*, on the way to Piazza Armerina (see p.270).

The villa and the mosaics

Conflicting theories surround the function of the **villa**, but the most convincing explanation of its deeply rural location is that it was an occasional retreat and hunting lodge. That theory is supported by the many mosaics of animals and birds, including two specific hunting scenes. It's also immediately clear from the extent of the remains that the villa complex belonged to an important owner, possibly Maximianus Herculeus, co-emperor with Diocletian between 286 and 305 AD. There are four separate groups of buildings, built on different levels of the hillside and connected by passageways, doors and courtyards. Nearly all of what you see would have been occupied by the family for which it was built – slaves' housing and other outbuildings are still to be excavated properly. Few enough examples survive of such splendid Imperial Roman wealth – and even fewer with such extraordinary interior decoration. The floors of almost the entire building are covered with bright **mosaics** of excellent quality, stylistically belonging to an early fourth-century Roman-African school, which explains many of the more exotic scenes and animals portrayed. Their design also contains several hints as to their period and patron, though given their extent they're likely to have taken fifty or sixty years to complete.

The villa's **main entrance** gives one of the best impressions of its former grandeur, with the approach leading through the remains of a columned arch into a wide courtyard. Today's site entrance, though, is through the adjacent **thermae** (or baths): a typical arrangement of dressing/massage rooms and plunge-baths around an octagonal **frigidarium**, its central mosaic a marine scene of sea nymphs, tritons, and little cherubs rowing boats and spearing fish. A walkway leads out of the baths and into the villa proper, to the massive central courtyard or **peristyle**. This is where guests would have been received, and the vestibule displays a badly fragmented mosaic depicting a formal welcome by an attendant holding an olive branch. The corridor around the four sides of the courtyard is covered with a series of animal-head medallions: snarling tigers, yapping dogs and unicorns. Just off here, a balcony looks down upon one of the most vivid pictures, a boisterous circus scene showing a chariot race. Starting in the top right-hand corner, the variously coloured chariots rush off, overtaking and crashing at the turns, until finally there's victory for the green faction. The next room's mosaic shows a family attended by slaves on their way to the baths. Period detail – footwear, hairstyles and clothes – helped archeologists to date the rest of the mosaics.

Small rooms beyond, on either side of the peristyle, reveal only fragmentary geometric patterns, although one displays a **small hunting scene**, an episodic adventure that ends with a peaceful picnic in the centre. Another room contains what is the villa's most famous image, a two-tiered scene of **ten girls**, realistically muscular figures in Roman "bikinis", taking part in various gymnastic and athletic activities. One of the girls, sporting a laurel wreath and a palm frond, is clearly the winner of the competition.

The peristyle is separated from the private apartments and public halls beyond by a long, covered corridor, which contains the best of the villa's mosaic works. The **great hunting scene** sets armed and shield-bearing hunters against a panoply of wild animals, on sea and land. Along the entire 60m length of the mosaic, tigers, ostriches, elephants and even a rhino, destined for the games back in Rome, are pictured being trapped, bundled up and down gangplanks and into cages. The caped figure overseeing the operation is probably Maximianus himself. Much of the scene is set in Africa, Maximianus's main responsibility in the Imperial Tetrarchy, while an ivy-leaf symbol on the costume of the attendant to his right is that of his personal legion, the Herculiani.

Family apartments and public halls beyond are nearly all on a grand scale. A large courtyard, the **xystus**, gives onto the **triclinium**, a dining room with three apses, whose mosaics feature the labours of Hercules. One bloody scene portrays his fight against the giants, all struck by arrows, who writhe and wail with contorted faces. A path leads around the back to the **private apartments**, based around a large basilica, with mosaics echoing the spectacular scenes of the main building: a **children's circus**, where the small chariots are drawn by colourful birds, and a **children's hunt**, the tiny tots being chased and pecked by the hares and peacocks they're supposed to snare.

Aidone and the site of Morgantina

The extraordinary remains of the Greek city of **Morgantina**, which was at its height in the fourth century BC, lie 15km northeast of Piazza Armerina. That it's not better known is a shame, but also a boon as your visit will be mercifully free of the tourist shenanigans associated with the famous Casale mosaics. Unfortunately, buses from Piazza Armerina (leaving from Piazza Senatore Mareschalci) only run as far as the pretty village of **Aidone** (site of Morgantina's museum), with the archeological site itself another 5km beyond. Drivers should turn off the SS117 for Aidone at the crossroads known as Madonna della Noce, where there's a large restaurant-pizzeria; it's then a twisting 7km ride through the trees to the village.

Aidone

With its quiet central square and thoroughly laid-back air, **AIDONE** is a charming little spot. There are a couple of agreeable bars on the square and a crumbling church, but the true reason for a visit is the **Museo Archeologico** (Tues–Sun 9am–7pm; €4, includes site of Morgantina), impressively housed in a former Capuchin monastery – it's signposted, right at the top of the village. It makes an indispensable adjunct to seeing the archeological site itself, since it's here that you'll find everything that was removed from the ancient city – from ceramics, statuettes and busts to coins, candle-holders and domestic artefacts. Aerial photos and plans also provide a useful idea of the layout of the site.

Morgantina

Five kilometres northeast of Aidone, at the end of a long cobbled lane, the **site of Morgantina** (daily 9am–1hr before sunset; €4, includes Museo Archeologico at

Aidone) occupies two quiet hillsides with gorgeous views of the valley below. The car park is just under the east hill, and it's around a 500m walk down to the main entrance and ticket office, where you're given a brochure and map: all the signs on the site are in Italian and English.

After its demise in around 211 BC, the city became buried and forgotten for almost two thousand years, and even after the site's discovery it wasn't identified as Morgantina until 1957. To date, only a fraction of the city has been excavated, but the finds have shed much light on the island's pre-Hellenic Sikel population, who inhabited central Sicily from the ninth century BC. In the sixth century BC, Chalcidian Greeks settled here and lived in harmony alongside the Sikels until the city became the centre of a revolt led by the Sikel leader Ducetius, who destroyed it in the mid-fifth century BC. Swiftly rebuilt on a grid-plan with walled and towered defences, Morgantina reached its apogee in the fourth and third centuries BC under the protection of Syracuse, and many of the surviving buildings date from this period. A couple of hundred years later the city was in decline and soon after was abandoned altogether.

Heading left into the site from the main entrance leads directly to Morgantina's most distinctive ruin, the **agora**, bounded by three stepped sides that served as seats for public meetings. The small **teatro** to its right was built in the third century BC, but reconstructed in Roman times. Concerts, Greek plays and modern drama are sometimes held here in the summer (you can check at the tourist offices in Enna or Piazza Armerina). Other buildings here include a fourth-century BC **santuario** of Demeter and Kore, while on the level ground behind the agora is a granary and square slaughterhouse, beyond which stretches the 100m-long **east stoa**. A great kiln, the **Fornace Grande**, is one of the biggest ancient kilns ever excavated, and probably produced heavy-duty roof tiles, massive storage jars and the like. Further up the hillside in the residential quarter stand the ruins of some Hellenic **houses**, with two mosaic floors. One, the "House of Ganymede", has an illustration of the youth Ganymede being carried away to Olympus by Zeus's eagle to become the cupbearer of the gods.

There's an awful lot more of the site to explore, though in summer the heat might dissuade you. A path leads up to excavations on the **west hill**, which, though less revealing, include the fairly substantial remains of houses, roads and walls in what was another large residential area. In recent years, the remains of a second temple and a spring and aqueduct have also been unearthed. Not far from the site entrance, the **bar-restaurant** *Eyexei* (T 0935.87.074) is a rustic place serving drinks, snacks and meals, theoretically year-round.

Caltagirone

One of the most ancient of Sicilian towns, settled well before the arrival of the Greeks, **CALTAGIRONE** is a curious place, with an Arabic name (from *kalat*, "castle" and *gerun*, "caves"), yet an overwhelmingly Baroque aspect, dating from the dramatic rebuilding after the 1693 earthquake that flattened the area. The Arabs, though, had one extraordinary and lasting influence on the town, introducing local ceramic craftsmen to the glazed polychromatic colours – in particular, blues and yellows – that subsequently became typically Sicilian in execution. Until the great earthquake, the town supported a population of around 20,000, of whom perhaps five percent were actively engaged in the tiled decoration of churches and public buildings. The Baroque rebuilding saw a further burst of creative construction, while later, during the nineteenth century, came the

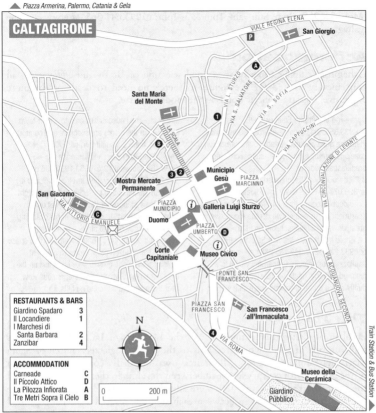

CALTAGIRONE

San Giorgio

VIALE REGINA ELENA

Santa Maria
del Monte

VIA L. STURZO

VIA S. SALVATORE

VIA S. SOFIA

VIA CAPPUCCINI

VIA CIRCONVALLAZIONE DI LEVANTE

LA SCALA

Municipio
Gesù

PIAZZA
MARCINNO

Mostra Mercato
Permanente

PIAZZA
MUNICIPIO

Galleria Luigi Sturzo

San Giacomo

VIA VITTORIO EMANUELE

Duomo

PIAZZA
UMBERTO

VIA ACQUANUOVA SECONDA

Corte
Capitaniale

Museo Civico

PONTE SAN
FRANCESCO

PIAZZA SAN
FRANCESCO

San Francesco
all'Immaculata

N

VIA ROMA

Museo della
Cerámica

Giardino
Púbblico

RESTAURANTS & BARS	
Giardino Spadaro	3
Il Locandiere	1
I Marchesi di Santa Barbara	2
Zanzibar	4

ACCOMMODATION	
Carneade	C
Il Píccolo Attico	D
La Pilozza Infiorata	A
Tre Metri Sopra il Cielo	B

0   200 m

Train Station & Bus Station

ENNA AND THE INTERIOR | Caltagirone

principal period of ceramic figurative work. Caltagirone's traditional industry is still flourishing, with scores of ceramicists displaying work at galleries across the town, while public buildings, churches, house balconies and gardens all feature ceramics in every nook and cranny – not to mention the famous tiled steps of La Scala that is Caltagirone's pride and joy. The old centre is small and easy to see in half a day, but there's an upbeat air here (and plenty of shopping opportunities) that makes a night an enjoyable prospect.

Arrival and information

Caltagirone is around 35km southeast of Piazza Armerina, or a 45-minute drive; it's also a handy stop en route to Gela on the south coast (40km) or Ragusa in the Baroque southeast (60km). The **bus station** and adjacent **train station** are in the lower town, a couple of kilometres below the old centre and connected to it by half-hourly local bus. Driving right into the upper town is best avoided, and **parking** is easiest at the large free space off Viale Regina Elena, near San Giorgio church. You can walk down Via Luigi Sturzo from here into the centre in five minutes or so. The main **tourist office** (Mon–Fri 8am–2.30pm & 3–6.30pm; ℗0933.53.809) is down an alley (Via Volta Libertini) just off Piazza Umberto, and there's a useful information desk inside Galleria Luigi Sturzo, Piazza Municipio

(Mon–Sat 9am–7pm, Sun 9am–1pm & 3–7pm; ☎0933.41.365, ⓌWww.comune
.caltagirone.ct.it).

Accommodation

Caltagirone's upper town offers a good selection of **B&Bs** and *affittacamere*, all
conveniently located for the sights, so there's no need to head for the more
expensive, less atmospheric hotels in the modern centre.

Carneade Via Vittorio Emanuele 96
☎0933.352.394, ⒺCarneade.rooms@tiscali.it.
Pleasant, quiet and comfortable *affittacamere* with
spacious, simply furnished en-suite rooms (no
breakfast served). ❷
Il Piccolo Attico Via Infermeria 82 ☎0933.21.588
or 320.077.3315, ⓌWww.ilpiccoloattico.it. One
large double room with a bathroom, and one attic
apartment composed of two double rooms, with
great views on all sides, taking in Etna. ❷
La Pilozza Infiorata Via San Salvatore 97
☎0933.22.162 or 339.735.2861, ⓌWww
.lapilozzainfiorata.com. Rather fancy B&B in a
restored "Liberty"-style *palazzo* with five individually styled en-suite rooms. There's no view to

speak of – the house is tucked into an old-town
street – but the rooms are spacious and comfortable, and there's a small terrace. ❸
🏃 **Tre Metri Sopra il Cielo** Via
Bongiovanni 72 ☎0933.193.5106 or
392.213.3228, ⓌWww.bbtremetrisoprailcielo.it.
Top B&B choice is this perfectly sited place right
on La Scala steps, near the top. Helpful owner
Gaetano has three simple rooms in his charming
house (you may have to share a bathroom,
depending on numbers), but he can also find space
in up to half a dozen other rooms in adjacent
buildings. Everyone gets to take breakfast on the
top-floor terrace, which has a stupendous view
over the town and surrounding hills. ❷

The Town

Emblem of Caltagirone is undoubtedly the 142 steps of **La Scala**, which cuts
right up one of the town's three hills to the sorely neglected church of Santa
Maria del Monte at the top. The staircase was originally conceived at the turn
of the seventeenth century as a road between the church, then the cathedral, and
the town centre below; the steps were added once it was clear that the incline
was too steep. The risers in between each step are covered with hand-painted
ceramic patterns, added in the 1950s, no two the same. Having puffed your way
up, your reward is the magnificent view down across town to the distinctive spire
of the Sicilian Baroque church of San Francesco all'Immacolata, with the plain
stretching away into the distance beyond. At night the steps are lit, and couples
and families spread out on them, chatting away. In May, there are floral decorations laid up the entire length, while on July 24 and 25 every year the steps are
lit by thousands of coloured paper lamps as part of the celebrations for the feast
of St James (San Giácomo).

All the way up the staircase, and in the alleys on either side, are found various
ceramicists' **workshops and galleries**, though you'll also find shops and
showrooms all over town. Some are huge warehouses, others just a room in an
old house, selling copies of traditional designs or original work – plates, vases,
jars, figurines – from just a few euros to a few thousand. The other Caltagirone
specialities are sculpted terracotta whistles and *presepi*, or Nativity crib scenes, and
again, you can find examples in shops and galleries all across town.

At the foot of the steps is the main old-town square of Piazza Municipio,
where the sturdy seventeenth-century **Corte Capitaniale**, decorated by the
Gagini family, is used for temporary exhibitions. Exhibitions are also held in
the modern **Galleria Luigi Sturzo**, named after the locally born Luigi Sturzo
(1871–1959), mayor, reformer and anti-Fascist. There's also a bar and a helpful
information desk inside here. Further down, off Piazza Umberto, the square

building with grilled windows and spike-studded metal doors was a Bourbon prison in the eighteenth century but now houses the **Museo Cívico** (Tues, Fri & Sat 9.30am–1.30pm & 4–7pm, Wed & Thurs 9.30am–1.30pm, Sun 9.30am–12.30pm & 4–7pm; €3). There's nothing essential to see inside, just the usual intriguing collection of local curios, folklore items and architectural fragments, plus paintings by the Vaccaro family who renovated the cathedral in the nineteenth century.

Beyond the museum, the road to the newer town crosses the **Ponte San Francesco** – studded with ceramic flowers and emblems – and then runs down towards the large public gardens (a 10min walk), where you'll find the last word on the 5000-year-old tradition of local ceramics in the **Museo della Cerámica** (entrance on Via Roma; daily 9am–6.30pm; €4). The gardens themselves are worth a whirl in any case, the centrepiece being a wonderful Art Nouveau bandstand, overlooked by a couple of kiosk cafés. This is one of several elegant examples in Caltagirone of the "Liberty" style – you'll also pass the Art Nouveau theatre outside the main entrance to the gardens.

Eating and drinking

There's not a great deal of choice of restaurants in the centre, but as you're unlikely to spend more than a night in town you should find something to suit.

Giardino Spadaro Via San Giuseppe 5. Lamp-lit garden bar just up an alley off the bottom of La Scala, which is cool and shady by day, often thronged in the evening when the music is turned up. Closed Tues.

Il Locandiere Via Luigi Sturzo 55 ☎0933.58.292. A tastefully restored old restaurant that's largely a fish place, though there are good vegetarian *antipasti* and pastas. The menu depends on what's off the boat, though fish couscous is usually available. Dishes €7–14. Closed Mon.

I Marchesi di Santa Barbara Via San Bonaventura 22 ☎0933.22.406. Located within a cavernous aristocratic mansion, with meals served in the echoing dining room or out

in the internal courtyard. There's an upmarket regional menu with reasonable prices (first courses €6–8, mains €10–16, and pizzas in the evening), offering things like pasta with pistachios and almonds or pasta *Marchese*, which is with tomatoes, wild fennel and breadcrumbs. Closed Mon.

Zanzibar Via Roma, at Via R. Tondo Vecchio ☎0933.58.661. The main attraction is the big outdoor terrace that catches the sunset, plus forty types of pizza (€4–8), a dozen crepes and a full menu besides (dishes €7–13), including a fair bit of fish. It's more of a locals' place than most, just out of the old centre, across the Ponte San Francesco.

A geometric diversion

Just fifteen minutes east of Caltagirone by train, twenty by car (Ragusa road), **Grammichele** ranks among the strangest and most ambitious of the new towns built after the 1693 earthquake that flattened much of this land. At its heart is a hexagonal design centred on an imposing central piazza with six radial streets, each bisected by secondary piazzas. The shape is no longer entirely perfect, due to a surfeit of new building around the edges of town, but it makes for an intriguing couple of hours' stroll, with all the streets in each segment corresponding exactly to their neighbours in dimension and appearance. It's disconcertingly easy to lose your bearings and, despite the grand design, Grammichele remains a predominantly rural-looking, old-fashioned town. Piazza Carafa, the main square, has a handful of *circoli*, or clubs, where most of the town's over-60s gather, while the *Jolly Café* has ringside seats for all the comings and goings.

Travel details

Trains

Caltagirone to: Catania (7–8 daily Mon–Sat; 1hr 40min); Gela (8–9 daily Mon–Sat; 40min); Grammichele (7–9 daily Mon–Sat; 15min).

Caltanissetta to: Agrigento (5–6 daily Mon–Sat, 2 daily Sun; 1hr 25min); Enna (7 daily Mon–Sat, 5 daily Sun; 35min); Gela (3–4 daily; 2hr); Licata (3–4 daily; 1hr 20min); Palermo (4 daily; 2hr).

Enna to: Caltanissetta (7 daily Mon–Sat, 5 daily Sun; 35min); Catania (6 daily; 1hr 20min); Palermo (2 daily Mon–Sat, 1 daily Sun; 2hr 20min).

Buses

Caltagirone to: Catania (1–2 hourly Mon–Sat, 4 daily Sun; 1hr 30min); Enna (2 daily Mon–Fri, 1 daily Sun; 1hr 25min); Gela (2 daily Mon–Sat; 1hr–1hr 10min); Grammichele (2 daily Mon–Sat; 30–40min); Piazza Armerina (5 daily Mon–Sat; 1hr–1hr 20min); Ragusa (2 daily Mon–Sat; 2hr).

Caltanissetta to: Agrigento (3–4 daily Mon–Sat, 1 daily Sun; 1hr 35min); Catania (13 daily Mon–Sat, 8 daily Sun; 1hr 35min); Enna (4–5 daily Mon–Sat; 50min); Palermo (7–10 daily Mon–Sat, 4 daily Sun; 1hr 40min); Piazza Armerina (5–8 daily; 30min).

Cesarò to: Catania (3 daily Mon–Sat; 2hr 15min); Randazzo (1 daily Mon–Sat; 1hr); Sant'Agata Militello (1 daily Mon–Sat; 1hr 45min).

Enna to: Agira (7 daily Mon–Sat, 2 daily Sun; 1hr); Calascibetta (8–12 daily Mon–Sat, 2 daily Sun; 30min); Caltagirone (2 daily Mon–Fri, 1 daily Sun; 1hr 25min), Caltanissetta (4–5 daily Mon–Sat; 55min); Catania (8–10 daily Mon–Sat, 5 daily Sun; 1hr 15min); Gela (3–4 daily; 1hr 15min); Leonforte (8 daily Mon–Sat, 2 daily Sun; 35–45min); Nicosia (3 daily Mon–Sat; 1hr 30min); Palermo (3–5 daily; 1hr 35min); Pergusa (4–9 daily Mon–Sat, 4 daily Sun; 20min); Piazza Armerina (4–6 daily; 30min).

Nicosia to: Catania (5 daily Mon–Sat, 1 daily Sun; 2hr); Enna (3 daily Mon–Sat; 1hr 30min); Gangi (4–7 daily Mon–Sat, 2 daily Sun; 40min); Leonforte (4–5 daily Mon–Sat, 1 daily Sun; 40min); Palermo (4 daily Mon–Sat, 2 daily Sun; 3hr 10min); Petralia Soprana (4–5 daily Mon–Sat, 2 daily Sun; 1hr 10min); Petralia Sottana (4–5 daily Mon–Sat, 2 daily Sun; 1hr 20min); Polizzi Generosa (2 daily; 2hr); Sperlinga (4–7 daily Mon–Sat, 2 daily Sun; 15min).

Piazza Armerina to: Aidone (6–13 daily Mon–Sat, 2 daily Sun; 15min); Caltagirone (5 daily Mon–Sat; 1hr–1hr 30min); Catania (3–6 daily Mon–Sat, 2 daily Sun; 1hr 40min); Enna (3–6 daily; 30min); Gela (3–4 daily; 40min); Palermo (3–5 daily; 2hr 15min).

8

The south coast

CHAPTER 8

Highlights

* **Museo Archeologico, Gela**
Stunning painted vases were
a speciality of Greek Gela,
and the town's museum holds
scores of fine examples.
See p.283

* **Valle dei Templi, Agrigento**
Take a walk through the distant
past at this archeological park,
dramatically sited between
town and sea. See p.290

* **Eraclea Minoa** A superb
sandy beach overlooked by
the impressive remains of a
Greek city. See p.296

* **Sciacca** Medieval buildings
and quirky stone heads at
Castello Incantato make
underrated Sciacca a
worthwhile stop. See p.297

* **Lampedusa** The rocky
shore, cliffs and grottoes of
Lampedusa are best seen
on a boat tour of the island.
See p.303

▲ Tempio di Giunone in Valle dei Templi

The south coast

The long south coast, from Gela to Sciacca, should be one of the most attractive parts of Sicily. Sparsely developed, it holds good beaches and some low-key Mediterranean ports and resorts that are barely known to Italians, let alone other tourists. However, sporadic concentrations of spectacularly ugly industrial development along the coast manage to put off many people, while the sea is heavily polluted in some areas, particularly around **Gela**, a large port and petrochemical town. To miss this coast altogether, however, would be to ignore some of the most important sights on the island. Gela itself retains its extensive Greek fortifications, while further west the hill-top town of **Agrigento** overlooks a series of splendid ancient temples, unrivalled in extent and preservation outside Greece.

Inland of Agrigento, the only place that merits more than a cursory glance is the village of **Sant'Angelo Muxaro**, whose 3000-year-old tombs dot the hill below. On the coast to either side of Agrigento, isolated sandy **beaches** – packed with locals on summer weekends – warrant the occasional trip off the busy main road, the SS115. One of the best lies just below another Hellenic site, **Eraclea Minoa**, while the port of **Licata** offers a few old-town diversions to go with its beach. Of the other coastal towns, **Sciacca** is perhaps the most enjoyable, a fishing port and summer resort with amazing cliff-top views, and from here you can make a couple of detours into the tall and craggy mountains that back this part of the coast. Or you might consider heading out to the **Pelágie Islands**: these barren spots in the Mediterranean are closer to Africa than Europe, yet are connected by regular ferry and hydrofoil with **Porto Empédocle**, near Agrigento.

Regular **train** and **bus** services link the coastal towns and villages, while less frequent services access the inland towns. **Hotel** accommodation is limited outside the major settlements, but there are plenty of opportunities to **camp** at sites along the coast.

Gela

GELA couldn't present a worse aspect on first sight: drivers have to negotiate a tangle of untidy backstreets, while the train line weaves through a mess of futuristic steel bubbles and pipes. Despite a few fine dune-backed beaches in the vicinity, it's no place to bathe; serious doubts surround the cleanliness of the water, and there's occasionally a chemical tang to the air. It was not always so. Gela was one of the most important of Sicily's Greek cities, founded in 688 BC, and under Hippocrates in the fifth century BC it rivalled even ancient Syracuse as the

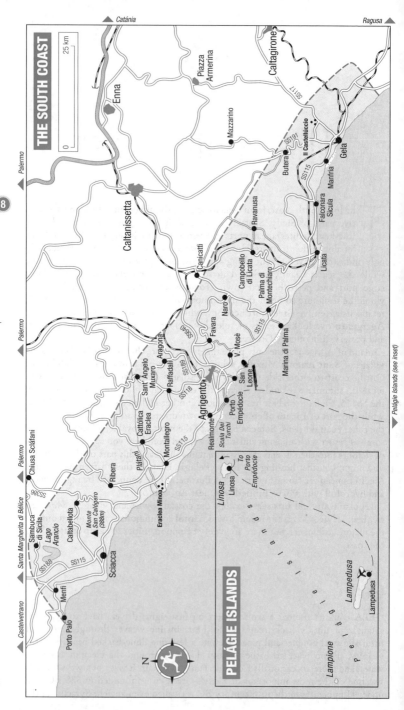

THE SOUTH COAST

25 km

0

▲ Catánia

Ragusa ▲

Piazza Armerina

Enna

Caltagirone

Mazzarino

SS117

Il Castelluccio

SS191

Butera

Gela

SS115

Manfria

Falconara Sicula

Ravanusa

Caltanissetta

Canicattì

Campobello di Licata

Palma di Montechiaro

Licata

Naro

Favara

V. Mosè

SS115

SS640

Marina di Palma

Aragona

Sant' Angelo Muxaro

Raffadali

SS189

SS118

San Leone

Cattolica Eraclea

Agrigento

Porto Empédocle

Plàtani

Montallegro

Realmonte

Scala Dei Turchi

SS115

Ribera

Chiusa Sciàfani

SS386

Sambuca di Sicilia

Lago Arancio

Caltabellota

Monte San Calógero (388m)

Eraclea Minoa

Santa Margherita di Bélice ▲

SS188

SS115

Sciacca

Menfi

Porto Palo

Castelvetrano ▲

Pelágie Islands (see inset) ▼

PELÁGIE ISLANDS

N

To Porto Empédocle

Linosa

Linosa

P e l á g i e   I s l a n d s

Lampione

Lampedusa

Lampedusa

February
First/second week Almond-blossom festival, the Sagra del Mandorlo in Fiore, at **Agrigento**: events take place in the Valle dei Templi – costumes, music and processions.

February/March
Carnevale at **Sciacca**, with participation of the entire town in five days of parades and competitions.

March/April
Easter Holy Week processions at **Agrigento**.

June
27–29 Sagra del Mare at **Sciacca**: a statue of St Peter is paraded on a boat at sea; there's a big fish fry-up and maritime-themed games at the port.

July
First/second Sunday Festival at **Agrigento** in honour of St Calógero.
Pirandello week Plays and concerts held at Pirandello's house at **Caos**, near **Agrigento**.

September
22 Pilgrimage and religious procession at **Lampedusa**, in honour of the Madonna di Porto Salvo.

island's political hub. Its artistic eminence attracted literary stars, most notably the dramatist Aeschylus, who, according to legend, met his end here when an eagle dropped a tortoise on him, apparently mistaking his bald head for a stone on which to dash its prey. However, Gela's heyday was short-lived. Hippocrates' successor, Gelon, transferred his power and half the city's population east to Syracuse in 485 BC, the deep-water harbour there being more to the tyrant's liking. Gela was later smashed by the Carthaginians and the Mamertines, its walls razed in the third century BC and abandoned to the encroaching sands. Modern Gela was the first Sicilian town to be liberated by the Allies in 1943, but otherwise – beyond an excellent archeological museum and a fine set of Greek defensive walls – is almost entirely without interest.

Gela's Greek remains

There's really no need to stay longer than half a day in Gela. That gives you enough time to see the only two sights, which lie at either end of the town's main Corso Vittorio Emanuele. At its eastern end, a twenty-minute walk from the centre, the **Museo Archeologico** (daily 9am–6pm; €4, includes entry to Greek fortifications) is notable largely for its important collection of painted vases upstairs. Mainly seventh- to fifth-century BC, the black and red jugs and beakers were Greek Gela's speciality: most major world museums tend to feature one or two, but the bulk are here. Other impressive finds include an animated sculpture of a horse's head (sixth century BC), and objects unearthed from necropolises belonging to Geloan dependencies. Outside the museum, a small **acropolis** has been uncovered, consisting of a few walls and a single temple column from the fifth century BC, though the small site is drained of all romance by the brooding, dirty industrial plant that dominates the beach below.

More archeological remains can be seen at **Capo Soprano**, at the western end of town. Head along the Corso and take a left fork (Via Manzoni), which runs parallel to the sea as far as the red gates of the site, a distance of almost 4km. The **Greek fortifications** here (daily: April–Oct 9am–6pm, Nov–March 10am–5pm; €4, includes entry to Museo Archeologico) date from the fourth century BC. Preserved by the sand dunes under which they were discovered, the walls stand nearly 8m high in parts, made up of perfectly fitted stone blocks topped by a layer of brick and now covered in protective glass panels. It's a beautiful site, and you're free to wander around the line of the walls: in some places you can make out the remains of watchtowers and gateways, while waves crash onto a duned stretch of beach below. If you've come this far out of town, you may as well nip around the corner (back towards the centre and left, by the hospital), to Via Europa, to see the remains of Gela's fourth-century BC **public baths**, the only ones from Greek times discovered in Sicily and still equipped with their original seats.

Practicalities

Driving into town, simply follow the signs for museum and fortifications – it's slow going on the SS115, which cuts right through the centre. **Buses** leave from directly outside the **train station** (tickets and information from the bar across the square); regular departures serve nearby towns, including Licata and Agrigento, Vittoria, Caltanissetta and Siracusa. From the station, turn right down the main road and, at the junction, bear right for the town centre and Corso Vittorio Emanuele.

Information can be obtained at the **tourist office** at Via Pisa 65, off Via Bresmes, which cuts across Corso Vittorio Emanuele (Mon–Fri 8am–2.15pm, plus Wed 2.45–6.15pm; ☎0933.913.788, ⓦwww.comune.gela.cl.it). You're unlikely to want to **stay** in Gela, but if you get stuck, the centrally located *Sole* on Via Mare 32 (☎0933.925.292, ⓦwww.hotelsolecl.com; ②) makes a useful stop, with air-conditioned, en-suite rooms, though it's somewhat run-down. A long row of bars, pizzerias and trattorias lines the endless lungomare.

Around Gela

With your own transport, you can pay a quick visit to Gela then strike off inland to the medieval hill-town of **Butera** or west along the coast to find a beach. Gela's surroundings don't improve until you're a good few kilometres out of town in any direction. Best for scenery are the two **inland** routes north: either up the SS191 to Butera, or northeast along the scenic SS117, which swoops towards Caltagirone and Piazza Armerina, following the line of the fertile Gela Valley. By car, you can be in either of the latter within the hour, the road taking you through rolling cornfields and vineyards. For the coast **west of Gela**, stick to the main SS115, which runs through town.

Inland to Butera

Around 8km out of Gela on the SS117, at a small road junction, a forlorn Norman keep – **Il Castellúccio** – sticks out on a hillock, in the middle of land keenly contested at the start of the Allied landings in Sicily in 1943. Defensive concrete pillboxes still stud the dirt-brown hillsides on either side of the keep.

From Il Castellúccio, a minor road runs 7km west to join the rather more direct SS191 from Gela, which runs to **BUTERA** in twenty winding kilometres. Important during the sixteenth century, under the control of the Barresi princes, Butera today idles along in its lofty, remote way, pulling in the occasional stray driver to Caltanissetta, another 50km north. It's a pretty little place, with the drive up alone revealing why Butera was once coveted by medieval overlords – the town sits on an impregnable crag, overseeing a patchwork of walled fields, burnt hillsides, bare peaks, regimented rows of vines and tomato plantations.

All traffic (including buses from Gela and Caltanissetta) pulls into Piazza Dante, the main square. From there, Via Aldo Moro leads up in five minutes to the **Castello dei Normanni**, a yellowing pile of which one battlemented wall and the central keep survive, incongruously tucked between modern apartment blocks. The terrace beyond enjoys tremendous views, to Gela and the coast.

Back in Piazza Dante, you can get a drink while contemplating the next move. *Il Portico dei Normanni* has outdoor seats, and doubles as an inexpensive pizzeria-restaurant (☎0934.346.146; closed Tues).

West along the coast to Falconara Sicula

The long, empty coastline **west of Gela** is dotted by more pillboxes left behind after the war. Following the SS115 from Gela, you come to a decent sand **beach** at **MANFRIA**, just off the main road. You won't get to stop here if you're travelling by train, however, as the tracks loop inland soon after Gela, and the next stop is at **FALCONARA SICULA**, a few kilometres beyond. Though neither place holds much apart from its respective beach, Falconara does boast a fourteenth-century castle, the private property of Palermitan aristocrats. It also has a **hotel**, the *Lido degli Angeli* (☎0934.349.054, ⓦwww.hotellidodegliangeli.it; ❷), with a ristorante/pizzeria, sports facilities and a **campsite** attached (☎0934.349.033; May–Oct), all right by the beach off the main SS115.

Licata and around

Ten kilometres further along the coast, the port of **LICATA** is the only other worthwhile coastal stop before Agrigento, though everything here can be seen in an hour or so. There's certainly nothing left of ancient Phintias, the settlement founded here in 280 BC by Greeks from Gela, whose own city had been destroyed in successive attacks. Instead, the centre of Licata is largely Baroque in character, with a lower town split into two distinct halves. Pavement cafés line the two wide avenues – Corso Roma and Corso Umberto – that form an L-shape at the heart of town meeting at Piazza Progresso. Behind here, the narrow crisscrossed alleys of the old town reach back to the harbour. There's a lido and **beach** just up from the harbour, though as Licata is still a working port, full of maritime hardware, it's not exactly enticing. For a view over the harbour, climb to the top of the town from the main Corso Roma and then work your way around the hill to reach an imposing sixteenth-century **castello**. Other strolls can take in the lively old-town **market** (over by 2pm), held in the cobbled square in front of the church, and some of Licata's good *palazzi*, the most prominent being the gargoyle-studded **Palazzo Canarelli** on Corso Roma. Housed in a sixteenth-century convent on Piazza Sant'Angelo, and reached by walking down Via Dante off Corso Umberto, the

Museo Archeologico displays a good deal of local prehistoric and Greek material, as well as medieval art, but was closed for renovation at the time of writing (when open, usually Mon–Sat 9am–1pm, also afternoons in summer; free).

Practicalities

Buses pull up on Corso Roma, right in the centre; the bar at no. 36 posts timetables and sells tickets for departures to Agrigento, Gela, Catania and Palermo. The **train station** is five minutes' walk away: go back down the Corso to the church, turn right down Via Giovanni Améndola, left at the bottom and then take the fifth right, down a little street called Via Stazione.

There's a great little **B&B** in town: *Antica Dimora San Girolamo*, Piazza San Girólamo (℡0922.875.010, ⓦwww.dimorasangirolamo.it; ➌), an old building full of character on an atmospheric square where, in fine weather, guests are served first-class breakfasts *al fresco*. You'll find slightly lower prices at *Al Faro*, Via Dogana 6 (℡0922.775.503, ⓦwww.alfarohotel.it; ➋–➌), a much blander hotel by the port and near the lido, with its own pizzeria/restaurant.

Licata also has some fine **dining** choices, including the pricey, double-Michelin-starred *La Madia*, Corso Re Capriata 22, off Corso Serrovia (℡0922.771.443; closed Sun eve & Tues, in Aug Sun lunch & Tues), where world-class dishes can be sampled on a tasting menu for €80. You'll find cheaper fare at *L'Oste e il Sacrestano*, a small, smart but unpretentious *hostaria* with moderate prices at Via Sant'Andrea 19 (℡0922.774.736; closed Sun eve & Mon, Aug open daily), near the Duomo and Corso Vittorio Emanuele, where a full meal should cost €40–45 without drinks. Otherwise, a few pizza joints are located by the lido, or try any of the bars on and around Piazza Progresso.

Palma di Montechiaro and Naro

If you're heading straight for Agrigento, it's quicker to pick up a direct bus at Licata than to stick with the train, which swoops inland to Canicattì before doubling back to the coast. If you're driving, though, you could make a couple of stops along the way.

From Licata, it's 20km to shabby **PALMA DI MONTECHIARO**, which lies just off the SS115; the Agrigento–Licata bus passes this way too. This was once the seat of the Lampedusa family, the last of whom – **Giuseppe Tomasi di Lampedusa** – wrote the acclaimed novel, *The Leopard*. He died in 1957 (*The Leopard* was published a year later), but the palace in Palma had lain derelict for a long time before that. Indeed, far more resonant for *Leopard* fans are the ruins in the western Sicilian town of Santa Margherita di Belice (see p.362). Today, the only echoes of the great feudal family recorded in the novel are to be found in Palma's imposing seventeenth-century **Chiesa Matrice**, built by one of Lampedusa's ancestors and approached by a wide flight of crumbling steps, and the ruined site of the **Castello di Palma**, a few kilometres west of town at the end of a small track. Four kilometres south of town, on the coast, **MARINA DI PALMA** has a strip of beach, mobbed by locals during summer weekends.

North of Palma, the road climbs 17km up to medieval **NARO**, whose thirteenth- and fourteenth-century buildings merit a look if you have time on your hands. SAIS **bus** services run here from Agrigento (Mon–Sat 3 daily, last one returning at 1pm; call ℡0922.29.324 for up-to-date schedules). The finest of the buildings are the Chiaramonte **castello** at Naro's highest point, and the nearby ruins of the old cathedral; other churches in this walled and battlemented town are emphatically Baroque. Architecturally harmonious though Naro is, the real attraction is not so much the end destination as the drive itself, from Palma and Agrigento, which is rewarded by extensive sweeping views down to the coast.

BxB Tranquillo Via Acrone 30

Agrigento and around

No one comes to **AGRIGENTO** for the town, though its worn medieval streets and buildings soak up thousands of tourists every year. The interest instead focuses on the substantial remains of **Akragas**, Pindar's "most beautiful city of mortals", a couple of kilometres below. Strung along a ridge facing the sea, its series of Doric temples are the most captivating of Sicilian Greek remains and are unique outside Greece.

In 581 BC, colonists from nearby Gela and Rhodes founded the city of Akragas between the rivers of Hypsas and Akragas. This was the concluding act of expansion that had seen Geloans spread west along the high points of their trade routes, subduing and Hellenizing the indigenous populations as they went. They surrounded the new city with a mighty wall, formed in part by a higher ridge where they placed the acropolis (and where, today, the modern town stands). The southern limit of the ancient city was a second, lower ridge, and it was here, in the so-called **Valle dei Templi** (Valley of the Temples), that the city architects erected their sacred buildings during the fifth century BC. They were – and are – stunning

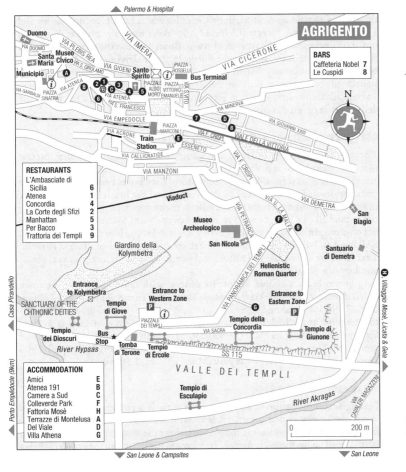

in their effect, reflecting the wealth and luxury of ancient Agrigento: "Athens with improvements", as Henry Adams had it in 1899.

As so often, however, Agrigento's Hellenic pre-eminence was no buffer against the cruel tide of Sicilian history. Conquered and sacked by successive waves of Carthaginians, Romans (twice), Saracens and Normans, the ancient city lost its status and many of its finest treasures. In a way, Agrigento never really recovered, and despite the undoubted modern pulling power of the temples, which fills the town with tourists throughout much of the year, it has little sense of purpose these days. Ugly modern suburban buildings and road viaducts on the coast below town lack all sense of proportion and are creeping ever closer to the temples themselves. Meanwhile, government statistics show Agrigento to be one of Italy's poorest towns. Consequently it comes as no surprise to learn that the Mafia has an undue local influence, not least in the sphere of speculative building projects.

Arrival

Public transport arrives in the centre of town. While you could easily jump straight on a bus to the Valle dei Templi archeological site, the town itself is worth exploring, and has some decent accommodation options. **Trains** pull in at the edge of the old town at Stazione Centrale, which has a beautiful garden and a number of luggage lockers (€3 for 12 hr) – don't make the mistake of getting out at Agrigento Bassa, 3km north of town. **Buses** arrive at the terminal in Piazza Rosselli, a few minutes' walk to the north. If you're **driving** into Agrigento, be warned that the one-way system in the old town is a nightmare. Some hotels are signposted, but you may well not be able to **park** anywhere near where you're staying (ask about *parcheggio* when you book). You can usually bag a space on Viale della Vittoria or Via F. Crispi.

City transport and information

The old town stretches west of the three main interlocking squares, piazzas Marconi, Aldo Moro and Vittorio Emanuele. Via Atenea is Agrigento's principal artery, running west from Piazzale Aldo Moro. **City buses** head from outside the train station on Piazza Marconi to the temples and the beach at San Leone; buy tickets prior to boarding from kiosks, *tabacchi* or the station bar (€1.10, or €3.30 for ticket valid all day); kiosks stand to either side of Piazza Marconi, though they're not always open on Sundays. You can buy single tickets on board the bus for €1.65. SAL buses to Porto Empédocle for the Pelágie Islands leave from Piazza Rosselli. **Taxi** ranks are at Piazzale Aldo Moro and outside the train station; for taxi phone numbers, see "Listings", p.294.

Agrigento holds a couple of **tourist offices**, with one focusing on the town at Via Atenea 272 (Mon–Fri 9.30am–1.30pm, also Tues & Thurs 3.30–7.30pm; ℡0922.596.168), and one covering the whole province located inside the Prefettura building at the back of Piazzale Aldo Moro (Mon–Fri 8am–2pm & 3–7pm, Sat 8am–1pm; ℡0922.593.227 or 800.236.837); both can supply useful maps and brochures. There's also a desk at Stazione Centrale (Mon–Fri 9am–1pm) and a kiosk at the Valle dei Templi car park (Mon–Sat 9am–1.30pm).

Accommodation

Finding **accommodation** in Agrigento itself is rarely a problem, although in peak season the nearby coastal resorts fill fast. All the budget choices, primarily small family-run establishments, are in the old town above the temples, and there are several B&Bs signed on the main Via Atenea. Tour groups tend to stay in the grander hotels a few kilometres east of town at **Villaggio Mosè**, an unattractive traffic-choked suburb on the coast road into Agrigento, though the hotels themselves – glossy, three- and four-star holiday palaces – are fine. The nearest **campsites** lie 6km south of town at the coastal resort of San Leone (see p.295), also the site of a good B&B.

Amici Via Acrone 5 ☎0922.402.831, Ⓦwww .hotelamici.com. Handy for the train station, the bright, air-conditioned rooms here have TVs, tiled floors and gleaming bathrooms. Some larger rooms sleep three and four; those on the ground level are smaller but have great coastal and valley views (especially rooms 101 and 102) and balconies. Breakfast can be poor. Free parking available. ❷

Atenea 191 Via Atenea 191 ☎0922.595.594, Ⓦwww.atenea191.com. A real find, this B&B on the main drag has huge, tastefully designed en-suite rooms, most with balconies offering distant views of the sea. One room has painted walls and ceiling. Breakfast is served on the roof terrace in summer. No a/c but ceiling fans. ❷

Camere a Sud Via Ficani 6 ☎349.638.4424, Ⓦwww.camereasud.it. This bijou B&B in an alley off Via Atenea has charming hosts, three vividly coloured en-suite rooms with a/c, paintings by Catanese artist Antonio Recca and a roof terrace for breakfasts. Internet access. No credit cards. ❷

Colleverde Park Via Panorámica dei Templi ☎0922.29.555, Ⓦwww.colleverdehotel.it. Large, modern hotel, halfway to the archeological zone, with English-speaking staff, wi-fi, parking and beautiful gardens. It's quite pricey, even given the location and facilities, but you'll find good rates online, and it's worth bargaining; valley-facing rooms cost most, the two fourth-floor rooms have wide roof-terraces, and there are cheaper town-facing rooms. ❺

Fattoria Mosè Via M. Pascal 4, Villaggio Mosè ☎0922.606.115, Ⓦwww.fattoriamose.com. On an estate run by the same family for 200 years, this *agriturismo* midway between the sea and

the temples (signposted from the SS115) offers a simple B&B option or else self-catering apartments in a converted stable block. Rooms are on the spartan side but there's a huge garden and a small swimming pool. Breakfasts and meals (€10 for lunch, €25 for dinner) are mostly home-produced and organic, and the family also run cookery courses. There's free internet and a laundry service. Closed Nov–Feb. ❸

Terrazze di Montelusa Piazza Lena 6 ☎0922.28.556, Ⓦwww.terrazzedi montelusa.it. Smart, clean and airy second-floor B&B at the far western end of the old town, with large, fully-equipped rooms and a charming, knowledgeable host who will offer useful tips for the area and even trot out a few tunes on the piano if you ask nicely. There are great views from the roof terraces, where a garden is being planned. Free internet. No credit cards. ❷

Del Viale Via del Piave 12 ☎0922.20.063, Ⓦhoteldelviale.it. A decent if unexciting mid-range hotel with clean, comfortable, air-conditioned rooms with private bathrooms and TVs. It's signposted off Piazza Cavour, behind an apartment block. Free parking is always available. ❷

Villa Athena Località Templi ☎0922.596.288, Ⓦwww.hotelvillaathena.it. The best reason to stay in this hotel is for its unrivalled location, just a brief stroll from the Valle dei Templi, with big windows soaking up the views. Service is prompt and efficient and there are landscaped grounds and a small pool, but the food and all the extras are horribly expensive, and it's a 30–40min march up to town. ❺–❼

The Town

It would be a mistake not to scout around the modern town of Agrigento. Modern only in comparison with the temples, it's thoroughly medieval at its heart. Unlike the mean streets of many less commercialized Sicilian towns, **Via Atenea**, the long main drag, flaunts a run of quality jewellers, trendy boutiques, bookshops and *pasticcerie*. Window-shopping here is a positive pleasure, especially in the late afternoon, when it's closed to traffic.

The streets off both sides revert to type, however, harbouring ramshackle *palazzi* and minuscule *cortili* (courtyards), among which a couple of specific buildings are worth seeking out. North of Via Atenea, the **Santo Spírito** church, at the end of Via Foderà, was built for Cistercian nuns in 1290. You can usually find someone to show you round, in return for a small tip. Inside, florid early eighteenth-century monochrome stuccoes by Serpotta sprawl across the walls and trompe l'oeil domed ceiling. Upstairs, you'll find some decorative nineteenth-century pictures of angels and saints inlaid with mother-of-pearl, and marvellous views of the temples across the fields. Back downstairs, if you ring the bell marked "monastero" and ask for "*dolci di mándorla*", a nun will bring you a tray of almond cakes, which are expensive, chewy, and worth the experience.

Via Atenea cuts right through the oldest part of town, at its most grand at the western end, around the **Municipio**, in Piazza Sinatra, housed inside a seventeenth-century convent. Next door to the tourist office here, the **Museo Cívico** (Mon–Sat 9am–1pm & 3.30–7.30pm; €2.50) contains a motley collection, from local artefacts – puppets, miniatures, ceramics – to contemporary art, with regular exhibitions. The narrowest and steepest of the streets spread up the hill from here, passing the church of **Santa Maria dei Greci**, built over a Greek temple of the fifth century BC. The flattened columns can be seen in the nave, while outside, visible from an underground tunnel in the flower-filled courtyard, the stylobate and column stumps are incorporated into the church's foundations. Inside are the remains of Byzantine frescoes; if the church is closed, you can get a key from the guardian at Via Santa Maria dei Greci 15, opposite. Just up from here, Via Duomo leads past a line of decrepit *palazzi* to the massive **Duomo**, set on a terrace at the top of the hill and fronting a spacious piazza below (9am–12.30pm & 4–6.30pm, closed during services).

The Valle dei Templi

A road winds down from Agrigento to the **Valle dei Templi**. Buses #1, #2 and #3 from outside the train station will drop you at a car park between the two separate sections of archeological remains, the eastern and western zones; a taxi will cost €10–15. You'll pass Agrigento's Museo Archeologico on the way; if you're intent upon doing the ancient site and museum in one go, you'll need a full day here. Take a picnic, or use the bar-*távola calda* at the car park. Entrance to both the eastern and western temple sites costs €10 including the museum (July & Aug Mon–Fri 8am–10pm, Sat & Sun 8am–midnight; Sept–June daily 8am–7pm). There's a useful audioguide (€5), and **guided tours** are offered in English – ask at the information kiosk in the car park for details. On August and September evenings, open-air **concerts** take place on the southeastern edge of the archeological zone at Piano San Gregorio, with tickets from €28, though the average price is nearer €50: phone ☎0922.20.500 for details of the programme, or ask at the tourist office.

The eastern zone

The **eastern zone** is the more popular, and is at its least crowded in the early morning or at night when floodlit in striking amber light. From the eastern entrance, a path climbs up to the **Tempio di Giunone** (Juno, or Hera), an engaging structure, half in ruins, standing at the very edge of the spur on which the temples were built. A long altar has been reconstructed at the far end of the temple; the patches of red visible here and there on the masonry denote fire damage, probably from the sack of Akragas by the Carthaginians in 406 BC.

Following the line of the ancient city walls that hug the ridge, Via Sacra leads west to the **Tempio della Concordia** (Concord), dating from around 430 BC. Perfectly preserved and beautifully situated, with fine views to the city and the sea, the tawny stone lends the structure warmth and strength. It's the most complete of the temples, and has required less renovation than the others, mainly thanks to its conversion in the sixth century AD to a Christian church. Restored in the eighteenth century to its (more or less) original layout, the temple has kept its simple lines and slightly tapering columns, although sadly it's fenced off from the public. Circle the temple at least once to get a decent view, and stand well back to admire its elegant proportions.

Via Sacra continues, past the site of the city's ancient necropolis and across what remains of a deep, wheel-rutted Greek street, to the oldest of Akragas's temples, the **Tempio di Ércole** (Herakles). Probably begun in the last decades of the sixth century BC, it's a long structure, with nine of the original 38 columns re-erected, and everything else scattered around like a half-finished jigsaw puzzle.

The western zone

The **western archeological zone** is less impressive, though still engaging – a vast tangle of stone and fallen masonry from an assortment of temples. Most notable is the mammoth pile of rubble that was the **Tempio di Giove** (Jupiter, or Zeus). The largest Doric temple ever known, it was never completed, left in ruins by the Carthaginians and further damaged by earthquakes and the removal of stone to build the port of Porto Empédocle to the south. Still, the stereobate remains, unnaturally huge in scale, while on the ground, face to the sky, lies an 8m-high telamone: a supporting column sculpted as a male figure, arms raised and bent to bear the weight of the temple. As excavations continue, other scattered remains litter the area, not least piles of great column drums marked with a U-shaped groove, which enabled them to be lifted with ropes.

Beyond, behind the excavated gates and walls of the Greek city, is the earliest sacred site, the Sanctuary of the Chthonic Deities, marked by two altars (one square and fire-reddened, the other round), dating from the seventh century BC, before the official foundation of the colony. This is also the site of the so-called **Tempio dei Dioscuri** (also known as Tempio di Castore e Polluce, or Castor and Pollux), rebuilt in 1832, its columns and corner-work actually made up of unrelated pieces from the confused debris on the ground.

Near here is the entrance to the **Giardino della Kolymbetra**, for which you need a separate ticket (daily: April–June 10am–6pm; July–Sept 10am–7pm; Oct to early Jan, Feb & March 10am–5pm; €3). Part of the city's irrigation system in the fifth century BC, it's now an extensive sunken garden, lush and green amid the aridity of the rest of the archeological zone. There is nothing monumental here, but it makes a pleasant relief from temple-touring, the olive, almond and citrus groves overlooked by honey-toned calcareous cliff walls draped with cactus and pitted with caves. It also holds banana, pistachio and pomegranate trees, all meticulously labelled and explained, and a reedy stream.

The Museo Nazionale Archeologico

The road that leads back to town from the car park, Via dei Templi, runs past the excellent **Museo Nazionale Archeologico** (Tues–Sat 9am–1pm & 2–7pm, Mon & Sun 9am–1pm; €8), outside which buses will stop on request. It holds an extraordinarily varied collection, devoted to finds from the temples, the ancient city and the surrounding area. There are brief notes in English throughout, and an informative audioguide €5). Count on spending two or three hours here, more if you combine it with seeing the remains of the residential area of the old city, just over the road.

Unusually for an archeological museum, much of what's here holds artistic merit as well as historical interest. You could skip most of the initial local prehistoric and Bronze Age finds, though in **room 1** look out for the gold signet rings, engraved with animals. **Rooms 3 and 4** feature an outstanding vase collection, beguiling sixth- to third-century BC pieces, one of which depicts the burial of a warrior. The highlight is a stunningly detailed white-ground *krater* from 440 BC portraying a valiant Perseus freeing Andromeda. But it's the finds from the temples themselves that make this collection come alive: leaving **room 4**, you'll pass a series of sculpted lion's-head water-spouts, a common device for draining the water from the roofs of the city's temples, while **room 6** is given over to exhibits relating to the Tempio di Giove, with three enormous stone heads from the temples sitting in the recessed wall. Some useful wooden model reconstructions help to make sense of the disjointed wreckage on the ground, although the prime exhibit is a reassembled telamon stacked against one wall: all the weather damage can't hide the strength implicit in this huge sculpture. The finest statue in the museum is in **room 10**, where the Ephebus, a naked Greek youth, displays a nerveless strength and power that suggests that the model was probably a soldier. Rooms beyond hold coins, inscriptions and finds from local necropolises; typical is an alabaster child's sarcophagus in **room 11** showing poignant scenes from his life, which was cut short by illness. The last couple of rooms contain finds from the rest of the province, one of which, in **room 15**, is the equal of anything that's gone before, amply demonstrating the famed Geloan skill as masters of vase-ware: a fifth-century BC *krater* displays a graphic scene from Homer in which Achilles slays the queen of the Amazons at the moment when he falls in love with her.

In the grounds of the museum, look out for the Gothic doorway of the adjacent church of **San Nicola**. From the terrace outside, you get an invigorating view over the temple valley, while just beyond is a small odeon (third-century BC) used for public meetings, during which the participants stood rather than sat in the narrow rows. Nip over the road on the way out of the museum, too: the **Hellenistic-Roman quarter** opposite (daily 9am–1hr before sunset; free) contains rows of houses, inhabited (on and off) until the fifth century AD, many with mosaic designs still discernible.

Other archeological remains

While you could see everything thus far described in four or five hours, without your own transport the archeological park's remaining sights mean a lot of extra walking. The quickest way to reach one of these, the **Tempio di Esculapio** (Asclepius), is to climb over the wall to the side of the Tempio di Concordia and scramble down to the SS115, from which a dusty track leads down to the under-sized temple, which has solid walls instead of a colonnade.

Back up towards the entrance to the western archeological zone, close to the cross-roads on the SS115, you can view the large two-storeyed Roman tomb known as the **Tomba di Terone** (75 BC), mistakenly named by historians after the Greek tyrant Theron. From the crossroads, Via Panorámica dei Templi heads up past the car park to another junction by the *Colleverde Park* hotel. Turn left here, then right onto Via Demetra, which leads to the Norman chapel of **San Biagio**, altogether around 3km from the Tomba di Terone. The tiny church was built over the visible remains of a temple that was contemporaneous with the ones below on the ridge. It's currently closed for restoration, but hang around and a custodian may appear to lead you down the cliff behind the chapel to the eerie **Santuario di Demetra** (be prepared to tip), where a stone-built chambered shrine hides two dingy caves that stretch 20m into the hillside. The thin corridor between building and caves was a sort of vestibule with niches for water so that worshippers could wash themselves. The most ancient of Agrigento's sacred sites, it was once devoted to the cult of Demeter and Persephone, and in use even before Akragas was founded. A mysterious and evocative place, it's at its best as the sun sets, when shadows flit across the dark and silent caves.

Eating and drinking

Agrigento has a fairly good choice of **restaurants**, many clustered around Via Atenea and offering some kind of *menu turístico*. Unsurprisingly, they tend to be a bit touristy, though prices are usually low. Only two or three places in town offer pizzas; most **pizzerias** are at Villaggio Mosè, east of town, below the temples, or at the coastal resort of San Leone (see p.295).

There are two distinct areas for **cafés and bars**. The town-centre *passeggiata* focuses on Via Atenea, and once the shops re-open in the late afternoon the whole street is packed. To watch the action, choose a seat at one of the little bars in Piazzale Aldo Moro, a nice place to sit in the early evening, despite the occasional burst of organ music from a local crooner. For sunsets and views, stroll along the leafy Viale della Vittoria, where four or five cafés cater to a local family crowd.

L'Ambasciate di Sicilia Via Giambertoni 2 ⊕0922.20.526. Fairly standard food in folksy surroundings, though tables on the outdoor terrace provide one of the few good views in town. The *antipasto rústico*, house pasta and *involtini* are good choices (mains €6–9 for meat, €12–17 for fish dishes). Closed Mon, but open Mon eve in Aug.

Atenea Via Ficani 12 ⊕0922.20.247. Family-run budget restaurant, set in a quiet courtyard with outdoor tables in summer. Expect simple, no-frills pasta, meat (around €6) and fish (€10) dishes of variable quality, or try the €14.50 tourist menu with wine. No credit cards. Closed Sun.

Caffeteria Nobel Viale della Vittoria 11. A relaxing spot for an ice cream or a beer under the shady trees of the avenue, open until late.

Concordia Via Porcello 8, opposite Via Atenea 61 ⊕0922.22.668. Tourist prices and clientele, with decent food, a chatty *padrone*, and an air-conditioned dining room with a bit of exposed ancient wall. In summer, you can eat outside in a private courtyard across the way. Spaghetti (*alle sarde*, pesto, or with prawns) or grilled fish are the best choices; first courses cost €7–9, mains €8–15, and meat and fish tourist menus €15 and €20 respectively (wine extra). Closed Sun lunch June–Sept.

La Corte degli Sfizi Cortile Contarini, opposite Via Atenea 169 ⊕349.579.2922 Little trattoria with a summer walled courtyard where you can eat tasty

pasta (like *cavatelli* with aubergines), or dishes such as grilled sausage or swordfish, and there's pizza in the evening. Nice staff and very reasonable food for the price. Fixed-price menus including wine cost €20 (meat) and €22 (fish). Closed Tues, but open Tues eve in summer.

Le Cuspidi Piazza Cavour 19. Come to this *gelateria* for the best ice creams in town – try the fresh ricotta, pistachio or almond.

Manhattan Salita Madonna degli Angeli 9 ⊕0922.20.911. Popular alleyway trattoria that serves a selection of fresh pastas (€5–10) and a lipsmacking fish soup (€15). The menu is pretty standard, but the food is nicely prepared. Usually busy at lunchtime. Closed Sun.

Per Bacco Vícolo Lo Presti ⊕0922.553.369. Fish dominates the menu in this small, smart trattoria favoured by locals. There's a good selection of salads (€5) and risottos (€7–9). Expect to pay around €30 for a full meal including drinks. Evenings only. Closed Mon.

Trattoria dei Templi Via Panorámica dei Templi 15 ⊕0922.403.110. Fresh seafood in a traditional restaurant halfway between town and the Valle dei Templi. Among their ample pasta dishes, opt for *panzerotti della casa* (ravioli with seafood sauce, €7), or splash out on the *fettuccine all'aragosta*, served with a chunk of lobster (€14). Closed Sun in summer, Fri rest of the year.

Listings

Banks and exchange ATMs at banks along Via Atenea (nos. 2, 15 and 145); on Piazza Vittorio Emanuele, and on Piazzale Aldo Moro 1. There's an exchange office at the post office.

Buses Services operating from the bus terminal at Piazza Rosselli include: Camilleri (⊕0922.29.136, ⊛www.camilleriargentoelattuca.it) and Cuffaro (⊕091.616.1510, ⊛www.cuffaro.info) to Palermo; Lattuca (⊕0922.36.125, ⊛www.autolineelattuca .it) to Sant'Ángelo Muxaro; SAL (⊕0922.401.360, ⊛www.autolineesal.it) to Licata, Gela, Palma di Montechiaro and Porto Empédocle; SAIS Trasporti

(⊕0922.29.324, ⊛www.saistrasporti.it) to Caltanissetta, Catania and Naro; Salvatore Lumia (⊕0922.20.414, ⊛www.autolineelumia.it) to Castelvetrano, Cattólica Eraclea (for Eraclea Minoa), Marsala, Mazara, Menfi, Sciacca and Trápani. There's a SAIS bus ticket/information office in the corner of the piazza. Otherwise, buy tickets on the bus. Timetables are posted in front of the various companies' stops.

Car rental Avis, Piazzetta San Calógero 11 (near train station) ⊕0922.26.353; Hertz, Via Empédocle 35 ⊕0922.556.090.

Ospedale Civile San Giovanni di Dio, Contrada Consolida, just outside town ℡0922.442.111, or for Pronto Soccorso (emergencies) ℡0922.591.221.

Internet Internet Train, Cortile Contarini, opposite *La Corte degli Sfizi* (Mon–Sat 9.15am–1.15pm & 3.30–9pm); you can also log on at the provincial tourist office in the Prefettura (first 15min free).

Pharmacies Averna, Via Atenea 325 ℡0922.26.093; Maria Teresa Indelicato, Piazza Vittorio Emanuele 13 ℡0922.23.889; Minacori, Via Atenea 91 ℡0922.25.089.

Police Call ℡112 or 113, or contact the Questura on Piazza Vittorio Emanuele ℡0922.483.111,

or the Carabinieri at Piazzale Aldo Moro 2 ℡0922.499.000.

Post office The circular building in Piazza Vittorio Emanuele (Mon–Fri 8am–6.30pm, Sat 8am–12.30pm).

Taxis You'll find ranks at Piazzale Aldo Moro (℡0922.21.899) and outside the train station (℡0922.26.670); otherwise call ℡347.339.4345.

Travel agents For ferry tickets to the Pelágie Islands and other services: Atenea Viaggi, Via San Francesco d'Assisi 3 ℡0922.26.333; Edrega Viaggi, Via Atenea 21 ℡0922.594.155.

Around Agrigento: Caos and Casa Pirandello

Southwest **of Agrigento,** at the end of the flyover leading out towards Porto Empédocle, the suburb of **Caos** was the birthplace of **Luigi Pirandello** and the inspiration for the Taviani Brothers' film, *Kaos*, based on four of his short stories. One of the greats of twentieth-century Italian literature, Pirandello is best known for his dramatic works, such as *Six Characters in Search of an Author* and *Henry IV*, though his 1934 Nobel Prize was awarded as much for his novels and short stories. He had a tragic life: his wife was committed to an asylum having lapsed into insanity following the ruin of her family and the birth of their third son, and for much of his life Pirandello was forced to write to supplement his frugal living as a teacher. His drama combines elements of tragedy and comedy with keenly observed dialogue, and the nature of identity and personality, reality, illusion and the absurd are all recurring themes. Pirandello's ideas – and innovations – formed the blueprint for much subsequent twentieth-century drama.

Although he left Agrigento while still young, Pirandello spent time here every summer at the **Casa Natale di Luigi Pirandello,** Contrada Caos, just off the SS115 and past the Valle dei Templi (daily 9am–1pm & 2–7pm; €4), and you can see the study where he wrote, crammed with foreign editions of his works. As well as a couple of murals he painted, it holds stacks of photos, including one sent by George Bernard Shaw, and a fifth-century vase, depicting a bearded man attacking a young woman, that was formerly used as an urn for Pirandello's ashes. After seeing the house, with its bamboo and daub interior, you can wander down through the grounds to where the writer's ashes are interred, though the views he once enjoyed over the sea are now ruined by a patch of industrial horror.

SAL buses stop here once or twice hourly between Agrigento's bus and train stations and Porto Empédocle (reduced services on Sun).

Porto Empédocle and around

Six kilometres southwest of Agrigento, **PORTO EMPÉDOCLE** is of main interest as the departure-point for ferries to the Pelágie Islands. Though it's an unprepossessing, functional port, much of it dominated by an enormous cement works, its workaday ambience makes it a welcome antidote to tourist-ridden Agrigento. If you're waiting for a ferry, you can enjoy a pleasant enough stroll along the central pedestrian walkway in town, or dine at good, inexpensive fish **restaurants** such as *La Lámpara*, in what looks like a long wooden shed a few minutes' walk along the seafront at Via F. Crispi 3 (☎339.490.6833), where an abundant three-course meal plus good local wine will cost around €25. SAL **buses** leave for the port once or twice hourly from Agrigento's bus and train stations, six times on Sunday (a 15–20min journey), dropping you in Piazza Italia, one block from the waterfront; the last bus from Agrigento leaves at 9pm (7pm on Sun). A **taxi** from Agrigento will cost about €25.

About 7km west of Porto Empédocle, following signs for Realmonte, you'll find a stunning sandy **beach** at the bottom of furrowed and gleaming-white cliffs at **Scala dei Turchi**. A hideous abandoned construction has defaced the magnificent landscape on one side of the beach, but the water is crystalline (beware the shoals of biting fish). At the top of the steps leading down to the beach, the *Lido Scala dei Turchi* (☎0922.814.563; closed Mon Sept–June) provides welcome sustenance in the form of delicious seafood **meals** for less than €25. There are no bus connections here from Agrigento.

San Leone ✓ 20 m'ns by bus

A far less spectacular but still decent beach lies east down the coast, 6km south of Agrigento, at the resort of **SAN LEONE**. With a handful of accommodation options, including the two campsites nearest to Agrigento (both open all year), this would make a good alternative to staying in Agrigento itself, to which it's connected by bus #2 from outside the train station (every 30min until 9pm); taxis from Agrigento charge around €30. Things get very lively here in summer, and there's a good choice of **places to eat**. The best of these is *Trattoria Caico*, Via Nettuno 35 (☎0922.412.788; closed Tues and Nov), in business for half a century, where you can dig into such dishes as *cavatelli alla Siciliana* (pasta with tomato and aubergine), ravioli *di cernia* (with grouper fish) or grilled meats and fish on the vine-shaded patio; main courses cost around €15, and pizzas from the wood-fired oven are available in the evening.

Hotels and B&Bs

Hotel Costazzurra Via delle Viole 2 ☎0922.411.222, ⓦwww.hotelcostazzurra.it. A 5min walk from the beach, this family-run hotel offers quiet, modern and spacious rooms with a/c, TV and wi-fi. There's a good restaurant, spa whirlpool, free bikes and diving courses. The bus stops right outside. ❹

Sabbia d'Oro Via Nettuno 19 ☎331.508.6842, ⓦwww.sabbiadoro.ag.it. Close to the beach and 20m from the bus stop for the temples and Agrigento, this B&B is smart and modern but the rooms – some on the small side, but all light and airy – are tastefully furnished with antiques. Breakfasts are simple: breads, yoghurt and coffee. Free wi-fi. ❷

Campsites

Nettuno Via Lacco Ameno 3 ☎0922.416.268, ⓦwww.campingnettuno.com. This is right by a sandy beach at the southern end of San Leone (2km from the centre), with pinewoods that provide shade for camping. There's a restaurant, pizzeria and store, and apartments sleeping two to four are available for weekly rent. Take bus #2 from Agrigento or San Leone to get here.

Valle dei Templi Viale Emporium 192 ☎0922.411.115, ⓦwww.campingvalledeitempli .com. A couple of kilometres from the temples and 700m from the sea (with a bus stop for Agrigento outside), this has a bar, restaurant and pizzeria, and ten bungalows (❶) that are usually booked up in high summer.

Sant'Ángelo Muxaro

Some 30km north of Agrigento, in the steeply sloping Plátani River valley, the small agricultural centre of **SANT'ÁNGELO MUXARO** boasts a number of local *tholos* (tombs) hollowed out of the rock in dome-shaped caves. The earliest date from the eleventh century BC, but most are from around the eighth to the fifth century BC, and recall Minoan and Mycenaean examples in design. You'll spot them as you approach the bare hillside on which the village stands: the road leads up past a ramshackle brick wall, beyond which a path heads along the sheer rock to the "beehive" caves. At the bottom, the largest is known locally as the **Tomba del Príncipe**: later converted into a Byzantine chapel, it's half-hidden by overhanging trees and you may have to backtrack to get inside. Like all the others, it's empty now, the finds scattered in various museums around Europe.

Practicalities

You can get to Sant'Ángelo by **bus** from Agrigento with the Lattuca line, leaving from Agrigento's Piazza Vittorio Emanuele (Mon–Sat at 10.30am, 2.10pm & 6.30pm; the last bus back leaves at 4pm). Drivers should take the SS189 branching off westward for Aragona and Sant'Ángelo, or choose the more wriggly but faster SS118 via Raffadali.

A great **accommodation** option, ⚒ *Val di Kam*, based in the centre of town at Piazza Umberto I 31 (☎0922.919.670 or 339.530.5989, ⓦwww.valdikam .it; ❷), offers en-suite rooms in different parts of the village. Breakfast is usually a grand affair with local delicacies, served in your room, and the agency can also arrange local dinners in private houses. *Val di Kam* also organizes hiking, caving and archeological trips around Sant'Ángelo, can arrange pick-ups from Agrigento and is a mine of useful information on the area.

Eraclea Minoa

Thirty-five kilometres along the coast northwest of Agrigento is the third important Greek site in this stretch of seafront, **ERACLEA MINOA**. According to the historian Diodorus, this was originally named Minoa after the Cretan king Minos, who chased Daedalus from Crete to Sicily and founded a city where he landed. The Greeks settled here in the sixth century BC, later adding the tag Heraklea. A buffer between the two great cities of Akragas, 40km to the east, and Selinus (Selinunte), 60km west, Eraclea was dragged into endless border disputes, but flourished nonetheless. Most of what's left dates from the fourth century BC, the city's most important period, three hundred years or so before it fell into decline.

It can be a challenge to **reach the site** without your own transport. In summer it's slightly simpler: regular Lumia buses from Agrigento go to Cattólica Eraclea, from which, between May and September, four Cacciatore buses run daily to Eraclea Minoa (9am, 11.30am, 2.30pm & 6.45pm; ☎0922.39.016) – the buses go direct to the main village by the sea, so for the site ask to get off at the turn-off from which it's a kilometre's walk. In other periods, you'll have to catch any bus between Agrigento and Sciacca and ask the driver to put you off at the turning for Eraclea Minoa on the SS115. The site is 3.5km distant from there, with the beach another 1km below. **Heading on** west from the site turn-off, you should be able to flag down a bus en route to Sciacca.

The site

The **site** (daily 9am–1hr before sunset, may close Sun in winter, call ☏0922.846.005 to check; €4) sits on a ridge high above a beautiful arc of sand, with the mouth of the River Plátani on the other side. Among the most attractive of all Greek sites in Sicily, it occupies a headland of which only around a third has so far been excavated. What there is to see is the fruit of successive excavations by foreign universities, who, together with the local *Comune*, have landscaped the remains to good effect. Don't stray too far off the paths, though, as snakes lurk in the undergrowth.

Apart from the city **walls**, once 6km long and with a good part still standing, the most impressive remains are of the sandstone **theatre**. Now restored to its former glory, after years of deterioration of the seats, which are made of very soft stone, the theatre is protected from the worst of the elements by a plastic roof. Evening concerts and classical **drama productions** are staged here in July and August, with tickets costing around €12: see ⓦcattolicaeracleaonline.it for information or call ☏0922.846.005.

Above the theatre, excavations have also revealed tombs and traces of a Greco-Roman temple, while below stand the ruins of a grand house, with fragments of Roman mosaics, though these are covered and inaccessible. Many of the finds are displayed in a small on-site **museum** (same ticket).

The beach

While you're here, you'll be hard put to resist a trip down to the **beach**, one of the finest on Sicily's southern coast, backed by pine trees, chalky cliffs and a strip of holiday homes. It's hideously busy in July and August; unless you get here early, you'll never find a space to park. You can rent loungers and parasols on the beach, which also holds a couple of good **bar-restaurants**: the *Sabbia d'Oro* (☏0922.846.066), which stays open all year and offers pasta and seafood dishes for around €10, and *Lido Garibaldi* (☏0922.846.061 or 339.813.7907), which has pizzas, pastas and good breakfasts. Next to the *Sabbia d'Oro*, the beach bar *Rotta Su Itaka* also has food and music until late (open summer only).

You'll find **rooms** and apartments advertised at *Lido Garibaldi* and *Sabbia d'Oro*, though in high season these are usually booked up. Alternatively, you can **camp** just steps from the sea at the pine-shaded *Eraclea Minoa Village* (summer ☏0922.846.023, winter ☏0922.29.101, ⓦwww.eracleaminoavillage.it), which also has one- and two-bedroom bungalows (❸) and a bar, pizzeria, restaurant and disco. There's a **supermarket** on the road running eastwards on the one-way system.

Sciacca

Just over 30km further up the coast from Eraclea Minoa, **SCIACCA** comes as a welcome surprise after the ugly industry around the southern coast's other towns. Although not immediately attractive – it is, after all, a working fishing port, and run-down in parts – it does have a good-looking upper town that's virtually untouched by tourism. A spa town for nearby Selinus in ancient times, it enjoyed great prosperity under the Arabs, from whom its modern name is thought to derive (the Arabic *xacca* meaning "from the water"). The town was at the centre of a feud between Catalan and Norman families that simmered on for a century, resulting in the deaths of a good half of the local population. Several notable buildings are scattered about, which infuse Sciacca's agreeable Mediterranean air with more than a passing historical interest and make for some pleasant strolling through the weaving streets.

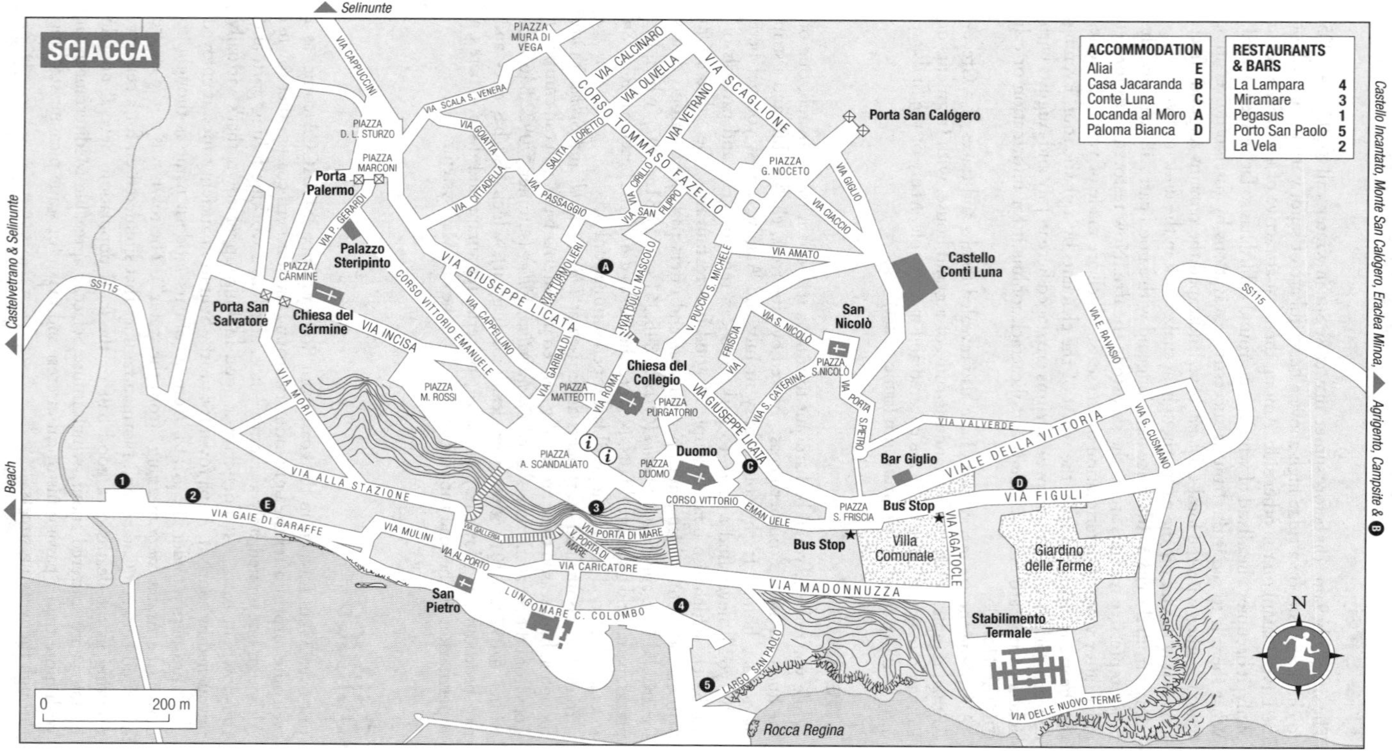

SCIACCA
ACCOMMODATION
Aliai E
Casa Jacaranda B
Conte Luna C
Locanda al Moro A
Paloma Bianca D
RESTAURANTS & BARS
La Lampara 4
Miramare 3
Pegasus 1
Porto San Paolo 5
La Vela 2
Selinunte
Castelvetrano & Selinunte
Beach
Castello Incantato, Monte San Calógero, Eraclea Minoa, Agrigento, Campsite & B
Porta San Calógero
Castello Conti Luna
San Nicolò
Chiesa del Collegio
Duomo
Bar Giglio
Bus Stop
Bus Stop
Villa Comunale
Giardino delle Terme
Stabilimento Termale
Porta Palermo
Palazzo Steripinto
Porta San Salvatore
Chiesa del Càrmine
San Pietro
Rocca Regina
VIA CAPPUCCINI
PIAZZA MURA DI VEGA
VIA CALCINARO
VIA OLIVELLA
VIA SCAGLIONE
CORSO TOMMASO FAZELLO
VIA VETRANO
VIA SCALA S. VENERA
PIAZZA D. L. STURZO
PIAZZA MARCONI
VIA GOIATTA
SALITA LORETTO
VIA CIRILLO
VIA SAN FILIPPO
VIA PASSAGGIO
VIA CITTADELLA
PIAZZA G. NOCETO
VIA GIGLIO
VIA CIACCIO
VIA AMATO
VIA P. GERARDI
PIAZZA CARMINE
VIA GIUSEPPE LICATA
VIA TURMOLIERI
VIA DULCI MASCOLO
V. PUCCIO S. MICHELE
CORSO VITTORIO EMANUELE
VIA CAPPELLINO
VIA INCISA
VIA GARIBALDI
VIA FRISCIA
VIA S. NICOLÒ
PIAZZA S.NICOLÒ
VIA S. CATERINA
VIA PORTA S.PIETRO
VIA E. RAVASIO
SS115
SS115
VIA MORI
PIAZZA M. ROSSI
PIAZZA MATTEOTTI
VIA ROMA
PIAZZA PURGATORIO
VIA VALVERDE
VIALE DELLA VITTORIA
VIA G. CUSMANO
PIAZZA A. SCANDALIATO
PIAZZA DUOMO
VIA FIGULI
VIA ALLA STAZIONE
CORSO VITTORIO EMANUELE
PIAZZA S. FRISCIA
VIA AGATOCLE
VIA GAIE DI GARAFFE
VIA MULINI
VIA GALLERIA
VIA PORTA DI MARE
V. PORTA DI MARE
VIA AL PORTO
VIA CARICATORE
VIA MADONNUZZA
LUNGOMARE C. COLOMBO
LARGO SAN PAOLO
VIA DELLE NUOVO TERME
N
0
200 m

The town is the main centre of **ceramic** production on Sicily's south coast, and you'll see colourful plates, vases and ornaments on sale everywhere.

Arrival and information

Buses pull up on Via Figuli and Via Agatocle, by the Villa Comunale (the town gardens) at the eastern end of Sciacca. Bus tickets are sold at the *Bar Giglio* on Viale della Vittoria for Lumia services to Agrigento, Caltabellotta, Castelvetrano and Trápani, and from the *Antico Chiosco* bar in the centre of Piazza Santa Friscia for Gallo services to Palermo. Parking is problematic in Sciacca – ask locals for advice. Both of the town's **tourist offices** – at Corso Vittorio Emanuele 84 (Mon–Fri 9am–1pm, also Wed 3.30–7pm; ☏0925.22.744, ☻www.servizioturistico regionalesciacca.it) and 94 (Mon–Fri 8am–2pm plus Tues & Thurs 3–6pm, extended opening in summer; ☏0925.20.478, ☻www.comunedisciacca.it) – can supply maps, public transport timetables, accommodation lists and information in English, though not everything is up to date.

Accommodation

While Sciacca itself offers a small selection of **hotels and B&Bs**, other resort-style hotels and campsites can be found out of town by the local beaches, for example at Contrada Sovareto, 5km east of town. A further 2–3km east of the centre in Contrada San Giorgio, the *Makauda Beach Residence* (☏0925.997.001, ☻www .makaudabeach.it; closed late Sept to late April) is a good **campsite** right on the beach, with apartments also available.

Aliai Via Gaie de Garaffe 60 ☏0925.905.388, ☻www.aliai.com. First-rate B&B facing the sea in the lower town. The smartly renovated rooms boast antique touches and free wi-fi, and one has its own terrace. ❷

Casa Jacaranda Via delle Sequoie, Contrada Isabella ☏392.812.3231, ☻www.casajacaranda .it. This ultramodern B&B lies 2km east of town, but just 30m from the bus stop for the frequent service into the centre. It has highly designed decor, boldly coloured rooms equipped with LCD TV, a/c, wi-fi and scented towels, and a gazebo in the semi-tropical garden where breakfast is served. No credit cards. ❸

Conte Luna Vícolo Gino 1 ☏0925.993.396 or 348.120.3647, ☻www.contelunasciacca .com. A welcoming B&B in an old *palazzo* in the heart of the upper town (off Via Licata), where two of the seven en-suite rooms have cooking facilities, and all have fridges and a/c. The top room is

best, with a large balcony and panoramic views. There's also a spacious lounge and a terrace, and in summer, a minibus service is available to carry guests to nearby beaches. Breakfast is at a nearby café. No credit cards. ❷

Locanda al Moro Via Liguori 44 ☏0925.86.756, ☻www.almoro.it. Set in a thirteenth-century Moorish tower but modern and clean within, this is an excellent B&B, in the heart of town run by a Sicilian-German couple. Local wine tours can be organized. The only downsides are the difficulty in finding it by car (ask directions and don't attempt to negotiate the surrounding narrow lanes) and the stairs. Rooms – some small – have a/c, and there's free internet. ❸

Paloma Bianca Via Figuli 5 ☏0925.25.130, ☻www.lapalomablanca.it. Plain, old-fashioned hotel close to the bus stop, adequate for a night or two. Half of the rooms have little balconies overlooking the street. ❷

The Town

Sciacca's still-walled upper town can be entered through any of the three grand gates remaining of the original seven. The westernmost, **Porta San Salvatore**, leads onto the **Chiesa del Cármine**, whose facade is lent a skew-whiff air by an off-centre Gothic rose window. Past the church, up Via P. Gerardi, the fifteenth-century **Palazzo Steripinto** is even more ungainly, its embossed exterior only partially offset by some slender arched windows.

Haunting heads

Just outside town, a couple of kilometres east of Sciacca, **Castello Incantato** on Via Ghezzi is a garden full of thousands of stone heads (Tues–Sun: April–Oct 9am–1pm & 4–8pm; Nov–March 9am–1pm & 3.30–7.30pm; €3). Carved in naive style over a period of fifty years by Filippo Bentivegna, their faces are serious, beautiful and disturbing. After being rejected by his girlfriend, then beaten up and left for dead on the streets of America, Bentivegna returned home to Sciacca and devoted his life to carving these heads, symbols of his imaginary enemies, until his death in 1967. The eccentric artist would walk the streets of Sciacca with a short stick and a sceptre, and liked to be addressed as "Your Excellency".

To get here, follow the yellow signs from Sciacca, or take bus #4 from Porta Palermo, the port area or the Villa Comunale.

From here, the main **Corso Vittorio Emanuele** runs right the way down to the lovely **Piazza A. Scandaliato**, a large terrace with some good cafés, enhanced by wide views over the port and distant bays. The most enduring Arab legacy in town is the street layout and, back from the piazza, above the **Duomo**, a Moorish knot of passages and steep alleys leads up to the rather feeble remains of the fourteenth-century **Castello Conti Luna**, which belonged to one of the feuding families that disrupted medieval Sciacca. A little way down from here, the twelfth-century church of **San Nicolò** is a tiny construction with three apses and some elegant blind arcading. Back up beyond the Duomo, at the end of Via Madonnuzza, are Sciacca's *Stabilimento Termale*, or **thermal baths** (Mon 3.30–7.30pm, Tues–Sat 9.30am–1.30pm & 3.30–7.30pm, Sun 9.30am–1.30pm; €6 for half a day, €9 all day), where you can take a cleansing dip in the therapeutic waters, while a range of massages and treatments are offered at the adjacent *Grand Hotel delle Terme* from €32, which should be booked (℡0925.23.133, ⓦwww .grandhoteldelleterme.com).

Steps from Piazza A. Scandaliato lead down the cliffside to the lower town and **port**, whose most distinctive feature is the hexagonally steepled modern church of San Pietro. Just north of the church you'll see further steps, each riser decorated with contemporary ceramic tiles, some depicting sea life, some just patterned, and each one different. Fishing vessels lie tied up at the quayside, lorries unload salt by the bucketful for anchovy- and sardine-processing, and repairmen, foundry workers and chandlers go about their business, breaking off work for a drink in some scruffy portside bar.

There's a decent arc of sandy **beach** a kilometre west of the centre at the end of Via Gaie di Garaffe.

Eating and drinking

Although there are a couple of decent pizza places in the upper town, along Viale della Vittoria and Corso Vittorio Emanuele, Sciacca's best **places to eat** are the fish restaurants down by the port. As for **bars**, check out *Pegasus*, by the seafront on Via Gaie di Garaffe, where you can sit outside until late sipping beers and nibbling crepes, ice creams or pastries; panini are also available.

La Lampara Lungomare C. Colombo ℡0925.85.085. Slightly pricier than some other places in the port, and better quality, with a fancy upstairs dining area where you can enjoy your meal overlooking the boats. First courses such as *pasta con sarde* and *risotto ai frutti di mare*

go from €10, fish mains start at around €12, and there's a good wine list. Closed Mon.
Miramare Piazza A. Scandaliato ℡0925.26.050. The main attraction in this upper-town restaurant is the terrace with its excellent panoramas; the food itself can be just mediocre, with fish the top choice

– count on around €40 for a meal. Pizzas are also available (weekends only in winter).

Porto San Paolo Largo San Paolo 1 ⊕ 0925.27.982. Come here for the fine views over the harbour from the terrace. Delicious dishes such as seafood risotto and lobster fettuccine are served, and you can get pizza in the evening. You'll pay around €35 for a full meal excluding drinks.

Arrive early for the best tables, and in any case book ahead in summer. Closed Wed except Aug.

La Vela Via Gaie de Garaffe 60 ⊕ 0925.23.971. This quayside eatery serves a €25 set menu, which includes two first and two second courses plus dessert but not drinks – all very abundant and usually exquisite. Booking advisable. Closed Wed except Aug.

Around Sciacca

If you have a car, Sciacca makes a good base for a day's circular drive, taking in a few minor **inland towns**, including the superbly sited village of **Caltabellotta**. Local buses also make certain simple excursions into hinterland possible.

Monte San Calógero

The easiest side-trip from Sciacca is to the vaporous caves at **Monte San Calógero** (388m), 8km north of town. Bus #5 runs here in ten minutes, leaving from Sciacca roughly every hour. Excavations and finds have shown that the site has been used as a place of healing since antiquity, though the mountain takes its contemporary name from the saint whose sanctuary is at the summit, near some natural caves.

Caltabellotta

Twenty kilometres northeast of Sciacca, the village of **CALTABELLOTTA** perches magnificently on three jutting fangs of rock 950m above sea level. Tremendous views stretch out on all sides, apparently taking in 21 villages. On the highest pinnacle, you can pass through the solitary surviving entrance of the Norman **castello** (always open; free) that once stood here, and climb up steep, rock-cut steps to the very top, from which the village below appears as a patchwork of grey roofs. The castle itself, ruined by an earthquake, was where the Angevins and Aragonese signed the peace treaty that ended the Wars of the Vespers in 1302. Immediately below sit the Norman **Chiesa Madre** and the Gothic **Chiesa di San Salvatore**, both wonderfully sited against a rocky backdrop.

Lumia **buses** run direct to Caltabellotta from Sciacca four times daily (not Sun), the last one back leaving at 3.40pm. It's an impressive ride, past sparkling fresh streams and jagged outcrops of rock. There's a **B&B** close to the castle entrance, for anyone interested in staying right off the beaten track: **Mulè**, Via Venezia 5 (⊕ 0925.951.145 or 320.812.5027; no credit cards; ❶), a typical village dwelling where the plain rooms share a bathroom. You can also taste and buy local oil and other rural products, and view changing collections of local arts and crafts.

Sambuca di Sicilia

Continue north from Caltabellotta onto the SS386, and turn west at Chiusa Sclàfani to reach the little town of **SAMBUCA DI SICILIA**, on a hill west of the Arancio lake, a total distance of nearly 50km. Sambuca's Arab past is just about discernible in its convoluted old-town layout. A sixteenth-century church in Piazza della Vittoria, the **Chiesa del Cármine**, is home of a statue that's reputed to be by Antonello Gagini, and you can **eat** at two or three very cheap trattorias. In addition, a 10km detour north enables you to see the low-key excavations (always open; free) at **Monte Adranone**, a Greek city of the sixth century BC which fell to Carthage in the fourth.

Menfi and Porto Palo

Ten kilometres west of Sambuca you join the main SS188 which sweeps back to Sciacca, though there are a couple of other diversions before that: either head north for 6km to Santa Margherita di Belice (see p.362), or south for 9km to **MENFI**, planned in the eighteenth century but devastated by an earthquake in 1968. Today Menfi presents a very mean aspect: lacerated churches on derelict central streets, a jumble of untidy prefab housing – still being used – and bland rebuilding on the outskirts.

If this is all a bit depressing, things improve when you drive on 7km to the coast at **PORTO PALO**, a fishing village and summer resort with a nice beach – the waters around here are classified among Sicily's cleanest. Though facilities are few, a first-class **restaurant** stands apart at the eastern end of the village, signposted at the end of a dirt lane: *Da Vittorio* (☎0925.78.381, ⓦwww.ristorantevittorio.it; closed Sun eve & Mon eve in winter), a fairly large place that's often completely full. Highly recommended, the food – almost exclusively seafood – is reasonably priced and abundant, with a set-price menu for €45. It's worth booking one of the tables on the broad covered terrace, right next to the beach, especially at weekends. You can also **stay** here in pleasant en-suite rooms with sea views for €85 per person, half board. If there's no room here, there's the simple *Miramare* hotel, Via Piemonte 34 (☎0925.78.211; ❷), with a beachside restaurant, obligatory half board in July and August comes to €65 per person.

Back at Menfi, it's just 20km to Sciacca, either along the minor road or the faster SS115.

The Pelágie Islands

The remote **Pelágie Islands** (Isole Pelágie) are little more than dry rocks set bang in the middle of the Mediterranean, over 200km from Sicily's south coast and lying even further south than Malta or Tunis. Throughout history they've been neglected, often abandoned or uninhabited, although the largest island, **Lampedusa**, now makes its living as a summer resort for an increasing number of Italians, who are attracted by its wonderfully clear waters and remote, end-of-the-line feel. Smaller, quieter, volcanic **Linosa** is generally hotter and less breezy than Lampedusa – both day-trips and overnight stays are possible – while the tiniest islet, **Lampione**, is uninhabited and mostly visited on dive and fishing trips.

Getting to the Pelágie Islands

The quickest way to Lampedusa is to **fly from Palermo or Catania** with Meridiana (ⓦwww.meridiana.it). Tickets cost from €60 one-way (cheapest booked online) and the flight takes just over an hour. Otherwise, there are ferries and hydrofoils **from Porto Empédocle** (6km southwest of Agrigento and connected to it by frequent buses). Siremar (ⓦwww.siremar.it) **ferries** leave Porto Empédocle year-round at midnight daily except Friday, calling at Linosa (5hr 45min) and Lampedusa (8hr 15min). You can buy tickets online, at the port or in travel agencies in Sicily, with one-way tickets starting at around €40 to Linosa, or €50 to Lampedusa, including use of a *poltrona* (reclining chair); shared and exclusive-use cabins are also available. Ústica Lines (ⓦwww.usticalines.it) operates **hydrofoils** six times a week (not Tues) from May to October, departing Porto Empédocle at 3pm and arriving in Linosa three hours later and Lampedusa about four hours later; one-way tickets are around €40 to Linosa, €60 to Lampedusa.

In 1943 the Allies bombed Lampedusa prior to springing into Sicily, and Colonel Gaddafi of Libya nearly gave a repeat performance in 1987 when he retaliated against the American bombing of Tripoli by targeting missiles at the US base on Lampedusa. Italian troops were mobilized and Sicily was on a virtual war-footing for three days, though in the event the missiles dropped into the sea short of the island. In recent years, the island has been the site of detention centres for enormous numbers of immigrants from Africa, either dumped here by unscrupulous people-traffickers, or intercepted at sea by naval vessels. Often they stay for months on end – kept firmly out of sight of tourists – until the legal processes for their inevitable repatriation are completed.

Lampedusa

LAMPEDUSA is the largest of the Pelágie Islands (23 square kilometres), inhabited by around 5000 people, mostly based in the town of the same name. Many still earn a living from fishing, but most depend on the influx of tourists who swell the population to around 20,000 every August. This is a comparatively recent phenomenon, since Lampedusa has either been largely uninhabited or long neglected by Sicily's rulers. In 1667 it passed into the hands of the Tomasi family (as in Giuseppe Tomasi di Lampedusa, of *The Leopard* fame), one of whose descendants attempted to sell the island to Queen Victoria in 1839 when it still had only twenty or so inhabitants. The queen lost out on the sale, at a cost of twelve million ducats, to Ferdinand II, the Neapolitan king, finally stirred into action at the prospect of losing such a scraggy but strategically important island.

Lampedusa is long, thin, flat and very dry, though the pristine waters offer some of the best swimming, snorkelling and diving in the Mediterranean. There are excellent beaches, almost all found on the south coast, and some fantastic swimming coves and grottoes. Dolphins are often seen, there's a sperm whale migration in March, and an offshore nature reserve where turtles come to lay their eggs. Bear in mind that it's a small, exposed island, so summer evenings are cooler than on the mainland. It's also not really somewhere you'd want to holiday in winter, when the wind whips across the barren landscape.

Arrival, information, transport and tours

Lampedusa's **airport** is on the edge of town, from where it's a ten-minute walk to Via Roma and the centre (most hotels have courtesy buses for guests). Arriving by ferry or hydrofoil at **Porto Vecchio**, it's a ten-minute walk around the harbour to the foot of town, or a good twenty- to thirty-minute walk west to the larger harbour of Porto Nuovo, near which is the main beach and the bulk of the resort hotels. A minibus meets harbour arrivals in summer, or you can jump in a taxi.

There's information (in Italian) on **websites** like Ⓦwww.lampedusa35.com and www.lampedusa.it, while on the island you can call in at the environmental agency, Legambiente, Via Vittorio Emanuele 25 (highly erratic hours, and usually closed in winter; ☏0922.971.611). Some English is spoken here, and you can pick up an island sketch map and information about the nature reserve and hiking trails.

The **bus station** is in the centre of the town, off Via Roma. Timetables are posted, but basically there are buses every hour (roughly 8am to 8pm) to Isola dei Conigli and the south coast, and to Cala Creta and the east coast. It's much easier to see the whole island by renting some form of **transport**, either a bike (from €6 a day), scooter or quad (from €25) or a mini-moke (€40), with all prices cheaper by the week or outside July and August. There are lots of rental agencies around town and harbour, or ask at your accommodation. **Bike rental** in particular is a great idea – you can easily do a complete circuit of the island in a day, and even in the hottest months a refreshing breeze blows constantly.

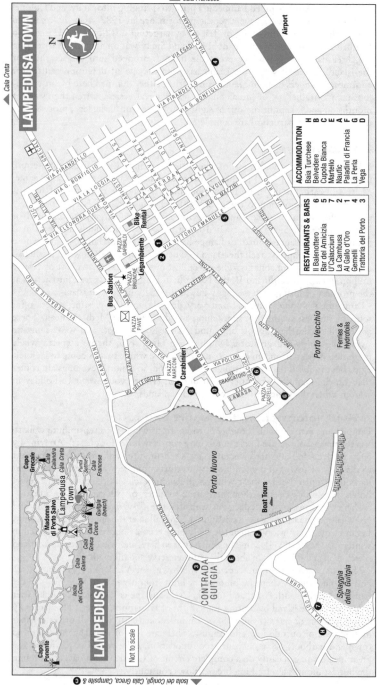

▲ Cala Francese

N

Airport

VIA DELLA CALA PISANA

VIA EGADI

▲ Cala Creta

VIA G. BONFIGLIO

VIA PIRANDELLO

VIA PIRANDELLO

VIA G. BONFIGLIO

VIA LA LOGGIA

VIA G. VICO

VIA ELEONORA DUSE

VIA ROMA

VIA B. CROCE

VIA MAZZINI

VIA VERGA

VIA ANTONIO

VIA CAVOUR

VIA G. MAZZINI

VIA VITTORIO EMANUELE

VIA OBERDAN

VIA ROSA

VIA F. PETRARCA

VIA A. VOLTA

VIA TASSO

VIA CRISPI

VIA TERRANOVA

VIA MEDAGLIE D'ORO

PIAZZA GARIBALDI

PIAZZA BRIGNONE

Bus Station

Bike Rental

Legambiente

★

PIAZZA PIAVE

VIA B. CROCE

VIA VERGA

VIA MACCAFERRI

VIA ENNA

VIA SAN ANTONIO

PIAZZA MARCONI

Carabinieri

VIA DELLE GROTTE

VIA ROMA

VIA PALAZZO

VIA CAMERONI

VIA MEDAGLIE D'ORO

VIA POLLINI

VIA SBARCATOIO

VIA LA MASA

VIA STRASACUSA

PIAZZA CASTELLO

Porto Vecchio

Ferries & Hydrofoils

LUNGOMARE RIZZO

Porto Nuovo

Boat Tours

VIA MADONNA

VIA VOLTA

CONTRADA GUITGIA

VIA LIDO AZZURRO

Spiaggia della Guitgia

▲ Isola dei Conigli, Cala Greca, Campsite & ▲

ACCOMMODATION

Baia Turchese	H
Belvedere	B
Cupola Bianca	C
Martello	E
Nautic	A
Paladini di Francia	F
La Perla	G
Vega	D

RESTAURANTS & BARS

Il Balenottero	6
Bar del Amicizia	5
U'Calacciuni	7
La Cambusa	2
Al Gallo d'Oro	1
Gemelli	4
Trattoria del Porto	3

A B D C E F G H

1 2 5 6 3 7

LAMPEDUSA

Not to scale

Capo Grecale

Cala Calandra

Cala Creta

Punta Sottile

Cala Francese

Lampedusa Town

Madonna di Porto Salvo

Guitgia (beach)

Cala Croce

Cala Greca

Cala Galera

Isola dei Conigli

Capo Ponente

THE SOUTH COAST

8

Boat trips and **cruises** (from €30–35 per person) mostly depart from the Porto Nuovo, particularly the part of the harbour by the petrol station below the *Hotel Martello*. Departures are usually around 10.30am, returning at 5.30pm, and options include round-island cruises with swimming stops and lunch included, or more specialist tours like dive trips to Lampione or night fishing for squid. You can also rent your own **self-drive motor boat** from various harbour agencies, which costs around €80 per day plus fuel.

Accommodation

The season on Lampedusa runs from Easter to the end of October, and you'll generally have no problem finding a room, save in **August**, when advance booking is essential. You may also be obliged to take your room with half or full board then too. There are several **hotels** in the town itself, another half a dozen within a stone's throw of the port and main beach (Spiaggia della Guitgia), and others just outside town and near Cala Creta. Self-catering accommodation (usually by the week) is available either in **apartments** or in one of Lampedusa's stone-built **dammusi** – updated versions of the traditional, dome-roofed, thick-walled shepherd's hut, typical of Sicily and North Africa. *Dammusi* are found all over the island, some in village-style developments, and prices vary wildly (some are very boutiquey in style) – there's more information from agencies like Servizi Mikael (Ⓦwww.servizimikael.com), Licciardi (Ⓦwww.lampedusa-licciardi.it), and Dammusi di Borgo Cala Creta (Ⓦwww.calacreta.com). There's also an island **campsite**, *La Roccia* (Ⓦwww.laroccia.net), a resort-style place with beach and bungalows 3km out of town at Cala Greca, but rocky, shadeless Lampedusa is not the first place you'd think of to go camping in Sicily.

Baia Turchese Via Lido Azzurro ℡0922.970.455, Ⓦwww.guitgia.com. This cheery four-star seaside hotel has the best location at the main beach, a skip across from the sands, which explains the high prices. Stays are always on a half-board basis, which in August jumps to at least €125 per person per night, and more like €160 if you want a terrace and sea view. ❺

Belvedere Piazza Marconi 4 ℡0922.970.188, Ⓦwww.hotelbelvedere lampedusa.it. In town, rather than by the beach, but it's a friendly, family-run place overlooking the harbour (rooms with a view cost extra), with a good panoramic dining room and terrace restaurant to boot. It's pretty good value for most of the year, though August room prices start at €130. Closed Nov–Feb. ❸

Cupola Bianca Via Madonna ℡0922.971.274, Ⓦwww.hotelcupolabianca.it. A luxury outfit 2km out of town, with a North African feel and plush rooms as well as upmarket *dammusi*-style accommodation. There's a fabulous pool and terrace, plus a restaurant and all sorts of boat trips and excursions available. At least half board is required, starting at €130 per person, *dammusi* accommodation from €180 (August from €170/220). Closed Nov–April. ❼

Nautic Via delle Grotte, off Via Roma ℡0922.971.531, Ⓦwww.lampedusanautic hotel.it. Classiest town-centre choice is this chic

little four-star hotel with only a dozen rooms and a light, stylish touch throughout. There's a decent restaurant too, with a corner terrace. Rooms for most of the year go for around €120, though expect to pay double in August. ❹

Paladini di Francia Via Alessandro Volta ℡0922.970.550, Ⓦwww.hotelpaladinidifrancia .it. Contemporary three-star resort hotel and restaurant on the harbour, close to the beach, with rooms set around bright, white courtyards, the four at the front with port-side balconies. It's part of a group, together with the neighboring, more traditional and cheaper *Martello* (Ⓦwww.hotelmartello .it), and the apartments and *dammusi*-style rooms at the out-of-town *Oasis* (Ⓦwww.oasisresort.it) resort, above the rocks at Cala Creta. There are flight-and-accommodation packages available by the week at any of the hotels, or otherwise it's B&B (from €90 per room) or half-board (from €65–80 per person), depending on hotel and season. Closed Nov–Feb. ❹

La Perla Via L. Rizzo 1, Porto Vecchio ℡0922.971.932, Ⓦwww.laperlahotel.net. Three-star hotel right on the harbourside, with rooms looking either on to the old port or the marina. Some have little balconies but the best are those on the top with full terraces and parasols. There's also a restaurant with a great raised terrace above the harbour. Prices are usually on a half-board basis, but B&B might be available outside July and August. Closed Nov–Feb. ❹

Vega Via Roma 19 ☏0922.970.099, ⓦwww.lampedusa-hotelvega.it. There's nothing wrong with the cheapest hotel in town – in fact, it's quite cheery, with perfectly decent en-suite rooms – but it just doesn't have much of an island or seaside feel. That said, B&B rates are always available, some rooms have distant port views, and it's ideally located in the middle of town for bars, restaurants and services. ❸

Lampedusa Town

Its location – set back from two curving harbours – is the best thing about **LAMPEDUSA TOWN**, as otherwise it is nothing special to look at. Low concrete buildings hug a dusty grid of streets between airport and harbours, though things improve along the wide, main **Via Roma**, which is largely closed to traffic and lined from top to bottom with gift shops, pavement cafés and restaurants. On summer evenings, as the temperature drops, out come the wicker café chairs, souvenir stalls, jewellery hawkers and fruit-and-veg stands, and a real street-market atmosphere develops. Indeed, there are far more people on the street at 11pm than 11am. You can buy the usual beach gear, postcards and T-shirts, but there's also a thriving trade in souvenirs like sea sponges, turtle carvings, sculpted beach rocks and hand-crocheted Arab caps. Enterprising local kids sell polished shells from the beach, while **island produce** – sun-dried tomatoes, mountain capers, wild oregano and fennel seeds, hand-made cheese – is widely available from stalls and grocery stores.

A twenty-minute walk around the large Porto Nuovo harbour leads to the busy main beach, **Spiaggia della Guitgia**, backed by bars, hotels and restaurants. There's a stretch of fine sand, and good swimming in gently shelving water, though it's always packed here in summer; for a change of view try the next bay west, **Cala La Croce**. The other place you can explore from town is the smaller harbour, **Porto Vecchio**, where the ferries and hydrofoils dock, which also has a few bars and restaurants, and fishing boats coming and going during the day.

Around the island

The best single beach destination is **Isola dei Conigli** (Rabbit Island), 5km to the west; there's an hourly bus service from town. From the cliff-top road you clamber down the jagged path to a stretch of fine, white sand and gorgeous aquamarine waters. Just offshore is the little island itself, which you can reach either on foot or by swimming, depending on the tide. Conigli island, and much of the rest of Lampedusa's **southern coast**, is protected as a nature reserve and there are various access places along the cliff-top road to viewpoints and short signposted footpaths. With a bike or scooter you can find more windswept vantage points and hidden bays if you continue along the road past Isola dei Conigli, or you can turn inland opposite the Conigli parking area and loop back towards town high above the **north coast**. However, you can only swim on the north side of the island from a boat – it's mostly sheer cliffs, tiered like a wedding cake, and pierced by deep gorges and grottoes.

The other excursion from town (and the other bus route) is up the east coast the 3km to **Cala Creta**. Off the road, and signposted down a dusty track, is a magnificent swimming cove, where steps lead from a tiny rock apron directly into stunning waters. Lots of people have the same idea in summer, but it's a pretty spot with a lovely beach bar on the rocks that's part of the fancy *Marina di Cala Creta* restaurant – a perfect place for a lazy lunch. The bottles of Veuve Cliquot on the bar shelf rather give the game away; Cala Creta is a cut above the other island beaches, overlooked by pristine *dammusi* and the Borgo Cala Creta holiday village (where there's another attractive restaurant, with garden dining, open to non-residents).

Wildlife and nature on Lampedusa

During the twentieth century Lampedusa was practically stripped of its natural vegetation, resulting in massive soil erosion that accounts for the arid state of the land. However, a progamme of conservation and reforestation is gradually having some effect and, while at first glance Lampedusa still appears devoid of greenery, a closer look reveals a wide range of **plant life**. Date palms are dotted along otherwise barren stretches, and, at Cala Galera in particular, look out for the Phoenician juniper, carob and wild olive trees, all survivors of the original blight. Rare plants include the *Caralluma europaea*, a cactus-like plant with star-shaped flowers, and the *Centaurea acaulis*, from the centaury family, while during spring the flowering squills, irises, crocuses, orchids, echinops and thyme make up a vibrant display. Meanwhile, the nature reserve of Isola dei Conigli is the only habitat in Italy of the *Psammodromus algirus* **lizard** – a common species in North Africa – and the only nesting place in Italy of the **turtle** *Caretta caretta*. During summer evenings, the turtles deposit between 100 and 150 eggs in deep holes, from which the babies stagger out after sixty days. The nests are individually fenced off, but that doesn't help protect them from peregrine falcons. Injured turtles are cared for at the World Wildlife Fund's **Centro Recupero Tartarughe Marine** (⊚ www.isolablu.org) on the island's east coast at Cala Creta, before being released back into the sea.

The only other diversion is the church of the **Madonna di Porto Salvo** (off the main road west out of town), its white steeple set in a little wooded valley, and the garden in front dripping with flowers and bougainvillea. A pilgrimage here every September commemorates a sixteenth-century Italian slave, captured by Saracens, who was shipwrecked on the island and made his way to the sanctuary here. Afterwards, he used the image of the Madonna on the sail of his makeshift raft to return safely to Liguria.

Eating and drinking

There are lots of **restaurants** in town, and more around the harbours, and while prices are much higher than on most of the Sicilian mainland, the quality is largely excellent. In fact, you're unlikely to have a bad meal, given the abundance of fresh-off-the-boat fish and the exacting standards of Italian holiday-makers. Specialities available everywhere include fish couscous, grilled tuna and swordfish (often simply served with a garlic, olive oil, lemon and parsley *salsa*), and whole sea bream or bass cooked in the oven with potatoes. At night, the whole of Via Roma is basically one long open-air café, with hundreds of chairs and tables spread out down the traffic-free road. Some places are more **bar** than café, with DJs and music, and it's a pretty lively scene until well into the small hours. Most cafés and restaurants close in the winter from mid-October to mid-May, but you'll find something open whenever you come.

Il Balenottero Via Sbarcatoio 40, Porto Vecchio ⊤0922.970.830. A family-run place near the old port that's nice and cool inside but also has an outdoor terrace. It's a standard seafood pasta and grilled fish place, with squid, shrimp, clams, mussels, tuna, swordfish and bream on the menu, and most dishes in the €10–15 range. Closed Dec–Feb.

Bar del Amicizia Via Vittorio Emanuele 34. Not exactly a secret, but you have to know it's here to come this far down the street. Inside is a huge array of stuffed pastries, simply amazing ice cream and a dozen flavours of *granita* (from strawberry to watermelon), plus a large terrace that overlooks Lampedusa's back gardens to the sea beyond.

U' Calacciuni Spiaggia della Guitgia ⊤339.435.0300. Summer-season beach-shack trattoria that's great for whiling away the hours over typical *lampedusani* dishes. There's no menu but you'll be offered pasta (say with clams and mussels, or *con le sarde*, with sardines and wild fennel), followed by the day's catch, like a slab of grilled tuna with a breadcrumb and pistachio crust. Dishes cost between €10 and €20. Closed Nov–April.

La Cambusa Piazza Municipio ☏ 0922.970.826. Cavernous underground restaurant down an alley just off Via Vittorio Emanuele that serves the best pizzas (€5–8) in town, straight from the wood-fired oven. It's also a fish place (dishes €8–16), though nearly everyone comes for the pizzas. Dinner only.

Al Gallo d'Oro Via Vittorio Emanuele 45 ☏ 0922.970.249. A cheerful trattoria, with seats inside and out, serving a fish and seafood menu that's a cut above most in town. Typical dishes are pasta tossed with fresh tuna, cherry tomatoes and parsley, followed by oven-roast bass with potatoes – expect to pay €30 ahead or so. Closed Nov–Easter.

Gemelli Via Cala Pisana 2 ☏ 0922.970.699. Near the airport, and worth the short walk for a menu full of Tunisian flavour – from appetizers like *brik* (stuffed savoury pastries) and *merguez* sausage to couscous. It's also excellent for fish, and well worth the higher-than-normal prices (*antipasti* and *primi* €10–16, *secondi* €20–35). Dinner only; reservations essential in Aug.

Trattoria del Porto Via Madonna 20 ☏ 0922.970.516. Best place on the main harbour, it has a great upper terrace with a breeze and a bird's eye view of the port. There's a summer salad menu for lunch, as well as a choice of classic fish and seafood dishes, from *spaghetti alle vongole* to marinated tuna with wild fennel (*primi* €7–12, *secondi* €15).

Listings

Airport Information ☏ 0922.970.006.
Banks There are ATMs along Via Roma.
Bike rental A recommended, central place for cheap bike rental is Noleggio Ecologico, Via S. Pellico 12 ☏ 333.324.6668, which rents bikes for €6 per day, scooters for €20.
Diving centres The larger hotels can all book you onto dive trips, or contact one of the operators direct, like Blue Dolphins (🌐 www.bluedolphins.it), Lo Verde Diving (🌐 www.loverdelampedusa.it), Mediterraneo Immersioni Club (🌐 www.mediterraneo immersionclub.it) or Moby Diving Center (🌐 www .mobydiving.it). Single dives are from €35, open-water dive courses from €350, and most places are open April–Nov.
Ferry/hydrofoil tickets The Siremar ferry (🌐 www.siremar.it) to Linosa/Porto Empédocle departs daily (not Sat) at 10.15am, with one-way tickets from around €50. The Ústica Lines

hydrofoil (🌐 www.usticalines.it) departs May–Oct daily except Tues at 7.30am (one-way tickets around €60). There's also an extra morning and afternoon hydrofoil to Linosa (6 times a week between April and October, and at least 4 times a week throughout the year; one-way ticket around €20). The summer hydrofoil to Pantelleria (July to mid-Sept) departs on Wed, Fri and Sun at 11.30am, price €30 one way. Full timetables available on the websites.
Hospital Via Grecale ☏ 0922.970.604.
Pharmacy Dottore Inglisa, Via Vittorio Emanuele 35 (Mon–Sat 9am–12.45pm & 5–7.30pm, Sun 10am–noon & 6–7.30pm; ☏ 0922.970.195).
Police Carabinieri, Via Roma 37 ☏ 0922.970.001 or 112.
Post office Piazza Piave (Mon–Fri 8am–1.30pm, Sat 8am–12.30pm).

Linosa

Fifty kilometres north of Lampedusa, **Linosa** is basically the tip of a submerged volcano, with four extinct craters and some lava beaches to explore, and not much else in the way of actual sights. It's much smaller than Lampedusa (just five square kilometres), and the only village has just a few hundred inhabitants, rather fewer cars and a minimal road system. Until the advent of tourism, the only time the tranquillity was disturbed was when the government in Rome sent their latest star Mafia prisoner to be detained on the island pending trial, a practice suspended since the holiday trade picked up. Some Italian families come here year after year, reveling in the peace and quiet. If you take the tracks that lead away from the brightly coloured houses on either side of the port, you can clamber around the cliffs and coves, and reach a couple of black-sand beaches with crystal clear water. Swimming and diving are, of course, fantastic, and operators like the Linosa Diving Centre (🌐 www.linosadivingcenter.it) or

Mare Nostrum (www.marenostrumdiving.it) offer all sorts of dive trips, courses and excursions.

Practicalities

You can see Linosa on a day-trip from Lampedusa, as it's only an hour away by Ústica Lines **hydrofoil**. There are two or three departures a day, the first at 7.30am or 8am, leaving six days a week (not Mon or Tues, depending on the service) from April to October and four days a week (not Tues, Thurs or Sun) from November to March; one-way tickets are around €15), leaving Lampedusa daily (not Sat) at 10.15am, arriving at noon. The hydrofoil **from Linosa to Porto Empédocle** leaves daily except Tuesday at 8.45am (May–Oct only), and the ferry (not Sat) leaves at 12.15pm.

You might find **B&B rooms** offered on arrival in the summer, and restaurants (including *Da Anna*, below) and tour operators have apartments for rent. Otherwise, the main choice is *Residence La Posta* (☎320.601.0556 or 339.741.0705, www.linosaresidencelaposta.it; closed Nov–March; ❸, July & Aug ❺), which has smartly furnished, air-conditioned accommodation in the heart of the village. There are half a dozen **trattorias, pizzerias and bars**, all closed in winter, notably the *Errera* (☎0922.972.041) and the rustic-style *Da Anna* (☎0922.972.048, www.linosavacanze.it) at the top of the village, which has good views. Note that there's no bank or ATM on the island.

Travel details

Trains

Agrigento to: Caltanissetta (5 daily Mon–Sat, 3 daily Sun; 1hr 30min); Canicattì (for Gela, 5 daily Mon–Sat, 3 daily Sun; 1hr); Enna (3 daily; 1hr 50min–2hr 25min); Palermo (12 daily Mon–Sat, 8 daily Sun; 2hr 15min).

Gela to: Catania (5 daily Mon–Sat; 2hr 10min–3hr 15min); Caltagirone (4 daily Mon–Sat; 35min); Canicattì (for Agrigento, 5 daily Mon–Sat; 1hr 25min); Licata (5 daily Mon–Sat; 30min); Ragusa (5 daily Mon–Sat; 1hr 30min); Vittoria (5 daily Mon–Sat; 30min).

Buses

Agrigento to: Caltanissetta (hourly Mon–Sat, 10 daily Sun; 1hr 15min); Catania (hourly Mon–Sat, 10 daily Sun; 2hr 50min); Cattólica Eraclea (for Eraclea Minoa, 6 daily Mon–Sat, 1 daily Sun; 1hr–1hr 30min); Gela (4 daily Mon–Sat; 1hr 40min); Licata (14 daily Mon–Sat; 1hr); Palermo (14 daily Mon–Sat, 5 daily Sun; 2hr); Palma di Montechiaro (14 daily Mon–Sat; 35min); Porto Empédocle (1–2 hourly Mon–Sat, 6 daily Sun; 20min); Sant'Ángelo Muxaro (3 daily Mon–Sat; 1hr 10min); Sciacca (11 daily Mon–Sat, 2 daily Sun; 1hr–1hr 40min); Trápani (3 daily Mon–Sat, 1 daily Sun; 3hr 20min–4hr).

Gela to: Agrigento (4 daily Mon–Sat; 1hr 45min); Caltagirone (2 daily Mon–Sat; 55min); Caltanissetta (7 daily Mon–Sat; 1hr 10min–1hr 40min); Catania (9–12 daily Mon–Sat, 6 daily Sun; 1hr 45min); Enna (5 daily Mon–Sat; 1hr 10min); Licata (10–11 daily Mon–Sat, 4 daily Sun; 45min); Palermo (3–4 daily; 2hr 45min); Piazza Armerina (4 daily; 1hr); Siracusa (2–3 daily Mon–Sat, 1 daily Sun; 3hr 40min–4hr 15min); Vittoria (3–4 daily Mon–Sat, 1 daily Sun; 40min).

Sciacca to: Agrigento (9 daily Mon–Sat, 2 daily Sun; 1hr 10min–1hr 40min); Caltabellotta (4 daily Mon–Sat; 45min); Castelvetrano (3 daily Mon–Sat, 1 daily Sun; 40–55min); Menfi (12 daily Mon–Sat, 1 daily Sun; 25–45min); Palermo (8–10 daily Mon–Sat, 5 daily Sun; 1hr 45min); Trápani (3 daily Mon–Sat, 1 daily Sun; 2hr–2hr 20min).

Ferries

Lampedusa to: Linosa (6 weekly; 1hr 45min); Pantelleria (July to mid-Sept 3 weekly; 2hr 45min); Porto Empédocle (6 weekly; 7hr 45min).

Linosa to: Lampedusa (6 weekly; 1hr 45min); Porto Empédocle (6 weekly; 5hr 45min).

Porto Empédocle to: Lampedusa (6 weekly; 8hr 15min); Linosa (6 weekly; 5hr 45min).

Hydrofoils

Lampedusa to: Linosa (2–3 daily, 4 to 6 days a week; 1hr); Porto Empédocle (May–Oct 6 weekly; 4hr 15min).
Linosa to: Lampedusa (2–3 daily, 4 to 6 days a week; 1hr); Porto Empédocle (May–Oct 6 weekly; 3hr).

Porto Empédocle to: Lampedusa (May–Oct 6 weekly; 4hr 15min); Linosa (May–Oct 6 weekly; 3hr).

Flights

Palermo to: Lampedusa (2–4 daily; 1hr).
Lampedusa to: Palermo (2–4 daily; 1hr).

Trápani and the west

CHAPTER 9

Highlights

* **Riserva Naturale dello Zíngaro** Hike the footpaths or swim from isolated pebble coves within Sicily's loveliest nature reserve. See p.320

* **Segesta** Perhaps the most romantic of all Greek sites on the island, beautifully positioned amid rolling hills. See p.321

* **Cable car to Érice** A stunning panorama opens up on this stately ascent from Trápani to the hilltop town of Érice. See p.330

* **Swimming at San Vito Lo Capo** Hidden away on Sicily's northwestern tip, this idyllic beach has a dramatic mountainous backdrop. See p.334

* **Hiking on Maréttimo** Panoramic walks, none too demanding, can be made on this, the remotest of the Égadi Islands, ideally ending with a fish supper overlooking the port. See p.345

* **Pantelleria** Without a beach in sight, this craggy island en route to Tunisia still makes an enticing place to unwind. See p.363

▲ Castello di Vénere, Érice

Trápani and the west

C loser to North Africa than the Italian mainland, Sicily's western reaches are traditionally poor and remote, the economy dependent on fishing and small-scale farming. Since the opening of the A29 autostrada, the region has become more integrated with the rest of Sicily than ever before, but even today, access by public transport is limited. Indeed, much of the appeal of the area lies in the fact that it's still very different from the rest of the island. Historically, the region has always been distinct, influenced by a strong Phoenician and Arab culture rather than the Greek and Norman traditions that prevail elsewhere in Sicily. The Arab influence can still be tasted in its food – couscous is a local favourite – and visually too, the flat land, dotted by white cubic houses, is strongly reminiscent of North Africa.

On the northern coast, the **Golfo di Castellammare** is only an hour's train ride from Palermo. Despite patches of industrial development along the gulf, it still manages to offer some empty beaches and a couple of unspoiled villages at its western end. In particular, the coastline between the old tuna-fishing village of **Scopello** and the resort of **San Vito Lo Capo** encompasses the beautiful **Zíngaro** nature reserve. The capital of the province that takes in this entire area, **Trápani**, is a congenial port town within sight of the flat saltpans on which its wealth was based. It is also a departure point for the **Égadi Islands**, and makes a good base for visiting the mountain town of **Érice** – originally a centre of Punic influence, though diverging from the region's dominant trend in its uniform Norman and medieval character. The pattern re-establishes itself a little way down the coast at **Mózia**, Sicily's best-preserved Phoenician site, while further south the Moorish imprint is discernible in the secretive alleys and courtyards of **Marsala** and **Mazara del Vallo**.

Although the Greeks never wielded much influence in the area, the Hellenic remains at **Segesta** and **Selinunte** (Selinus) count among the island's most stunning. Between the two, the Valle del Belice delineates the region struck by an earthquake in 1968, which left a trail of destruction still visible in many towns and villages. This is most notable at **Gibellina**, abandoned in its ruined state as a powerful reminder, and at the little town of **Santa Margherita di Belice**, whose once-proud palace and church were immortalized in that quintessential Sicilian novel, *The Leopard*. There could be no greater contrast to this disorder than the peaceful island of **Pantelleria**, a distant outpost just a short hop away from the African coast, mountainous and wind-blown, and adopted as a chic resort by a few high-profile glitterati.

You'll find **getting around** the coast a simple matter, as frequent buses and trains cover the short distances between all the towns and villages. There's much less public transport, though, if you strike off **inland**: what interior bus services there

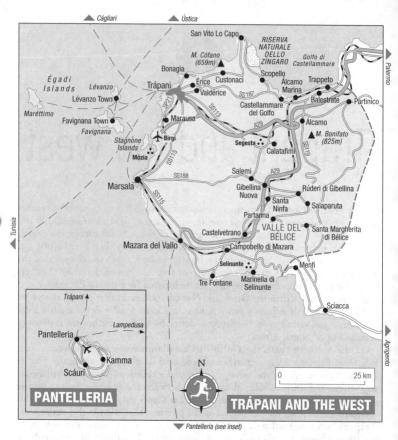

▼ *Pantelleria (see inset)*

are depart from Marsala or Castelvetrano. As for driving, apart from the two arms of the A29 autostrada there are only two other main roads, the SS115 following the coast between Trápani and Castelvetrano and the inland SS188 between Marsala and Salemi.

The Golfo di Castellammare

Backed by a forbidding wall of jagged mountains, the wide bowl of the **Golfo di Castellammare** is almost entirely made up of small holiday towns. Some are uncomfortably close to industrial plants, though these disappear as you progress west. The main train line from Palermo (and the SS187 road) skirts the bay from Trappeto to Castellammare del Golfo, but despite the ease of access and the consequent development the resorts have not entirely shrugged off their original role as fishing villages – though they have completely lost the mean look they had when fishing was the only source of income. If you're after a beach, some of these make a reasonable morning's halt, though be warned that in July and August it's slow going on the roads and the sands are packed. Otherwise, the train ride is as fair an entertainment, hugging the coast at the base of massive wedges of rock, often of a raw red colour, echoed by smaller, weathered nuggets poking out of the sea.

Trappeto, Balestrate and Álcamo Marina

Today, the two villages of **TRAPPETO** and **BALESTRATE**, just 5km apart (and both on the train line), display a tidy sense of well-being that's in sharp contrast to the poverty that Danilo Dolci found when he came to the region in 1952 (see box, p.316). Nowadays, things have dramatically improved, and the beaches on either side of the villages, backed by orange groves, are regularly visited by Palermitan holiday-makers. Both places hold popular summer pizzerias, fish restaurants and hotels, but there's no real reason to stay: in summer it's just too busy and in winter too funereal. There's more of the same 10km further west at **ÁLCAMO MARINA**, where a few more bars and restaurants provide sweeping views of the gulf.

Festivals

February
3 Festival of St Biagio in **Salemi**, with pasta figures given to children and a slippery-pole competition.

March
19 Festival of St Joseph at **Salemi**, with poetry recitals and sculptures of Jesus, Mary and Joseph made out of bread.

March/April
Good Friday Procession of the Misteri in **Trápani** and **Érice**.
Easter Thursday Enactment of the Passion in **Marsala**, in brightly jewelled processions with gorgeous finery.
Easter Sunday Symbolic meeting of statues of Christ and Mary in **Mazara del Vallo**.

May/June
La Mattanza tuna slaughter in **Favignana**; it hasn't taken place in recent years so check first with Favignana's tourist office.

June
19–21 Festival of Santa Maria dei Mirácoli at **Álcamo**, with a pilgrimage to Monte Bonifato.
29 Feast of Sts Peter and Paul in **Pantelleria**.

July
Music festival in **Trápani** at the Villa Margherita.
10–13 Feast of the Three Maries in **Pantelleria**.

August
Festival of modern Italian art in **Marsala**.
15 Horse race around Specchio di Vénere lake in **Pantelleria**.

September
Last week International couscous festival at **San Vito Lo Capo**.

December
24 Procession of characters from the Nativity story in **Salemi**.

Danilo Dolci: the "Sicilian Gandhi"

The social reformer **Danilo Dolci** (1924–97) was as close to a secular saint as Sicily can come. Born near Trieste, and having first worked among the poor in Tuscany, he moved to Trappeto in 1952, determined to settle in "the poorest place I had ever known". His *Sicilian Lives* records his first impressions of Trappeto: "Coming from the North, I knew I was totally ignorant. Looking all around me, I saw no streets, just mud and dust. Not a single chemist – or sewer. The dialect didn't have a word for sewer." He campaigned tirelessly but nonviolently (including by fasting and "reverse strikes") to draw attention to the local conditions, and to have a dam built outside nearby Partinico – something that was resisted at every turn by the Mafia and their political clients, who controlled the existing water supplies. Inevitably, he stirred up the opposition not just of the Mafia, but of the police, the church, and – eventually – even local people, who accused him of publicity-seeking and ill-conceived campaigns. Though twice nominated for the Nobel Peace Prize, he spent the last twenty years of his life in obscurity.

Álcamo

Inland, and just inside the Trápani provincial boundary, **ÁLCAMO** itself was founded by Frederick II early in the thirteenth century. Good wine is made from Álcamo grapes, and the town, spread across a low hill with views towards the coast, has also become known thanks to the atmospheric descriptions in **Mary Taylor Simeti**'s classic memoir *On Persephone's Island* (1986), much of which is set hereabouts. Otherwise, Álcamo will mainly be of interest to fans of medieval castles: adjacent to the broad main Piazza della Repubblica, the beautifully restored fourteenth-century **Castello dei Conti di Módica** in Piazza Castello (Mon–Sat 9.30am–12.30pm & 4.30–7.30pm, Sun 4.30–7.30pm; free) holds a small collection of archeological scraps and farming items as well as regular exhibitions; more museums are destined to be housed here. Álcamo also boasts some fine ecclesiastical architecture, its largely Baroque **churches** all found along and around the lengthy main street of the old town, Corso VI Aprile. The Chiesa Madre on the Corso is typical, with its bold frescoes and elaborate sculptures by members of the Gagini family.

Practicalities

Álcamo's **tourist office** is on Piazza Mercato, near Piazza Ciullo (Mon–Sat 9am–1pm, also Mon, Wed & Thurs 4–7pm, in winter 3.30–6.30pm; ☎0924.22.301, Ⓦwww.alcamo.tp-net.it). It's not practical to come here by train, since the nearest **train station** (Castellammare del Golfo) lies down on the coast with infrequent bus connections, but there are regular **buses** from Palermo and Trápani.

You're unlikely to want to stay over in Álcamo, but it does hold a handful of **hotels**, including a couple of cheapies, both west of the centre at the end of Corso VI Aprile: the small, plain *Miramare*, Corso Médici 72 (☎0924.21.197; no credit cards; ❶), which has en-suite, air-conditioned rooms, and the more up-to-date *La Principessa*, Via Canapè 5 (☎0924.507.789, Ⓦwww.albergolaprincipessa.it; ❷), geared towards business travellers.

Off Corso VI Aprile, the lovely pedestrianized square of Piazza Ciullo holds some pleasant **cafés** for a sit-down and snack, or try the *Moulin Rouge* bar on Piazza Libertà, a five-minute walk from the Corso down Via Vittorio Emanuele and Via Buonarroti. Round the corner from here at Via Libertà 1, *Salsapariglia* (☎0924.508.302; closed Mon) is a first-rate, moderately priced **restaurant** with pizzas in the evenings.

Monte Bonifato

Five kilometres south of Álcamo – a well-signposted climb up a corkscrew road – **Monte Bonifato** (825m) is worth the drive for the panoramic views from the top. The other local attraction is the **Stabilimento Termale Gorga** (☎0924.23.842, ⓦ www.termegorga.com), a thermal spa where you can bathe in the exquisitely hot pool for €7, or take other treatments, such as a mud bath (€15) or a sauna (€12). You can also stay comfortably here (❷) – guests have free access to the pool – and there's a ristorante-pizzeria. It's just a couple of hundred metres along the right-hand dirt track from the train station (don't go down under the bridge). At a second spa, **Terme Segestane** (☎0924.530.057; no credit cards), five to ten minutes' drive west, mud treatments (June to mid-Nov only) cost €20, and entrance to the pool (closed 2 weeks in Dec) is €7.

Castellammare del Golfo

CASTELLAMMARE DEL GOLFO is the last coastal stop on the gulf before the train line winds inland to Trápani. It's the biggest of the local fishing ports, entirely surrounded by high hills and built on and around a hefty rocky promontory that's guarded by a squat castle from which the town takes its name. Castellammare's incredible pedigree of bloodshed once gave it one of the worst reputations in Sicily for Mafia violence. The writer Gavin Maxwell, who lived locally during the 1950s, claimed that in that period eighty percent of the town's adult males had served prison sentences, and one in three had committed murder: coupled with this are the official statistics for the same period that classify one family in six as destitute. Needless to say, all of this is extremely hard to believe today: strolling down the sloping Corso Garibaldi towards the castle and harbour, past handsome *palazzi* interspersed with bars and shops selling beach gear, it seems a most benign place, ideal for a few days' relaxation.

Arrival and information

The local **train station** is 4km east of town; a bus meets arrivals and shuttles you into Castellammare, passing the campsite on the way. It drops you at the **bus station** in the upper part of the town on Via della Repubblica, which runs off Via Segesta. Regular services operated by Russo and (in summer) Tarántola run from here **to Scopello** (Mon–Sat, also Sun from mid-June to mid-Sept) and, in summer, on **to Lo Zíngaro**.

You'll find the **tourist office** inside the castle (Mon–Fri 9am–1pm & 3.30–7.30pm; ☎0924.30.217). **Banks** are on the main Corso Garibaldi.

Accommodation

Castellammare holds several good **accommodation** options, while the local **campsite**, *Nausicaa* (☎0924.33.030, ⓦ www.nausicaa-camping.it; closed Oct–March), a kilometre or so east, is small but clean, and has direct access to the beach.

Cala Marina Via Don Leonardo Zangara 1 ☎0924.531.841, ⓦ www.hotelcalamarina.it. In a prime position right by the marina and beach, this smart, modern hotel provides a relaxed atmosphere. Ask for one of the three bright rooms with balconies and sea views (costing extra). ❸

Case d'Anna Corso Garibaldi 120 ☎0924.31.101 or 339.661.0722, ⓦ www .casedanna.it. The large, clean rooms in this central *affittacamere* are beautifully and meticulously

decorated with Art Deco or Victorian furnishings, and come with a/c, minibars and wi-fi. You'll pick up loads of helpful tips from the friendly host family, and breakfast includes home-made pastries. No credit cards. ❷

Nonna Giò Via A. Mario 28 ☎334.594.1224, ⓦ www .sicilianelgolfo.it. Four good-value, en-suite and air-conditioned rooms are available in this place just up from Piazza Petrolo and the seafront. Breakfast is taken on the roof terrace. No credit cards. ❷

The Town

Originally Norman but much remodelled in later centuries, the **castello** today contains well-presented collections dedicated to the history, archeology and maritime culture of the area (Mon–Sat 9am–1pm & 3.30–7.30pm; free). Beneath the castle walls, on the harbourside, a row of cafés and restaurants face the fishing-boats, a nice place to kill time and eat lunch. There's a scrappy sand beach at the harbour, though you may prefer the fine sands 2km east of the centre, between the town and train station. Between June and September, you can also take a **boat tour** up the coast to Zíngaro and San Vito Lo Capo, leaving from the port every morning at 8.15am or 10.50am, returning at 4.15pm or 6.15pm (around €35 including lunch; ℡0924.34.222 or 331.868.6242).

Away from the sea, the pinewood slopes of **Monte Inici**, accessed from the SS187 2km west of town, are a popular spot for picnics and views. It provides some relief from the summer heat, and there is a restaurant here (listed below).

Eating and drinking

Most of the **restaurants** around the centre of Castellammare or down by the harbour feature *cuscus a pesce*. The harbour is also the place for an evening stroll and **drink**, with a selection of late-opening bars.

La Cambusa ℡0924.30.155 and **Salvinius** ℡0924.30.185 Cala Marina. The best of the harbourside eateries, these two restaurants next to each other offer very similar fare, prices and ambience, with a selection of the catch of the day displayed for your order. First and second courses in each are mostly €9–15, and pizzas are available. Arrive early or book for the best tables.
Michael's Contrada Belvedere ℡0924.35.230. Popular pizzeria-restaurant with tables under the trees below Monte Inici, on the main road west of town. Closed Mon–Thurs Oct–April; also daytime Oct–June.

🏃 **A Muciara du Rais** Via Don Sturzo 12 ℡0924.30.604. Backstreet trattoria just down the steps from the town gardens, with a vaulted stone interior and a few tables outside. Dishes have a pronounced North African influence (first courses €7–10, mains €10–12). Closed Mon Oct–May.

Scopello

The coastline northwest of Castellammare is perhaps the most beautiful in the whole of Sicily, abounding in unspoiled coves and gravel beaches, connected by paths to the road above. The road passes **Baia di Guidaloca**, a small scrubby bay with a stony beach with a stream running into it and pleasant swimming. Some people believe this to be the spot where Nausicaä found the naked, shipwrecked Odysseus and finally set him on the last leg of his journey home to Ithaca.

Soon after this cove, 10km from Castellammare, a turn-off leads to **SCOPELLO**, a tiny inland hamlet perched on a ridge a couple of hundred metres above the coastline where stands the old tuna fishery (*tonnara*) that the village once serviced.

Arrival

The **bus** from Castellammare drops you in Scopello's square; out of season, four services a day (Mon–Sat) run back to Castellammare, the last at 4.45pm. In summer, there are four additional services on Sunday; the last returns to Castellammare at 7pm.

Accommodation

Scopello can be rather an exclusive retreat, given the building restrictions that limit the accommodation choices. Book well in advance if you want to stay here in summer, and be prepared to accept half-board terms in the *pensioni*. Out of season you'll be able to pick and choose, and the prices drop a little too.

All the official **places to stay** are within a thirty-second walk of the square – if everything is booked up, you might find **rooms to rent** by asking around in the bars and shops. The nearest **campsite** is *Baia di Guidaloca* (☎ 0924.541.262, ⓦ www .campingguidaloca.com; closed mid-Sept to Easter), 3km south of Scopello and a stone's throw from Cala Bianca, a shady spot with a pizzeria-restaurant, shop and sports facilities.

Angelo Via Marco Polo 4 ☎ 338.697.4276, ⓦ www.angelobedandbreakfast.it. Small B&B with rooms with a/c and a terrace overlooking Piazza Fontana. Alternatively, ask here about *Casale Corcella*, 1km north of Scopello and ideal for walkers in the Zíngaro nature reserve. No credit cards. Both closed Nov–March; both ❷

La Tavernetta Via A. Diaz 3 ☎ 0924.541.129, ⓦ www.albergolatavernetta.it. Pleasant rooms in mellow colours, some small, and most with balconies and sea views. The food is recommended. Half board in Aug costs €85 per person. ❸

Torre Bennistra Via Natale di Roma 19 ☎ 0924.541.128, ⓦ www.hoteltorrebennistra.it. Though lacking warmth or character, this modern

hotel on the edge of Scopello has palatial public rooms and fully equipped, mostly spacious bedrooms, some (costing extra) enjoying glorious views over the coast. Worth taking half board here for the exceptional food. Rates plummet out of season. No credit cards. ❷–❸

La Tranchina Via A. Diaz 7 ☎ 0924.541.099, ⓔ pensione.tranchina @gmail.com. Comfortable *pensione* run by a friendly family that includes an English and Spanish speaker. It has plain, modern rooms and there's an open fire in winter (when the nights can get chilly). Great dinners are served too, and at least half board is required in summer at €72 per person. ❷

The village

The village of Scopello consists of little more than **Piazza Fontana** – a paved square and a fountain – and a couple of alleys running off it. On one side of the square sits the gateway and enclosed courtyard of the village's eighteenth-century **baglio**, or manor house, now the focus of local life. In here – centred on a huge eucalyptus tree – the courtyard buildings harbour a ceramicist's workshop, artist's studio, craft shop, a couple of bars and a pizzeria-restaurant. With the lights on and the wind rustling the leaves, it's a magical place at night, though in July and August – when every bar table is full and queues develop – you could be forgiven for wishing for more solitude. Outside high summer, traditional village life is more to the fore: men playing cards at the tables, people gossiping around the fountain and neighbours helping out in each other's fields.

Elsewhere in the village – you won't have to look far to find everything – there's an *alimentari*, a bakery, a butcher's shop, a couple of bars and a post office, and there's an ATM inside the *baglio* courtyard.

Three kilometres south of Scopello, the lovely bay of **Cala Bianca** offers some great swimming; the bus from Castellammare stops here.

Eating and drinking

For such a small place, Scopello has a profusion of **restaurants**, many of them tucked away in back lanes. At weekends, when booking is advisable, they can be full to bursting, while most places close out of season.

Il Baglio Baglio Isonzo 4 ☎ 0924.541.200. Extremely popular place for pizzas (€6–10), pastas (€10–16) and seafood dishes (€11–16), with attractive outdoor seating in the *baglio* courtyard. Eat early to avoid queues at weekends and in summer. Closed Nov–Feb.

Locanda Cantuccio Via Mazzarella. On a side street off the main square, this place with terrace seating specializes in fresh seafood and typical Roman dishes (the owner-chef is from Rome), as well as a range of antipasti. Expect to pay around €30 per person excluding drinks. Closed daytime May, June & Oct and all Nov–April.

La Tavernetta Via A. Diaz 3 ⓣ0924.541.129. Reliable pasta and fish dishes using local ingredients, doled out either inside or out on the terrace. A hearty three-course meal with local wine runs to around €35, though you could eat for less.

Torre Bennistra Via Natale di Roma 19 ⓣ0924.541.128. The accent here is on home-made pasta and the freshest fish. Prices are €5–10 for first courses, €8–16 for mains. Tables by the windows enjoy wonderful views over the *faraglioni*.

The Tonnara di Scopello

Just before Scopello on the road from Castellammare, a right-hand fork will bring you after a few hundred metres down to the coast and the **Tonnara di Scopello**, set in its own tiny cove. This old tuna fishery and its associated outhouses was where the writer Gavin Maxwell lived and worked in the 1950s, basing his *Ten Pains of Death* on his experiences there. It's almost too picturesque to be true – not least the row of abandoned buildings on the quayside, fronted by lines of rusting anchors, and the ruined old watchtowers tottering on knobbly columns of rock above the sea. From the shore, it's still precisely as Maxwell described it more than fifty years ago: "a sea of purple and blue and peacock green, with a jagged cliff coastline and great *faraglioni* (rock towers) thrusting up out of the water as pinnacle islands, pale green with the growth of cactus at their heads".

The *tonnara* remained in intermittent use until the 1980s. Although it's still privately owned, the gate is always open (free; beverage machines inside the building) to allow visitors to wander around the quayside – provided, according to the notice, they don't bring with them a whole host of proscribed items (dogs, radios, chairs, umbrellas). An injunction like this is usually as a red rag to a bull to your average Sicilian, and the place is regularly engulfed with all of the above on summer weekends – though more strictly enforced regulations may yet come into effect. Most visitors come to swim in the most crystal clear of waters off the tiny shingle **beach** here. Whether or not you indulge in a dip, it's a thoroughly photogenic spot (and scenes from the film *Ocean's Twelve* were shot here).

The Riserva Naturale dello Zíngaro

The coast road continues northwest of Scopello, affording wonderful views of the *tonnara*'s towers and the gulf beyond, and passing fairly unobtrusive holiday homes, fields of vines and grazing horses. Three kilometres beyond the *tonnara*, the road ends at the southern entrance to the **Riserva Naturale dello Zíngaro** (daily: April–Oct 7am–8pm; Nov–March 8am–4pm; €3; ⓣ800.116.616 or 0924.35.108, ⓦwww.riservazingaro.it), where you can proceed on foot through pristine country and past yet more extremely beautiful coves and beaches. This is not exactly unknown territory, since hundreds of Palermitani descend on Scopello and its surroundings on summer weekends, but at other times – and especially out of season – it's one of the most tranquil places in Sicily. In addition, since the whole area is regulated by building restrictions that actually seem to be enforced, the water quality – and hence the swimming – is excellent. In summer, Russo buses arrive here from Castellammare del Golfo.

The first nature reserve established in Sicily, Lo Zíngaro comprises a completely unspoiled 7km stretch of coastline backed by steep mountains. Its genesis was the proposal to force a coast road through from Scopello to San Vito, an idea that horrified environmentalists, who persuaded six thousand supporters to march in protest in May 1980. The road was scrapped and the reserve established, following which great efforts have been made to attract sympathetic visitors to the site. Most, it's true, come for the isolated cove **beaches**, which provide scintillating swimming, but since there's no vehicle access beyond the entrances it's not hard to escape the crowds by simply walking further into the reserve. Around forty different bird species nest and mate here, including the rare **Bonelli's Eagle**, and there are some six hundred species of plant. Apart from the wide variety of fauna and flora, there's great archeological interest in an area that supported some of Sicily's earliest prehistoric settlements. The waters around this coast are reckoned to be among the best in the region for **diving**, with wrecks and grottoes to explore; if you're interested, contact Cetaria, Via Marco Polo 3, Scopello (☏368.386.4808, ⓦwww.cetaria.it), for dives, excursions and equipment hire.

At the Scopello entrance, **Ingresso Sud**, there's a car park and an **information hut** where you can pick up a simple map showing the trails through the reserve. If you're heading off from the coastal path, treat the map with some scepticism and make sure you carry plenty of water – any water you see along the way may not be fit for drinking. There's a water fountain at the information hut and, in summer, a van selling ices and drinks.

Walking routes

The easiest and best-maintained of the network of **paths** through the reserve keep close to the coast. Of the two main routes, the **Sentiero Alto** is best in spring for the vegetation and natural life, while the **Sentiero Basso**, hugging the shore, is best in summer if you want to stop for swims. The mid- and high-mountain routes are favoured by well-prepared walkers and ornithologists; refuges here can be used at night, so long as you book ahead through the park authority.

Following the Sentiero Basso, it takes less than twenty minutes to reach the first beach, **Cala Capreria**, which can as a result be crowded at weekends and in July and August. When it's not, it's perfect: a tiny cove of white pebbles, azure water, shoals of little fish nibbling at the edge and baby squid darting in and out. A small **Museo Naturalístico** and visitor centre stands just above the beach. Three more museums (all open daily, roughly 10am–4pm, closing later in summer; free) are located further up the coast, one – above **Cala del Varo**, another twenty minutes or so onward – dedicated to manna and the flowering manna-ash, examples of which grow hereabouts.

Sticking with the coastal path, it's 3km from the southern entrance to the successive coves of **Disa**, **Berretta** and **Marinella**, which should be a little more secluded. The next cove, **Cala dell'Uzzo**, holds a museum of rural life, while the **Cala Tonnarella dell'Uzzo** (7km from the southern entrance) has a museum of fishing and other marine activity. Five hundred metres beyond here, at the **Ingresso Nord** – the northern, San Vito Lo Capo, park entrance – you'll find another **information hut**, water and, in summer, refreshments. If you're walking on to San Vito, note that it's another 11km from the entrance, and there's no public transport or facilities of any kind along the way.

Segesta and around

Set amid deserted green countryside, around 15km south of Castellammare del Golfo (and 30km east of Trápani), the remains of the ancient city of **Segesta** are among the most inspiring on the island. All that still stands is a Doric temple and a brilliantly sited theatre, relics of a city whose roots – like Érice's – lay back in the twelfth century BC. Unlike Érice, though, ancient Segesta was eventually

Hellenized and spent most of the later period disputing its border with Selinus. The temple dates from a time of prosperous alliance with Athens, but it was never finished – work on it was abandoned when a new dispute broke out with Selinus in 416 BC.

If you're driving, it's easiest to see the site en route between Palermo and Trápani, since it lies just off the motorway. By public transport, the best approach is by bus from Trápani. However you arrive, you'll find an overnight stop at **Calatafimi**, the nearest town to the ruins.

The site

The site of **SEGESTA** (daily 9am–1hr before sunset; last entry 1hr before closing; €9 including the ruins at Selinunte) is best seen early or late in the day, when visitors are fewer and the light less blanching in its effect. The **temple** itself, started in 424 BC, crowns a low hill beyond the café and car park. From a distance you could be forgiven for thinking that it's complete: the 36 regular stone columns, entablature and pediment are all intact, and all it lacks is a roof. However, get closer (and for once you're allowed to roam right inside) and you see just how unfinished the building really is: stone studs, always removed on completion, still line the stylobate, the tall columns are unfluted, and the cella walls are missing. In a way, this only adds to the natural grandeur of the site, and it's not too fanciful to imagine that the pitted and sun-bleached temple simply grew here – a feeling bolstered by the birds nesting in the unfinished capitals, the lizards scampering over the pale yellow stone, and, in spring, the riot of flowers underfoot.

From the main entrance, a road winds up through slopes of wild fennel to a small **theatre** on a higher hill beyond; if you don't relish the twenty-minute climb you can use the half-hourly **bus service** (€1.50). The view from the top is terrific, across green slopes and the plain to the sea, the deep blue of the bay a lovely contrast to the theatre's white stone – the panorama not much damaged by the motorway snaking away below. Behind the theatre, **excavations** (explained by information boards) have revealed the foundations of a mosque and Arab-style houses. These were pulled down in the thirteenth century when a Norman castle was erected on the high ground – though this itself lasted less than a hundred years, as political forces on the island waxed and waned. There are also the remains of a late medieval church, built for local shepherds and landholders and used, in one form or another, until the nineteenth century. Thus it is a site of enormous significance and utility, spanning generations.

Concerts and plays are staged at the theatre between mid-July and early September. Ask at the tourist offices in Palermo and Trápani for details, or call ☏800.904.560. Special excursion buses leave from both cities to coincide with the performances, and tickets for the various productions cost around €15.

Practicalities

Coming from Trápani or Palermo by car, the easiest way to Segesta is to take the A29 autostrada. Apart from the small café and shop at the site, the café-restaurant near the signposted turn-off is the only nearby place for refreshments.

To reach the site by **bus**, catch one of the Tarántola services from Piazza Malta in Trápani, which leave Monday to Saturday at 10am and 2pm, returning at 1.10pm, 5.10pm and 6.25pm; the only Sunday departure is at 10am, returning at 1.10pm. In summer, Tarántola also operates two daily buses from Castellammare del Golfo and one from Palermo. The **train** from Trápani to Álcamo/Palermo stops at Segesta-Tempio; it's a twenty-minute walk uphill to the site from here, with the temple up on the right. Services are infrequent though, just three or four times daily.

Calatafimi

The small town of **CALATAFIMI** lies 4km south of its train station, so it's better to come by bus – there are four services daily here from Trápani. Defended by a castle (hence the Arabic *kalat* of its name) whose remnants top a wooded hill, the town gained fame as the site of the first of Garibaldi's victories against the Bourbon forces in 1860, which opened the way to Palermo and hence the rest of Sicily. The battle took place on the Salemi road, around 1km south of Calatafimi and then 3km up a hill, the summit marked by a white obelisk. It's signposted "Ossario di Pianto Romana", and named as such because the bones of the fallen from the battle are collected here. They used to be on display in cases for the edification of the local population; now they're hidden behind commemorative tablets underneath an Italian flag. The custodian might attempt an explanation of the history if your Italian is up to it – a tip wouldn't go amiss. The views outside, to Calatafimi itself, Érice and the Castellammare gulf, are magnificent.

The old town isn't much more than a strip of development along a single main street, at the top of which stand the church and, just beyond, the only **hotel**, the modern *Mille Pini*, at Piazza F. Vivona 2 (T0924.951.260, W www.hotelmillepini .com; ●). This has ten simple rooms with balconies and valley views, and a **restaurant** where you can eat well for around €15 – overall, it's a very nice place for a quiet night in the sticks.

Trápani

Although predominantly modern, **TRÁPANI**, the first of three major towns on Sicily's western edge, has an elegant old centre that's squeezed into a narrow arm of land pointing out to sea. Lent an end-of-the-line feel by its port, the town's inconspicuous monuments give no great impression of its long history. Nonetheless, Trápani flourished as a Phoenician trading centre and as the port for Eryx, modern Érice, profiting from its position looking out towards Africa. As an important stopover on the sea routes linking Tunis, Naples and Aragon, the town played an enduring role throughout the Middle Ages, when Europe's crowned heads virtually passed each other on the quayside. The Navarrese king Theobald died here of typhoid in 1270; two years later Edward I of England touched down after a Crusade to learn he'd inherited the throne, while Peter of Aragon arrived in 1282 to claim the Sicilian throne, following the expulsion of the Angevin French. The city's growth over the last century has been founded on the development of salt, fishing and wine industries, though severe bombardment during World War II has given rise to miles of dull postwar building around the outskirts.

Still, as a **touring base** for the rest of the west, Trápani can't be beaten. It offers a good few accommodation possibilities, mostly in the old-town area; regular trains south to nearby Marsala and Mazara del Vallo; buses to Érice, the resort of San Vito Lo Capo and the more distant site of Segesta; and the nearest of the Égadi Islands is only twenty minutes away by hydrofoil.

The best time to visit Trápani itself is at **Easter**, to see the famous procession of the **Misteri** – eighteenth-century wooden images arranged in scenes representing the last days in the life of Christ. If you're aiming to be here then, make sure of a hotel room in advance, though you should have no problem finding space at any other time.

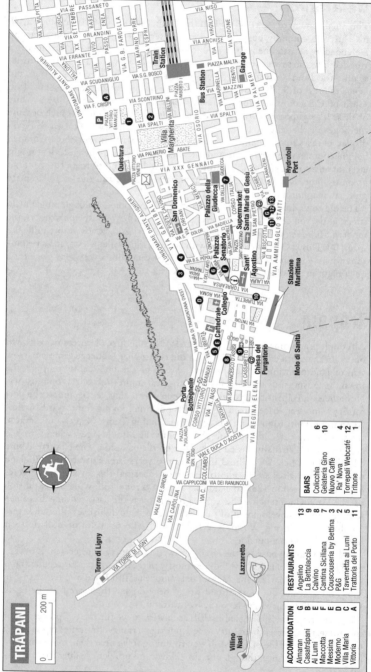

TRÁPANI

0 _____ 200 m

N

Villino Nasi

Lazzaretto

Torre di Ligny

▲ **B**, **C**, Museo Regionale Pépoli, Santuario dell'Annunziata & Cable-Car

► Égadi Islands, Pantelleria, Cágliari & Tunis

► Égadi Islands, Pantelleria, Ústica & Naples

ACCOMMODATION
Almaran	G
Casatrápani	B
Ai Lumi	E
Maccotta	F
Messina	E
Moderno	D
Villa Maria	C
Vittoria	A

RESTAURANTS
Angelino	13
La Bettolaccia	9
Calvino	8
Cantina Siciliana	7
Couscouseria by Bettina	3
P&G	2
Tavernetta ai Lumi	5
Trattoria del Porto	11

BARS
Colicchia	6
Gelateria Gino	10
Nuovo Caffè	4
Ra' Nova	12
Torrepali Webcafé	1
Tritone	1

Arrival and orientation

Trápani's **Vincenzo Florio airport**, 15km south of the city at Birgi, has international flights as well as connections with major Italian cities and Pantelleria, and there's an ATM, an information desk (see below) and car rental (see p.329). Hourly AST buses run to the train station and port (40min) until 11.30pm (Sun 12.30am) – buy tickets on board – while the more expensive Terravision buses have less frequent departures to Trápani's centre but take only 20 minutes. There are also shuttle services to take you directly to your hotel for around €10, or to San Vito Lo Capo for about €80. See p.329 for details of shuttle services and bus connections to other towns. **From Palermo airport** there are four daily Segesta services direct to Trápani (1hr).

The **train station** and main **bus station** (for regional buses) are at the edge of the modern part of town, in Piazza Umberto I and the adjacent Piazza Malta (also known as Piazza Montalto) respectively, about a fifteen-minute walk from the old centre. Buses from Palermo and Agrigento drop you either at the bus station or at the **hydrofoil** dock on Via Ammiraglio Staiti, or the **Stazione Maríttima** at Molo di Sanità, from where there are **ferries** to the Égadi Islands, Pantelleria, Ústica, Naples, Cágliari (Sardinia) and Tunis. See p.329 for all ticket office addresses.

It's pointless trying to **park** in the narrow lanes of the old town, part of which is pedestrianized, though you may find available spaces around the Stazione Maríttima on Via Regina Elena, where cars can be parked within the blue lines, displaying a ticket from the meter (Mon–Sat 8am–1pm & 3.30–8pm, also Sun June–Sept; €0.80/hr, free at other times). Alternatively, you can park for free at the expansive Piazza Vittorio Emanuele, off Lungomare Dante Alighieri in the modern town, about 15 minutes' walk from the old centre.

The narrow, irregularly shaped **old town** occupies around a square kilometre at Trápani's western end, centred on the main **Corso Vittorio Emanuele**. Everything in the old town is easily reachable on foot, though you'll need to catch a **city bus** to visit Trápani's museum, in the new part of the city: most routes depart from Piazza Vittorio Emanuele. Tickets are available from *tabacchi*, and are valid for one hour. During the day, **taxis** usually wait outside the train station – just make sure they switch on the meter, or you could be in for a surprise.

Information

There's a helpful **tourist office** at Florio airport, Birgi (daily 8am–midnight; ℡0923.842.502). In town, the office on Via Torrearsa, near the port (Mon–Sat 9am–1pm & 3.30–8pm, Sun 9am–1pm, reduced times in winter; ℡0923.544.533, ⓦwww.comune.trapani.it/turismo), has information on accommodation and services, and issues free maps.

Accommodation

Most of Trápani's **accommodation** is in the old town, where driving and parking can be difficult. Outside Easter, finding somewhere to stay is usually no problem. The nearest **campsites** are around 12km from Trápani, either north up the coast (see p.333) or south, near the airport (see *Villa Maria*, below).

Ai Lumi Corso Vittorio Emanuele 71 ℡0923.540.922, ⓦwww.ailumi.it. Superior B&B, carved from an eighteenth-century *palazzo* and entered through a lovely arcaded courtyard filled with plants. The four quiet and charming rooms with a/c and modern bathrooms are enhanced by restored tiles and painted wooden furniture, and apartments are available too, sleeping up to five (€100–165 per night). Breakfast – served in their own excellent restaurant (see p.328)

– is a better-than-usual spread of cheese, salami, preserves, fruit and yoghurt. English-speaking owner. ❸

Almaran Via San Cristoforo 8 ☏ 0923.549.847 or 349.611.0211, ⓦ www.almaran.it. Clean and pretty B&B close to the hydrofoil port; rooms have private bathrooms and a/c. The English-speaking owner is friendly and helpful, but breakfasts are basic. ❷

Casatrápani Via Livio Bassi 196 ☏ 333.532.2010, ⓦ www.casatrapani.it. In the modern town, but just 10 minutes' walk from the station, this friendly B&B offers great rates, a pick-up from the airport or station, clean, colour-themed en-suite rooms with a/c, and the use of a kitchen with a washing machine. No credit cards. ❷

Maccotta Via degli Argentieri 4 ☏ 0923.28.418, ⓦ www.albergomaccotta.it. Smart and friendly place behind the Palazzo Senatorio, holding spacious modern rooms with comfortable beds and a/c, but bathrooms are small, and it can be noisy. No breakfast. ❷

Messina Corso Vittorio Emanuele 71 ☏ 0923.21.198, ⓔ albergo.messina@libero.it. The city's cheapest option occupies the first floor of the eighteenth-century Palazzo Bernardo Ferro, and is entered through the same grand courtyard as *Ai Lumi*. The nine rooms, with shared bathrooms, are large and have sinks, fridges and balconies, though the owners can be grumpy. Nonetheless, it's often full. No breakfast. ❶

Moderno Via Ten. Genovese 20 ☏ 0923.21.247, ⓦ www.hotelmoderno.trapani.it. As you might imagine, the *Moderno* is no such thing, though it does have more character than some, housed in an old *palazzo* with a courtyard where limited parking is available. The simple rooms have a/c and some have little balconies over the street. No breakfast. ❶

Villa Maria Via Torre di Mezzo, Lido Marausa ☏ 0923.841.363 or 340.556.4225, ⓦ www .villamaria.marausa.it. With a basic but clean and shady campsite and six apartments to rent, this rural spot may be in the middle of nowhere but it's the nearest accommodation to the airport, one of the two closest campsites to Trápani (12km), and 200m from the sea. Facilities are clean and reliable, and the lovely old couple running it are tops. You'll need your own transport though – it's off the SP21. ❷

Vittoria Via Francesco Crispi 4 ☏ 0923.873.044, ⓦ www.hotelvittoriatrapani.it. In the new town, not far from the bus and train stations, this business-style hotel is reasonably priced, with fully equipped, wi-fi-enabled rooms and good views from the upper floors, though it has zero character. ❸

The City

Almost everything of interest in Trápani is found in the **old town**, west of the Villa Margherita gardens. Some churches and palaces have been renovated over the years, but off the main Corso and away from the central shopping streets there's a scruffy air to much of Trápani, with crumbling *palazzi* and layers of grime on the churches – though this does not necessarily detract from the city's charm.

The old town is most elegant along **Corso Vittorio Emanuele**, the pedestrianized main street, dominated at its eastern end by the pinkish marble front of the **Palazzo Senatorio**, the seventeenth-century town hall. With its twin clocks separated by an imperious eagle, it adds a touch of grandeur to the thin promenading strip, otherwise hemmed in by balconied *palazzi*, a couple of Baroque churches, and the **Cattedrale** on the right, with its Baroque portico, cupolas and vast interior. Dedicated to San Lorenzo, it has a *Crucifixion* inside, in the fourth chapel on the right, attributed to Van Dyck.

Changing its name along the way, the Corso runs almost to the end of the curving promontory from which the town took its Phoenician name of Drepanon (sickle). At its very tip is the **Torre di Ligny**, a squat Spanish fortification dating from 1671, now privately owned, but a good spot for a sit-down with a sandwich. On the way back into town, a walk down the north side of the promontory will show you what's left of the medieval city wall, the *bastione*, breached by the thirteenth-century **Porta Botteghelle**.

Back at the eastern end of the Corso, **Via Torrearsa** is one of the old town's main shopping streets. At its southern end, the church of **Sant'Agostino** on Piazzetta Saturno boasts a pretty fourteenth-century rose window of interlocking stone bands; the church is occasionally used as a concert hall (details of performances from the tourist office). Architecturally more appealing is the sixteenth-century church

One of Sicily's most evocative religious processions, held since the seventeenth century, takes place in Trápani at Easter, when the **Misteri**, extraordinary life-sized wooden statues depicting scenes from the Passion, are carried shoulder-high through the streets on Good Friday. The procession through the town takes ten hours, starting at 2pm and finishing back at the **Chiesa del Purgatorio** at midnight. Sculpted from cypress wood and cork in the eighteenth century, each of the twenty groups of chocolate-brown figures is associated with one of the town's trades – fishermen, metalworkers, saltworkers, and so on – whose representatives undertake to maintain them and, draped in cowls and purple robes, annually parade them. The rest of the time the statues are kept in the **Purgatorio church**, on Via Francesco d'Assisi, south of the main Corso. The church is usually locked, but when it's open, there should be a priest around to explain which of the trades is responsible for each of the sculpted groups, and what the particular figures represent – though most of the scenes are familiar enough. When it's closed, you can arrange admission at the Cattedrale office.

of **Santa Maria di Gesù**, on Via San Pietro to the east, whose two doors display a diversity characteristic of the town, the right-hand one Gothic, the other defiantly Renaissance, and there's a fine relief in the architrave. Inside, at the end of the nave, a terracotta *Madonna col Bambino* surrounded by angels, the work of Andrea della Robbia, shelters beneath a graceful marble canopy carved by Antonello Gagini.

There's little more to see in this part of town apart from a few unusual facades, one of them buried in the wedge of hairline streets and alleys north of Corso Italia, at Via della Giudecca 43, where the sixteenth-century **Palazzo della Giudecca** sports a plaque-studded front and some Spanish-style Plateresque windows. The building lies at the heart of Trápani's old **Jewish quarter**, an area dating from Trápani's medieval heyday at the centre of Mediterranean trade. From here, it's not far to the **Villa Margherita**, the shady town gardens (open dawn to dusk) which hold a small zoo and host summer concerts (information available from the tourist office).

The modern city

While Trápani's **modern city** mainly consists of a dull grid of right-angled streets, a trio of specific attractions are well worth seeking out. For two of these, drivers should follow Via Giovan Battista Fardella east, bearing right at Via Pépoli (by bus take #25, #28 or #30, or Circolare Villa Pépoli on Sun, from Piazza Vittorio Emanuele, Via Libertà or Via Garibaldi) to **Villa Pépoli**, a park. In front of it stands the lavishly decorated **Santuario dell'Annunziata** (daily 8am–noon & 4–8pm, closes 7pm in winter; free), a fourteenth-century convent and church whose cloisters incorporate the town's main museum. The sanctuary was rebuilt in 1760 and only the facade, with its Gothic portal and magnificent rose window, is original. Inside (entrance on Via Pépoli), you'll find a series of sumptuous **chapels**, two dedicated to Trápani's fishermen and seamen – one echoes the facade's shell motif around the sides of the room – and, best of all, the **Cappella della Madonna**, containing Trápani's sacred idol: the beautiful, smiling *Madonna and Child*, attributed to Nino Pisano in the fourteenth century. Responsible for a host of miracles, the statue is housed beneath a grandiose marble canopy sculpted by Antonello Gagini and surrounded by polychrome marble – as well, generally, as a crowd of hushed worshippers.

Adjacent, and entered through Villa Pépoli, the wide-ranging collection at the **Museo Regionale Pépoli** (Mon–Sat 9am–1.30pm, Sun 9am–12.30pm; €6) takes in everything from exemplary Gagini statuary to seventeenth-century coral

TRÁPANI AND THE WEST | Trápani

9

craftwork. Highlights downstairs include a little bronze horse and rider by Giácomo Serpotta and a sixteenth-century marble doorway by Berrettaro Bartolomeu, taken from the old church of San Giuliano, which, though badly worn in parts, displays a lively series of tableaux. Downstairs, too, bizarrely, is a grim wooden guillotine from 1789 with a basket for the head, and a coffin at the ready. The museum houses a good **medieval art** section – including a powerful *Pietà* by Roberto Oderisio, and a couple of fine fifteenth-century triptychs by the anonymous *Maestro del Políttico di Trápani*. Other displays include a coin collection, with Greek, Roman, Arab and Italian examples; an eighteenth-century majolica-tiled scene of *La Mattanza* (tuna slaughter), with the fishermen depicted corralling the fish in their boats; a small archeological section with a few finds from Selinunte and Mózia, though nothing outstanding, and some intricate coral work, including crib scenes with alabaster and shell decoration.

Eating and drinking

Eating out in Trápani is a real treat – you can get fresh fish and couscous almost everywhere, while the local pasta speciality, *alla trapanese*, is terrific – either spaghetti or home-made *busiate* served with a pesto of fresh tomato, basil, garlic and almonds. There are quite a few lively **bars** around, too, good for breakfast and snacks, and bustling at night with people stopping off from the clamorous *passeggiata* that fills Via Torrearsa and the bottom end of Corso Vittorio Emanuele.

Restaurants

Angelino Via Ammiraglio Staiti 87 ☎0923.26.922. Examine the mouthwatering displays in this fashionable *pasticceria-távola calda*, take a ticket, order at the bar and grab a table in the conservatory. You're spoiled for choice – *involtini* of aubergine rolled around spaghettini, stuffed sardines, rosemary-roast potatoes, lasagne and *focaccia*, all at extremely reasonable prices, with wine by the glass and coffee and delicious *dolci* to follow, if you can manage it. Closed Mon except Aug.

La Bettolaccia Via Gen. Enrico Fardella 25 ☎0923.21.695. Popular with locals, this modern *osteria* is known for its excellent risotto and *busiate* dishes (mainly seafood, though *alla trapanese* is recommended). Expect to pay €30–40 per head, including good local wine. Delicious desserts include *parfait al pistacchio*. The atmosphere is informal but sophisticated. Book, or arrive early. Closed Sat lunch & Sun.

Calvino Via N. Nasi 72 ☎0923.21.464. Renowned backstreet pizzeria, with Moorish cubbyhole rooms, a bit rough-and-ready but well worth a visit. The tasty pizzas come in four sizes, from *Píccola* (€5–6) to *Tripla* (€14–17), cut into bite-sized pieces and served on squares of greaseproof paper. Try the *Rianata*, made with fresh oregano, tomato, garlic, anchovies and pecorino cheese – a local speciality – and wash it down with cold beer. Book for a table, or be prepared to queue. No credit cards. Closed Tues.

Cantina Siciliana Via della Giudecca 32 ☎0923.28.673. In the old Jewish quarter, this cosy restaurant with blue-tiled walls is a great spot for a romantic dinner, though service can be poor. The menu features traditional Sicilian dishes as well as fish couscous, and desserts include a sublime lemon ice cream with limoncello. Pastas and meat and fish mains are all €8–12.

Couscouseria by Bettina Via Torrearsa 110. This unpretentious *távola calda* has low prices and lots of heart. You can pick up traditional *trapanese* snacks to take away or eat at a few tables inside; everything is authentic and delicious, from *couscous con pesce* to *caponata* and *involtini di melanzane*.

P&G Via Spalti 1 ☎0923.547.701. This long-established restaurant in the modern town has seen better days, but it still lays on a fine selection of *antipasti*, seafood and grilled meats. Among the pastas (€7–12), try the fresh *busiate casarecce*, with a pesto of anchovy, garlic, pine nuts and tomato. There are a few tables outdoors, and pizzas in the evening. Closed Mon.

Tavernetta ai Lumi Corso Vittorio Emanuele 71–77 ☎0923.872.418. The best restaurant in the old town occupies the brick-vaulted stables of an old palace – and there's a shady outdoor terrace for summer dining. A typical meal from the regional menu might be home-made pasta with zucchini and shrimp, followed by a seafood stew or braised rabbit, and the wine list features good Sicilian wines. It's not cheap, with most dishes €10–20. Closed Tues.

Trattoria del Porto Via Ammiraglio Staiti 45
☎0923.547.822. Friendly, family-run trattoria
(also known locally as *Da Felice*) opposite the
port with occasionally slow service but good food
and outdoor tables under the arches. Top choices
are the *spaghetti marinara*, fish couscous, roast
squid or, in season, *involtini di spada* (swordfish
roulades). Good-value tourist menus are €20 and
€30, otherwise all dishes are €9–12. Closed Mon
except July & Aug.

Bars, birrerias and cafés

Colicchia at the corner of Via delle Belle Arti
and Via Carosio, just off Via Torrearsa. Fine
bar-*pasticceria* with a super array of cakes; a good
place to sample a *granita*. No seats.
Gelateria Gino Piazza dalla Chiesa. Make a
beeline here for excellent ice cream and

frullati, from kiwi to coconut, and grab a table in
the piazza.
Nuovo Caffè Ra' Nova Via Garibaldi. Busy café
with a range of hot snacks and pastas, and a large
outdoor area on a traffic-free road. There's also a
huge array of ice creams and cocktails.
Torrepali Webcafé Via Ammiraglio Staiti 73.
Contemporary and chic bar opposite the hydrofoil
port for beers, cocktails and snacks. With
numerous terminals on hand, it's a relaxed spot to
catch up with your emails, and stays open 10pm,
later in summer.
Tritone Piazza Vittorio Emanuele 38. A congenial
place in the modern town opposite the public
gardens, where you can sip a drink or munch on
gelato while gazing upon palm trees, and ponder
on the strange creature perched on the head of
King Vittorio Emanuele's statue.

Listings

Airline tickets Egatour (see Travel agents), or
Airone ☎199.207.080, ⊛www.alitalia.com/ap_it;
Meridiana ☎892.928, ⊛www.meridiana.it; Ryanair
T899.018.880, ⊛www.ryanair.com.
Airport information For Trápani airport flight info,
call ☎0923.842.502 or check ⊛www.airgest.it.
Airport transport Hourly AST buses run from the
port and bus station to Trápani's airport at Birgi.
There are also regular Terravision buses from
Palermo to Trápani's airport and Segesta buses
from Trápani's bus station to Palermo airport.
Banks Banks with cashpoints (ATMs) on Piazza
Umberto I, Corso Italia, Via Garibaldi and at the
Stazione Maríttima.
Buses AST ☎0923.23.222, ⊛www.aziendasiciliana
trasporti.it, from Piazza Malta (for destinations within
the province, including Érice, Marsala, Mazara del
Vallo, Castelvetrano, Gibellina, San Vito Lo Capo,
Salemi, Trápani airport and Valderice); S. Lumia
☎0922.20.414, ⊛www.autolineelumia.it, from
Piazza Malta and Trápani airport (for Agrigento and
Sciacca); Segesta ☎091.342.525, ⊛www.segesta
.it, from Piazza Garibaldi (for Álcamo, Palermo and
Palermo airport); Salemi ☎0923.981.120, ⊛www
.autoservizisalemi.it, from Trápani airport (for
Marsala and Palermo); Tarántola ☎0924.31.020,
from Piazza Malta (for Segesta); Terravision
☎0923.981.120, ⊛www.terravision.eu from the
port, bus station and airport (for Palermo).
Car rental Europcar ⊛www.europcar.com,
Stazione Maríttima ☎0923.22.874, airport
☎0923.842.828; Serse, Via Passo Enea 30
☎0923.21.843, ⊛www.autonoleggioserse.com;
Sixt ⊛www.sixt.com, Via Marino Torre 21
☎0923.28.533 and airport ☎0923.030.554.

Ferries Grimaldi ☎0923.593.673, ⊛www
.grimaldi-lines.com (for Civitavécchia and Tunis);
Siremar ☎0923.24.968 or 892.123, ⊛www
.siremar.it (for the Égadi Islands and Pantelleria);
Tirrenia ☎892.123, ⊛www.tirrenia.it (for Cágliari);
Ústica Lines ☎0923.873.813, ⊛www.usticalines
.it (for the Égadi Islands and Ústica). All the ferry
companies have offices at the Stazione Maríttima,
Molo di Sanità, Via Ammiraglio Staiti.
Garage Bulgarella, a 10min walk from the dock at
Via Mazzini 17 ☎0923.547.022; €10–12 per day.
Hospital Ospedale S. Antonio Abate, Via Cosenza
☎0923.809.111.
Hydrofoil tickets Siremar (for the Égadi Islands);
Ústica Lines (for the Égadi Islands, Naples and
Pantelleria). Both companies have ticket booths on
the dockside, open 15min before departures. See
Ferries for contact details.
Internet Piazza Garibaldi 28 (closed Sun) and
Torrepali Webcafé, Via Ammiraglio Staiti 73 (open
till 10pm daily), opposite the ferry and hydrofoil
ports respectively.
Left luggage Top Transfer, near the hydrofoil port
at Via Ruggiero di Lauria 4–8, charges €4 per bag
until 7pm daily.
Markets There's a general market every Thursday
near the stadium on Via Ilio (follow Via A. Staiti and
Via Palmeri east), and a morning fish market on Via
Ammiraglio Staiti near the port.
Pharmacies Marini, Corso Vittorio Emanuele 117;
Occhipinti, Corso Italia 67, both open roughly
Mon–Sat 8.30am–1.30pm & 4.30–8pm.
Police Questura at Piazza Vittorio Véneto
☎0923.598.111; Carabinieri, Via Orlandini
☎0923.330.000.

The Funierice cable car to Érice

Even if it weren't the quickest means to reach Érice – far more convenient than driving or catching a bus – the Funierice **cable-car** (*funivia*) ride from Trápani would be worth the excursion. In fact the ascent, which takes about twelve minutes, constitutes one of the region's most memorable experiences, revealing a gradually expanding panorama that extends over the flat saltpans to the south, the mountainous coast north, and out over the narrow limb that holds the old city to the Égadi Islands and the blue sea beyond. By night, the scene is very different, with Trápani's lights sparkling under a starry sky.

From the Trápani terminal on Via Caserta, **departures** are continuous (Mon 2–8.30pm, Tues–Fri 7.30am–8.30pm, Sat & Sun 9.30am–midnight; @www.funiviaerice.it), with tickets costing €3.50 one way, €6 return. Note that the service may be cancelled if it's windy, in which case you'll have to take the AST bus from the stop on Via G.B. Fardella. Check whether the service is operating on ☎0923.869.720.

Driving to the cable-car station on Via Caserta, at the extreme eastern end of the modern city, is not straightforward: from the old centre, follow Via G.B. Fardella east, bear left at Corso Mattarella, keep straight along this and its continuation Via Manzoni (following signs for Érice), and turn left at the end into Via Fratelli Aiuto, from which it's a right turn into Via Caserta and the large car park. It's simpler **by bus**: take #21 or #23 from Piazza Vittorio Emanuele (direction Ospedale S. Antonio Abbate) and get off at the stop before the hospital, from where it's a short walk.

Post office At Piazza Vittorio Véneto, at the bottom of Via Garibaldi. Mon–Fri 8am–6.30pm, Sat 8.30am–1pm, but Aug Mon–Fri 8am–1.30pm, Sat 8.30am–1pm.
Supermarket Margherita Conad, Corso Italia 35, is a central supermarket for food, open Mon–Sat 8am–1.30pm & 5–8.15pm.
Taxis and transfers Ranks at train station and port. Call ☎0923.30.0051, 337.896.010 or 368.734.0893 (24hr). Top Transfer offers

airport shuttles and longer-distance transfers ☎0923.27.899 or 337.896.010, @www.toptransfer.it.
Train information FS information line is ☎89.20.21, @www.ferroviedellostato.it.
Travel agents Egatour Viaggi, Via Ammiraglio Staiti 13 ☎0923.21.754, can provide information and tickets for getting to Pantelleria, plus all other hydrofoil and ferry tickets, flights, train tickets and some bus tickets.

Érice

Despite being just a brief hop from Trápani and the coast, **ÉRICE** couldn't be further away in spirit. It's a walled mountain town – around 750m above sea level – thoroughly medieval, with its creeping hillside alleys, grey stone buildings and silent charm, but boasting a truly ancient lineage. Founded by Elymians, who claimed descent from the Trojans, the city was known to the ancient world as Eryx. A magnificent temple, dedicated to Aphrodite Erycina, Mediterranean goddess of fertility, once topped the mountain and was big enough to act as a landmark to sailors. According to legend, it was here that Daedalus landed, unlike his son Icarus who flew too near the sun, after fleeing from Minos; he presented the temple with a honeycomb made of gold as his gift to the goddess. Even though the city was considered impregnable, Carthaginian, Roman, Arab and Norman armies all forced entry over the centuries, but all respected the town's sanctity, the Romans rebuilding the temple and setting two hundred soldiers to serve as guardians of the shrine. Later, the Arabs renamed the town Gebel-Hamed, "Mohammed's mountain", while Count Roger called it Monte San Giuliano, a name that stuck until Mussolini returned its ancient moniker in 1934. Nowadays it's a centre for scientific conferences, and you're likely to see numbers of foreigners with labels on their lapels among the milling tourists.

Indeed, the constant tourist presence in this small town can be wearisome, especially in August when the streets are busy until late at night as trippers and sojourners negotiate the polished cobblestones. Though as people have always come to Érice to sightsee and worship, it seems churlish to resent these, and in any case, there are enough cobbled alleys and quiet spots to enable you to avoid the tour groups. Otherwise, the only modern blots in the town's otherwise homogeneous aspect are the pylons that tower above the grey walls. Beyond these, the views from Érice's terraces are superb, taking in Trápani, the Égadi Islands and even (allegedly) distant Cap Bon in Tunisia.

As well as summer, **Easter** is another popular time to visit, when the *Misteri* sculptures representing the Stations of the Cross are paraded through the streets on Good Friday.

Arrival and information

From Trápani, it's a twisty half-hour's **drive**, or a 45-minute **bus** ride, to Érice; the buses stop outside the Porta Trápani, where there's also a handy **car park** (don't even think of taking your car into the old-town streets). By far the most rewarding way to arrive, however, is by **cable car**, which takes less than fifteen minutes from the base station at Via Caserta in Trápani (see opposite for details). The upper terminal is right outside Porta Trápani.

The helpful **tourist office** (Mon–Fri 8am–2pm; ☏0923.869.388, ⓦwww .prolocovalderice.it) is just off Piazza Umberto I on Via Tommaso Guarrasi. The **post office** stands on Via G.F. Guarnotti (Mon–Fri 8am–1.30pm, Sat 8am–12.30pm), and there's a **bank** at the top of Via Vittorio Emanuele, by Piazza Umberto I – both have ATMs.

Accommodation

Staying the night in Érice is relatively expensive, and in summer, or at Easter and Christmas, you'd do well to book in advance. If you stay in the old town you'll have to park outside Porta Trápani and carry your luggage up. The other option is to stay in Valderice (see p.334), about twenty minutes' drive back down the mountain.

Il Cármine Piazza del Cármine 23 ☏ 0923.194.1532 or 328.445.5026, Ⓦ www.ilcarmine.com. This former Carmelite convent in the heart of town has been sympathetically restored, retaining its own tiny chapel. Rooms are spacious, bright and simply furnished, and come with separate private bathrooms. Wi-fi available. ❷

Edelweiss Cortile Padre Vincenzo 5 ☏ 0923.869.420, Ⓔ edelweiss@libero.it. Tucked up a cobbled alley off Piazza San Domenico, this *pensione* has plain, smallish rooms, all with shower. The staff are somewhat gloomy, but it'll do for a night. ❷

Elimo Via Vittorio Emanuele 75 ☏ 0923.869.377, Ⓦ www.hotelelimo.it. Beautifully restored building with a little courtyard garden. The luxurious rooms have great views – as does the quality restaurant where you take breakfast – though the overall tone is somewhat snooty. ❹

Moderno Via Vittorio Emanuele 63 ☏ 0923.869.300, Ⓦ www.hotelmodernoerice.it. The best aspect of the *Moderno* is its panoramic roof terrace, but the rooms (with en-suite shower-rooms and a/c) aren't so terrific, at least not for the price – rates are more reasonable in low season. ❸

Ulisse Via Santa Lucia ☏ 0923.860.155 or 389.985.6089, Ⓦ www.sitodiulisse.it. A great budget choice, this *affittacamere* offers rooms spread over two buildings, all with private bathrooms and some with a/c. Opt for those grouped around a peaceful central courtyard, where rugs and colourful ceramic floors lend a North African ambience. No credit cards. ❷

The Town

The greatest pleasure in Érice is simply to wander around. You'll soon get lost in the winding alleys, but the most convoluted of routes is only going to take a couple of hours, and every aspect is delightful. Square and solid from the outside, the houses hide pretty courtyards, and while most of the churches are locked, there's usually something to admire – a carved door, a cupola or a belltower. The number of tourists means a fair amount of tat in the souvenir shops, from tea towels to puppets, but **traditional industries** still flourish, in particular the making of ceramics, tapestries and *dolci di badia* (almond-paste sweets).

You enter through the Norman **Porta Trápani**, at the southwestern edge of town. Just inside is the battered stone **Chiesa Madre** (daily: March 10am–4pm; April–June & Oct 10am–6pm; July & Aug 10am–8pm; Sept 10am–7pm; Nov–Feb 10am–12.30pm; €2), dating from around 1314, though the massive Gothic entrance was added a century later and much of the structure was rebuilt in the nineteenth century. The neo-Gothic interior preserves some exceptional lace-like carving. To the left of the church, the stout, battlemented campanile owes its name, **Torre di Re Federico** II (same hours; €2), to its original role as a lookout tower for Frederick III of Aragon (Frederick II of Sicily), who made Érice his base during the Wars of the Vespers. Climb to the top for sublime views over village, mountains and sea. From the ticket office, you can acquire a Passe Partout ticket (€5) that allows entry to a handful of Érice's attractions, including these two.

From Porta Trápani, the main Via Vittorio Emanuele climbs steeply past houses, shops and *pasticcerie* to the pretty **Piazza Umberto I**, where café tables are strewn adventurously across the sloping cobbles. The small **Museo Córdici** (Mon–Fri 8.30am–1.30pm, Mon & Thurs also 3–5pm, also open Sat 9am–1pm in summer; free) here boasts a good *Annunciation* by Antonello Gagini and the pick of the local archeological finds. Further north, the medieval **Porta Cármine** marks the other end of town, from where the line of ancient **city walls** leads back to the Chiesa Madre.

Heading east instead from the Porta Trápani, along Viale Conte Pépoli, you get the best of the views across the plains and out to sea. You'll eventually come to the ivy-clad, twelfth-century **Castello di Vénere** (April–Oct daily 10am–1hr before sunset; Nov–March Sat & Sun 10am–4pm; €3), built on the site of the famed ancient temple of Aphrodite, chunks of which are incorporated into the walls. The castle is built on the most precarious of crags, offering grand views in all directions, though there's not much to see inside.

Below the castello are laid out the **Giardini del Balio** public gardens, in the middle of which sits a restored fifteenth-century tower, the **Torretta Pépoli**. From here, you can wind towards Piazza Umberto I, perhaps passing clifftop **San Giovanni Battista** and its distinctive dome before eventually negotiating the minuscule **Piazza San Domenico**, whose church and palace facade is one of the town's most harmonious sights. The *Antica Pasticceria del Convento* on one corner of the square does a roaring trade in locally produced sweets and pastries.

Eating and drinking

Though **restaurant** prices are a good bit higher in Érice than elsewhere in the region, you can still eat at a reasonable price if you stick to the set-price menus. Bring a picnic and you can sit in the shady Giardini del Balio, or there's a *panineria* on Via Vittorio Emanuele.

Restaurants

Monte San Giuliano Vícolo San Rocco 7 ☏0923.869.595. Entering this backstreet restaurant is like visiting a castle, through a stone archway and up steps. There's a sort of courtyard too, where tables are spread out amid plants with seaward views. Try the *ravioli védova allegra* ("happy widow"), with ricotta and squid ink. First courses are €8–10, mains are €10–18. Closed Mon plus 3 weeks in Nov & Jan.

La Pentolaccia Via G.F. Guarnotti 17 ☏0923.869.099. Housed in an old monastery, this popular restaurant specializes in home-made *busiate* with aubergine, basil, pine nuts and *ricotta salata*. Couscous is good too, or there are simple grills and cheap local wine. Pasta dishes cost €7–10, meat and fish €8–14. Closed Jan & Feb, and Tues rest of winter.

Ulisse Via Chiaramonte 45 ☏0923.869.333. Reached down the stepped Vico San Rocco, just off the main square, and with a pretty courtyard garden. The pizzas here (€5–8) are the best in town (and Sun sees a queue form early), while the regular menu is good too,

if on the pricey side. Gluten-free dishes are offered. Closed Thurs in winter.

La Vetta Via G. Fontana ☏0923.869.404. Signposted off Piazza Umberto I (and also called *Da Mario*), this place serves standard trattoria meals and evening pizzas, and fish couscous is prepared daily. Eat upstairs or at outdoor tables in the alley in summer. Closed Thurs in winter.

Cafés and bars

Pasticceria di Maria Grammático Via Vittorio Emanuele 14. Famous speciality cake shop/café selling marzipan fruits, *amaretti* and the like, a popular tourist-stop. Maria Grammático learned her trade as a girl in a convent, and has co-written a recipe book with writer Mary Taylor Simeti. You can admire the view from a minuscule balcony, and there's a more spacious garden with tables. The *Caffè Maria* is a few doors down at no. 4, and the sister *Antica Pasticceria del Convento* is on Piazzetta San Domenico. Closed Tues in winter.

Caffè San Giuliano Via G.F. Guarnotti 11. When the wind blows, retreat to this stone-walled bar, sip a marsala and nibble on *arancini*, panini or salads.

North to Custonaci

North of Trápani, the main attraction is the resort town of San Vito Lo Capo, though with a car you could explore the rugged coastline en route. Between Trápani and the cape, 40km away, two wide gulfs – Bonagia and Cófano – are backed by holiday homes and small plantations, overlooked both by the heights of

Érice and by its lower neighbour **VALDÉRICE**, a ribbon development occupying a prominent ridge. The buses from Trápani to Érice come this way. There's no real reason to stop, save for the coastal views from Valdérice's belvedere, although there are a couple of good **hotels**, both under the same ownership: *Érice Valle*, Via del Cipresso 1 (℡0923.891.133, Ⓦwww.bagliosantacroce.it; ❷), a modern place at the southern (Trápani) end of the main road, with rooms opening onto a Mediterranean garden, and, 5km out of Valdérice on the SS187 (and signposted), 𝒜 *Baglio Santa Croce* (℡0923.891.111, Ⓦwww.bagliosantacroce.it; ❹), a glorious renovation of a seventeenth-century stone-built estate, whose rooms have beamed ceilings, exposed walls, tiled floors and iron bedsteads (other rooms are in the modern annex) – there's a pool, a renowned restaurant and superb views to the coast.

From Valdérice, a minor road winds 5km down to the coast at **BONAGIA**, where the old tuna fishery has been transformed into another very stylish and swanky **hotel** with a pool and numerous other luxury facilities, the *Tonnara di Bonagia* (℡0923.431.111, Ⓦwww.tonnaradibonagia.it; ❻) – reasonably-priced packages are usually available. Nearby, boats bob in the small harbour, though the swimming isn't much good, thanks to the swathes of kelp which infest the coast. There's another other hotel here, right on the harbour: the smart, modern *Saverino* (℡0923.592.727, Ⓦwww.saverino.it; ❸), with much lower prices, clean, spacious rooms and a superb **restaurant** that's worth a stop in its own right (closed Mon).

A little further up the coast lies the *Lido Valdérice* **campsite** (℡0923.573.477 or 349.854.2190, Ⓦwww.campinglidovalderice.it; closed Nov–Feb), close to the sea and a couple of good bars; it's quite small, but clean and friendly, and there are apartments available (❷). It's one of the closest campsites to Trápani (12km), connected by up to six buses a day from Trápani's bus terminal, a thirty-minute ride, then a five-minute walk from the bus stop.

On from Bonagia, the road weaves under some of the gigantic outcrops of rock that characterize Sicily's west. The most spectacular, **Monte Cófano** (659m), is protected as a nature reserve. The village of **CUSTONACI**, 20km from Trápani and famous as a marble-cutting centre, nestles under here, slightly inland. The road then plunges east and inland – passing through purgatory (well, the settlement of Purgatorio) – to re-emerge beside sparkling clear water and more rocky beaches leading up to the San Vito cape, 40km from Trápani.

San Vito Lo Capo and around

With its dense ranks of trattorias, hotels and bars, **SAN VITO LO CAPO** is certainly geared to holiday consumers, but its comparative remoteness has helped to stave off the worst pressures of the tourist industry, even in high season. All the same, you'll have a lot more elbow-room outside the peak months – the best time to appreciate the presence here of one of Sicily's finest beaches.

Arrival and information

Regular daily AST **buses** run to San Vito from Trápani's bus terminal and Russo buses from Palermo's Piazza Marina; all stop on Via P.S. Mattarella, close to the seafront and three blocks up from the central Via Savoia. The last bus back to Trápani leaves at 7.40pm in winter, 8pm in summer (8.30pm Sun); it's a bit too far for a day-trip from Palermo. **Parking** is highly restricted during the summer months: your best bet is to search out one of the car parks on the edge of town, some free, others costing €5–6 per day. From the biggest of these, the free Parcheggio Comunale Sud (Villaggio Azzurro) – for which take an early right turn onto Via

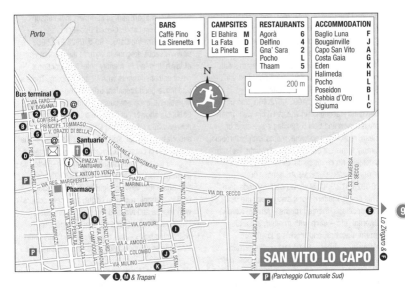

BARS	CAMPSITES	RESTAURANTS	ACCOMMODATION	
Caffè Pino 3	El Bahira M	Agorà 6	Baglio Luna	F
La Sirenetta 1	La Fata D	Delfino 4	Bougainville	J
	La Pineta E	Gna' Sara 2	Capo San Vito	A
		Pocho L	Costa Gaia	G
		Thaam 5	Eden	K
			Halimeda	H
			Pocho	L
			Poseidon	B
			Sabbia d'Oro	I
			Sigiuma	C

SAN VITO LO CAPO

La Piana as you enter town – a free shuttle runs to the centre in the summer months. Alternatively, you can park between the blue lines in a few more central areas (€1 per hour, buy a scratch-card from *tabacchi*).

The **tourist office** is at Via Savoia 61 in summer, in winter switching to Via Venza 12, directly behind it (June–Sept daily 9am–1pm & 5–11pm; Oct–May 9am–1pm & 4–8pm; ☎0923.974.300, ⓦwww.sanvitoweb.com). There are **banks** with ATMs on Via Savoia.

Accommodation

Accommodation in San Vito is plentiful and mostly central – as with all resorts, the nearer the sea, the more expensive the room. It's worth noting that in July and August and during the Cous Cous Fest of late September, many places virtually double their prices and demand a minimum stay of three days or a week. Furthermore, you'll almost always have to agree to half-board terms, and you're unlikely to find anything suitable without an advance reservation. In winter, you won't find many places open; ask around the bars in the centre if you get stuck. There are several **campsites** in the area and the "No camping" signs on the town beach should be heeded.

Hotels and B&Bs

Baglio Luna Via del Secco 11 ☎335.836.2856, ⓦwww.bagliolaluna.com. Seven kilometres out of town, on the Zingaro road and so ideal for forays into the reserve, this rural B&B boasts lofty views from its terrace, and complete tranquillity. The airy whitewashed interior with tiled floors has five simple rooms – those with sea views cost €10 extra. You'll need your own transport to stay here, and there's a two-night minimum stay in Aug. No credit cards. Closed Nov–March. ❸–❹

Bougainville Via Mulino 61 ☎0923.972.207, ⓦwww.sanvitoweb.com/bougainville. Quite a walk from the beach, this family-run place features climbing plants, five decent rooms and a spiral staircase leading to a roof terrace. Fridge available for guests. Closed Oct–March. ❷

Capo San Vito Via San Vito 1 ☎0923.972.122, ⓦwww.caposanvito.it. Right on the seafront, this top-of-the-range hotel has smart, modern rooms, those at the front (costing more) with balconies and sea views – those at the back can be noisy – and there's a spa (not included in the price). Meals are taken in the terrace restaurant, and a small garden gives on to the beach. ⑥

Costa Gaia Via Savoia 125–127 ☎0923.972.268, ⓦwww.hotelcostagaia.com. A good, central choice, though with only seven en-suite rooms this little *pensione* fills quickly. Half or full board only in July & Aug (half board €80 per person). ❸

Eden Via Mulino 58 ☎0923.972.460. One of the cheapest places in San Vito, a 10min walk from town centre and beach, holding a selection of clean, reasonably spacious rooms with bathrooms, simply furnished but perfectly adequate. Parking available. No credit cards. ❷

Halimeda Via Generale Arimondi 100 ☎0923.972.399, ⓦwww.hotelhalimeda.com. This small, modern hotel away from the sea has spacious, themed rooms – Arabic, Nordic, Oriental, etc – each with minibar, a/c and internet access, and there's a lovely Art Nouveau staircase. Breakfast on the terrace includes fresh *cornetti*, biscuits and local *dolci*. There's free parking too – a useful bonus in San Vito. Normally a week minimum stay in Aug. Closed Nov–Feb. ❹

Pocho Contrada Macari ☎0923.972.525, ⓦwww.pocho.it. Making the most of its coastal location, 4km south of town, this cliffside hotel-restaurant provides a stylish and soothing base for anyone with transport, with twelve quiet and elegant rooms with fridges and wi-fi (those sea views cost extra). The food is terrific too (see opposite), and there's access to the small rocky beach below. Closed Oct–March. ❹

Poseidon Via P.S. Mattarella 28 ☎0923.972.444, ⓦwww.poseidonresidence.com. Good for families, these stylish one- and two-room apartments have a/c, kitchenette and shower, plus parking. Ground-floor rooms have garden access but no views; you get more light and a balcony higher up. Prices are €400–850 weekly for a two-person apartment in summer; low-season rates are negotiable. Closed Dec–Feb.

Sabbia d'Oro Via Cavour 90 ☎0923.972.508, ⓦwww.sabbiadorohotels.com. At the eastern end of town, this family-friendly hotel has functional, air-conditioned rooms with TV and balcony. There's parking, a good breakfast using home-made ingredients, excellent suppers and a private patch of beach; shower cubicles are a bit cramped, however. You can spend a little less in the associated two-star *Spiaggia d'Oro* (❹), nearer the beach on Via Santuario, which has a small internal tropical garden. Both closed roughly Nov–Easter. ❺

Sigiuma Via Santuario 39 ☎0923.972.952 or 347.863.8967, ⓦwww.sigiuma.it. Very central B&B with ample rooms in bright, summery colours with fridges and a/c, and there's a patio (where breakfast is served) and a tranquil garden. The welcoming hosts – two brothers – are ready with local info and good advice. Closed Nov–March. ❸

Campsites

El Bahira Contrada Macari ☎0923.972.577, ⓦwww.elbahira.it. The largest and classiest of San Vito's sites, this "camping village" has a range of facilities as well as a private beach, but it's some way out of town, 4km south, and pricey. Caravans and apartments are available (€600–1000 per week in summer). Closed Oct–March.

La Fata Via P. Mattarella ☎0923.972.133, in winter 833.369, ⓦwww.trapaniweb.it/lafata. Most central and the smallest of San Vito's sites, just up from the bus stop, with minimal facilities – though there's a bar – and little shade.

La Pineta Via del Secco ☎0923.972.818, ⓦwww.campinglapineta.it. With a bar, pizzeria, a pool and bungalows to rent, this is the best of San Vito's campsites, shady and efficiently run, located a 10min walk from town east along the seafront.

The town and beach

Running down to the beach, San Vito's long shop- and restaurant-lined main strip, the pedestrianized **Via Savoia**, is the focus of the evening *passeggiata*, with its shops staying open late in summer. It holds one sight worth a glance: the curious, square and fortified-looking **church** (concerts are held outside in summer; check posters around town).

A pleasant promenade backs the **beach**, which stretches east of town. Framed by the looming cliffs behind and overlooked by jagged slabs of rock, the wide, curving stretch of white sand is ideal for swimming and sunbathing, though it gets pretty congested in August. Deck-chairs and parasols are available to rent (€10–12/day).

West of the main beaches, an old watchtower at the small harbour is destined to hold the **Museo del Mare**, holding sundry marine exhibits, though don't hold your breath – it could take years. A ten-minute walk past the harbour brings you to the point of **Capo San Vito** itself – a rocky and windswept plain on which a fenced-off lighthouse is perched. For views you need to climb above the town (bear left on the way out to the lighthouse), up a steep road leading to the top of the high cliffs and looking down over the Golfo di Castellammare. The other local walk is east to the Riserva Naturale dello Zíngaro, a nature reserve, covered in more detail on p.338.

Eating and drinking

Via Savoia and the lungomare are lined with **bars**, ice-cream parlours and pizzerias, and there's no shortage of fish **restaurants** either, most on the pricey side. Things get impossibly busy in August and during the **Cous Cous Fest** (ⓦ www.couscousfest .it), which takes place over six days in late September and includes free samplings of dozens of versions of the dish, as well as nightly concerts in Piazza Santuario and a fireworks extravaganza on the last night at midnight. In recent years, a **Cous Cous Preview** takes place over three days in early June, a sort of mini-version of the main event, while there are free concerts and more festivities around San Vito's day in mid-June. It's always worth booking during these periods, and restaurant queues are common. Most places stay open throughout the winter too.

Restaurants

Agorà Piazza Marinella 5 ☏ 0923.974.442. Always busy, this smart trattoria near the seafront has tables in the piazza and pastas for €10–12 and mains for around €13. The house speciality is *cassatelle Agorà*, fresh pasta stuffed with zucchini, pistachio and basil, served with mussels and shrimps (€12). Closed Wed in winter.

Delfino Via Savoia 15 ☏ 0923.972.711. A pizzeria-trattoria on the main street and near the beach, with smoked-fish *antipasti*, fresh pasta, couscous *di pesce* and a short list of decent pizzas to eat in or take away. One of the cheaper places in town, it offers tourist menus for around €12.

Gna' Sara Via Duca degli Abruzzi 6 ☏ 0923.972.100. A popular place for great pizzas (€6–8), fresh seafood pastas (€8–12) and excellent couscous. Mains are €8–18.

🏃 **Pocho** Contrada Macari ☏ 0923.972.525. Small and casually chic, and with an unparalleled location overlooking the rocky coast 4km south of town, this place has tables inside – where there's a collection of Sicilian puppets – and on a lovely panoramic terrace. Inventive dishes are available on a six-course set menu (€35 including drinks). The owner, Marilù, occasionally ends the evening with Sicilian songs. Closed lunchtime Mon–Sat and all Tues, but mid-June to mid-Sept closed lunchtime Mon–Sat and all Sun, and closed all Oct–March.

Thaam Via Duca degli Abruzzi 32–36 ☏ 0923.972.836. Elaborately decorated restaurant with a marked Tunisian influence, with *merguez*, kebabs and couscous (all €10) featuring alongside more mainstream Italian dishes. First courses cost €11–17, mains €13–18. The outdoor tables beneath a tent-like canopy fill fast, so book or arrive early.

Bars

Caffè Pino Via Savoia. A nice choice for breakfast, with friendly service and delicious cakes and pastries. Try the *torrone* ice cream. Closed Thurs Oct–June.

La Sirenetta Via Savoia, corner of Via Faro. *Gelateria* overlooking the beach, with a choice of twenty ice creams and a summer shaded terrace. Specialities are *gelsomino* (jasmine flower, summer only), *torrone* and *caldofreddo* (with hot chocolate sauce). Closed Tues Nov–March.

Listings

Bike rental Bikes can be hired May–Sept from various stalls behind the beach (usually €2.50 per hour or €5–10 per day).

Boat excursions Between May and September boats operated by several companies run daily to Zíngaro and Scopello, leaving at around 9.15am and 3.30pm, returning at 1.30pm and 7.30pm, with prices around €20. Try San Vito Travel Service,

Via Savoia 98 (☏ 328.827.2822). Ask at the tourist office about fishing trips.

Bus information AST (for Trápani and Bonagia) ☏ 0923.23.222, ⓦ www.aziendasicilianatrasporti .it; Russo (for Castellammare del Golfo and Palermo) ☏ 0924.31.364, ⓦ www.russoautoservizi.it.

Car and scooter rental Auto Vesco, Via Orazio di Bella 20 (☏ 388.140.8305, ⓦ www.autovesco.it), and Serse, Via Dogana 3 (℡0923.974.434, Ⓦwww.autonoleggioserse.com), have cars, motorbikes and scooters.

Diving Contact Argonauta, based in the summer at the port (℡331.561.6581, Ⓦwww.argonauta -divingcenter.com).

Internet You can log on and make long-distance calls at Internet Point, Via Orazio di Bella 17, off Via Savoia (daily 8am–1pm & 4pm–midnight,

reduced hours in winter), and there's internet access at Zona Bet, Via Flores (daily 10am–1pm & 4.30–7pm).

Pharmacy Via Regina Margherita 26 (Mon–Sat 9.30am–12.30pm & 4.30–8.30pm, reduced hours in winter).

Post office Via Savoia 58 (Mon–Fri 8am–1.30pm, Sat 8am–12.30pm).

Lo Zíngaro: the northern access

The **northern entrance** to the isolated **Riserva Naturale dello Zíngaro** (for full details, see p.320) is 11km southeast of San Vito. Accessible by your own transport or on a boat trip from San Vito Lo Capo, it's also a fine walk, initially following the road along the lungomare from San Vito and across the flat headland, before winding up into the mountains. In the higher reaches, the views are exhilarating, with the surrounding scenery almost alpine in character – fir trees, flowers edging the road, and the clank of bells from goats roaming the hillsides. Sadly, though, the road through this secluded and dramatic landscape offers few opportunities to descend to the alluringly deserted coves below.

The **access road** to the reserve is signposted just before the ruined Torre dell'Impiso, around a three-hour walk from San Vito. From the sign to the park entrance itself is about another 1km, following a gravel track and then a path, which runs down into the reserve, past the Tonnara dell'Uzzo. At the San Vito **entrance** (Ingresso Nord; daily: April–Oct 7am–8pm; Nov–March 8am–4pm; €3; ℡800.116.616 or 0924.35.108, Ⓦwww.riservazingaro.it), you'll find a car park and an info point where you can pick up a map of the various **trails** running through the reserve.

The beautiful little cove-beach below the entrance offers translucent water, with glorious peace and quiet all around – at least, whenever the first few little creeks here aren't inundated with bathers. Travel on for less crowded spots, or else take one of the higher paths for greater isolation. Scopello is a 10km walk south from the San Vito entrance. Hikers should note that there are no shops, bars or restaurants along the road from San Vito, or in the park itself (though there's usually a refreshment stall at the park entrance), and that shade and shelter are only sporadically available. In short, come prepared.

The Égadi Islands

Moored off the western coast, the three **Égadi Islands** (Isole Égadi) are the easiest of Sicily's offshore islands to visit – which accounts for the summer crowds that swarm over **Favignana**, the nearest of the Égadis to the Sicilian mainland. The other islands are much less affected, however, and if you come out of season things are noticeably quieter everywhere.

Before the advent of tourism, the economic success of the islands was largely based on a historical relationship with the northern Italian city of Genova, whose sailors plied the trading routes on which the Égadis stood throughout the Middle Ages. The link was formalized in the middle of the seventeenth century, when the Bourbon King Philip IV sold all the islands, in lieu of a debt, to Genoan businessmen. Then, as now, a major element in the local economy was the **tuna fish**, which congregate here to breed at the end of spring. Channelled through the

Ferries (operated by Siremar ☎0923.24.968, ⓦ www.siremar.it) and **hydrofoils** (operated by Siremar and Ústica Lines, ☎0923.873.813, ⓦ www.usticalines.it) depart several times daily **from Trápani**. They're more frequent between June and September, and most frequent in July and August. They generally call at Favignana, Lévanzo and Maréttimo, in that order, though Lévanzo is sometimes the first stop, and some services don't run as far as Maréttimo.

Ferries depart from the Stazione Maríttima in Trápani, and hydrofoils from further east along Via A. Staiti; you can buy **tickets** at booths on the dockside. Ferries are less frequent than hydrofoils and take at least twice as long, but they're cheaper. One-way ferry tickets from Trápani to Favignana and Lévanzo cost around €8.50, and to Maréttimo around €13, slightly less in low season; one-way hydrofoil tickets are around €10.50 and €18 respectively; all return tickets cost double. In summer, Siremar also runs fast ferries (*navi veloci*) to Favignana and Lévanzo, which may take half the time of a normal ferry, depending on the route.

Ústica Lines also operate a year-round hydrofoil service to the islands **from Marsala** and, in summer, from Ústica; see "Travel details" (p.372) for frequencies and journey times.

straits between the two main islands during their migrations around the Sicilian coast, they have traditionally been systematically slaughtered in an age-old rite known as **La Mattanza** – though in recent years the practice has been discontinued due to falling stocks and the efficiency of the offshore "factory ships".

Favignana, fifteen to forty minutes from Trápani by hydrofoil, is the biggest island and site of the main fishery. The Genovese link is most apparent in the island of **Lévanzo**, across the strait, which is named after a quarter in Genova and shelters the **Grotta del Genovese**, a cave in which a rich bounty of prehistoric cave paintings was discovered. These days, with the annual tourist influx, the greatest hope for peace and quiet lies in the furthest island, **Maréttimo**, whose rugged coasts are indented with a succession of coves, ideal for clean and secluded swimming. The island also offers a choice of **hikes** across its interior and along the rocky coasts.

You could easily see any of the islands as a **day-trip** from Trápani; seeing two on the same day is also feasible. If you want to stay longer, be warned that **accommodation** is extremely limited, and in summer you should phone ahead to reserve a room. It's certainly worth staying over, though you should also bear in mind that, in general, **prices** for rooms and food are higher than on the mainland.

Favignana

The main island, **FAVIGNANA**, has progressed over the years from tuna centre to prison, and now tourist resort. Shaped like a lopsided butterfly, the island is almost split in two, its narrow "waist" holding the port and most of the population. To the east lie Favignana's best swimming spots, the water accessible from a succession of rocks and inlets, while the western half of the island is only reachable along the southern coastal road, which tunnels through Favignana's sole hill, **Monte Santa Caterina** (300m). Its peak is topped by an abandoned Norman **castello**, floodlit at night, and reached by a crazy-paved stairway from the west side of town. Alternatively, follow the lower path over the mountain to a crest with views to Maréttimo. The path down the other side, however, is hard to follow and you may end up scrambling over walls and through fields to reach the road.

The port, **FAVIGNANA TOWN**, is the focus of most of the tourist traffic. As the archipelago's only town, it holds the island's main services and best choice of accommodation and restaurants, but otherwise there's no particular reason to hang around. The only distinctive feature is the imposing building near the port, the **Palazzo Florio**. Now part of the town hall, it was built by Ignazio Florio, an entrepreneur who took over the islands in 1874 and revitalized the fisheries; there's a statue of him in nearby Piazza Europa. His tuna fishery, **Stabilimento Florio**, is similarly impressive, its vaulted nineteenth-century buildings a solid counterpoint across the bay. It is currently open for visits (with a flexible timetable), and plans are afoot to open a marine and fishing museum here at some future date. Otherwise, all there is to do is window-shop in the many places selling "*prodotti tipici*"– traditional tuna products, of course, as well as *bottarga* (fish roe), oil, local dried herbs, wine and bloody postcards of *la Mattanza*.

The **rest of the island** is tidily cultivated, pitted with square white houses built from **tufa** quarried from curious pits all over the island – an export that has historically provided Favignana with a second source of cash (after fishing). One of the old quarries, behind the town church by the decrepit chapel of Santa Anna, has been landscaped and turned into a quirky sunken garden.

You can swim at the beach near the town, but the sandy beach at **Lido Burrone**, on the island's south side, is better, with a friendly pizzeria-restaurant-bar that rents out parasols and sun-loungers. Otherwise, just follow the coast roads and plunge in off the rocks, or settle down on one of the tiny handkerchiefs of sand. Call in at **Cala Azzurra**, below the lighthouse at the island's eastern end, where there's a beautiful blue bay, but little sand, or, just north, the spectacular **Cala Rossa**, where you can swim off rocks at the base of towering tufa cliffs. Its name – Red Cove – is said to derive from the blood washed ashore after the Roman defeat of the Carthaginians in a fierce sea battle in 241 BC. The road to Cala Rossa in particular is noted for its tufa quarries – just before the cove itself is a huge quarry where stacks of tufa and unexcavated pillars rise high from the gloomy depths. On the other side of the mountain, the best beach is at **Cala Rotonda**, where, local legend would have it, Odysseus washed up before being attacked by the Cyclops.

Arrival, information and transport

From the port, you can see the dome of the church: aim for that and you'll reach the main square, Piazza Madrice, with the **tourist office** at no. 25 (Mon–Sat 10am–12.30pm, usually closed Jan & Feb; ☏0923.921.647). Everything else is contained in the short streets between here and the nearby Piazza Europa. A useful website for Favignana and the whole archipelago is Ⓦ www.egadi.com.

The best way to **get around** the island is by bike, since the flat terrain and good road surfaces enable you to see the whole of Favignana in an afternoon. **Bike rental** shops are all over town, including down at the port – look for the words "*noleggio bici*". A **bus service** leaves from down by the port on three routes: #1 to Cala Azzurra, #2 to Punta Sottile, #3 to the turn-off for Cala Rossa. Departures are roughly hourly during the summer, much less frequent in winter; tickets on board (€1). **Boat tours** of the island's offshore grottoes are offered down at the port, costing €35 per person including lunch for a full day (less for a two- or three-hour excursion) – there's always someone around in summer, but you may have to ask in town at other times.

Accommodation

Favignana's **hotels** are not cheap, but still get packed out in peak season. You can find bargain rates at the few places remaining open in winter. The only **campsite** lies out of town, an easy bus ride or walk, and well signposted from the port. Most places are closed from November to March.

Hotels

Albergo Aegusa Via Garibaldi 11 ℡0923.922.430,
ⓦwww.aegusahotel.it. Central, clean and quiet
three-star hotel just off Via Roma. Rooms have a/c,
minibar and safe; some are in an annex, 100m
away. It's worth taking half board here, with a
rated garden restaurant. Closed Nov–March. ❹
B&B Favignana Via Roma 10 ℡392.725.2398,
ⓦwww.bbfavignana.com. One of the cheapest
choices on the island, this place has simple,
colour-themed rooms with private bathrooms and
a/c. It's a good choice if you want to stay centrally,
just minutes away from the port. Closed mid-Jan to
mid-March. No credit cards. ❷
Bouganville Via Cimabue 10 ℡0923.922.033,
ⓦwww.albergobouganville.it. This small, reasonably
priced hotel has spacious rooms and a restaurant in
the garden. It's near the beach on the southwestern
edge of town: follow Via Diaz and Via Battisti from the
centre, a 10min walk. Closed Dec–Easter. ❸

🏃 **Cave Bianche** Cala Azzurra ℡0923.925.451,
ⓦwww.cavebianchehotel.it. Favignana's
most striking accommodation is harmoniously built
within an abandoned quarry, with chic and minimalist
rooms. There's a pool, hydromassage and a great
restaurant, and scooters and bikes are available to
rent. It's about ten minutes from town by bike. Closed
Nov–March. ❺–❼

Hotel delle Cave Contrada Torretta
℡0923.925.423, ⓦwww.hoteldellecave.it. Like
Cave Bianche, this boutique hotel a couple of
kilometres east of town is built on the lip of an
abandoned quarry, with gardens, a hydromassage
pool and a restaurant inside the quarry itself. The
structure is severely functional, but the rooms are
full of designer features, and come with minibar,
a/c and wi-fi. Closed Nov–Easter. ❺–❻
Villa Antonella Via Punta Marsala
℡0923.921.073, ⓦwww.egadi.com/villantonella.
A few minutes southeast of town, and 300m from
the beach at Lido Burrone, this place has plain but
adequate rooms, run by a friendly local family who
can arrange to pick you up from the port. There's
a restaurant, and good-value self-catering mini-
apartments. No credit cards. ❸

Campsite

Camping Egad Contrada Arena ℡0923.921.555,
ⓦwww.campingegad.it. A little over 1km east of
town, and 500m from the beach at Lido Burrone,
this has a range of accommodation, including
rooms and igloo-type apartments sleeping four
(❶–❹). Facilities include bar, restaurant, store and
scooter and bike hire, and there's transport to and
from the port. Closed Nov–Easter.

Eating and drinking

Piazza Madrice, Piazza Europa and the surrounding streets are where you'll find
Favignana's **bars and restaurants**, but be warned: restaurant prices on the island
tend to be high. Excellent slices of pizza, *schiacciata* and the like are sold at the
bakery Costanza on Via Roma, just up from Piazza Madrice, or you may prefer
to **picnic** on the town beach. For picnic provisions, carry on past Costanza to the
Égadi **supermarket**, where the deli counter has local ricotta and a good range
of cheeses and hams. For ice cream and almond goodies try *Bar Albatros* at Via
Vittorio Emanuele 11, off Piazza Madrice, or join the locals sitting on rows of
chairs either side of the street at *Grammático* on Via Pilota di Garibaldi, just off
Piazza Europa.

🏃 **Amici del Mare** Piazza Marina
℡0923.922.596. Good-quality pasta and
superlative tuna and swordfish dishes, all within
view of the harbour. First courses are around €12,
mains about €15. Arrive early (or book) for one of
the terrace tables. Also good for drinks and snacks,
and there's an internet point.
La Bettola Via Nicotera 47 ℡0923.921.988. With
a terrace for eating *al fresco*, this popular spot
serves up a memorable *couscous di pesce*. As an
antipasto, the *fritelle di gámberi* (prawn fritters) are
also worth sampling. Prices are reasonable, with
starters at €5–10, mains €10–15. Closed Thurs in
winter & mid-Nov to Jan.

Due Colonne Piazza Madrice 76 ℡0923.922.291.
Just across from the church, this place has terrific
fish dishes (especially the *grigliata di pesce* and
anything with tuna) and tables outside, but it gets
very busy and service can be slow. Most main
courses are €12–15.
Pizza Pazza Via Mazzini 16, off Piazza Madrice. You
can pick up excellent and inexpensive pizzas here
from the wood-fired oven. Closed Tues in winter.
Pizzeria Salvador Via Nicotera 7 ℡0923.921.271.
This family-run place serves great pizza – but not
June–Sept, when other dishes come to the fore (all
€8–13), including local specialities like couscous.
In summer there's seating outside.

Listings

Airport transfer Siciltransfert (T 348.262.0089) arranges transport direct to Favignana from Palermo (€40 per person) and Trápani (€25) airports, including hydrofoil crossing and island taxi.

Banks The banks in Piazza Europa and Piazza Madrice both have ATMs.

Bike and scooter hire Isidoro, at Via Mazzini 40 T 347.323.3058, stays open all year; for a bike, expect to pay about €3 a day, or €5 in high season. Scooters are €20–25 a day, €35–40 in Aug.

Diving Progetto Atlantide (T 347.517.8338 or 347.050.4492, W www.progettoatlantide.com) offers courses and equipment hire.

Ferries and hydrofoils Siremar T 0923.921.368, W www.siremar.it; Ústica Lines T 0923.921.277, W www.usticalines.it.

Internet Elyos, Piazza Madrice 37 (April–Oct Mon–Sat 9am–1pm & 3–7.30pm, Sun 9am–1pm). You can also log on at the bar-restaurant *Amici del Mare*.

Pharmacy Abramo, Piazza Europa (English-speaking); Barone, Piazza Madrice; both open Mon–Fri 8.30am–1pm & 5–8.30pm. At other times see rota on the door.

Post office Via Marconi 2 (Mon–Fri 8am–1.30pm, Sat 8am–12.30pm).

Taxi T 347.479.6745 or 333.318.3112.

Lévanzo

LÉVANZO, 4km north of Favignana, is the smallest of the three main islands. Most of it is used to pasture sheep and goats, and, with its turquoise seas and white houses, it has very much the feel of a Greek island. Its population is concentrated in **LÉVANZO TOWN**, little more than a cluster of square houses and holiday homes around a tiny port, where you'll find the island's two hotel-restaurants and a couple of bars.

The coastline is rocky and largely inaccessible, but you can get around on foot by following the dirt paths along the shore and over the hills. Following the only road twenty minutes west of the port, you'll come to a rocky spire sticking out of the sea – the Faraglione – beyond which a rocky path leads north up the coast. On the island's northwest coast, on a slope overlooking the sea, the **Grotta del Genovese** is the main attraction for most visitors, famed for its prehistoric cave paintings.

The walls of the cave display some remarkable Paleolithic **incised drawings**, discovered in 1949, as well as later Neolithic pictures; they're mostly of animals, and are between six thousand and ten thousand years old. Despite their age, the evocative drawings retain their impact, drawn by prehistoric man in an attempt to harness and influence the power of nature: one lovely picture of a deer near the entrance dates from when the island was still connected to the Sicilian mainland.

Getting to the Grotta del Genovese

All visits to the **Grotta del Genovese** (W www.grottadelgenovese.it) have to be arranged at least a day in advance through the official custodian, Signor Natale Castiglione: either telephone T 0923.924.032 or 339.741.8800, or pass by at Via Calvario 11, above the quay. Tickets cost €20 each either by jeep or by boat. **By boat**, the round trip will take nearly two hours, usually departing at 10.30am and (if there's enough demand) 3pm. Note that the smallest swell may be enough to make it impossible for the boat to pull into the narrow rocky disembarkation point. You can also extend the tour by opting for the round-island trip (€25), taking up to three hours including a swimming stop.

By jeep, the two-hour round trip is roughly 10km, following an inland route through the valley in the centre of the island. The fairly difficult descent on foot to the grotto from where the jeep stops is not recommended for anyone infirm. You might negotiate a discount jeep fare if you feel like walking back. Booking for either route is essential. Winter tours only take place when the conditions are right – again, always telephone ahead.

The later Neolithic sketches are easy to pick out too; less well drawn, more stylized representations of men and even of tuna fish and a dolphin.

Many other grottoes on the island were formerly used by locals to hide from the corsairs who regularly called on raiding missions. To see a few, you might bargain for a **boat rental** at the port.

If you fancy stretching your legs in the island's lovely **interior**, walk west along the road from the port (towards the Faraglione), turning right up the steep tarmacked road. That becomes a stone and dirt track once it reaches the upper part of the valley. If you stick to it, it takes around an hour to reach the lighthouse at **Capo Grosso** at the northeastern point of the island.

On your way to the cape, you can swim at the lovely white **Tramontana bay**: just before you reach an old metal gate, a track leads down the red-earth mountainside, ending in an acute concrete slope, which you can just about slither down, though scrambling back up is hard work.

Tracing the coast eastwards from Lévanzo Town, you can reach **Cala Minnola** in about fifteen minutes – a lovely rocky cove ideal for swimming.

Practicalities

The **port** is just below the island's only road, Via Calvario. In summer both Siremar and Ústica Lines have ticket booths at the port; in winter, they move into the town, out of reach of stormy waves (precise locations vary from year to year). **Boat excursions** round the island are advertised here in summer.

There are just two **hotels** with a total of 25 rooms, so booking ahead is advisable; ask around, though, and you may find someone who'll rent you a **room**. Closest to the port, next to the bar, the *Paradiso* (℡0923.924.080, ⓦwww.albergoparadiso .eu; ❷) has a terrace-restaurant and marvellous sea views from the en-suite, air-conditioned rooms, some of which are a bit cramped. Just behind, the *Fenici* (℡0923.924.083, ⓦwww.albergodeifenici.com; ❷) is a little fancier and has the same good views. In summer, both hotels will usually require a week's minimum stay and only accept guests on half-board terms (respectively €80 and €70 per person), though as the only other options for food on the island are two bars, an *alimentari* and a bakery, this is no hardship. In any case, the food is good at both places. Alternatively, there's *Lisola Residence* (℡0923.194.1530 or 320.180.9090, ⓦwww.lisola.eu; closed Nov–March; ❷), seven apartments 400m outside the port sleeping between two and four, occupying simple tufa cottages originally built by nineteenth-century tuna-canning magnate Florio for his workers. Extras include a large pool with parasols and sun-loungers, and free transport to the port whenever you need it. There's a minimum stay of three nights or a week in summer.

Maréttimo

Wildest and furthest out from Trápani, **MARÉTTIMO** was claimed by Samuel Butler, in his *The Authoress of the Odyssey*, as the original Ithaca, home of Odysseus. Even more far-fetched, Butler also thought that Homer himself was the princess Nausicaä of ancient Trápani. These theories aside, there are compelling reasons to come to Maréttimo. Its spectacular fragmented coastline is pitted with rocky coves sheltering hideaway beaches, and numerous walks can take you all over the island. Even in high season, you're likely to have much of Maréttimo to yourself, as few tourists can be bothered to visit a place with limited accommodation and no more than half a dozen trattorias. That said, there are signs of heightened interest these days in the shape of a sprinkling of new holiday homes, while EU money has gone towards paving a couple of sections of track. However, such "improvements" are still fairly low-key and, at least for now, the island retains its air of being far off the beaten track.

Arrival, information and boat tours

There's no **information** office on Maréttimo, but you can gather details of accommodation, food, itineraries and transport from ⓦ www.marettimonline.it. Maréttimo's main street, Corso Umberto, is about a minute's walk from the harbour where the ferries and hydrofoils dock. It holds a **bank** with an ATM, a Siremar **ticket agency** and an Ústica Lines agency in a little shop just up from Piazza Umberto. Other services include a pharmacy, a couple of *alimentari*, a bakery and a **post office** above the port (Mon–Sat 9.30am–12.30pm).

Boat trips can be organized from *Rosa dei Venti* (see "Accommodation" below). Various options are possible: around the island to Cala Bianca for swimming costs €15 per person, or the same with a picnic, including home-cured fish, and local cheeses and wines is around €30 per person. On either, you can be left at a cove to swim and be collected an hour or so later. You can rent bikes from Sealife, Via Campi 5 (☎ 0923.923.288 or 347.542.9713, ⓦ www.sealifesnc.com) for around €10 a day.

Accommodation

Maréttimo offers a better choice of **accommodation** than Lévanzo, with a couple of B&Bs and a few apartments and holiday residences for weekly rents. If these are full, ask around in the bars and restaurants for **rented rooms**, but in any case it's always best to book before you come.

I Delfini Corso Umberto 34 ☎ 0923.923.137 or 339.239.9867, ⓦ www.idelfinimarettimo.it. Central B&B with great sea views on one side. Rooms are simple but clean and comfortable, with private bathrooms, and there's a roof terrace on which delicious breakfasts are served. No credit cards. Closed Nov–March. ❷

Maréttimo Residence Via Telégrafo 3 ☎ 0923.923.202, ⓦ www.marettimoresidence.it. Small resort-cluster of cottages above a stony beach south of the main port, available for B&B or weekly rental at €700–1000 for two in summer. Demand is high, but you'll find greater availability and much lower prices outside the summer period. ❹

Rosa dei Venti Punta Simone 4 ☎ 0923.923.249 or 333.675.8893, ⓦ www.isoladimarettimo.it. As well as operating various other tourist activities, this outfit has rooms and self-catering apartments dispersed around the island, also available for short stays. ❷

Sealife Corso Umberto and Via Tedesco ☎ 0923.923.288 or 347.542.9713, ⓦ www.sealifesnc.com. The two apartments are centrally located, accommodating two to five people usually by the week, though they'll let you have them for shorter periods if there are vacancies. One has a terrace, the other a small courtyard, and both are equipped with barbecues. For two people, they're €550 per week in high season, €300 at other times. ❷

🏃 **La Terrazza** Via G. Pepe 24 ☎ 0923.923.252 or 368.768.1571, ⓦ www.bedandbreakfastmarettimo.it. The best feature here is the wide, semi-shaded terrace, with terrific views over the castle and sea, where breakfast is served and which is free for guests' use all day. The four rooms are simply and tastefully decorated. No credit cards. Closed mid-Oct to March. ❷

Exploring the island

As you pull into port and explore its few streets, **MARÉTTIMO TOWN** appears almost North African in character, with its flat-roofed cube houses with blue shutters and painted tiles, and alleys full of tumbling bougainvillea. There's one main street, a little square and church, and a second harbour, the fishing port, just along from the main harbour.

Two of the island's most popular **bathing** spots are conveniently close, one near the main harbour, one near the fishing harbour, but you'll find other places on the way to destinations further afield – at Cala Sarde and Cala Nera on the south coast, or at the Saracen castle at the northeastern point of the island (see box opposite). None of the walks is particularly onerous, though you might have to scramble at times – and make sure you're carrying enough water at all times.

Outdoor adventures

Sicily is rightly known for its archeology, architecture and food, but holidays here are about more than just culture and cuisine. The largest island in the Mediterranean also has a long coastline, a mountainous interior of peaks, rivers and gorges, a dozen or more offshore islands and two of the world's most famous volcanoes – so you don't have to look far for an exciting Sicilian outdoor adventure.

Boat trips

Almost wherever there's a harbour (and that's a lot of Sicily) there's a boat waiting to show you the local coastline, whether on a scenic cruise or during a day's snorkelling or fishing. The most memorable experiences are on Sicily's outlying islands – visiting the grottoes and rock-stacks of Filicudi (p.143), for example, or spending the day floating about in the azure waters of Lampedusa (p.305). If you prefer sailing, catamarans and yachts can also be hired, with or without crew.

Even simply zipping by hydrofoil from one pin-prick island to another generates a rush of excitement – dolphins are commonly seen – and in the Aeolian archipelago there are seven different island destinations alone, each with local fishermen and boat operators waiting to show you hidden coves, soaring cliffs, smouldering volcanoes, tiny outer islets and idyllic bathing spots.

Sailing near San Vito lo Capo ▲

Alcántara river gorge ▼

Down the gorge

Sicily's ancient peoples buried their dead in rock-cut tombs in the deep gorges of the southeast, most famously at Pantálica (p.235), but also near lesser-known Íspica (p.244). In both places wonderfully atmospheric walking trails wind through the gorges, while closer to Noto a stepped path climbs down into Sicily's own Grand Canyon, the Cava Grande (p.242), at the foot of which are swimming holes and another delightful gorge walk along the Cassíbile river.

For more thrills, spend the day wading and splashing in the refreshingly cool falls and pools under the awe-inspiring basalt walls of the Alcántara river gorge (p.181), near Taormina – a great way to escape the intense Sicilian summer heat.

Volcano visits

The ascent of Mount Etna (p.207) is the single greatest outdoor adventure on the island, and there's a whole local industry devoted to getting you up and down safely what is one of the world's largest and most active volcanoes. Strómboli (p.141), too, has a wonderfully resonant name, and plenty more ways of getting up close and personal with an erupting volcano – it's hard to beat the drama of a night-time volcano-viewing cruise.

▲ Smoking volcano, Strómboli

The fires may have gone out on other Aeolian islands, like Salina and Alicudi, but the extinct volcanoes themselves still offer an energetic day's hiking, while on Vulcano (p.129) a wallow in the foul-smelling but supposedly very beneficial natural mud baths is the prelude to the climb up to the bubbling main crater.

On your bike

Although the Sicilian mainland does cyclists few favours (featuring congested towns and cities, unforgiving motorists and a sparsely populated mountainous interior), the more remote offshore islands are a different matter altogether. You can rent mountain bikes in many of the ports, and enjoy the largely traffic-free lanes of places like Ústica, or Vulcano in the Aeolians, at a leisurely pace. Cycling is also the best way to see the larger islands, since although there are bus services on Favignana or Lampedusa, for example, whizzing around the largely flat terrain on two wheels is far more fun – and you'll be able to make your own itineraries and discoveries without being at the mercy of a bus timetable.

▲ Mud baths, Vulcano

▼ Cyclists on traffic-free path

If you want to brave cycling in town, Siracusa is the place to do it, thanks to its city-wide bike-rental scheme (p.220).

Walking

Experiencing Sicily on foot can mean anything from negotiating the rugged interior in the Monti Madonie and Monti Nebrodi to leisurely strolls along paved coastal paths or ambling explorations of extensive ancient sites.

Cefalù seen from La Rocca ▲

Filicudi island ▼

Hiker in Lo Zingaro ▼

Sicily's ten best walks

▶▶ **Around Ústica** Take the beautiful coastal path around an island small enough to see entirely on foot in half a day. See p.90

▶▶ **La Rocca, Cefalù** A strenuous climb above the holiday town of Cefalù offers ancient ruins and spectacular views. See p.100

▶▶ **Filicudi** Remote Filicudi's island paths are a joy, including the enjoyable hike to the old village of Zucco Grande. See p.143

▶▶ **Ascent of Etna** The big one, not to be missed – the hike from Rifugio Sapienza to the craters on the summit of Mount Etna. See p.207

▶▶ **Ortigia, Siracusa** The old centre of Sicily's most attractive city is a warren of narrow streets and alleys that make for a great day out on foot. See p.222

▶▶ **Noto Antica** Explore the abandoned, overgrown town of ancient Noto, its ruins left to the lizards. See p.239

▶▶ **Valle dei Templi** There's no more dramatic walk into the past than along the path connecting the beautifully preserved Greek temples of Agrigento. See p.290

▶▶ **Zíngaro** Western Sicily's glorious coastal nature reserve has a network of fantastic beach and mountain hiking trails. See p.321

▶▶ **Maréttimo** For real off-the-beaten-track exploration, head for the least visited of the Égadi Islands and strike out on foot. See p.345

▶▶ **Pantelleria** An island retreat, halfway to Africa, with an unusual walk to a natural sauna hidden in the rocks. See p.371

Maréttimo hikes

To the Case Romane

Maréttimo's simplest walk takes you to some old **Roman defensive works**, which are still in pretty good condition. Climb up the road to the side of *Caffè Tramontana* and, at the top, scout around to the left and then right to find the signpost for the start of the walk. The remains are half an hour on, sitting next to a small and dilapidated church that shows marked Arab characteristics but is thought to have been built by Byzantine monks in the twelfth century.

To Cala Sarde and Cala Nera

Follow the road south of Maréttimo port, turning inland after about 1km where the path divides. There's a steep climb, with the town's cemetery below you, rising to about 300m. After about half an hour, you'll pass a pine forest and a small outhouse, looking out on views towards Tunisia; below is the **Cala Sarde**, a small bay reachable along a smaller path to the left in another half an hour.

Instead of descending to the bay, continue for about an hour on the main path along the island's rocky west coast. You'll pass a lighthouse and a route down to **Cala Nera**, where you can swim off the rocks in perfect isolation.

To the castle at Punta Troia

This walk follows the footpath all the way to the northeastern tip of the island, a hike that should take you around three hours; you'll need a head for heights in certain stretches. Go past the fishing harbour with the sea on your right, and keep to the coast along the path for about ten minutes, until the terrace wall on your left stops. When a sign here ("Castello Punta Troia") points to the left, cut up to find the main path on a small spur above you. This stretches along the whole length of the island about 100m above the sea, ending at some concrete steps that descend to a lovely secluded beach and the foot of the **castle**, perched on an impregnable rocky crag. This precipitous fortification was originally built by the Saracens, enlarged by Roger II, and further extended by the Spanish in the seventeenth century, when it became a prison, and acquired a dire reputation for cruelty.

Alternatively, you could take a three-hour **boat tour** of the island (a "*giro dell'isola*") from the main harbour, which allows you to see Maréttimo's entire rocky coastline and dive into otherwise inaccessible waters that are clean and clear and a joy for snorkellers.

Eating and drinking

Maréttimo offers a reasonable range of **eating** options, though prices are a little higher than on the mainland, given the cost of shipping in ingredients. Not all the places listed below stay open throughout the year, but there's always something open. There are two *alimentari* on Via Garibaldi, off the main drag, one of which has takeaway items.

Baia del Sole Piazza Umberto. Next to the Siremar office on the main road, this bar has a few tables and excellent ice cream and *granite*.

Il Pirata Via Scalo Vecchio ☎0923.923.027. *Pesce spada all'arancia* (swordfish with orange) and *pasta con le sarde* are among the specialities in this pleasant trattoria by the fishing harbour. First courses are around €10, mains €10–18.

La Scaletta Via Telegrafo. A good spot for an ice cream or *granita* overlooking the main port.

Caffè Tramontana Via Campi. On the road above the fishing harbour, people gather here for the superb sea views. Snacks available.

Il Veliero Corso Umberto ☎0923.923.274. Owned by a fisherman, this trattoria has excellent fresh seafood and a summer cane-and-fishing-trap-bedecked terrace by the harbour. Firsts, such as pasta with squid ink or *bottarga* (tuna roe), cost around €12; mains aren't much more. Closed Nov–Feb.

Mózia and around

Fifteen kilometres down the coast from Trápani, the uninhabited **Stagnone Islands** (Isole dello Stagnone) have been mostly given over to salt extraction since the fifteenth century. On the mainland opposite, several windmills still stand near the surviving **saltpans**, which form a crystalline patchwork between Trápani and Marsala. Offshore, the long, thin Ísola Grande shelters the only one of the Stagnone group that you can visit, San Pantaleo, in the middle of a shallow lagoon that is now the year-round scene of **windsurfing, kitesurfing and sailing**. You can hire the equipment from shacks strung along the coast road, some outlets also renting **canoes** for around €6 for half a day, allowing you to weave around the saltpans.

The big cultural attraction hereabouts, however, is on the isle of San Pantaleo, which holds the site of the ancient Phoenician settlement of Motya (or **Mózia** in Italian). Along with Palermo and Solus (Solunto), Motya was one of the three main Phoenician bases in Sicily, settled some time during the eighth century BC and completely razed to the ground by Dionysius I in 397 BC. It's the only one of the three sites that wasn't subsequently built over, though it remained undiscovered until the seventeenth century, and wasn't properly excavated until Joseph "Pip" Whitaker (amateur archeologist and member of one of the marsala wine dynasties) bought the island in the late nineteenth century and started to dig it up.

You reach the island site and its archeological museum by a short **ferry** ride from the mainland. Although the linguistic link between the archipelago's name (Stagnone) and our "stagnant" is not entirely coincidental, that doesn't deter some visitors from wading into the lagoon on the mainland side and crossing to Mózia in beachwear – the island museum, at least, has had enough and won't allow entry to anyone who's not properly clothed.

The island: the remains of Motya

Flat, cultivated and only 2.5km in circumference, **MOTYA** is one of the most manageable of Sicily's ancient sites, with the unique Phoenician ruins spread across the whole island. You could circle the perimeter in an hour or so, but it's more enjoyable to make a day of it and bring a picnic (and there's a bar with basic snacks on the island).

You buy **entrance tickets** (daily 9.15am–6.30pm; €9) on the way up the path to Joseph Whitaker's house – once incongruously furnished in Edwardian style and now converted to use as the **Museo Whitaker**. Outside stands an aristocratic bust of its founder, "Giuseppe" Whitaker, with a shaded picnic area under the trees nearby. You might as well call in to the museum first to see the finds from the island. Its cool rooms are packed with a beautiful collection of jewellery, arrowheads, terracotta figurines and domestic artefacts, with the earliest pieces dating from the eighth century BC. Pride of place goes to the magnificent fifth-century BC marble sculpture of a youth, *Il Giovinetto di Mózia*, sensual and self-assured in his pose. The identity of the subject is unknown, but he was likely to have been a high-ranking official, suggested by the subtle indentations round his head, indicating some kind of crown or elaborate headwear.

The remains on the ground start immediately outside the museum. In front and 100m to the left is the **Casa dei Mosaici**, two houses containing some faded black-and-white mosaics made from sea pebbles. One, probably belonging to a patrician, shows animal scenes; the other, thought to be a craftsman's, yielded numerous shards of pottery. Further along the path you come to the **cothon**, a small artificial boat dock built within the ancient town's walls and similar in style to a much larger one at Carthage itself.

The other way, back past the museum, leads along the rough tracks, set among flowering cacti and vine plantations, that were once the city's main thoroughfares, most of which end at one of the gates on Motya's formerly well-fortified shore. The once-strong **north gate**, now a ragged collection of steps and ruined walls – up beyond the museum and right – lies at the head of a causeway built by the Phoenicians in the sixth century BC to connect the island with the mainland (and a necropolis) at Birgi, 7km to the north. The road is still there, although these days it's submerged under the water. Left along the shore from the gate is the **Tophet** burial ground. Most of the information about day-to-day life in Motya has come from here, the sanctuary revealing a number of urns containing the ashes of animals sacrificed to the Phoenician gods (chiefly Baal Hammon) and of children, probably stillborn or who died of natural causes. A remarkable series of inscribed votive stele from the Tophet is on display in the museum. Just inland of the gate, the **Cappiddazzu** site shows the foundations of a large building, probably a temple, while between gate and Cappiddazzu is a Punic **industrial zone** that was dedicated to the production of pottery and ceramics. This was where the famous marble sculpture was found, probably hidden by the city's inhabitants as the Greeks stormed the island.

The saltpans and salt museum

Glistening in the shallows between Trápani and Marsala lie a series of **saltpans** that have been worked since Phoenician times. Barechested men toil with shovels, carting full wheelbarrows across from the pans to a rising conveyor belt that dumps 2m-high mounds of white salt along the banks. At different times of the day, as the light changes, there's a pink tint to the saltpans, while Maréttimo rises in the distance through the haze. On the mainland, just opposite Mózia, one of three windmills has been turned into a showroom and museum, the **Saline Ettore e Infersa** (April, May, Sept & Oct daily 9am–6.30pm; June–Sept 9.30am–8pm; call ☏0923.733.003 for winter visits; €5). It's free to enter if you just want to browse the locally produced foods and crafts, and you can pay €2 for an instructive audio-guided tour of the whole salt-making process.

Practicalities

From Marsala, take the local Linea D bus from Piazza del Pópolo to the Mózia ferry-landing. Return buses are on a similar schedule; a reduced service in either direction operates on a Sunday. **From Trápani**, you'll have to take the bus or the train first to Marsala.

Ferries out to the island are run by Arini & Pugliese (☏347.779.0218) and Mozia Line (☏329.476.0294) from two separate spots, about a kilometre apart. A steady flow of visitors ensures that there's usually a ferry waiting during the hours when the museum is open; tickets for the ten-minute crossing cost €5 return. **Parking** is available near the two embarkation points.

The northern embarkation point lies right next to the **bar-restaurant** *Mamma Caura*, by the windmill and saltpans, where you can eat well, and they also offer three **rooms** (☏0923.966.036; ❸–❹) and canoes to rent for €6 per hour, or €15 for three hours. Alternatively, you'll find first-class food and accommodation at the peaceful **agriturismo** *Baglio Vajarassa* (☏0923.968.628, ⓦwww.bagliovajarassa .com; no credit cards; ❷) at Contrada Spagnola 176, a couple of kilometres south of the ferry landing off SP21, which offers rooms furnished with antiques, typical local dishes for dinner around a communal table and a small museum of rural culture; half board costs €60 per person.

Marsala

When the island-city of Motya had been put to the sword by the Syracusans, the survivors founded Lilybaeum (modern **MARSALA**), 10km to the south. The main city of the Phoenicians in Sicily, and the only one to resist the Greek push westwards, Lilybaeum finally succumbed to Rome in 241 BC, and not long after was used as a springboard for an attack against the Carthaginian heartland itself. The town's position at Sicily's western tip later made it the main Saracenic base on the island, and it was renamed Marsah Ali, Arabic for the "port of Ali", son-in-law of the Prophet, from which its modern name derives.

The town scored a place in modern Italian history for its role in the saga of the **Risorgimento**, the struggle for Italian unity in the nineteenth century. It was here that Garibaldi kicked off his campaign to drive out the Bourbons, in the company of his red-shirted "Thousand". Until a planned Garibaldi museum on Marsala's southwestern seafront (on Via Scipione l'Africano) gets round to opening, memorials to the swashbuckling freedom-fighter are confined to a few statues and street names, and the nearby Porta Garibaldi, at the end of Via Garibaldi, which recalls the hero's entry into the town. Local enthusiasts clad in red shirts parade through the gate each year on May 11, in commemoration of the exploits of the "Thousand".

Arrival and information

Trains to Marsala, from Trápani in particular, are quicker and more frequent than buses. The **train station** is at the southeastern edge of town on Viale A. Fazio, a

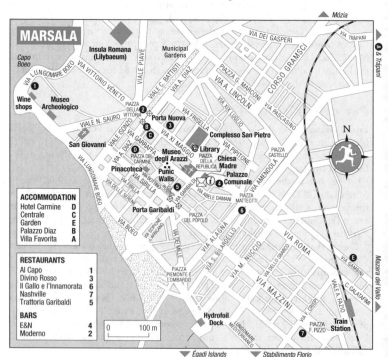

fifteen-minute walk from the centre. **Buses** arrive centrally at Piazza del Pópolo (also known as Piazza Marconi), near Porta Garibaldi. **Hydrofoil** services to and from the Égadi Islands are operated by Ústica Lines (☎348.357.9863) at the harbour, fifteen minutes' walk from the centre – you can buy tickets on the dockside.

There's a **tourist office** at Via XI Maggio 100, off Piazza della Repubblica near the Chiesa Madre (Mon–Sat 8am–1.30pm & 3–8pm; ☎0923.714.097). You'll find a **post office** on Via Garibaldi, and **banks** with ATMs along Via XI Maggio and Via Roma. The library on Via XI Maggio has cheap **internet** access (Mon–Fri 9am–1pm, also Thurs 3.30–5.30pm).

Accommodation

Marsala holds little budget **accommodation**, though it does offer a fine selection of mid- and upper-range hotels, any of which make a nice base for exploring the region.

Hotel Cármine Piazza del Cármine 16 ☎0923.711.907, ⓦ www.hotelcarmine.it. Very central, Marsala's most stylish hotel combines modernity with domed rooms, antique trimmings and fabulous breakfasts. The spacious rooms have exposed brickwork and wood or tiled floors, some with balconies, some overlooking the internal garden. ❸–❹

Centrale Via Salinisti 19 ☎0923.951.777, ⓦ www .hotelcentralemarsala.it. Plain but spacious and comfortable en-suite rooms with a/c and minibar, arranged around a courtyard. The hotel has a quiet location in the old town, and there's off-street parking. Breakfast is in a nearby bar. ❷

Garden Via Gambini 36 ☎0923.982.320, ⓦ www.albergogardenmarsala.it. The cheapest hotel in town, located behind the train station, is not great, but it's modern and clean enough, with

a/c. It only has nine rooms (five with bathroom), so ring ahead. There's parking, but no breakfast, and no credit cards. ❷

Palazzo Diaz Via Salinisti 22 ☎348.019.0662 or 329.216.3780, ⓦ www.palazzodiaz.com. This B&B in a converted 19th-century *palazzo* has large, airy rooms with a/c and en-suite bathroom, and there's a grand roof terrace where breakfast is served. ❷

Villa Favorita Via Favorita 27 ☎0923.989.100, ⓦ www.villafavorita.com. This beautiful secluded villa on the outskirts of town is set in its own gardens and has a pool, a tennis court and a restaurant, where the food and service alternate between superb and dire. Regular wedding receptions can disrupt the overall serenity of the place. It's signposted 2km northeast of the centre, off Via Trápani. ❹

The Town

Marsala's town centre is a predominantly Baroque assortment of buildings, though there are hints of the older town's layout in the narrow, largely traffic-free streets around the central **Piazza della Repubblica**. The elegance of the square is due to its two eighteenth-century buildings: the arcaded **Palazzo Comunale**, and the **Chiesa Madre** – dedicated to San Tommaso di Canterbury, patron saint of Marsala – from which four statues peer loftily down. The church's large but rather disappointing interior has a few Gagini sculptures.

Behind the Chiesa Madre, at Via Garraffa 57, the sole display at the **Museo degli Arazzi** (Tues–Sat 9.30am–1pm & 4–6pm, Sun 9.30am–noon; €2.50) is a series of eight enormous hand-stitched wool and silk tapestries depicting the capture of Jerusalem. Made in Brussels in the sixteenth century, they were the gift of the Spanish ambassador, who doubled as the archbishop of Messina, and are beautifully rich, in burnished red, gold and green. Further up Via Garraffa, you can view the remains of **Punic walls** and pavements from the Greco-Roman period in Piazza San Girólamo. Still further, a left turn leads into Piazza del Cármine, where a fourteenth-century convent has been stylishly renovated to hold the **Pinacoteca Comunale** (Tues–Sun 10am–1pm & 6–8pm, or 5–7pm in winter; free). Visitors can enjoy a good collection of art and regular exhibitions – mostly contemporary and with local connections.

The making of marsala wine

The Baglio Anselmi, which houses Marsala's archeological museum, is one of a number of old *bagli*, or warehouses, conspicuous throughout this wine-making region. Many are still used in the making of the famous dessert wine that carries the town's name. It was an Englishman, John Woodhouse, who first exploited the commercial potential of **marsala wine**, when he visited the town in 1770. Woodhouse soon realized that, like port, the local wine could travel for long periods without going off, when fortified with alcohol. Others followed: Ingham, Whitaker, Hopps and many more whose names can still be seen on some of the warehouse doors. Interestingly, it was the English presence in Marsala that persuaded Garibaldi to launch his campaign here rather than Sciacca (his first choice), judging that the Bourbon fleet wouldn't dare to interfere so close to Her Majesty's commercial concerns.

Marsala owes much of its current prosperity to the marketing of its wine, which is still a thriving industry, though no longer in British hands. You can visit some of the *bagli* and sample the stuff for free: try the **Cantine Montalto** (Mon–Fri 9am–1pm & 3–6pm, Sat 9am–1pm, other times can be booked at ☎0923.969.667) at Contrada Bérbaro, 3km along the road south towards Mazara del Vallo, reached along Lungomare Mediterraneo. Free guided tours and samplings are offered, and there's an **Enomuseum** where you can look over the old apparatus and techniques for wine-making. Otherwise, you'll find marsala or the sweeter *marsala all'uovo* (mixed with egg yolks) in every bar, enoteca and restaurant in town.

Parallel to Via Garraffa, threading up from Piazza della Repubblica, Via XI Maggio is lined with smart shops and *palazzi* with pretty courtyards. On the right you'll pass the **Complesso San Pietro**, a fifteenth-century monastery now fully restored as a cultural centre incorporating the **Museo Cívico** (Tues–Sat 9am–1pm & 4–8pm; €2), where you can see a selection of archeological items from the Punic, Greek and Roman eras and, more compellingly, rooms dedicated to Garibaldi's triumphant campaign in western Sicily, including letters, photos, arms and uniforms. The complex also contains the town library and a courtyard for occasional open-air performances.

At the far end of Via XI Maggio, through the eighteenth-century **Porta Nuova**, Piazza della Vittoria has a gate into the municipal gardens and a bar where you can sit and admire the austere Art Deco front of the Cine Impero, so out of keeping with the Baroque arch opposite. Beyond the piazza lies **Capo Boeo**, the western-most point of Sicily that was the first settlement of the survivors of annihilated Motya. All the town's major antiquities are concentrated here, including the old **Insula Romana**, closed to the public at present, but normally accessible from Via Vittorio Véneto. The site contains all that's been excavated so far of the city of Lilybaeum, though most of it is third-century BC Roman, as you might guess from the presence of a vomitorium, lodged in the most complete section of the site – the **edificio termale**, or bathhouse. There's some good mosaicwork here: a chained dog at the entrance and, much better, a richly coloured **hunting scene** in the atrium, showing a stag being savaged by a wild beast.

From Piazza della Vittoria, Viale N. Sauro leads to the church of **San Giovanni**, under which is a grotto reputed to have been inhabited by the sibyl Lilibetana, endowed with paranormal gifts. There's another slice of mosaic here, and a well whose water is meant to impart second sight. A pilgrimage takes place every June 24.

The Museo Archeologico

350

Beyond the church, one of the stone-vaulted warehouses that line the lungomare contains the **Museo Archeologico** (daily 9am–6pm; €4), mostly dedicated to a very skeletal but still surprisingly well-preserved warship from the classical period. Displayed in a heat- and humidity-regulated environment, it ranks as the only extant *liburnian*, a specifically Phoenician or **Punic warship**, probably sunk during the First Punic War in the great sea battle off the Égadi Islands that ended Carthage's rule of the waves. It was discovered in 1971 and brought here after eight years of underwater surveying by a British team working under the archeologist Honor Frost. Originally 35m long, nearly 5m wide and rowed by 68 oarsmen, the vessel has been the source of much detailed information on the period, including what the crew ate and the stimulants they chewed to keep awake. Scattered about lie ranks of amphorae and anchors, and other items found in or around the ship, plus photographs and explanations (in Italian and English) of the ship's retrieval from the sea.

On the left-hand side of the building is displayed a medley of archeological finds from various sites hereabouts, both on land and sea. Prize exhibit is a marble torso dredged up from the sea in 2005, the **Venus of Lilybaeum**: comparable in style to the more famous Venus Landolina in Siracusa, it's probably a Roman copy of a Hellenistic statue of the second century BC. Other items include more mundane ceramics from the Punic tophet ("sacrificial grounds") on Motya and other ancient necropolises in the neighbourhood, a good Roman mosaic and some colourful examples of Italian and North African pottery.

Eating and drinking

In the centre of Marsala at least, which empties of life after 9pm, **restaurants** can be hard to come by, but you'll eat well and relatively cheaply at the ones listed below. The couple of **bars** in Piazza della Repubblica are good for a *tè freddo alla pesca* (cold peach tea), accompanied by earnest discussion of lottery numbers – otherwise try the places listed below.

For general groceries, there's a lively daily **market** around the Porta Garibaldi, selling fresh fish as well as fruit and vegetables. To sample some **marsala wine**, visit either the *Enoteca Garibaldi*, Via Garibaldi 32, or one of two adjacent enoteca-souvenir shops in Via Lungomare Boeo, by the archeological museum.

Restaurants

Al Capo Via Lungomare Boeo 40 ☏ 328.862.8586. In a restored warehouse near the Museo Archeologico, this makes a handy pre- or post-museum lunch stop. Try the fresh *busiate* with swordfish and aubergine. There are pizzas in the evenings and fish couscous at weekends. Set-price menus are €15–25. Closed Wed in winter.

Divino Rosso Largo di Giròlamo ☏ 0923.711.770. Congenial pizzeria and wine bar where you can sit outside opposite a seventeenth-century *palazzo*. Snack on cheeses, cold meats, panini and salads, or go for a range of tasty pizzas (around €7). There are also some meat and fish dishes (€8–15), and a fantastic range of wines. Closed daytime, also Mon Nov–March.

Il Gallo e l'Innamorata Via S. Bilardello 18 ☏ 0923.195.4446. Small and friendly *osteria* with great food, including bruschetta with *bottarga* (fish roe), *busiate con ragù di tonno* (pasta with tuna sauce) and grilled fish. Prices are very reasonable – you can eat abundantly for €30 per head including drinks. Closed Tues.

Trattoria Garibaldi Piazza Addolorata 5 ☏ 0923.953.006. Cosy, upmarket trattoria in the centre. Fish and couscous are the specialities, though you'll spend less if you choose grilled meat. First courses are €6–10, mains €9–13. Closed Sat lunch & Sun eve.

Nashville Piazza F. Pizzo 24 ☏ 0923.951.826. Casual stop near the station, with tables in the square in summer, opposite what must be Italy's ugliest statue. The menu takes in pizzas (€4–6), meat and fish dishes (€10–13), and a fish buffet for €25. There are also set-price menus (minimum 2 people) for €10.50 (meat) and €13 (fish).

Bars and cafés

E&N Via XI Maggio 130. This classy *pasticceria* and *gelateria* has a small courtyard and a selection of snacks. Closed Wed.

Bar Moderno Piazza della Vittoria. Quiet spot outside the Porta Nuova for a sightseeing pause by day or a beer or ice cream after dinner.

Mazara del Vallo

The North African element in Sicily's cultural melange is at its strongest in the major fishing port of **MAZARA DEL VALLO**, 22km and a thirty-minute train or bus ride down the coast from Marsala. Under the Muslims, Mazara was one of Sicily's most prosperous towns and capital of the biggest of the three administrative districts, or *walis*, into which the island was divided – hence the "del Vallo" tag. The first Sicilian city to be taken by the Arabs, and the last they surrendered, Mazara's prosperity lasted for 250 years, coinciding with the height of Arab power in the Mediterranean. Count Roger's anxiety to establish a strong Norman presence in this Muslim power base ensured that Mazara's importance lasted long after his conquest of the city in 1087, and it didn't give up its rank as provincial capital until Trápani took over in 1817.

The Arab links have revived since the port became the prime Sicilian destination for Tunisian immigrants flocking across the sea to work in the vast fishing fleet – one of Italy's biggest. Indeed, wandering through Mazara's casbah-like backstreets, there are moments when you could imagine yourself to be in North Africa, passing Tunisian shops and a café plastered with pictures of the Tunisian president, and Arab music percolating through small doorways. For the visitor, the attraction of Mazara is its profusion of fine churches in a slowly reviving – though far from genteel – old town. The tree-shaded lungomare and seafront gardens add another facet to its character, and with a row of sea-view restaurants, Mazara is one of the few towns in the west to make the most of its coastal location.

Arrival and information

Buses stop at Via Salemi, either outside the **train station** or 200m up at Piazza Matteotti. Drivers will find **parking** spots on Lungomare Mazzini. Ústica Lines runs **fast ferries** in summer for Pantelleria from the port; tickets are sold at the

Formosa agency at Via Molo Caito 55 (℡0923.941.116), and at Giacalone, Via Fata Morgana 20 (℡0923.941.366).

The main **tourist office** is on Piazza Mokarta (Tues–Sat 8am–2pm & 3–8pm, Sun 8am–2pm; ℡0923.942.776), and there's also a Pro Loco in a gift shop at Via XX Settembre 5 (Mon–Sat 9am–1pm & 4–8pm, Sun 11am–1pm & 6–8pm; ℡0923.944.610). **Banks** with ATMs can be found on Piazza Mokarta and Corso Umberto I.

Accommodation

Mazara holds a small but varied array of **accommodation**, adequate for a night or two's stay. The local **campsite**, *Sporting Club* (℡0923.947.230, ⓦwww.sporting clubvillage.com; closed mid-Oct to March), at Località Bocca Arena, 3km southeast of the centre (signposted from the lungomare), is resort-like, with grassy pitches, and has a range of alternative accommodation for the tentless, starting at €80 per night for two, though a minimum stay may be required.

Foresteria Monastica ℡0923.906.565 or 347.722.5069, ⓦwww.foresteriasanmichele.com. Very plain but clean and quiet rooms are available in this old-town convent annexed to San Michele church. You probably won't see any sign of the seven Benedictine nuns who are resident here, and who make the local pastries served at breakfast, which costs €5. Closed Nov–Feb. **❶**

Hopps Hotel Via G. Hopps 29 ℡0923.946.133, ⓦwww.hoppshotel.it. Large resort-style three-star centred on a palm-fringed pool, five minutes' walk down the lungomare from the public gardens. Rooms are spacious if a bit dated, and breakfast is by the pool. All in all good value for what you get, though poolside entertainments in summer can be noisy. **❸**

Nosteon Via Plebiscito 9 ℡0923.651.619 or 347.571.8904, ⓦwww.nosteon.it. Great-value B&B off Piazza Plebiscito, with a double room and an apartment consisting of a double in the loft and a bunk downstairs, with a kitchen and bathroom. Breakfast is taken at the nearby *Bar Garden*. No credit cards. **❶**

Villa Altair Via Salemi 9 ℡0923.944.088 or 347.666.2963, ⓦwww.villaaltair.com. A couple of kilometres southeast of town (call for directions), this peaceful B&B occupies an old *baglio*, or farmhouse, in the middle of vineyards and olive groves. The five rooms have a/c and wi-fi connections, and the owners can arrange airport transfers, excursions and vehicle hire. **❷**

The Town

Mazara's **old town**, where all the interest lies, is bordered by the River Mázaro and sea on two sides and the main corsos – Umberto I and Vittorio Véneto – on the other two. At the southern end of Corso Umberto I, Piazza Mokarta holds the scant ruins of Count Roger's **castello**, magnificently floodlit at night, when the square is the focus of promenading crowds. Fronting the garden to one side of the piazza is the **Duomo**, originally Norman but completely remodelled in the late seventeenth century – though the relief over the main door showing a mounted Count Roger trampling a Saracen underfoot was carved in 1584. The light and airy interior reveals an almost indigestible profusion of stuccoed and sculptured ornamentation, including, behind the altar, a group of seven marble statues depicting the *Transfiguration*, carved by Antonello Gagini. To the right, a niche reveals a fragment of Byzantine fresco, dating from the end of the thirteenth century, while, through the marble doorway on the right side of the nave, you'll find some excellently chiselled Roman sarcophagi, with reliefs of a lively hunting scene and a battle, rich with confusion.

Outside the Duomo, **Piazza della Repubblica** heralds a harmonious set of Baroque buildings: the square itself is flanked by the elegant, double-storey porticoed facade of the **Seminario** and the **Palazzo Vescovile**, both eighteenth-century. In nearby Piazza del Plebiscito, the fifteenth-century church of Sant'Egido now houses the **Museo del Sátiro** (daily 9am–6pm; €6), whose centrepiece is a rather risqué fourth-century BC bronze satyr captured in the ecstatic throes of an orgiastic Dionysian dance. It was, quite literally, caught by a Mazara fishing-boat in the waters between Pantelleria and Cap Bon, Tunisia, in 1998. Sadly, as the fishermen hauled the catch aboard, one of the arms broke off and has yet to be recovered. A 25-minute video with English subtitles relates the story.

Less compelling archeological finds can be seen at two other ex-churches, San Bartolomeo off Via Porta Palermo, which holds **Mirabilia Urbis**, displaying a smattering of minor, mainly Roman, finds from the area, and San Carlo on Via San Giovanni, now holding the **Amphoreus**, which has amphorae, anchors and various other items hauled up from the deep (both Mon–Fri 8am–2pm; free). Rather different in tone, the engaging social club-cum-museum that is the **Museo Ornitológico**, opposite the public gardens on Via San Salvatore (daily 9.30am–12.30pm & 3.30–8.30pm; free), displays a roomful of stuffed and rather raggedy owls, ibises and herons, among other birds (nothing is labelled).

Many other Baroque constructions are tucked away in the intricate network of streets and squares that makes up Mazara's old town, including several monumental churches. **Santa Veneranda**, in the square of the same name, is perhaps the most beautiful of these, its twin belltowers styled with a jaunty twist. On the edge of the old town, on a platform overlooking the Mázaro River, the church of **San Nicolò Regale** has a more restrained air. A restored Norman church, it has strong Arab elements, with a honey-toned, battlemented exterior and a simple interior rising to a single cupola.

Most of the churches were built after Mazara's teeming Arab population had dwindled to nothing – but it's here in the old town, especially in the Pilazza neighbourhood, that their descendants have returned, making up a low-key **Tunisian quarter** centred on Via Porta Palermo and nearby Via Bagno. Stroll around the quiet alleys here and you'll pass authentic Tunisian cafés and shops, and the occasional social club resounding to Arab tapes and the clack of backgammon tables.

West of the quarter, the waters of the Mázaro River are hidden by the hulls of the two hundred-odd trawlers that clog Mazara's **port**. Heavy overfishing and the use of illegal explosives (dropped into the sea to stun the fish) have greatly decreased the catch in recent years, but the rich waters above the continental shelf have ensured that there are enough fish left to make it worthwhile for the fishermen to pursue their trade – at least, given the reduced wages that the Tunisians are prepared to accept.

Out of the centre: the beach and Santa Maria della Giummare

Crossing over the bridge further down the river, you can walk past the docks to Mazara's seafront, mostly sandy **beach**, though a good part of it is choked by seaweed. Things improve the further up you go, but bathers might bear in mind that the stretch between Mazara and the Stagnone Islands has suffered from intense pollution in the past. If you're looking for a **swim** you'd be better advised to drive or jump on a bus from Mazara's train station to the lidos a couple of kilometres south, or head for the white sands and clear waters of **Tonnarella Lido**, 3km northwest.

There's one more easy excursion out from the centre of Mazara – walkable this time – a couple of kilometres away on the outskirts of town, though drivers could see it on their way in or out by following Via Circonvallazione, the main SS115 running to Marsala. Signposted "Madonna del Alto", the chapel of **Santa Maria della Giummare** sits on a slight elevation on the right-hand side of the road (looking north). Built as a Basilian convent by a daughter of Count Roger's in 1103, its portal also shows a strong Saracen strain.

Eating and drinking

As you might expect in a Sicilian/Tunisian fishing port, you can eat well in Mazara. There's a line of **restaurants** near the public gardens, each offering variations of fish couscous and all with tables outside.

Restaurants

La Béttola Via Maccagnone 32 ☏ 0923.946.422. Near the train station, this simple, old-fashioned place is recommended for regional specialities, mainly seafood. All dishes cost around €12. Closed Wed.

Eyem Zemen Via Porta Palermo 36 ☏ 347.386.9921. Tiny place, with three or four tables outside and authentic and cheap Tunisian snacks – *brik* (fried pastry parcels), oily aubergine salads and couscous. You can eat well for €15. Closed Tues except July & Aug.

Alla Kasbah Via Itria 10 ☏ 0923.906.126. Don't be fooled by the name: apart from a very acceptable fish couscous, the food here is less North African than modern Sicilian specialities. You can just have *antipasto*, couscous and wine for €15 – other fixed-price menus are €20–25. The ambience is relaxed and friendly. Closed Mon Sept–June.

Lo Scoiáttolo Via N. Tortorici 9 and Lungomare Mazzini ☏ 0923.946.313. With tables outside, "The Squirrel" has a fine *antipasto* buffet and daily fish specials, though many locals come here at night for the huge choice of pizzas (€4–6). All other dishes cost €7–12. Closed Thurs.

Bars

Bar Garden Piazza della Repubblica. Facing the town's most harmonious buildings, this is a nice place for a breakfast or sit-down by day, and to soak up the weird green illuminations in the evening. Closed Mon.

Villa delle Rose Via Conte Ruggero. With tables under shady trees in the public gardens, this makes a pleasant retreat for a quiet drink at any time.

Zelig Via N. Tortorici and Lungomare G. Mazzini. *Birreria* with plenty of outdoor tables, rock videos and occasional live music. Snacks include panini and plates of spaghetti. Closed daytime & Mon.

Selinunte and around

SELINUNTE, the site of the Greek city of Selinus, lies around 30km east of Mazara del Vallo, stranded on a remote corner of the coast in splendid isolation. It's a crucial sight if you're travelling through the west of Sicily, its series of mighty temples lying in great heaps, where they were felled by earthquakes.

Most westerly of the Hellenic colonies, **Selinus** reached its peak during the fifth century BC. A bitter rival of Segesta, whose lands lay adjacent to the north, the powerful city and its fertile plain attracted enemies hand over fist, and it was only a matter of time before Selinus caught the eye of Segesta's ally, Carthage. Geographically vulnerable, the city was sacked by Carthaginians, any attempts at recovery forestalled by earthquakes, which later razed it altogether. However, people continued to live here until 250 BC, when the population was finally transferred to Marsala before the Roman invasion. The Arabs did occupy the site briefly, but the last recorded settlement at Selinunte was in the thirteenth century, after which time it remained forgotten until rediscovered in the sixteenth century. Despite the destruction, the city ruins have exerted a romantic hold over people ever since.

By **public transport**, it's easiest to approach from **Castelvetrano** (see p.359), which is about thirty minutes' ride from Mazara del Vallo by road or rail. Selinunte is another thirty minutes south from there, via buses that run two to eight times daily from the train station or Piazza Matteotti.

Marinella di Selinunte

The archeological site of Selinunte is situated just west of the modern village of **MARINELLA DI SELINUNTE**, which makes a far better base than Castelvetrano, and is also where the buses stop. Although it can get a bit hectic in summer, Marinella is an atmospheric place to spend a few hours. Its most appealing parts lie on and around the long, narrow road that winds down to the small harbour, where fishing boats are hauled up onto the sands by pulleys.

Arrival and information

Marinella's **bus station** is south of the entrance to the temple site, but most buses continue to the entrance as well. The small but obliging **tourist office** (summer daily 9am–7pm, winter Mon–Fri 9am–1pm; ☎0924.46.251), which is often thronged with visitors in summer, is on the roundabout near the entrance.

There's an **alimentari** nearby on Via Caboto, while beyond it, in the main residential district, you'll find a **supermarket** behind the *Alceste* hotel. Descending to the seafront, Via Caboto holds most of the hotels and restaurants, as well as a **bank** with ATM (there's another ATM in the entrance lobby of the archeological site). You can log on to the **internet** at Costa del Sole, Via Castore e Polluce 17 (☎0924.46.712 or 389.698.1058), which also rents out **bikes** (€10 for half a day, €13 for full day).

Accommodation

You may well be offered **rooms** as you get off the bus, which are worth accepting in summer when the hotels and pensions in the village fill rapidly. Two **campsites** stand virtually side by side on the main road, about 1.5km north of the village: the *Athena* (☎0924.46.132, ⓦwww.campingathenaselinunte.it), with a ridiculous temple facade and a good pizzeria, and *Il Maggiolino* (☎0924.46.044, ⓦwww.campingmaggiolino .it); the bus to and from Castelvetrano passes right by them.

Garzia Via A. Pigafetta 2 ☎0924.46.024,
ⓦwww.hotelgarzia.com. This large, Arabic-themed hotel on the seafront road lacks charm, but it has a wide range of rooms (some with sea-facing balconies), friendly staff and its own patch of beach. The restaurant offers good set-price menus. ❸

Il Pescatore Via Castore e Polluce 31
☎0924.46.303, ⓦwww.affittacamereil
pescatore.it. With a roof terrace that enjoys views over to the temples and sea, this place offers eight good-size rooms with private bathrooms and a/c or fans, breakfast (that includes fresh fruit) on the terrace plus use of a kitchen. Alternatively, you can sleep on the roof for €15, and there are also four self-catering apartments. No credit cards. ❶

Porta del Sole Via Apollonio Rodio 32
☎0924.46.035. A B&B offering four basic rooms with private or shared bathrooms, and there are five larger ones with balconies (not that there's a view) in the *Holiday House* across the road, run by the same family. Furniture and beds are from the visit-grandma school of comfort. No credit cards. ❶

Sicilia Cuore Mio Via della Cittadella 44
☎0924.46.077 or 336.612.769, ⓦwww
.siciliacuoremio.it. Right across from the archeo-logical site, and with a long terrace overlooking the sea in front, this friendly, modern B&B offers five rooms, three with a sea view and two of them in a separate building next door with a kitchen for guests' use. Closed Dec–March. ❷

The town and its beaches

Marinella is no longer the isolated place it used to be, with new buildings and streets in evidence everywhere, while the seafront has become top-heavy with trattorias, and shops selling Tunisian carpets, souvenirs and beachwear. But it remains an attractive place, of particular appeal if you're planning to use the fine sand **beach** that stretches west from the village to the ruins. The water isn't great to swim in, since it's often clogged with seaweed at the sand's edge, though this doesn't deter the kids. However, the surfing here can be good, and you can rent equipment in the summer, as well as pedalos, chairs, shades and all the usual beach paraphernalia. Another beach is located east of the village, **Mare Pineta**, backed by pine trees stretching into the distance; follow the road east of the port for ten minutes.

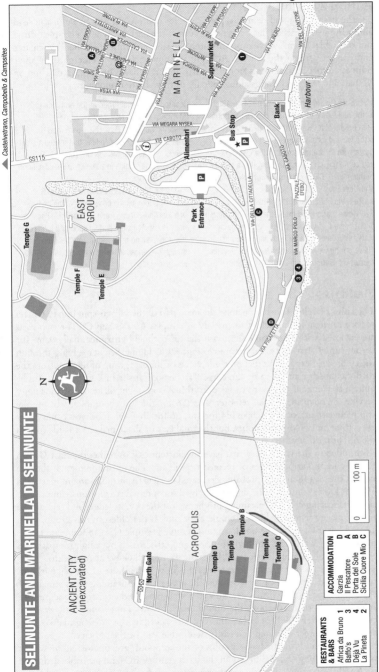

SELINUNTE AND MARINELLA DI SELINUNTE

▲ Castelvetrano, Campobello & Campsites

▲ ❷ & Mare Pineta

ANCIENT CITY
(unexcavated)

ACROPOLIS

North Gate

Temple D
Temple C
Temple B
Temple A
Temple O

EAST GROUP

Temple G
Temple F
Temple E

N

100 m
0

SS115

MARINELLA

VIA ARISTOTELE
VIA PLATONE
VIA CASSIOPEA
VIA CASTORE E POLLUCE
VIA APOLLONO
VIA SIRIO
VIA PERSEFONE
VIA ARGONAUTI
VIA VEGA
VIA CALIPSO
VIA CALLIOPE
VIA PEGASO
VIA NAUSICA
VIA ULISSE
VIA ANTIGONE
VIA PALINURO
VIA DEL CANTONE

VIA MEGARA NYSEA
VIA CABOTO

Supermarket
Alimentari
Bus Stop
Bank

Harbour

Park Entrance
VIA DELLA CITTADELLA
VIA MARCO POLO
VIA CABOTO
PIAZZALE EFEBO
VIA PIGAFETTA

▲ Santuario Malophoros (400m) & Antiquarium (600m)

RESTAURANTS & BARS
Africa da Bruno	1
Baffo's	3
Déjà Vu	4
La Pineta	2

ACCOMMODATION
Garzia	D
Il Pescatore	A
Porta del Sole	B
Sicilia Cuore Mio	C

Eating and drinking

All the best eating and drinking places are located on Via Marco Polo, the road above the west beach. That starts down at the little harbour where a couple of bars put out tables from which you can watch the sun set, while the fishermen chatter and dispute among themselves. At night in summer, visitors emerge from their holiday homes to join locals from the surrounding villages on foot, in cars and on Vespas, and the party chugs along merrily until well after midnight.

Africa da Bruno Via Alceste ☎ 0924.46.456. In the residential district, this cheerful trattoria with bright white walls offers superlative *antipasti* and locally inspired fish dishes, like pasta with tuna and capers. In the evenings, you can enjoy crispy pizzas cooked in a wood-burning oven. Closed Thurs except July & Aug, and Nov–Feb.

Baffo's Via Marco Polo 51 ☎ 0924.46.211. Sea views and a good menu that includes magnificent *forno a legna* pizzas (€6–8), a range of tasty fettuccine dishes (€8–9) and grilled fish. There are no views but better food at the sister restaurant, *Baffo's Castle* (☎ 0924.46.859),

located on the main road at the entrance to Marinella. Closed Nov–March.

Déjà Vu Via Marco Polo. Lively bar/*birreria* overlooking the sea, open late, that makes a great venue for watching the sun set. There are DJs most Saturday nights in summer, and cold snacks. Closed Oct–March.

La Pineta Mare Pineta ☎ 0924.46.820. This trattoria on the beach east of the harbour is a real find, serving fresh seafood including sea urchins (*ricci*). It's the perfect spot for a lunch or leisurely evening meal just metres from the sea, though overpriced (€10–18 for most dishes). Call ahead in winter.

Selinus: the site

The **ruins** of Selinus are back behind the main part of the village, split into two main parts with temples in each, known only as temples A to G and O. The two parts are enclosed within the same site, with the car park and **entrance** (daily 9am–1hr before sunset; last entry 1hr before closing; €9 including Segesta – lying through the landscaped earthbanks that preclude views of the east group of temples from the road. Selinus is claimed to be the biggest archeological site in Europe, so it can be quite a challenge if you want to see everything; you might make use of the buggy service, or **navetta**, for the remoter sites (€6 for the nearer temples, €12 for the complete circuit), or rent a bike (€4 for 1hr, €6 for 2hr). On foot, you could cover everything in two or three hours, but the total lack of shade makes for hard work in the full heat of summer.

Shrouded in the wild celery that gave the ancient city its name, the **East Group** temples are in various stages of reconstructed ruin. The most complete is the one nearest the sea (Temple E), probably dedicated to Hera (Aphrodite) and re-erected in 1958. A Doric construction, almost 70m by 25m, it remains a gloriously impressive sight, its soaring columns gleaming bright against the sky, its ledges and capitals the resting place for flitting birds. Temple F, behind, is the oldest in this group, from around 550 BC, while the northernmost temple (Temple G) is an immense tangle of columned wreckage, 6m high in places and crisscrossed by rough footpaths. In Sicily, the only temple larger than this is the Tempio di Giove at Agrigento.

The road leads down from here, across the (now buried) site of the old harbour, to the second part of excavated Selinus, the **acropolis**, containing what remains of the other temples (five in all), as well as the well-preserved city streets and massive stepped **walls** that rise above the duned beach below. These huge walls were all constructed after 409 BC – when the city was sacked by the Carthaginians – in an attempt to protect a limited and easily defensible area of the old city.

Temple C stands on the highest point of the acropolis, giving glorious views out over the sparkling sea. Built early in the sixth century BC (and probably dedicated to Apollo), it originally held the finest of the metopes (decorative panels) that are now in Palermo's archeological museum. Its fourteen standing columns were re-erected in the 1920s: other fallen columns here, and at the surrounding temples, show how they were originally constructed – the drums lying in a line, with slots and protrusions on either side that fitted into each other.

The buildings immediately behind temples C and D were shops, split into two rooms and with a courtyard each. At the end of the main street beyond stands the **north gate** to the city – the tall blocks of stone marking a gateway that was 7m high. Behind the north gate stood the rest of the ancient city, still largely unexcavated, though crisscrossed by little paths through the undergrowth. The **agora** was sited just north of here, and a necropolis further up, while to the west, across the Modione river, stood the **Santuario Malophoros**, part of a complex that marked the western boundary of the city. Animal sacrifices were performed at the small well in front of the structure. Beyond it, on the edge of the archeological zone, the **Antiquarium** holds statuettes and terracotta fragments, mostly excavated in the 1980s from a temple dedicated to Hera Matronale, south of the Malophoros.

Campobello and the Cave di Cusa

If you have your own transport, it makes some sense to call in at the quarries where the stone for the building of Selinus was extracted in the fifth century BC. They lie 3.5km south of the scruffy town of **CAMPOBELLO DI MAZARA**, deep in olive country. From Selinunte, a lovely 20km drive takes you along country roads lined with olive groves and vines. When you reach Campobello, take the road to Tre Fontane and follow the signs ("Cave di Cusa"), keeping your eyes peeled and fingers crossed.

At the site of the **Cave di Cusa** (9am–1hr before sunset; free), a path leads into a bucolic setting that is more reminiscent of English Romanticism than of ancient Greece. In early summer, workers fork hay into piles in between the rock ledges and tended shrubs, while behind them stretch shaded groves of olives. Everywhere, you can see the massive column drums and stumps lying randomly about, quarried and chiselled into shape here before being dragged to the ancient city on wooden carts, where they formed part of the great temple complex. There are examples of all the various stages of the process, with unfinished pieces poignantly abandoned, the work interrupted when Selinus was devastated in 409 BC. The most impressive pieces are those stone drums and column sections that remain in place where they were being excavated. A couple are 6m high and 2m across, with a narrow groove dug all the way around in which the stonemasons had to work – the reflected heat must have been appalling. Other rock sections indicate clearly where drums have already been cut – parts of the site look as though someone has been through with a giant pastry-cutter.

Castelvetrano and around

It's hard to recommend a visit to **CASTELVETRANO**, 15km inland from Campobello, for any reason other than to get the bus straight out again. A depressed town, it's lightened only marginally by an elegant if traffic-choked centre, where the **Teatro Selinus** – looking rather like a copy of a Greek temple – boasts a proud plaque commemorating Goethe's visit in 1787. Just around the corner stands a good-looking **Chiesa Madre** from the sixteenth century. The church's finely engraved doorway leads into an interior warmly illuminated by stained-glass windows – a rare thing in Sicily – and ornamented by a number of stuccoes by Serpotta and Ferraro. Off the adjacent square, Piazza Garibaldi, it's a short walk down to Via Garibaldi 50 and the **Museo Cívico** (Mon–Sat 9am–1pm & 3–6.30pm, Sun 9am–1pm; €2.50), home of the bronze *Éfebo di Selinunte*, a statue of a young man from the fifth century BC.

From behind the church, Via Vittorio Emanuele leads down towards Piazza Matteotti and the train station. Piazza Matteotti marks the end of Via Serafino Mannone, where aficionados of banditry can visit the courtyard in which the body of the island's most notorious outlaw, **Salvatore Giuliano** (see p.82), was found on July 5, 1950. The courtyard is between Via Mannone 92 and 100, though it's a rather less appealing spot than its legend might suggest.

Practicalities

To reach the town centre from the **train station**, in Piazza Améndola, walk up to the main road and turn left: it's just a few minutes to Piazza Matteotti, from where Via Vittorio Emanuele – the main shopping street – leads all the way to the rear of the Chiesa Madre church. **Buses** from Marsala and Trápani stop in Piazza Matteotti, and there's a **tourist office** at Piazza Carlo d'Aragona, below Piazza Garibaldi (Mon–Sat 8.30am–1.30pm & 4–7pm, also Sun in summer 9am–1pm; ℡0924.902.004). There are a few mediocre places around town for a snack or meal, and one exceptional **restaurant**: *Lu Disiu*, Via XXIV Maggio 14 (℡0924.907.321; closed Mon), near the bottom of Via Vittorio Emanuele, offering a great range of local specialities at very reasonable prices.

To **get to Selinunte** from Castelvetrano, take the bus for Marinella from outside the train station – a timetable is posted inside the station – or from piazzas Matteotti, Dante or Regina Margherita in town.

Santíssima Trinità di Delia

Three and a half kilometres west of Castelvetrano, a twelfth-century Norman church makes a pleasant rural excursion for anyone not in a blazing hurry. Head down Via Ruggero Séttimo from Piazza Umberto, along a country lane fringed by vineyards, keeping left where the road forks. The domed church, **Santíssima Trinità di Delia**, is signposted before you arrive at the artificial lake of Lago Trinità: ring the bell to the right of the church for the key. The small, square building, its four slender columns and triple apse reminiscent of Saracenic styles, was meticulously restored by two brothers, whose mausoleum the church has become. Their tombs, dominating the small interior, rival those of the Norman kings in Palermo for splendour.

Inland: Salemi, Gibellina and Santa Margherita di Belice

North of Castelvetrano and east of Marsala, the interior of Trápani province is intensely rural, its few small towns little changed by the coming of the A29 autostrada, which cuts across the region. The whole area is green and highly fertile, mainly given over to vine-growing; indeed, the wine around the **Salemi** district is among Sicily's best. But, hard though it is to believe, the entire region still hasn't recovered from the **earthquake** of January 15, 1968, which briefly spotlighted western Sicily, sadly more for the authorities' inadequate response to it than for the actual loss of life. Four hundred died and a thousand were injured, no great number by Sicilian standards, but it was the 50,000 left homeless that had the most lingering impact on this already depressed part of the island, and the effects of the earthquake are still evident everywhere. Ruined buildings and ugly temporary dwellings being used four decades later testify to the chronically dilatory response to the disaster, aggravated by private interests and particularly by the Mafia contractors who capitalized on the catastrophe. Even where rebuilding went ahead, such as in the new town of **Gibellina**, it's still possible to see the dread hand of inertia.

It goes without saying that this is a little-visited area of Sicily, but it's intriguing nonetheless. This is, after all, the part of the world known best to Giuseppe di Lampedusa, whose classic novel, *The Leopard*, is partly set in the little town of **Santa Margherita di Belice** – also badly damaged in 1968 but emerging slowly from the doldrums, and an essential stop for anyone who's read the book. Local buses run to all the towns in the region, but it's impossible to construct any kind of sightseeing itinerary using them – you have to have your own car, not least to avoid the possibility of getting stuck in backwaters with no accommodation.

Salemi

The town of **SALEMI**, 20km north of Castelvetrano and 30km east of Marsala, oddly enjoyed the privilege of being the first capital of a united Italy in 1860, albeit for only three days, as recorded by a plaque in front of its heavily restored thirteenth-century **castello** on Piazza Alicia, at the top of the town. Another plaque marks Garibaldi's declaration of a dictatorship, asserting that "in times of war, it's necessary for the civilian powers to be concentrated in the hands of one man" – namely Garibaldi himself, though King Vittorio Emanuele still gets a mention. On Via d'Aguirre, leading down from the piazza, the former Collegio dei Gesuiti houses a quintet of museums (all Tues–Sun 10am–1pm & 4–7pm; €5 for all). The **Museo del Risorgimento** holds assorted pieces of "Garibaldini" – letters, documents and arms connected with the town's finest hour; the **Museo Archeólogico** contains finds from local excavations including Monte Polizzo; the **Museo dell'Arte Sacra** gathers treasures from various local churches, including the cathedral destroyed in the earthquake; the **Museo del Paesaggio** explores aspects of the Sicilian landscape by means of videos, and the **Museo della Mafia** brings together films, photographs, recordings of interviews, and paintings and sculptures by local artists of prominent figures in the Mafia's history – including representations of the two assassinated anti-Mafia judges Falcone and Borsellino, plus work by a *pentito*, or informer. It's a pretty disparate mix, and fairly indigestible if you attempt to take them all in, but the collections are definitely worth putting aside a couple of hours for.

There's a **tourist office** at the bottom of the hill on Piazza Libertà (daily 9am–1pm & 4–8pm, or 3–7pm in winter; ☎0924.981.426), where buses stop.

Gibellina

Salemi escaped the earthquake lightly, even though a third of the population had to abandon their shattered homes. Other towns, like Gibellina, were completely flattened, and the population moved en masse to a site close to Santa Ninfa, reached from Salemi along the SS188. This is **GIBELLINA NUOVA**, a modern town that was once a symbol of progress in the region, its wide, empty streets adorned with numerous weird constructions and abstract sculptures designed by a handful of iconoclastic architects with big budgets. A vast stainless-steel star straddles the motorway where you exit for Gibellina, while elsewhere the town holds huge white spheres, giant ploughs, snails and much besides – some fifty constructions in all, though many of them are crumbling already (one church collapsed in 1994), and many of the designs themselves are embarrassingly frozen in the image of what appeared futuristic in the 1970s. The town, meanwhile, bakes in the summer sun, since all the modern piazzas are vast concrete spaces with little shade.

You can get a taste of what Gibellina is all about by driving to the main square – Piazza XV Gennaio 1968, in case there was any doubt about what's to blame for all this – where the arcaded City Hall is fronted by some particularly abstract examples, and the tall **Torre Belice** clocktower chimes four times a day with taped human voices instead of bells, a reminder of the earthquake victims. You'll find some respite and more substance at the cultural centre signposted just east of the centre, the **Baglio di Stéfano**, home to a couple of good museums (Tues–Sun 9am–1pm & 3–6pm; €5 for both), one containing contemporary art – mainly works by Italian painters, but the sculptor Arnaldo Pomodoro is also represented – the other, more gripping, dedicated to Mediterranean culture, from Spain to Turkey and from Corsica to Africa, taking in costumes, jewellery, ceramics, tapestries, calligraphy and carpets, all beautifully presented. A separate space here, the Atelier, holds pieces donated by the various sculptors and designers who contributed to Gibellina Nuova's townscape.

The Baglio di Stéfano complex also holds a theatre, which is the main venue for the **Orestiadi**, a series of classical and modern dramas, concerts and events performed almost nightly every July and August. As well as works by Euripides, Sophocles and others, there are modern interpretations by the likes of Jean Cocteau, Stravinsky and John Cage, plus a full programme of exhibitions, cinema and music. Tickets cost around €12; for more details, call ☎0924.67.844 or see ⓦwww.orestiadi.it.

For a **lunch** stop in Gibellina Nuova, seek out *La Massara*, Viale dei Vespri Siciliani 41 (☎0924.67.601; closed Mon), an inexpensive trattoria ten minutes' walk from the central piazza, where the very filling house pasta, *busiate napoleonica* (€6), is made with aubergines, tomato and sausage. Alternatively, pick up provisions from the supermarket on the parallel Viale Sturzo.

Old Gibellina

Eighteen kilometres east along the SS119 (through Santa Ninfa), overlooked by ranks of wind turbines, the old town of **RÚDERI DI GIBELLINA** complements the new: a mountain of rubble from which smashed and mutilated houses poke out, strewn over a green hillside. On the way into town, you'll pass what is ironically its best-preserved fragment: a shady cemetery stretching down the side of the valley, where the inhabitants of the new town return every year to remember the catastrophe. Further down, modernism has left its mark here too, in the form of a wide, grey-white mantle of concrete, **Il Cretto**, poured over one slope, and carved through by channels that recall the previous layout of streets. It's an arresting spectacle, not least for its sheer scale.

Everything else remains as it was after the earthquake struck: only a church has since been restored. Nearby, a jumble of scaffolding on a hummock cradles a stage that makes up one of the two venues for the **Orestiadi**, though it's only infrequently used.

Santa Margherita di Belice

Often ranked among the finest of all historical novels, Giuseppe di Lampedusa's *The Leopard* ("Il Gattopardo" in Italian) is a masterpiece of manners and morals, written by a Sicilian prince who only ever completed this one work. Set in 1860s Sicily, it draws heavily on Lampedusa's own experiences, not least the summers he used to spend in his grandmother's palace in **SANTA MARGHERITA DI BELICE**, a small village 35km east of Castelvetrano. This is the Donnafugata of the book – the fictional prince's summer home, a place cherished for the "sense it gave him of everlasting childhood". The 1968 earthquake, unfortunately, completely wrecked the seventeenth-century palace and church described so intently in the novel, though fragments of the palace have been incorporated in a gleaming new Town Hall (Municipio). This, with its cool internal courtyards and lovely garden to the side, at least echoes the spirit of the original. More poignant is all that's left of the adjacent Chiesa Madre – a two-storey corner open to the elements, displaying its elegant marble tracery and painted medallions to the birds. Having paid your literary dues, it's a quick matter to look around the rest of Santa Margherita, which shows a few signs of revival these days – there's a thoroughly modern church with a space-rocket spire, new extensions grafted onto older, damaged buildings, and a traffic-free stretch of street where you can grab a cold drink in the *Caffè Gattopardo*.

Pantelleria

With an area of 83 square kilometres, **PANTELLERIA** is the largest of Sicily's offshore islands. Forty kilometres closer to Tunisia than to Sicily, it has been occupied since early times by whichever power controlled the central Mediterranean. By the time of the Phoenicians, who colonized it in the seventh century BC, it was called Hiranin, "island of the birds", after the birds who still stop over here on their migratory routes; for the Greeks, it was Kossyra, or "small". Its present name probably derives from the Arabic *bint ar-riah* ("daughter of the winds"),

You can reach Pantelleria by (year-round) ferry or (summer-only) hydrofoil services from Trápani, and by fast ferries from Mazara del Vallo (June to mid-Oct). Flights from Trápani or Palermo taking under an hour are convenient if more extravagant alternatives – however, taking the overnight ferry on the way out effectively negates the longer journey time while saving a night's accommodation expense.

Siremar **ferries** do the journey in around six hours (June–Sept daily; Oct–May daily except Sat), leaving Trápani at midnight, for a deck-class fare of around €34 one way (slightly less in low season). For around €5.50 you can reserve a reclining chair (*poltrona*), an expense worth considering since the regular seats are difficult to sleep in and uncomfortably close to the TVs; or there are couchette-cabins for around €15 (without WC) or €21 (with WC) per person. **Tickets** are on sale in the Siremar office at the Stazione Maríttima in Trápani (☎0923.24.968, ⓦwww.siremar .it), right up until departure.

Ústica Lines (☎0923.873.813, ⓦwww.usticalines.it) runs **fast ferries** from Mazara del Vallo between June and mid-October, leaving daily except Monday at 11am and 5pm and taking roughly two hours, and from the island of Lampedusa between July and mid-September, leaving on Wednesday, Friday and Sunday at 11.30am, taking nearly three hours. Tickets for either route cost around €35 one way.

Pantelleria is just a forty-minute **flight** from Trápani (3 flights daily) or a fifty-minute flight from Palermo (2–3 flights daily) with Meridiana (☎892.928, ⓦwww.meridiana .it). One-way tickets are €40–85, depending on availability and flexibility (try ⓦwww .expedia.it and www.edreams.it) – it's worth booking some time in advance in summer. Between April and September, there are also direct flights from Milan, Bologna, Rome, Verona and Venice.

after the restless breezes that blow around the island's rugged shores. Despite its remote, rocky appearance, however, Pantelleria is not as unsophisticated as some of Sicily's other offshore islands – it's long been on the African shipping route and has proved a popular destination for celebs: former aficionados like Truman Capote and Aldous Huxley have been succeeded more recently by such A-listers as Madonna, Giorgio Armani and Sting, and parts of *Il Postino* (*The Postman*) were filmed here, too.

There are no beaches of any kind on Pantelleria, its rough black coastline consisting mainly of jagged rocks, but the swimming is still pretty good in some exceptionally scenic spots. Inland, the largely mountainous country offers plenty of rambling opportunities, all an easy moped or bus ride from the port, which holds most of the accommodation options. If you're spending any length of time on Pantelleria, a novel option is to rent one of the local *dammuso* houses: their strong walls and domed roofs keep the temperature down indoors.

The main drawback to spending time on Pantelleria is the **cost of living**: the few hotels are pricey, while food (and water) is mostly imported and therefore relatively expensive. However, a few days spent here will probably leave you wanting more. Best times are May/June or September/October, to avoid the summer's ferocious heat; try to book your accommodation before you arrive.

Pantelleria Town

As you arrive off the ferry at dawn, **PANTELLERIA TOWN**, the only settlement of any size on the island, has an undeniably romantic aura, revealing a spread of serene, white-painted cubes. Only close up do these emerge as modern rather than medieval, as most of the town was flattened during the last war when Allied bombers pulverized what had become one of the main German bases in the

Mediterranean. Consequently, much of the town has a homogenous appearance, its low-rise, concrete buildings spreading back two or three streets deep from the harbour. The only building that predates the war is the morose, black **Castello Barabacane** (Aug daily 6pm–midnight; free), a legacy of the Spaniards. Its partly restored interior is destined to hold an archeological museum, but in the meantime it's the venue for changing exhibitions and has photos and videos showing aspects of island history and culture, from World War II bombing to carnival celebrations. More in-depth **tours** of the castle can be arranged by calling ℡327.363.9284.

Otherwise the town is largely devoid of specific interest. But while it may not fit the stereotype of the idyllic island port, Pantelleria town has a certain appeal, and there's much to be said for simply observing the regular to-and-fro of delivery vessels and fishing smacks from one of the seafront café-bars, while the marina sees the manoeuvrings of some uncommonly flash yachts and even the odd schooner. Things get a bit livelier in the evening, when the harbourside fills with perambulating locals.

Arrival, information and transport

The **airport** is 5km southeast of town. A bus service runs into town four times daily – a 12-minute journey – from a stop outside, and taxis into town charge €10–15; alternatively, it's a 45-minute downhill walk. **Arriving by sea**, you'll disembark right in the centre of town, close to most of the bars, restaurants and hotels. In bad weather, you may be deposited instead at Scauri, a smaller port on the island's southwestern side, from where a bus takes foot passengers into town (remember to disembark promptly or it will leave without you). Both Siremar and Ústica Lines agencies are along Via Borgo Italia on the harbourfront.

There is a **tourist office** near the castle on Lungomare Borsellino (mid-May to mid-Sept Mon–Sat 10am–1pm & 6–8.30pm; ℡0923.911.838, ⓦwww.prolocopantelleria.it), and you can usually pick up a booklet (in Italian) packed with local information at La Cossira, a travel and accommodation agency at Via Borgo Italia 77. The Italian **websites** ⓦwww.pantelleria.it and www.tuttopantelleria.it are also useful.

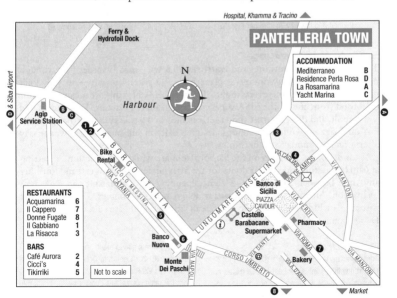

PANTELLERIA TOWN

ACCOMMODATION
Mediterraneo	B
Residence Perla Rosa	D
La Rosamarina	A
Yacht Marina	C

RESTAURANTS
Acquamarina	6
Il Cappero	7
Donne Fugate	8
Il Gabbiano	1
La Risacca	3

BARS
Café Aurora	2
Cicci's	4
Tikirriki	5

Not to scale

Local **buses** make regular departures from Piazza Cavour to all the main villages on the island, with reduced or no services on Sundays. Buy tickets in advance from any *tabacchi* for €1, or on the bus for €1.20. The tourist office has routes and timetables. For more independence, you might consider **renting a bike**, **scooter** or **car**: see "Listings" opposite for details.

Accommodation

While the town itself offers limited accommodation, other **hotels** – mostly quite pricey – can be found at Cuddie Rosse, Specchio di Vénere, Punta Fram and Bue Marino. Even in town prices are generally high, though low-season bargains are usually available. During July and August, some places impose a minimum stay of three days or even a week – at other times of the year, prices drop considerably. There's no **campsite** on the island, and camping rough is impractical given the terrain and lack of water. To rent one of the idiosyncratic **dammuso** houses dotted around the island, ask at the tourist office or contact one of the *dammuso* agencies listed opposite. Most *dammusi* are €300–1000 per week according to size and season (you may be able to book less than a week's rental in low season), and you'll usually need a car to get to and from them.

Mediterraneo Via Borgo Italia ☎0923.911.299, ⓦwww.pantelleriahotel.it. Immediately at the end of the dock, on the harbourfront, this three-star offers comfortable rooms and a pool. The restaurant at the top has great views (meals €20); a buffet breakfast is also served here. Free pick-up from the airport. ❺

Residence Perla Rosa Via Dante Alighieri, Contrada Itria ☎0923.912.114, ⓦwww.pantelleria hotel.it. Under the same management as the *Mediterraneo*, this place 500m from town and 100m from the sea has 18 one- and two-bedroom apartments sharing a pool, garden and BBQ facilities. They're on the cramped side, but rooms are air-conditioned and have TV. In summer there's

a minimum stay of three days (one week in Aug). Look out for any extras added to your final bill. ❸

🏃 **La Rosamarina** Via Sicania 10, off Via Villa ☎328.924.0159, ⓔlarosamarina@hotmail .it. You'll find the lowest prices on the island in this friendly B&B, a remodelled *dammuso* ten minutes from the port and 300m from the sea. The two rooms have warm colours and a/c, and one has cooking facilities. There's a terrace, a garden and sea views. No credit cards. ❸

Yacht Marina Via Borgo Italia ☎0923.913.649, ⓦwww.marinahotelpantelleria.com. Full of designer touches, this hotel has 37 rooms with a/c, satellite TV and internet access; the best, costing €20 extra, have a harbour-view balcony. ❸

Eating and drinking

There are several **restaurants and trattorias** in town – mostly rather flash, though not unaffordable. Many double as pizzerias – and good ones too – so you don't need to spend a fortune every night. If you're **self-catering**, you can buy your own food from any of the SISA supermarkets on Piazza Cavour, Via Catania and Via Nápoli, and there's a fruit and vegetable shop and a bakery, respectively on and just off Piazza Cavour. Most shops are open daily in summer, closed Wednesday afternoon and Sunday at other times.

As for drinking, the **bars** on the harbourfront are where all the action is, starting at 6am (when they open their doors for the arriving ferry passengers) and finishing any time between midnight and 2am depending on season and the manager's inclination. All have tables by the water, where prices are higher. The island's best pastries – including the typically Pantescan ricotta cakes – are sold at the *pasticceria* Da Giovanni on Piazza Cavour.

Restaurants

Acquamarina Via Borgo Italia 1 ☎0923.911.422. This trendy little joint is the best-placed restaurant in town, with large windows overlooking the

harbour. There's a long menu, including fish couscous (€14). Closed Sun Oct–May.

Il Cappero Via Roma 31 ☎0923.912.601. Just up from the main piazza, this popular place serves the local ravioli stuffed with *tumma* cheese, fresh fish (including large tuna steaks) and pizzas (also available to take away, *d'asporto*). There's a good *antipasto* table too. First courses are €8–12, mains €12–22.

Donne Fugate Corso Umberto I 10 ☎0923.912.688. Small, rather unprepossessing place where you can indulge in an excellent selection of *antipasti*, spaghetti *alla menta e gamberi* (with mint and prawns) and an unforgettable fish couscous (Thurs only). You'll pay around €40 for a full meal, drinks excluded. Closed daytime & Oct–May.

Il Gabbiano Via Trieste 5 ☎0923.911.909. Just off the seafront, this modest, white-walled and vaulted trattoria offers some of the cheapest food in town, nothing exceptional but the usual range of island specialities and a calm atmosphere. Pastas are around €9, seafood €10–12. Closed Wed in winter.

La Risacca Via Errera 18 ☎0923.912.975. At the end of the harbour, this busy ristorante-pizzeria with a terrace has an array of grilled seafood and outdoor seating. Try the ravioli *con pomodoro, burro e salvia* (with tomato, butter and sage), or, in the evening, fish couscous (€18). You'll pay around €10 for pastas, €10–20 for mains. Closed Mon in winter.

Bars

Café Aurora Via Borgo Italia 43. With a fine seating area overlooking the port, this bar serves classy aperitifs with olives and other nibbles.

Cicci's Via Cágliari. Just off the main piazza, this place has a lively evening crowd, musical accompaniment and snacks. Closed Sun.

Tikirriki Via Borgo Italia. Good snacks, pastries and ice cream, which you can eat by the harbour. Closed Sun in winter.

Listings

Airport ☎0923.911.172, ⊛www.pantelleriairport.it.

Banks ATMs at Banco di Sicilia, Piazza Cavour, Monte dei Paschi, Via Napoli 2, and Banco Nuova, Via Catania 5.

Boat tours Daily from the port in summer; a *giro dell'isola* (round-island tour) costs around €35 per person for a full day (leaving around 10am, returning at 4.30pm), including a spaghetti lunch. Call ☎0923.911.469 or 339.398.4810 for details.

Bike rental Viva Pantelleria, Vicolo Leopardi 5 (☎0923.911.078 or 349.619.9210, ⊛www.vivapantelleria.it) charges €12 for up to 2hr, €15 for half a day. Escorted bike tours and kayak rental also available.

Car and scooter rental Autonoleggio Policardo, Via Messina 31 and airport ☎0923.912.844, ⊛www.policardo.it. Expect to pay up to €65 per day for a Fiat 600, €60 per day for a scooter, lower prices outside high season.

Dammuso agencies La Cossira, Via Borgo Italia 77 ☎0923.911.078, ⊛www.lacossira.it; Dammusi di Rukia ☎335.120.6226, ⊛www.pantelleria.com; Pantelleria Travel ☎199.440.862, ⊛www.pantelleriatravel.com.

Diving Viva Pantelleria (see Bike rental, above) offers diving excursions and equipment hire.

Ferries and hydrofoils Siremar operates a ferry service to Trápani leaving at noon (June–Sept daily and Oct–May Fri & Sat) or at 10am (Oct–May Mon–Thurs); tickets from Agenzia Rizzo, Via Borgo Italia 22 ☎0923.911.120, ⊛www.siremar.it. Ústica Lines operates fast ferries to Mazara del Vallo (June to mid-Oct, leaving daily except Mon at 8am & 2.30pm) and to Lampedusa,

in the Pelágie Islands (July to mid-Sept, leaving Wed, Fri & Sun at 2.45pm); tickets from Agenzia Minardi, Via Borgo Italia 15 ☎0923.911.502, ⊛www.usticalines.it.

Hospital For first-aid and medical matters, go to the Ospedale B. Nagar, Piazzale Almanza ☎0923.910.234.

Internet Internet Point, Via Dante 7 (daily 8.30am–2pm & 4.30–9pm). Phone, fax and Western Union services also available here.

Market Every Tuesday and Friday morning on Via San Leonardo, at the end of Via De Amicis. Fresh fish is sold at stalls on the road to the hospital and the lighthouse, on the far side of the harbour from the dock.

Pharmacy Farmacia Greco on Piazza Cavour (Mon–Fri 8.30am–1pm & 5–8.30pm; ☎0923.911.310). Pharmacies operate on a rota outside normal opening hours, noted on the door.

Police Carabinieri, Via Trieste 29 ☎0923.911.109.

Post office The island's main post office is off Piazza Cavour on Via de Amicis (Mon–Fri 8am–1.30pm, Sat 8am–12.30pm).

Shopping A couple of good ceramicists work on Pantelleria, and shops at the harbour sell decent stuff. Look out for local Moscato and passito wines and capers. You can find these and much more, including home-made marmalade, olive paste, preserved seaweed and pasta sauces, at Emporio del Gusto on Via Catania.

Taxi Consolo, Piazza Castello ☎0923.912.716 or 339.715.7586.

Tours Excursions by jeep, on foot and on horseback are organized by the Gira l'Ísola agency at Vícolo Messina 21 (☎0923.913.254), from about €30 per person. Cooperativa Uros (☎ 327.363.9284) conducts tours all over the island, including archeological and gastronomic tours, from €15 per person.

Travel agency La Cossira, Via Borgo Italia 77 ☎ 0923.911.078 (for airline tickets).

Around the island

Surprisingly, most of Pantelleria's population of 8500 are farmers rather than fishermen. With a soil nourished by frequent past eruptions (the last in 1831), the islanders traditionally preferred tilling to risking life and limb in a sea swarming with pirates on the prowl. Farming on Pantelleria does have its problems, however, not least the numerous chunks of lava and basalt in the earth that preclude mechanical ploughing, not to mention the incessant wind, scorching sun and almost complete lack of water. The islanders have come up with methods of minimizing these disadvantages by some ingenious devices that would bring a gleam to an ecologist's eye. The prolific *zibbibo* vines are individually planted in little ridges designed to capture the precious rainwater; and the famous *giardini arabi* – high walls of stone built round orange trees and other plants – afford protection from the wind and the salt it carries with it. All over the island, various **cooperatives** (often signposted from the road) sell homegrown produce to visitors and locals – capers, wine, jojoba oil, honey and candles. If you want to buy, look for the words "*azienda agricola*".

Otherwise, it's a blackened landscape, thick with volcanic debris, in which the local **dammuso** houses, when whitewashed, provide some visual relief. Unembellished, these sombre cubic dwellings, unique to the island, blend in perfectly with their environment. These, too, are examples of technological adaptation, the thick walls and shallow-domed roofs designed to maintain a cool internal temperature, while ridges in the roofs catch the rain.

It's easy enough to get around the island by bus or bike, but to visit the isolated coves of the southeastern Dietro Ísola, and other good swimming spots, you'll need to **rent a boat**. There are notices in the agencies along the harbour, in every hotel, and on the boats themselves. If you don't want to navigate yourself, you'll find **boat tours** from the port.

Along the southwest coast

Up to nine daily buses run along the **southwest coast** to Scauri and Rekale. If you intend to walk any stretch, you're advised to take the bus first to Scauri (20min) and then walk back as far as the Sesi (see opposite), which takes a couple of hours or so.

Eating and drinking on Pantelleria

With its mix of Sicilian and North African elements, Pantelleria offers some unique gastronomic experiences. At some point, you ought to sample the locally produced ricotta-type cheese known as *tumma*, which is one of the ingredients of ravioli *con menta e ricotta*, a slightly bitter but fresh-tasting dish for which Pantelleria is famous. Pasta often comes served with *pesto pantesco*, a rough sauce of tomatoes, garlic and basil; while an *insalata pantesca* utilizes tomatoes, onions, cubes of boiled potato, herbs and local capers – the local capers are touted as the best in the Mediterranean.

The island's **wine** is well thought of too, made from the *zibbibo* grapes that grow well in this volcanic soil. The day-to-day drinking stuff – *vino pantesco* – is mostly white, with a nice fruity fragrance, while for something considerably stronger try the fortified Moscato, a sweet, amber-coloured dessert wine. Even better is the raisin wine, known generically as *passito*, which has a rich golden colour and a dry and heady flavour – the best-known variety is Tanit.

The route south of town is initially very unpromising, through an industrial wasteland of noisome and noisy factories, abandoned farmhouses and past a military barracks. Things pick up after a couple of kilometres at the **Cuddie Rosse**, volcanic red rocks that mark the site of a prehistoric cave settlement. There's nothing much to see, but the rocks are overlooked by the good-value *Cossyra Hotel* (☎0923.911.217, ⓦwww.mursiahotel.it; closed Nov–April; ❸), with a pool; half board is usually obligatory in August (€100 per person).

Fifteen minutes' walk further on, a signposted track on the left leads up 300m to the first of the island's strange **Sesi**, massive black Neolithic funeral mounds of piled rock, with low passages leading inside; a second one lies further up to the left. They're thought to be products of Pantelleria's first settlers, possibly from Tunisia. The main one here is 6m high, a striking sight, completely at one with its lunar-like environment. Scores of these must once have dotted the island, satisfying some primeval fears and beliefs. That so few survive is not so hard to understand when you take a look around at the regular-shaped stones from which the *dammuso* houses are built – centuries of plunder have taken their toll.

Beyond the Sesi, at **Punta Fram**, the posh *Villaggio Punta Fram* (☎0923.917.000, ⓦwww.aurumhotels.it; closed mid-Sept to mid-May), has a tennis court, a fine outdoor swimming pool and steps leading down to its own little rocky cove, where guests can swim happily. Full board is required, at €126 per person in high season. There's public access to the coast here, just back down the road a little way towards the Sesi; look for a footpath, marked "*Discesa a mare*", opposite a side road to a little tower.

On foot, it's just over an hour all told from the Sesi to **Sataria**, where concrete steps lead down to a tiny square-cut sea-pool, ideal for splashing around in. In the cave behind are more pools where warm water bubbles through, reputed to be good for curing rheumatism and skin diseases: a handful of people can usually be found jumping from pools to sea. There's room on the concrete apron around the pool to lay out a towel, and it's the only place for kilometres around with any shade – a nice place to eat your picnic.

From the port at **Scauri**, 2km (30min on foot) further on, you can see Cape Mustafa in Tunisia on a clear day. There's a nice **bar-restaurant** here, *La Vela* (☎0923.916.566; closed Nov–Easter), with a terrace right on the portside, where you can eat ravioli with ricotta and mint, grilled fish and sweet, ricotta-filled *baci*. The village itself is a steep twenty-minute walk above its harbour, and consists of no more than a minuscule church perched on a shelf of land, surrounded by a cluster of houses; it does at least hold a bakery and pharmacy, as well as an *alimentari* that does decent panini. On the way up, you'll pass *La Nicchia* (☎0923.916.342; closed lunchtime, also Wed except July & Aug, and all Nov–Easter), one of the island's most renowned eateries. You can dine inside or in the garden beneath the shade of an old orange tree, with such dishes as shrimps in a *zibbio* sauce and the island speciality, mint-and-*tumma*-stuffed ravioli bathed in sage butter. It's quite pricey, though, and worth dressing up for.

From here, the only other stop (and end of the bus line) is **Rekale**, an even smaller and more remote hamlet, beyond which the extensive southeastern segment of the island, the **Dietro Ísola**, curves round. Further hot springs at **Punto Nikà** are most easily reached by boat, though you can get there on foot.

The northeast coast

Eight or nine daily buses run along the northeast coast to both Khamma and Tracino. The latter village marks the end of the line, a thirty-minute ride from town.

Very early on you'll pass **Bue Marino**, which, though not the most striking part of this coast, has reasonable swimming from the rocks. It also offers accommodation, in the shape of the *Hotel Turistico Residenziale* (☏0923.911.054, ⓦwww.fortuna toerrera.it; ❸), each of whose 28 rooms has a fridge, terrace and independent entrance. The best swimming is actually a little further on, from the flat rocks below the road junction to Bugeber.

East of here lies the **Cala dei Cinque Denti**, where fantastic-shaped rocks jut out of the sea like monstrous black teeth – hence its name, "Bay of the Five Teeth" (though the rocks are really best seen from the sea). Just beyond, a minor road cuts away to the lighthouse at **Punta Spadillo**, where the cliff edges are covered with a carpet of surprising greenery that's somehow taken hold in the volcanic rocks.

At a fork further on in the road, the bus can drop you at the top of the smartly engineered route down into **Gadir**, one of the most perfect spots on Pantelleria. It's a small anchorage, with just a few houses hemmed in by volcanic pricks of rock, which – when the wind is up – can be battered and lashed by violent waves. At other times, people lay about on the flat concrete harbourside, and splash in the small thermal pools hereabouts.

The lower road from Gadir to Tracino is one of the loveliest on the island, following slopes that are terraced and corralled behind a patchwork of stone walls. Vines grow in profusion, with capers and blackberry bushes in the hedgerows. It's an easy, fairly flat hour's stroll to the charming **Cala Levante**, a huddle of houses around another tiny fishing harbour. There's good swimming from the rocks – provided the sea's not too rough – and a **bar-restaurant** above, the *Cala Levante* (☏0923.691.134; closed Oct–April), with a terrace overlooking the sea. Where the road peters out, bear right along the path at the second anchorage and keep along the coast for another five minutes to view the **Arco dell'Elefante**, or "Elephant Arch", named after the lovely hooped formation of rock that resembles an elephant stooping to drink. Again there's no beach, but it's a good place to swim anyway.

From the harbour, a stupendously steep road climbs all the way up to **Tracino** in around twenty minutes, passing old *dammusi*, newer holiday homes, and striking gardens of vines and flowers. The top of the road marks the centre of Tracino, where there's a small square and a bar-restaurant. It's difficult to see where Tracino ends and adjacent **Khamma** starts, though this matters little once you're on the bus back to town.

Keen **hikers** make Tracino the start of their route into the pretty **Piano Ghirlandia**. The road runs out the other side of Tracino and soon becomes a track, which continues all the way down to meet the road on the south coast near Rekale.

The Specchio di Vénere and Bugeber

From the first road junction on the northwest coast, it's a ten-minute walk up and around before you get the initial stunning views of the island's small lake, **Specchio di Vénere** (Venus's Mirror), shimmering below in a former crater. Though it glistens aquamarine in the middle, it has a muddy-brown edge, deposits of which you're supposed to apply to your body and allow to bake hard in the sun. Then you dive in and swim, washing all the mud off in the pleasantly warm water. A path skirts the edge of the lake, around which horse races take place every August as part of the *ferragosto* celebrations.

Beyond the lake, the road climbs up for another 2km to the hamlet of **Bugeber**, set amid tumbling fields of vines and craggy boulders. The bus back to town runs past here three times a day; alternatively, walk the 3km past the lake back to the main road, where you can pick up any of the buses from Tracino.

Siba and the Montagna Grande

The other inland destination is the highest reaches of Pantelleria's main volcano, the Montagna Grande, whose summit is the island's most distinctive feature when seen from out at sea. Buses (four daily Mon–Sat) run from the port, turning sharp left past the airport for the crumbly old village of **SIBA**, perched on a ridge below the volcano, with views over the terraced slopes and cultivated plains to the sea. Few of the ancient *dammusi* here are so much as whitewashed, let alone bristling with mod cons. Outside, large wooden water barrels sit on the mildewed dry-stone volcanic walls, while the hamlet's only services are an *alimentari* and a *tabacchino*. If time hasn't exactly stood still here, it's in no great hurry to get on with things either.

To climb the peak of **Montagna Grande** (836m), keep left at the telephone sign by the *tabacchino* here, and strike off the main road. The mountain's slopes afford the best views on the island, and are pitted by numerous volcanic vents, the **Stufe de Khazen**, marked by escaping threads of vapour.

From Siba, another (signposted) path – on the left as you follow the road through the village – brings you in around twenty minutes to a natural sauna, **Sauna Naturale** (or Bagno Asciutto), where you can sweat it out for as long as you can stand. It's little more than a slit in the rock-face, where you can crouch in absolute darkness, breaking out into a heavy sweat as soon as you enter. It's coolest at floor-level; raising yourself up is like putting yourself into a pizza oven, while the ceiling is so hot it's impossible to keep the palm of your hand pressed flat against it. Ten minutes is the most you should attempt the first time – emerging into the midday sun is like being wafted by a cool breeze. Bring a towel.

From the road that descends from Siba to Scauri and the coast, you can take a track off to the left that runs through the so-called **Valle Monastero**. This lovely route leads past the abandoned monastery which gives the valley its name. Make sure you carry enough water if you tackle this hike, which is best accomplished early in the day. The path meets the road midway between Scauri and Rekale.

Travel details

Trains

Castelvetrano to: Marsala (11 daily Mon–Sat, 5 daily Sun; 40min); Mazara del Vallo (11 daily Mon–Sat, 5 daily Sun; 20min); Palermo (6 daily Mon–Sat, 4 daily Sun; 2hr 30min–3hr; may involve change); Trápani (11 daily Mon–Sat, 5 daily Sun; 1hr 15min).

Marsala to: Castelvetrano (12 daily Mon–Sat, 6 daily Sun; 45min); Mazara del Vallo (12 daily Mon–Sat, 6 daily Sun; 20min); Palermo (6 daily Mon–Sat, 4 daily Sun; 3hr 10min; may involve change); Trápani (13 daily Mon–Sat, 5 daily Sun; 30min).

Mazara del Vallo to: Campobello di Mazara (13 daily Mon–Sat, 6 daily Sun; 10min); Castelvetrano (13 daily Mon–Sat, 6 daily Sun; 20min); Marsala (12 daily Mon–Sat, 5 daily Sun; 20min); Palermo (5 daily Mon–Sat, 4 daily Sun; 2hr 40min–3hr; may involve change); Trápani (12 daily Mon–Sat, 5 daily Sun; 50min).

Trápani to: Castelvetrano (11 daily Mon–Sat, 6 daily Sun; 1hr 10min); Marsala (13 daily Mon–Sat, 6 daily Sun; 30min); Mazara del Vallo (13 daily Mon–Sat, 6 daily Sun; 40min–1hr); Palermo (6 daily Mon–Sat, 4 daily Sun; 2hr 15min–4hr); Segesta-Tempio (3–4 daily; 25min).

Buses

Castellammare del Golfo to: Álcamo (12 daily Mon–Sat; 25min); Calatafimi (5–6 daily Mon–Sat; 30min); Palermo (5–9 daily Mon–Sat, 1–3 daily Sun; 1hr 10min–1hr 40min); San Vito Lo Capo (2–4 daily Mon–Sat, 1–3 daily Sun; 1hr–1hr 30min); Scopello (4–8 daily Mon–Sat, 4 daily Sun in summer; 30min); Segesta (2 daily; 40min); Trápani (4–5 daily Mon–Sat; 1hr–1hr 20min).

Castelvetrano to: Agrigento (3 daily Mon–Sat, 1 daily Sun; 1hr 40min–2hr 25min); Campobello (7–11 daily Mon–Sat, 4–6 daily Sun; 25min); Gibellina (1 daily Mon–Sat; 1hr); Marinella (for Selinunte, 5–8 daily; 25min); Marsala (9 daily Mon–Sat; 1hr–1hr 15min); Mazara del Vallo (9 daily Mon–Sat; 30–40min); Palermo (10 daily Mon–Sat, 2–3 daily Sun; 1hr 45min); Salemi (1 daily Mon–Sat; 1hr 15min); Sciacca (3 daily Mon–Sat, 1 daily Sun; 30–50min); Trápani (4 daily Mon–Sat; 2hr 15min).

Érice to: Trápani (7–8 daily Mon–Sat, 4 daily Sun; 45min).

Marinella/Selinunte to: Castelvetrano (5–8 daily; 30min).

Marsala to: Agrigento (3 daily Mon–Sat, 1 daily Sun; 2hr 25min–3hr); Campobello (4 daily Mon–Sat; 55min); Castelvetrano (7 daily Mon–Sat; 1hr 15min); Mazara del Vallo (1–2 hourly Mon–Sat, 4 daily Sun; 30min); Palermo (1–2 hourly Mon–Sat, 7–9 daily Sun; 2hr 30min); Salemi (2 daily Mon–Sat, 1 daily Sun; 35min); Sciacca (3 daily Mon–Sat, 1 daily Sun; 1hr–1hr 30min); Trápani (4 daily Mon–Sat; 55min–1hr 15min); Trápani airport (1–4 daily Mon–Sat, 2 daily Sun; 15min).

Mazara del Vallo to: Agrigento (3 daily Mon–Sat, 1 daily Sun; 2hr–2hr 40min); Campobello (3 daily Mon–Sat; 20min); Castelvetrano (3 daily Mon–Sat; 40min); Marsala (1–2 hourly Mon–Sat, 4 daily Sun; 30min); Palermo (8–14 daily Mon–Sat, 2–6 daily Sun; 2hr–2hr 35min); Trápani (4 daily Mon–Sat; 1hr 30min–1hr 45min).

Pantelleria Town to: Bugeber (3 daily; 20min); Khamma (9 daily Mon–Sat; 25min); Rekale (9 daily Mon–Sat; 20min); Scauri (9 daily Mon–Sat; 20min); Siba (4 daily Mon–Sat; 30min); Tracino (9 daily Mon–Sat; 30min).

San Vito Lo Capo to: Palermo (summer 3–4 daily; winter 1–2 daily; 2–3hr); Trápani (8–9 Mon–Sat, 4 daily Sun in summer; 1hr 20min).

Scopello to: Castellammare del Golfo (4–8 daily Mon–Sat, 4 daily Sun in summer; 40–55min).

Trápani to: Agrigento (3 daily Mon–Sat, 1 daily Sun; 3hr 10min–3hr 40min); Álcamo (2–3 daily Mon–Sat; 1hr); Bonagia (7 daily Mon–Sat, 3 daily Sun in summer; 25min); Castellammare del Golfo (5 daily; 1hr–1hr 20min); Castelvetrano (5 daily Mon–Sat; 2hr 15min); Érice (7–8 daily Mon–Sat, 4 daily Sun; 45min); Marsala (3 daily Mon–Sat; 45min); Mazara del Vallo (3 daily Mon–Sat; 1hr 30min); Palermo (1–2 hourly Mon–Sat, 14 daily Sun; 2hr); Palermo airport (4 daily; 1hr); San Vito Lo Capo (8–9 daily

Mon–Sat, 4 daily Sun in summer; 1hr 20min); Segesta (2 daily Mon–Sat, 1 daily Sun; 50min); Trápani airport (1–2 hourly; 20–40min).

Trápani airport to: Agrigento (3 daily Mon–Sat, 1 daily Sun; 2hr 45min–3hr 20min); Marsala (1–4 daily Mon–Sat, 2 daily Sun; 15min); Palermo (6–8 daily; 2hr 10min); Trápani (1–2 hourly; 20–40min).

Ferries

Pantelleria to: Trápani (1 daily June–Sept, 1 daily Mon–Sat Oct–May; 5hr 45min).

Trápani to: Cágliari (1 weekly; 10hr); Civitavécchia (1 weekly; 13hr 30min); Favignana (June–Sept 3 daily; Oct–May 1–2 daily; 1hr–1hr 25min); Lévanzo (3 daily June–Sept, 1–2 daily Oct–May; 50min–1hr 40min); Maréttimo (1 daily; 2hr 35min–2hr 50min); Pantelleria (1 daily June–Sept, 1 daily Sun–Fri Oct–May; 5hr 45min); Tunis (1 weekly; 7hr 30min).

Hydrofoils and fast ferries

Marsala to: Favignana (5 daily June–Sept, 3 daily Oct–May; 30min); Maréttimo (3 daily June–Sept; 1hr 10min–2hr 15min).

Mazara del Vallo to: Pantelleria (12 weekly June to mid-Oct; 2hr).

Pantelleria to: Lampedusa (July to mid-Sept 3 weekly; 2hr 45min); Mazara del Vallo (12 weekly June to mid-Oct; 2hr).

Trápani to: Favignana (hourly; 15–40min); Lévanzo (hourly; 20–40min); Maréttimo (4–5 daily; 1hr–1hr 25min); Naples (3–4 weekly June–Sept; 6hr 45min); Ústica (3–4 weekly June–Sept; 2hr 30min).

Flights

Pantelleria to: Palermo (2–3 daily; 50min); Trápani (3 daily; 40min).

Trápani to: Pantelleria (3 daily; 40min).

9

TRÁPANI AND THE WEST | Travel details

Contexts

Contexts

Sicily's history

S icily has a richer and more eventful past than any of the other islands
dotted around the Mediterranean. Its strategic importance made it the
constant prey of conquerors, many of whom, while contributing a rich
artistic heritage, also turned Sicily into one of the most desolate war zones
in Europe, their greed utterly transforming its ecology and heaping misery onto
the vast majority of its inhabitants.

Early times

Numerous remains survive of the earliest human settlements in Sicily. The most
interesting of these are the cave paintings in Addaura, on the northern face of
Monte Pellegrino, and those in the Grotta del Genovese, on Lévanzo in the Égadi
Islands, which give a graphic insight into late Ice Age **Paleolithic** culture, from
between 20,000 and 10,000 BC.

During the later **Neolithic period**, between 4000 and 3000 BC, a wave of
settlers arrived from the eastern Mediterranean, landing on Sicily's east coast and
in the Aeolian Islands. Examples of their relatively advanced culture – incised
and patterned pottery and simple tools – are displayed in the museum on Lípari
in the Aeolians. Agricultural advances, the use of ceramics and the domesti-
cation of animals, as well as the new techniques of metalworking imported
by later waves of Aegean immigrants in the **Copper Age** (3000–2000 BC),
permitted the establishment of fixed farms and villages. In turn, this caused
an expansion of trade, and promoted greater contact with far-flung Mediterranean cultures. The presence of Mycenaean ware from the Greek mainland
became more noticeable during the **Bronze Age** (2000–1000 BC), an era to
which the sites of Capo Graziano and Punta Milazzese on the Aeolian Islands
belong. In about 1250 BC, further population movements took place, this time
originating from the Italian mainland: the Ausonians settled in the Aeolians
and the **Sikels** in eastern Sicily, pushing the indigenous tribes inland. It was the
Sikels, from whom Sicily takes its name, who are thought to have first dug the
vast necropolis of Pantálica, near Siracusa. At about the same time, the Sicans,
a people believed to have originated in North Africa, occupied the western
half of the island, as did the **Elymians**, who claimed descent from Trojan
refugees: their chief city, Segesta, was alleged to have been founded by Aeneas'
companion, Acestes.

The Carthaginians and the Greeks

After about 900 BC, Mycenaean and Aegean trading contacts began to be
replaced by **Carthaginian** ones from North Africa, particularly in the west of
the island. The Carthaginians – originally Phoenicians from the eastern Mediterranean – first settled at Panormus (modern Palermo), Solus (Solunto) and Motya
(Mózia) during the eighth and seventh centuries BC. Their arrival coincided
with the establishment of Aegean **Greek colonies** in the east of Sicily, driven

by a shortage of cultivable land back home and beginning with the colonization of **Naxos** in 734 BC. The Chalcidinians and Naxians who founded this colony were quickly followed by Megarians at **Megara Hyblaea**, Corinthians at **Ortigia** (Siracusa), and Rhodians, Cnidians and Cretans in **Gela**. While continuing to have close links with their original homes, these cities became independent city-states and founded sub-colonies of their own, most important of which were **Selinus** (Selinunte) and **Akragas** (Agrigento). Along with the Greek colonies on the Italian mainland, these scattered communities came to be known as Magna Graecia, "Greater Greece".

The settlers found themselves with huge resources at their disposal, not least the island's fertility, which they quickly exploited through the widespread cultivation of corn – so much so that Demeter, the Greek goddess of grain and fecundity, became the chief deity on the island (the lake at Pergusa, near Enna, was claimed to be the site of the abduction of her daughter, Persephone). The olive and the vine were introduced from Greece, and commercial activity across the Ionian Sea was intense and profitable. The magnificence of the temples at Syracuse and Akragas often surpassed that of the major shrines in Greece.

But the settlers also imported their native rivalries, and the history of Hellenic Sicily is one of almost uninterrupted warfare between the cities, even if they did generally join forces in the face of common foes such as the Carthaginians. It was the alliance against Carthage of Gela, Akragas and Syracuse, and the resulting Greek victory at **Himera** in 480 BC, that determined the ascendancy of **Syracuse** in Sicily for the next 270 years. The defeat, in about 450 BC, of a rebellion led by **Ducetius**, a Hellenized Sikel, extinguished the remnants of any native resistance to Greek hegemony, and the century which followed has been hailed as the "Golden Age" of Greek Sicily.

The accumulation of power by Syracusan **tyrants** attracted the attention of the mainland Greek states; Athens in particular was worried by the rapid spread of Corinthian influence in Sicily. In 415 BC, Athens dispatched the greatest armada ever to have sailed from its port. Later known as the **Great Expedition**, the effort was in response to a call for help from its ally, Segesta, while at war with Syracuse-supported Selinus. By 413 BC Syracuse itself was under siege, but the disorganization of the attacking forces, who were further hampered by disease, led to their total defeat, the execution of their generals and the imprisonment of 7000 soldiers in Syracuse's limestone quarries. This victory represented the apogee of Syracusan power. Civil wars continued throughout the rest of the island, attracting the attention of the Carthaginians, who responded to attacks on their territory by sacking in turn Selinus, Himera, Akragas and Gela. A massive counterattack was launched by the Syracusan tyrant **Dionysius I**, or "the Elder" (405–367 BC). That culminated in the complete destruction of the Phoenician base at **Motya**; its survivors founded a new centre at Lilybaeum, modern Marsala, on the western tip of the island.

The general devastation in Sicily caused by these wars was to some extent reversed by **Timoleon** (345–336 BC), who rebuilt many of the cities and re-established democratic institutions. But the carnage continued under the tyrant **Agathocles** (315–289 BC), who was unrivalled in his sheer brutality. Battles were fought on the Italian mainland and North Africa, and the strife he engendered back in Sicily didn't end until **Hieron II** (265–215 BC) opted for a policy of peace-keeping, and even alliance, with the new power of the day, Rome.

The **First Punic War** – which broke out in 264 BC after the mercenary army in control of Messina, the **Mamertines**, appealed to Rome for help against their erstwhile Carthaginian protectors – left Syracuse itself untouched. It did however once again lead to the ruin of much of the island, before the final surrender of the Carthaginian base at Lilybaeum in 241. For Syracuse and its territories though, this was a period of relative peace, and Hieron used the breathing space to construct some of the city's most impressive monuments.

Roman Sicily

Roman rule in Sicily can be said to have begun with **the fall of Syracuse**. That momentous event became inevitable when the city, whose territory was by now the only part of Sicily still independent of Rome, chose to side with Carthage in the **Second Punic War**, provoking a two-year siege that ended with the sacking of Syracuse in 211 BC. For the next seven hundred years, Sicily was a province of Rome, though in effect a subject colony, since few Sicilians were granted citizenship until the third century AD, when all inhabitants of the empire were classified as Romans. The island became Rome's granary or, as Cato had it, "the nurse at whose breast the Roman people is fed". As a key strategic province, Sicily suddenly became susceptible to age-old Roman political intrigue, notably during the **civil war** between Octavian, the future Emperor Augustus, and Sextus Pompey, who seized Sicily in 44 BC. For eight years the island's crucial grain exports were interrupted, and the final defeat of Sextus – in a sea battle off Mylae, or Milazzo – was followed by harsh retribution.

Once Octavian was installed as emperor, in 27 BC, Sicily entered a more peaceful period of Roman rule, with isolated instances of imperial splendour, notably the extravagant villa at Casale, near Piazza Armerina. The island benefited especially from its important role in Mediterranean trade, and Syracuse, which handled much of the passing traffic, became a prominent centre of **early Christianity**, supposedly visited by Sts Peter and Paul on their way to Rome. Here, and further

Life in Roman Sicily

Much of the island's present appearance was determined during the Roman period. Forests were cut down to make way for grain cultivation, and the land was apportioned into large units, or **latifondia**, which became the basis for the vast agricultural estates into which Sicily is still to a certain extent divided. Conditions on these estates were so harsh that the second century BC saw two **slave revolts**, in 135–132 BC and 104–101 BC, involving tens of thousands of men, women and children, most of whom had been Greek-speaking citizens from all over Rome's newly won Mediterranean and Asian empire. These were isolated incidents, however, and on the whole Sicily benefited from the relative calm bestowed by the Romans. But little of the heavy tribute exacted by Rome was expended on the island itself and, though a degree of local **administration** existed, all important decisions were taken by the Roman Senate. That was represented on the island by two tax collectors, or quaestors, stationed in Syracuse and Lilybaeum, and a governor (praetor), who normally spent his year-long term extracting as much personal profit from the island as he could. The praetor **Verres** used his three terms of office, from 73 to 71 BC, to strip the countryside and despoil a large part of the treasure still held in the island's lavish temples. **Cicero's** prosecution of Verres, though undoubtedly exaggerated, constitutes our main source of information on Sicily under the Roman Republic: "When I arrived in Sicily after an absence of four years, it seemed to me a land in which there had been fought a prolonged and cruel war. Those fields and hills which I had seen bright and green I now saw devastated and deserted, and it seemed as if the land itself wept for its ancient farmers."

inland at Akrai, catacombs were burrowed from the third century AD onwards – and in caves throughout Sicily, Christian sanctuaries took their place alongside the shrines of the dozens of other cults prevalent on the island.

Barbarians, Byzantines and the Arabs

Though Rome fell to the Visigoths in 410 AD, Sicily became prey to another Germanic tribe, the **Vandals**, who launched their invasion from the North African coast. The island was soon reunited with Italy under the Ostrogoth Theodoric, but the barbarian presence in Sicily was only a brief interlude, terminated in 535 AD when the **Byzantine** general Belisarius occupied the island. Although a part of the population had been Latinized, Greek remained the dominant culture and language of the majority, and the island willingly joined the Byzantine fold.

Constantinople was never able to give much attention to Sicily, however. The island was perpetually harried by piratical attacks, particularly from North Africa, where the Moors had become the most dynamic force in the Mediterranean. In around 700, the island of **Pantelleria** was taken, and only discord among the Arabs prevented Sicily itself from being next. In the event, trading agreements were signed, Arab merchants settled in Sicilian ports, and a fully fledged **Arab invasion** did not take place until 827, when a Byzantine admiral rebelled against the emperor and invited in the Aghlabid Emir of Tunisia. Ten thousand Arabs, Berbers and Spanish Muslims (known collectively as **Saracens**) landed at Mazara del Vallo, and Palermo fell four years later, though the invading forces only reached the Straits of Messina in 965. As with the Roman invasion, however, the turning point came with the fall of Syracuse in 878, when its population was massacred and the city plundered of its legendary wealth.

Palermo became the capital of the **Arabs in Sicily**, under whom it grew to become one of the world's greatest cities, wholly cosmopolitan in outlook, furnished with gardens, mosques (more than anywhere the traveller Ibn Hauqal had seen, barring Cordoba) and luxurious palaces. The Arabs brought great benefits to the rest of the island, too, renovating and extending irrigation works, breaking down many of the unwieldy *latifondia* and introducing new crops, including citrus trees, sugar cane, flax, cotton, silk, melons and date palms. Mining was developed, the salt industry greatly expanded and commerce improved, with Sicily once more at the centre of a flourishing trade network. Many Sicilian place names testify to the extent of the Arab settlement of the island. Prefixes such as *calta* (castle) and *gibil* (mountain) are plentiful, while other terms still in use indicate their impact on fishing, such as the name of the swordfish boats prowling the Straits of Messina (*felucca*), or the tuna-fishing terminology of the Égadi Islands. Taxation was rationalized and reduced, and religious tolerance was greater than under the Byzantines (though non-Muslims were subject to a degree of social discrimination).

The Arabs were prone to divisive feuding, however, and when in the tenth century the Aghlabid dynasty was toppled in Tunisia and their Fatimid successors shifted their capital to Egypt, Sicily lost its central position in the Arab Mediterranean empire and was left vulnerable to external attack. In 1038, the Byzantine general **George Maniakes** attempted to draw the island back under Byzantine sway, but he was unable to extend his occupation much beyond Syracuse. The real threat came from western Europe, particularly from the **Normans**, some of whom had accompanied Maniakes and seen for themselves the rewards to be gained. One of these, William "Bras de Fer" ("Iron Arm"), who had earned his nickname by his slaying of the Emir of Syracuse with one blow, was the eldest of the Hauteville brothers, whose exploits were soon to change the map of southern Europe.

The Normans

The **Hauteville brothers** had long been active in southern Italy by the time the youngest of them, Roger, seized Messina in 1061 in response to a call for help by one of the warring Arab factions. It took another thirty years to take control of the whole island, in a series of bloody and destructive campaigns that often involved the enlistment of Arabs on the Norman side. In 1072 Palermo was captured and adopted as the capital of **Norman Sicily**, and was subsequently adorned with palaces and churches that count among their most brilliant achievements.

The most striking thing about the Norman period in Sicily is its brief span. In little more than a century, five kings bequeathed an enormous legacy of art and architecture that is still one of the most conspicuous features of the island. When compared with the surviving remains of the Byzantines, who reigned for three centuries, or the Arabs, whose occupation lasted roughly two, the Norman contribution stands out, principally due to its absorption of previous styles: the finest examples of Arab art to be seen in Sicily are elements incorporated into the great Norman churches. It was this fusion of talent that accounted for the great success of Norman Sicily, not just in the arts but in administration, justice and religious tolerance. The policy of integration was largely determined by force of circumstances: the Normans could not count on having adequate numbers of their own settlers, or bureaucrats to form a governmental class, and instead were compelled to rely on the existing framework. They did, however, gradually introduce a Latinized aristocracy and clerical hierarchy from northern Italy and France, so that the Arabic language was largely superseded by Italian and French by 1200.

The first of the great Sicilian-Norman dynasty was **Count Roger**, or Roger I. He was a resolute and successful ruler, marrying his daughters into two of the most powerful European dynasties, one of them to the son of the western (or Holy Roman) emperor Henry IV. Roger's death in 1101, followed soon after by the death of his eldest son, left Sicily governed by his widow Adelaide as regent for his younger son, who in 1130 was crowned **Roger II**. This first Norman king of Sicily was also one of medieval Europe's most gifted and charismatic rulers, who made the island a great melting pot of the most vigorous and creative elements in the Mediterranean world. He spoke Greek, kept a harem and surrounded himself with a medley of advisers, notably **George of Antioch**, his chief minister, or Emir of Emirs. Roger extended his kingdom to encompass all of southern Italy, Malta and parts of North Africa, and more enduringly drew up the first written code of law in the island.

His son, William I (1154–66) – "**William the Bad**" – dissipated these achievements by his enthusiasm for pleasure-seeking and his failure to control the barons, who exploited racial tensions to undermine the king's authority. During the regency that followed, the Englishman Walter of the Mill had himself elected archbishop of Palermo and dominated the scene for some twenty years, along with two other Englishmen, his brother Bartholomew and Bishop Palmer. This triumvirate preserved a degree of stability, but also encouraged the new king William II (1166–89), "**William the Good**", to establish a second archbishopric and construct a cathedral at **Monreale** to rival that of Palermo, just 10km away. The period saw a shift away from Muslim influence, though Arabs still constituted the bulk of the rural population and William himself resembled an oriental sultan in his style and habits, building a number of Arab-style palaces.

The death of William, aged only 36 and with no obvious successor, signalled a crisis in Norman Sicily. The barons were divided between **Tancred**, William's illegitimate nephew, and **Constance**, Roger II's aunt, who had married the Hohenstaufen (or Swabian) Henry, later to become the Holy Roman Emperor Henry VI. Tancred's election by an assembly was the first sign of a serious erosion of the king's authority: others followed, notably a campaign in 1189 against Muslims living on the island, which caused many of them to flee; and a year later the sacking of **Messina** by the English Richard I, on his way to join the Third Crusade. Tancred's death in 1194 and the succession of his young son, **William III**, coincided with the arrival in the Straits of Messina of the Hohenstaufen fleet. Opposition was minimal, and on Christmas Day of the same year Henry crowned himself king of Sicily. William and his mother were imprisoned in the castle at Caltabellotta, never to be seen again.

Hohenstaufen and the Angevins

Inevitably, Henry's imperial concerns led him away from Sicily, which represented only a source of revenue for him on the very outer limits of his domain. A revolt broke out against his authoritarian rule, which he repressed with extreme severity, but in the middle of it he went down with dysentery, died, and the throne passed to his three-and-a-half-year-old son, who became the emperor Frederick II, **Frederick I** of Sicily.

At first the running of the kingdom was entrusted to Frederick's mother Constance, but there was little stability, with the barons in revolt and a rash of race riots in 1197. Frederick's assumption of the government in 1220 marked a return to decisive leadership, with an immediate campaign to bring the barons to heel and eliminate a Muslim rebellion in Sicily's interior. The twin aims of his rule in Sicily were to restore the broad framework of the Norman state, and to impose a more imperial stamp on society, indicated by his fondness for classical Roman allusions in his promulgations and coinage. He allowed himself rights and privileges in Sicily that were impossible in his other possessions, emphasizing his own authority at the expense of the independence of the clergy and the autonomy of the cities. As elsewhere in southern Italy, strong **castles** were built, such as those at Milazzo, Catania, Siracusa and Augusta, to keep the municipalities in check.

A unified legal system was drawn up, embodied in his *Liber Augustales*, while his attempts to homogenize Sicilian society involved the harsh treatment of what had now become minority communities, such as the Muslims. He encouraged the arts, too, championing Sicilian vernacular poetry, whose pre-eminence was admitted by Petrarch and Dante. Frederick acquired the name **"Stupor Mundi"** ("Wonder of the World"), reflecting his promotion of science, law and medicine, and the peace that Sicily enjoyed during the half-century of his rule.

However, the balance of power Frederick achieved within Sicily laid the foundations for many of the island's future woes – for example, the weakening of the municipalities at a time when most European towns were increasing their autonomy. His centralized government worked so long as there was a powerful hand to guide it, but when Frederick died in 1250, decline set in, despite the efforts of his son **Manfred**, who strove to defend his crown from the encroachments of the barons and the acquisitiveness of foreign monarchs. New claimants to the throne were egged on by Sicily's nominal suzerain, the pope, anxious to deprive the Hohenstaufen of their southern possession, and he eventually auctioned it, selling it to the king of England, who accepted it on behalf of his 8-year-old son, Edmund of Lancaster. For ten years Edmund was styled "King of Sicily".

But a new French pope deposed Edmund, who had never set foot in Sicily, and gave the title instead to **Charles of Anjou**, brother of the French king, "St" Louis IX. Backed by the papacy, Charles of Anjou embarked on a punitive campaign against the majority of the Sicilian population, who had supported the Hohenstaufen. He plundered land to give to his followers, and imposed a high level of taxation, though in the end it was a grassroots revolt that sparked off the **Sicilian Vespers**, an uprising against the French that began on Easter Monday 1282; it is traditionally held to have started after the bell for evening services, or Vespers, had rung at Palermo's church of Santo Spírito. The incident that sparked it all off was an insult to a woman by a French soldier, which led to a general slaughter in Palermo, soon growing into an island-wide rebellion against the French. This was the one moment in Sicilian history when the people rose up as one against foreign oppression – though in reality it was more an opportunity for horrific butchery and the settlement of old scores than a glorious expression of patriotic fervour.

The movement was given some direction when a group of nobles enlisted the support of **Peter of Aragon**, who landed at Trápani five months after the initial outbreak of hostilities and was acclaimed king at Palermo a few days later. The ensuing **Wars of the Vespers**, fought between Aragon and the Angevin forces based in Naples, lasted for another 21 years, mainly waged in Spain and at sea, while, in Aragonese Sicily, people settled down to over five centuries of Spanish domination.

The Spanish in Sicily

Sicily's new orientation towards Spain, and its severance from mainland Italy, meant that the island was largely excluded from all the great European developments of the fourteenth and fifteenth centuries. Large parts of Sicily were granted to the Spanish aristocracy, meaning a continuation of suffocating feudalism, and little impact was made by the Renaissance, while intellectual life on the island was stifled by the strictures of the Spanish Inquisition.

Although Peter of Aragon insisted that the two kingdoms of Aragon and Sicily should be ruled by separate kings after his death, his successor James reopened negotiations with the Angevins to sell the island back to them. His younger brother Frederick, appointed by James as Lieutenant of Palermo, convened a "parliament", which elected him king of an independent Sicily as **Frederick II** (1296–1337). Factions arose, growing out of the friction between Angevin and Aragonese supporters, and open warfare followed until 1372, when the independence of Sicily was guaranteed by Naples. Under the terms of the subsequent treaty the island became known as **Trinacria** ("three-cornered"), an ancient name revived to distinguish the island from the mainland Regnum Siciliae, ruled by the kingdom of Naples.

The constant feuding had laid waste to the countryside and the interior of Sicily became depopulated and unproductive, exacerbated by the effects of the Black Death. The feudal nobility lived mainly in the towns, building wealthy mansions in the **Chiaramonte** or the later, richly ornate Catalan-Gothic styles. A tradition of artistic patronage grew up, though most of the artists operating in Sicily came from elsewhere – for example, Francesco Laurana and the Gagini family were originally from northern Italy. A notable exception was **Antonello da Messina** (1430–79), who soaked up the latest Flemish techniques on his continental travels. Following the closing off of the eastern Mediterranean by the Ottoman Turks in the fifteenth century, Sicily was isolated from everywhere except Spain – from which, after 1410, it was ruled directly. Sicily found itself on the very fringes of Europe, and the unification of Castile and Aragon in 1479, followed soon after by the reconquest of the whole Spanish peninsula from the Moors, meant that Sicily's importance to its Spanish monarchs declined even further. The island came under the rule of a succession of **viceroys**, who were to wield power for the next four hundred years. Few of these were Sicilian (none at all after the first fifty years), while the only Spanish king to visit the island during the entire viceregal period was Charles V, on his way back from a Tunisian crusade in 1535.

The island's political bond to Spain meant that its degeneration deepened in tandem with Spain's decline in the seventeenth and eighteenth centuries. There were occasional revolts against the excesses of the zealous Inquisition, but on the whole discontent manifested itself in a resort to **brigandage**, for which the forest and wild maquis of Sicily's interior provided an ideal environment. The mixed fear and respect that the brigand bands generated played a large part in the future formation of an organized criminal class in Sicily.

Already burdened by the ever-increasing taxes demanded by Spain to finance its remote religious conflicts (principally, the 1618–48 Thirty Years' War), the misery of the Sicilians was compounded at the end of the seventeenth century by two appalling natural disasters. The **eruption of Etna** in 1669 devastated a large part of the area around Catania, while the **earthquake** of 1693 – also in the east of the island – flattened whole cities, and killed around five percent of the island's population. With the death of Charles II of Spain in 1700 and the subsequent Wars of the Spanish Succession, the island once more took a back seat to mainland European interests. It was bartered in the **Treaty of Utrecht** that negotiated the peace, and given to the northern Italian House of Savoy, only to be swapped for Sardinia and given to Austria seven years later.

The **Austrian government** of the island lasted only four years, cut short by the arrival of another Spaniard, **Charles of Bourbon**, who claimed the throne for himself. Although he never visited Sicily again after his first landing, **Charles III** (1734–59) brought a refreshingly constructive air to the island's administration, showing a more benevolent attitude towards his new subjects. But, with his succession to the Spanish throne in 1759 and the inheritance of the Neapolitan crown by his son, **Ferdinand IV**, it was back to the bad old days. Any meagre attempts at reform made by his viceroys were opposed at every turn by the reactionary local aristocracy, who were closing ranks in response to the progress of the Enlightenment and the ideas unleashed by the French Revolution. When the ensuing **Napoleonic Wars** wracked Europe, Sicily, along with Sardinia, was the only part of Italy not conquered by Napoleon, while the Neapolitan *ancien régime* was further buttressed by the decision of Ferdinand (brother-in-law of Marie Antoinette) to wage war against the revolutionary French. He was supported in this by the British, who sustained the Bourbon state, so that when Ferdinand and his court were forced to flee Naples in 1799, it was **Nelson's** flagship they sailed in, accompanied by the British ambassador to Naples, Sir William Hamilton, and his wife Lady Emma. Nelson was rewarded for his services by the endowment of a large estate at Bronte, just west of Etna.

Four years later, Ferdinand was able to return to Naples, though he had to escape again in 1806 when Napoleon gave the Neapolitan crown to his brother Joseph. This time he had to stay longer, remaining in Palermo until after the defeat of Napoleon in 1815 – a stay that was accompanied by a larger contingent of British troops and a heavy involvement of British capital and commerce. **Liberalism** became a banner of revolt against the king's continuing tax demands, and Ferdinand's autocratic reaction provoked the British commander William **Bentinck** to intervene. Manoeuvring himself into a position where he was the virtual governor of Sicily, Bentinck persuaded the king to summon a new parliament and adopt a **constitution** whereby the independence of Sicily was guaranteed and feudalism abolished.

Although this represented a drastic break with the past, the reforms had little direct effect on the peasantry, and, following the departure of the British, the constitution was dropped and Ferdinand (now styling himself Ferdinand I, King of the Two Sicilies) repealed all the reforms previously introduced. Renewed talk of independence in Sicily spilled over into action in 1820, when a rebellion was put down with the help of Austrian mercenaries. The **repression** intensified after Ferdinand I's death in 1825, and the island's fortunes reached a new low under Ferdinand II (1830–59), nicknamed "Re Bomba" for his five-day **bombardment of Messina** following major insurrections there and in Palermo in 1848–49. Another uprising in Palermo in 1860 proved a spur for Garibaldi to pick Sicily as the starting point for his unification of Italy.

Unification and two world wars

On May 11, 1860, **Giuseppe Garibaldi** landed at Marsala with a thousand men. A professional soldier and one of the leading lights of **Il Risorgimento**, the movement for Italian unification, Garibaldi intended to liberate the island from Bourbon rule, in the name of the Piedmont House of Savoy. His skill in guerrilla warfare, backed by an increasingly cooperative peasantry, ensured that the campaign progressed with astonishing speed. Four days after disembarking, he defeated 15,000 Bourbon troops at **Calatafimi**, closely followed by an almost effortless occupation of Palermo. A battle at **Milazzo** in July decided the issue: apart from Messina (which held out for another year), Sicily was free of Spain for the first time since Peter of Aragon acquired the crown in 1282.

A **plebiscite** was held in October, which returned a 99.5 percent majority in favour of union with the new **kingdom of Italy** under Vittorio Emanuele II. The result, greeted by general euphoria, marked the official **annexation** of the island to the Kingdom of Savoy. Later, however, many began to question whether anything had been achieved by this change of ruler. The new **parliamentary system**, in which only one percent of the island's population was eligible to vote, made few improvements for the majority of people. Attempts at opposition were met with ruthless force, sanctioned by a distant and misinformed government convinced that the island's problems were fundamentally those of law and order. Sicilians responded with their traditional defence of *omertà*, or silent non-cooperation, along with a growing **resentment** of the new Turin government (transferred to Rome in 1870) that was even stronger than their distrust of the more familiar Spanish Bourbons.

A series of reports made in response to criticism of the Italian government's failure to solve what was becoming known as "**the southern problem**" found that the lot of the Sicilian peasant was, if anything, worse after Unification than it had been under the Bourbons. Power had shifted away from the landed gentry to the *gabellotti*, the middlemen to whom they leased the land. These men became increasingly linked with the **Mafia**, a shadowy, loosely knit criminal association that found it easy to manipulate voting procedures, while simultaneously posing as defenders of the people. At the end of the nineteenth century a new, more organized opposition appeared on the scene in the form of **fasci** – embryonic trade-union groups demanding legislation to protect peasants' interests. Violence erupted and the Italian prime minister, **Francesco Crispi** – a native Sicilian who had been one of the pioneers of the Risorgimento – dispatched a fleet and 30,000 soldiers to put down the "revolt", while also closing newspapers, censoring postal services and detaining suspects without trial.

Although there were later signs of progress, in the formation of worker cooperatives and in the enlightened land-reform programmes of individuals such as **Don Sturzo**, mayor of Caltagirone, the overwhelming despair of the peasantry was expressed in **mass emigration**. One and a half million Sicilians decided to leave in the years leading up to 1914, most going to North and South America. Many had been left homeless in the wake of the great **Messina earthquake** of 1908, in which upwards of 80,000 lost their lives. Though the high rate of emigration was a crushing indictment of the state of affairs on the island, it had many positive effects for those left behind, who benefited not only from huge remittances sent back from abroad but from the wage increases that resulted from labour shortages.

However, any advantages were offset by Italy's military adventures. The **conquest of Libya** in 1912 was closely followed by **World War I**, and both were heavy blows to the Sicilian economy. In 1922 **Mussolini** gained power in Rome and dispatched **Cesare Mori** to solve "the southern problem" by putting an end to the Mafia. Free of constitutional and legal restrictions, Mori was able to imprison thousands of suspected *mafiosi*. The effect was merely to drive the criminal class deeper underground, while the alliance he forged with the landed classes to help bring this about dissolved all the gains that had been made against the ruling elite, setting back the cause of agrarian reform. In the **1930s** Mussolini's African concerns and his drive for economic and agricultural self-sufficiency gave Sicily a new importance for Fascist Italy, the island now vaunted as "the geographic centre of the empire". In the much-publicized **"Battle for Grain"**, wheat production increased, though at the cost of the diversity of crops that Sicily required, resulting in soil exhaustion and erosion. Mussolini's popularity on the island is best illustrated by his order, in 1941, that all Sicilian-born officials be transferred to the mainland, on account of their possible disloyalty.

During **World War II**, Sicily became the first part of Europe to be invaded by the Allies, when, in July 1943, Patton's American Seventh Army landed at Gela, and Montgomery's British Eighth Army came ashore between Pachino and Pozzallo further east. This combined army of 160,000 men was the largest ever seen in Sicily, but the campaign was longer and harder than had been anticipated, with the Germans mainly concerned with delaying the advance until they had moved most of their men and equipment across the Straits of Messina. Few Sicilian towns escaped **aerial bombardment**, and Messina itself was the most heavily bombed of all Italian cities before it was taken on August 18.

Modern times

The aftermath of the war saw the most radical changes in Sicily since Unification. With anarchy and hunger widespread, a wave of banditry and crime was unleashed, while the Mafia were reinstated in their behind-the-scenes role as adjudicators and power-brokers, now allied to the landowners in the face of large-scale land occupations by a desperate peasantry. **Separatism** became a potent rallying cry for protesters of all persuasions, who believed that Sicily's ills could best be solved by cutting its links with the mainland. A Separatist army was formed, financed by some of the gentry, but it lacked the organization or resources to make any great impact. It was largely in response to this call for independence that, in 1946, Sicily was granted **regional autonomy**, with its own assembly and president. The same year saw the declaration of a republic in Italy, the result of a popular mandate.

Autonomy failed to heal the island's divisions, however, and brute force was used by the Mafia and the old gentry against what they perceived as the major threat to their position – **communism**. The most famous bandit of the time, **Salvatore Giuliano**, who had previously been associated with the Separatists, was enlisted in the anti-communist cause. He organized a campaign of bombings and assassinations, most notoriously at the 1947 May Day celebrations at Portella della Ginestra. Giuliano's betrayal and murder in 1950 was widely rumoured to have been carried out to prevent him revealing who his paymasters were, though it all helped to glorify his reputation in the popular imagination.

By the 1950s, many saw the **Christian Democrat** party, Democrazia Cristiana, as the best hope to defend their interests. Along with the emotional hold it exerted by virtue of its close association with the Church, the DC could draw on many of the Sicilians' deepest fears of change. And the party was too closely involved with business and the land-owning classes to have any real enthusiasm for genuine reform. All attempts at enterprise were channelled through the party's offices, and favours were bought or bartered. Cutting across party lines, political patronage, or **clientelismo**, grew to be stronger than ever. It still affects people's lives on every level today, especially in the field of work – from finding a job to landing a contract. The favours system was also evident in the workings of the island's sluggish **bureaucracy**, so that the smallest reforms often took years to effect. The essential problem is unchanged today, with the elaborate machinery of the civil service often exploited to accumulate and dispense personal power.

One area that managed to avoid bureaucratic control or planning of any sort was **construction** – one of Sicily's greatest growth industries, the physical evidence of which is among the visitor's most enduring impressions of the island. The building boom was inextricably connected with the Mafia's involvement in land speculation, and boosted by the phenomenal rate of urban growth all over Sicily. But in both the towns and rural areas, minimum safety standards were rarely met, as highlighted by the **1968 earthquake**, in which 50,000 were made homeless along the Valle di Belice in the west of the island. **Industry**, too, has been subject to mismanagement, and, apart from isolated cases, has rarely fulfilled the potential it promised after the discovery of oil near Ragusa and Gela in the 1950s, and the development of refineries and petrochemical plants along the Golfo di Augusta.

Substantial subsidies have been channelled into many ventures, largely from the **European Union**, which Italy joined in 1958. However, it's still the great urban centres in the north that flaunt their prosperity, while the south of Italy, known as Il Mezzogiorno, is left far behind. Conversely, the huge financial concessions made to Sicily have provoked resentment from Italy's more self-sufficient regions, who point to massive corruption and incompetence on the island. Few Sicilians would wholly deny this; a longer view, however, argues that Sicily's disadvantages are derived principally from the past misuse of resources, coupled with a culture and mentality that have never given much credence to collectivist ideals. There is more awareness, too, on the part of the state that the fight against **organized crime** requires more than moralistic speeches. Indeed, in 1992, following the murders of anti-Mafia investigators Falcone and Borsellino, the chief of police of Palermo was sacked, while 7000 troops were sent to the island to patrol prisons and search towns with a known Mafia presence. There have been significant breakthroughs, though these are mostly connected with a change in the public attitude towards criminality, resulting in part from a campaign to reform Sicily's dilapidated **education** system. In the 1990s, a campaign of anti-Mafia education began in Sicilian schools, aiming to cut the secondary-school drop-out rate by encouraging children away from the traditional path of corruption and crime.

Despite superficial improvements, the deep problems that have always bedevilled Sicily remain in some form. Unemployment is still high, and not helped by the diminishing opportunities for **emigration**, though a million still managed to escape the island between 1951 and 1971, along with the majority of Sicily's most outstanding artists and writers. Ironically, the late 1990s saw the problem of **immigration** hitting the agenda for the first time, as economic refugees from North Africa started to arrive by regular boatloads, particularly on the two southernmost islands of Lampedusa and Pantelleria. These *extracomunitari* (literally, "those from non-EU countries") are routinely rounded up and sent to crowded processing centres, where they languish for months, before almost all are eventually returned to their countries of origin. Others slip through and join the already strained jobs market. Despite harsh anti-immigration legislation introduced by the Italian government, illegal immigration continues to be a contentious issue that has affected Italy more than most EU countries.

In the long run, perhaps the greatest hope for Sicily lies in **tourism** and related services. Visitor numbers are growing (helped by budget airline routes to fast-growing Trápani airport), and there's an increasing emphasis on boutique and eco-tourism, in the shape of hundreds of new B&Bs, rural tourism ventures and outdoor activity operators. Many towns and resorts (particularly on the outlying islands) have a positively fashionable air – Madonna has holidayed on Pantelleria, no less – while more and more Italians are throwing off their distrust of the south and discovering the island's potential, especially its outdoor attractions, wildlife and crystal-clear seas. The creation of **regional parks** in Etna and the Nébrodi and Madonie ranges, and the **marine reserves** around Ústica and the Égadi and Pelágie islands, are a reflection of this, and an encouraging pointer for the future.

The Mafia in Sicily

n Sicily, there is "*mafiosità*" and there is "the Mafia". *Mafiosità* refers to a criminal mentality, the Mafia to a specific criminal organization. In Italy's deep south, a man can look *mafioso*, or talk like a *mafioso*, meaning he has the aura, or stench, of criminality about him, even though he has no explicit connection to the crime syndicate. And, while notions of family solidarity and the moral stature of the outlaw mean that *mafiosità* can never be completely extirpated from Sicilian society, the Mafia is an entity whose members can be eliminated and its power emasculated.

What has always prevented this is the shadowy nature of the organization, protected by the long-standing **code of silence**, or *omertà*, that invariably led to accusations being retracted at the last moment, or to crucial witnesses being found dead with a stone, cork or a wad of banknotes stuffed into their mouths, or else simply disappearing off the face of the earth. As a result, many have doubted the very existence of the Mafia, claiming that it's nothing more than the creation of pulp-thriller writers, the invention of a sensationalist press and the fabrication of an Italian government embarrassed by its inability to control an unusually high level of crime in Sicily.

The background

In 1982, however, proof of the innermost workings of the Mafia's organization emerged when a high-ranking member, **Tommaso Buscetta**, was arrested in Brazil, and – after a failed suicide attempt – agreed to prise open the can of worms. His reason for daring this sacrilege, he claimed, was to destroy the Mafia. In its stampede to grab huge drug profits, the "Honoured Society" (La Società Onorata) had abandoned its original ideals: "It's necessary to destroy this band of criminals", he declared, "who have perverted the principles of Cosa Nostra and dragged them through the mud." He was doubtlessly motivated by revenge: all of those he incriminated – Michele Greco, Pippo Calò, Benedetto Santapaola, Salvatore Riina and many others – were leaders of, or allied to, the powerful Corleone family who had recently embarked on a campaign of terror to monopolize the drugs industry, in the process eliminating seven of Buscetta's closest relatives in the space of four months, including his two sons.

Buscetta's statements to Giovanni Falcone, head of Sicily's anti-Mafia "pool" of judges, and later to the Federal Court in Manhattan, provided crucial revelations about the structure of Cosa Nostra. Mafia "families" are centred on areas, he revealed: villages or quarters of cities from which they take their name. The boss (*capo*) of each group is chosen by election, and appoints a lieutenant (*sottocapo*) and one or more *consiglieri*, or counsellors. Above the families is the *cupola*, or **Commission**, a governing body that includes representatives from all the major groupings. Democracy and collective interest, Buscetta claimed, had been replaced in the Commission by the greed and self-interest of the individuals who had gained control. Trials of strength alone now decided the leadership, often in the form of bitter feuds between rival factions – or *cosche* (literally, "artichokes", their form symbolizing solidarity).

The existence of the Commission sets the Mafia apart from the normal run of underworld gangs, for without a high level of organization the international trafficking in heroin in which they engage would be inconceivable. The route is circuitous, starting in the Middle and Far East, moving on to the processing plants in Sicily, and ending up in New York, where American Mafia channels are said to control sixty percent of the heroin market. This multimillion-dollar racket – known in the US as the "**Pizza Connection**", because Sicilian pizza parlours were used as covers for the operation – was blown apart chiefly as a result of Buscetta's evidence, and led to the trial and conviction of the leading members of New York's Mafia Commission in September 1986.

The history

The Mafia has certainly come a long way since its rustic beginnings in **feudal Sicily**. Although Buscetta denied that the word "Mafia" is used to describe the organization – the term preferred by its members is "Cosa Nostra" – the word has been in currency for centuries, and is thought to derive from the Arabic, **mu'afah**, meaning "protection". In 1863, a play entitled *Mafiusi della Vicaria*, based on life in a Palermo prison, was a roaring success among the high society of the island's capital, and gave the word its first extensive usage. When the city rose against its new Italian rulers three years later, the British consul described a situation where secret societies were all-powerful: "*Camorre* and *maffie*, self-elected juntas, share the earnings of the workmen, keep up intercourse with outcasts, and take malefactors under their wing and protection." Until then, *mafiosi* had been able to pose as defenders of the poor against the tyranny of Sicily's rulers, but in the years immediately following the toppling of the Bourbon state in Italy *mafiosi* were able to entrench themselves in Sicily's new power structure, acting as intermediaries in the gradual redistribution of land and establishing a modus vivendi with the new democratic representatives.

There is little documentary proof of the rise to power of the "Honoured Society", but most writers agree that between the 1890s and the 1920s its undisputed boss was **Don Vito Cascio Ferro**, who had close links with the American "Black Hand", a Mafia-type association of southern Italian emigrants. Ferro's career ended with Mussolini's anti-Mafia purges, instigated to clear the ground for the establishment of a vigorous Fascist structure in Sicily. **Cesare Mori**, the Duce's newly appointed Prefect of Palermo, arrived in the city in 1925 with the declared aim of "clearing the ground of the nightmares, threats and dangers which are paralyzing, perverting and corrupting every kind of social activity". This might have worked, but the clean sweep that Mori made of the Mafia leaders (in all, 11,000 cattle rustlers, thieves and "conspirators" were jailed during this period, often on the basis of flimsy hearsay) was annulled after World War II when the prisons were opened and Mafia leaders, seen as unjustly jailed by the Fascist regime, returned to their regular operations. In the confusion that reigned during Italy's reconstruction, crime flourished throughout the south, and criminal leagues regrouped in Naples (the Camorra) and Calabria ('ndrángheta). In Sicily, men such as **Don Calógero Vizzini** were the new leaders, confirmed in their power by the brief Anglo-American postwar administration, in return for their contribution towards the smooth progress of the Allied landings. One of them, **Lucky Luciano**, a founder member of the American Commission, was even flown out from prison in America to facilitate the invasion. Later he was alleged to be responsible for setting up the Sicilian-American narcotics empire, which was taken over at his death in 1962 by **Luciano Leggio**, who subsequently manoeuvred himself into the leadership of the Corleone family.

The new Mafia

The cycle was by now complete: the Mafia had lost its original role as a predominantly rural organization, and had transferred its operations to the cities, moving into entrepreneurial activities such as construction, real estate and, ultimately, drug smuggling. The growth of the heroin industry raised the stakes immensely, as shown by the vicious feuds fought over the division of the spoils, and the struggle for control of narcotics trafficking played a key role in the consolidation of power within the Mafia. The Italian state responded with an **anti-Mafia Parliamentary Commission** that sat from 1963 to 1976, and posed enough of a threat to provoke a change of tactics by the Mafia, who began to target important state officials in a sustained campaign of terror. In 1971, Palermo's chief public prosecutor, Pietro Scaglione, became the first in a long line of "**illustrious corpses**" – *cadáveri eccellenti* – which have included journalists, judges, lawyers, police chiefs and left-wing politicians. A new peak of violence was reached in 1982 with the murder in Palermo's city centre of **Pio La Torre**, regional secretary of the Communist Party in Sicily, who had proposed a special government dispensation to allow lawyers access to private bank accounts.

Among the mourners at La Torre's funeral was the new Sicilian prefect of police, **General Dalla Chiesa**, a veteran in the state's fight against the anarchist/terrorist Red Brigades. The prefect began to investigate Sicily's lucrative construction industry, and his scrutiny of public records and business dealings threatened to expose one of the most enigmatic issues in the Mafia's organization: the extent of corruption and protection in high-ranking political circles, the so-called "**Third Level**". However, exactly 100 days after La Torre's death, Dalla Chiesa himself was gunned down, together with his wife, in Palermo's Via Carini. The whole country was shocked, and the murder revived questions about the depth of government commitment to the fight. In his engagement with the Mafia, Dalla Chiesa had received next to no support from Rome, to the extent that Dalla Chiesa's son accused the mandarins of the Christian Democrat party – former prime minister Andreotti among them – of isolating his father. Nando Dalla Chiesa refused to allow many local officials to his father's funeral, including Vito Ciancimino, former mayor of Palermo and a Christian Democrat. Later, Ciancimino was accused, not just of handling huge sums of drug money, but of actually being a sworn-in member of the Corleone family. Those who were present at the funeral included the Italian president and senior cabinet ministers, all of them jeered at by an angry Sicilian crowd.

To ward off accusations of government inertia or complicity, the law that La Torre had demanded was rushed through Parliament soon afterwards, and was used in the **super-trials**, or *maxiprocessi*, that arose from the confessions of Buscetta and the other *pentiti* (penitents) who had followed his lead. The biggest of these trials, lasting eighteen months, started in February 1986, when five hundred *mafiosi* appeared in a specially built maximum-security bunker adjoining Palermo's Ucciardone prison. The insecurity felt by the Mafia was reflected in continuing bloodshed in Sicily throughout the proceedings, but the worst was to come after the trial closed in December 1986, starting right on the steps of the courthouse with the murder of one of the accused *mafiosi* – many of whom were freed after they had squealed on their accomplices. Of those that were convicted, 19 received life sentences, and 338 others sentences totalling 2065 years.

The fightback in the 1990s

The violence reached a new level of ferocity during the 1990s, starting in 1992 with a wave of assassinations of high-profile figures. In March, **Salvatore Lima**, a former mayor of Palermo who later became a Euro MP, was shot dead outside his villa in Mondello. Lima didn't have police bodyguards because he didn't believe he needed them; he had, in fact, been in the Mafia's pocket throughout his political career. His "crime" was his failure to fix the Supreme Court, which had gone ahead and confirmed the convictions of scores of *mafiosi* who had been incriminated in the super-trials of the 1980s.

This murder was followed by two more atrocities in quick succession: in May, the best-known of Sicily's anti-Mafia crusaders, **Giovanni Falcone**, was blown up by half a tonne of TNT on his way into Palermo from the airport, together with his wife and three bodyguards, while two months later his colleague, **Paolo Borsellino** (with five of his police guards), was the victim of a car-bomb outside his mother's house, also in Palermo. As ever, public opinion was divided over what it all meant. There were those who claimed that these murders were public gestures, while others saw in them increasing evidence of the panic percolating through the Mafia's ranks in the face of the growing number of defections of former members who were turning *pentiti*.

The carnage certainly propelled the state into action, and a dramatic breakthrough came shortly afterwards. In January 1993, **Salvatore Riina**, the so-called "Boss of all the Bosses", and the man held ultimately responsible for the murder of the anti-Mafia judges, was arrested. **Leoluca Bagarella**, Riina's successor and brother-in-law, and the convicted killer of the chief of the Palermo Flying Squad in 1979, was captured in 1995 (Bagarella's hideout turned out to be a luxury apartment overlooking the heavily guarded home of two of the judges who had helped catch him). Another of the Corleone clan, **Giovanni Brusca**, was arrested in 1996 – a particularly gratifying coup for the anti-Mafia forces, as Brusca was one of the organization's most ruthless hitmen, the mastermind behind Falcone's assassination and believed to have been responsible for the strangling of an informant's 11-year-old son, whose body was then disposed of in a vat of acid. Elsewhere, **Natale D'Emanuele**, alleged to be the financial wizard behind the Mafia in Catania, was arrested and charged with trafficking arms throughout Italy, using hearses and coffins to transport them in a throwback to 1930s Chicago.

On the political front, **Leoluca Orlando**, the mayor of Palermo who was forced out of office by his own Christian Democrat party in 1990, established an independent power base on an anti-Mafia ticket, at the head of his Rete (Network) party. Meanwhile, the confessions of Tommaso Buscetta began to provide evidence for the first time of the postwar alliance between Italy's former leading party and organized crime. Allegations inexorably focused on the very highest levels of government, and specifically on the relationship of Mafia stooge Salvatore Lima to his protector, **Giulio Andreotti**, the Christian Democrat leader and Italy's most successful postwar politician. Formerly considered untouchable, Andreotti finally bowed to increasing pressure to relinquish his parliamentary immunity and, in September 1995, aged 75, went on trial in Palermo for complicity and criminal association. Much fuss was made of the famous *bacio*, a kiss he was reported to have symbolically exchanged with Riina, according to *pentiti* revelations in 1994. However, the fact that most of the charges levelled against Andreotti were based on the testimony of Mafia informers (and therefore unreliable witnesses) led to Andreotti's complete acquittal in 1999. Many saw the result as simply further evidence of the famous cunning and survival skills of this political stalwart, which have given him the nickname *la volpe* ("the fox").

Statements by *pentiti* and others accused of Mafia associations were also at the bottom of investigations into the business dealings of the then-prime minister **Silvio Berlusconi**. This time they were considered serious enough to warrant a raid on Berlusconi's Milan headquarters by an elite anti-Mafia police unit in July 1998, and a hasty dash to Sicily by Berlusconi to defend himself against charges of money-laundering for Cosa Nostra. Despite these high-profile events, though, the very concept of Mafia involvement was becoming increasingly irrelevant to most Italians, as reports of political and business corruption began to dominate public life throughout the 1990s. As the mayor of Venice remarked, in response to whispers of Mafia involvement in the fire that destroyed La Fenice opera house in 1996, "claiming it was burnt by the Mafia is about as useful as saying it was attacked by alien spacecraft."

Contemporary events

Since the turn of the millennium, the violence has for the most part calmed down. While killings still occur, few political figureheads are targeted these days, perhaps because fewer are willing to take the visible risks that sealed the fate of crusaders like Falcone and Borsellino. More Mafia bosses have been jailed – **Bernardo Provenzano**, for thirteen years *capo dei capi*, was captured in 2006, quickly followed by 52 arrest warrants against the top echelons of Cosa Nostra in Palermo, while the man thought to be Provenzano's successor, **Salvatore Lo Piccolo**, was arrested in 2007. Perhaps more significantly, the last decade has seen the repossession by Palermo's anti-Mafia magistrate of billions of euros in assets held by *mafiosi*, largely from the real estate and construction industries.

The most important development, however, has been the growth of a new open attitude towards the Mafia, in contrast to the previous denial and *omertà*. One of the most watched TV programmes in Italy in recent years has been *La Piovra* ("The Octopus"), a drama series along the lines of *The Sopranos*, while in Corleone, an anti-Mafia centre has opened to educate both foreigners and Sicilians alike. Sicilians themselves are now bolder than ever in their public demonstrations of disgust at the killings and intimidation, and a new movement against paying **pizzo**, or protection money, has gathered force throughout the island. An increasing number of brave individuals are willing to make a stand: people such as Rita Borsellino, sister of murdered judge Paolo Borsellino and now an anti-Mafia figurehead, or Giovanna Terranova, widow of another "illustrious" victim, Judge Cesare Terranova (killed in 1979), who launched a women's movement against the Mafia with the words, "If you manage to change the mentality, to change the consent, to change the fear in which the Mafia can live – if you can change that, you can beat them."

It is precisely that element of "consent" among ordinary Sicilians that has always been the strongest weapon in the Mafia's armoury, indeed the very foundation of the Mafia's existence, bolstered by an attitude that has traditionally regarded the *mafioso* stance as a revolt against the State, justified by centuries of oppression by foreign regimes. This historical dichotomy is perhaps best expressed by one of Sicily's greatest writers, Leonardo Sciascia, who proclaimed, "It hurts when I denounce the Mafia because a residue of Mafia feeling stays with me, as it does in any Sicilian. So in struggling against the Mafia I struggle against myself. It is like a split, a laceration."

At least the problem is being confronted, and few Sicilians now hold any illusions about the true nature of the Mafia, shorn of its one-time altruistic ideals – if they ever existed. And crucially, the myth of the Mafia's invincibility has been irreparably dented.

Sicilian Baroque

Most of the church and civic architecture that you'll come across in Sicily, certainly in the east of the island, is Baroque in style. More particularly, it's of a type known as Sicilian Baroque. What follows is a brief introduction to the subject, designed to serve as a handy reference for some of the more important aspects of the style mentioned in the Guide.

Origins

To some extent, the qualities that attract art historians to the Sicilian Baroque – its "warmth and ebullience", "gaiety", "energy", "freedom and fantasy" – typify all **Baroque** architecture. The style grew out of the excesses of Mannerism, a distorted sixteenth-century mode of painting and architecture that had flourished in Italy in reaction to the restraint of the Renaissance. The development of a full-blown, ornate Baroque style followed in the late sixteenth century, again originating in Italy, and it quickly found a niche in other countries touched by the Counter-Reformation. The Jesuits saw in Baroque art and architecture an expression of a revitalized Catholicism, its theatrical forms involving the congregation by portraying spiritual ecstasy in terms of physical passion.

The origin of the word "Baroque" itself is uncertain: the two most popular theories are that it comes either from the seventeenth-century Portuguese *barroco*, meaning a misshapen pearl, or the term *barocco*, used by philosophers in the Middle Ages to mean a contorted idea. Whatever its origins, it was used by contemporary critics in a derogatory sense, implying odd or extravagant shapes, as opposed to the much-vaunted Classical forms of the Renaissance.

Although Baroque was born in Rome, the vogue quickly spread throughout Europe. Everywhere, the emphasis was firmly on elaborate ornamentation and spectacle, something that reflected the growing power of the aristocracy, who had begun to challenge the established wealth and tradition of the Church. The primary motivating force behind the decoration of the buildings was the need to impress the neighbouring gentry; building to the glory of God came a poor second.

Some of the finest examples of Baroque architecture are to be found in Sicily, although there's some debate as to the specific origins of the **Sicilian Baroque** style. During the eighteenth century alone, Sicily was conquered and ruled in turn by the Spanish Habsburgs, the Spanish Bourbons, the House of Savoy, the Austrian Habsburgs and the Bourbons from Naples, lending a particularly exuberant flavour to its Baroque creations – which some say was borrowed from Spain. Others argue that the dominant influence was Italian: Sicilian architects tended to train and to travel in Italy, rather than Spain, and brought home what they learned on the mainland, adapting prevalent Roman Baroque ideas to complement peculiarly Sicilian architectural traditions. Both theories contain an element of the truth, though perhaps more pertinent is Sicily's unique long-term history: two and a half millennia of invasion and domination have produced a very distinct culture and society – one that is bound to have influenced, or even produced, an equally distinct architectural form.

Baroque towns

Sicily's seismic instability has profoundly affected its architectural history. The huge **earthquake of 1693** that almost flattened Catania, and completely destroyed Noto, Ragusa, Ávola and Módica, provided a fantastic opportunity for local architects, who began massive rebuilding programmes in the southeast corner of Sicily. To them, a **Baroque town** aspired to be, and should be seen to be, a centre of taste and sophistication, They designed their new towns to delight their citizens, to encourage the participation of passers-by and to impress outsiders, with long vistas contriving to focus on the facade of a church or a palace, or an unexpected view of the sea. To enhance the visual effect even more, a building was designed to offer multiple, changing views from different angles of approach. This way, a completed plan might include all the buildings in a square or series of squares, and the experience of walking from place to place through varied but harmonious spaces was considered as important as the need to arrive at a destination. Moreover, as much of eighteenth-century Sicilian town-life took place outside, the facade of a building became synonymous with the wealth and standing of its occupant. External features became increasingly elaborate and specialized, and some parts of buildings – windows and staircases, for example – were often merely there for show. Invariably, what seem to be regular stone facades have been cosmetically touched up with plaster to conceal an asymmetry or an angle of less than ninety degrees: a self-conscious approach to town planning that can sometimes give the impression of walking around a stage set. Interestingly, this approach remained confined to the south and east of Sicily; outside the earthquake zone, in the west of the island, local architectural traditions continued to dominate in towns that hadn't had the dubious benefit of being levelled and left for the planners.

Ideally, where there was scope for large-scale planning, an entire city could be constructed as an aesthetic whole. As early as 1615 the Venetian architect and theorist **Vincenzo Scamozzi** published a treatise, *Dell'Idea dell'architettura universale*, in which he stated that the architectural harmony of the ideal city should reflect the perfect relationship between the prince, the judiciary, the Church, the marketplace and the populace.

Noto is an almost perfect example of Scamozzi's ideal city. After the 1693 earthquake, the old town was so devastated that it was decided to move its site and rebuild from scratch. The plan that was eventually accepted was nearly an exact replica of Scamozzi's. Noto is constructed on a grid-plan, traversed from east to west by a wide corso crossing a main piazza, which is itself balanced by four smaller piazzas. The buildings along the corso show remarkable balance and grace, while the attention of the Baroque planners to every harmonious detail is illustrated by the use of a warm, golden stone for the churches and *palazzi*.

Neighbouring towns in the southeast were also destroyed by the earthquake and rebuilt along similar lines. Both **Ávola** and **Grammichele** were moved from their hill-top positions to the coastal plain, and their polygonal plans were similarly influenced by Scamozzi. Grammichele, particularly, retains an extraordinary hexagonal layout, unique in Sicily. **Ragusa** is more complex, surviving today as two towns: the medieval Ragusa Ibla, which the inhabitants rebuilt after the earthquake, and the Baroque upper town of Ragusa, which is built on a sloping grid-plan, rather similar to Noto. Although Ibla isn't built to any kind of Baroque pattern, it does lay claim to one of the most spectacular of Sicilian Baroque churches.

Catania was not completely destroyed by the earthquake, but was instead rebuilt over its old site. Broad streets were built to link existing monuments and to facilitate rescue operations in case of another earthquake. The city is divided into four quarters by wide streets that meet in Piazza del Duomo, and wherever possible these spaces are used to maximize the visual impact of a facade or monument. The main Piazza del Duomo was conceived as a uniform set piece, while the main street, Via Etnea, cuts a swath due north from here, always drawing the eyes to Mount Etna, smoking in the distance.

On the other side of the island, Baroque **Palermo** evolved without the impetus of natural disaster. There's no comparable city plan, Palermo's intricate central layout owing more to the Arabs than to seventeenth- and eighteenth-century designers; what Baroque character the city possesses has almost entirely to do with its highly individual churches and palaces. These were constructed in a climate of apparent opulence but encroaching bankruptcy; as the Sicilian aristocrats were attracted to Palermo to pay court to the Spanish viceroy, they left the management of their lands to pragmatic agents, whose short-sighted policies allowed the estates to fall into neglect. This ate away at the wealth of the gentry, who responded by mortgaging their lands in order to maintain their living standards. The grandiose palaces and churches they built in the city still stand, but following the damage caused during World War II many are in a state of terrible neglect and near collapse; wild flowers grow out of the facades, and chunks of masonry frequently fall into the street below.

Specific features

Eighteenth-century aristocrats in Palermo escaped the heat to **summer villas** outside the city, and many of these still survive around Bagheria. The villas tend to be simply designed, but are bedecked with balconies and terraces for afternoon strolling, and were approached by long, impressive driveways. Above all, they are notable for their **external staircases**, leading to the main entrance on the first floor (the ground floor usually contained the kitchen and servants' quarters). It's typical of the Baroque era that an external feature should take on such significance in a building – and that they should show such a remarkable diversity, each reflecting the wealth of the individual owners. Beyond the fact that they were nearly always double staircases, symmetrical to the middle axis of the facade, each was completely different.

While **balconies** had always been a prominent feature of Sicilian domestic architecture, during the eighteenth century they became prolific. The balcony supports, or buttresses, were elaborately carved: manic heads, griffins, horses, monsters and mythical figures all featured as decoration, fine examples of which survive at Noto's **Palazzo Villadorata**, as well as in Módica and Scicli. The wrought-iron balustrades curved outwards, almost like theatre boxes, to allow room for women's billowing skirts.

Church building, too, flourished during this period. Baroque architects could let their imaginations run wild: the facade of the **Duomo** at Siracusa was begun in 1728, based on designs by Andrea Palma of Palermo, and the result is highly sophisticated and exciting. Other designs adapted and modified accepted forms for church architecture, as well as inventing new ones. In Palermo especially, typically Sicilian elements – like central circular windows – were used to great effect.

It was in the church **interiors**, however, that Sicilian Baroque came into its own, with tomb sculpture ever more ostentatious and stucco decoration abundant. Inlaid marble, a technique introduced from Naples at the start of the seventeenth century, became *de rigueur* and reached its prime during the second half of the century, when entire walls or chapels would be decorated in this way. Palermo fields some of the best examples of all these techniques, at their most impressive in the church of **San Giuseppe dei Teatini**, designed by Giacomo Besio, a Genovese who lived most of his life in Sicily. For real over-the-top detail, though, the churches of **Santa Caterina** and **Il Gesù**, also in Palermo, conceal a riot of inlaid marble decoration.

Architects and sculptors

Rosario Gagliardi was responsible for much of the rebuilding of Noto and Ragusa, and became known as one of the most important architects in southeast Sicily. Born in Siracusa in 1698, he worked in Noto as a carpenter from the age of 10, and was first acknowledged as an architect in 1726. Between 1760 and 1784 he was chief architect for the city of Noto, and during this time also worked on many different projects in Ragusa and Módica. As far as is known, he never travelled outside Sicily, let alone to Rome, yet he absorbed contemporary architectural trends from the study of books and treatises, and reproduced the ideas with some flair.

Gagliardi's prime interest was in facades, and his work achieved a sophisticated fusion of Renaissance poise, Baroque grandeur and local Sicilian ornamentation. He had no interest, however, in spatial relationships or structural innovation, and the interiors of his buildings are disappointing when compared to the elaborate nature of their exteriors. Perhaps his most significant contribution was his development of the **belfry** as a feature. Sicilian churches traditionally didn't have a separate belltower, but incorporated the bells into the main facade, revealed through a series of two or three arches – an idea handed down from Byzantine building. Gagliardi extended the central bay of the facade into a tower, a highly original compromise satisfying both the local style and the more conventional notions of design from the mainland. The belfry on the church of **San Giorgio** in Ragusa Ibla, Gagliardi's masterpiece, is an excellent example of this.

The principal architect on the design and rebuilding of Catania after the 1693 earthquake, **Giovanni Battista Vaccarini**, was born in Palermo in 1702. He trained in Rome and embraced the current idiom, working with such illustrious figures as Alessandro Specchi (who built the papal stables) and Francesco de Sanctis (designer of the Spanish Steps). In 1730 he arrived in Catania, having been appointed as city architect by the Senate, and at once began work on finishing the Municipio. Outside he placed a fountain, whose main feature is an obelisk supported by an elephant, the symbol of Catania – reminiscent of Bernini's elephant fountain in Rome.

Giacomo Serpotta, master of the Palermitan oratories, was born in Palermo in 1656. He cashed in on the opulence of the Church and specialized in decorating oratories with moulded plasterwork in ornamental frames. He would include life-sized figures of Saints and Virtues, surrounded by plaster draperies, trophies, swags of fruit, bouquets of flowers and other extravagances much beloved of the Baroque. Among his most remarkable works is the Oratory of the Rosary in the church of **Santa Zita**, where the end wall is a reconstruction of the Battle of Lépanto. Three-dimensional representation is taken to an extreme here, and actual wires are used as rigging.

Other Baroque architects are less well known, but are influential in Sicily all the same. **Giacomo Amato** (1643–1732) was a monk, sent to Rome in 1671 to represent his Order, where he came into contact with the works of Bernini and Borromini. Dazzled by what he'd seen, he neglected his religious duties after his return to Palermo in order to design some of the city's most characteristic churches, **Sant'Ignazio all'Olivell** and **San Domenico** among them. **Vincenzo Sinatra** had a more traditional career, starting as a stonecutter before working with Gagliardi in the 1730s as his foreman. In 1745 he married Gagliardi's niece, a move which did him no harm at all, since by 1761, when Gagliardi had a stroke, Sinatra was managing all his affairs. For ten years he directed the construction of Noto's Municipio, and during the rest of his life Sinatra worked in collaboration with the other city architects on a variety of projects. More important was **Giovanni Verméxio**, who was active in Siracusa at around the same time. His work graces the city's Piazza del Duomo, notably the **Palazzo Arcivescovile**, while he gets a couple of ornate-interior credits, too, in the shape of one of the Duomo's chapels, and the octagonal **Cappella di San Sepolcro** in the church of Santa Lucia in the Achradina quarter of Siracusa.

Books

Although only a few modern writers have travelled in and written about Sicily, the island has provided the inspiration for some great literature, by both Sicilians and foreign visitors. Translations of Italian and Sicilian classics are also often available at bookshops in major towns and resorts in Sicily.

Travel and general

Vincent Cronin *The Golden Honeycomb*. Disguised as a quest for the mythical golden honeycomb of Daedalus, this classic, erudite travelogue is a searching account of a sojourn in Sicily in the 1950s.

Duncan Fallowell *To Noto*. Follows the author's trip from London to Baroque Noto in an old Ford – a witty tale, complete with pithy observations on Sicily and the Sicilians.

Matthew Fort *Sweet Honey, Bitter Lemons*. Cheery food-writer Fort returns to the island he first visited in the 1970s, only this time he comes on a Vespa and eats his way around, from ice cream to anchovies.

Norman Lewis *In Sicily*. A sweeping portrait of the island which Lewis came to know well through his wife and her family. Subjects range from reflections on Palermo's ruined *palazzi* to the impact of immigration, and there's plenty on the Mafia.

Daphne Phelps *A House in Sicily*. An Englishwoman inherits a grand *palazzo* in Taormina in the late 1940s, and turns it into a guesthouse to make ends meet. Cue the usual cultural

misunderstandings while she learns to love the locals, leavened by vignettes of her eminent guests – including Bertrand Russell, Tennessee Williams and Roald Dahl.

Gaia Servadio *Motya*. On one level, an account of Phoenician history and culture as they relate to the excavated ruins of Motya – but in truth, so much more than that, as Servadio explores the fabric of Sicily and its people in uncompromising, enlightening detail.

Mary Taylor Simeti *On Persephone's Island: A Sicilian Journal*. Sympathetic record of a typical year in Sicily by an American who married a Sicilian professor and has lived in the west of the island since the early 1960s. It's full of keenly observed detail about flora and fauna, customs, the harvests, festivals and – above all – the Sicilians themselves.

Elio Vittorini *Conversations in Sicily*. A Sicilian emigrant returns from the north of Italy after fifteen years to see his mother on her birthday. The conversations of the title are with the people he meets on the way, and reveal a prewar Sicily that, while affectionately drawn, is ridden with poverty and disease.

History, politics and archeology

David Abulafia *Frederick II: A Medieval Emperor*. Definitive account of the Hohenstaufen king, greatest of the medieval European rulers, with much on his reign in Sicily. It's a reinterpretation of the received view

of Frederick, revealing a less formidable king than the omnipotent and supreme ruler usually portrayed. Also see the same author's *Italy, Sicily and the Mediterranean, 1100–1400*.

Brian Caven *Dionysius I: Warlord of Sicily*. The life of Dionysius I, by a historian who sees him not as a vicious tyrant but as a valiant crusader against the Carthaginians.

Christopher Hibbert *Garibaldi and His Enemies*. A popular treatment of the life and revolutionary works of Giuseppe Garibaldi, thrillingly detailing the exploits of "The Thousand" in their lightning campaign from Marsala to Milazzo.

R. Ross Holloway *The Archaeology of Ancient Sicily*. The standard work on the ancient monuments and archeological discoveries of Sicily, from the Paleolithic to the later Roman period.

John Julius Norwich *The Normans in Sicily*. Published together under one title, J.J. Norwich's *The Normans in the South* and *Kingdom in the Sun* tell the story of the Normans' explosive entry into the south of Italy, and their creation in Sicily of one of the most brilliant medieval European civilizations.

Steven Runciman *The Sicilian Vespers*. The classic account of Sicily's large-scale popular uprising in the thirteenth century. Runciman's *A History of the Crusades: 1, 2 & 3*, meanwhile, covers the Norman kings of Sicily, as well as the crusading Frederick II.

Crime and society

John Dickie *Cosa Nostra*. Dickie, an Italian professor at University College London, is an expert on the Mafia and its role in Sicilian society, and offers an in-depth look at the secret workings of the Mafia, from its early days in the mid-1800s to its current manifestation.

David Lane *Into the Heart of the Mafia*. The most recent look at life in the Italian south (published 2010) is a journey through corruption from Naples to Sicily, an essential counterpoint to any number of expat-life-in-a-vineyard experiences.

Norman Lewis *The Honoured Society*. Originally written in the 1960s, this is the most famous account of the Mafia, its origins, personalities and customs, and is still the most accessible introduction available to the subject.

Clare Longrigg *Boss of Bosses*. One of the Mafia's most notorious *capo dei capi* (Boss of Bosses), Bernardo Provenzano, was arrested in Sicily in 2006 after four decades spent evading the law. Longrigg's careful unravelling of his successful shifting of criminal enterprise into mainstream business explains the subtitle: *How One Man Saved the Sicilian Mafia*.

Gavin Maxwell *The Ten Pains of Death*. Maxwell lived in Scopello during the 1950s, and recorded the lives of his neighbours in their own words. There's much on Sicilian small-town life and poverty, and sympathetic portraits of traditional festivals and characters. His *God Protect Me from My Friends* is a sympathetic biography of the notorious bandit Salvatore Giuliano, ripe with intrigue and double-dealing.

Peter Robb *Midnight in Sicily*. The Australian Robb spent fifteen years in the Italian south tracing the contorted relations between organized crime and politics. Here, he focuses on the structure of the Mafia, the trials of the bosses in the 1980s, the high-profile assassinations that ensued, and the trial of Andreotti, providing deep insights into the dynamics of Sicilian society.

Alexander Stille *Excellent Cadavers*. An important book tracing the modern fight against the Mafia as led by Giovanni Falcone and Paolo Borsellino, whose assassinations in 1992 finally sparked the Italian state into action.

Novels about Sicily

Allen Andrews *Impossible Loyalties*. Fast-moving narrative of an Anglo-Sicilian family caught up in the turmoil of World War II, containing an authentic portrait of prewar Messina society.

Michael Dibdin *Blood Rain*. Dibdin's Venetian detective, Aurelio Zen, is an idiosyncratic loner, always up against the Italian state and society in an unequalled series of crime novels. Here, Dibdin sends him to Sicily, with dark consequences for all concerned.

Simonetta Agnello Hornby *The Marchesa; The Almond Picker*. From aristocratic nineteenth-century Palermo to 1960s' village life, Hornby's best-selling Sicily novels are full of subtle intrigue, voluptuous imagery and period detail.

Norman Lewis *The March of the Long Shadows*. An affectionate novel set in postwar Sicily, dealing with the Separatist movement, the bandit Giuliano and a whole cast of endearing characters. *The Sicilian Specialist* is Lewis's Mafia thriller, which flits from Sicily to the US to Cuba on the trail of a Mob assassin.

Dacia Maraini *The Silent Duchess*. The tale of a noble eighteenth-century family seen through the eyes of a young duchess – beautifully written and dripping with authentic detail. *Bagheria*, meanwhile, is a delightfully engaging memoir of Maraini's childhood in the town of the title.

Lily Prior *La Cucina*. Subtitled a "novel of rapture", this chronicles the romance between a spinster librarian from Castiglione and an enigmatic English chef. Drawn into the plot are the Mafia, copious recipes, and the convolutions of Sicilian family life.

Mario Puzo *The Godfather*. The New York Godfather – Don Corleone – was born in Sicily and the majestic book (a great read, even if you've seen the films) touches on all things Sicilian.

Sicilian literature

Gesualdo Bufalino *The Plague Spreader's Tale*, *Blind Argus*, *The Keeper of Ruins*, and *Night's Lies*. Bufalino arrived late on the literary scene, publishing his first novel, *The Plague Sower*, in his 60s. Subsequent publications enhanced the reputation made by this remarkable debut, notably *Night's Lies*, which won Italy's most respected literary award, the Strega Prize, in 1988. Bufalino himself – seeking to explain the Sicilian character – commented, "Don't forget that even our most obscene vices nearly always bear the seal of sullen greatness".

Andrea Camilleri *Inspector Montalbano Mysteries*. Born in Agrigento, Camilleri is one of Italy's favourite modern authors, though he writes in Sicilian dialect that not all Italians can understand. His intelligent, and often vulgar and graphic, crime novels have subsequently become hugely popular all over Europe. Inspector Montalbano delves deep into the folds of Sicilian culture in an ongoing series, starting with *The Shape of Water*.

Giuseppe di Lampedusa *The Leopard*. The most famous Sicilian novel, written after World War II but recounting the dramatic nineteenth-century years of transition from Bourbon to Piedmontese rule from an aristocrat's point of view. David Gilmour's *The Last Leopard: A Life of Giuseppe di Lampedusa*, is the first biography in English of Lampedusa, a readable account of the life of an otherwise rather dull man.

Sicilian cuisine and cookbooks

There are Sicilian recipes in all the major Italian cookbooks, starting with **Elizabeth David**'s classic *Italian Food* (published 1954), the book that introduced Mediterranean flavours and ingredients to Britain. (Olive oil, famously, was previously something you could only buy in chemists'.) **Antonio Carluccio**, Britain's avuncular Italian master, is good on Sicilian fish and snacks in his *Southern Italian Feast* – his *arancini* recipe is definitive – while *Southern Italian Cooking* by **Valentina Harris** has an excellent chapter on Sicilian cooking. However, there are also plenty of specifically Sicilian books on the market, notably ⋏ *Sicilian Food* by **Mary Taylor Simeti**, which combines recipes with fascinating detail about life and traditions on the island. Simeti also co-authored *Bitter Almonds: Recollections and Recipes from a Sicilian Girlhood*, alongside **Maria Grammatico**, who was raised in a convent where she learned the pastry-cooking skills that she employs in her outlets in Érice. For an anecdotal trawl through the classics and the lesser-known dishes, including several from out-of-the-way places like Pantelleria and Strómboli, consult *The Flavors of Sicily* by **Anna Tasca Lanza**, the respected owner of a cooking school established at her family estate on the island – hence also her *Heart of Sicily: Recipes and Reminiscences of Regaleali, a Country Estate*.

Luigi Pirandello *Six Characters in Search of an Author, Henry IV, The Late Mattia Pascal, Short Stories*. His most famous and accomplished work, *Six Characters…*, written in 1921, and his *Henry IV*, written a year later, contain many of the themes that dogged Pirandello throughout his writing career – the idea of a multiple personality and the quality of reality. *The Late Mattia Pascal* is an entertaining early novel (1904), though the collection of abrasive short stories is perhaps the best introduction to Pirandello's work.

⋏ **Leonardo Sciascia** *Sicilian Uncles, The Wine-Dark Sea, Candido, The Knight and Death, Death of an Inquisitor, The Day of the Owl, Equal Danger*. Sciascia's short stories and novellas are packed with incisive insights into the island's quirky ways, and infused with the author's humane and sympathetic view of its people. The first to describe the Mafia in Italian literature, he wrote metaphysical thrillers in which the detectives often turn out to be the hunted; the best known is *The Day of the Owl*.

Giovanni Verga *Short Sicilian Novels, Cavalleria Rusticana, Maestro Don Gesualdo, I Malavoglia* or *The House by the Medlar Tree, A Mortal Sin, La Lupa*, and *Sparrow*. Born in the nineteenth century in Catania, Verga spent several years in various European salons before coming home to write his best work. Much of it is a reaction against the pseudo-sophistication of society circles, stressing the simple lives of ordinary people, with much emotion, wounded honour and feuds to the death. D.H. Lawrence's translations are suitably vibrant, with excellent introductions.

Films

Though Sicily doesn't have its own motion picture industry, the island's stunning scenery has served as a backdrop to a number of very successful films. The Aeolian and Pélagie islands, in particular, have proved popular settings for some interesting films, a few of them now classics of Italian cinema.

Michelangelo Antonioni *L'Avventura* (1960). Shot on the barren rocks of Panarea's Lisca Bianca, this film notes the beginning of a marked change in postwar Italian social mores. When a group of friends get together for a day out in the islands, one gets lost, and the relationships between those remaining begin to fracture. Here, Antonioni focuses ingeniously on the internal responses of those affected.

Emanuele Crispalese *Il Respiro* (2002). Filmed on the southern island of Lampedusa, this is a timeless, well-constructed look at how an eccentric mother is misunderstood by other islanders. Crispalese's second film, it addresses the overwhelming patriarchy of Italian families and the sexual tension latent between family members.

Francis Ford Coppola *The Godfather* (1971). Mario Puzo's brilliant screenplay tells the story of how Don Vito Corleone, *capo* of the New York Sicilian Mafia, tries to maintain his hold on the family business and his old-world values, despite his renegade son Michael. Since the town of Corleone itself was far too developed for the period filming, much of it was shot in Savoca and Forza d'Agro, outside Taormina.

Pietro Giermi *Divorzio alla Siciliana* (1961). Proof that not all Sicilian films need be deep or cinematic, this is a hilarious and pointed satire of Italian marital conventions. Marcello Mastroianni plays a Sicilian nobleman trying to prove his wife unfaithful so he can kill her and marry his younger

cousin. Known as *Divorce Italian Style* in English, it was filmed in Íspica near Ragusa, and got Giermi nominated for a Best Director Oscar.

Nanni Moretti *Dear Diary* (1994). Moretti plays himself as he tours Italy on a Vespa, visiting all the Aeolian Islands, showing how the inhabitants of each differ in mentality and lifestyle. Mostly comic, but a real downer at the end.

Michael Radford *Il Postino* (1994). An international favourite, featuring a postman on a small island who learns to love poetry after befriending the exiled poet Pablo Neruda. The film was shot in the town of Pollara on Salina, leading to a dramatic increase in tourists to the region.

Roberto Rossellini *Stromboli: Terra di Dio* (1949). Starring Ingrid Bergman as a tormented young refugee who marries an Italian to escape the war, this is a sad story of solitude and cynicism, that received little praise in its home country. The real star, however, is the volcano itself, whose brooding presence undermines the illusion of an idyllic, happy island.

Giuseppe Tornatore *Cinema Paradiso* (1988). Though derided by critics for its saccharine storyline, this Oscar-winning film by Sicilian director Tornatore received popular acclaim the world over. Shot around Cefalù, it follows the friendship between a young boy and the local cinema projectionist, and is in many ways a homage to cinema itself.

Language

Language

Italian

The ability to speak English confers enormous prestige in Sicily, and plenty of locals – particularly returned *emigrati* – are willing to show off their knowledge. Few outside the tourist resorts, however, actually know more than a few simple words and phrases, more often than not culled from pop songs or films. To get the most from your visit, therefore, you'd do well to master at least a little Italian.

Some tips

Attempting to speak Italian brings instant rewards; your halting efforts will often be greeted with smiles and genuine surprise that an English-speaker should stoop to learn the language. In any case, Italian is one of the easiest European languages to learn, especially if you already have a smattering of French or Spanish, both of which are extremely similar grammatically. The best **phrasebook** is Rough Guides' own *Italian Phrasebook* (Penguin), while Collins publishes a comprehensive series of **dictionaries**.

Easiest of all is the **pronunciation**, since every word is spoken exactly as it's written, and usually enunciated with exaggerated, open-mouthed clarity. The only difficulties you're likely to encounter are the few **consonants** that are different from English:

c before **e** or **i** is pronounced as in **ch**urch, while **ch** before the same vowels is hard, as in **c**at.

g is soft before **e** and **i**, as in **g**entle; hard when followed by **h**, as in **g**arlic.

gn has the **ni** sound of our o**ni**on.

gl in Italian is softened to something like **li** in English, as in vermi**li**on.

h is not aspirated, as in **h**our.

sci or **sce** are pronounced as in **shee**t and **she**lter respectively.

When **speaking** to strangers, the third person is the polite form (ie *Lei* instead of *Tu* for "you"); using the second person is a mark of disrespect or stupidity. It's also worth remembering that Italians don't use "please" and "thank you" half as much as we do: it's all implied in the tone, though if you're in doubt, err on the polite side.

All Italian words are **stressed** on the penultimate syllable unless an **accent** denotes otherwise, although accents are often left out in practice. Note that the ending **–ia** or **–ie** counts as two syllables, hence *trattoria* is stressed on the i. We've put accents in, throughout the text and below, wherever it isn't immediately obvious how a word should be pronounced: for example, in *Maríttima*, the accent is on the first **i**; conversely *Catania* should theoretically have an accent on the second **a**. Other words where we've omitted accents are common ones (like *Isola*, stressed on the I), some names (*Domenico*, *Vittorio/-a*), and words that are stressed similarly in English, such as *Repubblica* and *archeologico*.

None of this will help very much if you're confronted with a particularly harsh specimen of the **Sicilian dialect**, which virtually qualifies as a separate language (see p.406). However, television has made a huge difference, and almost every Sicilian can now communicate in something approximating standard Italian.

For political reasons, all regional languages in Italy are considered dialects of Italian. In reality, however, each has its own history and influences, and the majority of them are, linguistically speaking, separate languages. During the 600-year-long Roman occupation of Sicily, Vulgar Latin became the lingua franca for the entire island, though it was highly influenced by close contacts with Arabic, Norman and Spanish languages. The grammar, lexicon and phonology of Sicilian thus differs immensely from modern standard Italian – so much so that during the American Mafia trials of the 1980s, the FBI had to enlist special agents fluent in Sicilian to translate the conversations of mafiosi based in New York. The Sicilian language even has its own regional dialects (*parrati*), though in general these are understood by all Sicilians.

Today nearly all Sicilians speak and understand standard Italian, though, unlike numerous other dialects spoken throughout Europe, the language is in no danger of extinction: in most towns, the younger generation prefers Sicilian to Italian, and almost everyone speaks Sicilian at home. While Sicilians are well known for using their hands and arms as much as their vocal cords to communicate, their language is rich in idioms and sayings. Below are some favourite Sicilian proverbs:

Si vo' passari la vita cuntenti, statti luntanu di li parenti.
If you want a quiet life, stay away from relatives.

Sciarri di maritu e mugghieri duranu finu a lu lettu.
Quarrels between wives and husbands always end in the bed.

Cu'arrobba pri manciari nun fa piccatu.
He who steals to eat is no sinner.

Cu'asini caccia e fimmini cridi, faccia di paradisu nun ni vidi.
He who seeks girls and asses will never reach heaven.

Camina chi pantofuli finnu a quannu non hai i scarpi.
Walk with your slippers until you find your shoes (ie make the best of a bad situation).

Cu' va a Palermu e nun va a Murriali, si nni parti sceccu e torna maiali.
He who visits Palermo and not Monreale arrives an ass and returns a pig.

A language guide

Basics

Good morning	Buongiorno	Thank you (very much)	Grázie (molte/mille grazie)
Good afternoon/ evening	Buonasera	You're welcome/ after you	Prego
Good night	Buonanotte		
Hello/goodbye	Ciao (informal; when speaking to strangers use the phrase above)	Alright/that's OK	Va bene
		How are you?	Come stai/sta? (informal/formal)
Goodbye	Arrivederci (formal)	I'm fine	Bene
Goodbye	Arrivederla (more formal)	Do you speak English?	Parla inglese?
		I don't speak Italian	Non parlo italiano
Yes	Sì	I don't understand	Non capisco
No	No	I haven't understood	Non ho capito
Please	Per favore	I don't know	Non lo so

Excuse me/sorry	Scusa (informal)	In the morning	Di mattina
Excuse me/sorry	Mi scusi (formal)	In the afternoon	Nel pomeriggio
Excuse me	Permesso (in a crowd)	In the evening	Di sera
I'm sorry	Mi dispiace	Tonight	Stasera
I'm here on holiday	Sono qui in vacanza	Here/there	Qui/là
I live in…	Abito a…	Good/bad	Buono/cattivo
I'm English	Sono inglese	Big/small	Grande/píccolo
I'm Welsh	Sono gallese	Cheap/expensive	Económico/caro
I'm Scottish	Sono scozzese	Early/late	Presto/ritardo
I'm Irish	Sono irlandese	Hot/cold	Caldo/freddo
I'm American	Sono americano/a (masculine/feminine)	Near/far	Vicino/lontano
		Vacant/occupied	Líbero/occupato
I'm Australian	Sono australiano/a (masculine/feminine)	Quickly/slowly	Velocemente/lentamente
		Slowly/quietly	Piano
I'm Canadian	Sono canadese	With/without	Con/senza
I'm from New Zealand	Sono neozelandese	More/less	Più/meno
I'm South African	Sono sudafricano/a (masculine/feminine)	Enough/no more	Basta
		Mr…	Signor…
Today	Oggi	Mrs…	Signora…
Tomorrow	Domani	Miss…	Signorina…
Day after tomorrow	Dopodomani	(il Signore, la Signora, la Signorina when speaking about someone else)	
Yesterday	Ieri		
Now	Adesso	First name	Primo nome
Later	Più tardi	Surname	Cognome
Wait a minute!	Aspetta!		

Accommodation

Hotel	Albergo	Do you have anything cheaper?	Ha niente che costa di meno?
Is there a hotel nearby?	C'è un albergo qui vicino?	Full/half board	Pensione completa/ mezza pensione
Do you have a room…	Ha una cámera…	Can I see the room?	Posso vedere la cámera?
for one/two/ three people	per una persona, due/ tre persone	I'll take it	La prendo
for one/two/ three nights	per una notte, due/ tre notti	I'd like to book a room	Vorrei prenotare una cámera
for one/two weeks	per una settimana, due settimane	I have a booking	Ho una prenotazione
with a double bed	con un letto matrimoniale	Can we camp here?	Possiamo fare il campeggio qui?
with a shower/bath	con una doccia/ un bagno	Is there a campsite nearby?	C'è un camping qui?
with a balcony	con una terrazza	Tent	Tenda
hot/cold water	acqua calda/fredda	Cabin	Cabina
How much is it?	Quanto costa?	Hostel	Ostello
It's expensive	È caro	Youth hostel	Ostello per la gioventù
Is breakfast included?	È compresa la prima colazione?		

Questions and directions

Where? (Where is/ are...?)	Dove? (Dov'è/ Dove sono?)
When?	Quando?
What? (What is it?)	Cosa? (Cos'è?)
How much/many?	Quanto/Quanti?
Why?	Perché?
It is/There is (Is it/Is there...?)	È/C'è (È/C'è...?)
What time is it?	Che ora è?/Che ore sono?
How do I get to...?	Come arrivo a...?
How far is it to...?	Quant'è lontano a...?
Can you give me a lift to...?	Mi può dare un passaggio a...?

Can you tell me when to get off?	Può dirmi quando devo scendere?
What time does it open?	A che ora apre?
What time does it close?	A che ora chiude?
How much does it cost?/do they cost?	Quanto costa?/ Quanto costano?
What's it called in Italian?	Come si chiama in italiano?
Left/right	Sinistra/destra
Go straight ahead	Sempre diritto
Turn to the right/left	Gira a destra/sinistra

Getting around

Aeroplane	Aereo
Bus	Autobus/Pullman
Train	Treno
Car	Mácchina
Taxi	Taxi
Bicycle	Bicicletta
Ferry	Traghetto
Ship	Nave
Hydrofoil	Aliscafo
Hitch-hiking	Autostop
On foot	A piedi
Bus terminal	Capolinea
Bus station	Autostazione
Train station	Stazione ferroviaria
Ferry terminal	Stazione maríttima
Port	Porto
A ticket to...	Un biglietto a...
One way/return	Solo andata/andata e ritorno
Can I book a seat?	Posso prenotare un posto?

What time does it leave?	A che ora parte?
When is the next bus/train/ferry to...?	Quando parte il próssimo pullman/ treno/traghetto per...?
Where does it leave from?	Da dove parte?
Which platform does it leave from?	Da quale binario parte?
Do I have to change?	Devo cambiare?
How many kilometres is it?	Quanti chilómetri sono?
How long does it take?	Quanto ci vuole?
What number bus is it to...?	Que número di autobus per...?
Where's the road to...?	Dov'è la strada a...?
Next stop, please	La próssima fermata, per favore

Signs

Entrance/exit	Entrata/uscita
Free entrance	Ingresso líbero
Gentlemen/ladies	Signori/signore
WC/bathroom	Gabinetto/bagno
Vacant/engaged	Líbero/occupato
Open/closed	Aperto/chiuso

Arrivals/departures	Arrivi/partenze
Closed for restoration	Chiuso per restauro
Closed for holidays	Chiuso per ferie
Pull/push	Tirare/spingere
Out of order	Guasto
Drinking water	Acqua potabile

Not for drinking	Non potabile	Do not touch	Non toccare
To let	Affitasi	Danger	Perícolo
Platform	Binario	Beware	Attenzione
Cash desk	Cassa	First aid	Pronto soccorso
Go/walk	Avanti	Ring the bell	Suonare il campanello
Stop/halt	Alt	No smoking	Vietato fumare
Customs	Dogana		

Driving

Parking	Parcheggio	Slow down	Rallentare
No parking	Divieto di sosta/	Road closed/damaged	Strada chiusa/guasta
	Sosta vietata	No through road	Vietato il transito
One-way street	Senso único	No overtaking	Vietato il sorpasso
Both sides of	Ambo i lati	Crossroads	Incrocio
the street		Speed limit	Límite di velocità
No entry	Senso vietato	Traffic light	Semáforo

Numbers and days of the week

1	Uno	20	Venti
2	Due	25	Venticinque
3	Tre	30	Trenta
4	Quattro	40	Quaranta
5	Cinque	50	Cinquanta
6	Sei	60	Sessanta
7	Sette	70	Settanta
8	Otto	80	Ottanta
9	Nove	90	Novanta
10	Dieci	100	Cento
11	Úndici	1000	Mille
12	Dódici	Monday	Lunedì
13	Trédici	Tuesday	Martedì
14	Quattórdici	Wednesday	Mercoledì
15	Quíndici	Thursday	Giovedì
16	Sédici	Friday	Venerdì
17	Diciassette	Saturday	Sábato
18	Diciotto	Sunday	Doménica
19	Diciannove		

Menu reader

Basics and snacks

Aceto	Vinegar	Burro	Butter
Aglio	Garlic	Caramelle	Sweets
Biscotti	Biscuits	Cioccolato	Chocolate

Focaccia	Savoury bread	Patatine	Crisps/potato chips
Formaggio	Cheese	Patatine fritte	Chips/French fries
Frittata	Omelette	Pepe	Pepper
Gelato	Ice cream	Pizzetta	Small cheese-and-tomato pizza
Grissini	Bread sticks		
Maionese	Mayonnaise	Riso	Rice
Marmellata	Jam	Sale	Salt
Olio	Oil	Uova	Eggs
Olive	Olives	Yogurt	Yoghurt
Pane	Bread	Zúcchero	Sugar
Pane integrale	Wholemeal bread	Zuppa	Soup
Panino	Bread roll		

Antipasti and starters

Antipasto misto	Mixed cold meats and cheese (plus a mix of other things in this list)	Melanzane alla parmigiana	Fried aubergine in tomato sauce with parmesan cheese
Caponata	Mixed aubergine, olives and tomatoes	Mortadella	Salami-type cured meat with nuggets of fat, often with pistachios
Caprese	Tomato and mozzarella cheese salad	Pancetta	Italian bacon
Insalata di mare	Seafood salad (usually squid, octopus and prawn)	Peperonata	Grilled green, red or yellow peppers stewed in olive oil
Insalata di riso	Rice salad	Pomodori ripieni	Stuffed tomatoes
Insalata russa	"Russian salad": diced vegetables in mayonnaise	Prosciutto	Ham
		Salame	Salami
		Salmone/tonno/ pesce spada/ affumicato	Smoked salmon/tuna/ swordfish

Pizzas

Biancaneve	"Black and white": mozzarella and oregano	Funghi	Mushroom: tinned, sliced button mushrooms unless it specifies fresh mushrooms, either **funghi freschi** or **porcini**
Calzone	Folded pizza with cheese, ham and tomato		
Capricciosa	"Capricious": topped with whatever they've got in the kitchen, usually including baby artichoke, ham and egg	Frutti di mare	Seafood: usually mussels, prawns, squid and clams
		Margherita	Cheese and tomato
		Marinara	Tomato and garlic
Cardinale	Ham and olives	Napoli/Napoletana	Tomato, anchovy and olive oil (often mozzarella too)
Diávolo	"Devil": spicy, with hot salami or Italian sausage		

Quattro formaggi	"Four cheeses": usually mozzarella, fontina, Gorgonzola and Gruyère			peppers, onion, mushrooms, artichokes, olives, egg etc
Quattro stagioni	"Four seasons": the toppings split into four separate sections, usually including ham,	Rianata	Fresh tomato, oregano, garlic and anchovy; a western Sicilian speciality
		Romana	Anchovy and olives

The first course (il primo): Soups

Brodo	Clear broth	Pastina in brodo	Pasta pieces in clear broth
Minestrina	Any light soup		
Minestrone	Thick vegetable soup	Stracciatella	Broth with egg
Pasta e fagioli	Pasta soup with beans		

Pasta

Cannelloni	Large tubes of pasta, stuffed	Ravioli	Ravioli (stuffed, square-shaped pasta)
Farfalle	Literally "bow"-shaped pasta; the word also means "butterflies"	Rigatoni	Large, grooved, tubular pasta
Fettuccine	Narrow pasta ribbons	Risotto	Cooked rice dish, with sauce
Gnocchi	Small potato and dough dumplings	Spaghetti	Spaghetti
Lasagne	Lasagne	Spaghettini	Thin spaghetti
Maccheroni	Macaroni (tubular pasta)	Tagliatelle	Pasta ribbons, another word for fettuccine
Pappardelle	Pasta ribbons	Tortellini	Small rings of pasta, stuffed with meat or cheese
Pasta al forno	Pasta baked with minced meat, eggs, tomato and cheese	Vermicelli	Very thin spaghetti (literally "little worms")
Penne	Smaller version of rigatoni		

Pasta sauces (salsa)

Aglio e olio (e peperoncino)	Tossed in garlic and olive oil (and hot chillies)	Carbonara	Cream, ham and beaten egg
		Frutta di mare	Seafood
Amatriciana	Cubed pork and tomato sauce, with onions and hot chillies (originally from Rome)	Funghi	Mushroom
		Panna	Cream
		Parmigiano	Parmesan cheese
		Pesto	Ground basil, pine nut, garlic and pecorino
Arrabbiata	Spicy tomato sauce, with chillies	Pomodoro	Tomato sauce
		Puttanesca	Tomato, anchovy, olive oil and oregano sauce (literally "whorish")
Bolognese	Meat sauce		
Burro e salvia	Butter and sage		

| Ragù | Meat sauce | Vóngole (veraci) | Clam and tomato |
| Trápanese | Cold puréed tomato, garlic and basil | | sauce (fresh clams in shells, usually served with oil and herbs) |

The second course (il secondo): Meat (carne)

Agnello	Lamb	Manzo	Beef
Bistecca	Steak	Ossobuco	Shin of veal
Cervello	Brain	Pollo	Chicken
Cinghiale	Wild boar	Polpette	Meatballs
Coniglio	Rabbit	Rognoni	Kidneys
Costolette/cotolette	Cutlets/chops	Salsiccia	Sausage
Fegatini	Chicken livers	Saltimbocca	Veal with ham
Fégato	Liver	Scaloppina	Escalope (of veal)
Involtini	Steak slices, rolled and stuffed	Spezzatino	Stew
		Tacchino	Turkey
Lepre	Hare	Trippa	Tripe
Lingua	Tongue	Vitello	Veal
Maiale	Pork		

Fish (pesce) and shellfish (crostacei)

Note that surgelato or congelato written on the menu next to a dish means "frozen" – it often applies to squid and prawns.

Acciughe	Anchovies	Orata	Gilthead bream
Anguilla	Eel	Ostriche	Oysters
Aragosta	Lobster	Pesce spada	Swordfish
Baccalà	Dried salted cod	Pólpo/pólipo	Octopus
Bottarga	Fish roe	Ricci di mare	Sea urchins
Calamari	Squid	Ricciola	Amberjack
Céfalo	Grey mullet	Rospo	Monkfish
Cernia	Grouper	Sampiero	John Dory
Cozze	Mussels	Sarago	White bream
Dattile	Razor clams	Sarde	Sardines
Déntice	Dentex (like sea bass)	Séppie	Cuttlefish
Gamberetti	Shrimps	Sgombro	Mackerel
Gámberi	Prawns	Sógliola	Sole
Gránchio	Crab	Spígola	Sea bass
Merluzzo	Cod	Tonno	Tuna
Nasello	Hake	Tótani	Species of squid
		Triglie	Red mullet
		Trota	Trout
		Vóngole	Clams

Vegetables (contorni) and salad (insalata)

Aspáragi	Asparagus	Carciofi	Artichokes
Basílico	Basil	Carciofini	Artichoke hearts
Bróccoli	Broccoli	Carotte	Carrots
Cápperi	Capers	Cavolfiori	Cauliflower

Cávolo	Cabbage	Melanzane	Aubergine/eggplant
Ceci	Chickpeas	Orígano	Oregano
Cetriolo	Cucumber	Patate	Potatoes
Cipolla	Onion	Peperoni	Peppers
Fagioli	Beans	Piselli	Peas
Fagiolini	Green beans	Pomodori	Tomatoes
Finócchio	Fennel	Radícchio	Red chicory
Funghi	Mushrooms	Spinaci	Spinach
Insalata verde	Green salad/mixed	Zucca	Pumpkin
/mista	salad	Zucchini	Courgettes

Desserts (dolci)

Amaretti	Macaroons	Torta	Cake, tart
Cassata	Ice-cream cake with candied fruit	Zabaglione	Dessert made with eggs, sugar and Marsala wine
Gelato	Ice cream		
Macedonia	Fruit salad	Zuppa Inglese	Trifle

Cheese

Caciocavallo	A type of dried, mature mozzarella	Provolone	Cheese with grooved rind, either mild or slightly piquant
Fontina	Northern Italian cheese used in cooking	Ricotta	Soft white cheese made from ewe's milk, used in sweet or savoury dishes
Gorgonzola	Soft, strong, blue-veined cheese		
Mozzarella	Soft white cheese, traditionally made from buffalo's milk	Vastedda Palermitana	Similar to Caciocavallo, but tastes slightly more acidic
Parmigiano	Parmesan cheese		
Pecorino	Strong-tasting, hard sheep's cheese		

Fruit and nuts

Albicocca	Apricot	Lemone	Lemon
Ánanas	Pineapple	Mándorla	Almond
Angúria/coccómero	Watermelon	Mela	Apple
Arancia	Orange	Melone	Melon
Banana	Banana	Néspola	Medlar
Cacco	Persimmon	Pera	Pear
Ciliegia	Cherry	Pesca	Peach
Fico	Fig	Pinolo	Pine nut
Fico d'India	Prickly pear	Pistacchio	Pistachio nut
Frágola	Strawberry	Chicco d'uva/uva	a grape/grapes

Cooking terms

Affumicato	Smoked	Al Marsala	Cooked with Marsala wine
Arrosto	Roast	Milanese	Fried in egg and breadcrumbs
Ben cotto	Well done		
Bollito/lesso	Boiled	Pizzaiola	Cooked with tomato sauce
Alla brace	Barbecued		
Brasato	Cooked in wine	Ripieno	Stuffed
Cotto	Cooked (not raw)	Sangue	Rare
Crudo	Raw	Allo spiedo	On the spit
Al dente	Firm, not overcooked	Stracotto	Braised, stewed
Ferri	Grilled without oil	Surgelati	Frozen
Al forno	Baked	In úmido	Stewed
Fritto	Fried	Al vapore	Steamed
Grattugiato	Grated		
Alla griglia	Grilled		

Sicilian specialities: starters and pasta

Arancini	"Little oranges": deep-fried rice balls with minced meat, cheese and peas
Caponata	Sautéed aubergine, olives and tomatoes; served cold
Cozze alla marinara	Mussels in a rich wine-based soup
Cozze pepata	Mussels in spicy tomato stock
Crocchè di patate	Potato croquettes
Insalata di arance	Orange salad, dressed with oil and parsley
Maccu	Fava-bean (like lima-bean) soup
Panelle	Chickpea fritters
Pasta con i broccoli arriminati	Pasta cooked with broccoli, anchovy paste, pine nuts and saffron
Pasta con la mollica	Pasta with oil and toasted breadcrumbs
Pasta con le sarde	Macaroni with fresh sardines, fennel, raisins and pine kernels; a speciality of Palermo
Penne all'arrabbiata	Short tubular pasta with spicy tomato sauce made with chillies (*arrabbiata* means "angry")
Peperonata	Peppers (capsicum) sautéed in olive oil until soft and sweet, either served as antipasto or as a vegetable
Spaghetti alla carrettiera	"Carter's spaghetti", cooked with garlic, oil, pecorino and salt and pepper; a dish traditionally cooked by roving carters, common in Catania province
Spaghetti alla Norma	Spaghetti with tomato sauce topped with fried aubergine and parmesan or pecorino cheese; a speciality of Catania, named after one of Bellini's operas
Spaghetti alla Trapanese	Spaghetti tossed with cold puréed tomatoes, basil and garlic; a pungent dish from Trápani
Uova/funghi in tegame	Eggs/mushrooms fried in olive oil, served at the table in a little metal pan

Sicilian specialities: main courses

Cuscus — Couscous, usually served with fish and vegetable sauce, sometimes meat; a common dish in western Sicily and on the islands of Lampedusa and Pantelleria

Fritto misto — A standard seafood dish; deep-fried prawns and squid rings in batter

Fritto di pesce — As above but also with other fried fish, like sardines and whitebait

Involtini di pesce spada — Slices of swordfish, stuffed, rolled and fried

Pesce spada alla Ghiotta — Swordfish cooked in spicy tomato sauce with capers and olives; from Messina province

Sarde a beccafico — Sardines stuffed with breadcrumbs, nuts, dried fruit and anchovies; a Palermitan speciality

Scaloppine di maiale al Marsala — Escalopes of pork cooked in Marsala wine; the most common way of cooking meat with this Sicilian wine

Stocca alla Messinese — Dried cod stewed with potatoes, olives, tomatoes, capers and celery; a speciality of Messina, although there are other regional variations

Zuppa di cozze/vóngole — A big dish of mussels/clams in rich wine-based soup

Zuppa di pesce — As above but usually with pieces of cod, squid and prawns, and served with fried bread

Sicilian specialities: desserts and festival food

Cannoli — Fried pastry stuffed with sweet ricotta and candied peel; a Carnevale speciality

Cassata — Ice-cream cake with candied fruit

Crispelle di riso — Sweet rice fritters

Frutti di Martorana — Marzipan-based confection shaped and coloured to look like fruit, vegetables, and even fish

Ossa dei morti — Literally "dead men's bones", a clove-flavoured, sugared pastry handed out to children on All Hallows' Eve (October 31), and almost identical to *Agnellini pasquali* (Easter lambs)

Sfinci — Fried pastry stuffed with ricotta; served at the festival of St Joseph (San Giuseppe)

Torrone di mándorle — Crystallized almonds and sugar, sold at markets around All Saints' Day

Drinks

Acqua minerale	Mineral water
Aranciata	Orangeade
Bicchiere	Glass
Birra	Beer
Bottiglia	Bottle
Caffè	Coffee
Cioccolata calda	Hot chocolate
Ghiaccio	Ice
Granita	Iced coffee/fruit drink
Latte	Milk
Limonata	Lemonade
Selz	Soda water
Spremuta	Fresh fruit juice
Spumante	Sparkling wine
Succo di frutta	Concentrated fruit juice with sugar
Tè	Tea
Tónico	Tonic water
Vino	Wine
Rosso	Red
Bianco	White
Rosato	Rosé
Secco	Dry
Dolce	Sweet
Litro	Litre
Mezzo	Half-litre
Quarto	Quarter-litre
Salute!	Cheers!

Glossaries

Artistic and architectural terms

Agora Square or marketplace in an ancient Greek city.

Apse Domed recess at the altar-end of a church.

Architrave The lowest part of the entablature.

Atrium Forecourt, usually of a Roman house.

Bothros A pit that contains votive offerings.

Campanile Belltower.

Capital Top of a column.

Catalan-Gothic Hybrid form of architecture, mixing elements from fifteenth-century Spanish and northern European building styles.

Cavea The seating section in a theatre.

Cella Sanctuary of a temple.

Cupola A dome.

Decumanus The main street in a Roman town.

Entablature The part of the building above the capital on a classical building.

Ex-voto Decorated tablet designed as thanksgiving to a saint.

Hellenistic period 323–30 BC (Alexander the Great to Augustus).

Hypogeum Underground vault, often used as an early Christian church.

Kouros Standing male figure of the Archaic period (700 BC to early fifth century BC).

Krater Ancient conical bowl with round base.

Loggia Roofed gallery or balcony.

Metope A panel on the frieze of a temple.

Naumachia Mock naval combat, or the deep trench in a theatre in which it took place.

Nave Central space in a church, usually flanked by aisles.

Odeon Small theatre, usually roofed, for recitals.

Orchestra Section of the main floor of a theatre, where the chorus danced.

Pantocrator Usually refers to Christ, portrayed with outstretched arms.

Pediment The triangular front part of a building, usually surmounting a portico of columns.

Polyptych Painting or carving on several joined wooden panels.

Portico The covered entrance to a building.

Punic Carthaginian/Phoenician.

Scene-building Structure holding scenery in Greek/Roman theatre.

Stelae Inscribed stone slabs.

Stereobate Visible base of any building, usually a temple.

Stoa A detached roofed porch, or portico.

Stylobate Raised base of a columned building, usually a temple.

Telamon A supporting column in the shape of a male figure.

Thermae Baths, usually elaborate buildings in Roman villas.

Triptych Painting or carving on three joined wooden panels.

Italian words

Aliscafo Hydrofoil.

Anfiteatro Amphitheatre.

Autostazione Bus station.

Autostrada Motorway.

Belvedere A lookout point.

Cappella Chapel.

Castello Castle.

Cattedrale Cathedral.

Centro Centre.

Chiesa Church (main "mother" church, Chiesa Matrice/Madre).

Comune An administrative area; also, the local council or the town hall.

Corso Avenue/boulevard.

Duomo Cathedral.

Entrata Entrance.

Faraglione Obelisk-shaped deposits of volcanic rock rising out of the sea.

Festa Festival, carnival.

Fiume River.

Fumarola Volcanic vapour emission from the ground.

Golfo Gulf.

Lago Lake.

Largo Place (like piazza).

Lungomare Seafront promenade or road.

Mare Sea.

Mercato Market.

Mongibello Sicilian name for Mount Etna.

Municipio Town hall.

Palazzo Palace, mansion or block (of flats).

Parco Park.

Passeggiata The customary early-evening walk.

Pedaggio Toll.

Piano Plain (also "slowly", "gently").

Piazza Square.

Pineta Pinewood.

Pro Loco Local office, usually funded by the Comune, overseeing cultural events and providing tourist information.

Santuario Sanctuary.

Sottopassaggio Subway.

Spiaggia Beach.

Stazione Station (train station, stazione ferroviaria; bus station, autostazione; ferry terminal, stazione marittima).

Strada Road/street.

Teatro Theatre.

Tempio Temple.

Torre Tower.

Traghetto Ferry.

Uscita Exit.

Vicolo/Vico Alley.

Via Road (always used with name, as in Via Roma).

Zona Zone.

Acronyms

ACI Italian Automobile Club.

FS Ferrovie Statali (Italian State Railways).

IVA Imposta Valore Aggiunto (VAT).

RAI The Italian state TV and radio network.

SP Strada Provinciale; a minor road, eg SP116.

SS Strada Statale; a main highway, eg SS120.

FAIR FARES from
NORTH SOUTH TRAVEL

Our great-value air fares cover the world, from Abuja to Zanzibar and from Zurich to Anchorage. North South Travel is a fund-raising travel agency, owned by the NST Development Trust.

ALL our profits go to development organisations.

Call 01245 608 291 (or +44 1245 608 291 if outside UK) to speak to a friendly advisor. Your money is safe (ATOL 5401). For more information, visit northsouthtravel.co.uk. Free Rough Guide of your choice for every booking over £500.

EVERY FLIGHT A FIGHT AGAINST POVERTY

Visit us online
www.roughguides.com
Information on over 25,000 destinations around the world

- **Read** Rough Guides' trusted travel info
- **Access** exclusive articles from Rough Guides authors
- **Update** yourself on new books, maps, CDs and other products
- **Enter** our competitions and win travel prizes
- **Share** ideas, journals, photos & travel advice with other users
- **Earn** points every time you contribute to the Rough Guide
  community and get rewards

ROUGH
GUIDES

BROADEN YOUR HORIZONS

Small print and

Index

A Rough Guide to Rough Guides

Published in 1982, the first Rough Guide – to Greece – was a student scheme that became a publishing phenomenon. Mark Ellingham, a recent graduate in English from Bristol University, had been travelling in Greece the previous summer and couldn't find the right guidebook. With a small group of friends he wrote his own guide, combining a highly contemporary, journalistic style with a thoroughly practical approach to travellers' needs.

The immediate success of the book spawned a series that rapidly covered dozens of destinations. And, in addition to impecunious backpackers, Rough Guides soon acquired a much broader and older readership that relished the guides' wit and inquisitiveness as much as their enthusiastic, critical approach and value-for-money ethos.

These days, Rough Guides include recommendations from shoestring to luxury and cover more than 200 destinations around the globe, including almost every country in the Americas and Europe, more than half of Africa and most of Asia and Australasia. Our ever-growing team of authors and photographers is spread all over the world, particularly in Europe, the US and Australia.

In the early 1990s, Rough Guides branched out of travel, with the publication of Rough Guides to World Music, Classical Music and the Internet. All three have become benchmark titles in their fields, spearheading the publication of a wide range of books under the Rough Guide name.

Including the travel series, Rough Guides now number more than 350 titles, covering: phrasebooks, waterproof maps, music guides from Opera to Heavy Metal, reference works as diverse as Conspiracy Theories and Shakespeare, and popular culture books from iPods to Poker. Rough Guides also produce a series of more than 120 World Music CDs in partnership with World Music Network.

Visit www.roughguides.com to see our latest publications.

Rough Guide credits

Text editor: Anna Streiffert Limerick
Layout: Nikhil Agarwal
Cartography: Swati Handoo
Picture editor: Michelle Bhatia
Production: Erika Pepe
Proofreader: Richard Lim
Cover design: Nicole Newman, Dan May
Photographer: Jon Cunningham
Editorial: **London** Andy Turner, Keith Drew,
Edward Aves, Alice Park, Lucy White, Jo Kirby,
James Smart, Natasha Foges, James Rice,
Emma Beatson, Emma Gibbs, Kathryn Lane,
Monica Woods, Mani Ramaswamy, Harry Wilson,
Lucy Cowie, Alison Roberts, Lara Kavanagh,
Eleanor Aldridge, Ian Blenkinsop, Joe Staines,
Matthew Milton, Tracy Hopkins; **Delhi** Madhavi
Singh, Jalpreen Kaur Chhatwal, Jubbi Francis
Design & Pictures: **London** Scott Stickland, Dan
May, Diana Jarvis, Mark Thomas, Nicole Newman,

Sarah Cummins; **Delhi** Umesh Aggarwal,
Ajay Verma, Jessica Subramanian, Ankur Guha,
Pradeep Thapliyal, Sachin Tanwar, Anita Singh,
Sachin Gupta
Production: Rebecca Short, Liz Cherry,
Louise Daly, Erika Pepe
Cartography: **London** Ed Wright, Katie Lloyd-
Jones; **Delhi** Rajesh Chhibber, Ashutosh Bharti,
Rajesh Mishra, Animesh Pathak, Jasbir Sandhu,
Deshpal Dabas, Lokamata Sahu
Marketing, Publicity & roughguides.com:
Liz Statham
Digital Travel Publisher: Peter Buckley
Reference Director: Andrew Lockett
Operations Coordinator: Becky Doyle
Operations Assistant: Johanna Wurm
Publishing Director (Travel): Clare Currie
Commercial Manager: Gino Magnotta
Managing Director: John Duhigg

Publishing information

This eighth edition published May 2011 by

Rough Guides Ltd,
80 Strand, London WC2R 0RL
11, Community Centre, Panchsheel Park,
New Delhi 110017, India
Distributed by the Penguin Group
Penguin Books Ltd,
80 Strand, London WC2R 0RL

Penguin Group (USA)
375 Hudson Street, NY 10014, USA

Penguin Group (Australia)
250 Camberwell Road, Camberwell,
Victoria 3124, Australia

Penguin Group (NZ)
67 Apollo Drive, Mairangi Bay, Auckland 1310,
New Zealand

Rough Guides is represented in Canada by
Tourmaline Editions Inc. 662 King Street West,
Suite 304, Toronto, Ontario M5V 1M7

Cover concept by Peter Dyer.

Typeset in Bembo and Helvetica to an original
design by Henry Iles.

Printed in Singapore
© Robert Andrews and Jules Brown, 2010
Maps © Rough Guides
No part of this book may be reproduced in any
form without permission from the publisher except
for the quotation of brief passages in reviews.
432pp includes index
A catalogue record for this book is available from
the British Library
ISBN: 978-1-84836-902-3

The publishers and authors have done their
best to ensure the accuracy and currency of all
the information in **The Rough Guide to Sicily**,
however, they can accept no responsibility for
any loss, injury, or inconvenience sustained by
any traveller as a result of information or advice
contained in the guide.

3   5   7   9   8   6   4   2

MIX
Paper from
responsible sources
FSC
www.fsc.org   FSC™ C018179

Help us update

We've gone to a lot of effort to ensure that the
eighth edition of **The Rough Guide to Sicily** is
accurate and up-to-date. However, things change
– places get "discovered", opening hours are
notoriously fickle, restaurants and rooms raise
prices or lower standards. If you feel we've got it
wrong or left something out, we'd like to know,
and if you can remember the address, the price,
the hours, the phone number, so much the better.

Please send your comments with the
subject line "**Rough Guide Sicily Update**" to
✉ mail@uk.roughguides.com. We'll credit all
contributions and send a copy of the next edition
(or any other Rough Guide if you prefer) for the
very best emails.
    Find more travel information, connect with
fellow travellers and book your trip on ✆ www
.roughguides.com

Acknowledgements

Robert Andrews: Quinn and Ev were entertaining and patient travelling companions, with superb navigational and culinary skills. Ros Belford provided interesting and insightful contributions as well as Aeolian hospitality – molte grazie. Extreme thanks are also due to Anna Streiffert Limerick for a meticulous and knowledgeable but thoroughly relaxed edit.

Jules Brown thanks all those who helped with the research and provided valuable assistance for this edition, especially Ros Belford and Rob, who both stepped in when the going got tough. And one day, Foxton and Ripley, you can come too.

Readers' letters

Thanks to all the readers who have taken the time to write in with comments and suggestions (and apologies if we've inadvertently omitted or misspelt anyone's name):

Mhairi Bremner, J. Michael Brotherton, René Brouwer, Madeleine Carpenter, Vivien Conrad, Joan Craig, Andrew Feldman, Jan and Dino Fracaro, Sandy & Pat Fraser, Angela Gheradi, Joe Hofmann, Roger Kennington, Roger Latham, Claudia Lopez, Paul McMaster & Liz, Daniele Martin, Peter Meijer, Deanna Morgan, Marcello Ranno, Urte Spaeth, John Spuches, K. Stoner, Susan Thomas, Isobel and Phillip Wilson.

SMALL PRINT

Photo credits

All photos © Rough Guides except the following:

Full page
Cala dei Turchi beach © Luis Alberto Aldonza/
photolibrary.com

Introduction
Sicilian folk art on a wooden cart © Funkyfood
London – Paul Williams/Alamy
San Paolo feast, Palazzolo Acreide © CuboImages
srl/Alamy
Ceramics shop Santo Stefano © David Lyons/
Alamy
Capo San Vito, Nature Reserve of the Zingaro
© René Mattes/Hemis/Corbis
Piazza IX Aprile in the evening, Taormina © Ingolf
Pompe 86/Alamy

Things not to miss
01 Lampedusa © Gabrio/Fotolia
02 Ortigia, Siracusa © CuboImages/photolibrary
.com
06 Byzantine Mosaic of Christ as Pantocrator in
Cefalù Cathedral © Gérard Degeorge/Corbis
07 Hydrofoil ferrying passengers between islands,
near Lipari © Guido Cozzi/Corbis
08 Landscape, Madonie mountain © CuboImages
srl/Alamy
10 Isole Egadi © Tunde Pecsvari/Fotolia
13 Fish, Catania © Ollirg/Fotolia
15 San Vito Lo Capo © Yohka91/Fotolia
19 Etna © Bastien Poux/Fotolia

Food and wine in Sicily colour section
Aeolian Island, grape baskets © John Ferro
Sims/Alamy
Fishmonger at market, Siracusa © Ingolf
Pompe 86/Alamy

Men selling prickly pears from a market stall
© David Pearson/Alamy
Pasta alla norma © Mario Matassa/photolibrary
.com
Mini ice cream cornets in Módica © Michael
Jenner/Alamy
Grape harvest, Salina Island © Riccardo
Lombardo/photolibrary.com

Outdoor adventures colour section
View over the beach at Isola Bella island,
Taormina © Yadid Levy/Alamy
Catamaran along coast at San Vito lo Capo
© Mario Cipriani/Corbis
Gola dell'Alcantara © DavidCameron/Alamy
Strómboli © Federico Raiser/photolibrary.com
Vulcano Island © Jonathan Blair/Corbis
Cyclists, Ragusa province © Plinthpics/Alamy
Cefalù from La Rocca © Danita Delimont/Alamy
Prehistoric village, Filicudi island © CuboImages
srl/Alamy
Hiker in Zingaro National Preserve © Loetscher
Chlaus/Alamy

Black and whites
p.94 Caccamo © Walter Bibikow/JAI/Corbis
p.148 Tíndari © cate1966/Fotolia
p.186 Etna © Tanguy de Saint Cyr/Fotolia
p.214 Piazza del Duomo, Siracusa © Visibilis/
Fotolia
p.312 Érice © baccos/Fotolia

SMALL PRINT

Index

Map entries are in colour.

Map symbols

maps are listed in the full index using coloured text

– – –	Chapter boundary	⬧	Point of interest
	Motorway	@	Internet access
	Major road	ⓘ	Tourist information
	Minor road	✉	Post office
	Viaduct	⊞	Hospital
⅏	Steps	◉	Accommodation
⊐······⊏	Underpass or long tunnel	▣	Restaurant
	Railway	⚠	Campsite
●- - -●	Cable car	∴	Ruins
- - - -	Footpath	⛢	Lighthouse
	River	▮	Tower
– –	Ferry route	⚘	Gardens
	Wall	✈	Airport
⊠—⊠	Gate	★	Bus stop
)(	Bridge	⚲	Church (regional maps)
≈	Pass	⛪	Monastery
⋀	Mountain range	🅿	Parking
▲	Mountain peak	☐	Market
	Cliff	▬	Building
	Rocks	⊞	Church (town maps)
	Gorge	⬭	Stadium
⊻	Viewpoint	⊹	Cemetery
⌂	Cave	░	Park
⬧	Museum	░	Beach

So now we've told you about the things not to miss, the best places to stay, the top restaurants, the liveliest bars and the most spectacular sights, it only seems fair to tell you about the best travel insurance around

WorldNomads.com
keep travelling safely

Recommended by Rough Guides

www.roughguides.com
MAKE THE MOST OF YOUR TIME ON EARTH

ROUGH
GUIDES